CROSSCURRENTS

Fifth Edition

INTERNATIONAL RELATIONS

EDITED BY

MARK CHARLTON
ST. MARY'S UNIVERSITY COLLEGE

NELSON / EDUCATION

NELSON EDUCATION

Crosscurrents: International Relations, Fifth Edition

Edited by Mark Charlton

Associate Vice President, Editorial Director:
Evelyn Veltch

Editor-in-Chief, Higher Education:
Anne Williams

Publisher:
Cara Yarzab

Marketing Manager:
Ann Byford

Developmental Editor:
My Editor Inc.

Permissions Coordinator:
Sandra Mark

Content Production Manager:
Susan Ure

Production Service:
Macmillan Publishing Solutions

Copy Editor:
Wendy Yano

Proofreader:
Dianne Fowlie

Senior Production Coordinator:
Ferial Suleman

Design Director:
Ken Phipps

Managing Designer:
Franca Amore

Interior Design:
Katherine Strain

Cover Design:
Peter Papayanakis

Cover Image:
J. A. Kraulis/Masterfile

Compositor:
Macmillan Publishing Solutions

Printer:
Webcom

Library and Archives Canada Cataloguing in Publication

Crosscurrents : international relations / [edited by] Mark Charlton. — 5th ed.

Includes bibliographical references.
ISBN 978-0-17-644084-8

1. International relations—Textbooks. I. Charlton, Mark, 1948–

D863.3.C76 2009   327
C2009-900435-6

ISBN-13: 978-0-17-644084-8
ISBN-10: 0-17-644084-4

Contents

Contributors

Lloyd Axworthy is a chancellor of the University of Winnipeg and a former minister of foreign affairs of Canada.

Jagdish N. Baghwati is a university professor of economics at Columbia University.

William W. Bain is a lecturer in international relations theory at the University of Wales at Aberystwyth.

Frank Biermann is the leader of the Global Governance Project at the Potsdam Institute for Climate Impact Research.

Jutta Brunnee is a professor at the Faculty of Law, University of Toronto.

Michael Byers holds a Canada Research Chair in International Law and Politics at the University of British Columbia.

R. Charli Carpenter is a professor of international affairs at the University of Pittsburgh.

Terrell Carver is a professor of political theory at the University of Bristol.

Douglass Cassel is the director of the Center for International Human Rights at Northwestern University School of Law in Chicago.

Lucille Charlton is an instructor of English at Mount Royal College, Calgary.

Michael Crosswell is a senior economist with the Office of the Director of Foreign Aid, U.S. State Department.

William Easterly is a professor of economics at New York University.

Robyn Eckersley is a professor in the School of Politics, Sociology and Criminology, University of Melbourne, Australia.

Denise Froning is a policy analyst with the Center for International Trade and Economics at the Heritage Foundation in Washington, D.C.

Stephen Gill is a professor of political science at York University.

Romilly Greenhill in an economist with Jubilee Research.

Robert Heubert is a professor of political science and Associate Director of the Centre for Military and Strategic Studies at the University of Calgary.

Naierossadat Daneshvar Hosseini teaches economics at the Islamic Azad University, Iran.

Gary Hufbauer is the Reginald Jones Senior Fellow at the Peterson Institute for International Economics.

Samuel Huntington is a professor of political science at Harvard University.

Rebecca Johnson is visiting professor at the Georgetown Public Policy Institute, Georgetown University.

Steven Meyer is a professor of political science at the Industrial College of the Armed Forces at the National Defense University in Washington, D.C.

Jerry Z. Muller is a professor of history at the Catholic University of America.

Adil Najam teaches international environmental policy at the Fletcher School of Law and Diplomacy at Tufts University.

Joanna R. Quinn is a professor of political science at the University of Western Ontario.

Richard Rosecrance is Senior Fellow at the Belfer Center for Science and International Affairs, Harvard University.

Douglas Alan Ross is a professor of political science at Simon Fraser University.

Alfred P. Rubin is a professor of international law at the Fletcher School of Law and Diplomacy at Tufts University.

Brett D. Schaefer is Jay Kingham Fellow in International Regulatory Affairs in the Margaret Thatcher Center for Freedom, a division of the Kathryn and Shelby Cullom Davis Institute for International Studies, at the Heritage Foundation.

Jan Aart Scholte is a professor of politics and international studies at the University of Warwick.

Vaughn P. Shannon is a professor of political science at the University of Northern Iowa.

Arthur Stein is a professor of political science at the University of California at Los Angeles.

Joseph E. Stiglitz is a university professor of economics at Columbia University.

Yvonne Terlingen heads Amnesty International's United Nations Office in New York.

Alexander Wendt is the Ralph D. Mershon Professor of International Security at the Mershon Center, Ohio State University.

Richard Ashby Wilson is the director of the Human Rights Institute at the University of Connecticut.

David Wingfield is a lawyer with the Toronto firm WeirFoulds.

Mark Woods is a professor of philosophy at the University of San Diego.

Micah Zenko is a research associate with the Belfer Center for Science and International Affairs.

Introduction

When the first edition of *Crosscurrents: International Relations* was published in 1993, the introduction began with the following words from Charles Dickens: "It was the best of times, it was the worst of times." Dickens wrote those words in response to the tumult of revolutionary France in the eighteenth century. His words seem even more apt for the current situation than when I cited them eleven years ago. For many, the past decade has been one of growing prosperity, expanding human rights, and progress toward democratization. The emergence of a global civil society and the "democratization" of foreign policy have enabled new actors on the global scene to achieve successes in promoting issues—such as a global ban on landmines and international debt relief—that were unheard of decades ago.

At the same time, others experienced the 1990s as a period of increased impoverishment and alienation. Resistance to the forces of globalization intensified and took more violent forms. Genocidal warfare in Rwanda and the former Yugoslavia challenged the ability of the international community to respond. Our entry into the new millennium has also brought new hopes and disappointments. As part of its Millennium Development Goals, the United Nations has planned to cut the amount of global poverty and hunger in half by the year 2015. In its 2004 annual review, the World Bank claimed that we are well on our way to meeting these targets. At the same time, the attacks on the United States on September 11, 2001, and the subsequent military interventions in Afghanistan and Iraq have heightened international tensions and fears. The conflicts and hatreds in the Middle East are more entrenched than ever. Terrorist attacks in countries that had not experienced them before have given new credence to talk of a "new world disorder." Indeed, "the best of times, the worst of times" continues to be an apt description of our entry into the new millennium.

As we reach the end of the first decade of a new century, we continue to be faced with a number of complex questions: Will ethnic differences be the major fault lines for future international conflicts? Do the forces associated with globalization threaten to undermine a more equitable distribution of resources and progress toward human rights? Have old institutions such as the NATO alliance become irrelevant in a new age of global terrorism? Will new institutions such as the International Criminal Court and the United Nations Human Rights Council provide the basis for building a more stable global society? Are new forms of international governance needed to address issues of international debt, human rights, and the environment? Are we moving toward some form of world state or world government?

THE DEBATE FORMAT

In preparing the fifth edition of *Crosscurrents: International Relations*, it is my hope that students will be challenged to wrestle with many of these questions. Students enrolling in introductory international relations courses generally do so in the hopes of gaining a better understanding of contemporary world issues and events. In contrast, many international relations texts focus on structures, abstract concepts, and theories that, while vital to the discipline, when taken alone fail to address students' interest in current world developments. The debate format in the *Crosscurrents* series, I believe, provides a structured way of relating topical information about current affairs to the broader concepts and theories of the discipline. By evaluating contending arguments concerning various global issues, students will be encouraged to analyze for themselves the relevance of different theories and concepts for explaining contemporary international developments.

While the debate format has its advantages, it sometimes limits the choice of readings. Thus, some of the more seminal pieces on particular topics were not included because they were not suitable to the debate format, or adequate companion pieces could not be found for them. In these cases, I have added them to the suggested readings list in the postscripts.

USAGE IN THE CLASSROOM

Crosscurrents: International Relations is designed as a flexible pedagogical tool that can be incorporated into courses in several ways.

i. Perhaps the most effective use of *Crosscurrents: International Relations* is to utilize the readings as a means of organizing weekly discussion sessions in a debate format. On each topic, two students may be asked to argue the case for the opposing sides, and these arguments could be followed by a group discussion. This format requires students to adopt a particular point of view and defend that position. Because the necessary background material is provided in the readings, this format is very easily adapted to large courses in which teaching assistants are responsible for weekly tutorial sessions.

ii. Some may wish to assign the chapters simply as supplementary readings reinforcing material covered in the lectures, and to use them as points of illustration in classroom lectures or discussions. In this way, the text can be used as a more traditional course reader, with the instructor having the option of assigning only one of the readings under each topic.

iii. Others may wish to use the readings as a point of departure for essay assignments in the course. In some cases, the readings and the postscript, with its suggestion of further readings, could simply serve as a starting point for researching the topic under discussion. In other cases, the instructor might want to encourage students to develop their critical skills by having them write an assessment of the arguments and evidence presented by the writers in a particular debate. Alternatively, students could select one side of the debate and write a persuasive essay developing their own arguments in favour of that point of view. I have included, as an appendix, instructions on writing an argumentative essay that should serve as a useful guide to students.

OTHER FEATURES

The availability of Internet resources and electronic journals has significantly expanded the range of materials at the disposal of students. To enhance the students' ability to find additional resources for both their participation in class discussions and for writing papers, I provide two useful features in addition to the list of suggested readings:

- **Web resources:** At the end of each postscript, I provide an annotated list of suggested website resources. The list is also available on the Nelson website for this book, at www.crosscurrents.nelson.com, where students can connect directly to the recommended sites. Instructors may also wish to have their students purchase Grant Heckman, *Nelson Guide to Web Research 2007–2008* (Scarborough: Nelson, 2008). This manual not only provides useful tips on conducting web research, but also includes information on citing web resources in both MLA and APA formats.

- **InfoTrac®:** Students purchasing this edition of *Crosscurrents: International Relations* will receive a free four-month subscription to InfoTrac® College Edition. This is an online library containing full-text articles from a large number of scholarly journals and popular news magazines. In each postscript, I have suggested some useful readings relevant to each topic. A separate *User Guide for Instructors* is available from Nelson.

ACKNOWLEDGMENTS

I would like to express appreciation to the reviewers who provided many valuable suggestions and comments: Aurélie Dépelteau-Lacassagne, Algoma University College; Leonard Friesen, Wilfrid Laurier University; Malcolm Grieve, Acadia University; and David Winchester, Capilano College. Appreciation is also expressed to the authors and publishers who have given permission to include their work in this volume. At Nelson, I would like to acknowledge the excellent and patient support of Bram Sepers, Katherine Goodes, and other members of the staff. A special words of thanks to Chris Charlton and Lucille Charlton who have provided research assistance on some of the issues in this volume.

Mark Charlton
St. Mary's University College
Calgary, Alberta

About the Editor

Mark Charlton is Vice-President Academic and Dean and Professor of Political Science at St. Mary's University College in Calgary, Alberta. He has written *The Making of Canadian Food Aid Policy* (1992) and has co-edited, with Paul Barker, *Crosscurrents: Contemporary Political Issues*, and with Paul Rowe, *Crosscurrents: International Development*. Dr. Charlton is also co-author of the *Thomson Nelson Political Science Writer's Guide*. He has also published a number of articles in *International Journal*, *Études Internationales*, and *The Canadian Journal of Development Studies*.

PART ONE

UNDERSTANDING OUR CHANGING WORLD

Is the World Fragmenting into Clashing Cultures?

Is a World State Inevitable?

Can a Non-Feminist Approach to Gender Issues Help Us to Better Understand Global Politics?

Is the World Fragmenting into Clashing Cultures?

✔ **YES**

SAMUEL HUNTINGTON, "The Clash of Civilizations? The Next Pattern of Conflict," *Foreign Affairs* 72, no. 3 (Summer 1993): 22–28

✘ **NO**

DOUGLAS ALAN ROSS, "Ten Years After: The Inevitable Waning of Huntington's Civilizational Clash Theory?"

As the Cold War drew to an end, international relations scholars began debating what the implications of this development would be for international politics. One of the first to address this issue was Francis Fukuyama in an article entitled "The End of History?" (*The National Interest* 16, 1989). Fukuyama argued that the end of the Cold War signalled the end of humankind's ideological evolution and the triumph of Western liberal democracy. He predicted that international conflict, especially between the major powers, would be significantly diminished—that we were moving to a new era of peace and stability. One of the scholars to respond to Fukuyama's thesis was Samuel Huntington, whose article "No Exit: The Errors of Endism" (*The National Interest* 17, 1989) challenged such an optimist assessment of the end of the Cold War.

Huntington was concerned with the growing preoccupation with "endism" or, as he put it, the view that "bad things are coming to an end." In particular, he feared that Fukuyama's optimistic predictions of a new era of expanding zones of peace and tranquility would tempt American policymakers into pursing a policy of retreat and isolationism. Huntington warned that the world was instead moving into a new era of possibly greater "instability, unpredictability, and violence in international affairs." In his article in *The National Interest*, he said that "endism" is "dangerous and subversive" because it "present[s] an illusion of well-being."

In making his case, Huntington noted that the structure of bipolarity and the presence of nuclear weapons had both defined the nature of and placed constraints on U.S.–Soviet rivalry. The end of the Cold War did not "mean the end of the struggle for power and influence." In fact, the end of the "balance of terror" between the two superpowers presaged a slide into a more chaotic and troubling time.

In 1993, Huntington published an article in which he sought to identify in clearer terms the sources of this increased instability and unpredictability. In this article, reproduced here, Huntington claims to be presenting students of international relations with a new and more comprehensive paradigm for understanding world politics. He stresses that rather than simply thinking about the structure of world politics in terms of polarity and balance of power between nation-states, we should take into account the relevance of civilizations and cultures in shaping international conflict, a dimension that has often been ignored in traditional realist analyses of world politics. This "new paradigm," he argues, is necessitated by the evolution of history. According to Huntington, the modern world has evolved through three phases of conflict, progressing from conflicts between princes to conflicts between nation-states and then to conflicts between ideologies. We are entering a new phase of human history in which conflict between civilizations will supplant ideological conflict as a dominant force in international politics.

In the future, Huntington contends, conflicts are most likely to develop between groups that are part of different civilizations. He argues that the cultural differences between the eight different civilizations he identifies will become more dangerous and entrenched than traditional ideological and economic clashes. Advances in communications technologies, and increased economic and social interaction, rather than creating a globalized culture, will magnify "civilizational consciousness" and exacerbate future conflicts. Because questions of identity, culture, and religion are more fundamental to people, future conflicts will be less amenable to negotiation and compromise. As Islamic and Confucian states increasingly challenge Western political, economic, and cultural dominance, the possibility of conflict on a global scale—the "West against the rest"—becomes increasingly likely. Accordingly, Huntington issues a call to the American policymakers to be vigilant and to maintain U.S. military and economic strength.

Huntington's "clash of civilizations" theory has been widely debated since it was first published. Many rejected his thesis outright, and some criticized its author for offering spurious academic arguments in order to justify increased defence expenditures in a period of growing peace and stability. However, the events of September 11, 2001, led many to take a renewed interest in Huntington's thesis. The bold attacks on the United States by Islamist radicals seem to give new impetus to his argument that we may be facing a new and more dangerous era of civilizational conflict. Clashes between Orthodox Russians and Muslims in Chechnya, between Christians and Muslims in Indonesia, and between Hindus and Muslims in India have, in the eyes of some, give greater credence to Huntington's argument.

Nevertheless, many are still skeptical about Huntington's thesis. Douglas Ross of Simon Fraser University critically examines the debate surrounding Huntington's writings and questions the usefulness of the "clash of civilizations" thesis in understanding international conflict and the evolving international system today.

✔ **YES**

The Clash of Civilizations? The Next Pattern of Conflict

SAMUEL HUNTINGTON

World politics is entering a new phase, and intellectuals have not hesitated to pro-liferate visions of what it will be—the end of history, the return of traditional rivalries between nation states, and the decline of the nation state from the con-flicting pulls of tribalism and globalism, among others. Each of these visions catches aspects of the emerging reality. Yet they all miss a crucial, indeed a cen-tral, aspect of what global politics is likely to be in the coming years.

It is my hypothesis that the fundamental source of conflict in this new world will not be primarily ideological or primarily economic. The great divisions among humankind and the dominating source of conflict will be cultural. Nation states will remain the most powerful actors in world affairs, but the principal con-flicts of global politics will occur between nations and groups of different civi-lizations. The clash of civilizations will dominate global politics. The fault lines between civilizations will be the battle lines of the future.

Conflict between civilizations will be the latest phase in the evolution of con-flict in the modern world. For a century and a half after the emergence of the modern international system with the Peace of Westphalia, the conflicts of the Western world were largely among princes—emperors, absolute monarchs, and constitutional monarchs attempting to expand their bureaucracies, their armies, their mercantilist economic strength and, most important, the territory they ruled. In the process they created nation states, and beginning with the French Revolution the principal lines of conflict were between nations rather than princes. In 1793, as R.R. Palmer put it, "The wars of kings were over; the wars of peoples had begun." This nineteenth-century pattern lasted until the end of World War I.

Then, as a result of the Russian Revolution and the reaction against it, the conflict of nations yielded to the conflict of ideologies, first among communism, fascism-Nazism, and liberal democracy, and then between communism and liberal democracy. During the Cold War, this latter conflict became embodied in the struggle between the two superpowers, neither of which was a nation state in the classical European sense and each of which defined its identity in terms of its ideology.

These conflicts between princes, nation states, and ideologies were primarily conflicts within Western civilization, "Western civil wars," as William Lind has labeled them. This was as true of the Cold War as it was of the world wars and the earlier wars of the seventeenth, eighteenth, and nineteenth centuries. With the end of the Cold War, international politics moves out of its Western phase, and its

4

centerpiece becomes the interaction between the West and non-Western civiliza-tions and among non-Western civilizations. In the politics of civilizations, the peoples and governments of non-Western civilizations no longer remain the objects of history as targets of Western colonialism but join the West as movers and shapers of history.

THE NATURE OF CIVILIZATIONS

During the Cold War the world was divided into the First, Second, and Third Worlds. Those divisions are no longer relevant. It is far more meaningful now to group countries not in terms of their political or economic systems or in terms of their level of economic development but rather in terms of their culture and civilization.

What do we mean when we talk of a civilization? A civilization is a cultural entity. Villages, regions, ethnic groups, nationalities, religious groups, all have distinct cultures at different levels of cultural heterogeneity. The culture of a vil-lage in southern Italy may be different from that of a village in northern Italy, but both will share in a common Italian culture that distinguishes them from German villages. European communities, in turn, will share cultural features that distin-guish them from Arab or Chinese communities. Arabs, Chinese, and Westerners, however, are not part of any broader cultural entity. They constitute civilizations. A civilization is thus the highest cultural grouping of people and the broadest level of cultural identity people have short of that which distinguishes humans from other species. It is defined both by common objective elements, such as language, history, religion, customs, and institutions, and by the subjective self-identification of people. People have levels of identity: a resident of Rome may define himself with varying degrees of intensity as a Roman, an Italian, a Catholic, a Christian, a European, a Westerner. The civilization to which he belongs is the broadest level of identification with which he intensely identifies. People can and do redefine their identities and, as a result, the composition and bound-aries of civilizations change.

Civilizations may involve a large number of people, as with China ("a civiliza-tion pretending to be a state," as Lucian Pye put it), or a very small number of people, such as the Anglophone Caribbean. A civilization may include several nation states, as is the case with Western, Latin American, and Arab civilizations, or only one, as is the case with Japanese civilization. Civilizations obviously blend and overlap, and may include subcivilizations. Western civilization has two major variants, European and North American, and Islam has its Arab, Turkic, and Malay subdivisions. Civilizations are nonetheless meaningful entities, and while the lines between them are seldom sharp, they are real. Civilizations are dynamic; they rise and fall; they divide and merge. And, as any student of history knows, civilizations disappear and are buried in the sands of time.

Westerners tend to think of nation states as the principal actors in global affairs. They have been that, however, for only a few centuries. The broader reaches of human history have been the history of civilizations. In *A Study of History*, Arnold Toynbee identified 21 major civilizations; only six of them exist in the contemporary world.

WHY CIVILIZATIONS WILL CLASH

Civilization identity will be increasingly important in the future, and the world will be shaped in large measure by the interactions among seven or eight major civilizations. These include Western, Confucian, Japanese, Islamic, Hindu, Slavic-Orthodox, Latin American, and possibly African civilization. The most important conflicts of the future will occur along the cultural fault lines separating these civilizations from one another.

Why will this be the case?

First, differences among civilizations are not only real; they are basic. Civilizations are differentiated from each other by history, language, culture, tradition, and, most important, religion. The people of different civilizations have different views on the relations between God and man, the individual and the group, the citizen and the state, parents and children, husband and wife, as well as differing views of the relative importance of rights and responsibilities, liberty and authority, equality and hierarchy. These differences are the product of centuries. They will not soon disappear. They are far more fundamental than differences among political ideologies and political regimes. Differences do not necessarily mean conflict, and conflict does not necessarily mean violence. Over the centuries, however, differences among civilizations have generated the most prolonged and the most violent conflicts.

Second, the world is becoming a smaller place. The interactions between peoples of different civilizations are increasing; these increasing interactions intensify civilization consciousness and awareness of differences between civilizations and commonalities within civilizations. North African immigration to France generates hostility among Frenchmen and at the same time increased receptivity to immigration by "good" European Catholic Poles. Americans react far more negatively to Japanese investment than to larger investments from Canada and European countries. Similarly, as Donald Horowitz has pointed out, "An Ibo may be . . . an Owerri Ibo or an Onitsha Ibo in what was the Eastern region of Nigeria. In Lagos, he is simply an Ibo. In London, he is a Nigerian. In New York, he is an African." The interactions among peoples of different civilizations enhance the civilization-consciousness of people that, in turn, invigorates differences and animosities stretching or thought to stretch back deep into history.

Third, the processes of economic modernization and social change throughout the world are separating people from longstanding local identities. They also weaken the nation state as a source of identity. In much of the world religion has moved in to fill this gap, often in the form of movements that are labeled "fundamentalist." Such movements are found in Western Christianity, Judaism, Buddhism, and Hinduism, as well as in Islam. In most countries and most religions the people active in fundamentalist movements are young, college-educated, middle-class technicians, professionals, and business persons. The "unsecularization of the world," George Weigel has remarked, "is one of the dominant social facts of life in the late twentieth century." The revival of religion, "la revanche de Dieu," as Gilles Kepel labeled it, provides a basis for identity and commitment that transcends national boundaries and unites civilizations.

Fourth, the growth of civilization-consciousness is enhanced by the dual role of the West. On the one hand, the West is at a peak of power. At the same time, however, and perhaps as a result, a return to the roots phenomenon is occurring among non-Western civilizations. Increasingly one hears references to trends toward a turning inward and "Asianization" in Japan, the end of the Nehru legacy and the "Hinduization" of India, the failure of Western ideas of socialism and nationalism and hence "re-Islamization" of the Middle East, and now a debate over Westernization versus Russianization in Boris Yeltsin's country. A West at the peak of its power confronts non-Wests that increasingly have the desire, the will, and the resources to shape the world in non-Western ways.

In the past, the elites of non-Western societies were usually the people who were most involved with the West, had been educated at Oxford, the Sorbonne or Sandhurst, and had absorbed Western attitudes and values. At the same time, the populace in non-Western countries often remained deeply imbued with the indigenous culture. Now, however, these relationships are being reversed. A de-Westernization and indigenization of elites is occurring in many non-Western countries at the same time that Western, usually American, cultures, styles, and habits become more popular among the mass of the people.

Fifth, cultural characteristics and differences are less mutable and hence less easily compromised and resolved than political and economic ones. In the former Soviet Union, communists can become democrats, the rich can become poor and the poor rich, but Russians cannot become Estonians and Azeris cannot become Armenians. In class and ideological conflicts, the key question was "Which side are you on?" and people could and did choose sides and change sides. In conflicts between civilizations, the question is "What are you?" That is a given that cannot be changed. And as we know, from Bosnia to the Caucasus to the Sudan, the wrong answer to that question can mean a bullet in the head. Even more than ethnicity, religion discriminates sharply and exclusively among people. A person can be half-French and half-Arab and simultaneously even a citizen of two countries. It is more difficult to be half-Catholic and half-Muslim.

Finally, economic regionalism is increasing. The proportions of total trade that were intraregional rose between 1980 and 1989 from 51 percent to 59 percent in Europe, 33 percent to 37 percent in East Asia, and 32 percent to 36 percent in North America. The importance of regional economic blocs is likely to continue to increase in the future. On the one hand, successful economic regionalism will reinforce civilization-consciousness. On the other hand, economic regionalism may succeed only when it is rooted in a common civilization. The European Community rests on the shared foundation of European culture and Western Christianity. The success of the North American Free Trade Area depends on the convergence now underway of Mexican, Canadian, and American cultures. Japan, in contrast, faces difficulties in creating a comparable economic entity in East Asia because Japan is a society and civilization unique to itself. However strong the trade and investment links Japan may develop with other East Asian countries, its cultural differences with those countries inhibit and perhaps preclude its promoting regional economic integration like that in Europe and North America.

Common culture, in contrast, is clearly facilitating the rapid expansion of the economic relations between the People's Republic of China and Hong Kong, Taiwan, Singapore, and the overseas Chinese communities in other Asian countries. With the Cold War over, cultural commonalities increasingly overcome ideological differences, and mainland China and Taiwan move closer together. If cultural commonality is a prerequisite for economic integration, the principal East Asian economic bloc of the future is likely to be centered on China. This bloc is, in fact, already coming into existence. As Murray Weidenbaum has observed,

> Despite the current Japanese dominance of the region, the Chinese-based economy of Asia is rapidly emerging as a new epicenter for industry, commerce and finance. This strategic area contains substantial amounts of technology and manufacturing capability (Taiwan), outstanding entrepreneurial, marketing and services acumen (Hong Kong), a fine communications network (Singapore), a tremendous pool of financial capital (all three), and very large endowments of land, resources and labor (mainland China). . . . From Guangzhou to Singapore, from Kuala Lumpur to Manila, this influential network—often based on extensions of the traditional clans—has been described as the backbone of the East Asian economy.[1]

Culture and religion also form the basis of the Economic Cooperation Organization, which brings together ten non-Arab Muslim countries: Iran, Pakistan, Turkey, Azerbaijan, Kazakhstan, Kyrgyzstan, Turkmenistan, Tadjikistan, Uzbekistan, and Afghanistan. One impetus to the revival and expansion of this organization, founded originally in the 1960s by Turkey, Pakistan, and Iran, is the realization by the leaders of several of these countries that they had no chance of admission to the European Community. Similarly, Caricom, the Central American Common Market and Mercosur rest on common cultural foundations. Efforts to build a broader Caribbean-American economic entity bridging the Anglo-Latin divide, however, have to date failed.

As people define their identity in ethnic and religious terms, they are likely to see an "us" versus "them" relation existing between themselves and people of different ethnicity or religion. The end of ideologically defined states in Eastern Europe and the former Soviet Union permits traditional ethnic identities and animosities to come to the fore. Differences in culture and religion create differences over policy issues, ranging from human rights to immigration to trade and commerce to the environment. Geographical propinquity gives rise to conflicting territorial claims from Bosnia to Mindanao. Most important, the efforts of the West to promote its values of democracy and liberalism as universal values, to maintain its military predominance, and to advance its economic interests engender countering responses from other civilizations. Decreasingly able to mobilize support and form coalitions on the basis of ideology, governments and groups will increasingly attempt to mobilize support by appealing to common religion and civilization identity.

The clash of civilizations thus occurs at two levels. At the micro-level, adjacent groups along the fault lines between civilizations struggle, often violently, over the control of territory and each other. At the macro-level, states from different civilizations compete for relative military and economic power, struggle over the control of international institutions and third parties, and competitively promote their particular political and religious values.

THE FAULT LINES BETWEEN CIVILIZATIONS

The fault lines between civilizations are replacing the political and ideological boundaries of the Cold War as the flash points for crisis and bloodshed. The Cold War began when the Iron Curtain divided Europe politically and ideologically; The Cold War ended with the end of the Iron Curtain. As the ideological division of Europe has disappeared, the cultural division of Europe between Western Christianity, on the one hand, and Orthodox Christianity and Islam, on the other, has reemerged. The most significant dividing line in Europe, as William Wallace has suggested, may well be the eastern boundary of Western Christianity in the year 1500. This line runs along what are now the boundaries between Finland and Russia and between the Baltic states and Russia, cuts through Belarus and Ukraine separating the more Catholic western Ukraine from Orthodox eastern Ukraine, swings westward separating Transylvania from the rest of Romania, and then goes through Yugoslavia almost exactly along the line now separating Croatia and Slovenia from the rest of Yugoslavia. In the Balkans this line, of course, coincides with the historic boundary between the Hapsburg and Ottoman empires. The peoples to the north and west of this line are Protestant or Catholic; they shared the common experiences of European history—feudalism, the Renaissance, the Reformation, the Enlightenment, the French Revolution, the Industrial Revolution; they are generally economically better off than the peoples to the east; and they may now look forward to increasing involvement in a common European economy and to the consolidation of democratic political systems. The peoples to the east and south of this line are Orthodox or Muslim; they historically belonged to the Ottoman or Tsarist empires and were only lightly touched by the shaping events in the rest of Europe; they are generally less advanced economically; they seem much less likely to develop stable democratic political systems. The Velvet Curtain of culture has replaced the Iron Curtain of ideology as the most significant dividing line in Europe. As the events in Yugoslavia show, it is not only a line of difference; it is also at times a line of bloody conflict.

Conflict along the fault line between Western and Islamic civilizations has been going on for 1,300 years. After the founding of Islam, the Arab and Moorish surge west and north only ended at Tours in 732. From the eleventh to the thirteenth century the Crusaders attempted with temporary success to bring Christianity and Christian rule to the Holy Land. From the fourteenth to the seventeenth century, the Ottoman Turks reversed the balance, extended their sway over the Middle East and the Balkans, captured Constantinople, and twice laid siege to Vienna. In the nineteenth and early twentieth centuries as Ottoman power declined, Britain, France, and Italy established Western control over most of North Africa and the Middle East.

After World War II, the West, in turn, began to retreat; the colonial empires disappeared; first Arab nationalism and then Islamic fundamentalism manifested themselves; the West became heavily dependent on the Persian Gulf countries for its energy; the oil-rich Muslim countries became money-rich and, when they wished to, weapons-rich. Several wars occurred between Arabs and Israel (created by the West). France fought a bloody and ruthless war in Algeria for most of the 1950s; British and French forces invaded Egypt in 1956; American forces went into Lebanon in 1958; subsequently American forces returned to Lebanon, attacked Libya, and engaged in various military encounters with Iran; Arab and Islamic terrorists, supported by at least three Middle Eastern governments, employed the weapon of the weak and bombed Western planes and installations and seized Western hostages. This warfare between Arabs and the West culminated in 1990, when the United States sent a massive army to the Persian Gulf to defend some Arab countries against aggression by another. In its aftermath NATO planning is increasingly directed to potential threats and instability along its "southern tier."

This centuries-old military interaction between the West and Islam is unlikely to decline. It could become more virulent. The Gulf War left some Arabs feeling proud that Saddam Hussein had attacked Israel and stood up to the West. It also left many feeling humiliated and resentful of the West's military presence in the Persian Gulf, the West's overwhelming military dominance, and their apparent inability to shape their own destiny. Many Arab countries, in addition to the oil exporters, are reaching levels of economic and social development where autocratic forms of government become inappropriate and efforts to introduce democracy become stronger. Some openings in Arab political systems have already occurred. The principal beneficiaries of these openings have been Islamist movements. In the Arab world, in short, Western democracy strengthens anti-Western political forces. This may be a passing phenomenon, but it surely complicates relations between Islamic countries and the West.

Those relations are also complicated by demography. The spectacular population growth in Arab countries, particularly in North Africa, has led to increased migration to Western Europe. The movement within Western Europe toward minimizing internal boundaries has sharpened political sensitivities with respect to this development. In Italy, France, and Germany, racism is increasingly open, and political reactions and violence against Arab and Turkish migrants have become more intense and more widespread since 1990. On both sides the interaction between Islam and the West is seen as a clash of civilizations. The West's "next confrontation," observes M.J. Akbar, an Indian Muslim author, "is definitely going to come from the Muslim world. It is in the sweep of the Islamic nations from the Maghreb to Pakistan that the struggle for a new world order will begin." Bernard Lewis comes to a similar conclusion:

> We are facing a mood and a movement far transcending the level of issues and policies and the governments that pursue them. This is no less than a clash of civilizations—the perhaps irrational but surely historic reaction of an ancient rival against our Judeo-Christian heritage, our secular present, and the worldwide expansion of both.[2]

Historically, the other great antagonistic interaction of Arab Islamic civilization has been with the pagan, animist, and now increasingly Christian black peoples to the south. In the past, this antagonism was epitomized in the image of Arab slave dealers and black slaves. It has been reflected in the on-going civil war in the Sudan between Arabs and blacks, the fighting in Chad between Libyan-supported insurgents and the government, the tensions between Orthodox Christians and Muslims in the Horn of Africa, and the political conflicts, recurring riots, and communal violence between Muslims and Christians in Nigeria. The modernization of Africa and the spread of Christianity are likely to enhance the probability of violence along this fault line. Symptomatic of the intensification of this conflict was Pope John Paul II's speech in Khartoum in February 1993 attacking the actions of the Sudan's Islamist government against the Christian minority there.

On the northern border of Islam, conflict has increasingly erupted between Orthodox and Muslim peoples, including the carnage of Bosnia and Sarajevo, the simmering violence between Serb and Albanian, the tenuous relations between Bulgarians and their Turkish minority, the violence between Ossetians and Ingush, the unremitting slaughter of each other by Armenians and Azeris, the tense relations between Russians and Muslims in Central Asia, and the deployment of Russian troops to protect Russian interests in the Caucasus and Central Asia.

Religion reinforces the revival of ethnic identities and restimulates Russian fears about the security of their southern borders. This concern is well captured by Archie Roosevelt:

> Much of Russian history concerns the struggle between the Slavs and the Turkic peoples on their borders, which dates back to the foundation of the Russian state more than a thousand years ago. In the Slavs' millennium-long confrontation with their eastern neighbors lies the key to an understanding not only of Russian history, but Russian character. To understand Russian realities today one has to have a concept of the great Turkic ethnic group that has preoccupied Russians through the centuries.[3]

The conflict of civilizations is deeply rooted elsewhere in Asia. The historic clash between Muslim and Hindu in the subcontinent manifests itself now not only in the rivalry between Pakistan and India but also in intensifying religious strife within India between increasingly militant Hindu groups and India's substantial Muslim minority. The destruction of the Ayodhya mosque in December 1992 brought to the fore the issue of whether India will remain a secular democratic state or become a Hindu one. In East Asia, China has outstanding territorial disputes with most of its neighbors. It has pursued a ruthless policy toward the Buddhist people of Tibet, and it is pursuing an increasingly ruthless policy toward its Turkic-Muslim minority. With the Cold War over, the underlying differences between China and the United States have reasserted themselves in areas such as human rights, trade, and weapons proliferation. These differences are unlikely to moderate. A "new cold war," Deng Xaioping reportedly asserted in 1991, is under way between China and America.

The same phrase has been applied to the increasingly difficult relations between Japan and the United States. Here cultural difference exacerbates economic conflict. People on each side allege racism on the other, but at least on the American side the antipathies are not racial but cultural. The basic values, attitudes, and behavioral patterns of the two societies could hardly be more different. The economic issues between the United States and Europe are no less serious than those between the United States and Japan, but they do not have the same political salience and emotional intensity because the differences between American culture and European culture are so much less than those between American civilization and Japanese civilization.

The interactions between civilizations vary greatly in the extent to which they are likely to be characterized by violence. Economic competition clearly predominates between the American and European subcivilizations of the West and between both of them and Japan. On the Eurasian continent, however, the proliferation of ethnic conflict, epitomized at the extreme in "ethnic cleansing," has not been totally random. It has been most frequent and most violent between groups belonging to different civilizations. In Eurasia the great historic fault lines between civilizations are once more aflame. This is particularly true along the boundaries of the crescent-shaped Islamic bloc of nations from the bulge of Africa to central Asia. Violence also occurs between Muslims, on the one hand, and Orthodox Serbs in the Balkans, Jews in Israel, Hindus in India, Buddhists in Burma, and Catholics in the Philippines. Islam has bloody borders.

CIVILIZATION RALLYING: THE KIN-COUNTRY SYNDROME

Groups or states belonging to one civilization that becomes involved in war with people from a different civilization naturally try to rally support from other members of their own civilization. As the post–Cold War world evolves, civilization commonality, what H.D.S. Greenway has termed the "kin-country" syndrome, is replacing political ideology and traditional balance of power considerations as the principal basis for cooperation and coalitions. It can be seen gradually emerging in the post–Cold War conflicts in the Persian Gulf, the Caucasus, and Bosnia. None of these was a full-scale war between civilizations, but each involved some elements of civilizational rallying, which seemed to become more important as the conflict continued and which may provide a foretaste of the future.

First, in the Gulf War one Arab state invaded another and then fought a coalition of Arab, Western, and other states. While only a few Muslim governments overtly supported Saddam Hussein, many Arab elites privately cheered him on, and he was highly popular among large sections of the Arab publics. Islamic fundamentalist movements universally supported Iraq rather than the Western-backed governments of Kuwait and Saudi Arabia. Forswearing Arab nationalism, Saddam Hussein explicitly invoked an Islamic appeal. He and his supporters attempted to define the war as a war between civilizations. "It is not the world against Iraq," as Safar Al-Hawaii, dean of Islamic Studies at the Umm Al-Qura University in Mecca, put it in a widely circulated tape. "It is the West against Islam." Ignoring the rivalry between Iran and Iraq, the chief Iranian religious leader, Ayatollah Ali Khamenei, called for a holy war against the West: "The struggle against American aggression, greed, plans and policies will be counted as a jihad, and anybody who is killed on that path is a martyr." "This is a war," King Hussein of Jordan argued, "against all Arabs and all Muslims and not against Iraq alone."

The rallying of substantial sections of Arab elites and publics behind Saddam Hussein caused those Arab governments in the anti-Iraq coalition to moderate their activities and temper their public statements. Arab governments opposed or distanced themselves from subsequent Western efforts to apply pressure on Iraq, including enforcement of a no-fly zone in the summer of 1992 and the bombing of Iraq in January 1993. The Western-Soviet-Turkish-Arab anti-Iraq coalition of 1990 had by 1993 become a coalition of almost only the West and Kuwait against Iraq.

Muslims contrasted Western actions against Iraq with the West's failure to protect Bosnians against Serbs and to impose sanctions on Israel for violating U.N. resolutions. The West, they alleged, was using a double standard. A world of clashing civilizations, however, is inevitably a world of double standards: people apply one standard to their kin-countries and a different standard to others.

Second, the kin-country syndrome also appeared in conflicts in the former Soviet Union. Armenian military successes in 1992 and 1993 stimulated Turkey to become increasingly supportive of its religious, ethnic, and linguistic brethren in Azerbaijan. "We have a Turkish nation feeling the same sentiments as the Azerbaijanis," said one Turkish official in 1992. "We are under pressure. Our newspapers are full of the photos of atrocities and are asking us if we are still serious about pursuing our neutral policy. Maybe we should show Armenia that there's a big Turkey in the region." President Turgut Ozal agreed, remarking that Turkey should at least "scare the Armenians a little bit." Turkey, Ozal threatened again in 1993, would "show its fangs." Turkish Air Force jets flew reconnaissance flights along the Armenian border; Turkey suspended food shipments and air flights to Armenia; and Turkey and Iran announced they would not accept dismemberment of Azerbaijan. In the last years of its existence, the Soviet government supported Azerbaijan because its government was dominated by former communists. With the end of the Soviet Union, however, political considerations gave way to religious ones. Russian troops fought on the side of the Armenians, and Azerbaijan accused the "Russian government of turning 180 degrees" toward support for Christian Armenia.

Third, with respect to the fighting in the former Yugoslavia, Western publics manifested sympathy and support for the Bosnian Muslims and the horrors they suffered at the hands of the Serbs. Relatively little concern was expressed, however, over Croatian attacks on Muslims and participation in the dismemberment of Bosnia-Herzegovina. In the early stages of the Yugoslav breakup, Germany, in an unusual display of diplomatic initiative and muscle, induced the other 11 members of the European Community to follow its lead in recognizing Slovenia and Croatia. As a result of the Pope's determination to provide strong backing to the two Catholic countries, the Vatican extended recognition even before the Community did. The United States followed the European lead. Thus the leading actors in Western civilization rallied behind their coreligionists. Subsequently Croatia was reported to be receiving substantial quantities of arms from Central European and other Western countries. Boris Yeltsin's government, on the other hand, attempted to pursue a middle course that would be sympathetic to the Orthodox Serbs but not alienate Russia from the West. Russian conservative and nationalist groups, however, including many legislators, attacked the government for not being more forthcoming in its support for the Serbs. By early 1993 several hundred Russians apparently were serving with the Serbian forces, and reports circulated of Russian arms being supplied to Serbia.

Islamic governments and groups, on the other hand, castigated the West for not coming to the defense of the Bosnians. Iranian leaders urged Muslims from all countries to provide help to Bosnia; in violation of the U.N. arms embargo, Iran supplied weapons and men for the Bosnians; Iranian-supported Lebanese groups sent guerrillas to train and organize the Bosnian forces. In 1993 up to 4,000 Muslims from over two dozen Islamic countries were reported to be fighting in Bosnia. The governments of Saudi Arabia and other countries felt under increasing pressure from fundamentalist groups in their own societies to provide more vigorous support for the Bosnians. By the end of 1992, Saudi Arabia had reportedly supplied substantial funding for weapons and supplies for the Bosnians, which significantly increased their military capabilities vis-à-vis the Serbs.

In the 1930s the Spanish Civil War provoked intervention from countries that politically were fascist, communist, and democratic. In the 1990s the Yugoslav conflict is provoking intervention from countries that are Muslim, Orthodox, and Western Christian. The parallel has not gone unnoticed. "The war in Bosnia-Herzegovina has become the emotional equivalent of the fight against fascism in the Spanish Civil War," one Saudi editor observed. "Those who died there are regarded as martyrs who tried to save their fellow Muslims."

Conflicts and violence will also occur between states and groups within the same civilization. Such conflicts, however, are likely to be less intense and less likely to expand than conflicts between civilizations. Common membership in a civilization reduces the probability of violence in situations where it might otherwise occur. In 1991 and 1992 many people were alarmed by the possibility of violent conflict between Russia and Ukraine over territory, particularly Crimea, the Black Sea fleet, nuclear weapons, and economic issues. If civilization is what counts, however, the likelihood of violence between Ukrainians and Russians should be low. They are two Slavic, primarily Orthodox peoples who have had close relationships with each other for centuries. As of early 1993, despite all the reasons for conflict, the leaders of the two countries were effectively negotiating and defusing the issues between the two countries. While there has been serious fighting between Muslims and Christians elsewhere in the former Soviet Union and much tension and some fighting between Western and Orthodox Christians in the Baltic states, there has been virtually no violence between Russians and Ukrainians.

Civilization rallying to date has been limited, but it has been growing, and it clearly has the potential to spread much further. As the conflicts in the Persian Gulf, the Caucasus and Bosnia continued, the positions of nations and the cleavages between them increasingly were along civilizational lines. Populist politicians, religious leaders, and the media have found it a potent means of arousing mass support and of pressuring hesitant governments. In the coming years, the local conflicts most likely to escalate into major wars will be those, as in Bosnia and the Caucasus, along the fault lines between civilizations. The next world war, if there is one, will be a war between civilizations.

THE WEST VERSUS THE REST

The West is now at an extraordinary peak of power in relation to other civilizations. Its superpower opponent has disappeared from the map. Military conflict among Western states is unthinkable, and Western military power is unrivaled. Apart from Japan, the West faces no economic challenge. It dominates international political and security institutions and with Japan international economic institutions. Global political and security issues are effectively settled by a directorate of the United States, Britain, and France, world economic issues by a directorate of the United States, Germany, and Japan, all of which maintain extraordinarily close relations with each other to the exclusion of lesser and largely non-Western countries. Decisions made at the U.N. Security Council or in the International Monetary Fund that reflect the interests of the West are presented to the world as reflecting the desires of the world community. The very phrase "the world community" has become the euphemistic collective noun (replacing "the Free World") to give global legitimacy to actions reflecting the interests of the United States and other Western powers.[4] Through the IMF and other international economic institutions, the West promotes its economic interests and imposes on other nations the economic policies it thinks appropriate. In any poll of non-Western peoples, the IMF undoubtedly would win the support of finance ministers and a few others, but get an overwhelmingly unfavorable rating from just about everyone else, who would agree with Georgy Arbatov's characterization of IMF officials as "neo-Bolsheviks who love expropriating other people's money, imposing undemocratic and alien rules of economic and political conduct and stifling economic freedom."

Western domination of the U.N. Security Council and its decisions, tempered only by occasional abstention by China, produced U.N. legitimation of the West's use of force to drive Iraq out of Kuwait and its elimination of Iraq's sophisticated weapons and capacity to produce such weapons. It also produced the quite unprecedented action by the United States, Britain, and France in getting the Security Council to demand that Libya hand over the Pan Am 103 bombing suspects and then to impose sanctions when Libya refused. After defeating the largest Arab army, the West did not hesitate to throw its weight around in the Arab world. The West in effect is using international institutions, military power, and economic resources to run the world in ways that will maintain Western predominance, protect Western interests, and promote Western political and economic values.

That at least is the way in which non-Westerners see the new world, and there is a significant element of truth in their view. Differences in power and struggles for military, economic, and institutional power are thus one source of conflict between the West and other civilizations. Differences in culture, that is basic values and beliefs, are a second source of conflict. V.S. Naipaul has argued that Western civilization is the "universal civilization" that "fits all men." At a superficial level much of Western culture has indeed permeated the rest of the world. At a more basic level, however, Western concepts differ fundamentally from those prevalent in other civilizations. Western ideas of individualism, liberalism, con-stitutionalism, human rights, equality, liberty, the rule of law, democracy, free markets, the separation of church and state, often have little resonance in Islamic, Confucian, Japanese, Hindu, Buddhist, or Orthodox cultures. Western efforts to propagate such ideas produce instead a reaction against "human rights imperi-alism" and a reaffirmation of indigenous values, as can be seen in the support for religious fundamentalism by the younger generation in non-Western cultures. The very notion that there could be a "universal civilization" is a Western idea, directly at odds with the particularism of most Asian societies and their emphasis on what distinguishes one people from another. Indeed, the author of a review of 100 comparative studies of values in different societies concluded that "the values that are most important in the West are least important worldwide."[5] In the polit-ical realm, of course, these differences are most manifest in the efforts of the United States and other Western powers to induce other peoples to adopt Western ideas concerning democracy and human rights. Modern democratic government originated in the West. When it has developed in non-Western societies it has usually been the product of Western colonialism or imposition.

The central axis of world politics in the future is likely to be, in Kishore Mahbubani's phrase, the conflict between "the West and the Rest" and the responses of non-Western civilizations to Western power and values.[6] Those responses gen-erally take one or a combination of three forms. At one extreme, non-Western states can, like Burma and North Korea, attempt to pursue a course of isolation, to insulate their societies from penetration or "corruption" by the West, and, in effect, to opt out of participation in the Western-dominated global community. The costs of this course, however, are high, and few states have pursued it exclu-sively. A second alternative, the equivalent of "bandwagoning" in international relations theory, is to attempt to join the West and accept its values and institu-tions. The third alternative is to attempt to "balance" the West by developing eco-nomic and military power and cooperating with other non-Western societies against the West, while preserving indigenous values and institutions; in short, to modernize but not to Westernize.

THE TORN COUNTRIES

In the future, as people differentiate themselves by civilization, countries with large numbers of peoples of different civilizations, such as the Soviet Union and Yugoslavia, are candidates for dismemberment. Some other countries have a fair degree of cultural homogeneity but are divided over whether their society belongs to one civilization or another. These are torn countries. Their leaders typically wish to pursue a bandwagoning strategy and to make their countries members of the West, but the history, culture, and traditions of their countries are non-Western. The most obvious and prototypical torn country is Turkey. The late-twentieth-century leaders of Turkey have followed in the Attaturk tradition and defined Turkey as a modern, secular, Western nation state. They allied Turkey with the West in NATO and in the Gulf War; they applied for membership in the European Community. At the same time, however, elements in Turkish society have supported an Islamic revival and have argued that Turkey is basically a Middle Eastern Muslim society. In addition, while the elite of Turkey has defined Turkey as a Western society, the elite of the West refuses to accept Turkey as such. Turkey will not become a member of the European Community, and the real reason, as President Ozal said, "is that we are Muslim and they are Christian and they don't say that." Having rejected Mecca, and then being rejected by Brussels, where does Turkey look? Tashkent may be the answer. The end of the Soviet Union gives Turkey the opportunity to become the leader of a revived Turkic civilization involving seven countries from the borders of Greece to those of China. Encouraged by the West, Turkey is making strenuous efforts to carve out this new identity for itself.

During the past decade Mexico has assumed a position somewhat similar to that of Turkey. Just as Turkey abandoned its historic opposition to Europe and attempted to join Europe, Mexico has stopped defining itself by its opposition to the United States and is instead attempting to imitate the United States and to join it in the North American Free Trade Area. Mexican leaders are engaged in the great task of redefining Mexican identity and have introduced fundamental economic reforms that eventually will lead to fundamental political change. In 1991 a top adviser to President Carlos Salinas de Gortari described at length to me all the changes the Salinas government was making. When he finished, I remarked: "That's most impressive. It seems to me that basically you want to change Mexico from a Latin American country into a North American country." He looked at me with surprise and exclaimed: "Exactly! That's precisely what we are trying to do, but of course we could never say so publicly." As his remark indicates, in Mexico as in Turkey, significant elements in society resist the redefinition of their country's identity. In Turkey, European-oriented leaders have to make gestures to Islam (Ozal's pilgrimage to Mecca); so also Mexico's North American–oriented leaders have to make gestures to those who hold Mexico to be a Latin American country (Salinas's Ibero-American Guadalajara summit).

Historically Turkey has been the most profoundly torn country. For the United States, Mexico is the most immediate torn country. Globally the most important torn country is Russia. The question of whether Russia is part of the West or the leader of a distinct Slavic-Orthodox civilization has been a recurring one in Russian history. That issue was obscured by the communist victory in Russia, which imported a Western ideology, adapted it to Russian conditions, and then challenged the West in the name of that ideology. The dominance of communism shut off the historic debate over Westernization versus Russification. With communism discredited, Russians once again face that question.

President Yeltsin is adopting Western principles and goals and seeking to make Russia a "normal" country and a part of the West. Yet both the Russian elite and the Russian public are divided on this issue. Among the more moderate dissenters,

Sergei Stankevich argues that Russia should reject the "Atlanticist" course, which would lead it "to become European, to become a part of the world economy in rapid and organized fashion, to become the eighth member of the Seven, and to put particular emphasis on Germany and the United States as the two dominant members of the Atlantic alliance." While also rejecting an exclusively Eurasian policy, Stankevich nonetheless argues that Russia should give priority to the protection of Russians in other countries, emphasize its Turkic and Muslim connections, and promote "an appreciable redistribution of our resources, our options, our ties, and our interests in favor of Asia, of the eastern direction." People of this persuasion criticize Yeltsin for subordinating Russia's interests to those of the West, for reducing Russian military strength, for failing to support traditional friends such as Serbia, and for pushing economic and political reform in ways injurious to the Russian people. Indicative of this trend is the new popularity of the ideas of Petr Savitsky, who in the 1920s argued that Russia was a unique Eurasian civilization.[7] More extreme dissidents voice much more blatantly nationalist, anti-Western, and anti-Semitic views, and urge Russia to redevelop its military strength and to establish closer ties with China and Muslim countries. The people of Russia are as divided as the elite. An opinion survey in European Russia in the spring of 1992 revealed that 40 percent of the public had positive attitudes toward the West and 36 percent had negative attitudes. As it has been for much of its history, Russia in the early 1990s is truly a torn country.

To redefine its civilization identity, a torn country must meet three requirements. First, its political and economic elite has to be generally supportive of and enthusiastic about this move. Second, its public has to be willing to acquiesce in the redefinition. Third, the dominant groups in the recipient civilization have to be willing to embrace the convert. All three requirements in large part exist with respect to Mexico. The first two in large part exist with respect to Turkey. It is not clear that any of them exist with respect to Russia's joining the West. The conflict between liberal democracy and Marxism-Leninism was between ideologies which, despite their major differences, ostensibly shared ultimate goals of freedom, equality, and prosperity. A traditional, authoritarian, nationalist Russia could have quite different goals. A Western democrat could carry on an intellectual debate with a Soviet Marxist. It would be virtually impossible for him to do that with a Russian traditionalist. If, as the Russians stop behaving like Marxists, they reject liberal democracy and begin behaving like Russians but not like Westerners, the relations between Russia and the West could again become distant and conflictual.[8]

THE CONFUCIAN–ISLAMIC CONNECTION

The obstacles to non-Western countries joining the West vary considerably. They are least for Latin American and East European countries. They are greater for the Orthodox countries of the former Soviet Union. They are still greater for Muslim, Confucian, Hindu, and Buddhist societies. Japan has established a unique position for itself as an associate member of the West: it is in the West in some respects but clearly not of the West in important dimensions. Those countries that for reasons of culture and power do not wish to, or cannot, join the West compete with the West by developing their own economic, military, and political power. They do this by promoting their internal development and by cooperating with other non-Western countries. The most prominent form of this cooperation is the Confucian–Islamic connection that has emerged to challenge Western interests, values, and power.

Almost without exception, Western countries are reducing their military power; under Yeltsin's leadership so also is Russia. China, North Korea, and several Middle Eastern states, however, are significantly expanding their military capabilities. They are doing this by the import of arms from Western and non-Western sources and by the development of indigenous arms industries. One result is the emergence of what Charles Krauthammer has called "Weapon States," and the Weapon States are not Western states. Another result is the redefinition of arms control, which is a Western concept and a Western goal. During the Cold War the primary purpose of arms control was to establish a stable military balance between the United States and its allies and the Soviet Union and its allies. In the post–Cold War world the primary objective of arms control is to prevent the development by non-Western societies of military capabilities that could threaten Western interests. The West attempts to do this through international agreements, economic pressure, and controls on the transfer of arms and weapons technologies.

The conflict between the West and the Confucian–Islamic states focuses largely, although not exclusively, on nuclear, chemical, and biological weapons, ballistic missiles and other sophisticated means for delivering them, and the guidance, intelligence, and other electronic capabilities for achieving that goal. The West promotes nonproliferation as a universal norm and nonproliferation treaties and inspections as means of realizing that norm. It also threatens a variety of sanctions against those who promote the spread of sophisticated weapons and proposes some benefits for those who do not. The attention of the West focuses, naturally, on nations that are actually or potentially hostile to the West.

The non-Western nations, on the other hand, assert their right to acquire and to deploy whatever weapons they think necessary for their security. They also have absorbed, to the full, the truth of the response of the Indian defense minister when asked what lesson he learned from the Gulf War: "Don't fight the United States unless you have nuclear weapons." Nuclear weapons, chemical weapons, and missiles are viewed, probably erroneously, as the potential equalizer of superior Western conventional power. China, of course, already has nuclear weapons; Pakistan and India have the capability to deploy them. North Korea, Iran, Iraq, Libya, and Algeria appear to be attempting to acquire them. A top Iranian official has declared that all Muslim states should acquire nuclear weapons, and in 1988 the president of Iran reportedly issued a directive calling for development of "offensive and defensive chemical, biological and radiological weapons."

Centrally important to the development of counter-West military capabilities is the sustained expansion of China's military power and its means to create military power. Buoyed by spectacular economic development, China is rapidly increasing its military spending and vigorously moving forward with the modernization of its armed forces. It is purchasing weapons from the former Soviet states; it is developing long-range missiles; in 1992 it tested a one-megaton nuclear device. It is developing power-projection capabilities, acquiring aerial refueling technology, and trying to purchase an aircraft carrier. Its military buildup and assertion of sovereignty over the South China Sea are provoking a multilateral regional arms race in East Asia. China is also a major exporter of arms and weapons technology. It has exported materials to Libya and Iraq that could be used to manufacture nuclear weapons and nerve gas. It has helped Algeria build a reactor suitable for nuclear weapons research and production. China has sold to Iran nuclear technology that American officials believe could only be used to create weapons and apparently has shipped components of 300 mile-range missiles to Pakistan. North Korea has had a nuclear weapons program under way for some while and has sold advanced missiles and missile technology to Syria and Iran. The flow of weapons and weapons technology is generally from East Asia to the Middle East. There is, however, some movement in the reverse direction; China has received Stinger missiles from Pakistan.

A Confucian–Islamic military connection has thus come into being, designed to promote acquisition by its members of the weapons and weapons technologies needed to counter the military power of the West. It may or may not last. At present, however, it is, as Dave McCurdy has said, "a renegades' mutual support pact, run by the proliferators and their backers." A new form of arms competition is thus occurring between Islamic–Confucian states and the West. In an old-fashioned arms race, each side developed its own arms to balance or to achieve superiority against the other side. In this new form of arms competition, one side is developing its arms and the other side is attempting not to balance but to limit and prevent that arms build-up while at the same time reducing its own military capabilities.

IMPLICATIONS FOR THE WEST

This article does not argue that civilization identities will replace all other identities, that nation states will disappear, that each civilization will become a single coherent political entity, that groups within a civilization will not conflict with and even fight each other. This paper does set forth the hypotheses that differences between civilizations are real and important; civilization-consciousness is increasing; conflict between civilizations will supplant ideological and other forms of conflict as the dominant global form of conflict; international relations, historically a game played out within Western civilization, will increasingly be de-Westernized and become a game in which non-Western civilizations are actors and not simply objects; successful political, security, and economic international institutions are more likely to develop within civilizations than across civilizations; conflicts between groups in different civilizations will be more frequent, more sustained, and more violent than conflicts between groups in the same civilization; violent conflicts between groups in different civilizations are the most likely and most dangerous source of escalation that could lead to global wars; the paramount axis of world politics will be the relations between "the West and the Rest"; the elites in some torn non-Western countries will try to make their countries part of the West, but in most cases face major obstacles to accomplishing this; a central focus of conflict for the immediate future will be between the West and several Islamic–Confucian states.

This is not to advocate the desirability of conflicts between civilizations. It is to set forth descriptive hypotheses as to what the future may be like. If these are plausible hypotheses, however, it is necessary to consider their implications for Western policy. These implications should be divided between short-term advantage and long-term accommodation. In the short term it is clearly in the interest of the West to promote greater cooperation and unity within its own civilization, particularly between its European and North American components; to incorporate into the West societies in Eastern Europe and Latin America whose cultures are close to those of the West; to promote and maintain cooperative relations with Russia and Japan; to prevent escalation of local inter-civilization conflicts into major inter-civilization wars; to limit the expansion of the military strength of Confucian and Islamic states; to moderate the reduction of Western military capabilities and maintain military superiority in East and Southwest Asia; to exploit differences and conflicts among Confucian and Islamic states; to support in other civilizations groups sympathetic to Western values and interests; to strengthen international institutions that reflect and legitimate Western interests and values and to promote the involvement of non-Western states in those institutions.

In the longer term other measures would be called for. Western civilization is both Western and modern. Non-Western civilizations have attempted to become modern without becoming Western. To date only Japan has fully succeeded in this quest. Non-Western civilizations will continue to attempt to acquire the wealth, technology, skills, machines, and weapons that are part of being modern. They will also attempt to reconcile this modernity with their traditional culture and values. Their economic and military strength relative to the West will increase. Hence the West will increasingly have to accommodate these non-Western modern civilizations whose power approaches that of the West but whose values and interests differ significantly from those of the West. This will require the West to maintain the economic and military power necessary to protect its interests in relation to these civilizations. It will also, however, require the West to develop a more profound understanding of the basic religious and philosophical assumptions underlying other civilizations and the ways in which people in those civilizations see their interests. It will require an effort to identify elements of commonality between Western and other civilizations. For the relevant future, there will be no universal civilization, but instead a world of different civilizations, each of which will have to learn to coexist with the others.

NOTES

1. Murray Weidenbaum, *Greater China: The Next Economic Superpower?* St. Louis: Washington University Center for the Study of American Business, Contemporary Issues, Series 57, February 1993, pp. 2–3.

2. Bernard Lewis, "The Roots of Muslim Rage," *The Atlantic Monthly*, vol. 266, September 1990, p. 60; *Time*, June 15, 1992, pp. 24–28.

3. Archie Roosevelt, *For Lust of Knowing*. Boston: Little, Brown, 1988, pp. 332–33.

4. Almost invariably Western leaders claim they are acting on behalf of "the world community." One minor lapse occurred during the run-up to the Gulf War. In an interview on *Good Morning America*, Dec. 21, 1990, British Prime Minister John Major referred to the actions "the West" was taking against Saddam Hussein. He quickly corrected himself and subsequently referred to "the world community." He was, however, right when he erred.

5. Harry C. Triandis, *The New York Times*, Dec. 25, 1990, p. 41, and "Cross-Cultural Studies of Individualism and Collectivism," *Nebraska Symposium on Motivation*, vol. 37, 1989, pp. 41–133.

6. Kishore Mahbubani, "The West and the Rest," *The National Interest*, Summer 1992, pp. 3–13.

7. Sergei Stankevich, "Russia in Search of Itself," *The National Interest*, Summer 1992, pp. 47–51; Daniel Schneider, "A Russian Movement Rejects Western Tilt," *Christian Science Monitor*, Feb. 5, 1993, pp. 5–7.

8. Owen Harries has pointed out that Australia is trying (unwisely in his view) to become a torn country in reverse. Although it has been a full member not only of the West but also of the ABCA military and intelligence core of the West, its current leaders are in effect proposing that it defect from the West, redefine itself as an Asian country and cultivate close ties with its neighbors. Australia's future, they argue, is with the dynamic economies of East Asia. But, as I have suggested, close economic cooperation normally requires a common cultural base. In addition, none of the three conditions necessary for a torn country to join another civilization is likely to exist in Australia's case.

✗ NO

Ten Years After: The Inevitable Waning of Huntington's Civilizational Clash Theory?

DOUGLAS ALAN ROSS

The publication of Samuel Huntington's "clash of civilizations" hypothesis in 1993[1] generated a spirited debate about the plausibility and accuracy of his strategic "climate forecast" for the globe. Many critics from across the analytical spectrum leapt into the intellectual fray eager to criticize a paradigm that sympathetic observers thought might become the doctrinal successor to George Kennan's containment theory. Just as Kennan's 1947 "X" article had shaped American foreign policy thinking for most of the Cold War,[2] so too, some argued, might Huntington's cautionary warning concerning allegedly impending "fault line wars"—the only conflicts that he believed had the potential to spawn the next "world" war. Huntington's declaration that there was an urgent need to unify the Western countries against what soon might become an implacably hostile world as "the West" duelled with "the rest" was interpreted as a profoundly pessimistic (some said paranoid[3]) basis for the formulation of American foreign policy.

Over the ensuing decade, Huntington rejected such allegations, pointing out that many of his critics had failed to notice the question mark at the end of the title of his 1993 article. Where Kennan at the outset of the Cold War saw no alternative to the firm, patient, and active containment of an unremittingly hostile, authentically paranoid, opportunistically expansionist, and ideologically obsessed Soviet state, Huntington at least decreed that the cultural differences between various civilizations need not inevitably lead to war, nor even hostility and distrust. Major inter-civilizational war was a contingent risk, not a certainty. Cultural differences with the potential for catalyzing global war might possibly be managed, Huntington claimed, by civilizational "core states," who possessed a sensible disposition to compromise, a modicum of geopolitical self-restraint, and a political-diplomatic capacity to manage the bellicose impulses of their respective cultural satellites. So long as the leaders of the major civilizations respect a principle of non-interference in each others' cultural spheres of influence, so long as they act promptly to mediate jointly whenever fault line wars develop, and so long as they follow Lester Pearson's advice to promote mutual cultural understanding and learning, the avoidance of major wars is conceivable.[4] To the extent that such wisdom is absent in the twenty-first century, the risk of major inter-civilizational war will rise accordingly.

The body of this essay reviews the criticism that has been directed at Huntington's clash thesis since it first was published. It also provides some supplementary information about Huntington's views as they developed subsequent to the original article in both his 1996 book, titled *The Clash of Civilizations and the Remaking of World Order*, and several additional articles. Huntington's clash paradigm has evolved over the past eleven years, but the changes have been modest. His thinking has demonstrated remarkable consistency and internal coherence, and his pessimism about both global relations and, even more, the foolhardy risks taken by successive American administrations in trying to project American values onto unreceptive cultures and societies remains unaltered by the passage of time. Following the summary of a decade of critical responses to Huntington's thought, some concluding observations about Huntington's role as a strategic analyst are provided, and some additional criticism directed toward the clash thesis from a "grand strategy" perspective—a vantage point rarely heard in international security debates outside of the United States. In the words of one of his greatest admirers, Robert Kaplan, Samuel Huntington is "someone who combines liberal ideals with a deeply conservative understanding of history and foreign policy." Greatly influenced by Reinhold Niebuhr, Huntington shares a similar "tragic sensibility" that is embodied in all Niebuhr's thought, sensibility that "is the key to Huntington's definition of conservatism."[5]

The clash debate is unlikely to wane any time soon because Huntington is determined to continue to play the role of a responsible public intellectual warning against what he sincerely believes is the triumph of illogic, arrogance, and self-delusion in American foreign policy. Following the events of 11 September 2001, the overthrow of the Taliban regime in Afghanistan by American and NATO forces in 2002, and the invasion and occupation of Iraq by George W. Bush's "coalition of the willing" in March and April of 2003, Huntington's clash theory gained a new lease on life. In all probability, his writings have an even greater readership in 2004 than they did in the mid-1990s. Huntington somewhat coyly stated in 1996 that his clash writings were not meant to be taken as political science—without stating in precisely what category of analysis they should be placed. Clearly that field is strategy and international security studies, a domain that is far more "art" than "science." Notwithstanding this fact, it has generally been only analysts and social scientists in international relations who have taken up the challenge of debating the clash thesis. This is unfortunate.

In the words of one of Britain's foremost strategic thinkers, Colin Gray, strategy is "the use that is made of force and the threat of force for the ends of policy."[6] Huntington's work is at its core an exercise in threat analysis and national security policy planning—albeit in the very long term. As such, his work is most appropriately viewed within the debate on American "grand strategy," which may be defined as the formulation of feasible, long-term, security-enhancing political goals in conjunction with the coordination and management of national and allied resources and capabilities so as to promote the achievement of those goals.[7] Britain's greatest twentieth-century strategic analyst, Basil H. Liddell Hart, observed more than a half a century ago that "the realm of grand strategy is for the most part *terra incognita*—still awaiting exploration, and understanding."[8] Huntington sallied forth into that unknown country. The product of his threat analysis and strategic "climate" forecast is highly debatable and to be sure "unscientific" (as are all long-term threat forecasts), but to the extent that he has challenged Americans and others to engage in their own informed speculation about our common future, he has done the global academic community an important service. The third part of this essay comments on where his analysis may be correct and where he may be quite mistaken.

HUNTINGTON'S MANY CRITICS

Neoliberals attacked Huntington's pessimism because it implied a need for clear limits to global economic integration, if not a wholesale scaling back of American involvement in the world economy, so as to preserve American and Western scientific, technical, and economic advantages over rising civilizational competitors. A benign world congenial to ever-expanding trade and unimpeded flows of investment under the transcendent guidance of the multinational corporate managerialists was clearly a vision of the future in no way shared by Huntington, who at root is an unabashed American economic nationalist. For defenders of international corporate governance, the steady rise in incomes in many developing countries[9] has invariably produced pressure for some form of liberal democratic governance and enhanced personal freedom. Thus it is no surprise that authoritarian regimes have been everywhere in retreat since the early 1980s. To neoliberals in the business community and government, this suggests that the Western "model" of development may in fact be of near universal appeal—contrary to one of Huntington's central themes. With English spreading worldwide as the preferred language of trade and investment, with American popular culture spreading just as quickly (the twin engines of Barber's McWorld), and with global economic interdependence evolving quickly, assisted by the rapid spread of new information technologies to almost all countries, is it really plausible to suppose that deep antagonisms to the West will be felt in most of the other "civilizations"?[10] While not overtly protectionist in his call for setting national and Western alliance-wide limits to technology transfers to other rival civilizations, Huntington has implied unambiguously that the days of unfettered decisionmaking by the international corporate elite should end soon. For Huntington, the international corporate elite, including the now largely deracinated American corporate managers, has become a *de facto* alien threat to the citizenry of both the United States and other Western countries—in effect, "an emerging global superclass."[11] Most neoliberal analysts who might have detected such thinking in Huntington's various writings would therefore dismiss his increasingly explicit anti-elitist, anti-globalization critique as utterly antediluvian, nostalgic conservatism.

Constructivist writers in international relations were appalled to find that Huntington was claiming that "culture does matter," but that allegedly immutable cultural differences were deepening and setting the stage not for cooperation through a constructivist program founded on the willful rejection of the tenets of statist "realism," but rather for the potential stimulation of both intense intra-state and inter-civilizational conflict not seen since the European religious wars of the early seventeenth century or the crusades of the Middle Ages. For constructivist analysts in international relations, Huntington's clash model is a central challenge to their belief in the steady enhancement of transcultural communication and thus the rosy prospects for multicultural tolerance and growing international cooperation.[12] For postmodernist, postcolonial analysts such as the late Edward Said, Huntington's civilizational categories of analysis are grotesque, cartoon-like caricatures of what in fact are incredibly complex interwoven cultures where most individuals' identities are constantly reshaped.[13]

Early critiques also focused on Huntington's impressionistic but still expansive concept of civilizations and their allegedly new capacities for provoking war. In a comment that would be repeated subsequently by many other realist critics, Fouad Ajami expressed astonishment that any observer with Huntington's years of scholarly analysis of the role of the state could assert that these mysterious civilizational entities would soon displace states as the most important organizing force in the international system. States make wars, not civilizations, said Ajami, and they do so with an "unsentimental and cold-blooded nature."[14] A politically destabilizing "indigenization" or introversion of culture in India, China, and the Islamic world is extremely unlikely to happen, Ajami argued, because these societies already have been penetrated and transformed by "modernity and secularism." The strife of industrialization and modernization in countries such as Turkey, Algeria, Egypt, and Iran will only rarely produce theocratic rule. The forces representing religious repression and extremist anti-Western hysteria across the Islamic world are unlikely to broaden their appeal. The sensational press accounts of televisions being thrown from windows by angry mullahs, or nightclubs being attacked, or women being forced into Taliban-style, burka-bound subjugation will remain the exception. Much of the highly differentiated Islamic world has already undergone dramatic modernization, especially the Gulf states and the Muslim countries of Southeast Asia. While the sensationalist press may give undue attention to religious reactionaries and extremists (what Said saw as the equivalent of the Branch Davidians or Aum Shinrikyo), they are in fact symptomatic of "panic and bewilderment and guilt that the border with 'the other' has been crossed."[15] Ajami added, "it is hard to think of Russia, ravaged as it is by inflation, taking up the grand cause of a 'second Byzantium,' the bearer of the orthodox-Slavic torch."[16] And India's leaders will not jeopardize their country's attainment of great power status by a detour into the past; Bollywood and continued market liberalization and technical modernization, not Hindu drives for political purification along ethnic lines, will surely prevail.

For Ajami there was no credible basis for Huntington to assert that Saddam's Iraq had taken up the banner of Islam successfully. Saddam, a long-time student of Stalin, opportunistically tried to recreate himself as a standard bearer for Islam in

1990–91. The exercise was a transparent sham to everyone across the Middle East, hence the denunciations fired at him from Islamic religious leaders in Egypt and Saudi Arabia, as well as the complete absence of any support from Iran for Saddam in the leadup to the fighting in early 1991. So Iraq was left to confront not only American military might but also American troops from Saudi Arabia, Egypt, Turkey, and Syria. Only the desperate Palestinians rallied to Saddam's call for support, with very negative consequences for them in the aftermath of the war. The Gulf War demonstrated that a Pax Americana had replaced the Pax Britannica, but the rules of state behaviour and imperial interventionary practice had not changed: "The new power standing sentry in the gulf belonged to the civilization of the West, as did the prior one. But the American presence had the anxious consent of the Arab lands of the Persian Gulf. The stranger coming in to check the kinsmen."[17]

Jeane Kirkpatrick, President Reagan's former secretary of state, objected to Huntington's identified list of major civilizations. Why separate Latin American countries from North America and Western Europe, she asked, given the common cultural origins of all these regions? Why was Russia not considered "Western" too for that matter? Slavic Orthodox Christianity is hardly sufficiently different to warrant its own status separate from Europe.[18] And she might have added, on what basis can Japan be said to constitute a "civilization" in isolation? And why has Israel not been included in the West, given the heavy strategic and economic involvement of that country with the United States since its birth in 1948? Over the past four centuries, Kirkpatrick noted, and most especially during the twentieth century, the most violent major wars and genocidal assaults on people all occurred "within" civilizations, not between them: purges by Stalin and Mao, the Nazi and Khmer Rouge holocausts, the "European civil war" of World War I, and certainly the allied war against Nazi Germany were all "internal" to the classificatory divisions that Huntington formulated.[19] On what basis then can Huntington forecast a radically different risk of organized mass violence against human beings during the coming century?

Following the publication of *The Clash of Civilizations and the Remaking of World Order* in 1996, a second wave of criticism concentrated on Huntington's sweeping generalizations and his provocatively realist premises. For Barry Buzan, Huntington's "civilisational realpolitik" was based on a territorialization of civilizational cultures that is quite inappropriate. Historically, great cultural inventions and grand civilizational norms have transcended state boundaries and informed and influenced many societies for decades, centuries, or millennia after they were first formulated.[20] The rule of law is not confined to the states of the West, nor is the practice of democracy once literacy levels surpass fifty percent of national populations and once mass media communications are widely distributed. As Gwynne Dyer put it, when societies can in a practical way "talk things over," there is no need to rule by terror or authoritarian means; the adoption of some form of democracy becomes inevitable.[21]

Huntington's concept of a pivotal role for "core states" in each civilization was also greeted with skepticism by Buzan. The appeal of Islam in recent decades has been growing without any sponsoring "core state" promoting it. Buddhist religion and concepts spread over much of Asia and made inroads into Western states without any political or material territorial base pushing it forward. So too did Protestant Christianity spread to Asia, Africa, and Latin America during the twentieth century, long after the European and American governments ceased to promote it. Western ideas, ideals, and social, economic, and political norms also have spread far beyond their Western European region of origin. State sovereignty, market economics, nationalism, the scientific method, and the idea of progress itself—all the key elements of "modernity," said Buzan, are now the globalized foundations for all other civilizations: "the fact that so many fundamental Western ideas have become universal more than outweighs the fact that some, most notably human rights and individualism, are still hotly contested."[22] The vast scale of the cultural impact of the West on the rest of the world is, he noted, not without precedent:

> Over 2,300 years ago, five centuries of classical Greek civilisation transformed itself into the much wider-ranging Hellenistic period, which lasted for nearly two millennia until Byzantium fell, and profoundly changed its Greek heartland in the process. Now the five-century run of classical Western civilisation is similarly transforming itself into a wider Westernistic world, which will also feed many new forces into the old West. Although Atlanticism is a useful contribution to global stability, the West does not need to retreat into the Atlanticist bunker that Huntington thinks is its last best hope.[23]

G. John Ikenberry criticized what he saw as Huntington's "wildly overstated" warnings of inter-civilizational war. To assume now that international relations will turn out very badly in the twenty-first century and to take precautionary security measures now to try to weaken potential adversaries and build up one's own military capabilities while constraining theirs certainly will risk inducing a self-fulfilling prophecy. Huntington's urgent plea to reunify the countries of the Atlantic alliance would likely prove to be a massive geostrategic blunder, said Ikenberry:

> Declaring civilizational divides would invite counter-groupings and risk triggering precisely the types of antagonisms that Huntington anticipates. This is the civilizational equivalent of the "security dilemma"—Huntington wants the West to defensively guard against the coming clash, but to other powers like China and Japan the circling of the Western wagons will look like a declaration of a new Cold War.[24]

Both Ikenberry and Buzan evinced concern about the inherently policy-oriented character of Huntington's analytical perspective. Concerns about the neo-isolationist pessimism implicit in Huntington's work was developed in other critiques as well. In a previous commentary on Huntington's paradigm,[25] I noted that his policy prescriptions entailed a number of very troubling and very specific foreign policy recommendations for the United States:

- Withdrawal of the American security guarantee to Japan, the expansion of security ties with the "kin" countries of Western Europe, and the enlargement of NATO to include all European states that are "Western in their history, religion and culture." Countries that have been "primarily Muslim or Orthodox" were to be denied membership. Huntington claimed that over time one should expect Turkish and Greek membership to "weaken . . . come to an end or become meaningless."[26]

- Forging a strategic relationship of convenience with some combination of India, Russia, or Japan, or all three if possible, so as to be able to spread the burden of containing both China and the countries of the Islamic world.[27]

- Termination of American support for international intervention to prevent human-rights abuses ("promiscuous intervention" wastes resources and will generate needless inter-civilizational conflict[28]). By implication, the provision of international development assistance should also be cut back or eliminated because it too would counterproductively strengthen the economies of other civilizations while depleting Western strength.

- Reduction of the American effort to promote international treaties that will effectively regulate or ban nuclear, biological, or chemical weapons. "Universalist" arms control and disarmament treaties aimed at reducing the threat posed by weapons of mass destruction (WMDs) were instruments of the Cold War, said Huntington. Trying to eliminate WMDs in the early twenty-first century would be an error. Now that the United States is involved in a long-term struggle to maintain its scientific and military superiority over more populous rivals whose economies may surpass that of the U.S. in a few decades (China, India, and possibly Europe too, if the Franco-German partnership decides to leave the Euro-American, Atlanticist civilizational bloc), agreeing to forego WMDs could well be something that future American governments would greatly regret. Accordingly, treaty instruments like the foundational Russian–American Anti-Ballistic Missile Treaty of 1972 was something that should be jettisoned as soon as possible because it inhibited research and development in an area of American technological strength.[29] Nor should any tears be spilled over the decreasing respect for the Nuclear Non-Proliferation Treaty (NPT). The covert arms trade and weapons technology sharing that occurred among China, North Korea, Pakistan, Iraq, Iran,

Libya, and Syria was extensive through the 1990s and was the most tangible proof of "Confucian–Islamic" collusion to spread WMDs. Their successful collusion illustrated the inherent unworkability and unreliability of global disarmament measures.[30] It would only be a matter of time before the West was subject to direct terrorist threats involving mass destruction technologies.[31]

- Relative American disengagement from the Middle East. While the status of Israel apparently was not discussed systematically by Huntington in any of his writings on the clash thesis, again by implication (Israel is not included among the Western states in the maps in his 1996 book) his views can be inferred from indirect comments. Given Huntington's premise of an inherently adversarial character of the Islamic–Western relationship for some time to come, and given its current condition of what Huntington terms "quasi war,"[32] the U.S. should sensibly retrench from its overexposed position in the Middle East as a supporter of Israel. While there might be some value in the U.S. playing a role as an external balancer power to try to shore up the nuclear-biological-chemical (NBC) peace, there would be uncertain political-strategic gain and the certainty of immense costs and unwarranted risks in any attempt to democratize the Islamic world by trying to impose it on Iraq or Iran by force—especially in an era when terrorists may be able to acquire nuclear, radiological, or biological weapons. In 2002, Huntington counselled against American military intervention in Iraq.[33] He thereby anticipated (and possibly influenced) a similar judgment of several other prominent American realist international relations scholars who opposed the attack on Saddam's regime.[34]

- The end of any sort of governmental policies of multicultural accommodation and their replacement by intensely assimilationist measures for all recent immigrants now inside the U.S. Assimilationism would be assisted by a drastic reduction of Hispanic immigration that Huntington felt threatened the integrity of the dominant Protestant Christian ethos of American society. Continued high immigration from Mexico would be very dangerous in the long term, potentially setting the stage for future Mexican "revanchism" with respect to the American southwestern states.[35] What the U.S. had conquered in the nineteenth century might be lost in the twenty-first. In the same vein, Huntington applauded Western European efforts to slow dramatically the entry into the EU of illegal Muslim migrants, who threatened to turn European states into "cleft" societies.[36] The effective management of immigration flows and the fostering of institutions able to acculturate them to existing norms and values was critical, he argued, to the very survival of the West. Its elites should not forget that "the export of people was perhaps the single most important dimension of the rise of the West between the sixteenth and twentieth centuries."[37]

The net effect on American thinking of Huntington's multidimensional inventory of policy prescriptions is unclear. Few American analysts seem inclined to accept his "decline of the West" thesis, although some may privately agree that American strength of character has been badly corroded. Huntington's policy message has been termed nationalist at best and irrationally nativist at worst. No doubt many American academics see him as a national embarrassment—about as politically incorrect as one could be. He would return the favour and likely denounce them in return as "dead soul" traitors to core American values.[38] Attacking people of colour as culturally subversive to American values in general, and Hispanic migrants in particular as a *de facto* fifth column preparing for a demographic takeover of the American southwest, is not something that can be articulated in polite liberal or social democratic discourse.

Huntington's analysis also has prompted quantitatively based criticism by several researchers. Their criticism has been very limited, however, in its impact, largely because of their very narrowly circumscribed analysis. Russett, Oneal, and Cox published a lengthy study in 2000. They looked at patterns of conflict from 1950 to 1992 and concluded that "civilizational differences have no significant effect on the probability that a dyad will become involved in conflict once either realist or liberal theories are taken into account."[39] In this study, countries with democratic governance and high levels of trade were seen to have had a lower incidence of disputes. When allowance was made for these factors and for the variable of geographical contiguity, civilizational difference had no statistically significant impact on the incidence of conflict. The study also indicated that "civilizational conflicts did not increase as the Cold War waned."[40] Overall, the researchers found that "military, political and economic interests measured by our realist and liberal variables provide a substantially better account of interstate violence than does Huntington's theory."[41] They then asserted that "policymakers should focus on what they can do: peacefully extending democracy and economic interdependence to parts of the world still excluded. . . . Strengthening the liberal forces for peace can mitigate what might otherwise appear to be the clash of civilizations."[42]

The persuasiveness of the Russett, Oneal, and Cox study was undercut, however, by their own acknowledgment that "if the clash thesis is simply a prophecy about what may happen in the 21st century, that would immunize it to any current empirical test."[43] Throughout his book, Huntington indeed argued that future conflicts will arise from fundamentally different causes than in the past. He repeatedly claimed that there is an almost organic, evolutionary process at work in social relations worldwide, and that the historical epoch of nation-states is destined to give way to civilizational rivalries and manoeuvring, as people worldwide identify with ever larger socio-political collectivities, continuing a millennia-long process. While one can see hints of future behaviour in some of the conflicts of the 1990s and earlier, the full pattern of conflict causation in the next century is only now in the process of being revealed.[44] What is clear, Huntington believes, is that the two principal threats to the United States and the West will arise from a fully modernized China and a Muslim world experiencing a still more fully developed "Islamic Resurgence." For a Western world in relative demographic and economic decline, not to speak of the internal moral crisis of social decay and disorder that Huntington also laments,[45] the power capabilities of the West will have to be carefully monitored and protected by a governing elite with far more judgment, circumspection, and prudence than has been demonstrated thus far in the post–Cold War era. Thus, the most important specific predictions about future conflict were not and could not have been tested by Russett and his colleagues. Their findings may be quite accurate, but Huntington can with some justification dismiss them as irrelevant.

A second quantitatively based analytical investigation of Huntington's clash theme was produced shortly after the events of 9/11. Pippa Norris and Ronald Inglehart examined data from the World Values Survey, 1995–2001, and found that "when political attitudes are compared (including evaluations of how well democracy works in practice, support for democratic ideals, and disapproval of strong leaders), far from a 'clash of values,' there is minimal difference between the Islamic world and the West." Of the regions assessed only post-Communist Eastern Europe lagged substantially in support of democratic values. Popular attitudes in Islamic countries were much closer to those in Western Europe and North America. The most important finding indicated that the largest cultural cleavage between the West and the Islamic world concerned "social beliefs about gender equality and sexual liberalization." On these issues, the authors noted, "the West is far more egalitarian and liberal than all other societies, particularly Islamic nations. Moreover cohort analysis suggests that this gap has steadily widened and the younger generation in the West has gradually become more liberal in their sexual mores while the younger generation in Islamic countries remains deeply traditional."[46] Sexual liberalization as represented by greater social and economic equality for women, permissiveness toward homosexuality, serial marriage and divorce, abortion, and the sexualization of mass advertising and popular entertainment together constitute the truly great divergence from the values of Islamic societies—not any alleged divergence in levels of popular respect for democratic principles.

The Norris and Inglehart study is significant in that it suggests that democracy may indeed be in the offing for Islamic societies, but that such democracy would not be socially liberal and would probably be characterized by a highly constrained involvement of women. But Norris and Inglehart presume too much in suggesting that their findings throw substantial doubt on Huntington's diagnosis. Indeed, it is highly doubtful that he would find anything in their findings really surprising. Dislike of democracy was not the core of what Huntington identified as the heart of the Islamic opposition to the United States; rather, it was the sense of frustration with what most people in Islamic states saw as American manipulation of their societies and governments and their collective determination to assert their own path and priorities, domestically and internationally.[47] Islamic opposition to human-rights pressure from the U.S. and other Western states may very well be founded on the rejection of social, economic, and political equality for women. Equality for women plus equality for homosexuals is simply too much to bear for highly traditional cultures where the political left has been largely discredited and the liberal centre has had a hopeless task in trying to promote human rights as understood in Western countries, just as Huntington pointed out.[48]

A decade of critical responses to Huntington's thinking has not really dampened his enthusiasm for proclaiming the demise of the West, the arrogance and insensitivity of American foreign policy, and the stupidity of the neoliberal "imperialist" managerialists in Washington, most of whom seem to subscribe implicitly to some version of hegemonic stability theory. In sum, none of the critical reflections on Huntington's clash thesis have inflicted mortal damage on his broader argument and concerns, primarily because the criticisms are very limited in their applicability or, at their worst, they are little more than *ad hominem* attacks on Huntington and his conservative, nationalist values. But does he offer a sensible "grand strategy" for the countries of the West? What alternatives are available?

A WORLD OF WMD-ARMED CIVILIZATIONAL RIVALS OR AN ERA OF "COOPERATIVE SECURITY"?

What has happened on the ground since 1993? In China, both the suppression of Tibetan Buddhism and the tactics of demographic engulfment of the Tibetan people through forced migration was continued. Chinese repression of the Turkic-Muslim minority peoples in the far west of the country apparently intensified in the years after 9/11 as leaders in Beijing came to fear the prospect of an evermore coordinated Islamist terrorist insurgency. The protracted fight for independence in East Timor met unexpectedly with success against a shaky Indonesian elite; an uncompromising secessionist movement in Chechnya against the Russian Federation did not. The Islamic world continued to be involved in a large number of conflicts: Sudan, Pakistan, Turkey, Thailand, Indonesia, and the Philippines all saw substantial fighting and acts of terrorism over the past decade. Al Qaeda–linked terrorism spread to Southeast Asia after 9/11, leading to many victims in Indonesia and the Philippines. Jemaah Islamiya, a regional offshoot of Al Qaeda, proclaimed the goal of creating an Islamic Southeast Asian superstate living under *sharia*. Islamic extremists, after losing their principal training site when the U.S. deposed the Taliban, continued to organize and fight in western Pakistan and eastern Afghanistan to try to prevent the creation of a stable, more or less democratic government in Kabul. Islamic extremists undoubtedly rallied to the anti-American fight inside occupied Iraq in 2003–04 and may have begun a concerted campaign to try to topple the Saudi dynasty and the Jordanian monarchy.

Huntington thus appears to have been correct in forecasting a continuation of ethnically driven or exacerbated wars and intra-state civil strife. But to reiterate, to date there has been no evidence of an *intensification* of such violence. Violence overall does appear to have de-escalated globally, with the number of insurgencies falling gradually but steadily. As Ted Gurr noted, political accommodation techniques for economically and socially disempowered minorities do seem to be improving across the globe.[49] Huntington's prediction of more and more "fault line wars" has yet to be borne out.

On the WMD proliferation front, Huntington's pessimism has received greater validation. But that is due in part to American actions and policies, not merely the drive for WMD "autonomy" by smaller states or would-be rivals to American military hegemony. Despite the reduction in the number of operational nuclear warheads worldwide from roughly 70 000 in the mid-1980s to some 20 000 currently, there have been major setbacks to the cause of global nuclear disarmament. The ability to build weapons of mass destruction continued to proliferate over the decade, with North Korea, Pakistan, and China continuing to engage in the dissemination of ballistic missiles, development of uranium enrichment capacity, and possibly development of biological weapons capacity too. Iran continued covert efforts to acquire nuclear weapons and to extend the range of its ballistic missiles, even though it agreed in principle to accept more intensive IAEA inspections to verify its nuclear weapon-free status. Iraq's covert programs, if they existed by the late 1990s, were either destroyed or driven far underground (or out of the country) by the American invasion and occupation after March 2003. The solitary success of the Bush administration in disarming Libya in early 2004 was an important achievement for its counterproliferation policy. But that success was offset by the North Koreans' formal renunciation of membership in the NPT in 2002 and their declaration of intent to expand their small arsenal of a handful of atomic weapons quickly. The Bush administration has responded with further high-tech reinforcement of its sizeable conventional forces in South Korea, indicating that a military confrontation remains a serious risk.[50]

Although the potential nuclear successor states of Ukraine, Kazakhstan, and Belarus all opted for non–nuclear weapon state status and transferred their nuclear warheads and launchers to Russia in the mid-1990s, both India and Pakistan abandoned policies of "nuclear opacity" and publicly tested over a dozen nuclear devices in the summer of 1998. Tensions over Kashmir nearly flared into major warfare in 1999 and 2000 (including near use of nuclear weapons) between an Indian government composed of Hindu nationalists and a Pakistani Muslim government. Both Russia and China have begun what are likely to be large nuclear modernization programs in response to the Bush administration's decision to press forward with its ABM deployments in 2004 and beyond, to develop new nuclear warhead designs, and to develop "an ability to fight into, through and from space," while at the same time forging ahead relentlessly with its effort to widen American conventional military superiority over all other potential rivals. In view of American, Russian, and Chinese nuclear modernization, the cuts in the British and French nuclear arsenals implemented over the past decade may well be reversed in coming years.

Over the past decade, Russian security fears were heightened by NATO's two rounds of geographic expansion (under unilateral American direction) to include most of the countries to the west of the "Velvet Curtain of culture"—a move that Huntington endorsed in his 1993 article. Poland, the Czech Republic, and Hungary were admitted in March 1999, followed by the Baltic states of Slovakia, Slovenia, and Romania in April 2004.[51] Whether Huntington's strategic advice in this regard influenced Clinton and Bush administration officials is not known. But his analysis and recommendations probably helped smooth the path of domestic public opinion for such expansion.

Huntington's intellectual aid and comfort to those in Washington who have been pressing for permanent military superiority over all potential challengers cannot but be of deep concern to those who still hold to a liberal-internationalist perspective on world affairs. Huntington's grand strategy vision is the very antithesis of working for an evolving, multilateral "cooperative security" approach that would seek to build a broad international coalition of countries who would work jointly to eliminate the threat posed by nuclear and biological weapons of mass destruction. Only "cooperative security" holds out real promise for halting and then reversing the development of WMDs.[52] Huntington's primacist policy recommendations, if they all were to be implemented, would first commit the U.S. to retaining a significant margin of military superiority against all potential peer competitors. This is a formula for a renewed multilateral arms race. American efforts to develop new nuclear weapons and to achieve military control of space would threaten the NPT and likely stimulate still more nuclear proliferation. Second, a primacy-seeking grand strategy would carry the risk, as Ikenberry noted above, of creating an image of "circling the wagons" and awakening foreign fears that time was running out before the big shoot-out. American governments that seek perpetual military and economic "primacy" as recommended by Huntington (and others)—an approach that has been publicly endorsed by the Bush administration[53]—would almost certainly provoke retaliatory "balancing" by the other major powers in the system.

In a Huntingtonian approach to grand strategy, an American retreat from its security guarantees to Japan and South Korea might also catalyze the start of both Japanese and Korean nuclear weapons programs. The Bush administration's 2002 *National Security Strategy*, with its strong endorsement of preventive war ("preemption" is a polite euphemism) and the "dissuasion" of potential peer competitors militarily,[54] certainly helped provoke the North Koreans into a sprint to build a small but credible nuclear arsenal. That same document and those same policies of military and strategic preeminence will almost certainly drive Chinese and Russian military spending to levels much higher than they would otherwise be while poisoning the well for nuclear and other greatly needed disarmament measures.

Samuel Huntington's "clash" strategic package has a profound potential for destabilizing world politics. Its bleak vision of the future should be rejected. Liddell Hart's short chapter on grand strategy included the observation that "the object in war is to attain a better peace—even if only from your own point of view. Hence it is essential to conduct war with constant regard to the peace you desire."[55] Part of Huntington's vision of the future *does* include the real possibility of an eventual mutually constructive dialogue of civilizations (recall his question mark). Mutually tolerant and cooperative relations do need to be, and can be, established. Huntington's invocation of Lester Pearson's wise words recognize that fact. But one cannot build trust and tolerance or promote mutual learning in the long term by retreating into a heavily armed "Atlanticist bunker" and being ready to rain down destruction from the heavens at the push of button, as Buzan rightly noted. There are far better strategic alternatives than what Huntington has offered. Huntington is not "wrong" about his choice of ends—just seriously misguided in his selection of means.

NOTES

1. Samuel Huntington, "The Clash of Civilizations? The Next Pattern of Conflict," *Foreign Affairs*, v. 72 n. 3 (Summer 1993), 22–49; cited hereafter as Huntington, "Clash."

2. "X" (George F. Kennan), "The Sources of Soviet Conduct," *Foreign Affairs*, v. 26 (July 1947).

3. Kishore Mahbubani, "The Dangers of Decadence: What the Rest Can Teach the West," *Foreign Affairs*, v. 72 n. 4 (September/October 1993), 12. See also the angry denunciation of Huntington by the late Edward W. Said, who termed the clash thesis the work of an ideologist and propagandist—a collection of "vast abstractions that may give momentary satisfaction but little self-knowledge or informed analysis." Said, "The Clash of Ignorance," *The Nation*, 22 October 2001; accessed online 28 April 2004, at www.thenation.com/doc.mhtml?i=20011022&ts=said; cited hereafter as Said, "Ignorance."

4. Samuel P. Huntington, *The Clash of Civilizations and the Remaking of World Order* (New York: Simon and Schuster, 1996), 320–21; cited hereafter as *Remaking of World Order*.

5. Robert D. Kaplan, "Looking the World in the Eye," *The Atlantic Monthly* (December 2001); from *The Atlantic Online*, accessed 17 October 2002, at www.theatlantic.com.

6. Colin S. Gray, *Modern Strategy* (Oxford: Oxford University Press, 1999), 17.

7. This definition is a modified version of the elements brought together by Basil H. Liddell Hart. See B.H. Liddell Hart, *Strategy*, 2nd rev. ed. (New York: Signet/New American Library, 1974), 322.

8. Ibid.

9. According the chief economist of the World Bank, the proportion of people living on less than $1 per day worldwide declined from 40% to 21% between 1981 and 2001. The number of people living in extreme poverty apparently fell from 1.5 to 1.1 billion, although in sub-Saharan Africa the number of extremely poor people increased from 164 to 314 million, or rate of 47% of the region's population. Rapid growth in China and India generated most of the good news—a fall in extreme poverty in China from over 60% to under 20% and in India from over 55% to just over 30%. The World Bank analysts attribute these two countries' success to their internal economic reforms diminishing the role of government, far greater reliance on market allocation, and greatly increased openness to foreign trade and competition. See Francois Bourguignon, "A Wealthier World," *National Post*, 24 April 2004; also, Joseph Brean, "Global Poverty in Steep Decline," *National Post*, 24 April 2004.

10. Robert L. Bartley, "The Case for Optimism: The West Should Believe in Itself," *Foreign Affairs*, v. 72 n. 4 (September/October 1993), 16–17. Simon Murden observed that the "biggest omission" in Huntington's model is the lack of a plausible discussion of the pacifying impact of the world market economy. See his concluding comment in Murden, "Review Article: Huntington and His Critics," *Political Geography*, v. 18 (1999), 1022; cited hereafter as Murden, "Huntington and Critics."

11. See his attack on the systemic disengagement of, and loss of patriotic sentiment by, the American corporate "cosmopolitan" class as well as liberal or left-wing academics in Samuel P. Huntington, "Dead Souls: The Denationalization of the American Elite," *The National Interest*, n. 75 (Spring 2004), 8; cited hereafter as Huntington, "Dead Souls."

12. For a discussion of the responses of several constructivists and critical theorists, see Murden, "Huntington and Critics," 1017–20.

13. Said, "Ignorance."

14. Fouad Ajami, "The Summoning," *Foreign Affairs*, v. 72 n. 4 (September/October 1993), 2.

15. Ibid., 3–4.

16. Ibid., 7.

17. Ibid., 8–9.

18. Jeane J. Kirkpatrick, "The Modernizing Imperative," *Foreign Affairs*, v. 72 n. 4 (September/October 1993), 22–23. For Kirkpatrick, "orthodox theology and liturgy, Leninism and Tolstoy are expressions of Western culture."

19. Ibid.

20. Barry Buzan, "Civilisational *Realpolitik* as the New World Order?" *Survival*, v. 39 n. 1 (Spring 1997), 180–81; cited hereafter as Buzan, "Realpolitik."

21. This point is made very effectively in Gwynne Dyer's four-part film production *The Human Race* (Montreal: National Film Board of Canada/Gree Lion Productions, 1994); cited hereafter as Dyer, *Human Race*.

22. Buzan, "Realpolitik," 183.

23. Ibid.

24. G. John Ikenberry, "Just Like the Rest," *Foreign Affairs*, v. 76 n. 2 (March/April 1997), 163.

25. Douglas Ross, "Despair, Defeatism, and Isolationism in American 'Grand Strategy': The Seductive Convenience of Huntington's 'Civilizational Clash' Thesis," in Mark Charlton, ed., *Crosscurrents: International Relations in the Post-Cold War Era*, 2nd ed.

(Toronto: ITP Nelson, 1999), 55–72. While this article stressed the exceptionally blunt implications of Huntington's analysis for American international security policy, one of the senior editors for *Business Week* declared that Huntington's writing "offers virtually no guidance in applied foreign policy." See Bruce Nussbaum, "Capital, Not Culture," *Foreign Affairs*, v. 76 n. 2 (March/April 1997), 165.

26. Samuel P. Huntington, "The West: Unique, Not Universal," *Foreign Affairs*, v. 75 n. 6 (November/December 1996), 45.

27. Huntington, *Remaking of World Order*, 241–45.

28. Ibid., 316.

29. Huntington, "Clash," 46; also Huntington, *Remaking of World Order*, 309.

30. Huntington, *Remaking of World Order*, 188–89.

31. Ibid., 187–88.

32. See his trenchant summation of the state of this "quasi war" in *Remaking of World Order*, 216–18. American moralizing, crusading, and interventionism is as much to blame for the strife as Islamic rage: "The underlying problem for the West is not Islamic fundamentalism. It is Islam, a different civilization whose people are convinced of the superiority of their culture and are obsessed with the inferiority of their power. The problem for Islam is not the CIA, or the U.S. Department of Defense. It is the West, a different civilization whose people are convinced of the universality of their culture and believe that their superior, if declining, power imposes on them the obligation to extend that culture throughout the world. These are the basic ingredients that fuel conflict between Islam and the West."

33. Beth Baker, Huntington's assistant, confirmed to Ann Kooy that Huntington did speak out against U.S. military intervention in Iraq in 2002. My thanks to Ms. Kooy, an M.A. candidate in political science at SFU, for sharing this information. Daniel Pipes noted that Huntington will soon publish another study explaining why the present American government's "imperialist" effort to remake the Middle East through enforced democratization starting with Iraq is unlikely to succeed. See Pipes, "Bringing Democracy to Iraq beyond Reach of U.S.," *Chicago Sun-Times*, 28 April 2004; accessed online 3 May 2004, at www.chicagosuntimes.com/output/otherviews/cst-edt-pipes28.html.

34. See, for example, John J. Mearsheimer and Stephen M. Walt, "An Unnecessary War," *Foreign Policy* (January/February 2003), 50–59; also, Richard K. Betts, "Suicide From Fear of Death?" *Foreign Affairs*, v. 82 n. 1 (January/February 2003), 34–43.

35. Huntington, *Remaking of World Order*, 206.

36. Ibid., 204–6.

37. Ibid., 198.

38. Huntington, "Dead Souls," 9–10.

39. Bruce M. Russett, John R. Oneal, and Michaelene Cox, "Clash of Civilizations, or Realism and Liberalism Déjà Vu? Some Evidence," *Journal of Peace Research*, v. 37 n. 5 (2000), 595.

40. Ibid., 600.

41. Ibid., 602.

42. Ibid.

43. Ibid.

44. For the same reason, Huntington probably would dismiss the findings of Ted Robert Gurr that the incidence of ethnic conflict was declining worldwide throughout the decade of the 1990s. Gurr's study is nevertheless very important. See Gurr, "Ethnic Warfare on the Wane," *Foreign Affairs*, v. 79 n. 3 (May/June 2000), 52–64. Another study attacking the notion of cultural differences inciting conflict challenged the characterization of the breakup of Yugoslavia and the slaughter in Rwanda as "ethnic wars." John Mueller's iconoclastic but still compelling case study treatment of these two conflicts deserves a close reading. See Mueller, "The Banality of 'Ethnic War,'" *International Security*, v. 25 n. 1 (Summer 2000), 42–70.

45. Huntington sees the increased unwillingness of Americans to pay taxes and their declining willingness to have citizens die for national interests as significant indicators of national moral decline. A reluctance to fund public institutions and programs and to fight for the country are, he believes, grave symptoms of social malaise.

46. Pippa Norris and Ronald Inglehart, "Islam & the West: Testing the 'Clash of Civilizations' Thesis," Faculty Research Working Paper Series, April 2002, RWP02-015, Kennedy School of Government, Harvard University; accessed online 3 May 2004, at ksgnotes1. harvard.edu/research/wpaper.nsf/rwp/RWP02-015/$File/rwp02_015_norris_rev1.pdf.

47. This point is central to Huntington's denunciation of the Clinton administration's efforts to impose its own ideas of order on most of the world, leading to virtually all other regional powers viewing the U.S. as a "rogue superpower" that had to be contained. See Samuel P. Huntington, "The Lonely Superpower," *Foreign Affairs*, v. 78 n. 2 (March/April 1999), 40–44.

48. Huntington, *Remaking of World Order*, 111–14.

49. See Gurr, "Ethnic Warfare on the Wane," 63–64.

50. See Robert Wall, "Strategy in Korea: Better Defense, Better Offense," *Aviation Week and Space Technology*, 12 April 2004.

51. The inclusion in the 2004 expansion of eastern Romania and Bulgaria are modest exceptions to the Velvet Curtain boundary Huntington specified, but can be justified, if only on grounds of geographic contiguity and ease of defence.

52. "Cooperative security" as a strategy has been summarized usefully and compared with alternative 'grand strategy' approaches in Barry R. Posen and Andrew L. Ross, "Competing Visions for U.S. Grand Strategy," *International Security*, v. 21 n. 3 (Winter 1996/97), 5–53. For a discussion of its relevance to Canadian international security policy, see Douglas A. Ross, "Canada's International Security Policy in an Era of American Hyperpower and Continental Vulnerability," *International Journal*, v. 58 n. 4 (Autumn 2003), 533–69.

53. See *The National Security Strategy of the United States*, September 2002; available online at the White House website, at www.whitehouse.gov/nsc/nssall.html; accessed 22 August 2003.

54. Ibid., 30.

55. Hart, *Strategy*, 353.

POSTSCRIPT

Interestingly, even though many in the administration of President George W. Bush were sympathetic to Huntington's thesis, the president himself was reluctant to use the language of civilizational conflict in public statements. In the period following September 11, 2001, President Bush repeatedly stated that the United States was not engaged in a war with Islam itself and focused instead on arguing that radical Islamists represented a distortion of Islam, which he called a religion of peace. It appears that the president feared that if the label of civilizational conflict is applied to the "war on terrorism," it might constitute a self-fulfilling prophecy.

Today, it is difficult not to read this debate in the context of the American war on terrorism and the apparent escalating conflict between Islamic and Western forces in many parts of the world. In recent times, we have seen growing conflicts between Muslims and Christians in Nigeria and Indonesia, between Muslims and Buddhists in Thailand, and between Hindus and Muslims in India. How do we interpret Huntington's civilizational clash in the post–September 11 era? Do these recent conflicts give greater credence to his theory? Does the theory provide a framework for understanding the major fault lines of conflict today? If not, what alternative explanations may be offered? Huntington argues that civilizational conflict will be more intractable and less easy to resolve by conflict and negotiation. If this is true, what implications does this have for the foreign policy of our governments?

Suggested Additional Readings

Abrahamian, Ervand. "The US Media, Huntington and September 11." *Third World Quarterly* 24, no. 13 (June 2003): 529–44.

Aysha, Emad El-Din. "Huntington's Shift to the Declinist Camp: Conservative Declinism and the 'Historical Function' of the Clash of Civilisations." *International Relations* 17, no. 4 (December 2003): 429–52.

Chiozza, Giacomo. "Is There a Clash of Civilizations? Evidence from Patterns of International Conflict Involvement, 1946–9." *Journal of Peace Research* 39, no. 6 (November 2002): 711–35.

Cox, Robert. "Civilisations: Encounters and Transformations." *Studies in Political Economy* 47 (Summer 1995): 7–31.

Falk, Richard. "False Universalism and the Geopolitics of Exclusion: The Case of Islam." *Third World Quarterly* 18, no. 1 (March 1997): 7–24.

Henderson, Errol A., and R. Tucker. "Clear and Present Strangers: The Clash of Civilizations and International Conflict." *International Studies Quarterly* 45, no. 2 (June 2001): 317–38.

Kurtz, Stanley. "The Future of 'History.'" *Policy Review* 113 (June–July 2002): 43–58. Available at www.policyreview.org/jun02/kurtz.html.

Lewis, Bernard. "I'm Right, You're Wrong, Go to Hell." *Atlantic Monthly* 291, no. 4 (May 2003): 36–42.

Norris, Pipa, and Ronald Inglehart. "Islamic Culture and Democracy: Testing the 'Clash of Civilizations' Thesis." *Comparative Sociology* 1, no. 3–4 (August 2002): 235–64.

Rajendram, Lavina. "Does the Clash of Civilizations Paradigm Provide a Persuasive Explanation of International Politics post September 11th?" *Cambridge Review of International Affairs* 15, no. 2 (July 2002): 217–33.

Russett, Bruce M., John R. Oneal, and Michaelene Cox, "Clash of Civilizations, or Realism and Liberalism Déjà Vu? Some Evidence," *Journal of Peace Research* 37, no. 5 (2000): 538–608.

Vasillopulos, Christopher. "Clash of Civilizations: Prophecy or Contradiction in Terms?" *Arab Studies Quarterly* 25, no. 1–2 (Winter–Spring 2003): 89–100.

InfoTrac® College Edition

Search for the following articles in the InfoTrac® database:

Fox, Jonathan. "Ethnic Minorities and the Clash of Civilizations: A Quantitative Analysis of Huntington's Thesis." *British Journal of Political Science* 32, no. 3 (July 2002): 415–34.

Inglehart, Ronald, and Pippa Norris. "The True Clash of Civilizations." *Foreign Policy* 135 (March–April 2003): 63–70.

Kibble, David G. "The Attacks of 9/11: Evidence of a Clash of Religions?" *Parameters* 32, no. 3 (Autumn 2002): 34–45.

Morgan, Matthew J. "The West's Last Chance: Will We Win the Clash of Civilizations?" *Parameters* 38, no. 2 (Summer 2008): 125–27.

Walker, Christopher J. "Friends or Foes? The Islamic East and the West." *History Today* 57, no. 3 (March 2007): 50–57.

Web Resources

For current URLs for the following websites, visit www.crosscurrents.nelson.com.

CLASH OF CIVILIZATIONS: A READING GUIDE

http://www.csmonitor.com/specials/sept11/flash_civClash.html

Prepared by *The Christian Science Monitor*, this site contains a good collection of academic articles debating Huntington's thesis, along with links to articles discussing the concept in relation to the war on terrorism.

PEW FORUM ON RELIGION AND PUBLIC LIFE

http://pewforum.org/events/index.php?EventID=125

Samuel Huntington is interviewed as part of a forum entitled "Five years after 9/11, the Clash of Civilizations Revisited."

DAVID SKIDMORE, "HUNTINGTON'S CLASH REVISITED," *JOURNAL OF WORLD-SYSTEMS RESEARCH* 4, NO. 2 (FALL 1998)

http://www.jwsr.ucr.edu/archive/vol4/v4n2r2.php

This book review offers a critical look at Huntington's *The Clash of Civilizations and the Remaking of World Order.*

Is a World State Inevitable?

✔ **YES**
ALEXANDER WENDT, "Why a World State Is Inevitable," presented as the Twenty-Seventh Annual G. Theodore Mitau Endowed Lecture at Macalester College, April 2, 2008

✘ **NO**
VAUGH P. SHANNON, "Wendt's Violation of the Constructivist Project: Agency and Why a World State Is *Not* Inevitable," *European Journal of International Relations* 11, no. 4 (2005): 581–87

The concept of the state has always been central in thinking about international relations. Scholars date the modern international system of states from the Peace of Westphalia in 1648. This agreement, designed to bring an end to the Thirty Years War, signified both the secularization of politics and the rise of the territorial state as the principal unit of political organization. The peace redrew the map of Europe into a society of legally equal states. Each claimed to exercise sovereignty within fairly well-defined frontiers and acknowledged no authority above itself. Inherent in this notion was the claim that each state has the right to non-interference by others in its domestic affairs.

Since 1648, the territorial state has become the principal vehicle for organizing humankind into political communities. The composition of the international system has grown from a handful of European states in the seventeenth century to over 200 states and territorial entities today. States remain the highest level of political authority. Decisions made by bodies such as the United Nations and the International Court of Justice in the Hague are adhered to by states only on a voluntary basis. There has yet to emerge anything like a global state or world government.

Given the power and importance of sovereign states, it is perhaps not surprising that scholars have traditionally focused on a "state-centric" approach to the study of international politics. According to this view, the focus of the study of international relations is really *interstate* relations. Although there may be many other "actors" on the global scene, states remain the dominant actors because they alone can claim monopoly of legal authority within their territory and of the use of military force within and beyond that territory.

Why have states emerged as the predominant form of political organization? John Herz argues that the strength of states lies in their capacity to perform two major functions: defend those citizens who live within their borders and promote the economic well-being of their citizens. States have been successful to the extent that they have been able to build a "hard shell" of impermeability around themselves while ensuring a degree of self-sufficiency and autonomy.

In the twentieth century, there have been frequent predictions that the notion of the sovereign, territorial state is in demise. Herz himself, in the aftermath of World War II, predicted the imminent end of the territorial state. The development of instruments of total war, especially nuclear weapons, demonstrated that no state could any longer claim to provide a hard shell of security for its citizens. Herz later retracted his gloomy prediction in the wake of postwar decolonization and the birth of dozens of new states. He pointed out the "synthetic" quality of these states and argued for an international role in their "hardening" over time (John Herz, *The Nation-State and the Crisis of World Politics* [New York: David McKay, 1976]).

However, recently new concerns have been raised by those who believe that the forces of globalization now threaten the future of the nation-state. These analysts argue that since the early 1970s the international political economy has been experiencing a profound transformation. The idea of national economies, enclosed by national borders and controlled by national governments, is being rendered nearly meaningless by a globalized economy. As a result, the modern state is faced with an increasing inability to provide economic prosperity within its borders. In a global marketplace, few states can claim economic autonomy or self-sufficiency. The prosperity of citizens is now to a large extent determined beyond their national borders, rather than by any decisions made by their national governments. Those who believe that the state is in decline argue that students of international relations need to broaden their focus beyond an analysis of state behaviour, to the growing role played by transnational corporations, non-governmental organizations (NGOs), and international institutions. As a result, many analysts have focused on newly emerging complex networks of "global governance" which involve an array of state and non-state actors.

At the same time, there are some scholars who believe that the future lies neither with the continuation of the current nation-state system nor with new forms of complex global governance. Rather, they see the likely, indeed necessary, emergence of some sort of world state or global government as inevitable. Two scholars who argue this point of view are David Deudney and Alex Wendt. To some extent both authors begin by accepting the realist assumption that it is the anarchical nature of the international system which makes it a dangerous place to live. But, rather than accepting the notion that the nation-state is inevitable and that the only hope is that a strong hegemonic state (like the United States) maintains order, Deudney and Wendt argue that the very "logic of anarchy" calls for the creation of some kind of world state.

In a recent book entitled *Bounding Power: Republican Security Theory from the Polis to the Global Village* (Princeton, N.J.: Princeton University Press, 2006), Deudney argues that modern international war has become so dangerous and expensive that it is necessary to consider alternative means of ordering the world. Although he does not argue that the world state is inevitable, he contends that the ever-present threat of nuclear extermination makes it imperative that world leaders consider the possibility of forming some world republic. Thus, *Bounding Power* sets out the case for establishing a form of world republic, based on the republican notions of diffusing and decentralizing power, which inspired the founders of the American republic.

Alex Wendt goes further than Deudney in arguing that the emergence of a world state is not just a possibility, but may well be inevitable. Although he acknowledges that this step is not imminent and may take considerable time to accomplish, he argues that states should begin shaping their policies with the notion that it will be the inevitable outcome of the evolution of the international system. Although Wendt initially set out this argument in a lengthy article in the *European Journal of International Affairs*, he presented a briefer summary of his theory in a lecture at his aluma mater, Macalester College, in April 2008, which is reprinted here.

Vaughn Shannon provides a response to Wendt's argument. He focuses in part on a seeming contradiction between Wendt's argument regarding the inevitably of a world state and his previous writing as an international theorist. Wendt is most noted for his contributions in developing a "constructivist" approach to the study of international relations. This approach arose as a response to the dominance of realist perspectives in international relations theory in the United States. In particular, constructivists like Wendt argued against the realist assumption that it is the structure of the system itself which determines the interests of international actors. Instead, the constructivist perspective argues that ideas play a critical role in both defining and transforming the organization of world politics and also in helping to define the identity and interests of states. Thus, Shannon argues, Wendt's focus on the inevitability of the world state and his argument that it is product of the logic of the anarchical system itself violates Wendt's previous arguments about the nature of international politics.

✔ **YES**
Why a World State Is Inevitable
ALEXANDER WENDT

[. . .] My talk this evening [. . .] takes up one important element of "common sense" that I think is problematic. Namely, that the future of international politics will be just like the past, and specifically in the sense that the international system will remain forever an anarchy—a system in which sovereignty is decentralized to territorial states—rather than evolve into a universal or world state. Today there are over 190 of these territorial sovereigns, each, like the United States, with the independent, constitutional authority to make war and peace. The number of states might go up or down in the future, but the conventional wisdom is that there will never be a world state. After all, think of what that would mean—that the sovereignty of today's states, the sovereignty of America, is *temporary*, like the sovereignty of ancient Sparta or Rome, and will one day be subsumed by a universal sovereignty, the black helicopters of an all-powerful United Nations. What American President, or citizen, would ever let that happen?

Granted, we will not truly know what the international system will become in the future until we get there, and that is probably some time off. However, our expectations about the future still matter, since they orient our practice in certain directions rather than others, and that will in turn help create whatever future comes to pass, in a kind of self-fulfilling prophecy. And I think it is part of the collective unconscious of American citizens that our state will "live forever"—or at least, that is what we are implicitly taught, since I have never seen a high school history book making the case that American sovereignty is temporary. Quite the contrary, we are taught that as good citizens it is our responsibility to help make America immortal, rather than prepare ourselves for eventual submission to a world state. Since citizens everywhere are taught a similar principle for their states, this bit of common sense is I think highly consequential for the practice of contemporary politics, for what is on, and off, the table.

Quite apart from common sense, however, international relations (or IR) scholars known as "Realists" argue that there is a compelling *theoretical* reason to think that a world state is impossible, which is what they call the "logic of anarchy." According to Realists like John Mearsheimer, the anarchic character of the international system creates a self-help world in which there is no "911" for states to call in an emergency. Left to fend for themselves, in the realist view states need to be self-interested in their dealings with each other, jealously guarding their sovereignty and national interests, lest other states take advantage of them. The resulting "logic" of anarchy is a competitive, dog eat dog world of power politics in which only the fittest—the meanest and most powerful—states survive. For realists a world state might be desirable, if it would end the carnage, but because of anarchy we can't get there from here. History is cyclical rather than progressive, with periods of peace followed inevitably by war, and as such what was true of world politics 3000 years ago will still be true 3000 years hence.

There is another group of IR scholars, however, known as Liberals, who are more optimistic than Realists, at least about the prospects for cooperation among sovereign states. By spreading democracy and capitalism, and building international institutions like NAFTA and the WTO, Liberals believe that the negative consequences of anarchy can be mitigated and even self-interested states learn to cooperate. For inspiration here Liberals look to Immanuel Kant, who envisioned a "perpetual peace" of republican states under cosmopolitan law, a vision that seems to be becoming a reality in Europe today with the EU. Interestingly, however, Kant did not argue for a world state, which he thought would be impractical and tyrannical, and neither do contemporary Liberals. For them, as for Realists and all good citizens of nation-states, the "end of history" in Hegel's terms includes no expectation that the sovereignty of the state would, or should, ever be subsumed under a universal sovereignty.

It is against this common sense that I would like to argue this evening, by making the case that a world state is inevitable, whether we like it or not. Since the argument is hard enough to make as it is, I will not hazard a prediction as to when this is going to happen. My personal belief is that it will take 100 to 200 years, but nothing in my argument below turns on that prediction. The claim is only that a world state is "eventually" inevitable, barring planetary acts of God like an asteroid impact or pandemic that wipes out the human race.

Empirically, the claim that a world state is inevitable is actually not as quixotic as it might first appear. In particular, Robert Carneiro has estimated that in the year 1000 B.C. there were 600,000 independent political communities (in effect, states) in the world, whereas today there are less than 200. Even if Carneiro's estimate is off by a factor of 10, it is clear that in the past 3000 years there has been a tremendous consolidation of political authority worldwide. The trend is not perfectly smooth, and in the 20th century the number of states has actually grown with decolonization. However, if we factor in the growth of regional integration like the European Union the overall direction of history seems unmistakable. In this light, how could a world state *not* be inevitable?

Still, there is that Realist skepticism about the logic of anarchy, and it is an alternative to that skepticism that I want to offer tonight. In my earlier work I have criticized Realism on the grounds that "anarchy is what states make of it," and as such has no single logic. More recently, however, I have come to the view that anarchy does have a logic, but it is to produce a world state. The reason, I will argue, is that the most important thing that human beings want from each other is recognition of their rights, both individual and collective, and in the ensuing "struggle for recognition" we will all learn that this need can only be satisfied globally, in a world state.

I first published this argument in an article back in 2003, but even then I knew it would take a book to really make the case. So although that book is currently on the back burner, I continue to take notes and develop the ideas.[. . .]

For the rest of my talk, then, I will do four things: first, define what I mean by a world state; then, talk about the struggle for recognition; third, develop my alternative logic of anarchy, which has five distinct stages; and finally, I will conclude by considering the policy implications of this argument for both states and citizens.

DEFINING THE WORLD STATE

As any political scientist will tell you, there are many ways to define the state—Liberal, Marxist, Weberian, and so on—and this will in turn affect how we define the world state. Whatever their other merits, among these definitions I think we should choose the one that makes the case for a world state as difficult as possible, since only such a "hard case" will tell us whether my argument really holds up. And to my mind, the hard case for a theory of world state formation is provided by Max Weber's definition of the state as a monopoly on the legitimate use of organized violence. This is the hard case because it is the right to engage in organized violence to which modern territorial states cling most tightly, and which has led to so much death and destruction in the past.

Applying Weber's definition to a world state, then, implies that in a world state the right to engage in organized violence—in effect, to kill without accountability—would no longer be "privatized" to territorial states, as it is today, but collectivized to the whole system. All legitimate organized violence would be authorized by the global sovereign, even if in practice it is sub-contracted out to local forces. What makes such global authorization of organized violence a particularly hard problem politically is that it requires not just that little states like the Bahamas or Belgium give up their sovereignty over violence, but that Great Powers like the U.S. or China must as well. That obviously pushes back the date at which we can expect the world state to arrive, but I do not think we will have a proper world state until it can prevent illegitimate violence by "rogue" Great Powers, by force if necessary.

Although we are some distance from such a world today, I think we should also be flexible about what a world state might look like in practice. In particular, it need not be identical in form to the highly centralized, bureaucratic states of today, nor, conversely, would it necessarily mean the abolition of national administrative units or countries. All that matters is that a global monopoly on the legitimate use of organized violence somehow be achieved, which might be done in various ways and which could still leave substantial autonomy in the hands of national administrations. The European Union, for example, I would argue is halfway toward this goal on a regional basis, so that if the international system as a whole eventually resembled a "completed" EU, this would constitute a world state by my definition. That said, however, I will leave the precise content of the world state up to your imagination, since it does not affect what follows. Let me turn now to my causal argument, which works on two levels, a micro- or bottom-up level and a macro- or top-down level, that I will take up in turn.

THE STRUGGLE FOR RECOGNITION

The starting point for my argument is an assumption about human motivation. In IR scholarship three motivations get most of the attention: security, power, and greed or wealth. Of these security is probably seen as the most fundamental, since you cannot enjoy wealth if you're not secure, and desires for power for its own sake are usually seen as aberrations. The conventional picture of international politics, therefore, is one of a "struggle for security."

I agree that people and states want security, and wealth and sometimes even power. Indeed, I would argue that the desire for wealth and probably also for security themselves point toward a world state, although I will not make that argument here. Rather, I want to emphasize a fourth human motivation that has received much less attention, but whose importance in the contemporary world I think is very clear: the desire for recognition of identities.

Recognition presupposes difference, the fact that human beings and states are distinct individuals. Human beings are individuals by virtue of their physical bodies, and states are individuals by virtue of the social boundaries they draw between themselves and other states. "Recognition" of these individuals is a social act by which one actor accepts another actor's individual difference as legitimate. What this legitimacy means in practice is that the Other (the recognizee) is acknowledged to have certain rights that should not be violated by the Self (the recognizer), which leads to an internalized self-restraint toward the Other. To see how such recognition can matter consider the example of the U.S. recognition of Canada and its non-recognition of Native Americans in the past. Canada the U.S. let live, even though it could have been conquered without difficulty; the Native Americans the U.S. did conquer, with considerable effort, because they were not recognized as having any right to the land.

Now, according to Hegel and other recognition theorists, recognition of one's identity by the Other is a precondition for freedom and even for being a proper Self at all. (On an everyday level, think of the identity of professor, which cannot be sustained without recognition from one's students). So at a fundamental level human beings *need* recognition, and will therefore struggle for it, even to the death, when they do not get it. And indeed, when I look out on world politics today it is a struggle for recognition that I mostly see, whether in the form of violent resistance by groups like al-Qaeda or Hamas, or non-violent efforts by NGOs to promote human rights. Although these struggles are undoubtedly motivated by many considerations, at bottom they seem to be struggles for respect, not just security, wealth, or power.

Needs for recognition come in various forms, most of which, like being an esteemed professor or a good dad, are not relevant to the state. But there is one kind of recognition that implicates the state directly, and that is recognition of one's legal standing as a bearer of rights. Legal standing is important because it means (or should mean) that one's rights will be enforced by the collective—the state—rather than left up to the whim of the Other. Since this in turn means that individuals have incentives to band together, the implication is that it is the mutual recognition of difference or individuality, not its suppression, which enables people to form community.

In Western and most non-Western states today most people already enjoy such legal recognition, and thus one might argue that all we need today are a few more rule of law states and the struggle for legal recognition will be over, without culminating in a world state. In a sense this was Hegel's own conclusion when he rejected the idea of a world state, arguing instead that the end of history is the nation-state (although some scholars have argued that his reasoning here is inconsistent, and that he should have argued for a world state).

Be that as it may, I argue that the territorial, nation-state does not fully satisfy the desire for legal recognition, for two reasons. First, as long as states retain the sovereignty to wage war against other states, the citizens of those states are not recognized by each other as having legal standing, and may therefore be killed without accountability. Think of the difference between murder and killing in war. Physically the two behaviors are identical, but domestically killing is considered a crime because we all recognize each other's legal rights; internationally, in contrast, the very same physical act of killing is considered "war" and thus perfectly legitimate. Not until no one has to be murdered in war will the desire for legal recognition be satisfied universally. Second, a crucial part of individuals' sense of Self is their national or group identity, which means that if our state is not fully recognized by other states, then that collective aspect of our individual identity is not fully recognized either. The upshot of this is that states have needs for recognition too, not just people, and as such the struggle for recognition always plays itself out on two levels simultaneously, the group and the individual.

A skeptic might object here that if this account of human motivation is true, why do people not simply create a world state today, rather than fighting to the death for their territorial ones? The answer is that the struggle for recognition is about *getting* recognition, not giving it, and the political difference is significant. Giving recognition is in effect to make one's own actions accountable to law, and that is something which most people today are loathe to do for foreigners. The attitude is rather that if—for example—Americans feel that we need to go to war and kill foreigners to protect our national security, then that is what we must and will do, and we do not want that decision or those killings to be accountable to our victims, much less second-guessed by the ICC. In this light, therefore, the challenge of world state formation is to move from a situation in which everyone is clamoring to get recognition from everyone else to one where everyone is also willing to give it to everyone else. And because that involves giving up national sovereignty (or certain forms of it, anyway), it is something people and states will only do when they have no choice.

THE LOGIC OF ANARCHY

This brings me to the macro-level or top-down aspect of my argument, which concerns the logic of anarchy rather than individual motivation, and gives the struggle for recognition its directionality toward a world state. This logic has two dynamics, a material and a normative one.

The material dynamic comes from Realist theory, which tells us that the power politics characteristic of anarchies generates a tendency for military technology to get more destructive over time. In competitive security environments states have an incentive to develop new military technologies, and those that succeed will tend to win their wars. Proven successful, those innovations will then be copied by other states in order to keep up, ushering in yet another round of innovation. In this way the destructive potential of war is ratcheted up over time, to the point that today some states have the capacity to destroy humanity many times over.

We can draw two important conclusions from this material dynamic within anarchy. First, improvements in military technology will gradually increase the spatial scale upon which it is possible to organize a state, since state power is a lot harder to project in a world of bows and arrows than of GPS satellites and cruise missiles (ancient Rome notwithstanding). So as weapons technology improves, other things being equal we can expect a corresponding long-run tendency for states to expand the size of their territories, and by implication a tendency for the number of states to fall.

Second, improvements in technology will also tend to make the cost of war—at least among equals—greater over time, giving states a corresponding incentive to settle their conflicts peacefully. The same cannot be said, of course, of so-called "asymmetric wars" between Great Powers and small states or terrorist groups, where a state like the U.S. is virtually invulnerable to attack (9/11 notwithstanding), and capable of using overwhelming violence with unprecedented precision. Yet, like a rising tide lifting all boats, as the level of technology rises and diffuses in the system, weaker actors will gain access to better technologies too, a pattern already seen in the "Kalashnikov Revolution" and probable efforts by terrorist groups to acquire weapons of mass destruction. In the long run, therefore, *all* war will become more costly, not just Great Power war.

Beyond the material dynamics of anarchy, I believe there is also a second, ideational or normative dynamic in the system, which is rooted in the power of liberal ideas. Because this dynamic only really becomes significant toward the later stages of the process of world state formation, however, let me turn first to what I see as its five distinct stages overall, focusing on how the micro and macro levels interact to channel and propel the system forward toward a world state. By 'stage' I mean a temporary equilibrium in the system that may last for a long time. In order to get a world state, therefore, I have to explain why these equilibria eventually become unstable, and then requires progress toward the next stage, and on up to the end.

First is the Hobbesian stage, in which actors do not recognize each other at all. In the ensuing "war of all against all," states and their citizens therefore routinely get killed. Human history suggests that the Hobbesian stage can last a long time, but eventually it became unstable. Relatively equal states emerge that balance each other's power, and wars become increasingly costly due to technological change. Through costly wars of recognition Hobbesian states wear each other down, and once they are exhausted they agree to give each other at least the minimal recognition embodied in the right to "life" (sovereignty). Or at least, that is how I would gloss the Peace of Westphalia in 1648, a key turning point in the evolution of the international system that ushered in the second, Lockean stage.

The Lockean stage is Hedley Bull's "society of states." War remains a regular recourse for states in such a world, but not wars of extermination; states' recognition of each other's sovereignty ensures that they exercise a certain amount of self-restraint in war: states no longer try to "kill" each other, just beat each other up. However, this stage too is unstable because the cost of war keeps going up. This is problematic not only for states but also for their citizens, who have no legal standing in the international system except as soldiers who can be killed. So as the costs of war go up individuals press for more recognition in the system, and specifically for non-violent settlement of disputes.

This leads to the third stage, "world society." Here states' recognition of each other's sovereignty has deepened to the point that war is no longer considered an acceptable form of dispute resolution. Instead of a balance of power system states form what IR scholars call a "security community," where peace is the expectation and norm, not war. Today the zone of the "democratic peace" in the West clearly constitutes such a community, but I would argue that its norms are spreading well beyond those boundaries, suggesting that much of the contemporary international system has reached this stage. However, even though war is now effectively off the table, there are still sources of instability in the system. The issue now is the lack of collective protection against possible aggressors, or the "fox in the henhouse" problem. Namely, even if most states at any given time are pacific "hens," as long as states retain their sovereignty there is always the possibility of rogue "foxes" emerging which reject non-violence and proceed to attack the good states. (This is the international analogue to the problem of crime domestically.) In the absence of collective guarantees of their security each good state would then have to fend for itself, which in turn threatens to reignite the competitive power politics of the Realist's self-help world.

This instability therefore leads to the fourth stage in the struggle for recognition, the Kantian stage of collective security. Here states identify with each other sufficiently deeply that a threat to one is seen as a threat to all, and so good states never have to fight alone. This gives teeth to the mutual recognition of states and their citizens, protecting everyone against international "crime," and I believe this is where the West is at today. Note that this stage is not yet a world state, since states retain sovereignty. Nor, moreover, is it immediately clear why the system would have to proceed beyond this stage, since the desire for recognition of both states and individuals seems now fully satisfied. What more could be needed?

I see the transition from the Kantian, collective security stage to a world state as the hardest step in my argument. I don't think it is quite there yet, but here is what I have so far, which might be thought of as a "demand side" and a "supply side" argument.

On the demand side, the problem with collective security, which ultimately makes it unstable, is that it cannot compel its members to fight on each other's behalf, or even to stay in the system. That is because Kantian states still retain final sovereignty over their weapons. Thus, while they might be good international citizens today that could not imagine betraying other states, by retaining final sovereignty they retain the legal right to change their minds down the road, and to do so unilaterally. In contrast to the state's authority domestically, in other words, which is compulsory, collective security remains fundamentally voluntary. And that, it seems to me, amounts to a failure to fully recognize the Other, because it does not make one's commitment to the Other an obligation for which the Self can be held accountable, but relies instead on the Self's charity and good faith. So in a collective security system one can expect both individuals and states to continue their struggle for recognition, for full constitutionalization and enforcement of their rights on a global scale.

On the supply side, in turn, in place of the material dynamics of military competition that I emphasized earlier, at this stage a normative dynamic becomes the main driver in the system's progress. Namely, given the kind of more or less liberal and democratic world that would underpin the Kantian stage, there is no good reason *not* to cede one's sovereignty to a global authority. For if sovereignty is ultimately the right to make war on outsiders without accountability, what moral justification exists for such a right in a liberal world? If we really are liberals, how can we draw a boundary between "Us" and "Them" and then claim the right to kill them when we say so? That sounds more like communalism than liberalism to me. From a consistently liberal perspective I see no justification for the sovereign territorial state after the Kantian stage has been fully institutionalized. Liberalism, in short, entails a world state.

Accepting this logic will be hardest for the Great Powers, ironically perhaps especially in the West, because of all states they have the most freedom of unilateral action to lose—and the greatest ability to "just say no" to a world state, if necessary violently. But as the potential for catastrophic violence continues to diffuse throughout the system, both to smaller states and down toward individuals in the form of transnational terrorism, I don't see how even the Great Powers can resist the demand for constitutionalization of their power. For, it is only when the rights of all individuals and groups are enforceable against everyone else that the struggle for recognition—in its violent form, anyway—will come to an end.

CONCLUSION

That's the argument. It has a lot of moving parts, and I know there are many questions one might ask; some I have probably heard before, others I am sure you will come up with tonight. Rather than try to anticipate your questions, therefore, I want to conclude by assuming for a moment that the argument is true, and considering what I see as its implications for foreign policy.

Ideally, foreign policies should be based on expectations about what the future of world politics will be like. Thus, when Realists advise American policymakers to pursue the national interest and only the national interest, they are doing so in part because they think the international system not only is but will remain a "Realist" world. Given that expectation, it makes sense to hold that the responsibility of American foreign policy makers is nothing more than to help Americans compete selfishly in the system as best we can, as well as to avoid binding multilateral commitments that might eat away at our sovereignty and power.

But what if our expectation is that the logic of anarchy is actually to create a world state? A lot would depend, of course, on how long we think it is going to take; if it is 1000 years then even if a world state is inevitable, it would have no practical meaning for us today. However, if we are talking about less than 200 years, then America's life as a sovereign state would already be half over, and it might make sense to start planning for retirement. The way to do that, in my view, is to "get with the program," going with the flow of history rather than against it, and thereby ensure that we get the best deal we can from the emerging global constitutional order. Conceptually that means rethinking our national interests in light of long-term global interests, or collectively rather than always self-interestedly. And politically it means binding ourselves to multilateral institutions and international law, rather than seeing these only as threats to our sovereignty.

Such a policy might seem like a utopian prospect, especially for Great Powers who have so much to lose. However, there is already a model for it in world politics today: Germany in the EU. After two horrific wars trying to impose its interests on everyone else, Germany has subordinated its national interests and sovereignty to the European interest—and in so doing made itself the heart of the European project. The German case obviously has exceptional historical roots, including American occupation, and indeed there is very little evidence that the U.S. government or public today is ready to follow a similar path with the UN.

Nevertheless, working within the UN system, in effect trying to "capture" it, seems like a better way to advance our long-term interests than fighting an ultimately losing battle to preserve our sovereignty.

In the end, of course, we have no idea what the future will bring, and as such this is all very speculative. However, I do hope I have convinced you of one thing, which is that the future is a self-fulfilling prophecy, something based on expectations that human beings create in the course of their action, rather than something that just happens to us. To be sure, individuals acting individually cannot control our collective future, but those acting collectively certainly can. And that is an idea of citizenship with which I suspect Professor Mitau would have agreed.

✗ NO
Wendt's Violation of the Constructivist Project: Agency and Why a World State Is *Not* Inevitable
VAUGHN P. SHANNON

There is a saying in the US that 'In this world nothing is certain but death and taxes.' The certitude of death remains something beyond the power of human free will and social construction, but very little else does. But Alexander Wendt would add a third inevitability of life—the coming world state. Wendt's article, 'Why a World State is Inevitable' in *EJIR* 9(4), argues for a teleological theory that the 'logic of anarchy' and the 'struggle for recognition' push humanity inexorably toward a single global state with a monopoly on legitimate force. I contend that Wendt's argument suffers from irreconcilable neglect and reliance on agency. Below, I am not addressing the philosophy of teleology per se, nor am I taking on Hegel's writings about the 'struggle for recognition'. My focus is on three points related to the need to retain agency in Wendt's, or any, theorizing:

(a) Agency conceptually is denied by the logic of inevitable, progressive change, but internal to his logic Wendt is forced to rely on agency and the choices of actors, a paradox he does not reconcile.

(b) Wendt's agents are reduced to a new motivational monocausality of a kind; the struggle for recognition becomes virtually the sole force of politics in his model.

(c) By focusing on the inevitable World State, Wendt detracts from debate about agency and conditionality that could make a world state *possible*.

The first of these points critiques the internal logic of Wendt's theory, the second addresses both internal logical flaws and the premises of the theory itself, and the third addresses the extent to which Wendt's intellectual experiment is also an advocacy piece on world state formation.

WITHER AGENCY?

Wendt's teleology goes through five stages—(1) from a Hobbesian 'system of states'; (2) to a Lockean 'society of states' who 'live and let live'; (3) to a 'world society', marked by non-violent dispute resolution of a universal pluralistic security community 'no longer free to make war'; (4) to a 'collective security' system of one for all and all for one; and finally (5) to a world state—whereby the authority to use force and recognize peoples resides with a world government alone.

In arguing for an inevitable world state (WS), Wendt, one of the founding fathers of constructivist International Relations in the 1980s, abandons the spirit of the constructivist project in favor of a top-heavy structuralism. With teleology comes the concomitant withering of agency and the core constructivist insight that *nothing is inevitable*—human history may move forward or backward. To a constructivist, a world state is possible but by no means inevitable. Constructivism's promise relates to the role of both agent and structure in explaining world politics. Structures constrain and shape actor identity and behavior, while the possibility of free will permits structural change, not mere reproduction. Wendt, though, argues for unintentional change through material forces of recognition, anarchy and increasingly destructive weapons technology.

Constructivist or not, how does Wendt's argument fare on its merits? Though Wendt insists that 'human agency matters' (p. 491), he does not reconcile this conceptually. Wendt provides agency only with a 'reduced role' in the process of reaching the inevitable outcome—a World State via the 'multiple realizability' of agency (p. 501). But if agency is granted a free hand in crafting the future, that future must be contingent and open-ended. Wendt's argument is ultimately structural determinism, premised on materialist forces.

Furthermore, his stories of the movement from one stage to the next belie his own claims of teleology, as he is forced to confront the choice of states to progress from one level to the next. Rather than grapple with the complex options the multitude of states can take (not to mention the actions historically, empirically taken at junctures of world history),[1] he is forced into assuming that all actors would behave in a certain way. Consider the following:

From Stage 2 to Stage 3, it is assumed that the public will make states 'learn to desist from war altogether' (p. 519)—a classic liberalist aspiration that rational war-averse people will force elites to adapt 'non violent alternatives' to conflict resolution. Those studying the monadic democratic peace have learned that claims about the 'obsolescence of war' in the public mind is premature.

From Stage 4 to Stage 5, Wendt suggests that states will forfeit sovereignty to a WS due to the 'painful memories' of life under anarchy (p. 523). This implies that life and history so far have been widely accepted to be awful and traumatic with no redeeming aspects. But states and people may not share the author's woeful view of life under anarchy. Surely many have suffered from war and insufficient 'recognition', but enough to compel all humanity into submission to a global government? Wendt asserts that Stage 5 will come because a 'move back is less attractive than a move forward' (p. 523). This is taking objectivist liberties of 'knowing' what is desired or attractive to states, rather than asking states themselves. Wendt does acknowledge that the 'greatest hurdle to WS formation' is the Great Powers (p. 524). This introduces a paradox Wendt does not resolve in a convincing fashion—*Those most suffering and pained by anarchy and non-recognition are those least capable of forcing systemic change; those most capable of pushing a world state in terms of power have the least incentive to forfeit sovereignty, influence and autonomy.* Wendt's answer is simply:

> If the choice is between a world of increasing threats as a result of refusing to fully recognize Others . . . versus a world in which their desires for recognition are satisfied, it seems clear which decision rational Great Powers should make. (p. 525)

This quote introduces contingency, agency and choice, violating the notion of inevitability, since 'choice' and 'if' and 'should' are markers of agency and, thus, indeterminate outcomes. If states have choice, Wendt must concede that such states may choose *not* to create a WS. He cannot have it both ways and sustain his argument.

From Stage 3 to Stage 4, Wendt merely asserts that 'the desire to reproduce world society will induce it to develop even farther'. It does not follow that reproducing a favored system should lead to something new, much less 'inevitably'. Wendt allows for 'degeneration' to previous stages, but that 'there are good reasons to move forward' (p. 521) and thus he presumes that states will 'advance' to *his* next level. Wendt does not permit the possibility that human history is cycles of nonlinear change, caught between the tug of change, the pull of sovereignty and the myriad other forces of politics that make 'inevitability' problematic. There is no reason why such cycles of advancement and degeneration do not go on forever.

Consider the following path of Wendt's teleological trajectory. In five stages, the system evolves as such:

12345

Or, allowing for occasional historical 'degeneration', perhaps it looks like this:

121232345

Either way, Stage 5 is the inexorable conclusion. But what if, due to contingencies related to the rise and fall of different actors with different conceptions of order, preferences and identity, history instead reflects numerous steps forward and back, with nothing pregiven and the outcome unknowable? History may look like this:

1212321232143 . . . *ad infinitum*

Leaving aside empirical assessments of history to date, the point here is that agency is both necessary and neglected in Wendt's formulation. There is enough agency to allow his conception to unfold plausibly, but not enough agency to allow actors to choose other plausible futures.

MOTIVATIONAL MONOCAUSALITY

One reason why Wendt can elide serious treatment of agency is that he reduces all politics, history and war to 'struggles for recognition' (p. 528), which is never clarified beyond the search for 'full subjectivity'. While this is an interesting motivation that deserves attention and study, Wendt's oversimplification of all international relations to the pursuit of subjectivity under anarchy is a new example of 'motivational monocausality', simplicity and immutability (Cottam, 1977: 16). All inexorable forces moving history along toward a WS are about finding the 'solution to the struggle for recognition'. This presumes (1) that the struggle for recognition matters to all actors to the degree and breadth that Wendt claims; and (2) that it alone matters or is paramount to other interests, preferences and motivations. While I am sympathetic to the politics of identity—a hallmark of agentic studies—the primacy of the struggle for recognition granted in this conceptualization is undefended. Wendt mentions a catalog of 'other things to struggle over', but somehow these (and numerous other motivations) do not introduce contingency in the inexorable quest for recognition via WS formation.

Internal to his argument, recognition struggles work against the very forces of world unification he argues to be inevitable. Wendt's reference to nationalism acknowledges both the influence of non-state agents and the potential for system disintegration, yet he tries to reconcile this with his teleology by claiming that such a 'step back' is a 'precondition for moving forward' (p. 529). In fact, Wendt says a WS is 'only possible if it embraces nationalism', which seems contradictory since nationalism is about self-rule and statehood. So fragmentation is rewritten as evidence of consolidation, raising falsifiability problems as well as the logical conundrum of why new nationalist groups achieving independence from tyranny would turn and submit to another superstate.

On this last point of submission to a world state, Wendt faces unresolved problems related to Kant's skepticism regarding a world state—the potential that states will not want to give up sovereignty, and that a world state would be despotic. Sovereignty, Wendt reports, is the right to decide unilaterally to revoke an actor's recognized status and kill them. Two problems arise here—the one-sided view of sovereignty as bad, and the presumed benign nature of a world state. But sovereignty is also the right to guarantee your own recognized status against others. And why would a world state not be equally capable of unilateral right to de-recognize and kill subgroups? The WS has the power to 'enforce recognition' but also to deny it. One wonders if Israeli Jews, given their history of oppression, are comfortable with such forfeiture of autonomy, placing trust in the benign nature of an overarching superstate to uphold their identity.

Wendt does not help his cause to point out that, once a world state is formed, 'individuals and groups continue to evolve and might decide that what satisfied their desires for recognition in the past no longer do so'. This reminds us that what motivates identity groups varies spatially and temporally. If such dynamics operate *after* the creation of a WS, why do they also not inhibit the formation of the WS in the first place? If not all seek a WS, they will have to be forced into submission by somebody to accomplish it. That requires power, particularly if the resistance is from a China or United States or similar large power.

In sum, while the search for recognition is one motivation, it is clearly not the only or the most important one to all actors. To assume such is the same objectivist fallacy taken by rationalists—that situations can be characterized 'objectively' by the analyst rather than presented 'as it appears subjectively to the actor' (Simon, 1985: 298; see also Monroe, 1995). Agentic theories remind us that agents are capable of reflection, forethought and the processing of environmental pressures in ways that cannot be predicted deterministically (Jervis, 1976; Bandura, 2001). Wendt acknowledges intentionality of agency, but does not allow the implications to lead to their logical conclusion—a WS is contingent at best.

THE POSSIBILITY OF A WORLD STATE

A world state *is* a *possible* future, but it is a Herculean task given the primacy of sovereignty today. To understand its prospects, one must embrace agency and the complex motivations of actors—state and non-state. Wendt does not do this. Instead, he claims that a WS 'will emerge whether or not anyone intends to bring this about' (p. 529). He suggests a non-intentional, materialist argument that the logic of anarchy creates violence and military destructiveness that breaks the notion of self-sufficient state identity, 'enabling development of supranational we-feeling' (p. 516). Enabling such a development, however, does not determine its inevitable outcome.

He argues that the 'inevitability' may inspire supporters to work toward it, but if it is inevitable why need anybody worry? The fact that he references those actors 'globally oriented' and who '*believe* in the inevitability of a' WS (emphasis mine), shows that WS-building is in the hands of those whose identities and beliefs are so inclined, suggesting many others who are not so. Only if one recognizes it as contingent do proponents get motivated to work to persuade others of the virtues and form of a viable WS. It will require persuasion and power to construct such a wildly new world order, and teleology forecloses the discussion on the *conditions* for a world state—requirements of change brought about by willful agents. Such studies exist, the World Order Models Project (WOMP) being just one.

Wendt's article is commendable on at least three grounds. It reintroduces teleology as a plausible path for theorizing that, while I am not persuaded here, could be useful in other applications. It focuses on the 'struggle for recognition'. Identity politics is important and underexamined outside some constructivism and political psychology. Wendt's problem is that he reduces all world politics virtually to this one factor, belying the multiple motivations that define actors and their behaviors. Finally, it revisits the possibilities of a world state and reminds us that anarchy is not itself inevitable. But he commits the reverse error, for a world state is by no means inevitable either. If 'anarchy is what states make of it', that must allow for states to make it anything they want.

Agent-based IR theorizing has been swept under the carpet of structuralism since at least Waltz's *Theory of International Politics*. While solely focusing on agents is 'reductionist', to deny them *their* subjectivity—as perceivers with multiple interests, identities and motivations—does no justice to IR theorizing or the task of building a world state. World political systems are dynamic arenas of power and identity. The continued diversity of ideas and identities ensures that agency matters and that the future is up for grabs. A world state, however potentially desirable, is far from inevitable. To the extent that it is *possible*, it is through making agents believe what Wendt has argued. That is the task, and it is no small feat.

NOTE

Thanks for the comments of Ted Hopf and anonymous reviewers in improving this manuscript. Thanks also to Vasbjlt Banerjee for assistance in gathering materials for this project, and to Leah Strifling for pointing me to various world order projects referenced in the article.

1. Though Wendt's analysis is 'conceptual, not historical' (p. 516), history has shown cycles and 'backward' tendencies. The Concert of Europe in the wake of the Napoleonic Wars looked like regional 'Stage 3', but the Crimean and Franco–Prussian wars, and World War I push the system back to Stage 2 or 1. From the ashes of World War I comes the League of Nations experiment, à la Stage 2 or 3, but the 1930s beggar-thy-neighbor competition and the carnage of World War II revert us to Stage 1 or 2. The post-war headiness of the UN system represents Stage 3 logic, only to be undermined in a Cold War rivalry akin to Stage 2. At the same time, parts of the world arguably approach Stages 3 and 4 in terms of community and collective security—notably the EU and NATO. The end of the Cold War and the rise of unipolarity have left the trends ambiguous, as some 'friends' fear and compete with the US, and instability spreads throughout the world. Teleology is easy; historical reality is much messier and nonlinear.

REFERENCES

Bandura, Albert (2001) 'Social Cognitive Theory: An Agentic Perspective', *Annual Review of Psychology* 52: 1–26.

Cottam, Richard (1977) *Foreign Policy Motivation: A General Theory and a Case Study.* Pittsburgh, PA: University of Pittsburgh Press.

Jervis, Robert (1976) *Perception and Misperception in International Politics*. Princeton, NJ: Princeton University Press.

Monroe, Kristen Renwick (1995) 'Psychology and Rational Actor Theory', *Political Psychology* 16(1): 1–21.

Simon, Herbert (1985) 'Human Nature in Politics: The Dialogue of Psychology with Political Science', *American Political Science Review* 79: 293–304.

Waltz, Kenneth N. (1979) *Theory of International Politics*. New York: Random House.

Wendt, Alexander (2003) 'Why a World State is Inevitable', *European Journal of International Relations* 9(4): 491–542.

POSTSCRIPT

Many critics of the notion of some form of world state or government focus on the questions of practicality. Is it conceivable that major powers will actually surrender their sovereignty to some higher authority? Would such a move even be desirable? Critics often cite the fact that many current international institutions suffer from a "democratic deficit." Thus, they wonder how such a world state could be held accountable to the global populace and whether such a world state would be tyrannical and oppressive in nature. A critic like Robert Kagan would argue that it is better to put your faith in a benevolent hegemon like the United States, with its democratic traditions and institutions, than take the chance of an oppressive world government. In contrast, both Wendt and Deudney seem to think that that it is possible to have a liberal, republican form of world state in which power is still held in check and is made accountable to the public. Which do you find more convincing?

Liberal critics of world state argue that greater attention should be focused on improving existing forms of global governance, which are looser and more informal in nature. Most global problems, they would argue, can be addressed by working through existing liberal international institutions like the World Trade Organization or global non-governmental organizations. But, just as in the case of a world state, the challenge of how you diminish the "democratic deficit" and make these organizations accountable to the grass roots public still remains.

Suggested Additional Readings

Beitz, Charles. "Cosmopolitan Liberalism and the States System." In Chris Brown (ed.), *Political Restructuring in Europe: Ethical Perspectives*. London: Routledge, 1994.

Brown, Chris. "International Political Theory and the Idea of World Community." In K. Booth and S. Smite (eds.), *International Relations Theory Today*. University Park, Pa.: The Pennsylvania State University Press, 1995.

Copeland, Dale. "The Constructivist Challenge to Structural Realism: A Review Essay." *International Security* 25, no. 2 (Autumn, 2000): 187–212.

Deudney, Daniel. *Bounding Power: Republican Security Theory from the Polis to the Global Village*. Princeton, N.J.: Princeton University Press, 2006.

Deudney, Daniel. "Geopolitics and Change." In M. Doyle and G.J. Ikenberry (eds.), *New Thinking in International Relations Theory*. Boulder, Colo.: Westview Press, 1999.

Falk, Richard. *On Humane Governance: Toward a New Global Politics*. University Park, Pa.: Pennsylvania State University Press, 1995.

Lu, Catherine. "World Government." In Edward N. Zalta, (ed.), *The Stanford Encyclopedia of Philosophy* (Winter 2006 Edition). Available at http://plato.stanford.edu/entries/world-government/.

Nielsen, Kai. "World Government, Security, and Global Justice." In Steven Luper-Foy (ed.), *Problems of International Justice*. Boulder, Colo.: Westview Press, 1988, 263–82.

Wendt, Alex. "Why a World State Is Inevitable." *European Journal of International Relations* 9, no. 4 (2003): 491–542.

InfoTrac® College Edition

Search for the following articles in the InfoTrac® database:

Campbell, Craig. "The Resurgent Idea of World Government." *Ethics & International Affairs* 22 (Summer 2008): 133–42.

Etzioni, Amitai. "Forming a Global Authority: A World-Government Response to Terrorism." *The Futurist* 38, no. 6 (Nov.–Dec. 2004): 12–13.

Yunker, James. "Rethinking World Government: A New Approach." *International Journal of World Peace* 17, no. 1 (March 2000): 3–33.

Web Resources

For current URLs for the following websites, visit www.crosscurrents.nelson.com.

WORLD FEDERALIST MOVEMENT
http://www.wfm.org/site/index.php/pages/1

The World Federalist Movement was started in the 1930s following the failure of the League of Nations. World federalists support the creation of democratic global structures directly accountable to the citizens and call for the division of international authority among separate agencies, a separation of powers among judicial, executive, and parliamentary bodies. This site contains a wide variety of resources arguing in support of a federalist approach to world government.

WORLD BEYOND BORDERS
http://www.worldbeyondborders.org/index.htm

This site contains a number of articles and other resources both outlining the case for world government and discussing what it might look like in reality.

ONE WORLD TRUST
http://www.oneworldtrust.org

The One World Trust was founded in 1947 in the United Kingdom by the All Party Parliamentary Group for World Government. It is now an active NGO with consultative status at the United Nations and provides research and educational materials on the idea of a world government.

Can A Non-Feminist Approach to Gender Issues Help Us to Better Understand Global Politics?

✔ **YES**

R. CHARLI CARPENTER, "Gender Theory in World Politics: Contributions of a Nonfeminist Standpoint," *International Studies Review* 4, no. 3 (2002): 153–65.

✗ **NO**

TERRELL CARVER, "Gender/Feminism/IR," *International Studies Review* 5, no. 2 (2003): 287–302.

In the first two issues in this volume we have given attention to realist, liberal, and social constructivist approaches to the understanding of international relations. The addition of a feminist critique to the study of international relations is a relatively new development in the history of the discipline. Women have been largely absent from the principal canonical texts upon which the study of international relations has been founded. However, beginning in the late 1980s, an emerging generation of feminist scholars began asking, "Where are the women?" Women were absent both as analysts and as subjects of study in international politics.

Scholars argued that women were really not absent from world politics; indeed, they often played significant roles. But rather, the theories and methods that underlay the study of international relations made women largely invisible because the study of international relations, particularly within mainstream realist approaches, has been dominated by masculine reasoning. The concepts of power politics, sovereignty, autonomy, and anarchy, it is argued, rest on an inherently "masculine" view of the world. In an important early essay in feminist international relations scholarship, J. Ann Tickner took the famous "six principles of political realism" developed by Hans Morgenthau, the founding father of the realist approach to the study of international politics, and showed how each of Morgenthau's "objective" principles in fact reflected male values and perceptions of reality. Consequently, many feminists question whether mainstream IR scholarship has the ability to step out of the traditional masculine assumptions inherent to the IR field and to examine issues from a gender perspective.

As a result of some of the pioneering studies by feminist international scholars such as Cynthia Enloe, J. Ann Tickner, and Sandra Whitworth, the study of international relations has been enriched by a variety of theoretical and normative research surrounding the roles of women and gender issues in the IR field. Feminist scholars have pressed the discipline to give greater attention to such issues as the tremendous gender gap that exists in most of the world's government and power structures, the masculinity of conflict, and the effects of conflict on women. From a theoretical perspective, feminist critiques have opened conversations about the impact of capitalist systems on women and the impact of learned social constructs on human behaviour as well as the inherent masculinity in realist theoretical paradigms.

Although these studies have emphasized the point that gender is important to the study of international relations, there is no single dominant feminist approach to the study of international relations. Instead, within the literature, the reader can find a variety of approaches such as liberal feminism, socialist/Marxist feminism, standpoint feminism, and post-modern feminism. While these approaches are in agreement in focusing attention to gender and women as important themes in the study of international relations, they also differ on a number of fundamental issues leading to significant debates within feminism itself.

One such debate focuses on the question of relationship between feminism as a normative commitment and gender as an analytical category. Can gender be "mainstreamed" into the study of IR? If so, to what extent? Feminist scholars have criticized the mainstream for being dominated by masculine reasoning. They argue that since the study of IR tends to be controlled by "masculine" approaches, it is doubtful that mainstream IR scholarship has the ability to step out of the traditional masculine assumptions inherent to the IR field when examining issues from a gender perspective. Thus, as an alternative to mainstream approaches which provide a male understanding of the world, it is necessary to step aside and take a feminine perspective as a means to analyze and criticize traditional perspectives on IR.

However, some scholars feel that this approach poses the danger of "ghettoizing" the study of gender in international relations and associates it too closely with a feminist agenda. Rather than encouraging a greater focus on gender issues in international issues, it encourages mainstream scholars to continue seeing gender as an only of concern to those committed to the feminist project or to make the false assumption that the study of gender deals only with "women's issues."

This position is reflected in the first reading by Charli Carpenter. In her essay, Carpenter reflects on a number of recently published books dealing with feminism and gender in the study of IR. Carpenter is concerned that while the rise of feminist IR has made many significant advancements, the study of gender as an analytical category has still not made significant inroads into the mainstream of international relations theories. The fault lies not just with the "masculine" nature of conventional IR theories, but with feminist IR itself. She notes that sometimes the normative commitment of feminist scholars to the emancipation of women has contributed the perception of gender studies is only about "women's issues" and therefore discouraged non-feminist scholars from including gender considerations in their study. At the same time, Carpenter suggests that feminist scholars themselves have not been sympathetic to those scholars who, while not sharing a commitment to the feminist project, nevertheless want to include gender as a focus of their analysis. This has resulted, Carpenter contends, in a loss of some important insights into the nature of international relations and has narrowed the field of topics considered within the domain of gender studies. As a result, Carpenter calls for an end of the "monopoly of feminist IR of gender studies in IR theory" and the encouragement of what she labels as a non-feminist "gender constructivism." Such an approach, she believes, can fill some of the gaps left by IR feminism, and expand the study of gender to men, children, and non-feminist women's issues.

In the second reading, Terrell Carver responds to Carpenter's thesis and queries the idea of gender as an analytical category of analytical analysis, detached from normative commitments. For Carver, gender can be either *explanandum* (the thing to be explained) or *explanans* (whatever does the explaining) or both. Carver sees the conflict over gender IR theory as a part of a greater theoretical divide between those who are the "guardians of scientific objectivity," who believe in the development of analytical concepts and methods that are value-free, and those who believe that there is "an intrinsic connection between their work and their values." Carver sides with the latter position, arguing that " 'Nonfeminist gender studies' is virtually an oxymoron."

✔ **YES**

Gender Theory in World Politics: Contributions of a Nonfeminist Standpoint

R. CHARLI CARPENTER

While critical feminist theories of international relations (IR) have generated a burgeoning literature on gender in world politics, mainstream international relations theory remains largely silent on gender. This is an unfortunate state of affairs because mainstream scholars both deprive themselves of an important conceptual instrument and deprive knowledge on gender of nonfeminist insights. Although incorporating gender (and sex) would enrich all strands of IR theory, the absence of gender analyses within the emerging literature on norms and identities is particularly conspicuous. If reality is socially constructed and material outcomes depend largely on shared beliefs, the ubiquity and salience of beliefs about sexual difference in areas relevant to IR are worthy of study.

The books discussed here provide illustrative maps of the current terrain in approaches to gender in IR, while demonstrating the gaps within feminist thinking on the subject and the possibilities for generating meaningful dialogue with nonfeminist scholars. IR feminists, most recently exemplified by Ann Tickner's *Gendering World Politics*, argue that epistemological and normative differences prevent the mainstream from "taking gender seriously." Yet feminist IR also contributes to this marginalization by resisting the co-optation of gender as an explanatory framework separate from feminist normative commitments.

The edited book on gender and armed conflict, *Victims, Perpetrators or Actors?*, illustrates some of these discursive tendencies within feminist approaches to gender. While ostensibly about *gender*, the contributions actually focus on *women* and their struggles: there is little effort to broaden the scope of gender in such a way as to draw in diverse perspectives. While attempting to transcend the stereotype that women are always victims in armed conflict, many of the articles nonetheless rely on normative assumptions that women's empowerment (rather than promoting gender equality per se, or understanding the character of armed conflict) is the raison d'être of the research.

The question for "mainstreaming" gender in IR is how to put the analytical category of gender to work on topics that are not specifically feminist, without undermining the IR feminist agenda. In *War and Gender*, Joshua Goldstein attempts such a synthesis. His work compiles substantive knowledge on how gender and the war system constitute one another. But his goal is not to understand, problematize, or alleviate women's subordination. Instead, he analyzes the gendered underpinnings of the war system to identify leverage points for social and political change. This ambitious project breaks new ground in setting the stage for "conventional" empirical analyses of gender in world politics, but it does not situate gender firmly within conventional IR theory.

To engender dialogue, it would seem that conventional gender theory must be both "conventional" and "theory." How do we build an integrated framework in such a way as to complement, rather than co-opt, critical feminist theories of gender? I conclude by advocating the integration of gender into "conventional constructivist" literature on norms and identities in world politics.

GENDERING WORLD POLITICS: A FEMINIST PROJECT?

In many ways, *Gendering World Politics* exemplifies feminist IR at its best. It is understandable, grounded in empirical references, and semantically consistent. Tickner speaks to the IR community on its own terms while deconstructing such "gendered" ideas as the state, the nation, and anarchy. She demonstrates the diversity and recent evolutions within IR feminist thought and in the context of the changing issues in the broader discipline. Tickner emphasizes security, political economy, and democratization, and uses a "gender lens" to challenge nearly all the key assumptions in international theory and discourse.

Tickner informs the topic by what she has always framed as a puzzle: the seeming inability of "conventional IR" to engage meaningfully with feminists. She begins the book with theory: far more than a discussion of feminism, she provides a concise summary of the entire disciplinary landscape of IR. Feminist approaches are situated on the critical side of the continuum and in contrast to conventional IR, with its commitment to empiricism, data-based methods, value-neutrality, and substantive assumptions of states operating under anarchy (p. 149). Critical approaches (including postmodernism, critical theory, historical sociology, and normative theory) see different realities and draw on reflective and interpretive epistemologies. All critical theory contains an emancipatory agenda, as does feminism, yet feminism is distinctive insofar as all feminists "use gender as a central category of analysis" (p. 5).

While IR feminists have defined gender in different ways (and often inconsistently), Tickner views gender primarily as an analytical category. She is *not* referring to coding male and female, as the label is sometimes misappropriated by terms like the "gender gap" and the "gendered division of labor." Hers is a social constructivist view of gender that locates "genderedness" in the distributions of ideas regarding men and women—the cultural attributes associated with masculinity and femininity—that prop up the world system. Understanding how it operates—by channeling men and women disproportionately into different institutions, by devaluing attributes and behaviors associated with the feminine, and by underwriting discourses of international affairs—is a key component of understanding world politics per se. "Gendering is a mechanism for distributing social benefits and costs; therefore it is crucial for analyzing global politics and economics" (p. 134).

The puzzle is why so few theorists interested in understanding the world are willing to accord to gender the causal and constitutive role it plays. Tickner argues that even as feminism is increasingly paid lip service and given a respectable nod by the "mainstream," a healthy engagement between feminists and others is still absent. For Tickner, this can be explained by the gendered nature of the discipline itself, the masculinism of conventional approaches, and very different agendas that feminists and conventional scholars bring to the discipline. Certainly some of this is accurate.

But the answer Tickner does not consider lies in the paradox of IR feminism itself. Although she implicitly offers gender as an *explanatory* theory of world politics, she simultaneously locates gender in IR *feminism* (pp. 5, 11). If gender theory is inherently feminist, then feminist theory, as a critical theory concerned with emancipation, is explicitly normative: "the key concern for feminist theory is to explain women's subordination . . . and to seek prescriptions for ending it" (p. 11; also pp. 63, 137).

If gender is seen as synonymous with feminism,[1] this suggests that to take gender seriously means to subscribe to the prescriptive agenda of feminism, an implication that surely plays a role in silencing comments about gender by those who do not self-identify as feminists within the discipline. Moreover, it does not logically follow: the explanatory claim "gender matters" need not constitute a feminist prescriptive claim and in fact can do the opposite. For example, the claim that beliefs about sexual difference affect social behavior underlies antifeminist arguments for the exclusion of women from nuclear submarine duty.

Framing gender analysis as feminism, in which Tickner is not the only participant, has reduced incentives for scholars not committed to feminism to take gender seriously.[2] The mainstream IR scholar, even if s/he finds arguments about gender compelling, faces an apparent choice between adopting feminist theory to study gender (migrating from establishment to fringe) or joining in the collective marginalization of gender as an explanatory variable and feminism as a normative perspective. Scholars who have engaged or even used gender in their work without subscribing to the feminist agenda have received an icy reception from feminists.[3] It may be, in addition to the limited interest from the mainstream Tickner cites, that not all feminist scholars are as open-minded as Tickner about the utility of cross-turf dialogue. Perhaps this is one impediment to conversations about gender with nonfeminists that Tickner has underemphasized.

The need to fit scholarship on gender into the axiological mold of feminist theory not only has kept nonfeminists out, but also has affected both the substance of IR gender research and its discursive structure. Women's subordination and victimization is too often assumed by feminists rather than examined contextually, and there is little substantive work on how gender constrains the life chances of "people called men" in different contexts or affects political outcomes more generally. A reading of Tickner's text, with an eye to the hidden assumptions within feminist discourse, reveals a perpetuation rather than a questioning of certain gender stereotypes. This is indicative not so much of Tickner's substantive summary but of the linguistic and philosophical structure of the feminist subfield.

For example, the notion that women but not men are located as caretakers (pp. 50, 106) is a gendered construction that should be destabilized, perhaps through an emphasis on "parents" rather than "mothers." The trope "civilians now account for about 90 percent of war casualties, the majority of whom are women and children" (p. 6) is a gendered construction of the "civilian" that flies in the face of, among other things, refugee statistics and the widespread targeting of civilian men and boys for massacre in armed conflicts around the world.[4] Men as gendered subjects seldom appear in feminist work: of the now numerous IR feminist books on "gender and world politics," almost none deal explicitly with men and masculinity.[5] When "masculinities" are dealt with, they are conceptualized as a social problem; conversely, "femininities" have been greatly undertheorized, often dropping out of phrases like "men and masculinities . . . and women" (p. 134).[6]

Where the term "gender violence" is used to mean "violence against women" (p. 114), other forms of gender violence—such as against gays, against male partners by women or men, or against children deemed "illegitimate" by a patriarchal system—are rendered invisible, thus truncating the use of gender analytically.[7] When "family violence" is portrayed as violence against women and children, it obscures abuse of children at the hands of female adults (pp. 63, 113).

The fact that, as Tickner writes, "feminists have been reluctant to take on the question of paid domestic service . . . since it is women who usually employ, and often exploit, other women" suggests the quandary that feminists encounter as simultaneously normative and explanatory researchers. Writing with a declared agenda for promoting the interests of all women, feminists run up against empirical and theoretical difficulties when the results of gender in operation conflict with their normative agenda. Tickner's comments on the "democratic family," for example (p. 123), have important implications not just for husband/wife relations, but also for the license women may take with their children. Therefore, it may not follow that understanding gender and overcoming the hierarchies it generates may always coincide with promoting the liberties of women or the "satisfaction of women's needs" in every context.[8]

If IR feminism is focused more on some areas of political life than on others, this should not be read as an indictment of the subfield. Like other critical theorists, feminists would be the first to emphasize that no theory is value-neutral and detached from its political agenda. If feminist theory is for the purpose of exposing, addressing, and ending women's subordination, it will naturally be constructed and channeled in accordance with that agenda. *This is not a criticism of feminism (for this agenda is entirely legitimate) so much as it is a challenge to the monopoly of feminist IR on gender studies in IR theory.* It is not for feminists to change more than is digestible within the emancipatory framework to which they are committed, but it is the task of those not writing within that framework to recognize and appropriate gender as an analytical instrument, separate from feminism as a critical discourse, within the scope of their own analyses.

Yet many feminists are skeptical of the possibility of nonfeminist gender theory. Such developments have been seen as attempts to "co-opt feminist analyses and to accommodate women within the prevailing conception of IR [that] feminists must resist."[9] This sentiment has been echoed repeatedly in feminist work, especially in response to those few nonfeminist attempts to bring gender into the mainstream. According to this perspective, attempts to incorporate feminism into the mainstream "can be understood as an attempt to favor (certain parts of) the mainstream by dividing and conquering the new opposition."[10]

Research on gender in IR faces a conundrum. Feminist approaches—while rich, diverse, and a much needed critique—are substantively narrow as their emphasis is women in world affairs rather than international politics itself. Yet scholars working in nonfeminist traditions face disciplinary barriers to appropriating "gender" in conventional frameworks. Given the significance of gender in world politics and some of the limitations to feminist approaches described above, there are two questions for IR feminists and the broader community: Can IR feminists adjust their frameworks to generate more inclusive analyses while retaining their focus on women's emancipation? Can nonfeminist scholars interested in gender create a space for generating their own theories of gender in world politics while engaging with rather than substituting for the insights of feminist theory?

Two recent books provide clues. The collection edited by Caroline Moser and Fiona Clark begins by questioning some of the stereotypes in earlier IR feminist work on gender. The editors wish to go beyond the essentializing of women as victims and men as perpetrators of violence, a view that they argue denies women agency, as well as obscures the complexity of gender in armed conflict. The book "aims to contribute to a more comprehensive, global understanding of the complex roles, responsibilities and interests of women and men, whether as victims, perpetrators or actors, in armed conflict and political violence" (p. 4).

A promising agenda, but how well do the chapters in this book actually follow through? Of all the articles, only one chiefly concerns men and masculinity; only two have a roughly balanced gender analysis that emphasizes the effects of armed conflict on the well-being of both men and women. Although "gender" is in the title, it seems that women and women's mobilization remain the dependent variables. Lip service is given to the notion that gender affects men equally or that men may be victims as well as perpetrators. But disproportionately little empirical work here concerns men, children, or gender as it affects any other aspects of the war and peace process;[11] and comments such as the goal being "a peaceful existence for women" (Simona Sharoni, p. 99) or "although war affected men and women alike, for women the losses are innumerable" (Ibanez, p. 117) are hidden among the talk of theoretical advancement.[12]

Despite Cynthia Cockburn's remarkably coherent explanatory framework, articulated in the first chapter, few of the chapters follow through on a systematic analysis of gender. Instead, most of the authors confuse sex and gender (pp. 10, 30, 92). What is left is a great deal of descriptive research on sex-differentiated behavior, impacts, and issues in armed conflict but little explanatory analysis of how *gender* (identities, beliefs, and discourses) constructs these outcomes or how best to target those attitudes for change.

The book remains a solid feminist description of women's troubles, with some attention given to the conjoint difficulties men face and a positive spin on how women can mobilize to create solutions. For example, Sharoni's chapter on women activists on both sides of the Northern Ireland conflict and in Palestine examines variation in the impact of national struggles on women's liberties. Donny Meerten's analysis of displacement in Colombia celebrates women's coping strategies as a buffer against the struggles of urban existence. Urvashi Butalia's work on women's feminist and antifeminist mobilization in India both undermines the idea of a generic pan-female solidarity and explains the paradox of female support for bloody communalism and suttee. These chapters indeed move feminist work on political violence beyond simple formulas, capturing situational nuance and providing new puzzles and new answers.

Yet the book does little to generate an inclusive agenda for showing how gender affects political outcomes in general. Thus the book, while an excellent contribution to scholarship on *women*, leaves out much that could have been discussed pertaining to *gender* as it affects not women per se, but patterns of armed conflict and political violence generally.

Where the Moser and Clark book tries to transcend feminist biases while retaining a focus on women, Goldstein brings feminist theories to bear on the "conventional" agenda of IR: the war system. His task is not to critique or engage but to test hypotheses: sociocultural versus sociobiological approaches to explaining male predominance in organized warfare.

War and Gender does not read like Francis Fukuyama's facile argument about the relative utility of one side in the nature/nurture debate.[13] Goldstein sees value in both approaches and wishes to capture the interplay between sex and gender, between biology and culture, which are both interdependent and mutually constitutive: "biology provides diverse potential, and cultures limit, select and channel them" (p. 2).

Goldstein compiles, sorts, and analyzes evidence for or against a long list of hypotheses drawn from evolutionary biology and feminist theories (essentialist and constructivist). His survey is remarkably thorough, accounting both for sex differentiation in the location of human beings in institutions of war and peace and for the gendered cultural constructions that sustain them. The work will be important in placing "gender" in the feminist sense on the agenda of those interested in understanding the social dynamics of warfare. Moreover, *War and Gender* will become an important teaching resource in undergraduate IR courses, which may do more than anything to mainstream concepts of gender in the discipline.

Goldstein's work is groundbreaking as an example of how gender as an explanatory instrument may be combined with a conventional IR agenda using empirical science rather than interpretivism. He avoids engaging with current theoretical debates, but his work demonstrates that the disjunction Tickner identifies is one between feminism and conventional IR, not between gender theory and IR. According to Goldstein, gender can and should be deployed in conventional analysis to understand precisely the "real world issues . . . of war in and between states" that feminists wish to push beyond.[14]

Yet this work is only a first step toward integrating gender as a theory into conventional IR. On the subject of how gender may best intersect with contemporary debates, Goldstein has little to say. He represents a voice in an emerging "conversation" but does not lay out parameters for the conversation itself. Relative to the complexity of feminist approaches to gender, Goldstein's analytical framework seems oversimplified.

For example, while his hypotheses can be categorized according to whether they assign causal value to culture or biology, Goldstein denies that these are separate analytically. In using "gender to cover masculine and feminine roles and bodies alike" (p. 2), he is doing reflectively what many writers and policymakers do subconsciously. This enables Goldstein to provide some important insights, such as destabilizing the notion that biology is deterministic and cultural malleable: "In truth, scientists understand, control and change biology much more easily . . . than social scientists or politicians understand and control culture and social relationships, including gender and war" (p. 131). Laying out the multiple points of overlap between bodies and ideas is an important contribution because so much literature continues to posit a false dichotomy between them. Nonetheless, the distinction between sex and gender remains important for operationalizing the two, and the intelligibility of Goldstein's analysis, particularly to the lay reader, suffers as a result of this conflation.

Moreover, Goldstein sets up male predominance in organized fighting as a constant rather than exploring what variation exists. He then seeks to explain it by referring to configurations in physiology and culture that actually do vary greatly. What is lacking is reference to specific research agendas within mainstream theory: the democratic peace, ethnic conflict, nuclear proliferation, collective security. Goldstein has demonstrated the breadth of intersections among sex, gender, and the war system and has demonstrated that objective empirical theory on gender is possible in IR. But gender as an analytical category must also be welded to the mainstream IR agenda of explaining variation in international political outcomes. The remaining section sketches such a possible marriage of explanatory gender theory with "conventional constructivism."

TOWARD "GENDER CONSTRUCTIVISM" IN IR?

Paraphrasing Sandra Whitworth, Tickner claims theories that incorporate gender must satisfy three criteria: "1) they must allow for the possibility of talking about the social construction of meaning; 2) they must discuss historical variability; and 3) they must permit theorizing about power in ways that uncover hidden power relations" (p. 27).

Nothing in this formula requires gender theories to be explicitly normative, as Tickner and others claim feminism must be (p. 2).[15] Moreover, although Tickner begins by situating all IR scholarship on norms and social values in IR as "constitutive" versus "explanatory" theory (p. 27), much of the social constructivist work on norms and identities actually claims to share an epistemological framework with those traditions Tickner considers conventional while possessing the ontological orientation that Whitworth claims is necessary for gender theory.[16]

If gender as an explanatory framework is to be incorporated into mainstream IR epistemologies, conventional constructivism—or what Tickner later calls "bridging theories" (p. 46)—appear to be the obvious entry point. Scholars such as Ronald Jepperson, Peter Katzenstein, and Alexander Wendt are committed to an identity-based ontology but, according to Tickner, "stay within the traditional security agenda, a focus on states and explanatory social science" (p. 45). Given constructivism's emphasis on norms and identity in world politics, it is surprising that this school has not already begun to build on feminist gender theories; this may reflect, as Tickner argues, a systematic gender bias.

Yet it does not result from theoretical incompatibility. This variant of constructivism *is* ontologically suited to studying gender norms and identities, as a specific component of the broader category of social relations composing world politics. While Locher and Prugl correctly have pointed out that constructivists would epistemologically approach gender in a different way than feminists, it does not mean, as they conclude, that constructivists must incorporate feminist epistemologies to study gender.[17] It only means that the two sorts of gender theory will be somewhat different; the study of gender norms and international policy should be no more an epistemological problem for constructivists than the study of nuclear weapons taboos or humanitarian intervention. Martha Finnemore and Kathryn Sikkink's examination of the spread of women's suffrage as a norm of civilized society may be an example of such scholarship—a work that is absent from Tickner's bibliography of scholarship on gender.[18] This is less a matter of inherent incompatibility than of feminists and constructivists overcoming the notion that gender studies is a feminist preserve.

What could this explanatory gender theory look like, and how could it contribute to understanding gender and world politics? It could do so in three ways: conceptually, substantively, and analytically.

Conceptually, a conversation between nonfeminist and feminist gender theories would help refine much of the loose and inconsistent terminology pertaining to gender as a concept. For example, one outcome of such a conversation might be to clarify the sex/gender distinction. Much feminist theory routinely conflates these two concepts, either for theoretical reasons[19] or because of the way gender has been appropriated in colloquial usage.[20] Yet to destabilize the assumption that embodied men and women correlate to gendered ascriptive and prescriptive notions, it seems that sex and gender must be discussed separately in scholarly literature.

Although operationalizing sex versus gender in this way does abstract away from some of the issues that postmodernists point to, and from certain anomalies in human biology, it usefully maps onto the constructivist distinction between "material forces" and "ideas." For example, John Searle has distinguished between "brute facts" (objects that exist in the real world like tanks, nuclear weapons, or people with uteruses) and "social facts" like money, Christmas, marriage, or misogyny, which require intersubjective agreement on their existence and consti-tution.[21] It is an empirical fact that human beings are divided into roughly two categories based on biological roles and reproduction; this would still be true whether gender ideologies that assign social importance to this distinction exist or not. The existence and nature of those gender ideologies are separate from the sheer physiology of humans; gender ideologies, institutions, and identities built on them are social facts.

That the social and material interrelate does not mean, as Goldstein insists, that the distinction is analytically irrelevant. It may be true, for example, that nuclear weapons would have no actual destructive power without institutional and social arrangements that make it possible to actually deploy them.[22] But this does not mean that nuclear weapons are not objectively real. It is an analysis of the mutual interaction of the social and material worlds that is the task of constructivist IR in its critical and explanatory versions. An engagement of conventional con-structivists with these operationalization questions is certain to generate inter-esting dialogue between mainstream and feminist IR.

Substantively, "gender constructivism" can fill some of the niches left by IR feminism mentioned above. Beyond expanding the study of gender to men, chil-dren, and nonfeminist women's issues, nonfeminist social constructivists' main niche to be filled is in generating a richer body of literature in which the inter-national system is the dependent variable. Feminist IR has already created a large body of work to draw on in this capacity, emphasizing links between masculinism and militarism, the role of gender in constructing national identities and interests, the embeddedness of gendered thinking in foreign policy discourses and its influ-ence on political action, and the importance of gender beliefs in sustaining the international political economy. But the key purpose of feminist theory is to investigate and argue for improvements in the well-being of *women.* As Tickner emphasizes, it is women, not interactions between states, that are the primary dependent variable in feminist IR (p. 139). Conversely, gender constructivists can use the analytical category feminists have developed to understand the IR agenda as conventionally defined.

A rich variety of questions pertinent to mainstream IR theory is possible. Were American women allowed to fight in the Gulf War for manpower reasons, to satisfy domestic women voters, or as a part of psychological warfare against the opponent's male-dominated forces? Were these strategies effective, or does increasing hostility among allied Middle Eastern publics constitute a variety of "blowback" effect? Do the strategic advantages of shifts of sex composition of modern militaries outweigh the social and institutional challenges? How best can states uphold morale among soldiers programmed with militarized identities while successfully achieving the pacifist imperatives of humanitarian interventions? Can assumptions about gender embedded in international custom help explain patterns of intervention? How do gender relations influence the personality and the behavior of political leaders during international events? Is there no apparent relationship? How do sea changes in ideologies about gender relations change the political arena in which states must secure legitimacy?

Analytically, gender theory in IR would benefit from the development of distinctions between different causal and constitutive pathways by which gender affects world politics. Much of this also could map onto models used in conventional constructivism to explain how norms and identities operate. These could include distinctions among *gender identity* (individual beliefs about one's masculinity or femininity), *gender ideology* (principled beliefs about relations between men and women), and *gender structure* (distribution of embodied men and women into social and political institutions). All three of these influence and are manipulated by *gender norms* (collectively held causal and prescriptive beliefs regarding gender roles), and all constitute and reinforce a global (but changing) *gender regime.* Specifying and generating explanatory models for how these interrelate in different contexts, with reference to specific issue areas relevant to studying world politics, can do much more than advance knowledge on women's subordination. It can advance knowledge on IR itself.

If we accept that feminism is inherently critique but that gender per se is simply an analytical category, then scholarship on gender may—indeed must—be undertaken not only by feminists interested in "generating demands for change" (Cockburn, p. 16), but also by "conventional" scholars who wish to understand the world as it is. If we take the explanatory claims of IR feminism seriously—as I believe we must—then conventional IR theorists must recognize gender, whether or not they wish to be feminists, in the course of furthering their own agenda. This research should be undertaken in such a way as to complement and engage, rather than substitute for, feminist IR theory. Perhaps this could engender the substantive dialogue between feminists and "the mainstream" that Tickner so fervently seeks.

NOTES

1. The converse is not so obvious: all IR feminists have not relied on gender as an analytical category; some simply focus on women, and as Tickner describes, the earliest phase of IR feminism took precisely this "add women and stir" approach. One might speak of *gender feminists* and *nongender feminists*. The issue here is that there seem to be few examples of *nonfeminist gender theory*. By this, I mean scholarship that utilizes gender in analysis while lacking one or both other components of feminist theory: an emphasis on women and a critical/interpretive epistemology. See Adam Jones, "Gender and Ethnic Conflict in Ex-Yugoslavia," *Ethnic and Racial Studies* 17 (1994), which uses gender as critique but emphasizes men's in addition to women's issues; and Laura Miller and Charles Moskos, "Humanitarians or Warriors: Race, Gender and Combat Status in Operation Restore Hope?" *Armed Forces and Society* 21 (1995); Mary Caprioli, "Gendered Conflict," *Journal of Peace Research* 37, No. 1 (2000); Mark Tessler et al., "Further Tests of the Women and Peace Hypothesis," *International Studies Quarterly* 43, No. 3 (1999). These authors use gender as an instrument in empirical, explanatory analysis within a conventional IR agenda.

2. For example, see Marysia Zalewski, "Well, What Is the Feminist Perspective on Bosnia?" *International Affairs* 71 (1995), p. 341; V. Spike Peterson, "Introduction," in V. Spike Peterson, ed., *Gendered States: Feminist (Re)Visions of International Relations Theory* (Boulder, Colo.: Lynne Reinner, 1992), p. 1; Sandra Whitworth, *Feminism and International Relations* (New York: St. Martin's Press, 1994), p. 39.

3. See Cynthia Weber, "Good Girls, Little Girls and Bad Girls," *Millennium: Journal of International Studies* 23 (1994), pp. 337–348; Terrell Carver et al., "Gendering Jones: Feminisms, IRs, Masculinities," *Review of International Studies* 24, No. 2 (1998), pp. 283–297.

4. Adam Jones, "Gendercide and Genocide," *Journal of Genocide Research* (2000); Charli Carpenter, "Innocent Women and Children: Gender in Discourses of Justified Intervention," paper presented to the American Political Science Association, September 2001.

5. See, however, Marysia Zalewski and Jane Parpart, eds., *The Man Question in International Relations* (Boulder, Colo.: Westview, 1998), and Charlotte Hooper, *Manly States* (New York: Columbia University Press, 2000). That Charlotte Hooper would need to justify the study of masculinity, and would do so in terms of "understanding the enemy," is indicative of the norm within feminist gender theories to focus on women. See Hooper, "Masculinities in Transition," in Marianne Marchand and Anne Sisson Runyan, eds., *Gender and Global Restructuring* (New York: Routledge, 2000).

6. See Cynthia Enloe's analysis of militarized femininities: *Maneuvers: The International Politics of Militarizing Women's Lives* (Berkeley: University of California Press, 2000).

7. A few exceptions to this trend include Dubravka Zarkov, "The Body of the Other Man," *Victims, Perpetrators or Actors?* (London: Zed Books, 2001), and Charli Carpenter, "Surfacing Children: Limitations of Genocidal Rape Discourse," *Human Rights Quarterly* 22, No. 2 (2000), pp. 428–477.

8. Cynthia Cockburn, "The Gendered Dynamics of Armed Conflict and Political Violence," *Victims, Perpetrators or Actors?* (London: Zed Books, 2001), p. 16.

9. Sarah Brown, "Feminism, International Theory, and International Relations of Gender Inequality," *Millennium* 17, No. 3 (1989), p. 461.

10. Craig Murphy, "Seeing Women, Recognizing Gender, Recasting International Relations," *International Organization* 50 (1996), p. 530. See also Christine Sylvester, *Feminist Theory and International Relations in a Postmodern Era* (Cambridge, U.K.: Cambridge University Press, 1994), p. 41, and Marysia Zalewski, "Feminist Standpoint Theory Meeting International Relations Theory," *Fletcher Forum* 17, No. 2 (1993), pp. 13–32.

11. See Zarkov's chapter, "The Body of the Other Man," on the portrayals of male war rapes in the Croatian press during the Balkans wars. This chapter addresses men as both victims and perpetrators and provides explanatory analysis of how gender constructs militarized ethnicity.

12. Emphasis added by author.

13. Francis Fukuyama, "Women and the Evolution of World Politics," *Foreign Affairs* 77, No. 5 (1998).

14. Tickner, *Gendering World Politics*, p. 138.

15. Whitworth, *Feminism and International Relations*, p. 2; Brown, "Feminism," p. 472; Jill Steans, *Gender and International Relations* (New Brunswick, N.J.: Rutgers University Press, 1998) p. 15.

16. See Jeffrey Checkel, "The Constructivist Turn in IR Theory," *World Politics* 50 (1998), pp. 324–348. See also Ted Hopf's distinction between "conventional" and "critical" constructivism: "The Promise of Constructivism in IR Theory," *International Security* 23 (1998), p. 181. Because all critical theories take for granted that reality is socially constructed, the label "constructivism" is redundant for critical theory. I use the term only to refer to conventional or "bridging" social theories of IR.

17. Birgit Locher and Elisabeth Prugl, "Feminism and Constructivism: Worlds Apart or Sharing the Middle Ground?" *International Studies Quarterly* 45, No. 1 (2001), pp. 111–130.

18. Martha Finnemore and Kathryn Sikkink, "International Norm Dynamics and Political Change," *International Organization* 52 (1998), pp. 887–917.

19. Postmodern scholars in particular claim that the category of "male" or "female" is more a social than a biological reality, and to define sex as biological and only gender as social is to ignore an important role gender plays: the construction of male/female difference. For example, "it is the firmly held belief that there are two and only two sexes that explains the relative ease with which initial sex assignment is achieved." See Candace West and Sarah Fenstermaker, "Power, Inequality and the Accomplishment of Gender," in Paula England, ed., *Theory on Gender, Feminism on Theory* (New York: Aldine de Gruyter, 1993), p. 135.

20. This includes coding "male vs. female" to operationalize gender and using terminology such as "gendered" to describe sex distributions rather than distributions of ideas. For example, see Spike Peterson and Anne Sisson Runyan, *Global Gender Issues* (Boulder, Colo.: Westview, 1993), p. 45; Mary Meyer and Elisabeth Prugl, *Gender Politics in Global Governance* (Lanham, Md.: Rowman and Littlefield, 1999), p. 25; Peter Beckman, "Realism, Women and World Politics," in Francine D'Amico and Peter Beckman, eds., *Women, Gender and World Politics* (Westport, Conn.: Bergin and Harvey, 1994), p. 26.

21. John Searle, *The Construction of Social Reality* (New York: Free Press, 1995).

22. See Carol Cohn, "Clean Bombs and Clean Language," in Jean-Bethke Elshtain and Sheila Tobias, eds., *Women, Militarism and War* (Lanham, Md.: Rowman and Littlefield, 1990).

REFERENCES

Goldstein, Joshua. *War and Gender: How Gender Affects the War System and Vice-Versa* (Cambridge, U.K.: Cambridge University Press, 2001).

Moser, Caroline O. N., and Fiona C. Clark, eds. *Victims, Perpetrators or Actors? Gender, Armed Conflict and Political Violence* (London: Zed Books, 2001).

Tickner, J. Ann. *Gendering World Politics* (New York: Columbia University Press, 2001).

✗ NO

Gender/Feminism/IR
TERRELL CARVER

USING GENDER

Gender is not going to be "an explanatory framework" (Carpenter 2002:154). Rather, it is going to figure into the explanatory frameworks that people already have, and into the ones that international relations (IR) theorists think that they should have. Gender is not either explanandum (the thing to be explained) or explanans (whatever does the explaining). It could be either or both, on its own or in conjunction with other factors. Clearly some researchers are going to need persuading that gender matters at all in what they study. Typically gender is going to be in both explanandum and explanans, rather as cause and effect are linked, and, indeed, that linkage is likely to play a part in what convinces us that the explanation is a good one. For example, voting Republican or Conservative (an effect) is probably going to have something to do with having Republican or Conservative values or beliefs (a cause), but of course it could also be explanatorily linked with income and wealth as well as with parental voting (Republican or Conservative), with geographical residence (where there are lots of Republicans or Conservatives), and so on. Gender can function within a framework, but it is not the framework itself. Putting gender into the explanandum or explanans, or having it figure in some different way in both, may be said "to gender" a study and "to gender" an explanatory framework.

The above is intended to explain some shorthand usage and to help clarify situations in which researchers talk past one another (Carver forthcoming). It does not, of course, describe the only situation in which researchers talk past one another. Consider another. For some researchers the fact–value dichotomy is central and a cornerstone of science and objectivity whereas for others the dichotomy is not only nonexistent but an illusion with an ideological function. Communication across this divide is notoriously difficult. Few philosophers of social science today hold to anything like the Humean orthodoxy that "you cannot derive values from facts" and that "true facts are value-neutral." Such would require facts to be established by researchers who are (through some means or procedure) objective and detached in their professional roles. Weaker senses of objectivity rely on disclosure of values, concepts of balance, and a belief that literal language can exclude values sufficiently to offer a universality of truth to any and all who are rational and open-minded. This position obviously relies on views about language (that it can be literal and therefore value-free) and consciousness (that it can be detachedly objective apart from privately held views) that are well understood in theory but controversial in principle and in practice. The opposite view—that no literal language is possible and that value-free consciousness as a scientist is not only impossible but perniciously ideological—relies on philosophical positions that are rather more recent (post-"linguistic turn"), overtly critical rather than disengaged, and even more controversial to defend intellectually and politically. The debates continue, and the divide persists.

The methodological divide sketched above is a major one in IR and directly affects the gender question precisely because raising gender as an issue has been regarded as a major challenge to the discipline as such. Any discipline has boundaries setting out its self-definition. Arguably IR has been substantively defined at such a level of generality and abstraction that gender (as human sexual difference, we might say for the moment) could simply be ruled out altogether. Conversely those arguing that gender should be substantively included in explanandum or explanans (indeed that all previous IR content should be "gendered") have been perceived as radical challengers to an agreed upon or traditional core in the field (agreed upon by whom and when are, of course, further relevant difficulties here). Indeed, some of those arguing for the necessity and sometimes the centrality of gender have adopted the role of challenger quite self-consciously. For unsurprising reasons, the "gendering" of IR has been associated with, and the project of, a number of feminists, who have generally (though not completely) fallen on the side of the methodological divide that views the fact–value dichotomy with grave suspicion and overt hostility. Conversely those inclined to defend the so-called standard substance of IR have tended (though not exclusively) to be those using a methodology founded on the fact–value distinction (see Jones 1996, 1998; Carver, Cochran, and Squires 1998). The upshot here is that the "gendering" of IR has been attacked by disciplinary guardians and by guardians of scientific objectivity, whereas "gendered" IR has generally been pursued by feminists usually avowing an intrinsic connection between their work and their values, and often arguing for a transformation of the discipline in terms of substance. "Gendering IR" is thus a project; "gendered" IR is an outcome.

Nonetheless, some brave attempts at dialogue and crossover have occurred. To some extent this space is occupied by newish methodologies (for example, constructivism), containing and maintaining ambiguities that bridge the divides of substance and methodology. These meeting places allow newish topics to accrete to IR as a discipline and, thus, to gain inclusion of a sort (which may mean marginalization). There is, in effect, a kind of practical getting-on-with-it that may not please ruthlessly logical philosophers of science (who like to emphasize unbridgeable logical differences) or stern guardians of the discipline (who dislike accretions, particularly that one). But as a form of liberal pressure group and transformative identity politics, it clearly has advantages. Even though this account has emphasized (and oversimplified) intellectual issues, additional generational, geographical, cultural and—dare we say—gender issues about IR as a profession have considerable salience in the story (Carver 1998:351).

WHAT IS GENDER? WHAT IS SEX?

Recent debates about what gender is have complicated matters still further, particularly among feminists, who started the debates (Connell 2002). Joan Scott (1999) has argued that as a term "gender" tends to signal our desire to show that some aspects of our bodily and behavioral selves are malleable and, therefore, cultural products, whereas other aspects belong to "the natural," which is taken to be fixed. Sex as male–female differences and sexuality as desire and practices generally cover the bodily features and behavioral forms to which we call attention when "gendering" anything, and within which we commonly deploy the natural–cultural boundary line. Hardly anyone wants to claim that everything about sex and sexuality is cultural and therefore malleable, and almost no one regards everything in sex and sexuality as completely fixed biologically by nature.

While working to center "woman" as a valid object of study and to validate women as "knowers" and "speakers" generally, feminists have understandably developed a view of men (distinguishing here between a generic human "man" and man-as-male) that sees them benefiting from the masculine codings of so many of the resources and activities in society in a power-hierarchy over women. Gender researchers in men's studies and masculinities have contributed a theoretical and descriptive understanding of the gender categories (in terms of bodily stereotyping and sexuality policing) of advantage and disadvantage among men. Some of this work has occurred within a frame described as feminist or feminist-friendly (see Carver forthcoming). With reference to IR, these latter issues concerning men have recently surfaced in discussions about how to "gender" IR. Feminist and so-called non-feminist researchers in the field have approached the issue by tracking the distinctions described above (see Jones forthcoming). Given the number of dichotomies involved, the output matrix of possible positions is highly complex!

Gender is "marked" on women and on "woman" as female. It is often difficult to persuade men that they have any gender or that gender is of any relevance or interest, other than as something that women do, about women (or "woman"). Bringing men-as-men into gender studies and into a "gendered" IR is, therefore, quite tricky for two reasons. First, feminism is an ongoing political project about gender oppression that must be noticed and not lightly dismissed or marginalized, say, on methodological grounds, such as occurs in the push to be value-neutral. Second, notions that "gendering" IR must involve "balance" or "equality" are gendered notions in themselves, and gendered masculine, because they erase the hierarchy that exists within the binary and simple duality of "sex" (as male versus female) and the history of female oppression (Jones 2000; Carver 2002).

KNOWING GENDER

Feminist theory, feminist values, and feminist scholarship, although understandably focusing on women, have in no way resisted the consideration of men-as-men and masculinities as features of world politics, nor have they argued that feminists make gender into a synonym for women such that men-as-men get erased (see Jones 1996, 2000, 2002). The author's (Carver 1996) critical barb in his book title, *Gender Is Not a Synonym for Women*, was directed at men! Mainstreaming a feminist-informed concept of "gender" in any area or methodology in IR would hardly undermine the feminist agenda, and if any feminists think so, it is up to them to say rather than for anyone to presume that this process will ipso facto be a problem for nonfeminist IR (Carpenter 2002:154). Moreover, nonfeminist IR had better know what it is talking about when it "genders" its research!

Doing the "gendering" well would mean a thorough acquaintance with feminist literatures on gender beyond what is summarized in feminist IR, and a similarly thorough appreciation of how feminist thinking has created contemporary gender studies by fostering diversity and critique. "Nonfeminist gender studies" is virtually an oxymoron. Does nonfeminist IR have a concept of gender derivative of some "nonfeminist" conceptions that would stand up to scrutiny today in social scientific or theoretical circles? Even though it might be possible to adapt feminist-informed concepts of gender to political agendas that are feminist or even feminist-friendly, it is difficult to visualize an IR that is nonfeminist and credible in the sense of writing off feminist-informed concepts of gender as politically biased in favor of some nonfeminist concepts that are not. In sum, the urge to create a nonfeminist IR marks an interesting strategy of "othering" feminist IR yet again. What exactly has IR got to lose? Does feminist IR like its ghetto? Surely IR is broad enough to encompass feminist-informed and feminist-friendly concepts of gender on both sides of any ideological or political divides.

REFERENCES

Carpenter, R. Charli. (2002) Gender Theory in World Politics: Contributions of a Nonfeminist Standpoint? *International Studies Review* 4(3): 153–165.

Carpenter, R. Charli. (2003) Women and Children First: Gender, Norms, and Humanitarian Evacuation in the Balkans 1991–1995. *International Organization* 57(4).

Carver, Terrell. (1996) *Gender Is Not a Synonym for Women.* Boulder: Lynne Rienner.

Carver, Terrell. (1998) Gendering IR. *Millennium* 27: 343–351.

Carver, Terrell. (2002) Men and IR/Men in IR. In *Gendering the International*, edited by Louiza Odysseos and Hakan Seckinelgin. Basingstoke: Palgrave/Macmillan.

Carver, Terrell. (Forthcoming) Men and Masculinities in Gendercide/Genocide. In *Gendercide and Genocide*, edited by Adam Jones. Nashville, TN: Vanderbilt University Press.

Carver, Terrell, Molly Cochran, and Judith Squires. (1998) Gendering Jones. *Review of International Studies* 24: 283–297.

Connell, Robert W. (2002) *Gender.* Cambridge: Polity.

Jones, Adam. (1996) Does Gender Make the World Go Round? Feminist Critiques of International Relations. *Review of International Studies* 22: 405–429.

Jones, Adam. (1998) Engendering Debate. *Review of International Studies* 24: 299–303.

Jones, Adam. (2000) Gendercide and Genocide. *Journal of Genocide Research* 2: 185–211.

Jones, Adam. (2002) Gender and Genocide in Rwanda. *Journal of Genocide Research* 4: 87–89.

Jones, Adam, ed. (Forthcoming) *Gendercide and Genocide.* Nashville, TN: Vanderbilt University Press.

Scott, Joan Wallach. (1999) *Gender and the Politics of History.* New York: Columbia University Press.

POSTSCRIPT

Carpenter argues that by linking gender studies so closely with the feminist project and its focus on the emancipation of women, the field of IR has been deprived of some valuable insights that gender analysis can offer. What would a non-feminist gender analysis look like? In addition to the work of Joshua Goldstein cited by Carpenter, it is useful to look at the work of Adam Jones on gender and gendercide. In a book entitled *Gendercide and Genocide* (Nashville, Tenn.: Vanderbilt University Press, 2004), Jones argues that "gender studies" of civil wars, humanitarian crises, and genocide have focused primarily on the victimization of women. This de-emphasizes a critical dimension that is common to almost all cases of genocide—the deliberate targeting and killing of battle-aged men. The gender nature of targeting men has, in Jones's view, "attracted virtually no attention at the level of scholarship and public policy" (p. 2). Thus, by applying the concept of gender to the study of genocide, from a non-feminist perspective, Jones argues that he has opened up a deeper understanding of the phenomenon of genocide overlooked in previous studies. Students who wish to pursue this example further will find an interesting chapter by Terrell Carver in Jones's book critiquing the manner in which he uses the term "gender" and discussing some of the problems in applying gender to the study of genocide.

Suggested Additional Readings

Andrew, J. *American Empire: The Realities and Consequences of US Diplomacy.* Cambridge, Mass.: Harvard University Press, 2002.

Carpenter, Charli R. "Stirring Gender into the Mainstream: Constructivism, Feminism and the Uses of IR Theory." *International Studies Review* 5, no. 2 (June 2003): 287–302.

Carver, T. "Gender and International Relations." *International Studies Review* 5, no. 2 (June 2003): 287–302.

Jones, Adam. "Does Gender Make the World Go Round? Feminist Critiques of International Relations." *Review of International Studies* 22 (1996): 405–29.

Kinsella, H. "For a Careful Reading: The Conservativism of Gender Constructivism." *International Studies Review* 5, no. 2 (June 2003): 287–302.

Locher, Birgit, and Elisabeth Prugl. "Feminism and Constructivism: Worlds Apart or Sharing the Middle Ground?" *International Studies Quarterly* 45, no. 1 (2001): 111–30.

Peterson, V. Spike. "Feminist Theories Within, Invisible, and Beyond International Relations." *Brown Journal of World Affairs* 10, no. 2 (Winter/Spring 2004): 35–45.

Sylvester, Christine. *Feminist Theory and International Relations in a Postmodern Era*. Cambridge, U.K.: Cambridge University Press, 1994.

Tickner, J. Ann. *Gendering World Politics*. New York: Columbia University Press, 2001.

Tickner, J. Ann. "The Growth and Future of Feminist Theories in International Relations." *Brown Journal of World Affairs* 10, no. 2 (Winter/Spring 2004): 47–55.

Wibber, Annick, T.R. "Feminist International Relations: Old Debates, New Directions." *Brown Journal of World Affairs* 10, no. 2 (Winter/Spring 2004): 97–114.

Zalewski, M. "Women's Troubles Again in IR." *International Studies Review* 5, no. 2 (June 2003): 287–302.

InfoTrac® College Edition

Search for the following articles in the InfoTrac® database:

Paterson, Ruth. "Towards a Feminist International Political Economy." *Melbourne Journal of Politics* 26 (1999): 1–26.

Tickner, J. Ann. "Feminism and International Relations: Towards a Political Economy of Gender in Interstate and Non-Governmental Institutions." *American Political Science Review* 89, no. 3 (September 1995): 814–16.

de Volo, Lorraine Bayard. "Feminist Theory and International Relations in a Postmodern Era." *Journal of Interamerican Studies and World Affairs* 38, no. 4 (Winter 1996): 179–89.

Web Resources

For current URLs for the following websites, visit www.crosscurrents.nelson.com.

WOMEN WATCH
http://www.un.org/womenwatch
This site is operated by the United Nations Inter-Agency Network on Women and Gender Equality. It serves as an internet gateway to a variety of resources dealing with the issues regarding the advancement and empowerment of women.

FEMINIST THEORY AND GENDER STUDIES SECTION/INTERNATIONAL STUDIES ASSOCIATION
http://ftgss.blogspot.com/
This site is the official blog of the Feminist Theory and Gender Studies Section of the International Studies Association, the largest professional association of international relations scholars in the world.

CHARLI CARPENTER HOMEPAGE

http://www.people.umass.edu/charli/

This homepage of Dr. Charli Carpenter contains a number of the author's own papers as well as links relating to gender issues and international relations.

SANDRA WHITWORTH HOMEPAGE

http://www.yorku.ca/sandraw/

Dr. Sandra Whitworth has published extensively on the issues of feminism, gender, and international relations. Her homepage contains links to many of her papers and essays on these topics.

PART TWO

Is Ethnic Conflict Inevitable?

Did the War against Iraq Violate International Law?

Has NATO Become Irrelevant in an Age of Terrorism?

Should Canadian Troops be Deployed to Darfur Rather than Afghanistan?

Is Ethnic Conflict Inevitable?

✔ **YES**

JERRY Z. MULLER, "Us and Them: The Enduring Power of Ethnic Nationalism," *Foreign Affairs* 87, 2 (March/April 2008): 18–35

✗ **NO**

RICHARD ROSECRANCE AND ARTHUR STEIN, "Separatism's Final Country," *Foreign Affairs* 87, 4 (July/August 2008): 141–45

With the end of the Cold War in 1989, a period of optimism reigned in the Western world. A number of theorists suggested that we were entering into a new and more peaceful era of international politics. The symbolic dismantling of the Berlin Wall, the collapse of the once formidable Soviet Union, and the growing list of countries committing themselves to liberal democracy and open market economies suggested that a fundamental shift was taking place. Theorists writing primarily from a liberal perspective sounded a particularly optimistic note about what this new world would look like. Two writers in particular captured this optimism: John Mueller and Francis Fukuyama.

In 1989, John Mueller published a book entitled *Retreat from Doomsday: The Obsolescence of Major War* (Basic). He argued that we had reached a decisive stage in human history when the notion that war might be used to resolve conflicts had been "discredited and abandoned." In looking at the evolution of events in the twentieth century from the horrors of World War I and II to the tensions of superpower nuclear confrontation, Mueller argued that the horrendous costs of modern warfare were making major warfare largely unthinkable. Mueller challenged conventional realist and neorealist arguments that war is an inescapable feature of an anarchical international system that seeks power and security, and therefore war is the byproduct of the structure of international power. Rather, he suggested that war begins in the minds of humans and that is where it will end. As the attitudes to war as a viable instrument of state power change, war will become increasingly obsolete, just as in the cases of slavery and duelling, which were once socially acceptable institutions.

Francis Fukuyama sounded a similarly optimistic note in an article entitled "The End of History?" (*The National Interest* 16, 1989). He argued that we were witnessing the end of humankind's ideological evolution and that the principles of Western liberal democracy and liberal capitalism had finally triumphed. With no ideological rivals in sight, liberal economic and political values would now prevail globally. Since liberal democratic nations rarely go to war with each other, some liberal theorists suggested that the spread of democratization would contribute to a new era of peace and stability. In addition, with the spread of liberal capitalism through the process of economic globalization and its accompanying benefits of economic growth and increased wealth, nations would have a powerful material incentive to find constructive ways to resolve their conflicts and avoid violent confrontations. Thus, what came to be labelled as the "democratic theory of peace" seemed poised to offer a plausible alternative to the more pessimistic realist theories of international relations.

Despite the initial optimism of the immediate post–Cold War period, the events of the next two decades seemed to suggest that warfare was not so much in the process of disappearing, but that the pattern of warfare was shifting. Superpower confrontation, nuclear arms races, and military alliances were being replaced by regional conflicts, militant fundamentalism, and ethnic violence. The conflicts of the post–Cold War era tended to be intra-state wars rather than inter-state wars. This in turn shifted the attention of many analysts away from the structure of the international system itself to societal-level sources of conflict, such as ethnic rivalry, poverty, resource scarcities, and environmental degradation.

This led some analysts to posit a much more pessimistic picture of our future. Writing in 1994, Robert Kaplan published an article in the *Atlantic Monthly* entitled "The Coming Anarchy." Kaplan focused attention on the many parts of the developing world that were facing collapse and disintegration following the end of the Cold War. At a time when the capacities of many states were in severe decline, Kaplan warned of a new era where ethnic clashes and conflicts over resources would dominate. The world was potentially facing a new Hobbesian era of global anarchy in which life would be "nasty, brutish, and short." Such pessimistic scenarios would give credence to Robert Kagan's argument in his book, *Dangerous Nation,* that the world needs a strong hegemonic power to maintain a degree of peace and stability.

These quite different interpretations of the future of international conflict renewed interest in discussions about the likely future sources of international conflict. Will future conflicts be triggered by resource scarcities and environmental degradation, by rogue states seeking upset of the prevailing international order, or by centuries-old religious rivalries?

An important area of discussion is the role that ethnic identity and ethnonationalism will play in future conflicts on both the international and domestic levels. Here again, two quite different positions can be observed. Liberal analysts committed to a democratic theory of peace believe that ethnonationalism is likely to be a spent force in the future. They argue that we are entering in a new, postnational phase of human history. As people become increasingly connected through a global economic and communications networks and democratically accountable global institutions become more entrenched, individuals will more often identify themselves as cosmopolitan citizens of the world, whose common interests transcend differences in language, race, religion, and culture. In turn, parochial attachments to ethnic, linguistic, or religious groups will fade as the cosmopolitan values of a global civil society take root. As such parochial attachments diminish, factors like ethnic identity or religious affiliation will also disappear as a source of national and international conflict. The parochialism, self-interest, and exclusiveness often associated with nationalism will be replaced by a commitment to universal principles of human rights and a sense of global civic identity. According to this view then, the many outbursts of ethnic conflict that have appeared in areas such as the Balkans, Africa, or Asia during the past two decades are just part of a transitional phase and not an inevitable part of our future. The transitional processes of modernization, globalization, and democratization have brought new social groups, often with quite divergent interests, into the national and global political arena precisely at a time when the institutional capacity of the states to respond to conflicting demands has been strained. As a result, the creation of "winners and losers" through the process of social change and globalization has made many individuals and groups feel vulnerable. This has created an opportunity for some political elites to appeal to these insecurities as well as more traditional ethnic and religious ties as a means to mobilize support for political advantages. However, it is argued that if greater attention is given to the more equal distribution of the benefits of economic globalization, the reduction of the "democratic deficits" in global institutions like the United Nations, and the cultivation of a set of universal cosmopolitan civic values, nationalism in general, and ethnic nationalism in particular, will disappear as a feature of international politics.

An alternative perspective on the future of ethnonationalism is presented by Jerry Muller, an historian at the Catholic University America. He suggests that the commitment that many have to multiculturalism and cosmopolitan values has made it difficult for them to see the role that ethnonationalism has played and will continue to play in international politics. He makes his case by giving an alternative reading to the history of nationalism in the recent development of the international system and suggests that forms of ethnic nationalism will continue to be an important force in the years to come. In contrast, Richard Rosecrance and Arthur Stein argue that the world will not continue to fragment into a growing number of ethnic-based nation-states.

✔ **YES**

Us and Them: The Enduring Power of Ethnic Nationalism
JERRY Z. MULLER

Projecting their own experience onto the rest of the world, Americans generally belittle the role of ethnic nationalism in politics. After all, in the United States people of varying ethnic origins live cheek by jowl in relative peace. Within two or three generations of immigration, their ethnic identities are attenuated by cultural assimilation and intermarriage. Surely, things cannot be so different elsewhere.

Americans also find ethnonationalism discomfiting both intellectually and morally. Social scientists go to great lengths to demonstrate that it is a product not of nature but of culture, often deliberately constructed. And ethicists scorn value systems based on narrow group identities rather than cosmopolitanism.

But none of this will make ethnonationalism go away. Immigrants to the United States usually arrive with a willingness to fit into their new country and reshape their identities accordingly. But for those who remain behind in lands where their ancestors have lived for generations, if not centuries, political identities often take ethnic form, producing competing communal claims to political power. The creation of a peaceful regional order of nation-states has usually been the product of a violent process of ethnic separation. In areas where that separation has not yet occurred, politics is apt to remain ugly.

A familiar and influential narrative of twentieth-century European history argues that nationalism twice led to war, in 1914 and then again in 1939. Thereafter, the story goes, Europeans concluded that nationalism was a danger and gradually abandoned it. In the postwar decades, western Europeans enmeshed themselves in a web of transnational institutions, culminating in the European Union (EU). After the fall of the Soviet empire, that transnational framework spread eastward to encompass most of the continent. Europeans entered a postnational era, which was not only a good thing in itself but also a model for other regions. Nationalism, in this view, had been a tragic detour on the road to a peaceful liberal democratic order.

This story is widely believed by educated Europeans and even more so, perhaps, by educated Americans. Recently, for example, in the course of arguing that Israel ought to give up its claim to be a Jewish state and dissolve itself into some sort of binational entity with the Palestinians, the prominent historian Tony Judt informed the readers of *The New York Review of Books* that "the problem with Israel . . . [is that] it has imported a characteristically late-nineteenth-century separatist project into a world that has moved on, a world of individual rights, open frontiers, and international law. The very idea of a 'Jewish state' . . . is an anachronism."

Yet the experience of the hundreds of Africans and Asians who perish each year trying to get into Europe by landing on the coast of Spain or Italy reveals that Europe's frontiers are not so open. And a survey would show that whereas in 1900 there were many states in Europe without a single overwhelmingly dominant nationality, by 2007 there were only two, and one of those, Belgium, was close to breaking up. Aside from Switzerland, in other words—where the domestic ethnic balance of power is protected by strict citizenship laws—in Europe the "separatist project" has not so much vanished as triumphed.

Far from having been superannuated in 1945, in many respects ethnonationalism was at its apogee in the years immediately after World War II. European stability during the Cold War era was in fact due partly to the widespread fulfillment of the ethnonationalist project. And since the end of the Cold War, ethnonationalism has continued to reshape European borders.

In short, ethnonationalism has played a more profound and lasting role in modern history than is commonly understood, and the processes that led to the dominance of the ethnonational state and the separation of ethnic groups in Europe are likely to reoccur elsewhere. Increased urbanization, literacy, and political mobilization; differences in the fertility rates and economic performance of various ethnic groups; and immigration will challenge the internal structure of states as well as their borders. Whether politically correct or not, ethnonationalism will continue to shape the world in the twenty-first century.

THE POLITICS OF IDENTITY

There are two major ways of thinking about national identity. One is that all people who live within a country's borders are part of the nation, regardless of their ethnic, racial, or religious origins. This liberal or civic nationalism is the conception with which contemporary Americans are most likely to identify. But the liberal view has competed with and often lost out to a different view, that of ethnonationalism. The core of the ethnonationalist idea is that nations are defined by a shared heritage, which usually includes a common language, a common faith, and a common ethnic ancestry.

The ethnonationalist view has traditionally dominated through much of Europe and has held its own even in the United States until recently. For substantial stretches of U.S. history, it was believed that only the people of English origin, or those who were Protestant, or white, or hailed from northern Europe were real Americans. It was only in 1965 that the reform of U.S. immigration law abolished the system of national-origin quotas that had been in place for several decades. This system had excluded Asians entirely and radically restricted immigration from southern and eastern Europe.

Ethnonationalism draws much of its emotive power from the notion that the members of a nation are part of an extended family, ultimately united by ties of blood. It is the subjective belief in the reality of a common "we" that counts. The markers that distinguish the in-group vary from case to case and time to time, and the subjective nature of the communal boundaries has led some to discount their practical significance. But as Walker Connor, an astute student of nationalism, has noted, "It is not what is, but what people believe is that has behavioral consequences." And the central tenets of ethnonationalist belief are that nations exist, that each nation ought to have its own state, and that each state should be made up of the members of a single nation.

The conventional narrative of European history asserts that nationalism was primarily liberal in the western part of the continent and that it became more ethnically oriented as one moved east. There is some truth to this, but it disguises a good deal as well. It is more accurate to say that when modern states began to form, political boundaries and ethnolinguistic boundaries largely coincided in the areas along Europe's Atlantic coast. Liberal nationalism, that is, was most apt to emerge in states that already possessed a high degree of ethnic homogeneity. Long before the nineteenth century, countries such as England, France, Portugal, Spain, and Sweden emerged as nation-states in polities where ethnic divisions had been softened by a long history of cultural and social homogenization.

In the center of the continent, populated by speakers of German and Italian, political structures were fragmented into hundreds of small units. But in the 1860s and 1870s, this fragmentation was resolved by the creation of Italy and Germany, so that almost all Italians lived in the former and a majority of Germans lived in the latter. Moving further east, the situation changed again. As late as 1914, most of central, eastern, and southeastern Europe was made up not of nation-states but of empires. The Hapsburg empire comprised what are now Austria, the Czech Republic, Hungary, and Slovakia and parts of what are now Bosnia, Croatia, Poland, Romania, Ukraine, and more. The Romanov empire stretched into Asia, including what is now Russia and what are now parts of Poland, Ukraine, and more. And the Ottoman Empire covered modern Turkey and parts of today's Bulgaria, Greece, Romania, and Serbia and extended through much of the Middle East and North Africa as well.

Each of these empires was composed of numerous ethnic groups, but they were not multinational in the sense of granting equal status to the many peoples that made up their populaces. The governing monarchy and landed nobility often differed in language and ethnic origin from the urbanized trading class, whose members in turn usually differed in language, ethnicity, and often religion from the peasantry. In the Hapsburg and Romanov empires, for example, merchants were usually Germans or Jews. In the Ottoman Empire, they were often Armenians, Greeks, or Jews. And in each empire, the peasantry was itself ethnically diverse.

Up through the nineteenth century, these societies were still largely agrarian: most people lived as peasants in the countryside, and few were literate. Political, social, and economic stratifications usually correlated with ethnicity, and people did not expect to change their positions in the system. Until the rise of modern nationalism, all of this seemed quite unproblematic. In this world, moreover, people of one religion, language, or culture were often dispersed across various countries and empires. There were ethnic Germans, for example, not only in the areas that became Germany but also scattered throughout the Hapsburg and Romanov empires. There were Greeks in Greece but also millions of them in the Ottoman Empire (not to mention hundreds of thousands of Muslim Turks in Greece). And there were Jews everywhere—but with no independent state of their own.

THE RISE OF ETHNONATIONALISM

Today, people tend to take the nation-state for granted as the natural form of political association and regard empires as anomalies. But over the broad sweep of recorded history, the opposite is closer to the truth. Most people at most times have lived in empires, with the nation-state the exception rather than the rule. So what triggered the change?

The rise of ethnonationalism, as the sociologist Ernest Gellner has explained, was not some strange historical mistake; rather, it was propelled by some of the deepest currents of modernity. Military competition between states created a demand for expanded state resources and hence continual economic growth. Economic growth, in turn, depended on mass literacy and easy communication, spurring policies to promote education and a common language—which led directly to conflicts over language and communal opportunities.

Modern societies are premised on the egalitarian notion that in theory, at least, anyone can aspire to any economic position. But in practice, everyone does not have an equal likelihood of upward economic mobility, and not simply because individuals have different innate capabilities. For such advances depend in part on what economists call "cultural capital," the skills and behavioral patterns that help individuals and groups succeed. Groups with traditions of literacy and engagement in commerce tend to excel, for example, whereas those without such traditions tend to lag behind.

As they moved into cities and got more education during the nineteenth and early twentieth centuries, ethnic groups with largely peasant backgrounds, such as the Czechs, the Poles, the Slovaks, and the Ukrainians found that key positions in the government and the economy were already occupied—often by ethnic Armenians, Germans, Greeks, or Jews. Speakers of the same language came to share a sense that they belonged together and to define themselves in contrast to other communities. And eventually they came to demand a nation-state of their own, in which they would be the masters, dominating politics, staffing the civil service, and controlling commerce.

Ethnonationalism had a psychological basis as well as an economic one. By cre-ating a new and direct relationship between individuals and the government, the rise of the modern state weakened individuals' traditional bonds to intermediate social units, such as the family, the clan, the guild, and the church. And by spurring social and geographic mobility and a self-help mentality, the rise of market-based economies did the same. The result was an emotional vacuum that was often filled by new forms of identification, often along ethnic lines.

Ethnonationalist ideology called for a congruence between the state and the ethnically defined nation, with explosive results. As Lord Acton recognized in 1862, "By making the state and the nation commensurate with each other in theory, [nationalism] reduces practically to a subject condition all other nationalities that may be within the boundary. . . . According, therefore, to the degree of humanity and civilization in that dominant body which claims all the rights of the community, the inferior races are exterminated, or reduced to servitude, or outlawed, or put in a condition of dependence." And that is just what happened.

THE GREAT TRANSFORMATION

Nineteenth-century liberals, like many proponents of globalization today, believed that the spread of international commerce would lead people to recognize the mutual benefits that could come from peace and trade, both within polities and between them. Socialists agreed, although they believed that harmony would come only after the arrival of socialism. Yet that was not the course that twentieth-century history was destined to follow. The process of "making the state and the nation commensurate" took a variety of forms, from voluntary emigration (often motivated by governmental discrimination against minority ethnicities) to forced deportation (also known as "population transfer") to genocide. Although the term "ethnic cleansing" has come into English usage only recently, its verbal correlates in Czech, French, German, and Polish go back much further. Much of the history of twentieth-century Europe, in fact, has been a painful, drawn-out process of ethnic disaggregation.

Massive ethnic disaggregation began on Europe's frontiers. In the ethnically mixed Balkans, wars to expand the nation-states of Bulgaria, Greece, and Serbia at the expense of the ailing Ottoman Empire were accompanied by ferocious interethnic violence. During the Balkan Wars of 1912–13, almost half a million people left their traditional homelands, either voluntarily or by force. Muslims left regions under the control of Bulgarians, Greeks, and Serbs; Bulgarians abandoned Greek-controlled areas of Macedonia; Greeks fled from regions of Macedonia ceded to Bulgaria and Serbia.

World War I led to the demise of the three great turn-of-the-century empires, unleashing an explosion of ethnonationalism in the process. In the Ottoman Empire, mass deportations and murder during the war took the lives of a million members of the local Armenian minority in an early attempt at ethnic cleansing, if not genocide. In 1919, the Greek government invaded the area that would become Turkey, seeking to carve out a "greater Greece" stretching all the way to

Constantinople. Meeting with initial success, the Greek forces looted and burned villages in an effort to drive out the region's ethnic Turks. But Turkish forces eventually regrouped and pushed the Greek army back, engaging in their own ethnic cleansing against local Greeks along the way. Then the process of population transfers was formalized in the 1923 Treaty of Lausanne: all ethnic Greeks were to go to Greece, all Greek Muslims to Turkey. In the end, Turkey expelled almost 1.5 million people, and Greece expelled almost 400,000.

Out of the breakup of the Hapsburg and Romanov empires emerged a multitude of new countries. Many conceived of themselves as ethnonational polities, in which the state existed to protect and promote the dominant ethnic group. Yet of central and eastern Europe's roughly 60 million people, 25 million continued to be part of ethnic minorities in the countries in which they lived. In most cases, the ethnic majority did not believe in trying to help minorities assimilate, nor were the minorities always eager to do so themselves. Nationalist governments openly discriminated in favor of the dominant community. Government activities were conducted solely in the language of the majority, and the civil service was reserved for those who spoke it.

In much of central and eastern Europe, Jews had long played an important role in trade and commerce. When they were given civil rights in the late nineteenth century, they tended to excel in professions requiring higher education, such as medicine and law, and soon Jews or people of Jewish descent made up almost half the doctors and lawyers in cities such as Budapest, Vienna, and Warsaw. By the 1930s, many governments adopted policies to try to check and reverse these advances, denying Jews credit and limiting their access to higher education. In other words, the National Socialists who came to power in Germany in 1933 and based their movement around a "Germanness" they defined in contrast to "Jewishness" were an extreme version of a more common ethnonationalist trend.

The politics of ethnonationalism took an even deadlier turn during World War II. The Nazi regime tried to reorder the ethnic map of the continent by force. Its most radical act was an attempt to rid Europe of Jews by killing them all—an attempt that largely succeeded. The Nazis also used ethnic German minorities in Czechoslovakia, Poland, and elsewhere to enforce Nazi domination, and many of the regimes allied with Germany engaged in their own campaigns against internal ethnic enemies. The Romanian regime, for example, murdered hundreds of thousands of Jews on its own, without orders from Germany, and the government of Croatia murdered not only its Jews but hundreds of thousands of Serbs and Romany as well.

POSTWAR BUT NOT POSTNATIONAL

One might have expected that the Nazi regime's deadly policies and crushing defeat would mark the end of the ethnonationalist era. But in fact they set the stage for another massive round of ethnonational transformation. The political settlement in central Europe after World War I had been achieved primarily by moving borders to align them with populations. After World War II, it was the populations that moved instead. Millions of people were expelled from their homes and countries, with at least the tacit support of the victorious Allies.

Winston Churchill, Franklin Roosevelt, and Joseph Stalin all concluded that the expulsion of ethnic Germans from non-German countries was a prerequisite to a stable postwar order. As Churchill put it in a speech to the British parliament in December 1944, "Expulsion is the method which, so far as we have been able to see, will be the most satisfactory and lasting. There will be no mixture of populations to cause endless trouble. . . . A clean sweep will be made. I am not alarmed at the prospect of the disentanglement of population, nor am I alarmed by these large transferences." He cited the Treaty of Lausanne as a precedent, showing how even the leaders of liberal democracies had concluded that only radically illiberal measures would eliminate the causes of ethnonational aspirations and aggression.

Between 1944 and 1945, five million ethnic Germans from the eastern parts of the German Reich fled westward to escape the conquering Red Army, which was energetically raping and massacring its way to Berlin. Then, between 1945 and 1947, the new postliberation regimes in Czechoslovakia, Hungary, Poland, and Yugoslavia expelled another seven million Germans in response to their collaboration with the Nazis. Together, these measures constituted the largest forced population movement in European history, with hundreds of thousands of people dying along the way.

The handful of Jews who survived the war and returned to their homes in eastern Europe met with so much anti-Semitism that most chose to leave for good. About 220,000 of them made their way into the American-occupied zone of Germany, from which most eventually went to Israel or the United States. Jews thus essentially vanished from central and eastern Europe, which had been the center of Jewish life since the sixteenth century.

Millions of refugees from other ethnic groups were also evicted from their homes and resettled after the war. This was due partly to the fact that the borders of the Soviet Union had moved westward, into what had once been Poland, while the borders of Poland also moved westward, into what had once been Germany. To make populations correspond to the new borders, 1.5 million Poles living in areas that were now part of the Soviet Union were deported to Poland, and 500,000 ethnic Ukrainians who had been living in Poland were sent to the Ukrainian Soviet Socialist Republic. Yet another exchange of populations took place between Czechoslovakia and Hungary, with Slovaks transferred out of Hungary and Magyars sent away from Czechoslovakia. A smaller number of Magyars also moved to Hungary from Yugoslavia, with Serbs and Croats moving in the opposite direction.

As a result of this massive process of ethnic unmixing, the ethnonationalist ideal was largely realized: for the most part, each nation in Europe had its own state, and each state was made up almost exclusively of a single ethnic nationality. During the Cold War, the few exceptions to this rule included Czechoslovakia, the Soviet Union, and Yugoslavia. But these countries' subsequent fate only demonstrated the ongoing vitality of ethnonationalism. After the fall of communism, East and West Germany were unified with remarkable rapidity, Czechoslovakia split peacefully into Czech and Slovak republics, and the Soviet Union broke apart into a variety of different national units. Since then, ethnic Russian minorities in many of the post-Soviet states have gradually immigrated to Russia, Magyars in Romania have moved to Hungary, and the few remaining ethnic Germans in Russia have largely gone to Germany. A million people of Jewish origin from the former Soviet Union have made their way to Israel. Yugoslavia saw the secession of Croatia and Slovenia and then descended into ethnonational wars over Bosnia and Kosovo.

The breakup of Yugoslavia was simply the last act of a long play. But the plot of that play—the disaggregation of peoples and the triumph of ethnonationalism in modern Europe—is rarely recognized, and so a story whose significance is comparable to the spread of democracy or capitalism remains largely unknown and unappreciated.

DECOLONIZATION AND AFTER

The effects of ethnonationalism, of course, have hardly been confined to Europe. For much of the developing world, decolonization has meant ethnic disaggregation through the exchange or expulsion of local minorities.

The end of the British Raj in 1947 brought about the partition of the subcontinent into India and Pakistan, along with an orgy of violence that took hundreds of thousands of lives. Fifteen million people became refugees, including Muslims who went to Pakistan and Hindus who went to India. Then, in 1971, Pakistan itself, originally unified on the basis of religion, dissolved into Urdu-speaking Pakistan and Bengali-speaking Bangladesh.

In the former British mandate of Palestine, a Jewish state was established in 1948 and was promptly greeted by the revolt of the indigenous Arab community and an invasion from the surrounding Arab states. In the war that resulted, regions that fell under Arab control were cleansed of their Jewish populations, and Arabs fled or were forced out of areas that came under Jewish control. Some 750,000 Arabs left, primarily for the surrounding Arab countries, and the remaining 150,000 constituted only about a sixth of the population of the new Jewish state. In the years afterward, nationalist-inspired violence against Jews in Arab countries propelled almost all of the more than 500,000 Jews there to leave their lands of origin and immigrate to Israel. Likewise, in 1962 the end of French control in Algeria led to the forced emigration of Algerians of European origin (the so-called pieds-noirs), most of whom immigrated to France. Shortly thereafter, ethnic minorities of Asian origin were forced out of postcolonial Uganda.

The legacy of the colonial era, moreover, is hardly finished. When the European overseas empires dissolved, they left behind a patchwork of states whose boundaries often cut across ethnic patterns of settlement and whose internal populations were ethnically mixed. It is wishful thinking to suppose that these boundaries will be permanent. As societies in the former colonial world modernize, becoming more urban, literate, and politically mobilized, the forces that gave rise to ethnonationalism and ethnic disaggregation in Europe are apt to drive events there, too.

THE BALANCE SHEET

Analysts of ethnic disaggregation typically focus on its destructive effects, which is understandable given the direct human suffering it has often entailed. But such attitudes can yield a distorted perspective by overlooking the less obvious costs and also the important benefits that ethnic separation has brought.

Economists from Adam Smith onward, for example, have argued that the efficiencies of competitive markets tend to increase with the markets' size. The dissolution of the Austro-Hungarian Empire into smaller nation-states, each with its own barriers to trade, was thus economically irrational and contributed to the region's travails in the interwar period. Much of subsequent European history has involved attempts to overcome this and other economic fragmentation, culminating in the EU.

Ethnic disaggregation also seems to have deleterious effects on cultural vitality. Precisely because most of their citizens share a common cultural and linguistic heritage, the homogenized states of postwar Europe have tended to be more culturally insular than their demographically diverse predecessors. With few Jews in Europe and few Germans in Prague, that is, there are fewer Franz Kafkas.

Forced migrations generally penalize the expelling countries and reward the receiving ones. Expulsion is often driven by a majority group's resentment of a minority group's success, on the mistaken assumption that achievement is a zero-sum game. But countries that got rid of their Armenians, Germans, Greeks, Jews, and other successful minorities deprived themselves of some of their most talented citizens, who simply took their skills and knowledge elsewhere. And in many places, the triumph of ethnonational politics has meant the victory of traditionally rural groups over more urbanized ones, which possess just those skills desirable in an advanced industrial economy.

But if ethnonationalism has frequently led to tension and conflict, it has also proved to be a source of cohesion and stability. When French textbooks began with "Our ancestors the Gauls" or when Churchill spoke to wartime audiences of "this island race," they appealed to ethnonationalist sensibilities as a source of mutual trust and sacrifice. Liberal democracy and ethnic homogeneity are not only compatible; they can be complementary.

One could argue that Europe has been so harmonious since World War II not because of the failure of ethnic nationalism but because of its success, which removed some of the greatest sources of conflict both within and between countries. The fact that ethnic and state boundaries now largely coincide has meant that there are fewer disputes over borders or expatriate communities, leading to the most stable territorial configuration in European history.

These ethnically homogeneous polities have displayed a great deal of internal solidarity, moreover, facilitating government programs, including domestic transfer payments, of various kinds. When the Swedish Social Democrats were developing plans for Europe's most extensive welfare state during the interwar period, the political scientist Sheri Berman has noted, they conceived of and sold them as the construction of a folkhemmet, or "people's home."

Several decades of life in consolidated, ethnically homogeneous states may even have worked to sap ethnonationalism's own emotional power. Many Europeans are now prepared, and even eager, to participate in transnational frameworks such as the EU, in part because their perceived need for collective self-determination has largely been satisfied.

NEW ETHNIC MIXING

Along with the process of forced ethnic disaggregation over the last two centuries, there has also been a process of ethnic mixing brought about by voluntary emigration. The general pattern has been one of emigration from poor, stagnant areas to richer and more dynamic ones.

In Europe, this has meant primarily movement west and north, leading above all to France and the United Kingdom. This pattern has continued into the present: as a result of recent migration, for example, there are now half a million Poles in Great Britain and 200,000 in Ireland. Immigrants from one part of Europe who have moved to another and ended up staying there have tended to assimilate and, despite some grumbling about a supposed invasion of "Polish plumbers," have created few significant problems.

The most dramatic transformation of European ethnic balances in recent decades has come from the immigration of people of Asian, African, and Middle Eastern origin, and here the results have been mixed. Some of these groups have achieved remarkable success, such as the Indian Hindus who have come to the United Kingdom. But in Belgium, France, Germany, the Netherlands, Sweden, the United Kingdom, and elsewhere, on balance the educational and economic progress of Muslim immigrants has been more limited and their cultural alienation greater.

How much of the problem can be traced to discrimination, how much to the cultural patterns of the immigrants themselves, and how much to the policies of European governments is difficult to determine. But a number of factors, from official multiculturalism to generous welfare states to the ease of contact with ethnic homelands, seem to have made it possible to create ethnic islands where assimilation into the larger culture and economy is limited.

As a result, some of the traditional contours of European politics have been upended. The left, for example, has tended to embrace immigration in the name of egalitarianism and multiculturalism. But if there is indeed a link between ethnic homogeneity and a population's willingness to support generous income-redistribution programs, the encouragement of a more heterogeneous society may end up undermining the left's broader political agenda. And some of Europe's libertarian cultural propensities have already clashed with the cultural illiberalism of some of the new immigrant communities.

Should Muslim immigrants not assimilate and instead develop a strong communal identification along religious lines, one consequence might be a resurgence of traditional ethnonational identities in some states—or the development of a new European identity defined partly in contradistinction to Islam (with the widespread resistance to the extension of full EU membership to Turkey being a possible harbinger of such a shift).

FUTURE IMPLICATIONS

Since ethnonationalism is a direct consequence of key elements of modernization, it is likely to gain ground in societies undergoing such a process. It is hardly surprising, therefore, that it remains among the most vital—and most disruptive—forces in many parts of the contemporary world.

More or less subtle forms of ethnonationalism, for example, are ubiquitous in immigration policy around the globe. Many countries—including Armenia, Bulgaria, Croatia, Finland, Germany, Hungary, Ireland, Israel, Serbia, and Turkey—provide automatic or rapid citizenship to the members of diasporas of their own dominant ethnic group, if desired. Chinese immigration law gives priority and benefits to overseas Chinese. Portugal and Spain have immigration policies that favor applicants from their former colonies in the New World. Still other states, such as Japan and Slovakia, provide official forms of identification to members of the dominant national ethnic group who are noncitizens that permit them to live and work in the country. Americans, accustomed by the U.S. government's official practices to regard differential treatment on the basis of ethnicity to be a violation of universalist norms, often consider such policies exceptional, if not abhorrent. Yet in a global context, it is the insistence on universalist criteria that seems provincial.

Increasing communal consciousness and shifting ethnic balances are bound to have a variety of consequences, both within and between states, in the years to come. As economic globalization brings more states into the global economy, for example, the first fruits of that process will often fall to those ethnic groups best positioned by history or culture to take advantage of the new opportunities for enrichment, deepening social cleavages rather than filling them in. Wealthier and higher-achieving regions might try to separate themselves from poorer and lower-achieving ones, and distinctive homogeneous areas might try to acquire sovereignty—courses of action that might provoke violent responses from defenders of the status quo.

Of course, there are multiethnic societies in which ethnic consciousness remains weak, and even a more strongly developed sense of ethnicity may lead to political claims short of sovereignty. Sometimes, demands for ethnic autonomy or self-determination can be met within an existing state. The claims of the Catalans in Spain, the Flemish in Belgium, and the Scots in the United Kingdom have been met in this manner, at least for now. But such arrangements remain precarious and are subject to recurrent renegotiation. In the developing world, accordingly, where states are more recent creations and where the borders often cut across ethnic boundaries, there is likely to be further ethnic disaggregation and communal conflict. And as scholars such as Chaim Kaufmann have noted, once ethnic antagonism has crossed a certain threshold of violence, maintaining the rival groups within a single polity becomes far more difficult.

This unfortunate reality creates dilemmas for advocates of humanitarian intervention in such conflicts, because making and keeping peace between groups that have come to hate and fear one another is likely to require costly ongoing military missions rather than relatively cheap temporary ones. When communal violence escalates to ethnic cleansing, moreover, the return of large numbers of refugees to their place of origin after a cease-fire has been reached is often impractical and even undesirable, for it merely sets the stage for a further round of conflict down the road.

Partition may thus be the most humane lasting solution to such intense communal conflicts. It inevitably creates new flows of refugees, but at least it deals with the problem at issue. The challenge for the international community in such cases is to separate communities in the most humane manner possible: by aiding in transport, assuring citizenship rights in the new homeland, and providing financial aid for resettlement and economic absorption. The bill for all of this will be huge, but it will rarely be greater than the material costs of interjecting and maintaining a foreign military presence large enough to pacify the rival ethnic combatants or the moral cost of doing nothing.

Contemporary social scientists who write about nationalism tend to stress the contingent elements of group identity—the extent to which national consciousness is culturally and politically manufactured by ideologists and politicians. They regularly invoke Benedict Anderson's concept of "imagined communities," as if demonstrating that nationalism is constructed will rob the concept of its power. It is true, of course, that ethnonational identity is never as natural or ineluctable as nationalists claim. Yet it would be a mistake to think that because nationalism is partly constructed it is therefore fragile or infinitely malleable. Ethnonationalism was not a chance detour in European history: it corresponds to some enduring propensities of the human spirit that are heightened by the process of modern state creation, it is a crucial source of both solidarity and enmity, and in one form or another, it will remain for many generations to come. One can only profit from facing it directly.

✘ NO
Separatism's Final Country
RICHARD ROSECRANCE AND ARTHUR STEIN

Muller argues that ethnonationalism is the wave of the future and will result in more and more independent states, but this is not likely. One of the most destabilizing ideas throughout human history has been that every separately defined cultural unit should have its own state. Endless disruption and political introversion would follow an attempt to realize such a goal. Woodrow Wilson gave an impetus to further state creation when he argued for "national self-determination" as a means of preventing more nationalist conflict, which he believed was a cause of World War I.

The hope was that if the nations of the Austrian, Ottoman, and Russian empires could become independent states, they would not have to bring the great powers into their conflicts. But Wilson and his counterparts did not concede to each nation its own state. They grouped minorities together in Hungary, Italy, and Yugoslavia, and the Soviet Union ultimately emerged as a veritable empire of nationalities. Economists rightly questioned whether tiny states with small labor forces and limited resources could become viable, particularly given the tariffs that their goods would face in international trade.

More important, the nationalist prospect was and remains hopelessly impractical. In the world today, there are 6,800 different dialects or languages that might gain political recognition as independent linguistic groups. Does anyone seriously suggest that the 200 or so existing states should each, on average, be cut into 34 pieces? The doctrine of national self-determination reaches its reductio ad absurdum at this point.

Furthermore, the one-nation, one-state principle is unlikely to prevail for four good reasons. First, governments today are more responsive to their ethnic minority communities than were the imperial agglomerations of yesteryear, and they also have more resources at their disposal than their predecessors did. Many provinces populated by discontented ethnic groups are located in territories adjacent to national capitals, not overseas. And many governments in this era of globalization have annual budgets equivalent to nearly 50 percent of their GDPs, much of which is spent on social services. They can—and do—accommodate the economic needs of their states' differentiated units. They also respond to those units' linguistic requests. Basques, Bretons, Punjabis, Québecois, and Scots live quite well inside the bonds of multinational sovereignty and in some cases better than residents of other provinces with no claims of being a distinct nation.

Second, the achievement of separate sovereignty today depends on external recognition and support. Prospective new states cannot gain independence without military assistance and economic aid from abroad. International recognition, in turn, requires the aspiring nationalist movement to avoid international terrorism as a means of gaining attention. If a separatist group uses terrorism, it tends to be reviled and sidelined. If an ethnic group does not have enough support to win independence by peaceful electoral means inside its country, its resorting to terrorism only calls into question the legitimacy of its quest for independence.

Recognizing this, the Québecois abandoned the terrorist methods of the Quebec Liberation Front. Most Basques castigate Basque Homeland and Freedom (known by its Basque acronym ETA). Enlightened Europeans have withdrawn their support for the Chechen rebels. And the continued terrorist shelling of Israeli cities from a Hamas-dominated Gaza might undermine the previous international consensus in favor of a two-state solution to the Palestinian problem, or at least warrant an exceptional approach to Gaza.

With the possible exception of the Palestinians, the notion that any of these peoples would be better off in smaller and weaker independent states in a hostile neighborhood is unrealistic. Occasionally, dissidents make the case that if they were to leave the state unit, they would be taken into the comforting embrace of the European Union or the North American Free Trade Agreement, thereby gaining access to a large market. But that would depend a great deal on outsider support for their cause. The United Kingdom might not wish to see Scotland in the EU and would be in a position to veto its membership. The United States and Canada might not agree to let an independent Quebec join NAFTA. The belief that when a tiny nation is born it falls automatically into the loving hands of international midwives is questionable. The truth varies from case to case.

Third, although globalization initially stimulated ethnic discontent by creating inequality, it also provides the means for quieting discontents down the road within the fold of the state political system. Distributed economic growth is a palliative for political discontent. Indonesia, Malaysia, Singapore, and Thailand contain different ethnic groups that have largely profited from the intense economic resurgence of their states stimulated by globalization. Northern and southern Vietnam are culturally different, but both have benefited from the country's economic growth. Cambodia has a diverse population, but it has gained greatly from China's move to externalize some of its production.

Fourth, a discontented population may react to ethnic discrimination, but it also responds to economic need, and whatever its concerns, it does not always have to seek independence to alleviate them. It has another safety valve: emigration to another country. The state of Monterrey has not sought independence from Mexico; rather, many of its inhabitants have moved, legally or illegally, to the United States. The huge emigration from the Maghreb to France and Italy reflects a similar attitude and outcome; the dissatisfied populations of North Africa can find greater welfare in Europe. And when Poles move to France or the United Kingdom, they do not secede from the mother country but demonstrate greater satisfaction with French or British rule. Emigration is the overwhelming alternative to secession when the home government does not sufficiently mitigate economic disparities.

Even where the central government has used force to suppress secessionist movements, it has offered carrots at the same time that it has yielded sticks. The province of Aceh has been coaxed, even as it has been subjected to threats, to remain inside the Indonesian republic. Kashmir, facing a balance of restraints and incentives, is unlikely to emerge as an independent state in India. And the Tamil Tigers have lost the sympathy of the world by their slaughter of innocent Sinhalese.

The recent formation of an "independent" Kosovo, which has not yet been recognized by various key countries, does not foretell the similar arrival of other new states. It is unlikely that Abkhazia or South Ossetia, although largely autonomous in fact, will gain full and formal independence from Georgia or that the Albanian areas of Macedonia will secede. Rather, prospective secessionists, dissuaded by both central governments and the international community, are likely to hold back. Indeed, the most plausible future outcome is that both established states and their international supporters will generally act to prevent a proliferation of new states from entering the international system.

Much empirical work, which shows that a province's aspirations for sovereign status can be confined within a state if the province has access to monies from the central government and is represented in the governing elite, supports this conclusion. The Sikh party Akali Dal once sought Punjab's independence from India, but to little effect, partly because Punjabis are heavily represented in the Indian army and because fiscal transfers from New Delhi quieted dissidence in the region. The Québecois benefit from financing from Ottawa, elite connections, flows of private capital into Quebec, and the Canadian government's acceptance of bilingualism in the province. Chechnya remains poor, but if it seeks to remedy its relative neglect through a strategy of terrorism, it will undercut its own legitimacy. Lacking external support, and in the face of Russia's continued firmness, Chechnya has settled into a degree of political stability. In all three cases, the maintenance of the existing national boundaries seems likely, and so, too, does it seem likely in other cases.

The apostles of national self-determination would do well to consider a still more important trend: the return to bigness in the international system. This is happening not only because great powers such as China, India, and the United States are now taking on greater roles in world politics but also because international economics increasingly dwarfs politics. To keep up, states have to get bigger. The international market has always been larger than the domestic ones, but as long as international openness beckoned, even small powers could hope to prosper and attain some degree of economic influence. In the past decade, however, the tariff reductions proposed in the Doha Round of international trade negotiations have failed, industrial duties have not fallen, and agriculture has become even more highly protected than it was in the nineteenth century.

Globalization has clearly distributed economic boons to smaller countries, but these states still require greater political scale to fully realize globalization's benefits. To generate scale, states have negotiated bilateral and multilateral trade preferences with other states regionally and internationally, thereby gaining access to larger markets. The EU has decided to make up in the enlargement of its membership and a bigger free-trade area what it lacks in internal economic growth. The 27 countries of the EU currently have a combined GDP of over $14 trillion, besting the United States' $13 trillion, and the union's expansion is not over yet.

Europe never faced the limits on "manifest destiny" that confronted the United States—the shores of the Pacific Ocean. Charles de Gaulle was wrong when he heralded a "Europe from the Atlantic to the Urals": the EU has already expanded into the Caucasus. And with at least eight new members, it will proceed into Central Asia. As the borders of Europe approach Russia, even Moscow will seek de facto ties with the increasingly monolithic European giant.

In Asia, current tensions between China and Japan have not prevented proposals for a free-trade zone, a common currency, and an investment bank for the region. Chinese in Indonesia, Malaysia, the Philippines, Singapore, Taiwan, and Vietnam draw their adopted countries toward Beijing. China will not expand territorially (except titularly when Taiwan rejoins the mainland), but it will move to consolidate an economic network that will contain all the elements of production, except, perhaps, raw materials. Japan will adjust to China's primacy, and even South Korea will see the writing on the wall.

This will leave the United States in the uncomfortable position of experiencing unrealized growth and the possible failure of new customs unions in the Western Hemisphere. NAFTA may have been deepened, but a Free Trade Area of the Americas now seems beyond reach because of opposition from Argentina, Bolivia, Brazil, and Venezuela. U.S. politics has also turned, temporarily at least, against such ventures. South American nations have, in recent years, been far more responsive to China and Europe than to the United States. The U.S.-Central American Free Trade Agreement, now in the making, may be the only likely new string to the current U.S. bow.

Some economists contend that great size is not necessary in a fully open international economic system and that even small countries can sell their wares abroad under such conditions. But the international economic system is not open, and the future resides with broad customs unions, which substitute expanded regional markets for restricted international ones. China is seeking bilateral preferential trade arrangements with several other states, and so is the United States. Prospective secessionists will not prosper under such circumstances. They have to depend on international assistance, membership in trade pacts, and the acquiescence of their mother countries. They may have none of these, and they will fail if they use terrorism to advance their causes.

Under the present circumstances, secessionists will generally be better off remaining inside existing states, if only because the international system now advantages larger agglomerations of power. Economies of industrial scale are promoting economies of political size. In U.S. politics, the problem of outsourcing gets much political attention, but how is it possible to prevent that activity when national production and the national market are too small? Only larger political entities can keep production, research and development, and innovation within a single economic zone. Big is back.

POSTSCRIPT

At the end of their article, Rosecrance and Stein state that "big is back." They do not believe that there will continue to be a fragmentation of the international system into an increasing number of smaller states based on ethnic lines. Rather, they argue that the benefits to be derived from globalization will only be achieved by a scaling up of the size of political entities. This raises a related question of whether the international system would benefit more from a reduced number of larger scale political entities, rather than a growing number of smaller, self-governing states.

The rise of nationalism provided an important component to the process of state-building as the modern nation-state emerged in the seventeenth and eighteenth centuries. Nationalist sentiments were critical to the formation of a sense of common identity and shared consciousness of being part of one nation. By the nineteenth century, nationalism became an increasing source of conflict as industrializing states sought to extend their territorial reach.

Leaders such as Woodrow Wilson advocated a policy of self-determination of all peoples, based on the belief that an international system populated by a growing number of self-governing, sovereign republics would lead to a more peaceful world. When the United Nations first met in 1946, 51 nations attended. Today, there are 192 members. Wilson's dream seems to have been met.

Nevertheless, the fear of some analysts is that the continuing proliferation of states is not a reflection of a more just and stable international order. Rather, the addition of a greater number of smaller states may lead only to greater disorder and disharmony. It leaves us with the question: Can a small number of large political unities create greater order and stability than a large number of small states that accommodate a variety of ethnic and cultural differences?

Suggested Additional Readings

Bowen, John Richard. "The Myth of Global Ethnic Conflict." *Journal of Democracy* 7, no. 4 (October 1996): 3–14.

Ozkirimli, U. *Nationalism and Its Futures*. London: Palgrave, 2003.

Rose, W. "The Security Dilemma and Ethnic Conflict: Some New Hypotheses." *Security Studies* 9, no. 4 (2002): 1–51.

Smith, Anthony D. *The Ethnic Origins of Nations*. Cambridge, Mass.: Blackwell, 1986.

Smith, Anthony D. *Nations and Nationalism in a Global Era*. Cambridge: Polity Press, 1995.

Stavenhagen, Rodolfo. *Ethnic Conflicts and the Nation-State.* New York: St. Martin's Press, 1996.

Varshney, Ashutosh. "Ethnic Conflict and Civil Society: India and Beyond." *World Politics* 53, no. 3 (April 2001): 362–98.

InfoTrac® College Edition

Search for the following articles in the InfoTrac® database:

Collier, Paul. "Ethnic Civil Wars: Securing the Post-conflict Peace." *Harvard International Review* 28, no. 4 (Winter 2007): 56–60.

Csergo, Zsuzsa, and James M. Goldgeier. "Virtual Nationalism." *Foreign Policy* 125 (July 2001): 76.

Fenton, Steve. "Beyond Ethnicity: The Global Comparative Analysis of Ethnic Conflict." *International Journal of Comparative Sociology* 45, no. 3–4 (July–September 2004): 179–94.

Fuller, Graham E. "Redrawing the World's Borders." *World Policy Journal* 14, no. 1 (Spring 1997): 11–21.

Harish, S.P. "Ethnic or Religious Cleavage? Investigating the Nature of the Conflict in Southern Thailand." *Contemporary Southeast Asia* 28, no. 1 (April 2006): 48–69.

Kaufmann, Chaim. "A Security Dilemma: Ethnic Partitioning in Iraq." *Harvard International Review* 28, no. 4 (Winter 2007): 44–49.

Web Resources

For current URLs for the following websites, visit www.crosscurrents.nelson.com.

THE NATIONALISM PROJECT/NATIONALISM STUDIES INFORMATION CLEARINGHOUSE
http://www.nationalismproject.org/
The Nationalism Project provides users with a clearinghouse of scholarly information on the study of nationalism, including leading definitions of nationalism, book reviews, web links, subject bibliographies, as well as a bibliography of more than 2000 journal articles.

ETHNICITY, NATIONALISM AND MIGRATION SECTION OF THE INTERNATIONAL STUDIES ASSOCIATION (ENMISA)
http://isanet.ccit.arizona.edu/sections/enm/
ENMISA is comprised of scholars interested in the study of a variety of issues related to questions of ethnicity and nationalism. They vary quite widely in there theoretical approaches, methodologies, and empirical interests.

THE ERNEST GELLNER RESOURCE PAGE
http://www.lse.ac.uk/collections/gellner/index.htm
The late Ernest Gellner was one of the leading scholars on the subjection of nationalism, ethnicity, and conflict. This website contains a number of resources relating to his thoughts and ideas on the relationship between nationalism and modernity.

THE SOLOMON ASCH CENTER FOR THE STUDY OF ETHNOPOLITICAL CONFLICT
http://www.brynmawr.edu/aschcenter/online/index.htm
The Solomon Asch Center promotes training and research in the areas of ethnic group conflict and violence. The site contains a variety of resources including links to a number of other organizations and institutions conducting research on ethnopolitical conflict.

Did the War against Iraq Violate International Law?

✔ **YES**
JUTTA BRUNNEE, "The Use of Force against Iraq: A Legal Assessment," *Behind the Headlines* 59, no. 4 (Summer 2002): 1–8

✗ **NO**
DAVID WINGFIELD, "Why the Invasion of Iraq Was Lawful," *Behind the Headlines* 59, no. 4 (Summer 2002): 10–16

On March 19, 2003, the United States launched a cruise missile attack against targets in Baghdad in an attempt to "decapitate" the regime of Saddam Hussein. Failing in its attempt to kill the Iraqi leaders, American and allied armed forces crossed the Iraqi–Kuwait border and began moving toward Baghdad, while stealth bombers and cruise missiles pummelled targets throughout the country. Within a few weeks, the United States and its allies succeeded in removing the Hussein regime from power and occupied Iraq.

The war on Iraq was a culmination of a series of events that began with President Bush's speech to Congress in January 2002, in which he identified the "axis of evil" countries of special concern to the United States: Iraq, Iran, and North Korea. The president warned that in the face of the growing threat posed by these states, the United States was willing to take preemptive action if needed. In the following months, he laid the basis for what would become known as the Bush Doctrine, which called for the United States to take unilateral, preemptive action if necessary in order to protect itself from potential threats to its security. Iraq, it turned out, would be the first real test of the doctrine.

As the debate on the Bush Doctrine unfolded, considerable attention was focused on the status of the concept of preemptive war under international law. In order to understand this debate and its implications for the war on Iraq, it is useful to look carefully at the Charter of the United Nations.

When states join the United Nations, they pledge not to use armed force "save in the common interest" (Preamble to the UN Charter). Article 2 of the Charter stipulates that all members renounce the "use of force against the territorial integrity" of other states while pursuing peaceful means for the resolution of all disputes.

Under international law, two exceptions to this principle have been recognized. Article 51 states that "nothing in the present Charter shall impair the inherent right of individual or collective self-defence if an armed attack occurs against a

Member of the United Nations." But the assumption here is that a state will unilaterally act in self-defence only until the UN Security Council has been able to organize a response. Any subsequent use of force must by authorized by the Security Council.

International law has also allowed an exception for "humanitarian intervention." This type of intervention has traditionally been interpreted in a rather restrictive fashion, limiting military intervention in any country only to cases where the intervening state is acting to rescue its own nationals or acting at the invitation of the local government authorities. Despite the great loss of human life under the genocidal regime of Pol Pot, the international community, including Canada and the United States, widely condemned Vietnam for invading in order to "liberate" the Cambodian population from the Khmer Rouge. Vietnam was punished by having comprehensive economic sanctions imposed against it for this violation of another state's sovereignty. Similarly, the Tanzanian government was condemned for sending in troops to overthrow the brutal regime of Idi Amin, even though it claimed that it was acting for humanitarian reasons. Thus, international law provides a very limited basis for justifying military assaults against another state.

In the months following the Iraq invasion, the Bush administration gave several different legal justifications for a war against Iraq. At times, it argued that the Iraqi government was in "material breach" of previous resolutions passed by the Security Council. Following the 1991 war against Iraq for its invasion of Kuwait, the Security Council called on Saddam Hussein to renounce and dismantle all programs for developing chemical, biological, and nuclear weapons. Although Hussein refused to renounce such efforts, UN weapons inspectors could find no evidence that the regime either possessed or was continuing to develop such weapons. The Bush administration denounced the UN weapons inspection process as a failure while arguing that previous Security Council resolutions (such as resolutions 687 and 1441) gave the United States the legal basis to take military action against Iraq in face of clear evidence that it had not complied.

At other times, the Bush administration evoked the principle of humanitarian intervention, citing the terrible human rights abuses by the Iraqi government and its use of chemical weapons against its own civilians during the Iran–Iraq war. The Bush administration argued that the irrational and egomaniacal nature of Saddam Hussein made him dangerous and untrustworthy. Bush warned that once Hussein had weapons of mass destruction in his hands, the United States was in danger of attack at any time. Thus, the U.S. was justified in launching a preemptive strike against the Iraqi regime.

Finally, the Bush administration argued that Saddam Hussein had ties with al-Qaeda. These ties made Iraq an accomplice to the attacks of September 11 and therefore a legitimate target for a war of self-defence.

In the following readings, the debate over the legality of U.S. actions against Iraq is taken up by two Canadian experts in international law. Jutta Brunnee examines the various options for justifying the war against Iraq under international law. After weighing the evidence, she argues that under current international law the war against Iraq was illegal. David Wingfield carefully examines the wording of the Charter of the United Nations and argues that a clear legal basis for the American actions can be found.

✔ YES
The Use of Force against Iraq: A Legal Assessment
JUTTA BRUNNEE

Against the backdrop of two world wars, one of the overriding objectives in creating the United Nations in 1945 was, as outlined in the preamble to the UN charter, to 'save succeeding generations from the scourge of war.' To that end, article 2(4) provides a general prohibition of the threat or use of armed force against other states. An exception to this prohibition is provided only in article 51: pursuant to their 'inherent right of individual or collective self-defence,' states may use force to respond to an 'armed attack.' Arguably, in limited circumstances involving imminent threats, the right to self-defence also encompasses anticipatory action. In all other cases of threats to international peace and security, resort to force must be collective. That means that, outside the ambit of individual states' rights to self-defence, the use of force must be authorized by the United Nations Security Council.

In September 2002, the government of the United States published the much-quoted 2002 *National Security Strategy*, which promotes the adaptation of the rules on the use of force to permit pre-emptive strikes against 'emerging threats' posed by 'rogue states' with weapons of mass destruction.[1] That same month, President George W. Bush took his case for military action against Iraq to the United Nations. Since then, international law has enjoyed unusual popularity as a topic of discussion and concern. Politicians, pundits, and the proverbial people on the street have debated the rules of self-defence and the merits of a doctrine of pre-emptive strike, discussed the 'material breach' of UN Security Council resolutions, or opined on the need for additional resolutions explicitly authorizing the use of force against Iraq. The war in Iraq has generated many strongly held views and much heated rhetoric. This essay aims to look beyond the rhetoric to shed some light on the legality of the Iraq campaign. It provides a review of the three potential legal justifications for the use of force and explains why none of them ultimately supports the US–British intervention.

First, given the US rhetoric regarding the threat posed by Iraq, one might think that self-defence or pre-emptive self-defence was one of the justifications advanced for the intervention. Yet, while the US government may have deployed the language of self-defence at a political level, it was not invoked for purposes of legal justification. It is worth taking a closer look at this fact.

In situations of self-defence, states can act unilaterally. They must simply notify the Security Council that they are acting in self-defence. For example, in the case of military action in Afghanistan in 2001, the US reported to the Council that it had 'initiated actions in the exercise of its inherent right of individual and collective self-defense following armed attacks that were carried out ... on September 11,

2001.'[2] Given the political differences over intervention in Iraq, a self-defence argument would have had the advantage, from a US standpoint, that action could have been taken without Security Council approval. The fact that the US did not invoke self-defence, then, speaks for itself. A case of self-defence simply could not be made. Iraq had not attacked the US, and an attack by Iraq (or attributable to Iraq) was not imminent.

What is perhaps most noteworthy is that the US government refrained not only from making a self-defence argument, but also from relying on the pre-emptive strike doctrine promoted in its *National Security Strategy*. This doctrine has raised concerns because it would leave virtually no standard capable of providing normative guidance or constraining unilateral assessments. In the 1962 Cuban Missile crisis, the United States refrained from invoking pre-emptive self-defence for this very reason.[3] In 2003, one might have expected the Bush administration to make Iraq, a 'rogue state' alleged to have weapons of mass destruction and ties to global terrorism, the test case for the pre-emptive strike doctrine. It did not. In fact, the State Department's legal adviser took pains to bring pre-emption within the confines of the 'traditional framework,' stressing that 'a preemptive use of proportional force is justified only out of necessity.' He added that 'necessity includes both a credible, imminent threat and the exhaustion of peaceful remedies.' Indeed: 'While the definition of imminent must recognize the threat posed by weapons of mass destruction and the intentions of those who possess them, the decision to undertake any action must meet the test of necessity ... in the face of overwhelming evidence of an imminent threat, a nation may take preemptive action to defend its nationals from unimaginable harm.'[4] Three observations can be made. First, it appears that the US acknowledges that a sweeping right to pre-emptive military strikes does not exist under current international law. Second, in outlining criteria to reign in the overbroad concept of 'emerging threat' contained in the *National Security Strategy*, the United States appears to acknowledge the need for standards of review. Third, political rhetoric notwithstanding, the US government did not seem to think that these standards had been met in the case of Iraq.

A second justification for the invasion of Iraq that has received some attention is that of 'humanitarian intervention.'[5] Again, it is important to separate rhetoric designed to sway public opinion from legal argument. With the onset of hostilities, there was certainly a noticeable shift in the 'packaging' of the Iraq war for public consumption. The US and, to a lesser extent, Britain emphasized the liberation of the Iraqi people from dictatorship.[6] As a legal matter, however, no attempt was made to cast the war as a humanitarian intervention. Once again, the absence of legal argument speaks volumes. It speaks to the fact that there is no firm legal basis for asserting a right of individual states to intervene forcibly in other countries on humanitarian grounds. To be sure, there is a current of opinion suggesting that, in exceptional circumstances, armed force may be used when it is the only means to forestall an immediate, overwhelming humanitarian disaster.[7] It was this idea that animated the NATO intervention in Kosovo in 1999. But even in that case of extreme crisis, the balance of opinion remains that the notion of human-itarian intervention did not provide a legal justification for the use of armed force.[8] It is therefore hardly surprising that there was no attempt by the US or Britain legally to justify the Iraq war as a humanitarian intervention. In any case, even if one were to accept in principle that humanitarian interventions are legal in a narrow range of extreme circumstances, Iraq did not fall into that range. There is little doubt that the Iraqi government repressed and brutalized its citi-zens. The recent discoveries of mass graves bear witness to the regime's brutality.[9] However, there was no urgent humanitarian crisis that necessitated immediate use of force, and none was alleged by the US or British governments. In short, while the liberation of the Iraqi people may have been a positive side-effect of 'Operation Iraqi Freedom,' under existing international law it cannot convert other-wise illegal use of force into lawful action.

This takes us to the last possible legal basis for the Iraq intervention, and to the arguments that were actually deployed by the US and Britain to justify it. In essence, the argument is that the Security Council had authorized the use of force through a set of resolutions, encompassing resolution 678 (29 November 1990), resolution 687 (3 April 1991), and resolution 1441 (8 November 2002).[10] To appre-ciate the purchase of this argument, it is necessary to consider the relevant reso-lutions in some detail.

Iraq invaded Kuwait on 1 August 1990. In resolution 660 of 2 August, the Security Council called upon Iraq to withdraw from Kuwait 'immediately and unconditionally.' In light of Iraq's refusal to heed this and other calls by the Council for withdrawal, the preamble to resolution 678 'recalled and reaffirmed' a series of resolutions pertaining to Iraq, beginning with resolution 660 and ending with resolution 677 (1990). It then noted Iraq's refusal 'to comply, with its obligation to implement resolution 660 (1990) and the abovementioned subse-quent resolutions.' In paragraph 2 of resolution 678, the Council therefore autho-rized 'Member States cooperating with the Government of Kuwait ... to use all necessary means to uphold and implement resolution 660 (1990) and all subse-quent relevant resolutions and to restore international peace and security in the area.' Several weeks later, in January 1991, 'Operation Desert Storm' was under-taken to expel Iraq from Kuwait.

Upon completion of 'Desert Storm,' resolution 686 of 2 March 1991 outlined an initial, provisional ceasefire. Resolution 687 followed to provide for a permanent ceasefire, which was contingent upon Iraq's unconditional acceptance of various conditions, including extensive disarmament obligations. In paragraph 33 of the resolution the Security Council declared that 'upon official notification by Iraq ... of its acceptance of the provisions above, a formal ceasefire is effective between Iraq and Kuwait and the Member States cooperating with Kuwait in accordance with resolution 678 (1990).' In paragraph 34 of the resolution, the Council decided 'to remain seized of the matter and to take such further steps as may be required for the implementation of the present resolution and to secure peace and security in the area.'

As is well known, Iraq's compliance with its obligations under resolution 687 and a series of subsequent resolutions was less than satisfactory. Notably its compliance with disarmament obligations and its co-operation with UN weapons inspectors left much to be desired. In September 2002, the Bush administration vowed to put an end to a 'decade of deception and defiance.'[11] The administration called on the Security Council to enforce Iraqi compliance, if necessary through military means. However, other members of the Security Council were reluctant to set the tracks toward a military solution. After intense negotiations, a compromise was finally enshrined in resolution 1441.

The Council found that 'Iraq has been and remains in material breach of its obligations under relevant resolutions, including resolution 687' (paragraph 1) and gave Iraq a 'final opportunity to comply with its disarmament obligations' (paragraph 2). Any further non-compliance would 'constitute a further material breach,' which would be 'reported to the Council for assessment' (paragraph 4). Based on the reports of Iraq's performance, the Council would convene immediately 'in order to consider the situation and the need for full compliance ... in order to secure international peace and security' (paragraph 12). The resolution recalled 'that the Council has repeatedly warned Iraq that it will face serious consequences as a result of its continued violations of its obligations' (paragraph 13). Finally, the Council decided 'to remain seized of the matter' (paragraph 14).

In the weeks following the adoption of resolution 1441, the Security Council was not able to agree on whether Iraq's conduct warranted an armed intervention, and no resolution explicitly authorizing such intervention was adopted. The US and Britain have maintained that an additional resolution providing specific authorization of force was not required. If they had entertained discussions on a 'second resolution,' they argued, it was for political not legal reasons. According to the US government, taking action against Iraq was a question merely of will, not of authority.[12] The three resolutions outlined above—678, 687, and 1441—were said to provide all the authority needed to enforce Iraqi compliance. The argument goes roughly like this: resolution 678 authorized force against Iraq, for purposes that included restoring peace and security in the area. Resolution 687 suspended the authority provided in resolution 678, but did not terminate it. Rather, the ceasefire was contingent upon Iraq's compliance with the various conditions in resolution 687. If Iraq were in material breach of this arrangement, the authority to use force under resolution 678 would be revived. Resolution 1441 confirmed that Iraq was and continued to be in material breach. Resolution 1441 required reporting to and discussion by the Security Council of Iraq's breaches, but not an express further decision to authorize force.[13]

This line of argument has been rejected by an overwhelming majority of international lawyers, who have spoken out on the matter in unusual numbers.[14] Indeed, a senior legal adviser to the British foreign secretary resigned over the issue.[15] Why?

Security Council resolutions are carefully crafted compromises, often the product of delicate diplomatic tangos behind closed doors. But, like all treaty-based arrangements, they ultimately must be measured against the standard of the ordinary meaning of the language employed and interpreted in good faith. Add to that the fact that the Security Council has explicitly authorized the use of force only twice in its history—once during the Korean War in 1950 and once in response to Iraq's invasion of Kuwait in 1990. Given the reluctance of the Council to authorize forcible measures, it is difficult to see how resolutions 678, 687, and 1441 could in good faith be interpreted as an open-ended authorization of the use of force against Iraq. A closer look at the excerpts from these resolutions highlighted above further supports this conclusion. A number of points can be made in that regard.

First, the authority to use force provided by resolution 678 was quite clearly focused on Iraq's invasion of Kuwait. For better or for worse, it took this dramatic a transgression by Iraq to prompt the Security Council to authorize 'all necessary means.' But this authority related to compliance with resolution 660 and a specified set of subsequent resolutions relating to Iraq's invasion of Kuwait—not an indeterminate set of future resolutions on Iraq. Similarly, the phrase 'restore peace and security' was carefully chosen to confine the authority provided.

Second, the ceasefire effected pursuant to resolution 687 was contingent only upon Iraq's formal acceptance of the conditions set out in the resolution. Nowhere does the resolution indicate that the ceasefire merely suspended paragraph 2 of resolution 678 (the authorization of force), or that it could be terminated in case of Iraqi non-compliance. This silence stands in marked contrast to resolution 686, the earlier provisional ceasefire arrangement, which explicitly recognized that paragraph 2 of resolution 678 remained valid during the period required for Iraq to comply with the terms of the provisional ceasefire. In any event, a termination of the ceasefire would be a matter for the Security Council, not for individual states. Paragraph 34 of the resolution makes this plain through the decision of the Council that it will 'remain seized of the matter' and 'take such further steps as may be required.' Further, resolution 687 speaks of a ceasefire between Iraq, Kuwait, and 'Member States cooperating with the Government of Kuwait.' The latter terminology refers to the coalition of states that had pledged to assist Kuwait in collective self-defence against Iraq's invasion and that had been authorized to use force in resolution 678. This coalition of states no longer exists, and it is difficult to see how authority to use force or to end the ceasefire with Iraq could now rest with the United States or with Britain.

Third, authority for the use of force against Iraq cannot be found in resolution 1441. Yes, paragraph 13 reminds Iraq that it would face serious consequences as a result of its continued non-compliance. But, given the deep disagreements that led to the adoption of this compromise resolution, it is impossible to read this paragraph as an express or even an implied authorization of force. It is also true that resolution 1441 did not expressly require an additional resolution authorizing force, but no conclusions can be drawn from that fact. If the Council had indeed previously authorized the use of force, as the US and Britain maintain, no such additional decision, and therefore no reference to it, was needed. Conversely, if previous resolutions did not provide authority, as other Security Council members asserted, there was no need for resolution 1441 to state the obvious—that an authorizing resolution was required for lawful use of force. With respect to the question of force, then, resolution 1441 was simply a place holder. It allowed the UN process to proceed in the hope that it would resolve the Iraq situation through renewed weapons inspections. In the meantime, it preserved the legal status quo.

In short, resolution 1441 did not authorize the US and Britain to take military action against Iraq. The legality of their intervention in Iraq therefore turns on whether resolutions 678 and 687, adopted more than a decade earlier in the aftermath of Iraq's invasion of Kuwait, provided open-ended authority to enforce Iraqi disarmament with 'all necessary means.' They did not.

The UN charter has not accomplished the ambitious goal of eliminating war. Nonetheless, the rules on the use of force have done important work. They have served to constrain the resort to force by states, notably by providing a normative framework against which actions must be justified and can be assessed. In the case of the war against Iraq, neither justifications based on UN Security Council authorization, nor arguments based on self-defence or humanitarian intervention can carry the day. One may hold any number of opinions on whether or not the war against Iraq was necessary and appropriate, and even on whether or not international law should accommodate this type of intervention. But we should all be clear that, under existing international law, the use of force against Iraq was illegal.

NOTES

1. *The National Security Strategy of the United States of America*, September 2002, 13–16; available at www.whitehouse.gov.nsc/nss.pdf

2. 'Letter dated 7 October 2001 from the Permanent Representative of the United States of America to the United Nations addressed to the President of the Security Council'; available at www.un.int/usa/s2001–946.htm

3. See Abram Chayes, *The Cuban Missile Crisis: International Crisis and the Role of Law* (London and NY: Oxford University Press 1974), 63–6.

4. William Taft, IV, 'Memorandum: The Legal Basis for Preemption,' 18 November 2002; available at www.cfr.org/publication.php?id=5250

5. Ed Morgan, 'Use of force against Iraq is legal,' *National Post*, 19 March 2003.

6. 'Village by village, city by city, liberation is coming. The people of Iraq have my pledge: Our fighting forces will press on until their oppressors are gone and their whole country is free.' President Bush, Radio Address, 5 April 2003; available at www.whitehouse.gov/news/releases/2003/04/20030405.html. See also the 'Liberation Update'; available at www.whitehouse.gov/news/releases/2003/05/iraq/20030506-19.html

7. For a thoughtful treatment, see International Commission on Intervention and State Sovereignty, *The Responsibility to Protect* (December 2001); available at www.dfait-maeci.gc.ca/iciss-ciise/report-en.asp

8. See Nico Krisch, 'Legality, morality and the dilemma of humanitarian intervention after Kosovo,' *European Journal of International Law* 13(no 1, 2002); available at www3.oup.co.uk/ejilaw/hdb/ Volume_13/Issue_01/

9. See Patrick E. Tyler, 'An open secret is laid bare at mass grave in Iraqi marsh,' *New York Times*, 14 May 2003; available at www.nytimes.com/2003/05/14/international/worldspecial/14GRAV.html

10. Security Council resolutions can be accessed at www.un.org/Docs/sc/unsc_resolutions.html

11. See *A Decade of Deception and Defiance*, 12 September 2002; available at www.whitehouse.gov/news/releases/2002/09/iraq/20020912.html

12. President Bush, *Address to the Nation*, 17 March 2003; available at www.whitehouse.gov/news/releases/2003/03/20030317-7.html

13. On the US position, see 'Letter dated 30 March 2003 from the Permanent Representative of the United States of America to the United Nations addressed to the President of the Security Council'; available at www.un.int/usa/s2003_351.pdf. On the British position, see Attorney General, Lord Goldsmith, 'Legal basis for use of force against Iraq,' 17 March 2003; available at www.pmo.gov.uk/output/Page3287.asp

14. See, for example, 'Howard must not involve US in an illegal war,' 26 February 2003; available at www.theage.com.au/articles/2003/02/25/1046064031296.html (Australia); 'War would be illegal,' *Guardian*, 7 March 2003; at education.guardian.co.uk/Print/0,3858,4620124,00.html (Britain); Peter Slevin, 'Legality of war is a matter of debate—many scholars doubt assertion by Bush,' *Washington Post*, 18 March 2003; at www.commondreams.org/headlines03/0318-05.htm (US); Jeff Sallot, 'Legal experts say attack on Iraq is illegal,' *Globe and Mail*, 20 March 2003, A10 (Canada).

15. Ewen MacAskill, 'Adviser quits Foreign Office over legality of war,' *Guardian*, 22 March 2003, available at http://politics.guardian. co.uk/iraq/story/0,12956,919647,00.html

✗ NO
Why the Invasion of Iraq Was Lawful
DAVID WINGFIELD

When the United States, Britain, Australia, and their allies invaded Iraq, they claimed that they were acting in accordance with international law because resolutions passed by the United Nations Security Council had authorized the war. Many countries and international lawyers disagree. They claim that no resolution of the Security Council authorized the war and that as a consequence the invasion was illegal. Who is right?

The debate is reminiscent of Humpty Dumpty's debate with Alice. Humpty Dumpty said that when he uses a word 'it means just what I choose it to mean—neither more nor less.' In response to Alice's question of whether he could make words mean different things, Humpty Dumpty replied 'the question is, which is to be master—that's all.' Stripped to its core, the debate over the Iraq war was, and continues to be, a debate over who is to be master of the interpretation of Security Council resolutions—those countries that used force or those countries that opposed the use of force.

Democracies resolve debates within their borders about the meaning of words in statutes or other legal documents by referring the matter to a court. The international community cannot do so, however. It has no court that operates like a domestic court in a Western democracy. (The International Court of Justice can only decide disputes that the concerned states agree be submitted to it.)

For this reason, the legality of the invasion of Iraq cannot be tested in a court of law. It can be tested only by reference to reason: is there a rational basis for concluding that the invasion of Iraq was lawful under international law? If so, then the right of the United States, Britain, Australia, and their allies to invade Iraq must be conceded and the debate moved to the political question of whether the invasion was a smart thing to do. After all, international law exists for the benefit of the United States, too. The US should not be prevented from acting in accordance with its security needs by appeals to international law if it can make a rational case of legality.

The charter of the United Nations authorizes the use of force under chapter VII, which permits war under two circumstances. One circumstance is individual or collective self-defence pursuant to article 51. Countries that are attacked have the inherent right to defend themselves by war. The other is when the Security Council, on behalf of the international community, authorizes the use of force against another country.

The use of force under the charter begins with a 'determination' under article 39, the first article of chapter VII. Under article 39, the Security Council may 'determine the existence of any threat to the peace, breach of the peace, or act of aggression.' The wording of article 39 is very broad. The article gives the Security

Council the power to determine that a threat short of an actual breach of peace and security exists, that a breach of peace and security short of an act of aggression exists, that an act of aggression short of an attack on another country exists, or that an actual attack has taken place. Obviously in the last case the country that is the object of the attack has the right to defend itself by force, independent of any Security Council determination under article 39.

It is interesting that article 39 does not stipulate that the threat to or breach of the peace has to be committed by a sovereign nation. Although it is doubtful that the framers of the charter of the United Nations had in mind state-sponsored terrorists when they drafted the language of the charter, article 39 is written in language that is broad enough to encompass threats or breaches to the peace by states that sponsor terrorists but which otherwise do not overtly threaten any other country.

After the Security Council makes a determination under article 39 it has two choices. One choice, pursuant to article 41, is to decide on 'measures' that do not involve the use of armed force in order to give effect to its decisions. Economic sanctions, for example, are a permitted 'measure' under this article. The second choice, pursuant to article 42, is to take 'action by air, sea, or land forces as may be necessary to maintain or restore international peace and security.'

Sharp-eyed lawyers will notice the disjunctive 'or' in article 42 between the nouns air, sea, and land and between the verbs maintain and restore. Consequently, by combining articles 39 and 42, it is clear that force can lawfully be used in anticipation of a breach of international peace and security or as a reaction to such a breach. The threat or breach can come from the direct or indirect action of a country and the response can take any form of military action that is necessary either to maintain existing peace and security or to restore the peace and security that has been threatened or disrupted. In other words, pre-emptive attacks are perfectly lawful under international law providing that the Security Council has first 'determined' that another country threatens international peace and security and has authorized 'action' against that country to restore international peace and security.

The only limit on the degree of force to be used under article 42 is that the force must be 'necessary' to maintain or restore international peace and security. The whole point of using force under the charter of the United Nations is to change the behaviour of a state. Sometimes the force necessary to change a state's behaviour will consist of limited bombing of some military or political targets. Often, though, it will be necessary to destroy completely a hostile state's ability to use military power or to control territory. It is to this latter activity that one customarily applies the concept 'war.'

Lawyers look to precedent to guide their interpretation of the law. The Security Council has twice authorized war: in 1950 when North Korea invaded the Republic of Korea and forty years later when Iraq invaded Kuwait. Therefore, to understand what the Security Council must say in order to authorize war and what it does to wage that war, the best places to look are its resolutions authorizing the Korean and Gulf wars.

Of course, the United Nations does not possess its own military forces, and therefore it cannot itself wage war. Long before President George W. Bush coined the phrase 'coalition of the willing,' the Security Council had adopted the concept. When the Security Council declares war it requests and authorizes a 'coalition of the willing' to fight and allows that coalition to determine the tactics and strategy of the war, as well as its aims, as it did in both the Korean war and the Gulf war.

The Korean war was conducted essentially under three resolutions, resolutions 82, 83, and 84, which were enacted in June and July 1950. In those resolutions, the Security Council 'determined' that North Korea's attack on the Republic of Korea constituted a breach of the peace. The Council then 'called' upon the member states to provide assistance in enforcing these resolutions and 'recommended' that the member states assist the Republic of Korea in restoring international peace and security to the area. It is important to note that the Security Council recommended that those countries that were willing to provide military assistance should do so under United States command. Although the resolutions did not expressly refer to chapter VII or to any article of that chapter, it is clear from their language that they were enacted under that chapter. The 'determination' was obviously made pursuant to article 39, and 'calling' on all other countries to restore international peace and security was obviously an 'action' under article 42.

After China entered the Korean war, the Security Council enacted a resolution removing the complaint of aggression that had given legal sanction to the war from the list of matters of which the Council was then seized. In effect, the Council said that North Korea's breach of the peace was now off its plate. Nevertheless, the Korean war continued for almost another two-and-a-half years without any further Security Council resolutions authorizing its continuation. The Korean experience demonstrates that, once the Security Council authorizes 'action' to restore international peace and security, the actions taken under that authorization remain lawful until the countries taking those actions are satisfied that they should stop fighting or until the Security Council enacts a resolution determining that international peace and security have been restored in the area. Any such resolution would make the continuation of hostilities illegal for those countries engaged in them.

Following Iraq's invasion of Kuwait in 1990, the Security Council did not initially authorize war, although Kuwait, of course, had the right to defend itself by war. Rather, the Security Council passed resolution 660 under articles 39 and 40 of chapter VII in which the Council 'determined' that the Iraqi invasion of Kuwait was indeed a breach of international peace and security. This determination, which has been recalled in all subsequent resolutions, allowed the Security Council to decide what should be done about Iraq so that international peace and security could be restored.

What the Security Council decided to do was to pass resolution 678, which demanded that Iraq fully comply with resolution 660 and all subsequent resolutions of which it was in breach. The Security Council gave Iraq until 15 January 1991 to comply with those resolutions. If it did not do so, resolution 678 authorized the member states 'to use all necessary means' to 'restore' international peace and security and to ensure compliance with the resolutions Iraq had breached. Using 'all necessary means' is obviously an 'action' under article 42. The Security Council also requested in resolution 678 that the member states provide appropriate support for the 'actions' to restore international peace and security in the area. Unlike the Korean war resolutions, resolution 678 was expressly enacted under chapter VII of the charter in its entirety. Resolution 678 was unambiguously a declaration of war, albeit a conditional one.

As with the Korean war, the first Gulf war did not technically end. The hostilities ceased with an armistice, or a ceasefire in modern parlance, not with a treaty of peace or its Security Council equivalent. The United States, North Korea, and China, not the United Nations, agreed to the Korean war armistice. However, in the Gulf war the Security Council, not the belligerent states, enacted its terms.

The terms of the Gulf war ceasefire can be found in resolutions 686 and 687, which were enacted (as were all the other resolutions relating to Iraq's invasion of Kuwait) under chapter VII of the charter in its entirety, including the articles authorizing the use of force. Resolution 686 notes that combat operations by the coalition forces had been 'suspended,' not that the authority for those operations had been set aside. Resolution 687, which enacted the formal terms of the ceasefire, ordered Iraq unconditionally to destroy all its chemical, biological, and nuclear weapons and not to acquire new ones or the means of making new ones, amongst other things. It is clear from the terms of resolutions 686 and 687 that if Iraq was to breach the ceasefire the war could lawfully resume as if hostilities had never ceased in 1991. Indeed, the contrary cannot logically be argued.

As we all know, Iraq did breach the terms of the ceasefire and subsequent resolutions. In response to some of its more flagrant breaches, such as ejecting the weapons' inspectors in 1998, the United States and Britain bombed Iraq's military and security infrastructure. Nevertheless, over time, the Security Council ignored Iraq's non-compliance with the terms of the ceasefire. But the Council never enacted a resolution declaring that international peace and security had been restored to the area, or even a resolution similar to that which the Council enacted in January 1951 to remove the issue of Korea from its plate. Rather, in each of the resolutions it enacted, it recalled that Iraq was and remained a threat to world peace and security; the Council remained seized of the problem that Iraq presented.

In November 2002, the Security Council enacted resolution 1441, the resolution that contains the phrase 'serious consequences.' Resolution 1441 was enacted to remedy the Security Council's lack of action over Iraq's non-compliance with Security Council resolutions going all the way back to the ceasefire in 1991. In effect, the Security Council wanted to ensure that no one could argue that the legal effect of its previous resolutions had lapsed through lack of deliberate action to enforce them. Legally, this resolution was probably unnecessary. Over a dozen other resolutions enacted under chapter VII, stretching back to the ceasefire resolutions, re-affirmed the right to wage war by 'recalling' the earlier resolutions that had authorized the first Gulf war.

Thus, in resolution 1441 the Security Council was simply reaffirming that the legal basis for its declaration of war remained in effect. It did so by expressly recognizing under chapter VII that Iraq's non-compliance with the previous resolutions posed a 'threat to international peace and security.' It specifically recalled that the ceasefire declared in resolution 687 depended on Iraq's compliance with the terms of the ceasefire resolution and 'decided' that Iraq remained in breach of those terms. The Security Council then gave Iraq a 'final' opportunity to comply. Just to be sure that no one misses the point, at the end of all of this the Security Council 'recalled' that Iraq would face 'serious consequences' if it continued to violate its obligations under the many earlier resolutions. Serious consequences are, of course, 'actions.' In other words, in resolution 1441 the Security Council expressly re-affirmed the language that is its code for war and re-affirmed the right to resume the war should Iraq not immediately comply with its obligations. Short of saying 'any country that wishes to do so may attack Iraq again if it does not immediately comply with the earlier resolutions,' the meaning of resolution 1441 could not be clearer.

After resolution 1441 was passed, the Security Council authorized inspectors to enter Iraq to certify whether or not Iraq had fully complied with its disarmament obligations. The weapons' inspectors were unable to certify that Iraq had done so, thus confirming that Iraq remained in breach of its obligations. Therefore, the position of the United States, Britain, Australia, and their allies, that is, that Iraq remained in breach of the terms of ceasefire and other resolutions up to the moment of invasion, is unassailable. Iraq's breaches of the resolutions gave the coalition a rational basis in international law for resuming hostilities against Iraq for the purpose of destroying its military capability and changing its political leadership so that it would cease to threaten international peace and security. The legal basis for this war, for example, is much sounder than the legal basis for the military action against Serbia over Kosovo, which of course was not supported by any Security Council resolution before battle was joined.

The debate over the invasion of Iraq raised, and continues to raise, many fundamental questions relating to the use of power, the best way to create a secure and stable international order, the control of weapons of mass destruction, the legitimacy of the use of force to protect or promote human and political rights, the effectiveness of Security Council resolutions, and the right of the United States to use its military forces against another country unilaterally. In the context of the invasion of Iraq, these are all political not legal questions. Dressing them in legal garb does not make them any less political. The legal issue is quite narrow and straightforward: can a rational case be made that the invasion of Iraq was supportable under international law? Such a case can be made, and therefore the debate over this war should stay where it belongs: in the arena of politics, not that of law.

POSTSCRIPT

One problem that emerges from this debate is the growing gap between international law and the actual behaviour of states. This gap is particularly evident in relation to the expectation stated in the Charter of the United Nations that all members renounce war except in the "common interest" and under Security Council authorization. Critics are quick to point out that more than 126 members of the United Nations have been involved in interstate conflicts costing well over 22 million lives. How does one respond to this widening gulf between the expectations of international law and state behaviour?

One approach is to argue that we should discard international law along with the pretence that it constrains behaviour of states. In an increasingly dangerous and hostile world, those that pose the greatest danger (terrorist groups or "rogue" states) already totally disregard international laws. Thus, states must be willing to take whatever actions, unilaterally and without further authorization if necessary, in order to protect themselves. This appears to be partly the premise of the *National Security Strategy* and the Bush Doctrine. While the Bush administration was willing to seek endorsement of the Security Council for its actions, it was quite willing to act without such authorization. This reasoning is also reflected in the Bush administration's decision to withdraw from the International Criminal Court, an issue addressed later in this book.

A second approach seeks to make international law more relevant by broadening the definitions inherent in it. According to this view, we must legitimize those actions of states that must be taken as a matter of necessity in order to ensure their survival. Thus, international law must be changed to more "realistically" reflect the actual world. This perspective is adopted by those supporters of the Bush Doctrine of preemptive war who argue that the traditional definitions of self-defence need to be revised and updated to take into account present realities. Only by broadening its categories and recognizing the right to a preemptive strike in self-defence will international law be seen as legitimate and relevant in the future.

A third approach is to find new and better ways to hold states accountable to current international laws. The failure is not in the laws themselves, but in the inadequacies of current mechanisms for implementing and enforcing them. The international community must work toward building stronger international institutions, such as an International Criminal Court, while pressuring all states to continue to work within international law. Critics such as Noam Chomsky argue that the real "rogue" state is not Iraq, Iran, or North Korea, but the United States, because it insists on acting outside international law. Some of these issues will be raised again when we examine the case for an International Criminal Court in Issue Fifteen.

Suggested Additional Readings

Byers, Michael. "The Shifting Foundations of International Law: A Decade of Forceful Measures against Iraq." *European Journal of International Law* 13, no. 1 (February 2002): 21–41.

Cassese, Antonio. "Terrorism Is Also Disrupting Some Crucial Legal Categories of International Law." *European Journal of International Law* 12, no. 5 (December 2001): 993–1001.

Chace, James. "Present at the Destruction: The Death of American Internationalism." *World Policy Journal* 20, no. 1 (Spring 2003): 1–4.

Falk, Richard. "What Future for the UN Charter System of War Prevention? Reflections on the Iraq War." In Irwin Abrams and Wang Gungwu, (eds.), *The Iraq War and Its Consequences: Thoughts of Nobel Peace Laureates and Eminent Scholars.* New Jersey: World Scientific, 2003: 195–214.

Farer, Tom. "The Prospect for International Law and Order in the Wake of Iraq." *American Journal of International Law* 97, no. 3 (July 2003): 621–27.

Foster, Charles. "International Law: Another Casualty of the Iraq War?" *Contemporary Review* 283, no. 1651 (August 2003): 76–78.

Gray, Christine. "From Unity to Polarization: International Law and the Use of Force against Iraq." *European Journal of International Law* 13, no. 1 (2002): 1–19.

Kampfner, John. "War and the Law." *New Statesman* 133, no. 4678 (March 8, 2004): 21–22.

Lobel, Jules, and Michael Ratner. "Bypassing the Security Council: Ambiguous Authorizations to Use Force, Cease-Fires and the Iraqi Inspection Regime." *American Journal of International Law* 93, no. 1 (January 1999): 124–54.

Valasek, Tomas. "New Threats, New Rules: Revising the Law of War." *World Policy Journal* 20, no. 1 (Spring 2003): 17–24.

Williams, Jody. "Iraq and Preemptive Self-Defense." In Irwin Abrams and Wang Gungwu, (eds.), *The Iraq War and Its Consequences: Thoughts of Nobel Peace Laureates and Eminent Scholars.* New Jersey: World Scientific, 2003: 17–48.

Yoo, John. "International Law after the War in Iraq." *American Journal of International Law* 97, no. 3 (July 2003): 563–75.

InfoTrac® College Edition

Search for the following articles in the InfoTrac® database:

Bellamy, Alex J. "International Law and the War with Iraq." *Melbourne Journal of International Law* 4, no. 2 (October 2003): 497–520.

Gordon, Joy. "Accountability and Global Governance: The Case of Iraq." *Ethics & International Affairs* 20, no. 1 (March 2006): 79–99.

Kaufman, Whitley. "What's Wrong with Preventative War? The Moral and Legal Basis for the Preventive Use of Force." *Ethics & International Affairs* 19, no. 3 (December 2005): 23–39.

Podhoretz, Norman. "Stopping Iran: Why the Case for Military Action Still Stands." *Commentary* 125, no. 2 (February 2008): 11–20.

Web Resources

For current URLs for the following websites, visit www.crosscurrents.nelson.com.

THE WAR ON IRAQ: LEGAL ISSUES
http://www.hrcr.org/hottopics/Iraq.html
This site is maintained by the Arthur W. Diamond Law Library at Columbia Law School. It contains an extensive collection of documents, articles, and links relating to the legal aspects of the Iraq war.

ELECTRONIC IRAQ
http://electroniciraq.net/
Electronic Iraq is a news portal on the U.S.–Iraq crisis published by Middle East alternative news publishers. The site contains publications dealing with the legality of the war.

RICHARD FALK AND DAVID KRIEGER, (EDS.), "THE IRAQ CRISIS AND INTERNATIONAL LAW," NUCLEAR AGE PEACE FOUNDATION BRIEFING BOOKLET (JANUARY 2003)
http://www.wagingpeace.org/menu/resources/publications/2003_01_iraq-reader.pdf
This booklet contains a good collection of full-text articles and documents on the topic.

Has NATO Become Irrelevant in an Age of Terrorism?

✔ **YES**

STEVEN MEYER, "Carcass of Dead Policies: The Irrelevance of NATO," *Parameters* 33, no. 4 (Winter 2003–04): 83–97

✗ **NO**

REBECCA JOHNSON AND MICAH ZENKO, "All Dressed Up and No Place to Go: Why NATO Should Be on the Front Lines in the War on Terror," *Parameters* 32, no. 4 (Winter 2002–03): 48–63

On March 29, 2004, the leaders of seven states—Bulgaria, Estonia, Latvia, Lithuania, Romania, Slovakia, and Slovenia—met in Washington, D.C., to present their "instruments of accession" to the North Atlantic Treaty Organization. With the addition of these states, the membership in NATO is now twenty-six, an increase of ten members since the end of the Cold War. Representatives from three other countries hoping to join the alliance organization in the future—Albania, Croatia, and Macedonia—also attended the ceremonies.

In a speech marking the event, U.S. secretary of state, Colin Powell, recalled that NATO was originally founded to provide "defense of a common territory." Now, he proclaimed, "our enemies seek not only the death of multitudes but the death of liberty itself . . . we stand united in the global war against terrorism, a war that compels the resistance of all free peoples and must be won by free peoples together in alliance." Secretary Powell noted that rather than simply preventing aggression, the future role of NATO would be "to promote freedom, to extend the reach of liberty, and to deepen the peace." He concluded, "I am confident that with the new energy that these seven nations bring to our alliance, our alliance will be as successful in the future as it has been in the past." Secretary Powell's prediction of a positive and expansive future for NATO stands in contrast to the view held by many others who have increasingly questioned the relevance of NATO, especially in an age of terrorism, when the principal threat to security comes from non-state actors. It also appears to stand in contrast to the policies of an American administration that has emphasized its willingness to act unilaterally to protect its national interests. In order to understand this debate, it is useful to briefly recall the history of NATO.

Founded in 1949, NATO originally consisted of ten European nations, Canada, and the United States. The original European members (Belgium, Britain, Denmark, France, Iceland, Italy, Luxembourg, the Netherlands, Norway, and

Portugal) were later joined by Greece, Turkey, West Germany, and Spain. NATO forces are composed of members' armed forces, while the United States, as the dominant partner in the alliance, provides the Allied Commander, Europe. Political accountability is assured through the North Atlantic Council, composed of ministers from each member state and a permanent ambassador in residence in Brussels, Belgium, the location of NATO headquarters.

From its inception, the major purpose of NATO was to deter, and repel if necessary, an armed attack on Western Europe by the Soviet Union and its allies in the Warsaw Pact. In this sense, NATO was a classical defensive alliance. It existed principally because of the perceived threat from the Soviets. In addition, NATO was intended to foster political cooperation and reduce conflict within Europe so that the Soviets could not take advantage of any perceived weaknesses in Western solidarity.

When the Soviet Union collapsed and the Cold War came to an end, the future of NATO came increasingly into question. If the U.S.S.R. is no longer a security threat, from whom is NATO protecting Europe? Without a clear security threat to consolidate support from its members, can NATO hope to survive at all? One response to these questions has been to identify a broader field of concern for NATO security interests. In 1993, the NATO alliance agreed to the general principle of participating in peacekeeping operations outside its traditional sphere of influence. It was argued that unless NATO played some role in helping to mitigate regional hostilities, the ethnic conflicts in the Balkans, Southern and Eastern Europe, and Russia itself could drag the neighbouring NATO members into a wider European war. As a result, when the former Yugoslavia disintegrated into ethnic fighting, NATO became involved in both Bosnia and Kosovo, launching military strikes and later providing ground forces in an attempt to quell the fighting. These interventions were seen by many as a test to demonstrate the future relevance of NATO. To some, this intervention showed that NATO was willing to respond to security threats on its perimeter, while others perceived it as demonstrating the limitations of the NATO alliance for responding to the "new" threats. For example, some American military officials complained that the lengthy time that it took to obtain approval from all of the participants for every list of bombing targets had severely damaged the effectiveness of NATO actions.

The terrorist attacks on the United States on September 11, 2001, raised new questions about the future relevance of NATO. Article 5 of the North Atlantic Treaty, which states that an attack against any member is an attack against all members, was invoked by NATO for the first time in response to these attacks. However, all of the subsequent military actions in relation to Afghanistan, Iraq, and more generally as part of the "war on terrorism" have been organized by the United States through an ad hoc "coalition of the willing" and not under the aegis of NATO. In fact, the opposition of key NATO members such as France and Germany to the war in Iraq has revealed deep divisions with the alliance itself.

The new Bush Doctrine, while mentioning the continuing importance of alliances, placed significant weight on the necessity of taking unilateral actions in order to secure the national interest.

Despite these concerns about the future role of NATO, expansion of membership in the alliance itself has remained a high priority. In January 1994 at the NATO summit, allied leaders committed themselves to accepting new members into the alliance, as provided for under article 10 of the North Atlantic Treaty. The 1994 Brussels Declaration of NATO Heads of State and Government affirmed that membership in the alliance was open to other European states, as long as they were willing to contribute to the security of the North Atlantic area and to further the principles of the Washington Treaty. In other words, they must be committed to democratization. After a series of negotiations, in 1999, three former Warsaw Pact members—Hungary, Poland, and the Czech Republic—joined the alliance. The ceremonies in Washington in March 2004 marked the second round of membership expansion since the end of the Cold War.

Does this continued expansion of membership mark the beginning of a new and hopeful future for the NATO alliance? Or does it just mask the ongoing irrelevance and decline of an outdated artifact of the Cold War? In the following essay, Steven Meyer argues that NATO has become largely irrelevant in the current security context. He contends that it is time for members of NATO to admit to the myth of the alliance's continuing relevance and to dissolve the organization. In response, Rebecca Johnson and Micah Zenko argue that NATO is far from being irrelevant and that more attention should be invested in giving it a larger role in facing the new security threats. They call on the members of NATO to take their potential role in the war on terrorism more seriously and on the United States to invest more attention in supporting such a role for the alliance.

✔ **YES**

Carcass of Dead Policies: The Irrelevance of NATO*

STEVEN MEYER

In 1877, Lord Salisbury, commenting on Great Britain's policy on the Eastern Question, noted that "the commonest error in politics is sticking to the carcass of dead policies."[1] Salisbury was bemoaning the fact that many influential members of the British ruling class could not recognize that history had moved on; they continued to cling to policies and institutions that were relics of another era. Salisbury went on to note that the cost was enormous because this preoccupation with anachronism damaged Britain's real interests. Despite Salisbury's clever words, his observation is nothing new. Throughout Western history policymakers often have tended to rely on past realities, policies, and institutions to assess and deal with contemporary and future situations.

Post-Cold War American policymakers have not been immune from falling into this trap. Indeed, this inertial approach, characterized by Washington's unbending support for NATO and its expansion, has defined American foreign and security policy since the collapse of the Soviet Union and the bipolar world. During the Cold War, NATO provided the proper linchpin of American—and West European—security policy, and served as a useful, even fundamental deterrent to Soviet military might and expansionism. However, NATO's time has come and gone, and today there is no legitimate reason for it to exist. Although the strong differences exhibited in the Alliance over the war against Iraq have accelerated NATO's irrelevancy, the root causes of its problems go much deeper. Consequently, for both the United States and Europe, NATO is at best an irrelevant distraction and at worst toxic to their respective contemporary security needs.

THE INERTIAL IMPERATIVE

The end of the Cold War presented a problem similar to the one faced by post-World War II American leaders. A tectonic shift had occurred that required innovation, creativity, and a real understanding of the evolving world. For some experts—both in government and academia, as well as on both sides of the Atlantic—the collapse of the Soviet Union and the Warsaw Pact called into question the need for NATO. They recognized that an era had ended and the time was ripe for a basic debate about the future of NATO and Western security policies and structures.

---

*The views expressed in this article are personal ones and do not reflect the official policy or position of the National Defense University, the Department of Defense, or the U.S. Government.

Unfortunately, the policymakers in Washington who established the priorities for the post-Cold War era reacted quite differently from their predecessors. A small, influential coterie of policymakers in the elder Bush and then the Clinton administrations reacted reflexively and inertially, cutting off what should have been useful debate on the future. Moreover, virtually all of the officials who helped define the foreign and security policy in the Bush "41" Administration have resurfaced in the current Bush Administration. According to them, the existence and viability of NATO was not to be questioned. It was to remain basically the same successful alliance of American and European foreign and security policy that it had been since 1949. But a fundamental change was taking place in the post-Cold War security environment. In 1949, a genuine, measurable security threat justified NATO for all its members. Now, with the end of the Cold War, the inertial attachment to NATO meant that the alliance had to seek or invent reasons to justify its existence and relevance.

American officials recognized the threats to the alliance. NATO needed props. Expansion into the former Warsaw Pact was one. Not only did expansion provide a whole new raison d'etre for the alliance, but—perhaps more important—it spawned a large new bureaucracy and the accompanying "busyness" that provide the lifeblood of institutions trying to justify their existence. At the same time, the theological mantra changed. Since there was no longer an enemy, NATO could not be described as a defensive alliance, it now was to be a combination of a wide-ranging political and collective security alliance. There were only two avenues the countries of Central and Eastern Europe could take if they wanted to join the West: NATO for security interests, and the European Union for economic interests. No other avenues were acceptable.

Consequently, in 1999 Poland, Hungary, and the Czech Republic joined NATO, and in November 2002 the Baltic countries, Slovakia, Slovenia, Bulgaria, and Romania accepted invitations to join the alliance.

In addition to expansion, the crisis in the Balkans also came to NATO's rescue. For the Clinton Administration, the former Yugoslavia was never really the most important point. NATO credibility was. This distinction is fundamental because policies that were designed to justify NATO were not necessarily the same as those that would deal successfully with issues in the former Yugoslavia. Clinton Administration spokesmen often pointed out that our vital interest was in preserving the alliance and vindicating our leadership of it. [. . .]

Although the current Bush Administration's focus has been riveted on the post-9/11 war on terrorism and Iraq, it has remained staunchly committed to NATO and its expansion. In its approach to the NATO Summit in Prague in November 2002, the alliance's serious problems were ignored, downplayed, or glossed over. For example, in congressional testimony in February 2002, a high-level Administration official said that NATO expansion was an exercise in "how much we can do to advance the cause of freedom," and that we must strengthen NATO's military capability and political solidarity.[2] In October 2002, in an address to the NATO Parliamentary Assembly, another Administration official noted that NATO "remains the essential link between Europe and North America—the place for free nations to secure peace, security, and liberty."[3]

But no one explains what all of this means—whose freedom, peace, security, and liberty are endangered? Who, after all, is the enemy? How is it possible to argue that there is any sense of political solidarity in the wake of the alliance's deep split over Iraq? NATO enthusiasts repeat their mantra by rote, but none of it justifies supporting a failing alliance.

INEVITABLE DECLINE

There are five interrelated reasons why post-Cold War rhetoric and inertial symbolism no longer conform to reality.

- *First, the legitimate threat that justified NATO really is gone.* All three US administrations since the collapse of the Soviet Union have paid lip service to this aphorism. For more than a decade, US security has advocated cooperation with Russia, but the structural and functional reality is quite different. Essentially, we are following a modified version of the post-World War I model, which excluded the defeated Germany from European and Western councils, rather than the more positive post-1815 and post-1945 models of including former enemies as quickly and completely as possible into the new security system. Consequently, the NATO-Russia Founding Act, the old Permanent Joint Council, and the new NATO-Russia Council speak more to separation and isolation than they do to cooperation and inclusion. They reinforce the fault line in Europe, unnecessarily dividing the continent into "ins" and "outs," with Russia clearly still "out."[4]

  The fundamental problem has been the inability of the post-Cold War American—and European—leadership to move beyond old organizations, policies, and philosophies to build organizations, policies, and philosophies that are more appropriate to the current age. Ever since the end of the Cold War and the ascendancy of the United States as the world's only superpower, American foreign policy has been formulated and controlled by a very small coterie of elites from both the Democratic and Republican parties who share a remarkable synonymy of interests, values, and outlooks, differing only at the margins.

- *Second, the whole nature of contemporary European politics has changed so fundamentally that it has outgrown NATO-type alliances.* For the first time in about 1,800 years, there is no world-class threat to or from any European state or combination of European states that requires a wide-ranging, comprehensive alliance such as NATO.[5] For the most part, borders are set, uncontested, and peaceful. Aggressive nationalism (although not nationalism itself) and the race for arms and empire that so dominated the politics of every major power from the 16th through the early 20th centuries are gone.

In Western Europe, the political struggle has replaced many of the characteristics of Westphalian sovereignty with a more intricate system of regions, states, and supranational organizations. The "constitutional conference" launched in March 2002 ultimately may determine what happens to the residue of traditional sovereignty in Western Europe. The situation is different in Central Europe, where states are trying to reestablish democracy and civil society after years of Nazi and communist tyranny, while at the same time struggling to meet the requirements to join the European Union. And the collapse of the Stalinist system has resolved the "Soviet Question" that dominated much of the second half of the 20th century. Although we can't predict Russia's future exactly, it is highly unlikely that the Stalinist system will be reestablished, and by including Russia as an equal we greatly enhance her prospects for a stable political order and a more traditional, non-antagonistic relationship with the United States and the rest of the West.

The modern sense of security in Europe not only is broader than what even the new form of NATO is built for, it is different in *kind*, and it is best summarized in the (Maastricht) Treaty on European Union (1990–92) and the follow-up Treaty of Amsterdam (1997). These treaties speak to an understanding of security that includes issues of justice, environment, ethnicity, economic development, crime, and terrorism, in addition to references to more narrowly military definitions of security. In those sections of the Maastricht and Amsterdam treaties that deal with a "common foreign and security policy," NATO is not mentioned, but several references are made to the Western European Union. Neither treaty envisions NATO as an integral part of Europe's security future, and a major reason it has been so difficult to implement the "common foreign and security policy" parts of these treaties is because NATO stands as both an impediment and an intimidation to Europe's future.

Of course, the United States does have interests in common with the Europe that is emerging, but without the kind of overall mutual threat we faced in the past, they are much more issue-specific. For example, economic ties now provide America's single most important relationship with Europe—both as partner and competitor. However, we are doing much less than we should do to prepare for the future of this relationship, in part because we are distracted by an anachronistic security relationship. We also have other common interests in such areas as the environment, terrorism, and others, none of which are particularly well suited to resolution by NATO or any other like alliance. Occasionally, the United States and specific European countries or groups of countries may need to engage in joint military activities—the Gulf War in the early 1990s and the more recent war in Afghanistan provide two excellent examples. In both cases coalitions were put together to deal with specific issues and, during both, NATO was little more than a "truck stop." But these conflicts were unique. It was impossible to recreate the Gulf War alliance to confront Iraq in 2003, and within a year or two we probably will be saying the same thing about multilateral cooperation in Afghanistan. At the same time, there also are strong differences between the United States and much of Western Europe on a growing number of issues—such as how to deal with Iraq, the Israeli-Palestinian horror, abrogation of the ABM Treaty, disagreement over the Kyoto Treaty, and accusations in the European press and among European officials about "American hegemony" or "American hyperpower."

As Robert Kagan argues, the differences between the United States and Europe go to much deeper philosophical and anthropological levels.[6] As the US view of engaging the world has become increasingly ideological, that of the Europeans has become increasingly pragmatic. Both sides retain a sense of superiority and arrogance when dealing with the third world. For the Europeans, however, this tends to be more cultural, while for the United States it is a divine mission. Consequently, the United States takes more seriously what Anthony Padgen describes as the "vision of a single 'orbis terrarum'"—the notion "of a presumed right of lordship over the entire world," which, ironically, had been a hallmark of the European empire in America.[7]

In an environment of shifting interests and philosophies between Europe and the United States, Americans and Europeans still share—at least in theory— a respect for democratic values. But that is not enough to hold NATO together. There also is a growing transatlantic split over a range of primary issues: the size, sophistication, and use of military power; environmental issues; budget priorities, including welfare expenditures; the role of state sovereignty, involving especially the evolution of the European Union; and more.[8]

- *Third, as NATO's relevance has declined as a security organization in the West, it also has become less important for Russian security interests.* For a while after the Cold War, NATO enlargement was a top Russian foreign policy concern, and Russia's leaders almost uniformly opposed enlargement as a direct threat to their country's vital interests.

But while opposition to NATO remains strong in the Russian military, for President Putin and his primary leadership circle, the salience of NATO for Russia's security interests has declined dramatically since the 9/11 terrorist attacks. For example, the opposition of Putin and other Russian officials to the inclusion of the Baltic states in NATO—a crisis in Russian-Western relations just a few years ago—has become virtually a non-issue. The Putin government supported the establishment of US military bases in Central Asia after 9/11, an area still considered part of the Russian "near abroad," which was unthinkable before the terrorist attacks. In addition, there has been only mild opposition to the Bush Administration's decision to abrogate the 1972 ABM Treaty. Finally, the serious bickering between the United States and NATO partners in "Old

Europe" over Iraq apparently has convinced Putin that Russian interests are best served by holding the alliance at arm's length. [. . .]

For most Russian leaders—more so than for their American counterparts — the events of 11 September 2001 finally brought the Cold War to an end. Concern about terrorism has prompted Putin to seek a new strategic relationship with the West that preferably would replace NATO and end the artificial divide between east and west. Shortly after 9/11, Putin observed that "all nations are to blame for the terrorist attacks on the United States because they trust outdated security systems. . . . [W]e have failed to recognize the changes of the last 10 years."[9] [. . .]

- *Fourth, expansion to the east actually damages the legitimate interests of the new NATO members.* NATO membership does not protect the countries of Central and Eastern Europe from any recognizable security threat. The usual argument advanced by NATO enthusiasts is that the new members will become "consumers" of security rather than "providers" of security. But, again, security against or from what? What, for example, is the security threat to Hungary, or Slovenia, or the Czech Republic, or even Poland that requires NATO membership? There is no traditional security threat to these countries that could not be handled by the Europeans themselves—if they have the political will to do so. [. . .]

Enlargement puts the Central and East European members in an unnecessary and rapidly debilitating political and financial position. In particular, the countries of Central and Eastern Europe are becoming increasingly enmeshed in a conflict of loyalty between NATO and the European Union. Despite the propaganda that NATO and the EU are two legitimate, complementary avenues of development, in fact they are becoming increasingly competitive—for attention, loyalty, and resources. Although this problem is gaining momentum in Western Europe, it is becoming especially acute in Central and Eastern Europe, where the resource base is considerably smaller and political affiliations more fragile.

As a result, "since their accession on March 12, 1999, Poland, Hungary, and the Czech Republic have all experienced integration difficulties,"[10] because the real demands of economic and social issues lead to "economic constraints" and "a failure of political will."[11] And still, NATO and EU authorities continue to press these strapped economies to live up to difficult and at times mutually exclusive commitments that undermine pressing economic and social programs. [. . .]

In addition, NATO membership—including vulnerability to Western arms merchants—damages the ability of these countries to deal with genuine emerging security issues. Issues of social and economic justice, crime and corruption, environmental degradation, and ethnic reconciliation bear more directly on the security futures of these countries than does their struggle to satisfy NATO's arcane demands for membership. Consequently, instead of pressing these countries to spend scarce resources on NATO, Washington should encourage them to focus exclusively on European and regional organizations that are better geared to help address the real, pressing interests of the countries of Central and Eastern Europe.[12]

- *Fifth, since the end of the Cold War, NATO's programs and instruments have expanded seemingly exponentially, and its organizing rationale has changed.* Virtually every summit—especially since the fall of communism—has been concerned with attempts to "redefine" or "reinvent" NATO in an effort to ignore history and make NATO relevant to the new reality. [. . .]

As the Cold War faded into history, NATO enthusiasts began to argue that the very nature of the alliance had to change if it was to continue to exist. Consequently, as Henry Kissinger noted, NATO "has become more akin to a collective security organization, like the United Nations, than to a traditional alliance."[13] If the alliance was to survive, it had to find a rationale that did not depend on a clearly defined enemy, or even a potential enemy. A loosely formed "collective security organization" was the answer.

In reality, these two types of alliances represent a distinction without a difference. Even in a collective "security alliance," there must be at least some overriding common security bond that holds the participants together. As noted before, quite the opposite is happening—not only on security issues, but in the political realm as well. The NATO that has emerged since the end of the Cold War does not satisfy even the most rudimentary tests of what an alliance is supposed to do. For example, it fails both Stephen Walt's "five . . . explanations for international alliances" and Glenn Snyder's theory of alliance formation and management.[14] And, the further we get from the Cold War, the more serious those frictions will become as the nexus of values and interests between the United States and Europe continues to widen. Two recent examples illustrate the point.

First, after 9/11, NATO's European members declared "Article 5" support for the United States in its war against terrorism generally and the military action in Afghanistan. This was the first time in NATO's history that Article 5 had been formally invoked—and it is likely to be the last, despite the argument that "modern-day terrorism and WMD proliferation are 'Article 5 threats.'"[15] The United States spurned the European action, and in doing so Washington signaled that it did not need NATO and that the European allies counted for little in the greatest threat to US vital interests since perhaps the attack on Pearl Harbor.

Second, differences over Iraq illustrate the widening gap in interests and values between the United States and several important European countries, especially France and Germany. These differences are not superficial; they are rooted in a basic philosophical divergence that will not be explained away by the normal admonition that "there have always been differences among NATO countries." This time, the political survival of the German—and perhaps the French—government depends on it. In both cases, political success depends increasingly on disagreeing with Washington on many of the most important international issues. At the same time, US policy—either by design or by accident—is dividing Europe and thereby damaging the Europeans' efforts to find common ground on the future of Europe and underscoring Europe's irrelevancy for US security interests.

GETTING PAST THE PAST

The Europeans will have to take the initiative to move beyond security anachronisms such as NATO, because it will not happen as a result of US leadership. Washington will cling to NATO even more desperately and continue to manufacture complicated, ineffective, even deleterious mechanisms to "prove" NATO's importance and viability. For Washington, NATO is the security institution that best exemplifies the static world it prefers—it makes no difference that the alliance no longer serves any useful security function. The American political class will not be voluntarily shaken from that perspective, no matter how much the world changes.

The Europeans, on the other hand, have been more ready to recognize and embrace the changes that are taking place in the structure of the international system. They are struggling with the transition and are more fully engaged in the transformation than is the United States. The Europeans have reached a critical juncture in the construction of the "European space." Certainly, questions of "widening versus deepening," problems of a multiple-speed Europe, the lasting soundness of the Euro, the equity of the Common Agricultural Policy, and even issues of consensus versus majority rule are very important, and they will be handled one way or another in time. But the critical issue that will ultimately define the nature and character of European cooperation is the whole arena of foreign and security policy—an issue that the Europeans currently are not handling very well.

If the United States is blinded by its own self-righteousness, the Europeans are crippled emotionally by their timidity. For different reasons, then, both sides are unable to shed NATO's Cold War grip, despite the Europeans' greater potential to break this inertia. To do so, they will have to recognize that the conduct of foreign and security policy is perhaps the most fundamental arena that defines any polity. The Europeans are now "a de facto military protectorate of the United States,"[16] unable to fully provide for their own relations with other states and other political organizations on the international stage. To have one's security and foreign policy agenda set by another is the height of servitude.

The Europeans have made a halting start by trying to construct the Common Foreign and Security Policy (CFSP) and the European Security and Defense Policy (ESDP). Efforts in both areas have a long history, beginning in the 1960s and 1970s when the "member states of the European community cooperated and endeavored to consult with one another on major international problems."[17] These efforts progressed through the Single European Act in 1986, received a major boost in the Maastricht Treaty of 1993 and the Amsterdam Treaty of 1999, the Nice Treaty in 2001, and, in security specifically, at the 1999 Cologne Council meeting (including the Petersburg tasks), and the Helsinki Headline Goals (HHG), which are supposed to be achieved by 2003.[18]

But the effort has stalled, and it is likely to remain stalled as long as the Europeans are tied to the myth that NATO and its lore is the appropriate linchpin for the future. Although discussion under the current European Constitutional Convention does not presently provide a major role for foreign and security policy, there is no reason it cannot be extended to do so.[19] The platform and the precedent are available; only the political will is lacking. The Europeans should begin to chart their own course now by exercising their option under Article 13 of the NATO Treaty and announcing their intention to withdraw from the alliance. Ironically, the bitter transatlantic dispute over Iraq may already have started the process.

NOTES

1. David Steele, *Lord Salisbury—A Political Biography* (New York: Routledge, 1999), p. 121.

2. Comments by Undersecretary of Defense for Policy, Douglas Feith; see the Armed Forces Press Service, 28 February 2002.

3. Statement by Undersecretary of State for Political Affairs, Marc Grossman; see *Department of State Bulletin*, 9 October 2001.

4. *The Financial Times*, 15 May 2002.

5. Terrorism does not fit the bill because it is diffuse, sporadic, and of much less salience in Europe than in the United States. All of this requires a different kind of response than NATO can provide. In short, NATO does not have the tools to fight terrorism.

6. Robert Kagan, "Power and Weakness," *Policy Review*, No. 113 (June & July, 2002).

7. Anthony Padgen, *Lords of All the World—Ideologies of Empire in Spain, Britain, and France (1500–1800)* (New Haven, Conn.: Yale Univ. Press, 1995), pp. 5, 8.

8. Clearly, as disagreements within Europe over Washington's Iraq policy demonstrate, European countries are not always of one mind on all transatlantic issues. But intra-European divisions do not undermine the basic point, and once the immediate crisis over Iraq fades, the centrifugal issues separating the United States from the Europeans will accelerate.

9. BBC World News Report, 25 September 2001.

10. Jeffrey Simon, "NATO's Membership Action Plan and Defense Planning," *Problems of Post-Communism*, 48 (May–June 2001), 28.

11. Ibid., p. 30.

12. Although the EU is the most important organization for the future of Central and Eastern Europe, other organizations, such as the Southeast Europe Brigade (SEE-BRIG) and the Southeastern Europe Defense Ministerial (SEEDM) process are potentially more important to the specific security issues of these countries than is NATO.

13. "A Dangerous Divergence," *The Washington Post*, 10 December 2002, op-ed.

14. Stephen M. Walt, *The Origins of Alliances* (Ithaca, N.Y.: Cornell Univ. Press, 1987), ch. 2; Glenn H. Snyder, *Alliance Politics* (Ithaca, N.Y.: Cornell Univ. Press, 1997), chs. 2, 6.

15. Richard L. Kugler, "Preparing NATO to Meet New Threats: Challenge and Opportunity," US Department of State, International Information Programs, 27 March 2002, http://usinfo.state.gov/topical/pol/nato/02032800.htm.

16. Zbigniew Brzezinski et al., "Living With the New Europe," *The National Interest*, No. 60 (Summer 2000).

17. Council of the European Union, "Common Foreign and Security Policy/European Security and Defense Policy," http://ue.eu.int/pesc/pres.asp?lang=en.

18. Some scholars argue that European efforts to find common ground in foreign and security policy can be traced back to the European Defense Community idea (Pleven Plan) of 1966–67.

19. Title III, Article 13, of the preliminary draft Constitutional Treaty provides ample justification for bold moves in the area of foreign and security policy.

✗ NO

All Dressed Up and No Place to Go: Why NATO Should Be on the Front Lines in the War on Terror
REBECCA JOHNSON AND MICAH ZENKO

Following the 2000 American presidential election, some analysts worried that transatlantic relations would be strained by the policies proposed by the incoming Bush Administration. From disagreements over the Kyoto Treaty to the decision to proceed quickly with the deployment of ballistic missile defenses, a functional split between America and its European allies threatened to emerge.[1] While the attacks of 11 September 2001 changed US interests and priorities overseas, these disagreements will not dissolve completely. They have receded, however, in immediate importance to the American goal of fighting terrorists with a global reach. As European officials were quoted to have told an American official after 9/11, "Kyoto is an issue you argue about when all else is well."[2]

Retaining the commitment of a broad-based coalition is critical to the success of America's evolving war against terrorism. Although the North Atlantic Treaty Organization (NATO) is an obvious hub from which to organize this coalition, and alliance members have shown their eagerness to respond to common threats such as terrorism, Washington has held true allied support at arm's length. While officials in Washington have endorsed NATO's invocation of Article 5 for the first time in the alliance's history and accepted limited contributions of troops and equipment for the military campaign and later support for the restricted peacekeeping mission in Afghanistan, they have refused to allow NATO to engage in the sort of operations the alliance embraced when it affirmed its Article 24 commitments in April 1999. This refusal, while puzzling given the consistent willingness of the European allies to contribute troops and resources, is even more surprising when one remembers that it was the United States, not Europe, that initially pushed for the inclusion of Article 24 during the Washington Summit in April 1999.[3]

This article argues that the United States should work with its NATO allies in fulfilling their Article 24 commitments. It is organized in three sections. First, we examine the decisionmaking procedures immediately following 9/11 to determine the reasons behind the Bush Administration's opposition to a muscular NATO presence in the war against terrorism. In this section we answer Washington's objections that an active NATO role would undermine US operational autonomy and reveal stark inequalities in alliance readiness.

In the second section we argue the advantages of coordinating the war through NATO under the auspices of Article 24. First, given the undeniable links between al Qaeda and terrorist networks operating in Europe and elsewhere around the globe, it is important that the US campaign is not isolated to a few obvious spots in Afghanistan and Iraq. To do the job right, American military, diplomatic, and intelligence services will need serious, coordinated support from their allies, and working through—rather than past—NATO would help to ensure that important information does not slip through the cracks. Second, in its capacity as the pre-eminent institution for collective defense, NATO provides the support the United States needs to conduct such a comprehensive campaign. NATO has the mandate through its Article 24 provisions; it has the experience of running a coordinated campaign through its missions in Bosnia, Kosovo, and Macedonia (where alliance troops face many of the same issues of porous borders, trafficking, and militancy that must now be addressed in Afghanistan); and it has the will of its European members. Finally, in the conclusion we offer suggestions for what a NATO-centered effort would look like in practice, drawing from the alliance's ongoing operations in the Balkans.

NATO'S NEWEST CHALLENGE

Since the collapse of the Soviet Union in 1991, NATO has undertaken a series of missions unprecedented in the alliance's history. The alliance conducted military strikes and later provided ground forces for peace support operations in Bosnia and Kosovo, created institutional arrangements to engage with former Warsaw Pact countries, and expanded its membership to include three historically pivotal states of Central Europe—the Czech Republic, Hungary, and Poland.

Some have debated whether this expansion of NATO's responsibilities, combined with the disappearance of the unifying threat portrayed by the Soviet Union, could harm the centrality of NATO's mission—providing for the collective defense of all its members.[4] NATO's response to 9/11 has shown how quickly the alliance can refocus its sprawling interests when one member faces a direct attack.

Within 30 hours of the attacks on New York and Washington, the alliance invoked Article 5 of the North Atlantic Treaty. Article 5 states quite simply that "an armed attack against one or more of" the NATO members "shall be considered as an attack against them all." Though its original intent changed dramatically with the end of the Cold War, it has remained a core element of NATO's raison d'etre. The new rationale for Article 5 was found in the Strategic Concept statement released during NATO's 50th Anniversary Washington Summit in April 1999. An update of the first Strategic Concept publicly released in 1991, the 1999 version went further than the alliance's previous doctrinal declarations in embracing out-of-area operations of a sort that differed from the traditional understanding of defending against a Soviet invasion. Article 24 of the Strategic Concept declared:

> Any armed attack on the territory of the allies, from whatever direction, would be covered by Articles 5 and 6 of the Washington Treaty. However,

alliance security must also take account of the global context. Alliance security interests can be affected by other risks of a wider nature, including acts of terrorism, sabotage, and organized crime, and by the disruption of the flow of vital resources.[5]

While far-reaching, the declaration was actually a scaled-back compromise from language that the United States initially hoped to introduce regarding the declaration of new purposes.[6] European governments sought to limit the Strategic Concept to deal with threats directly related to Europe—including those originating in the Balkans and the Mediterranean. The United States pushed for an expansive declaration to consider threats from organized crime, terrorism, and especially weapons of mass destruction.[7]

When NATO officials met in Brussels on 12 September 2001 to discuss the alliance's response to the attack on America, 18 of the 19 NATO nations were prepared to fulfill the commitments laid out in Article 24. While the attacks were carried out on the territory of the United States, alliance members recognized that they were all vulnerable to future acts of terrorism. America absorbed the attacks, but the loss to the world included citizens of 80 countries. Within the alliance itself, all but three of its 19 member nations lost citizens either in Washington or New York. Direct threats to the European continent and its periphery included the US Embassy in Paris, synagogues in Strasbourg and Tunisia, Jewish and American properties in Germany, the water supply system in Morocco, and several other sites not revealed by European police for fear of making them more attractive.[8] Furthermore, there is evidence that NATO itself was threatened. Quoting sources within the German police agency (BKA), the newsmagazine *Stern* reported that NATO headquarters was itself the target of an attack similar to the ones committed on 11 September in the United States.[9]

THE WAR AGAINST TERRORISM: NATO ON THE SIDELINES

The only state that hesitated to embrace NATO's decision was the United States— the same state that had lobbied so forcefully for the creation of the new NATO mandate two years earlier. Two concerns featured prominently in the minds of decisionmakers in Washington: Washington's reluctance to cede operational autonomy, and its concern that the European allies lack the capabilities to conduct a military campaign outside the North Atlantic theater.

Washington's hesitancy to jeopardize operational control was evidenced in its response to the alliance's decision to invoke Article 5 in September. According to one NATO official, the allies requested "a commitment to be consulted by Washington before anything happens" in return for invoking Article 5.[10] European governments had sought enhanced consultations from the United States over a number of international issues long before the arrival of the Bush Administration, and they did not waste this opportunity to increase their leverage.

The reaction in Washington was quick and decisive—NATO could not be allowed to reign in any US response. According to a senior State Department official speaking to reporters after the first emergency meeting on 12 September, the United States was pushing for a resolution that would mention that the article could be invoked, without actually voting on the measure itself. A senior Administration official said that it was the Europeans who were "desperately trying to give us political cover and the Pentagon was resisting it." Eventually, Secretary of Defense Rumsfeld relented and agreed to accept the clause.[11]

Even in agreeing to the invocation of Article 5, Secretary Rumsfeld tried to distance himself from the NATO alliance, however, stating publicly to its members, "The mission determines the coalition. The coalition doesn't determine the mission."[12] The reason for America's tentative approach to accepting the invocation of Article 5 is most certainly related to the US desire to retain maximum flexibility in its military planning and operations. This concern would turn out to be overblown in that even after Rumsfeld relented, the alliance left it up to Washington to determine the nature of the response and whether the United States would need NATO assistance.[13]

Since it began planning a global response to the terror attacks of September 2001, the Bush Administration has worked from the assumption that at some point in the future America might have to operate alone.[14] During the Afghanistan operations, the United States relied primarily on its own capabilities for conducting the military strikes and allowed European peacekeepers to oversee the International Security Assistance Force (ISAF), the stability force sanctioned by the UN Security Council.

While placing NATO on the sideline may have been necessary for military efficiency and to avoid politically difficult decisions, Europe's ancillary role has meant that since the initial outpouring of support immediately following the attacks there has been less sympathy and support from mainstream society on the continent. As the war against terrorism verges further from one of specific military goals in Afghanistan to one of crucial global financial, intelligence, and legal cooperation, European governments may feel less attachment to what has been largely a unilateral American mission. Consequently, the United States may not be able to quickly enlist the support of its allies whenever its needs to, as some have suggested.[15] This has been most clearly visible in the allies' stark opposition to America's stated intention to pursue Saddam Hussein as part of its broader campaign.

Overriding and related to the American decision to operate outside of NATO's command structure is the fact that few NATO allies have the military capability to conduct combat operations outside the North Atlantic theater. None of the European allies possesses long-range strike attack aircraft that do not require forward basing, such as the American B-52H, B-1, and B-2 bombers. Meanwhile, the United States maintains over 150 such bombers in service.[16]

Europe also has severe limitations in its power-projection capabilities, with few assets in the fields of strategic air and sealift, air-to-air refueling, and reconnaissance and strategic intelligence. [. . .]

This is not to say that the European NATO members have had no military role in the first stages of the campaign against global terrorism. The most significant contribution has come from the NATO ally with the greatest capacity to provide the United States support for its operations in Afghanistan—the United Kingdom. Reflecting their long-standing special relationship with the United States, the British have been the most vocal American ally in the aftermath of the attacks, with Prime Minister Tony Blair at times appearing out in front of Washington in his condemnation and demands of the Taliban and the al Qaeda terror network. Militarily, the British provided three nuclear-powered submarines armed with precision-guided munitions, tactical fighter aircraft, 600 Royal Marine Commandos, and permission to use its strategically important air base on Diego Garcia. All told the British have contributed more than 6,000 military personnel to the South Asian theater of operations during the military campaign, with 1,700 infantry troops committed to Operation Jacana in the mountainous regions along the Afghan-Pakistani border.[17] The British also led the initial International Security Assistance Force that provided stability during the transition period for the interim government in Kabul.

The importance of this contribution should not be overlooked. According to Anthony Cordesman, senior scholar at the Center for Strategic and International Studies in Washington, "The US and British experience in Afghanistan may indicate that the US and NATO have overstressed the high technology and high investment aspects of coalition warfare and interoperability, and paid too little attention to the value of being able to draw on a pool of highly trained lighter forces, like the SAS, or their Australian, Canadian, German, and other equivalents."[18] Not only have British troops played a critical role in strategic operations on the ground in Afghanistan, they also have taken the lead in reconstruction efforts and are responsible for rebuilding airfields, de-mining large segments of land in and around Kabul, and rebuilding roads from the capital to the countryside.[19]

The rest of the NATO alliance also has participated in the war against terrorism in smaller though still important ways.[20] Although they were not included directly in combat operations in Afghanistan, as Colin Powell noted, "Not every ally is fighting, but every ally is in the fight."[21] [. . .]

The European military contribution has been useful to backfill those US forces that are needed to operate in the theater surrounding Afghanistan. Seven German-based AWACS planes, with Germans composing one-third of those on board, were deployed to America to relieve similar US assets, providing air interdiction support on the East Coast and other areas of interest.[22] Before the mission's termination in late April, the alliance's crew, including ground support for the AWACS operation, reached 830 personnel from 13 countries.[23] NATO also has dispatched seven frigates, a destroyer, and an auxiliary oiler to the Mediterranean to take the place of American naval assets there that moved into the Indian Ocean closer to Afghanistan.[24] And NATO forces will likely replace low-intensity, high-demand American forces in the Balkans in order to free them up for operations elsewhere.[25]

WASTED POTENTIAL

But NATO's contribution to the evolving effort should be greater than providing special forces for reconnaissance and limited combat in Afghanistan, and for keeping the peace in Afghanistan's capital. The alliance publicly codified its need to adapt its capabilities in the new fight against terrorism in its 18 December 2001 statement, but its troops and assets have largely been made to cool their heels.[26]

One need look only to alliance efforts in the Balkans to understand NATO's capacity to undertake operations like those needed to eradicate terrorist networks. Currently, NATO has troops involved in peacekeeping missions in Bosnia, Kosovo, and Macedonia, with European members providing roughly 80 percent of the forces for these missions.[27] The United States contributes around 5,000 of the 42,000 troops in KFOR,[28] and 3,100 of the 18,000 troops in Bosnia.[29] NATO's deployment in Macedonia is far smaller; a 3,000 troop, British-led operation finished in September 2001; that was followed by a 1,000 troop, German-led follow-on mission; in late June 2002, the mission was extended through October, with the number of German troops being reduced and the Netherlands taking over the lead nation role. Each of these missions must coordinate with the other international agencies at work in the area in order to control the region's porous borders and corrupt institutions that facilitate the development of transnational organized crime and extremist groups.

These missions are no longer combat missions; they more closely resemble the sort of low-intensity, on-the-ground, long-term engagement the United States has committed itself to in the current phase of Operation Enduring Freedom and must undertake in other areas if it realistically hopes to eradicate terrorism. It is important to be clear on this point. There are two components to the current war against terrorism, just as there were two components to NATO's interventions in the Balkans: a large-scale military engagement, and a long-term policing and reconstruction mission. [. . .]

The links between terrorist organizations like al Qaeda and regional crime syndicates in southeastern Europe have been trumpeted by specialists in Washington at luncheon talks and in the news since 9/11.[30] But the NATO troops on the ground in the Balkans realized long ago that these networks are the main obstacles to peaceful and sustainable reconstruction. Indeed, these networks are even more corrosive to the region than any lingering ethnic radicalism. According to British defense sources, "All NATO troops in the Balkans will be contributing to the campaign [against terrorism] because a lot of terrorist activity is funneled through the region in terms of arms-trafficking, money-laundering, and drugs."[31]

In addition, these troops themselves are targets in the region. According to a report from the International Crisis Group, "Given the presence of ex-mujahidin in Bosnia, the tens of thousands of former military and paramilitary fighters in Bosnia, Kosovo, and Macedonia who are Muslims by tradition, if not for the most part by observance, and the large deployments of US and other troops in the region, some (though by no means all) senior Western sources describe the potential terrorist threat as significant."[32]

So long as these criminal networks are allowed to operate in the Balkans, Western Europe remains vulnerable to attack. One common practice, "identity laundering," allows potential extremists to slip into Western Europe virtually unseen. In one striking example, British peacekeepers in Bosnia helped track down Bensayah Belkacem, one of Osama bin Laden's key associates who may have been responsible for obtaining the Western passports used by the terrorists in the attacks in the United States.[33]

Al Qaeda singled out Europe as the launching point for its terrorist attacks against the West. Islamic militants targeted ghetto Arab immigrant communities to propagate the radical message of bin Laden, recruited foot soldiers in slums and mosques, and used this foothold in Europe to plan their attacks.[34] Once mid-level al Qaeda officials had fomented sufficient human and financial support inside a city, compartmentalized sleeper cells were left in place awaiting opportunities to strike.[35] Despite vigorous efforts by local law enforcement officials in Germany, Spain, Italy, Britain, and the Netherlands, many of these cells may still exist unnoticed and be awaiting their signal to act.[36]

Europe has pursued its investigations on terrorism with an eye to integrating Muslim communities and protecting civil and human rights. National and continental-wide police forces have made renewed efforts to target potential suspects and break up radical Islamic networks. Despite these increased investigations into Islamic fundamentalism on the continent and arrests of suspected terrorists, however, after three months of the policing effort, an estimated 60 percent of radical Islamic networks were yet to be discovered, according to Western European intelligence officials.[37] Furthermore, law enforcement officials believe that European-based militants who trained and fought in Afghanistan have returned to the continent with the intent of conducting additional terrorist operations.[38]

Lord Robertson has called Afghanistan a "black hole" that lacks any sustainable state structure, and has argued, "That is why NATO is engaged in South-East Europe—to prevent such black holes from emerging on our doorstep."[39] He is right, and in order to avoid having the Balkans serve as the same sort of fertile breeding ground for extremism that is present in Afghanistan, a coordinated approach must be developed to respond effectively to these concerns.

This approach exists in the Balkans. NATO troops operate alongside representatives of the UN, the Organization for Security and Cooperation in Europe (OSCE), and the European Union (EU), as well as aide workers from numerous international relief agencies. In Bosnia and Kosovo, NATO takes responsibility for security, policing, and border monitoring.[40] The UN runs civil administration; the OSCE is in charge of democratization and institution-building; and the EU takes the lead in reconstruction and economic development. One can see how these missions overlap—civil administration and effective institution-building rely on security, and economic development relies on effective policing. For all the criticism levied against civil reconstruction campaigns in Bosnia and Kosovo, the parties are closer to a peaceful, stable existence than at any time in the past decade. NATO security forces are conducting an effective campaign to combat criminal and extremist networks in the region.

But localized success in some areas in the Balkans is not sufficient. If either mission—the war on terrorism or peacekeeping in the Balkans—is to be successful, the two need to be better integrated, not dissociated. The United States needs to remain active in both, not just in the assault on Afghanistan, and the European allies need to coordinate planning and intelligence on a scale larger than the Balkans. They should employ the lessons they have learned from their operations in the Balkans to coordinate efforts with other international institutions. This means capitalizing on strong communications networks, launching an aggressive outreach campaign with Muslim countries through the Euro-Atlantic Partnership Council (EAPC), and retaining operating autonomy to ensure that individual missions can be carried out with minimal bureaucratic delay. In brief, they should take their experience from the Balkans—both the successes and the failures—and adopt operational procedures that closely resemble the procedures and structures witnessed in the terrorist networks they are trying to combat.

PUTTING NATO ON THE FRONT LINES

The first of these procedures that should be adopted is operational autonomy. Effective coordination will be the linchpin of the international war against terrorism, and this coordination will fail unless each of the components is allowed to carry out its tasks unimpeded. By making NATO the hub that synchronizes the array of international institutions that will contribute to this effort, operational autonomy will be enhanced.

Skeptics will argue that the need for unimpeded action is precisely why the United States should lead the international effort. They will contend that placing NATO front and center in the international response will only stymie action. But while the United States may be able to carry out a military campaign in Afghanistan largely on its own, it is not able to fight the kind of war that is needed to cripple international terrorism. This "war" has many fronts, arguably the least important of which is being conducted south of Tajikistan today. An effective campaign against terrorism requires accurate and timely intelligence to locate cells and their planned activities. It requires alert, trained law enforcement, immigration services, and border patrols, as well as flexible teams ready to respond when important information is revealed. Finally, it requires time, dedication, and resources. With its membership, partners, and shared experience, NATO can commit each. The alliance might not be the most efficiently run organization, but it has both the breadth and depth to make it the best suited for the job of ringleader.

What does this mean in practice? John Arquilla and David Ronfelt have released a new edited volume on networks and "netwars."[41] A network is a distinct organizing concept that has developed along with technological advances. It requires not just that individuals' interactions link them in a network, but that they recognize and foster their form of organization (in contrast to a traditional, hierarchical form of organization). A network is generally characterized by diffuse clusters of individuals who relate to one another through hubs. The authors of the RAND study argue, "The West must start to build its own networks and must learn to swarm the enemy, in order to keep it on the run or pinned down until it can be destroyed."[42] "Swarming" refers to attacking the enemy in different ways simultaneously. Small, nimble networks are key to this endeavor, which means that NATO will be called on to operationalize smaller, more adaptable units operating with a large degree of autonomy to respond to their environments. This is not to advocate the abolition of traditional military force structures (corps, divisions, brigades, regiments, etc.), but to suggest NATO can best fulfill its Article 24 provisions by positioning itself at the center of the war against terrorism within its existing commitments. NATO forces tracking small arms in Bosnia should be given the discretion to make changes to their mission to respond to developments on the ground. Likewise, NATO troops working with Uzbekistan and Turkmenistan on border security through the Partnership for Peace program should be given leeway in how they carry out their missions.[43] So long as the contingents that are deployed to any one mission are all of the same nationality, there should be few problems concerning how changes in orders travel up the chain of command.

While the OSCE and the EU will likely fight having some of their core responsibilities usurped, NATO should take the lead in military, anti-crime, and border activity. The OSCE's track record on combating trafficking is poor, and a concerted policing effort is needed to counter the trails of drugs, arms, and people that snake across Central Asia, Russia, and the Balkans into Western Europe. NATO, with contributions from its member countries and support from its partners, has the heft that is needed to undertake this important job. Without question the alliance should consult closely with the OSCE and the EU to ensure that their security, political, and economic programs reinforce, not undermine, each other, but the programs all should be engineered with attention to shutting down transnational crime and building stable governments and economies. The OSCE lacks the institutional capacity to carry out this critical task, and NATO should take it over. While some may worry that EU and OSCE countries would resist NATO's enhanced role, these countries recognize that they are out of the loop in the war against terrorism. By positioning NATO at the hub of European anti-terror efforts, it would provide them with a voice in the planning and implementation of these efforts, as well as bring them in contact with the alliance's substantial assets and capabilities.

Working through NATO also gives the alliance the opportunity to continue to build strong working bonds with Russia. It is true that many in Russia still hold lingering suspicions about the alliance's true intentions, but NATO and Russia have been able to work very well together on joint missions in Bosnia and Kosovo. SFOR and KFOR are enduring examples of the good that can come from NATO-Russian cooperation, and the West should not shrink from using NATO as the center for the international response merely because they fear opposition from Moscow.

Luckily this is precisely what the alliance has undertaken with the new relationship that will be embodied in the NATO-Russian Council, or "NATO at 20."[44] The West can learn much more from Russia than the lessons of its military experiences in Afghanistan. Russian police also face traffickers transiting their territory; they contribute soldiers to secure Tajikistan's border with Afghanistan; and they still retain intelligence sources across the globe. NATO should work with Moscow to help neutralize the networks operating in Russia at the same time that they employ Russian assets to the larger military, police, and intelligence effort.[45]

Seen in this way, NATO would serve as the hub of an international network against terrorism. It would coordinate its own military and policing missions within Europe and offer training, intelligence, and potentially troops or logistical support to out-of-area efforts. [. . .]

The effectiveness of this coordination will rest on intelligence sharing. Before 9/11, NATO members were already providing relatively good intelligence estimates about terrorist threats to the United States. [. . .]

The future burden will be on the allies to more quickly process the analyses provided by US and European intelligence sources. Institutionally, the alliance needs to create mechanisms that assure such sharing will not be done in an ad hoc manner, in response to specific threats and crises, but as a part of the normal operating procedure of a network that faces transnational threats. [. . .]

NATO's ability to work with the other dominant European institutions has been battle-tested and improved throughout the 1990s with the alliance crisis management efforts in the Balkans. This high level of coordination will need to be even further enhanced by expanding ties outside Europe.

One of the most important institutions that NATO will need to coordinate with is the OSCE. Mircea Geoana, the Romanian Foreign Minister and former holder of the OSCE's rotating chairmanship, announced that the 55 OSCE member states had adopted an action plan against terrorism at their meeting in Bucharest on 3–4

December 2001.[46] While this plan was little more than a gesture, it can have important symbolic meaning in enhancing solidarity in the American-led campaign. Speaking at the meeting, US Secretary of State Colin Powell called the document "a resolute expression of our collective will."[47]

Reports are growing more insistent that in the war against terror, "Washington employs the rhetoric of political multilateralism, on the one hand, and the reality of military unilateralism, on the other."[48] If the operation in Afghanistan becomes associated with mere retaliation, or even worse, aggression, US goals become compromised and US interests become even more endangered. The Muslim countries in the Balkans, Central Asia, and the Caucasus are all members of the OSCE. Incorporating their support of this effort through their commitment to the action plan at the December 2001 meeting was an important step to gaining greater legitimacy. [. . .]

CONCLUSION

Although the 9/11 attacks on the United States were horrific and unprecedented, a worst-case scenario could arise in which America's European allies remember 11 September as an once-in-a-lifetime event. Even only a few months after the attacks there was evidence that Europe was viewing them as "an aberration that is now behind us."[49] Should the world be so fortunate that another large-scale unconventional attack does not occur, Washington will have to reinvigorate allied enthusiasm to make sure Brussels does not lose focus in the fight against terror. If no more attacks happen, and Europe loses its concentration, the American-led campaign could look increasingly like a global version of the decade-long enforcement of the no-fly-zones over Iraq, where all the allies dropped out except for Great Britain. For America's European allies to express outrage against terrorism but then forget the horror would send the wrong message to the world, and could be the source of the perpetually feared rift within the alliance.

A better course of action would be for the NATO allies to endorse a mission that retains transatlantic cohesion and that builds on the strengths of the alliance—its ability to work in conjunction with other organizations, its strong communications network, its reach into the Muslim world through the EAPC, and its ability to provide wide operating autonomy to coalition partners. To combat transnational terrorist networks effectively, NATO should more closely resemble a network itself. It has taken the initial steps in this direction following the end of the Cold War, and it should make further progress now and after the coming Prague summit if it is to retain a central role in the new security environment.

It has always been a central maxim of Brussels that the solidarity of the alliance is more important that the concerns of any single country. The threat of terrorism is a threat to the entire world, let alone NATO, and the victory over global terrorism is not inevitable, nor probable in the short-term. Thus, the alliance needs to maintain its solidarity in the face of this threat. It should find a way to do so, however, that does not undermine NATO's current missions or long-term health. This will require that the United States dedicate significant attention and resources to the alliance at precisely the time that its attention is being pulled elsewhere. For the continuing stability of Europe and lasting strength of the alliance, one hopes that the United States will make this necessary investment.

NOTES

1. Lord George Robertson, "The Future of the Transatlantic Link," Lisbon, Portugal, 24 October 2001.

2. Dana Milbank and T. R. Reid, "New Global Threat Revives Old Alliance," *The Washington Post*, 16 October 2001, p. A10.

3. Suzanne Daley, "Europeans Pledge Troops, if Necessary," *The New York Times*, 9 October 2001, p. B8; Alan Sipress and Vernon Loeb, "U.S. Welcoming Allies' Troops," *The Washington Post*, 11 November 2001, p. A38.

4. David S. Yost, *NATO Transformed: The Alliance's New Roles in International Security* (Washington: United States Institute of Peace Press, 1998).

5. NATO, "The Alliance's Strategic Concept," Press Release NAC-S(99)65, 24 April 1999.

6. Richard Sokolsky, Stuart Johnson, and F. Stephen Larrabee, eds., *Persian Gulf Security: Improving Allied Military Contributions* (Santa Monica, Calif.: RAND, 2000), p. 40.

7. Shahram Chubin, Jerrold Green, and F. Stephen Larrabee, *NATO's New Strategic Concept and Peripheral Contingencies: The Middle East*, workshop proceedings, 15–16 July 1999 (Santa Monica, Calif.: RAND, 1999); and William Drozdiak and Thomas W. Lippman, "NATO Widens Security 'Map,'" *The Washington Post*, 25 April 1999, p. A1.

8. Phillip Jaklin and Hugh Williamson, "Terror Suspects Detained in Germany," *Financial Times*, 24 April 2002, p. 6; Richard Bourdeaux, "4 Terror Suspects Arrested in Italy," *Los Angeles Times*, 21 February 2002, p. A1; and Barry James, "17 Suspected of Qaeda Links Arrested Across Europe," *International Herald Tribune*, 25 April 2002, p. 4.

9. Florian Gless and Regina Weitz, "Explodiert die Welt?" *Stern*, 20 September 2001.

10. Bruce Wallace, "We'll Stand Behind the U.S.," *The Gazette* (Montreal), 13 September 2001, p. B5.

11. Suzanne Daley, "After the Attacks: The Alliance," *The New York Times*, 13 September 2001, p. A17; and Elaine Sciolino and Steven Lee Myers, "Bush Says 'Time is Running Out'; U.S. Plans to Act Largely Alone," *The New York Times*, 7 October 2001, p. B5.

12. Martin Fletcher, Michael Evans, and Damian Whitworth, "U.S. Warns of Possible London Attack," *The Times* (London), 19 December 2001, p. 1.

13. Daley, "After the Attacks: The Alliance," p. A17.

14. Bob Woodward and Dan Balz, "At Camp David, Advise and Dissent," *The Washington Post*, 31 January 2002, p. A1.

15. Jim Hoagland, "Enlist America's Allies," *The Washington Post*, 13 January 2002, p. B7; and Martin Walker, "New Europe: Uneasy, Necessary Ally," *San Diego Union Tribune*, 30 December 2001, p. G5.

16. International Institute for Strategic Studies, *The Military Balance: 2000–2001* (Oxford, Eng.: Oxford Univ. Press, 2000), p. 30.

17. Michael R. Gordon, "Britain Allots Troops for Afghan Ground Combat, and Australia is Contributing, Too," *The New York Times*, 27 October 2001, p. B2; and Richard Norton-Taylor, "1,700 UK Troops to Fight in Afghan War," *The Guardian*, 19 March 2002, p. 1.

18. Anthony Cordesman, "The Lessons of Afghanistan: Warfighting, Intelligence, Force Transformation, Counterproliferation, and Arms Control," Center for Strategic and International Studies, Washington, D.C., 28 June 2002.

19. Interview with Julian Lindley-French, Senior Research Fellow, Institute for Security Studies, Paris, 16 July 2002.

20. For an accounting of these contributions through June 2002, see Anthony Cordesman's "The Lessons of Afghanistan," pp. 26–35.

21. Robin Wright, "NATO Promises Cohesive Stand Against Terrorism," *Los Angeles Times*, 7 December 2001.

22. Haig Simonian, "Berlin Flexes its Muscles," *Financial Times*, 13 October 2001, p. 13; and "NATO Adds Planes For U.S. Sky Patrols," *USA Today*, 17 January 2002, p. 8.

23. NATO, "Statement by the Secretary General on the Conclusion of Operation Eagle Assist," press release (2002) 057, 30 April 2002.

24. Norman Kempster, "NATO Sends Military Planes to U.S.," *Los Angeles Times*, 11 October 2001, p. A4; Paul Mann, "Europe Wary Of Prolonged Bombing," *Aviation Week and Space Technology*, 22 October 2001, p. 32.

25. Keith B. Richburg and DeNeen L. Brown, "NATO to Send Radar Planes to Patrol U.S. Coast," *The Washington Post*, 9 October 2001, p. B9.

26. NATO, "Statement on Combating Terrorism: Adapting the Alliance's Defence Capabilities," press release (2001) 173, 18 December 2001.

27. Charles Grant, "Does this War Show that NATO No Longer has a Serious Military Role?" *The Independent*, 16 October 2001, p. 4.

28. "French General Takes over Command of NATO-Led Force in Kosovo," *Agence France Presse*, 3 October 2001.

29. James Dao, "Americans Plead to Remain in Bosnia," *The New York Times*, 22 October 2001, p. B3.

30. Misha Glenny, "Balkan Instability Could Create a Terrorist Haven," *The New York Times*, 16 October 2001, p. A31; Judy Dempsey, "EU in Wrangle on Balkan Stability Pact," *Financial Times*, 30 October 2001, p. 12; and NATO/SFOR Press Conference, 25 September 2001.

31. Michael Evans, "British Soldiers Leaving Balkans," *The Times* (London), 27 September 2001, p. 13.

32. "Bin Laden and the Balkans: The Politics of Anti-Terrorism," ICG Balkans Report No. 119, 9 November 2001.

33. Daniel McGrory, "Bin Laden Aide Arrested in Bosnia," *The Times* (London), 11 October 2001, p. 9.

34. Sam Dillon with Emma Daly, "Spain Pursues Terrorists Among Its Muslim Immigrants," *Los Angeles Times*, 4 December 2001; Sebastian Rotella, "Europe Holds

Fertile Soil for Jihads," *Los Angeles Times*, 5 December 2001; Susan Sachs, "North Africans in Europe Said to Preach War," *The New York Times*, 11 December 2001, p. B2; and Steven Erlanger and Chris Hedges, "Terror Cells Slip Through Europe's Grasp," *The New York Times*, 28 December 2001, p. A1.

35. Sebastian Rotella and David Zucchino, "Hunt Is On for Middle Managers of Terrorism," *Los Angeles Times*, 23 December 2001, p. A1.

36. Edmund Andrews, "German Officials Find More Terrorist Groups, and Some Disturbing Parallels," *The New York Times*, 26 April 2002, p. A12.

37. Bob Drogin and Paul Watson, "Battlefield Clues Key to Bush's Next Step," *Los Angeles Times*, 9 December 2001.

38. Erlanger and Hedges, "Terror Cells Slip Through Europe's Grasp"; and Vivienne Walt, "Terrorists 'Spread all Over Europe,'" *USA Today*, 22 July 2001, p. A4.

39. Theodor Troev and Stefan Wagstyl, "NATO Plans Eastward Shift," *Financial Times*, 6 October 2001, p. 3.

40. Lord George Robertson, "Kosovo One Year on: Achievement and Challenge," NATO, 21 March 2000, internet, http://www.nato.int/kosovo/repo2000/index.htm, accessed 12 September 2002.

41. John Arquilla and David Ronfelt, eds., *Networks and Netwars: The Future of Terror, Crime, and Militancy* (Washington: RAND, 2001).

42. Ibid., p. 369.

43. Because of its recent civil war, Tajikistan is currently not a member of the Partnership for Peace (PfP) program. Given their crucial position in Central Asia and the porous nature of their shared border with Afghanistan, Tajikistan should be allowed to become a PfP member.

44. Michael Wines, "Accord is Near on Giving Russia a Limited Role in NATO," *The New York Times*, 23 April 2002, p. A3.

45. Of course a large component of the war against terrorism is financial. We omit it here only because NATO has no particular role to play in that area. Efforts to block terror financing will be complex and long-lasting.

46. "OSCE Ministerial Ends with Anti-Terror Declaration, Action Plan," US State Department website, 4 December 2001, http://usinfo.state.gov/topical/pol/terror/01120404.htm, accessed 11 September 2002.

47. Quoted in BBC News, "OSCE Moves Against Terror," 4 December 2001, internet, http://news.bbc.co.uk/1/hi/world/europe/1689179.stm, accessed 11 September 2002.

48. Julian Lindley-French, *Terms of Engagement: The Paradox of American Power and the Transatlantic Dilemma post-11 September*, Chaillot Paper No. 52 (Paris: Institute for Security Studies, May 2002), p. 14. See also Donald McNeil, "More and More, Other Countries See the War as Solely America's," *The New York Times*, 4 November 2001, p. B1.

49. Suzanne Daley, "Many in Europe Voice Worry U.S. Will Not Consult Them," *The New York Times*, 31 January 2002, p. A12.

POSTSCRIPT

This debate has focused primarily on the future of permanent multilateral military alliances, particularly NATO. An alliance generally involves making a formal commitment, usually through a treaty, to come to the aid of fellow members if they are attacked. As in the case of NATO, an alliance can take on a degree of permanence through the development of formal bureaucratic institutions and structures. To the extent that alliance members share a common set of cultural values and interests, the cohesion of the alliance will be strengthened. Thus, even when the threat that led to the formation of the alliance recedes, the alliance structure itself may continue, often searching for new tasks or missions.

An alternative to an alliance is the formation of more informal coalition. By definition, coalitions are temporary combinations of states that come together to address an immediate threat. Because a coalition, unlike NATO, lacks an institutional base, it may be harder to sustain for very long, especially as the security situation evolves. Therefore, coalitions are highly dependent on some combination of diplomatic pressures and financial rewards and punishments to maintain them. In the case of the "war on terrorism," for example, where the enemy is virtually unseen, clear victories are few, and the conflict may be long-term, the challenge of maintaining the cohesiveness of a coalition is enormous.

Nevertheless, some analysts suggest that international coalitions are more likely to be the wave of the future than permanent alliances such as NATO. They note that the two wars in Iraq, the war in Afghanistan, and the war against terrorism have all been fought by broad-based coalitions. The Bush Doctrine, while making reference to multilateral alliances, seems to rely more on a combination of temporary international "coalitions of the willing," bilateral alliances, and a willingness to act unilaterally. However, given their fluidity and the high investment required to maintain their cohesiveness, are such international coalitions likely to replace permanent multilateral alliances altogether in the future?

Suggested Additional Readings

Asmus, Ronald D. "Rebuilding the Atlantic Alliance." *Foreign Affairs* 82, no. 5 (September–October 2003): 20.

Davis, Jacquelyn K. *Reluctant Allies and Competitive Partners: U.S.–French Relations at the Breaking Point?* Herndon, Va.: Brassey's, 2003.

Dibb, Paul. "The Future of International Coalitions: How Useful? How Manageable?" *The Washington Quarterly* 25, no. 2 (Spring 2002): 131–32.

Gvosdev, Nikolas K. "Diplomatic Gobblygook: Alliances and the National Interest." *The National Interest* 2, no. 27 (July 9, 2003). Available at www.inthenationalinterest.com/Articles/Vol2Issue27/Vol2Issue27Realist.html.

Hanson, Victor Davis. "So Long to All That: Why the Old World of Bases, Alliances, and NATO Is Now Coming to an End." *National Review Online* (January 31, 2003). Available at www.nationalreview.com/hanson/hanson013103.asp.

Jentleson, Bruce W. "Tough Love Multilateralism." *The Washington Quarterly* 27, no. 1 (Winter 2003–04): 7–24.

Kolko, Gabriel. "Iraq, the United States, and the End of the European Coalition." *Journal of Contemporary Asia* 33, no. 3 (2003): 291–98.

Legault, Albert. "The Aftermath of the War: New Tasks for the Institutions." *European Foreign Affairs Review* 8, no. 4 (December 2003): 505–08.

Pasicolan, Paolo, and Balbina Y. Hwang. "The Vital Role of Alliances in the Global War on Terrorism." Washington, D.C.: The Hertiage Foundation, Backgrounder no. 1607 (October 24, 2002). Available at www.heritage.org/Research/NationalSecurity/bg1607.cfm.

Tertrais, Bruno. "The Changing Nature of Military Alliances." *The Washington Quarterly* 27, no. 2 (Spring 2004): 135–50.

Walt, Stephen M. "Why Alliances Endure or Collapse." *Survival* 39, no. 1 (Spring 1997): 156–79.

Yost, David S. *NATO Transformed: The Alliance's New Roles in International Security.* Washington, D.C.: Institute of Peace Press, 1998.

InfoTrac® College Edition

Search for the following articles in the InfoTrac® database:

Asmus, Ronald D. "Europe's Eastern Promise: Rethinking NATO and EU Enlargement." *Foreign Affairs* 87, no. 1 (Jan–Feb 2008): 95–107.

Gordon, Philip H. "NATO and the War on Terrorism: A Changing Alliance (The Shock Wave Abroad)." *Brookings Review* 20, no. 3 (Summer 2002): 36–38.

Hendrickson, Ryan C. "The Miscalculation of NATO's Death." *Parameters* 37, no. 1 (Spring 2007): 98–115.

Kwok, James. "Mending NATO: Sustaining the Transatlantic Relationship." *Harvard International Review* 27, no. 2 (Summer 2005): 36–40.

Valasek, Tomas. "The Fight against Terrorism: Where's NATO?" *World Policy Journal* 18, no. 4 (Winter 2001): 19–25.

Web Resources

For current URLs for the following websites, visit www.crosscurrents.nelson.com.

NORTH ATLANTIC TREATY ORGANIZATION
http://www.nato.int

The official website of the NATO contains many official documents of the organization, texts of speeches, and news updates.

CENTRE FOR EUROPEAN SECURITY AND DISARMAMENT
http://www.cesd.org

This site contains many resources on NATO from a European perspective. In the past, the organization published a regular newsletter called *NATO Notes*, which contains articles discussing developments in NATO.

GLOBAL BEAT RESOURCES ON NATO
http://www.nyu.edu/globalbeat/nato.html

Maintained by the Center for War, Peace and the News Media at New York University, this website contains resources relating to NATO, especially on the topic of expansion.

CENTRE FOR RESEARCH ON GLOBALIZATION
http://www.globalresearch.ca

The Centre for Research on Globalization is an independent group of scholars and writers who research numerous global issues. This website contains various resources on NATO.

Should Canadian Troops Be Deployed to Darfur Rather than Afghanistan?

✔ **YES**
MICHAEL BYERS, "Afghanistan: Wrong Mission for Canada"

✗ **NO**
ROBERT HUEBERT, "The Debate Between the Canadian Commitment to Afghanistan and the Sudan: The Need to Consider All Costs," *Calgary Papers in Military and Strategic Studies* 1 (2007)

The deployment of the Canadian Armed Forces to Afghanistan represents the largest military, humanitarian, and diplomatic engagement undertaken by Canada in the post–Cold War era. Canada's involvement in the region began in the aftermath of the terrorist attacks on the United States on September 11th, 2001. In the wake of these attacks, President Bush launched Operation Enduring Freedom, a military invasion of Afghanistan with the purpose of capturing the al-Qaeda forces responsible for the attacks and toppling the Taliban government which had given them safe refuge.

Although it did not participate in the opening days of the invasion, Canada sent 40 members of its elite Joint Task Force Two (JTF2) to Afghanistan in December 2001. In January 2002, the first regular land troops were deployed as Canada's contribution to Operation Anaconda, an American-led operation to destroy al-Qaeda and Taliban forces in the Shakri-Kot Valley and Arma mountain region. Later in 2003, Canadian forces were moved into the northern city of Kabul where they took command of the International Security Force (ISAF). The ISAF is a NATO-led security and development mission established by a resolution of the United Nation's Security Council. Its primary purpose is to secure Kabul and the surrounding areas from the Taliban and al-Qaeda forces and to allow the Afghan Transitional Administration, headed by Hamid Karzai, to get established. The mandate of the ISAF was later expanded by the Security Council to cover all of Afghanistan. Subsequently, leadership of the mission in Kabul was turned back to the Americans while Canadian troops were redeployed to the volatile province of Kandahar.

When the initial goal of toppling the Taliban from power was achieved, the focus of the intervention shifted toward the task of reconstruction, including rebuilding roads, schools, and clinics; supervising democratic elections; managing of the return of millions of displaced refugees; and delivering humanitarian relief to vulnerable populations. The Security Council hoped that these efforts at peace-building and post-war reconstruction would lay the foundation for a more stable and democratic Afghanistan where all parties could soon shift toward longer term goals of building a democracy and implementing a transition from humanitarian relief to development assistance.

Canada has participated significantly in this broadened mandate in Afghanistan. In 2003, Operation Athena was launched as part of Canada's contribution to the ISAF. Operation Athena included not only security patrols but also well digging and the reconstruction of buildings destroyed by the fighting. Canadian involvement expanded further when Operation Athena was replaced by Operation Archer in February 2006. Canada has played a major role in this operation, deploying 2300 troops in Kandahar and serving as commander of the Multinational Brigade in the region.

On one level some significant progress has been made as a result of the intervention. An internationally supervised election put in place the first popularly elected and functional parliament. The new government developed the Afghanistan Nation Development Strategy (ANDS), which was endorsed by international donors. All international military forces operating in Afghanistan were brought under NATO command. Improvements in some sectors, such as education, communications, and investment, began to be evident.

However, the task of rebuilding any war-torn country is always an enormously complex task. In the case of Afghanistan, previous attempts by both foreign powers and Afghan elites to modernize the country have largely failed. The present task of rebuilding Afghanistan has been complicated by the difficult topography of the country, its long history of warlordism and regionally divided politics, and ongoing insecurity. Despite some early successes, the Taliban began to reassert itself in the south and east portions of the country, creating new fears of insecurity. The slow pace of reconstruction has meant that the economic dependence of many peasants on the poppy has grown. As a result, opium production, once almost eliminated by the Taliban, has grown exponentially. The power of many regional warlords remains unchecked and corruption is widespread. As a result of the deteriorating security situation, the attention of the foreign forces has shifted from reconstruction to counter-insurgency efforts. As the pace of reconstruction has slowed and the security situation has become more tenuous, Afghans have become more skeptical of the benefits of the intervention.

As a result of these developments, the initial short-term intervention has become a longer term commitment. Despite earlier promises to withdraw Canadian forces by 2006, the Canadian government announced that it would extend its commitments a further two years. In making this commitment, the government reiterated that this was not simply a combat operation but part of a multi-faceted peace-building effort including not only armed forces personnel, but also officials from Foreign Affairs, the Canadian International Development Agency, and the Royal Canadian Mounted Police.

Nevertheless, opposition to Canadian involvement in Afghanistan has grown. Some critics argue that this has not been a peace-building mission focusing on reconstruction and development, but rather a counter-insurgency combat mission in support of American foreign policy objectives. As the number of Canadian casualties and the cost of the mission has escalated, many critics called for a withdrawal of Canadian forces. Despite these criticisms, in January 2008, Prime Minister Stephen Harper announced that he would further extend its military mission in Afghanistan to 2011 on the condition that other NATO members stepped up their commitment of troops in the more dangerous sections of the country.

In the first reading, Michael Byers offers a critical perspective on Canada's involvement in Afghanistan. He portrays the involvement as primarily a counter-insurgency combat mission which betrays Canada's long commitment to peace-keeping. He believes that Canada should shift its attention to areas like Darfur, Sudan, where a significant humanitarian crisis has largely been ignored by the international community. Byers believes this change would better match both Canada's traditional role as peacekeeper and the capabilities of our military forces. In the second article, Rob Heubert discusses the implications that a withdrawal from Afghanistan and a refocusing on Sudan would have. He fears that suggestions such as Byers' are based more on wishful thinking than on a careful calculation of the costs involved.

✔ YES

Afghanistan: Wrong Mission for Canada

MICHAEL BYERS

We are approaching the five-year mark of Canada's military involvement in Afghanistan.

Joint Task Force 2, Canada's special-forces unit, has been active in that country since shortly after the terrorist attacks of Sept. 11, 2001. We know that JTF-2 soldiers transferred detainees to U.S. custody in January 2002, participated in an attack at Tora Bora in December 2002, and transferred detainees to U.S. custody again during the summer of 2005.

The first deployment of regular soldiers came in January 2002, when 750 infantry from the Princess Patricia's Regiment were sent to Kandahar as part of an U.S. counter-insurgency task force. Four of these soldiers were killed, and eight others injured, in a "friendly fire" incident in April 2002.

Then, over a two-year period from August 2003 to October 2005, some 6,000 Canadian soldiers were rotated through Kabul as part of a UN-authorized, NATO-led "international security assistance force" providing security and stability for Afghanistan's new government.

In late 2005, the focus of Canada's military effort reverted to the counter-insurgency mission in Kandahar. The U.S. government, bogged down in Iraq, and with an eye to next month's mid-term elections, was keen to reduce its troop levels. NATO responded by scaling up its presence from 9,000 to around 20,000 soldiers, with most of the new troops coming from Britain, Canada, Denmark and The Netherlands.

Originally, the plan was to expand NATO's responsibilities to include southern Afghanistan by early 2006. But the transition was delayed by concerns, in Paris, Berlin and elsewhere, over the tactics employed in the counter-insurgency mission. For the better part of a year, Canada's soldiers operated as part of the U.S.-led *Operation Enduring Freedom*, where, despite being placed in charge of ground operations in Kandahar, they remained under more general U.S. operational control. In the end, the French and Germans refused to deploy into the south.

Kandahar is the stronghold of the Taliban, the nearby mountains bordering Pakistan provide a refuge for Al-Qaeda, and the agricultural lowlands are dominated by drug barons. Canada's soldiers face ever-increasing risks as these various forces copy their Iraqi counterparts by using roadside explosives and suicide bombs while, at the same time, coalescing into organized groups of guerrilla fighters. To some extent, the risks have been exacerbated by heavy-handed U.S.-led tactics, especially the use of air power against villages when Taliban or Al-Qaeda members are believed to be present. Hundreds, perhaps thousands of innocent civilians have died in such strikes, prompting angry family members and friends to join the insurgency.

BEYOND 'FIRST SIGN OF TROUBLE'

In March 2006, Prime Minister Stephen Harper said: "Canadians don't cut and run at the first sign of trouble."

Yes, indeed. But surely we're beyond the "first sign of trouble" now?

At least 39 Canadian soldiers have lost their lives in Afghanistan, along with one diplomat. There have likely been additional losses among our special forces, who operate behind a veil of secrecy that extends to the reporting of casualties. Then, there are the hundreds of seriously wounded Canadian soldiers, with lost limbs, blindness, brain damage or other forms of severe psychological harm.

These numbers are sobering. And let's be honest: whatever our political inclination, we all have a tipping point at which we'd call for Canada's troops to be brought home. Nobody—not even General Pervez Musharraf of Pakistan—is willing to argue that the counter-insurgency mission in Afghanistan would be worth the lives of 1,000 Canadian soldiers.

On that basis, it's time to assess where our national tipping point should be. Let's begin by considering the arguments in favour of the mission.

THE ARGUMENTS IN FAVOUR

First, it's argued that the mission is necessary to protect Canadians from the threat posed by the Taliban and Al-Qaeda. This is a serious argument, but it can be exaggerated. The Taliban do not pose a threat to the existence of Canada. They're not about to invade. Nor are they developing weapons of mass destruction and missiles capable of reaching North America.

The Al-Qaeda elements sheltering behind the Taliban do not pose an existential threat to Canada either. They certainly provide moral and perhaps technical support to aspiring terrorists elsewhere. But if the threat were truly serious, Washington would not have shifted its focus to Iraq. Nor would General Musharraf be allowed to conclude deals with pro-Taliban militants along the border of Afghanistan, while denying NATO forces access to that region.

Clearly, we do have a national interest in containing Al-Qaeda. Yet even if that interest was worth 39 Canadian soldiers' lives, it's not clear that the counter-insurgency mission is making progress towards this goal. After five years of efforts by American, British and Canadian troops, southern Afghanistan has become significantly more dangerous.

Second, it's argued that the counter-insurgency mission is needed to restrict the production of opium. Illegal narcotics are certainly a concern. But despite the presence of Canadian troops, opium production has increased dramatically.

Third, it's argued that the counter-insurgency mission is needed to protect the Afghan people. But, again, are we actually achieving this goal? Today, the average life expectancy in Afghanistan is less than 45 years, and 1,600 mothers out of 100,000 die during childbirth (compared to six out of 100,000 in Canada). What's more, some of the most important posts in the Afghan government are held by former warlords. Some of them stand accused—by international human rights organizations and other, elected members of the parliament—of heinous crimes, and of siphoning off billions of dollars of foreign aid.

Fourth, it's argued that NATO's credibility is at stake. But if that's the case, why have so many NATO members refused to step up to the plate? There are 26 NATO countries, and Canada—with our relatively small population and military—has made the third-largest contribution to the counter-insurgency mission.

And how much does NATO's credibility matter? Fifteen years after the collapse of the Soviet Union, NATO is simply a collection of countries that may or may not choose to co-operate in any given situation. When the United States intervened in Afghanistan in 2001, it chose not to call on NATO for help.

Fifth, it's argued that Canada's credibility would suffer if we withdrew from the counter-insurgency mission. It's certainly true that, within NATO circles, we'd be expected to provide reasonable notice. And so we should. But does anyone regard France or Germany as less credible because they refused to deploy into southern Afghanistan? Does anyone regard Spain or Italy as less credible because they chose to withdraw from Iraq? As Senator Roméo Dallaire has explained, the biggest blow to Canada's credibility today is occurring elsewhere, as we allow a genocide to continue in Darfur.

Sixth, it's argued that Canada's credibility in Washington would suffer. This is a serious argument. But it's also the same argument that was advanced by those who thought Canada should join in the Vietnam War. It's the same argument that was advanced by those who thought Canada should join in the 2003 Iraq War. All of which goes to show that Canadians are better judges of the Canadian national interest than Americans. As long as we provide reasonable notice, Washington has no reason to complain.

THE ARGUMENTS AGAINST

Let's turn to the arguments against the counter-insurgency mission. What are the costs—above and beyond the all-important cost in lost and shattered young Canadian lives?

There are financial costs. In August 2006, the Polaris Institute estimated that the counter-insurgency mission would cost Canadian taxpayers around $4 billion over two years. That, of course, works out to $2 billion per year. This compares to the $1 billion, over ten years, that Canada is providing for reconstruction and development in Afghanistan, which works out to $100 million per year—or five per cent of what we're spending on the military mission.

These financial costs also constitute opportunity costs. Four billion dollars could provide a massive amount of development and humanitarian assistance, and not just in Afghanistan.

Wisely spent, this money could save millions of lives, especially in disease and famine-ridden sub-Sahara Africa.

Opportunity missed: Lebanon. Another form of opportunity cost concerns the other missions that the Canadian Forces cannot fulfil because of their current engagement.

Take Lebanon, for instance. On August 11, 2006, the UN Security Council imposed a ceasefire on Hezbollah and Israel. It authorized a peacekeeping operation of 15,000 soldiers with a robust mandate to "use all necessary action in areas of deployment of its forces and as it deems within its capabilities, to ensure that its area of operations is not utilized for hostile activities of any kind."

Many of the peacekeepers have been provided by France, Italy and Spain. Belgium, Finland, Norway and Poland are sending smaller contingents, with Germany and Denmark providing maritime support. Canada is conspicuously absent. Yet Canada has a clear national interest in maintaining the ceasefire between Hezbollah and Israel, since the Middle East conflict has the potential to escalate into a highly destabilizing war with Iran involving attacks on nuclear facilities. Moreover, far more Canadians have personal connections with Israel and Lebanon than with Afghanistan. Last but not least, Canadian soldiers are uniquely suited to peacekeeping in Lebanon. In addition to their considerable experience and training for such missions, the Canadian Forces have the necessary language skills to communicate with Israelis (most of whom speak English) and Lebanese (most of whom speak French).

Opportunity missed: Darfur. Violence-wracked Darfur is another place Canadian peacekeepers could usefully be deployed. Since 2003, more than 200,000 people have been killed, countless women have been raped, and several million people have been forced from their homes. The agents of this destruction—the Janjaweed (who ride camels and horses) and the Sudanese military (which pushes crude barrel bombs out of the back of cargo planes)—would be no match for a well-trained, well-equipped Western military.

In May 2006, African countries recognized that they weren't up to the task. The African Union urged the commencement of a UN peacekeeping operation in Darfur "at the earliest possible time." In response, the UN Security Council requested that Secretary General Kofi Annan provide recommendations "on all relevant aspects of the mandate of the United Nations operation in Darfur" including "additional force requirements" and "potential troop-contributing countries." Mr. Annan's office immediately indicated that any force deployed to Darfur would have to include soldiers from developed countries.

Three months later, the Security Council adopted Resolution 1706, formally authorizing the creation of a peacekeeping force for Darfur. It did hold off deploying the force while last-ditch efforts were made to obtain Sudanese consent, but let's be clear: Resolution 1706 authorizes a muscular intervention in Darfur with or without the consent of Khartoum. In the circumstances, a declared willingness to deploy one or two thousand highly trained infantry and the Canadian Army's fleet of Griffin helicopters—which are not being used elsewhere—could be just what is needed to create the political will for the deployment to move forward.

Some have argued that Canada's national interest is not engaged in Darfur, at least not as much as it is in Afghanistan. But the argument overlooks two critical points. First, Canada does have an interest in protecting fundamental human rights, and there is no more fundamental right than being protected from genocide. Second, the degree of national interest that we have in any given situation must be balanced against the likely costs, including lost Canadian lives. And as I've said, neither the Janjaweed nor the Sudanese military constitute a serious fighting force.

THE CASE FOR "PEACEKEEPING"

Some people might decry the opportunities in Lebanon and Darfur as unsuitable for Canadian troops because they constitute "mere" peacekeeping. For almost a decade, Canada's generals, along with a growing collection of politicians and pundits, have asserted that peacekeeping is *passé* and counter-insurgency wars are the new reality. Yet the turn away from peacekeeping has been a matter of choice rather than necessity. In January 2002, *The Globe and Mail* reported that "Canada decided to send its troops into a combat mission under U.S. control in Afghanistan rather than participate in the British-led multinational force because it is 'tired' of acting as mere peacekeepers, according to a senior British defence official."

Since when have the generations of Canadian soldiers who risked their lives patrolling the world's conflict zones become "mere" peacekeepers? Yes, peacekeeping requires diplomacy and restraint, but it also takes courage. The myth that peacekeeping is "for wimps" originates in the United States, where it found its ultimate expression in Condoleezza Rice's October 2000 comment that "We don't need to have the 82nd Airborne escorting kids to kindergarten." Every time I read about the death and destruction in Iraq, I think of this comment, and wish the world had more properly trained and experienced peacekeepers.

COSTS TO CANADA

Reputation. Wrapped up in the distinction between the peacekeeping opportunities in Lebanon and Darfur and the counter-insurgency mission in Afghanistan is the additional issue of reputation costs, most notably the cost to Canada's international reputation for independence and objectivity, and thus our ability to lead and persuade on a wide range of issues. Where would we gain the most in terms of our international reputation: continuing with a failing counter-insurgency mission in Afghanistan, or leading a humanitarian intervention to stop the genocide in Darfur?

Security. There may even be a security cost to the counter-insurgency mission. Recently foiled terrorist plots in Toronto and London were reportedly motivated, at least in part, by anger at the presence of Western troops in Afghanistan. Canada's Chief of Defence Staff, Rick Hillier, hasn't helped matters by publicly characterizing the insurgents as "detestable murderers and scumbags." One wonders how Muslims around the world feel when they hear language like this being used on Canada's behalf.

Foreign stance. General Hillier's language points to another problem. The counter-insurgency mission in Afghanistan could, over time, lead to the development of a Canadian Forces that is focused almost entirely—in its training, ethos and equipment—on counter-insurgency missions conducted alongside or for the United States. The long-term consequences of this would be significant, especially for Canadian foreign policy.

And let's be clear, our current policy orientation is leading inexorably to a much longer engagement in the counter-insurgency mission. In August 2005, Canadian Major-General Andrew Leslie said that helping Afghanistan break out of "a cycle of warlords and tribalism" was a "20-year venture." In March 2006, Chief of Defence Staff Rick Hillier said: "From NATO's perspective, they look at this as a 10-year mission, right? Minimum. There's going to be a huge demand for Canada to contribute over the longer period of time."

Complicit in crime. It's even possible that Canada's involvement in the counter-insurgency mission is contributing to a decline in this country's commitment to strong rules of international humanitarian law.

In 2002, Canadian soldiers in Afghanistan were ordered by their American commander to lay anti-personnel landmines around their camp. When the Canadians refused—citing our obligations under the 1997 Ottawa Landmines Convention—American soldiers, who are not subject to the same restrictions, laid the mines for them. More recently, Canadian forces in Kabul and Kandahar have benefited from the protection provided by anti-personnel landmines laid by Soviet forces during the 1980s. The Canadian government argues that the Landmines Convention has not been violated, since the prohibition on the "use" of anti-personnel mines does not extend to reliance on mines laid by others. This is a strained interpretation, and one that hardly reinforces our claim to be the leading proponent of the total elimination of these devices.

Also in 2002, Canadian soldiers in Afghanistan captured detainees and transferred them to U.S. custody. The transfers took place despite the fact that U.S. Defence Secretary Donald Rumsfeld had publicly refused to convene the "status determination tribunals" required by the Third Geneva Convention of 1949, to investigate whether individuals captured on the battlefield are prisoners of war. Canada, by choosing to hand the detainees over in these circumstances, also violated the Third Geneva Convention. But the transfers did not undermine the prohibition on torture, since there was—at that time—no reason to believe that U.S. forces would mistreat the detainees.

Today we know better. The photographs from Abu Ghraib were only the first pieces of a growing body of evidence indicating that, at best, the U.S. military failed to educate its soldiers about international humanitarian law. At worst, the revelations—including a series of leaked legal memoranda that seek to justify torture—suggest a policy of law-breaking that extends all the way up the chain of command, to the Secretary of Defence and perhaps the commander-in-chief himself.

The full scope of the Geneva Conventions no longer applies to Canada's operations in Afghanistan, because our soldiers are there with the full consent of the sovereign government in Kabul. But Canada is still bound by a provision, "Common Article 3," that applies to armed conflicts that are "not of an international character occurring in the territory of one of the High Contracting Parties." It stipulates that "persons taking no active part in the hostilities, including members of armed forces who have laid down their arms," are absolutely protected from "violence to life and person, in particular murder of all kinds, mutilation, cruel treatment and torture." Common Article 3 also proscribes "outrages upon personal dignity, in particular, humiliating and degrading treatment." Canada, by transferring detainees to a foreign military that has recently committed violations of precisely this kind, has been risking complicity in breaches of the Geneva Conventions.

We've also been taking chances with the 1984 Torture Convention. Article 3 of this treaty decrees that "no state party shall expel, return or extradite a person to another state where there are substantial grounds for believing that he would be in danger of being subjected to torture." Given what we now know about practices at Abu Ghraib and elsewhere, the possibility that our detainees will be tortured in U.S. custody is real—as real, perhaps, as if we sent them to Syria.

What's more, the UN Committee on Torture has stated that the term "another state" in Article 3 of the Torture Convention encompasses any additional country to which a prisoner might subsequently be transferred. For this reason, transferring detainees to Afghan custody instead of U.S. custody cannot relieve Canada of responsibility, since Kabul may be expected to comply with a U.S. request for a further, onward transfer. Yet that's precisely what Canada has been doing since December 2005, when Chief of Defence Staff Rick Hillier signed a detainee-transfer agreement with the defence minister of Afghanistan.

Under the agreement, Afghanistan committed to the humane treatment of any individuals received, and to allow representatives of the International Committee of the Red Cross to visit them. At the same time, the agreement explicitly envisages that some detainees will be transferred onwards to the custody of a third country, and does nothing to guard against that country being one in which detainees are at risk of being tortured or otherwise abused. Professor Amir Attaran of the University of Ottawa has accurately described the document as a "detainee laundering agreement," for it enables Canada to move its detainees indirectly into U.S. custody without the scrutiny and approbation that might attach to direct transfers.

Canadians' self-image. These last concerns about international humanitarian law lead into my final point, which concerns the effect that the counter-insurgency character of our mission in Afghanistan might have on how Canadians think of themselves. We like to think that we are "global citizens" uniquely placed to promote a more peaceful, just, inclusive and law-abiding world, but how can engaging in search-and-destroy missions with and for the United States foster this self-identity? Wouldn't stopping genocide be more consistent with how Canadians have, traditionally, preferred their country to behave?

Have we reached our national tipping point with regard to the counter-insurgency mission in Afghanistan? Having done my best to assess the arguments for and against, the conclusion, to me, is obvious.

✗ NO
The Debate Between the Canadian Commitment to Afghanistan and the Sudan: The Need to Consider All Costs
ROBERT HUEBERT

With increasing attention being paid to international efforts to resolve the violence in the Sudan, Canada has been under mounting pressure to join these efforts. Combined with the recent Canadian military casualties in Afghanistan and the accompanying opinion polls showing decreased Canadian support for that mission, a debate regarding Canadian military action there has ensued. The emerging position is that Canada should mount a significant deployment to the Sudan. While few have come out and specifically stated it, the underlying assumption is that such a mission would be preferable to the current Kandahar mission. This debate is both illustrative and disturbing with respect to what it suggests about the public's current understanding of Canadian defence and foreign policy.

The fact that Canadians are discussing and debating overseas deployments to these failed and failing states is an important indication of Canadians' caring nature. There are few other states that have either the will or the capacity to offer such assistance. These deployments are expensive in terms of both personnel and resources. Given their expense, it is imperative that the debates be based on a full and complete understanding of the facts, rather than on wishful thinking.

The argument that Canada should commit resources to the Sudan contains four highly suspect assumptions. The first is that Canada is morally obligated to stop the genocide and the other horrific actions that have taken place there. It is often implied that this is in keeping with the Canadian tradition of support for "human security," which some suggest has always been the raison d'etre of Canadian defence. A second assumption is that the mission to the Sudan will be conducted as a "peacekeeping" operation as opposed to the "peace enforcement" nature of the Afghanistan operation. A third is that the Sudan mission is preferable to the current Afghanistan operation because America's participation has not yet been proposed. The belief that Canada can deploy troops to both Afghanistan and the Sudan in a meaningful fashion comprises the last supposition.

Let us begin with the first of these four assumptions. As important as peacekeeping has been in the minds of the Canadian public, the reality is that Canadian forces have been built and designed to fight wars against enemies. To a large degree, the most successful Canadian peacekeeping deployments have been to ensure that inter-allied relations are protected in the face of an adversary. Canadian involvement in the Suez crisis in 1956 focused on helping the

Americans, the British, and the French to resolve their differences. The commitment to Cyprus was also about ensuring that the Greek and Turkish allies did not go to war with each other over the island. While Canadian forces were deployed to other peacekeeping operations and made important contributions, none of these other operations come close to equalling Canada's contribution to the Cyprus and Suez deployments. Also forgotten in the understanding of Canadian forces is that Canadian forces perform so well in traditional peacekeeping operations because they have been highly trained for war-fighting against the USSR and its allies. Canada's peacekeeping success was built on Canada's requirement to ensure that its commitment to NATO remained strong and that NATO itself remained strong. The assumption that the current Canadian deployment fighting alongside its allies is at odds with Canadian history is simply wrong. If anything, the Canadian contribution of war-fighting troops deployment is actually much more in keeping with the traditional uses of the Canadian military since the end of the Second World War.

A second assumption that is building in the push for making the commitment to the Sudan is that it will be a traditional peacekeeping operation. This is based on the belief that current negotiations will lead to a peaceful settlement between the rebels and the government; it is to believe that there are two sides that need to be separated so peace can be enforced in the region. Unfortunately, this belief flies directly in the face of all precedents of the current Khartoum regime. There is no evidence that they have any intention of giving up their genocidal, destructive polices any time soon. Indeed, why would they? If they were reasonable men concerned about the violence, there would not be a crisis in the Sudan. The sad reality is that they will not end their horrific policies unless and until they are forced to. Any solution to Sudan's "problem" will require the use of military force. And even if the government was somehow convinced to change its policies, the militias would still need to be brought under control, once again requiring military force. Thus, any action directed to truly resolving the policy of genocide, rape, and destruction in the Sudan will require the extensive use of military power; any meaningful Canadian deployment would probably be even more violent and dangerous than our current deployment in Afghanistan.

Wending its way into the arguments of those strongly supporting an intervention in the Sudan is the third assumption, that is, that it can/will be done without the Americans. It is the probable absence of the Americans that causes some commentators to openly state that the Sudanese mission is preferable to the current Afghanistan deployment. Regardless of one's view of current American foreign policy and leadership, the reality is that if the United States does not commit troops to the Sudan, any mission is likely to fail. Canada has already discovered that it cannot deploy by itself as it attempted to do in Central Africa. Previous African efforts in the Sudan have likewise been unsuccessful, and the Europeans have shown no willingness to deploy on their own. The power needed to successfully force the government to stop its horrific actions and to stop the militias' actions could only come from the United States, assuming it is willing to deploy. If the crisis is to be resolved, America must be involved.

A fourth assumption many adhere to is that Canada can support both the Afghanistan mission and a deployment to the Sudan. However, a meaningful Canadian commitment to both, as opposed to mere tokenism, is just not possible. Starting with the cuts to the military made by the Trudeau government, continued by the Mulroney administration, and accelerated by the Chrétien government, successive Canadian governments decided to increase the number of overseas deployments while simultaneously and substantially reducing the size of the Canadian forces. This has created a situation wherein the forces' members are asked to shoulder an increasingly heavy work load with increasingly smaller numbers. Thus, with a few notable exceptions such as Bosnia, the Canadian commitment to international conflicts became smaller and ultimately less effective. Only in very recent years has it been recognized politically that Canadian contingents cannot be everywhere at the force levels that they have been reduced to. Had the forces been maintained at 80,000 rather than reduced to 50,000, it might be possible to talk of both a meaningful Afghanistan and a meaningful Sudanese mission. But with today's numbers, Canada has just two options. Either we pull out of Afghanistan completely when our official commitment ends in February 2009 and redeploy to the Sudan, or we maintain both by prioritizing one mission and sending only a token force to the other.

The costs of not renewing our commitment to Afghanistan should be clarified. First, there is a very real possibility that other contributing states might then also re-examine their decision to stay. A Canadian withdrawal might well be interpreted by the fundamentalist forces in that country as a victory. Whether valid or not, the decision to redeploy will be interpreted as a reaction to the recent Canadian casualties. Any Canadian withdrawal will be attributed to those events and perceived as a victory; the Taliban and Al Qaeda will view our withdrawal as validation of their recent attacks on Canadian forces. If Al Qaeda comes to believe that Canada is a "soft target," they may be encouraged to mount an attack on Canada itself in the future.

By the same token, a Canadian decision not to participate in an international peacemaking/enforcement effort in the Sudan will hurt efforts to bring peace to that country. Canadian forces, when properly supported and concentrated, have shown that they are capable of playing a significant role in robust missions that border on war-fighting, rather than peacekeeping mandates. Canada is seen as a leader and its absence would be felt. But Canada cannot do it alone.

Overall, the discussion regarding committing forces to the Sudan is understandable. Canadians do not want to see the Sudanese people's agony prolonged. But the price of providing real assistance comes at a cost that is not yet fully comprehended. Had the decision to reduce the number of Canadian forces not been made by successive governments, it might have been possible to commit to both actions. But the cuts were made, and Canadian forces cannot support both tasks in a meaningful manner. Likewise, those who call for a deployment to the Sudan also must recognize that this mission will be every bit as dangerous as the current mission in Afghanistan (and possibly even more hazardous). In all likelihood, a traditional peacekeeping deployment will accomplish little apart from making the contributing countries feel good. To stop those willing to commit themselves to genocide and rape, force is needed. And historically, the participation of the United States is necessary to generate enough force to complete that mission. This is not the scenario portrayed by those advocating Canada's commitment to the Sudan, but it is a necessary precondition for a successful outcome. Until Canada succeeds in rebuilding its forces (assuming that it is allowed to continue to do so), it must make some hard decisions. The commitment to remedy the crisis in the Sudan is noble, but most Canadians are unaware of the inherent expense. If this decision is made, it must be based on the facts, not on wishful thinking.

POSTSCRIPT

The debate over Afghanistan and Sudan highlights the shadow that the events of September 11th has cast over discussions of the appropriateness of humanitarian intervention. Following the end of the Cold War and the emergence of humanitarian crises as a result of the collapse of "failed states" such as Sudan, there was a growing interest in the adoption of a new international norm recognizing the right, and even obligation, of states to forcefully intervene in a country to protect civilian populations from acts of genocide or gross human rights abuses.

This position was most clearly articulated in a 2001 report of the International Commission on Intervention and State Sovereignty (ICISS) entitled *The Responsibility to Protect*. In its report, the Commission argues that while states bear the primary responsibility to protect their own citizens, when they fail to do so then "the principle of non-intervention yields to the international responsibility to protect." Further, the report suggests that this responsibility includes not only the need to respond to humanitarian crises, but also a responsibility to prevent crises from emerging and a "responsibility to rebuild" failed states.

How does the notion of "responsibility to protect" apply to the two situations in Afghanistan and Darfur? Is the intervention in Afghanistan primarily an act of self-defence on the part of the United States' "war on terror," or is it a humanitarian intervention designed to rescue the people of Afghanistan from the oppressive grip of the Taliban? Given that the United States and other western countries have been reluctant to intervene either in Darfur or the Democratic Republic of the Congo, where an even larger scale humanitarian disaster has taken place, have the strategic demands of the "war of terror" trumped a commitment to those areas facing the greatest humanitarian need?

In reviewing this debate, students will want to give particular attention to the clear definition of terms. Note that Byers repeatedly refers to Canada's involvement in Afghanistan as a "counter-insurgency combat" mission in contrast to a "peacekeeping" mission in Sudan. Heubert questions the appropriateness of using the term "peacekeeping" to describe a potential mission in Sudan and suggests that it would be more accurately described as a "peace enforcement" mission, a term which could equally be applied to the mission in Afghanistan. How does terminology shape the way we evaluate the value and legitimacy of the intervention?

Suggested Additional Readings

Black, David. "The Responsibility to Engage: Canada and the Ongoing Crisis in Darfur." *Behind the Headlines* 64, no. 4 (July 2007): 17–23.

Boivin, Marc André. "The Afghan Mission is in Canada's National Interest." *Inroads* 20 (Winter/Spring 2007): 31–41.

Fraser, Derek. "Failed States: Why They Matter and What We Should Do About Them." *International Insights* 5, no. 2 (2007): 1–6.

Hampson, Fen Olser. "Intervention and Conflict Management in a Changing World." *Behind the Headlines* 64, no. 4 (July 2007): 3–18.

Matthews, Robert O. "Sudan's Humanitarian Disaster: Will Canada Live up to its Responsibility to Protect?" *International Journal* 60, no. 4 (Autumn 2005): 1049–66.

Nossal, Kim Richard. "Ear Candy: Canadian Policy Toward Humanitarian Intervention and Atrocity Crimes in Darfur." *International Journal* 60, no. 4 (Autumn 2005): 1017–32.

Regehr, Ernie. "Canada Ignoring Its Own Advice." *Inroads* 20 (Winter/Spring 2007): 62–71.

Riddell-Dixon, Elizabeth. "Canada's Human Security Agenda: Walking the Talk?" *International Journal* 60, no. 4 (Autumn 2005): 1067–92.

Rubin, Barnett, "Saving Afghanistan," *Foreign Affairs* 86, no. 1 (January/February 2007). Available at http://www.foreignaffairs.org/20070101faessay86105/ barnett-r-rubin/saving-afghanistan.html.

Wright, James. "Canadian Policy Towards Fragile, Dangerous, and Failed States." Conference on Fragile States, Dangerous States and Failed States, 25–27 November 2005, University of Victoria. Available at http://www.failedstates.org/documents/keynote_asdelivered.pdf.

InfoTrac® College Edition

Search for the following articles in the InfoTrac® database:

Black, David. "The Responsibility to Engage: Canada and the Ongoing Crisis in Darfur." *Behind the Headlines* 64, no. 4 (July 2007): 17–23.

Regehr, Ernie. "A Peace to Keep in Afghanistan." *Ploughshares Monitor* 29, no. 1 (Spring 2008): 3–7.

Siebert, John. "From Manley Report to Sustainable Peace in Afghanistan: You Can't Get There from Here!" *Ploughshares Monitor* 29, no. 1 (Spring 2008): 8–10.

"The Recommendations of the Manley Report." *Ploughshares Monitor* 29, no. 1 (Spring 2008): 11.

Web Resources

For current URLs for the following websites, visit www.crosscurrents.nelson.com.

PEACE OPERATIONS MONITOR/CIVILIAN MONITORING OF COMPLEX PEACE OPERATIONS
http://www.pom.peacebuild.ca/

The Peace Operations Monitor is a project sponsored by the Peace Operations Working Group (POWG), which is affiliated with the Canadian Peacebuilding Network. This website takes an "integrated mission" perspective with the aim of compiling information on the various military, civilian, police, humanitarian, and diplomatic components of current peace operations in which Canada is involved. Particular attention is given to both Afghanistan and Sudan.

UNITED NATIONS ASSISTANCE MISSION IN AFGHANISTAN
http://www.unama-afg.org/Index.htm

This site provides ongoing news updates on the situation in Afghanistan with particular focus on UN-related activities. It provides additional background on the conflict and a link to relevant publications and UN documents.

PROJECT PLOUGHSHARES/CANADA'S ROLE IN AFGHANISTAN
http://www.ploughshares.ca/libraries/Reduce/CanadaInAfghanistan.htm

This site provides a compilation of documents related to Canada's role in Afghanistan, including submissions to the Independent Panel on Canada's Future Role in Afghanistan.

CANADA: ACTIVE IN SUDAN
http://geo.international.gc.ca/cip-pic/sudan/menu-en.asp

The Canadian government provides links to a variety of materials on Canada's role in Sudan and its current stance on the situation in Darfur. Links are also provides to both parliamentary and senate debates on Sudan.

PART THREE

GLOBAL POLITICAL ECONOMY

Can Trade Liberalization Benefit Both Rich and Poor?

Has Globalization Been Detrimental to Women?

Was the "Battle in Seattle" a Significant Turning Point in the Struggle Against Globalization?

Is Development Assistance Effective?

Will Debt Relief Address the Needs of Highly Indebted Countries?

Can Trade Liberalization Benefit Both Rich and Poor?

✔ **YES**

GARY HUFBAUER, "Free Trade," *The National Interest* 95 (May/June 2008): 15–18

✗ **NO**

JOSEPH E. STIGLITZ, "Fair Trade," *The National Interest* 95 (May/June 2008): 19–24

There is little doubt that the globalization of the world's economy is taking place at an extraordinarily rapid pace. World merchandise exports have expanded at an average annual rate of approximately 6 percent since 1950, compared with a 4.5 percent rate in world output. In 1913, the entire flow of goods in world trade totalled only U.S. $20 billion. In contrast, today's international trade in goods and services stands at about U.S. $6 trillion a year. Foreign direct investment (FDI) has been growing at an even faster pace than trade. During recent decades, FDI has been reported to have expanded by 27 percent per year, representing an average growth of U.S. $205 billion a year. Today, there are more than 2000 large multinational corporations (operating in six or more countries) and well over 8000 smaller ones. Together, these 10 000 multinationals are estimated to control over 90 000 subsidiaries.

At the same time, technology has been undergoing a similar process of globalization. Miniaturization and computerization have speeded up communications and transportation times while reducing costs. Rapid developments in communications, when combined with the globalization of financial markets, have led to a sharp increase in the movement of capital. Together, these developments have helped propel an expansion of the global economy, which is not limited by traditional geographical constraints. Factors such as geography and climate no longer give a particular region a comparative advantage.

For some observers, the rapid pace of economic globalization is a welcome trend. The lowering of economic barriers, greater openness to competitive market forces, and the reduction of artificial market restraints are seen as promoting higher economic growth and prosperity. Consumers have access to cheaper, more diverse, and more advanced products. Expansion of trade and investment generates jobs. At the same time, globalization is said to generate positive political dividends. States that adjust to the changing market are able to generate higher rates of economic growth and technological innovation. They have more resources to deploy in the international arena to both promote and defend their interests. Countries that are linked by economic ties and have a mutual interest in promoting economic growth are more likely to seek stable, peaceful, and cooperative ties with other states. Similarly, firms and workers with a stake in trade advancement and economic growth are more likely to be supportive of active and constructive foreign policies that are aimed at maintaining these benefits. Edward Mansfield, in *Power, Trade, and War* (Princeton, N.J.: Princeton University Press, 1994), suggests that the data clearly support the contention that trade and peace are closely related—higher levels of freer trade are usually associated with lower levels of international hostility and antagonism.

Despite this optimistic picture, economic globalization clearly has its downside. An increasingly liberalized economic world imposes severe adjustment burdens on certain segments of workers and firms. The distribution of wealth, both within and between states, has become more unequal. Exposure to the uncertainties and insecurities of foreign competition has led to demands for protectionist measures and the abandonment of multilateral cooperation. Critics are concerned that unfettered global competition creates overwhelming pressures to abandon domestic social policies, environmental regulations, and human-rights protections.

Such concerns have in turn given rise to a growing backlash against globalization itself. Globalization for many people, it is argued, has become a "race to the bottom." At the heart of globalization is growing poverty and inequality, which can be reversed only if the forces of globalization themselves are curtailed. As the massive demonstrations at several international summits have shown, anti-globalization movements have grown significantly in recent years.

The following essays discuss the implications of globalization and trade liberalization. In the first essay, Gary Hufbauer argues that trade liberalization benefits both developed and developing countries. His essay was written during the primaries leading up to the November 2008 U.S. presidential election. In the debates between Hillary Clinton and Barack Obama, the candidates focused on the negative impact that free trade was having on workers in the "rust belt" states. Hufbauer rejects these concerns, arguing that citizens in both wealthy industrialized countries and poorer developing countries ultimately benefit from the expansion of trade liberalization. In contrast, Joseph Stiglitz discusses the negative costs associated with trade liberalization as it has been practised by countries like the United States. He focuses on trade reforms that he argues would promote fair trade, for both rich and poor countries, rather than free trade.

✔ YES

Free Trade

GARY HUFBAUER

Free trade can benefit everyone—the developed and developing world. In large part because of open markets, the global economy is experiencing its greatest half century. In fact, free trade has increased American household income by lowering costs of products, increasing wages and making more-efficient American companies. And even though open markets may come with costs, the gains of globalization exceed them five times over. So, this means when there are burdens to be borne at home, Congress can well afford to help spread the benefits as workers transition. And if done right, free trade benefits the developing world, too, helping bring states out of poverty, allowing them to bargain on equal terms with far-larger countries and potentially stemming state failure.

Yet, the Democrats have splattered their primaries with nonsense about a "time-out" from trade agreements and "opting out" of the North American Free Trade Agreement (NAFTA). As president, neither Senator Hillary Clinton (D-NY) nor Senator Barack Obama (D-IL) could indulge such foolishness. The purpose of their catchy phrases, as everyone knows, is to snare convention delegates, not make policy. But enthusiastic supporters will call their candidate to account if he or she reaches the Oval Office.

Throughout the history of the world trading system—which is to say since the end of the Second World War—the twin objectives of U.S. commercial policy have been to foster economic prosperity and promote U.S. political alliances. These objectives will not vanish when a new president enters the White House in January 2009.

"Opting out" of NAFTA is the sort of ludicrous suggestion that can only surface on the campaign trail. Trade between the United States and its NAFTA partners represented almost 30 percent of total U.S. trade with the world in 2007. U.S. exports to Canada and Mexico totaled $378 billion in 2007, and some of this trade would be jeopardized—to the consternation of American farmers, industrialists and their congressmen. The United States needs the cooperation of Canada and Mexico on multiple fronts, from energy supplies to missile defense. Retreating from NAFTA would not only imperil relations with close neighbors, it would severely diminish U.S. credibility around the world.

Trade is almost miraculous in its effects. Even before NAFTA, the General Agreement on Tariffs and Trade (GATT—now the World Trade Organization, WTO) was born in Havana in 1947, part of a grand design to ensure European economic recovery. The GATT's role was to slash the protectionist thicket that sprang from the Depression and political divisions in the 1930s. During its first year, the GATT sponsored negotiations among twenty-three countries that led to forty-five thousand tariff concessions, covering 20 percent of world trade. Since then, seven successive "rounds" have reduced barriers on a progressively wider scope of commerce, now including more than 150 countries and reaching 90 percent of trade in the global marketplace. The payoff from GATT far exceeds the wildest expectations of those delegates meeting at Havana over a half century ago. World trade has expanded twenty-seven times between 1950 and 2005 (adjusted for inflation), and the world economy has enjoyed the best fifty years in recorded history.

Opposition to free trade is shortsighted—forgivable perhaps for an unemployed machinist in Ohio, but hardly the stuff of presidential policy. Free trade boosts growth and provides meaningful employment. A serious danger in the decades ahead is cascading violence in regions of low development, countries often characterized by political instability and feeble growth. Collectively, they are home to billions of people. Some of them, like Mexico and Colombia, are fighting drug lords and insurgents. Others, like Pakistan and Afghanistan, are fighting al-Qaeda. These are precisely the countries that will benefit the most from open trade and investment policies. Yet many of these countries have either marginalized themselves by erecting one barrier after another to world commerce or have been marginalized not only by the restrictive practices of the United States, Europe and Japan, but also by their own peers in the developing world.

Thus, for example, Tunisia maintains an import-weighted average tariff wall of 20 percent, which, among other harmful effects, slashes trade with its neighbors in the Middle East and North Africa as well as the rest of the world. In a perfect stroke of trade-policy inequity, the United States collects about the same tariff duties annually (approximately $400 million) from impoverished Cambodia as from wealthy Britain, even though Britain exports more than twenty times as much as Cambodia to American shores each year ($57 billion versus $2.5 billion). An outstanding example of the power of open markets is South Korea, a country that has handsomely prospered. In contrast, North Korea, which has followed a path of isolation, remains mired in poverty.

A country that accedes to the WTO, such as Ukraine is now doing, must first undertake a series of legislative and structural reforms to bring its trade regime up to par with the practice of other WTO members. This process gives the newly admitted states the basis for a stronger economy, thanks to the spillover effects to commercial law, property rights and many other areas. Over past decades, many developing countries have prospered from these disciplines. Once in, the country can join negotiations with other members and bring trade complaints to the WTO's dispute-settlement body. The new inductee becomes a full-fledged member of the WTO "club," with all the attendant rights and privileges. Thus, tiny Antigua won an important case against the mighty United States, and midsized Peru was victorious over the European Union.

Put simply, the World Trade Organization engages countries of all economic sizes and political shapes in a cooperative setting designed to liberalize commerce to their mutual advantage. It is hard to imagine President Obama or President

Clinton paying serious attention to naysayers such as Senator Sherrod Brown (D-OH) or Lou Dobbs, who would have the United States turn its back on the most successful piece of economic architecture since 1945.

Furthermore, Democratic and Republican presidents alike have often pushed the free-trade agenda to buttress their foreign-policy objectives. Foreign policy was a core reason why President Harry Truman supported the GATT in the late 1940s in the face of opposition from leading Republicans, notably Senator Robert Taft (R-OH and intellectual godfather of the aforementioned Senator Sherrod Brown). Truman wanted to banish the specter of American isolationism in the Great Depression and forge an enduring transatlantic alliance. More recently, trade agreements have changed the political tenor with partners as varied as our immediate neighbors to the north and south, and China, our potential peer to the east.

Foreign-policy logic has thus informed many of the U.S. trade-policy choices that find expression in free-trade agreements (FTAs), beginning with Israel (1958), then Canada (1989) and Mexico (1994), and more recently Jordan (2000), Chile (2004), Australia (2004), Bahrain (2004), Morocco (2004) and Peru (2007). In each of these cases, the goal was to strengthen political relations as well as boost two-way trade and investment. Likewise, the two FTAs now awaiting congressional ratification with South Korea and Colombia are motivated by hopes of cementing alliances—in Asia where U.S.-Korea military ties are gradually supplanted by economic alliances and in South America where the overarching U.S. priorities are to root out terrorism and drug trafficking and establish a bulwark against Venezuela's Hugo Chávez. But FTAs are not just foreign-policy tools; FTA partners now buy more than 42 percent of total U.S. exports.

Our memories of the vital role played by trade diplomacy during the cold war are now fading. Even as we expand our global commerce, and even when rising exports are offsetting economic weakness at home, public support has slipped—both for the WTO and for other parts of the free-trade agenda. Polls suggest that U.S. popular opinion has swung into opposition; NAFTA and China have become metaphors for all that is supposedly wrong with globalization. But, no other tools of foreign policy—from traditional diplomacy to military operations—have the same change-making potential as trade. When properly implemented, in association with market reforms, free trade can lift the lives of hundreds of millions of people.

Still, economists teach that there is no such thing as a free lunch, and this is just as true of free trade as anything else. Dismantling trade barriers almost always entails adjustment costs as workers and firms change their jobs and products. This applies to the United States just like other countries. Moreover, gains are spread widely across the American population while costs are concentrated on older workers in less-dynamic industries (think clothing and auto parts)—a severe political handicap. But serious analysis shows that gains exceed costs by *at least* five to one. In fact, U.S. gains from globalization are so large that Congress could easily afford to quintuple the size of our meager trade-adjustment programs (now under $1 billion a year), in order to cover far-more impacted workers in manufacturing and service industries with much-better transition assistance.

The important point is that free trade is not some sort of "gift" to foreign countries; it pays off for the United States as well, to the tune of $10,000 annually for each American household. U.S. firms and consumers alike benefit from low prices. U.S. companies and their employees gain new access to markets abroad. More efficient U.S. firms thrive and expand, and in this way, trade creates new and higher-paying jobs for American workers.

In the heated Ohio primary, one of the presidential candidates tossed out bogus numbers about "jobs lost" on account of NAFTA (supposedly a million) and trade agreements in general (supposedly millions). The image evoked by these sound bites—huge annual permanent job losses with no offsetting job gains—has no foundation in economics and can best be attributed to poetic license.

The challenge awaiting the next president, in contrast to the current presidential contestants, is to move forward, not backward. NAFTA will be fifteen years old in January 2009, and improvements based on experience would be a tonic for North American relations. Labor provisions could be given sharper teeth; and the North American partners could pioneer sensible measures to address climate change, energy needs and security concerns. If Senator Obama or Senator Clinton should reach the White House, the NAFTA sound bite should be transformed by political alchemy from "opt out" to "upgrade."

Apart from NAFTA, the next president will be faced with multiple challenges outlined by U.S. Trade Representative Susan Schwab. The most important items on the agenda will be a successful conclusion of the Doha Development Round; the ratification of pending free-trade agreements with, namely, South Korea and Panama; and engaging U.S. partners on issues ranging from currency values to climate change. Some features of life in the White House seldom change, and one of them is the essential role of trade policy in international diplomacy.

✘ NO
Fair Trade
JOSEPH E. STIGLITZ

It has become commonplace for politicians of both political parties to trot out rhetoric about how we need free-but-fair trade. Expanding markets through trade liberalization, it is urged, is a win-win situation. How is it, then, that in spite of assertions that *everyone* benefits from trade, there is so much opposition, in both developed and developing countries? Is it that populists have so misled ordinary citizens that, though they are really better-off, they have come to believe they are doing worse?

Or is it because trade liberalization has, in fact, made many people worse off, in developed and developing countries alike? Not only can low-skilled American workers lose their jobs or be paid less, those in developing countries suffer, too. They end up having to take the short end of the stick time and time again in trade agreements because they have little leverage over the big boys. And the links between trade liberalization and growth are far weaker than liberalization advocates claim.

A closer look at both data and standard economic theory provides further insight into the strength of the opposition to trade liberalization. In most countries around the world, there is growing inequality. In the United States, not only is there a steady uptick in poverty, but median household income has been falling for at least eight years. There are many factors contributing to these changes: technology, weakening of social mores, labor unions and, lest we forget, trade liberalization. More than sixty years ago, prominent economists Paul Samuelson and Wolfgang Stolper explained that trade liberalization in high-income countries would lower wages of unskilled workers. The economists showed that even a movement toward free trade brought wages of unskilled workers around the world closer together, meaning, for example, that America's unskilled workers' pay would fall toward that of India and China. Although their model stems from the mid-twentieth century, some of its assumptions hold even more true today. In particular, globalization has greatly reduced disparities in knowledge and technology between the developed and developing world. Lower-paid workers in the developing world now often have the tools, and increasingly, even the education, to perform the same tasks as their counterparts in developed countries. American workers simply get paid more to do the same task. Quite obviously, this can hurt even the higher-paid skilled American worker.

More generally, *standard* economic theory does not say that everyone will be better-off as a result of trade liberalization, only that the winners *could* compensate the losers. They could take a portion of their gains, give it to the losers and *everyone* could be better-off. But, of course, the winners, which in much of America are the very well-off, haven't compensated the losers; indeed, some have been arguing that to compete in the new world of globalization requires cutbacks in government spending, including programs for the poor. The losers then lose doubly.

These results of traditional economic theory are based on assumptions like perfect information, perfect-risk markets, perfect competition and no innovation. But, of course, we do not live in such a perfect world. Modern economic theory has shown that in the imperfect world in which we live, trade liberalization can actually make *everyone* worse off. For instance, trade liberalization may expose individuals and firms to more risk. In the absence of adequate insurance markets, firms respond by shifting production away from high-return risky activities to safer, but lower-return areas, thereby lowering national income.

Careful studies have found, at best, weak links between trade liberalization and growth. Many studies do show that countries that have increased their levels of trade—China is a good example—have grown faster. But these countries did not liberalize in their earlier stages of development. They promoted exports and restricted imports. And this export promotion worked.

A standard argument for reducing tariffs is that it allows resources, especially labor, to move from lower-productivity sectors into higher-productivity ones. But all too often, it results in moving workers from low-productivity employment into zero-productivity unemployment. For example, workers in Jamaica's dairy industry cannot compete with America's highly subsidized milk exports, so when Jamaica liberalized, opening up its markets to these subsidized imports, its dairies were put out of business. But the dairy workers didn't automatically get reemployed elsewhere. Rather, they simply added to the already-high unemployment rolls. In many countries, where there is high unemployment, there is no need to "release" resources to expand exports. There are a variety of impediments to expanding exports—including internal barriers to trade (such as the absence of infrastructure, which highlights the need for aid-for-trade) and, on an even-more-basic level, the absence of capital. Ironically, under today's rules, trade liberalization may again make matters worse. That is because countries are being forced to open up their markets to foreign banks, which are more interested in lending to multinationals and national monopolies than to local small- and medium-sized businesses, the sources of job creation.

WAXING POLITIC

The case for trade liberalization is far weaker than most economists will admit. Those who are more honest fall back on political arguments: it is not that trade liberalization is such a good thing; it is that protectionism is such a bad thing. Inevitably, it is argued, special interests prevail. But in fact, most successful economies have evolved with at least some protection of new industries at critical stages of their development. In recent work, my colleague from Columbia University, Bruce Greenwald, and I have built on that idea by developing an "infant-economy argument" that looks at how using protection as countries grow can encourage the industrial sector—the sector most amenable to learning and technological progress. The benefits of that support then diffuse throughout the economy. Such policies do not require governments to "pick winners," to identify which particular industries are well suited to the country. These policies are based on a recognition that markets do not always work well, particularly when there are externalities, where actions in one part of the economy affect another. That there are huge spillovers from successful innovation is incontrovertible.

Politicians, of course, are not constrained by economics and economic logic. Even if we see in our model that safeguarding nascent sectors is the best way to support economic growth, trade advocates claim, for instance, that trade creates jobs. But exports create jobs; imports destroy them. If one justified trade liberalization on the basis of job creation, one would have to support export expansion but simultaneously advocate import restrictions—these days, typically through nontariff barriers called dumping and countervailing duties. This is the curious position taken by many politicians who *say* they favor free trade. George W. Bush, for instance, while bandying about terms such as free trade and free markets, imposed steel tariffs at a prohibitive level even against desperately poor and tiny Moldova. This in spite of the fact that Moldova was struggling to make the transition from communism to a market economy. American steel producers could not compete and demanded these kinds of tariffs—they couldn't compete, not because of unfair competition from abroad, but rather because of failed management at home. In this case, eventually the World Trade Organization (WTO) ruled against the United States, and this time, the United States complied.

The important point missed by these politicians—and the economists who serve them ill by using such arguments—is that trade is not about job creation. Maintaining the economy at full employment is the responsibility of monetary and fiscal policies. When they fail—as they have now done once again—unemployment increases, *whatever the trade regime*. In reality, trade is about standards of living. And that raises an important question: whose standards of living, exactly?

DOUBLE STANDARDS

In developing countries, there is another set of arguments against the kind of trade liberalization we have today. The so-called free-trade agreements being pushed by the Bush administration are, of course, not free-trade agreements at all. If they were, they would be a few pages long—with each party agreeing to eliminate its tariffs, nontariff barriers and subsidies. In fact, they go on for hundreds of pages. They are *managed*-trade agreements—typically managed for the special interests in the advanced industrial countries (especially those that make large campaign contributions, like the drug industry). The United States keeps its agricultural subsidies, and developing countries are not allowed to impose countervailing duties. And the agreements typically go well beyond trade, including investment agreements and intellectual-property provisions.

These investment agreements do far more than just protect against expropriation. In a perfect show of how all of this is supporting the developed countries while hurting the developing, they may even give American firms operating overseas protections that American firms operating domestically do not have—such as against loss of profits from new regulations. They represent a step backward in creating a rule of law: disputes are adjudicated in processes that fall far short of the standards that we expect of others, let alone of ourselves. Even worse, the ambiguous provisions can put countries in crisis in an impossible bind. They have given rise to large lawsuits, forcing developing countries to pay out hundreds of millions of dollars. In a particularly egregious example, Indonesia was forced to pay compensation for profits lost when it abrogated an almost-surely corrupt contract that then-President Suharto signed. Even though the abrogation of the agreement took place when Indonesia was falling into crisis and receiving support from the International Monetary Fund, the country was still held responsible for repayment of *anticipated* profits, which were unconscionably large because of the very corruption that many believe contributed to the country's problems in the first place.

In addition, beyond the terms of the investment agreements, the intellectual-property provisions, too, are onerous on developing countries. In fact, the intellectual-property-rights regime that is being foisted on developing countries is not only bad for developing countries; it is not good for American science and not good for global science. What separates developed from less-developed countries is not only a gap in resources but a gap in knowledge. The intellectual-property provisions reduce access to knowledge, making it more difficult to close the knowledge gap. And even beyond their impact on development, the provisions make it more difficult for developing countries to gain access to lifesaving medicines by making it harder for them to obtain generic drugs, which sell for a fraction of the price of the brand-name ones. The poor simply cannot afford brand-name prices. And because they cannot afford these prices, thousands will needlessly die. At the same time, while the drug companies demand these high prices, they spend little on the diseases that afflict the poor. This is hardly surprising: the drug companies focus on profits; one of the problems of being poor is that you have no money—including no money to buy drugs. Meanwhile, the drug companies have been reluctant to compensate the developing countries adequately for the genetic material that they obtain from them that often provides the basis of new drugs; and the intellectual-property regimes almost never provide any protection for developing countries' traditional knowledge, giving rise to worries about biopiracy. The United States, for instance, granted patents for basmati rice (which had been consumed in India for generations), for the healing properties of turmeric and for many uses of neem oil. Had India recognized and enforced these patents, it would have meant, for instance, that every time an Indian had eaten his traditional staple basmati rice, or used turmeric for healing an ailment, he would have had to send a check to the United States in payment of royalties.

Recent bilateral trade agreements are, of course, even worse in many respects than the earlier multilateral ones: how could one expect a developing country to have much bargaining power when negotiating with the United States? As several trade negotiators have told me bluntly, the United States demands, and they either take it or leave it. The United States says, if we make a concession for you, we would have to make it for everyone. In addition, not only does the array of bilateral and regional agreements undermine the multilateral trading system, but it also weakens market economics, as countries must look not for the cheapest inputs, but for the cheapest inputs satisfying the rules of origin. A Mexican apparel firm might be able to produce shirts more cheaply using Chinese buttons, but if he turns to the lowest-cost provider, his shirt will no longer be considered sufficiently "Mexican" to warrant duty-free access to the United States. Thus, the bilateral trade agreements actually impede global trade.

In both the multilateral and bilateral agreements, there has been more of a focus on liberalization and protection of capital than of labor; the asymmetry alters the bargaining power of labor versus capital because firms threaten that if the workers don't accept wage cuts, they will move elsewhere, contributing to the growing inequality around the world.

The cards are stacked against the developing countries in other ways as well. The WTO was a step in the right direction, creating an international rule of law in trade; even an unfair rule of law may be better than no rule of law at all, where the big countries can use their economic muscle without constraints. But the legal process is expensive, and this puts poor countries at a disadvantage. And even when they win, there is little assurance of compliance. Antigua won a big case against the United States, but has no effective way of enforcing its victory. The WTO has ruled that American cotton subsidies are illegal, yet the United States continues to provide them—twenty-five thousand rich American farmers benefit at the expense of millions of very poor people in the developing world. It is America's and Europe's refusal to do anything about their agricultural subsidies, more than anything else, that has stalled the so-called Doha Development Round.

But even in its conception, the Doha Development Round was a development round in name only; it was an attempt by the developed countries to put old wine into new bottles while hoping the developing countries wouldn't notice. But they did. A true development round—a trade regime that would promote development—would look markedly different.[1] It would, for instance, allow freer movement of labor—the global gains from labor-market liberalization are in fact much greater than from the liberalization of capital. It would eliminate agricultural subsidies.

It would reduce the nontariff barriers, which have taken on increasing importance as tariff barriers have come down. What the trade ministers from the advanced industrial countries are trying to sell as a development round looks nothing like what a true development round would look like.

TRADE AGREEMENTS AND AMERICA'S NATIONAL INTEREST

The gap between American free-trade rhetoric and the unfair managed-trade reality is easily exploited by the critics of markets and of America. It provides an all-too-easy target. In some countries, America's trade agreements have helped promote democracy: citizens have been so aroused by America's unfair bilateral trade agreements that they have activated civil society, uniting disparate groups to work in unison to protest against the United States. The reason we wanted a trade agreement with Morocco was not because of the importance of our trade relations but because we wanted to build better relations with a moderate Arab country. Yet, by the time the U.S. trade representative put forth his largely nonnegotiable demands, the country had seen its largest street protests in years. If building good-will was the intent of this and other trade agreements, the effect has been, at least in many cases, just the opposite.

None of this is inevitable. We could easily manage trade liberalization in a way in which there are more winners and fewer losers. But it is not automatic, and it is not easy. We have to devise better ways of safeguarding the losers—we need social protections, not protectionism. To take but one example: America is one of the few advanced industrial countries where there is reliance on employment-related health insurance, and it has, at the same time, a poor unemployment-insurance system. A worker who loses his job, whether as a result of foreign competition or technological change, loses his health insurance; and the paltry sums he gets in unemployment insurance make private purchase unaffordable for most. It is understandable why Americans are worried about losing their jobs as the economy slips into recession. But with most Americans today worse off than they were eight years ago, this recession is beginning even before fully recovering from the last; Americans are seeing their life savings being wiped away by the ever-declining price of housing (their one and only asset). It provides these Americans little comfort to know that someone making more than $100,000 a year, who has just gotten big tax breaks in 2001 and again in 2003, may be better-off as a result of trade liberalization. Vague promises that in the long run they, too, will be better-off provide little comfort—as Keynes quipped, "in the long run we are all dead." The median American male in his thirties has a lower income today than his counterpart thirty years ago. Trade may not have been the only reason for the decline, or even the most important one, but it has been part of the story. Individuals can't do anything about technology; they can do something about trade. If there are benefits from trade and the winners want to sustain support for trade liberalization, they must be willing to share more of the gains with the losers.

If more developing countries are to benefit more from trade liberalization, we need a fairer trade regime; and if more people are to benefit from trade liberalization, we need to manage trade liberalization better. The United States should move toward a more comprehensive agenda for fairer trade and better-managed trade liberalization.[2] This agenda will ensure that the fruits of trade are shared by both the poor and the rich, in both the developing and developed countries. Without it, we should not be surprised about the backlash we are seeing, both in the United States and abroad.

NOTES

1. In my book with Andrew Charlton, *Fair Trade for All* (Cambridge: Oxford University Press, 2005), we describe in more detail what this regime would look like.

2. I explain this agenda further in my book *Making Globalization Work* (New York: W. W. Norton, 2006).

POSTSCRIPT

The above debate highlights the importance of language and the importance of understanding what is meant by a term. Stiglitz points out that those who often use the term "free trade" are often referring to something that in practice is something different than free trade. Often "free trade agreements," he notes, contain additional barriers to trade rather than meaning a reduction of all barriers to trade. Hence, he advocates instead for what he calls "fair trade."

Fair trade can also have different connotations. Here, Stiglitz discusses changes to the international trading regime that is fairer to all trading partners. The term has also come to refer to a social movement that seeks to establish alternative trade channels by which developing country producers can receive fairer wages for their produce. While still campaigning for changes in the rules and practice of conventional international trade regimes, the fair trade movement focuses on developing trading partnerships with non-governmental organizations or providing certification that a product has been fairly traded. A perspective on this approach to fair trade can be found in Laure Waridel, *Coffee with Pleasure: Just Java and World Trade* (Montreal: Black Rose Books, 2002).

Suggested Additional Readings

Bakan, Joel. *The Corporation: The Pathological Pursuit of Profit and Power.* Toronto: Penguin Canada, 2004.

Bello, Walden. *The Future in the Balance: Essays on Globalization and Resistance.* San Francisco: Food First and Focus on the Global South, 2001.

Birdsall, Nancy. "Life Is Unfair: Inequality in the World." *Foreign Policy* 111 (Summer 1998): 76–93.

Brecher, Jeremy, and Tim Costello. *Global Village or Global Pillage: Economic Reconstruction from the Bottom Up.* New York: South End Press, 1994.

Deaton, Angus. "Is World Poverty Falling?" *Finance & Development* 39, no. 2 (June 2002): 4–7.

Friedman, Thomas L. *The Lexus and the Olive Tree.* New York: Farrar, Straus and Giroux, 1999.

Grieder, William. *One World, Ready or Not—The Manic Logical of Global Capitalism.* New York: Simon and Schuster, 1997.

Martin, Hans-Peter, and H. Schumann. *The Global Trap: Globalization and the Assault on Prosperity and Democracy.* London: Zed Books, 1997.

Scott, Bruce R. "The Great Divide in the Global Village." *Foreign Affairs* 80, no. 1 (January–February 2001): 160–77.

Stiglitz, Joseph. *Making Globalization Work.* New York: W.W. Norton, 2006.

Stiglitz, Joseph, and Andrew Charlton. *Fair Trade for All.* Cambridge: Oxford University Press, 2005.

InfoTrac® College Edition

Search for the following articles in the InfoTrac® database:

Amann, Edmund, and Werner Baer. "Neoliberalism and Its Consequences in Brazil." *Journal of Latin American Studies* 34, no. 4 (November 2002): 945-59.

Bachelet, Michelle. "For Global Progress, Focus on Fair Trade." *Christian Science Monitor* 9 (January 2006): 9.

"Globalization and Inequality: A Norwegian Report." *Population and Development Review* 26, no. 4 (December 2000): 843.

Miles, Mark A. "Trade and Justice." *Harvard International Review* 28, no. 2 (Summer 2006): 78-79.

Nuruzzaman, Mohammed. "Economic Liberalization and Poverty in the Developing Countries." *Journal of Contemporary Asia* 35, 1 (March 2005): 109-19.

Web Resources

For current URLs for the following websites, visit www.crosscurrents.nelson.com.

ELDIS

http://www.eldis.org

This "gateway to development information" hosted by the Institute of Development Studies (at the University of Sussex) provides access to an extensive range of materials relating to trade, development, and globalization. Look for its useful research subject guides, including one on globalization.

RÓBINSON ROJAS ARCHIVE

http://www.rrojasdatabank.org/dev3000.htm

The Róbinson Rojas website archives a large collection of material on various aspects of globalization and international political economy.

GLOBALISATION GUIDE

http://www.globalisationguide.org

The site poses a number of questions that relate to the relationship between global poverty, trade liberalization, and globalization. It also contains numerous links and other resources.

POVERTY, INEQUALITY, AND GLOBALIZATION
http://are.berkeley.edu/~harrison/globalpoverty

This website, maintained by Professor Ann E. Harrison at the University of Berkeley, offers an extensive collection of papers and lectures on the relationship of globalization and poverty. It is a good starting point for research on globalization and poverty.

CENTER FOR TRADE POLICY STUDIES/CATO INSTITUTE
http://www.freetrade.org/

The CATO Institute promotes a libertarian perspective on a variety of issues. Its Center for Trade Policy Studies provides a variety of materials advocating for the pursuit of greater free trade.

Has Globalization Been Detrimental to Women?

✔ **YES**
NAIEROSSADAT DANESHVAR HOSSEINI, "Globalization and Women: Challenges and Opportunities," *International Business & Economics Research Journal* 5, 3 (March 2006): 35–40

✗ **NO**
JAGDISH N. BAGHWATI, "Women: Harmed or Helped?" In *In defense of Globalization,* Oxford: Oxford University Press, 2004: 73–91

As the forces of globalization have intensified in recent decades, so too has the debate regarding the positive and negative impacts of these changes. One central question is the impact that globalization has on the distribution of global wealth and poverty. Authors like Gary Hufbauer in Issue Eight argue that globalization has contributed to increased economic growth and created new opportunities for both rich and poor countries. Greater openness to international trade, investments, and technology has accelerated the pace of economic growth, contributing to a decline in both poverty and inequality. Much of the inequality that continues to exist in the world is the result of flawed domestic policies and failure to take advantage of the opportunities that globalization presents.

In contrast, anti-globalists see globalization as a largely negative and destructive force that is responsible for fostering increased levels of inequality and an overall decline in human welfare. Globalization has largely been a zero-sum game, in which a few have benefited from the changes taking place at the direct expense of the poor. Critics of globalization argue that globalization has produced not only greater inequality between rich and poor nations and within developing countries, but also with industrialized countries as well. While the world boasts a record number of millionaires and billionaires, disparities between high- and low-income groups continue to grow.

Even the defenders of globalization are concerned about the danger posed by increasing levels of inequality. As inequality increases, nations may be tempted to adopt protectionist measures and seek to disengage from the global economy. Growing economic inequalities can contribute to environment degradation and the spread of infectious diseases, as poor populations have inadequate social and health facilities or engage in survival strategies that damage the local ecology.

The process of democratization may be slowed down in many countries, as the poor withdraw from political participation as their access to education, health care, and other services diminish.

An important element of the debate on globalization is its impact specifically on women and on the attempts to promote gender equality. The United Nations has committed itself to improving the status of women worldwide. In 1979, the General Assembly of the United Nations adopted the Convention on the Elimination of All Forms of Discrimination against Women (CEDAW). The Convention vowed to guarantee women equal rights with men in all spheres of life, not only in the exercise of political rights but also in the areas education, employment, and health care. In 1985, as part of the its "Decade for Women," the United Nations adopted the Nairobi Forward-Looking Strategies for the Advancement of Women with the aim of achievement of full women's equality by the year 2000. Ten years later, the Fourth World Conference on Women was held in Beijing to examine the progress that had been made. As a result, the Conference issued the Beijing Platform for Action which hoped to reinvigorate the international community's commitment to gender equality. And when the UN adopted its Millennium Development Goals in 2000, it placed important priority on gender equality and the empowerment of women. As part of the Millennium Goals, the United Nations committed itself to monitoring the various indicators of gender equality such as female school enrollment, participation in the workplace, and representation in political institutions.

Defenders of globalization have suggested that the changes taking place in association with globalization have contributed to greater gender equality. The gender gap in areas such a political participation, education, and health care are lowest in countries that have integrated into the global economy. Countries that remain the least globalized also tend to have much higher levels of inequality. In cases where women may have experienced discrimination under traditional, patriarchal divisions of labour, globalization has created new opportunities and has had a liberating, equalizing effect.

However, others fear that globalization has only served to exacerbate gender inequality. As the forces of globalization have marched forward, women particularly in the poorer countries are often marginalized in unpaid or informal labour sectors, forced to work in low-wage sweatshops, and excluded from political decision-making.

In the following readings, we find two quite different perspectives on this debate. First, Naierossadat Daneshvar Hosseini, an Iranian economist, outlines what she sees as the negative impact of globalization and the struggle for equality. In response, one of the prominent defenders of globalization, Jagdish N. Baghwati, argues that when all the factors are taken into account, globalization is more likely to benefit women than harm them.

✔ YES

Globalization and Women: Challenges and Opportunities
NAIEROSSADAT DANESHVAR HOSSEINI

INTRODUCTION

While one interpretation of globalization has to do with equal exchange and sharing of goods and services between countries and cultures, the reality of a globalized world is much different. Globalization is a phenomenon that crosses and erases geographical and political borders and makes all countries start to look the same. As a result of globalization, local products, services, and cultures disappear into a global culture, a culture defined not by the global citizenry but rather the world's economic and political superpowers—mostly North America-owned corporations. Because of globalization, people on every continent are exposed to and consumed by a North American culture defined by Nike running shoes, MTV, Coca-Cola, and McDonald's. Some people have re-named the process of globalization and called it McDonaldization or CocaColonization.

WOMEN AND GLOBALIZATION

The issue of women and globalization is one that concerns all mankind: men and women. The subject of globalization and its impact on women has been of considerable interest in most countries. Tackling this question reveals that two views are existent. The first considers that globalization has been a source of more pressures and responsibilities on women, while the second views globalization as a source of several advantages for women. In fact, both trends are bearing non-negligible traits of reality. The primary results of studies on globalization and women reveal two divert directions:

The first believes that globalization will inflict more pressure and responsibilities on women, while others believe that there are many positives or advantages for women. In the political field, some studies concluded that women's political role will be marginalized in developing countries; on the contrary, others conclude that political participation of women will be increased and that women issues will be in the center of human rights issues. As for the economic side, women will be excluded from the market because of their lack of skills and experience; and because of strong competition women will be marginalized and impoverished. On the contrary in western countries, where women have more experience and qualifications, they are expected to have more opportunities to compete in the market. Some social studies empathize that the role of women in raising children will shrink causing family system to break down. Other social studies come to the opposite conclusion.

GLOBALIZATION, CULTURE, AND GENDER INEQUALITY

In regards to culture, there are three main issues concerning women and globalization. The first concerns the relationship between the particularity of the national culture and the international thought, because of the growing international concern of women's issues and which dealt with this relationship and the different national identities. There is a contradiction between the two extremes: some consider international thought and culture as a form of alienation; others look at the cultural identity as a form of self-inclusion. This contradiction is considered one of the wide gaps that need to be overcome and reconciled. The second issue is how to encourage the moderate and open-minded elucidation of the religious scripts. It is important to find continuous motives and incentives for religious interpretations in women issues. The third issue is the relationship between the future perspective of women's issues within the framework of globalization and the process of modernization of the society in a comprehensive way.

In some countries, globalization has resulted in serious gender imbalances. The extent of this imbalance depends largely on the level of gender equality prevailing in the norms, institutions, and policies of a country at the time when integration into the global economy takes place. In addition, women from different social groups in a particular country are affected differently. Nevertheless, in many developing countries deep-rooted and long-standing gender inequalities have meant that the social cost of globalization has fallen disproportionately on women.

There is a growing body of evidence illustrating the ways in which substantial a number of women have been adversely affected by globalization, both absolutely as well as in relation to men. For instance, trade liberalization has often allowed the import of subsidized agricultural products and consumer goods that have wiped out the livelihoods of women producers. The increased entry of foreign firms has often had a similar effect through, for example, displacing farming women from their land or out-competing them for raw materials essential to their productive activities. At the same time, women producers face formidable barriers to entry into new economic activities generated by globalization. This is often because of biases, either against women directly or against the micro- and small enterprise sector in which they predominate, in the policy and regulatory environment.

WOMEN AND CONSUMPTION PATTERNS

Another negative impact of globalization is spreading the culture of consumer entertainment through television, films, and advertisements, which serves big companies while destroying domestic social values and traditions. Globalization changes the consumption patterns of the family life and creates a tendency for unilateral consumption pattern. The problem of unlimited consumption is a problem facing households all over the world. Therefore, the question is how can we rationalize the consumption behaviour of the household. Since unlimited consumption will deprive the next generations from their rights in consumption, women can play a very important role in the rationalization of consumption as they are responsible for household expenditure and budget, but of course women alone can not do this. This emphasizes the importance of the role of all sectors of the state to help women rationalize domestic consumption.

WOMEN IN AGRICULTURAL SECTOR

Economic globalization—the process of opening up regional markets for global consumption—has played a major role in the transformation of agriculture from family gardens to a huge industry characterized by agribusinesses. Commercialized agriculture relies just as heavily on the work of women as did the family farm. "Women are cogs in the machine of a globalized agriculture industry: picking tomatoes in Mexico, harvesting rice in India, planting tea in Uganda, packing peaches in Ontario and fish in Nova Scotia. But while women still play a role in agricultural production, women's control over the means of food production has been significantly weakened. The forced migration, environmental contamination, and hunger that have resulted from this transformation, have been devastating."[1] Globalization has also severely impacted women's relationship to food and the production of food. The liberalization of trade and the subsequent global spread of a market economy in which inequalities between countries have become greater, has forced many impoverished countries to stop growing food for themselves in favour of growing food for export. As mentioned this has led to greater food insecurity, reduced nutrition, and has moved women in exporting countries into low-paying, undervalued agricultural work.

WOMEN IN INDUSTRIAL SECTOR

The increase of industrial exports in developing countries was accompanied by an increase in the demand for female employment, because industrialization under the present international conditions in the developing countries depended on female labour. Therefore, the new female employment opportunities depended on the expansion of industrial export. The participation of women in the industrial sector was much higher than on the national level in the formal sectors, and in the industrial sector female employment was concentrated in the export sector. Empirical evidence proved that industrialization in low income countries depended on women, just like export production; and that the increase in the income of many women is due to the expansion of trade. The expansion of export industries was the main reason for women to enter the market economy. For example, the number of the fabric factories in Bangladesh increased from four factories in 1978 to 2400 factories in 1995, with 1.2 million workers, 90% of them women under the age of 25. Many other countries share the same experience such as Indonesia, Tunisia, and Taiwan to name a few.

WOMEN IN THE SERVICE SECTOR

The service sector offers regular paid contract jobs to women more than any other sector. This increases women's employment opportunities, which is strongly connected to their contribution to family expenses especially for education and health of their children. Women's income support the creation of new human resources and raises the level of human development.

The service sector is considered one of the strongest sectors at the present time, as it clearly expanded very rapidly to the extent that it is getting more similar to the progress achieved by the industrial sector, specially in the field of communication and information technology. The service sector includes many activities, starting from domestic services and small trade, government administration, social service sector (education and health), and project services (accounting, counseling services, law and information processing). This sector is considered the largest sector of all the economic sectors in terms of its output, and the employment opportunities which it provides in many countries. Working in the service sector especially small businesses is considered the most important income source for poor women.

Modern information and communication technology, especially the Internet, and the growing trans-continental employment opportunities brought about many new opportunities for women. However women who will benefit from these advantages are mostly those who are well educated and who belong to high-income classes, while women who are not well educated or are illiterate are marginalized, usually these are over 35 years old and are working in sectors which suffer from declining demand.

Although technology is increasing the number of women working in the information and communication sector, and the wide rapid development of this technology in all possible languages, mean that poor people specially women in developing countries face the danger of being left out of production or knowledge and information exchange, and in many other aspects of life.

A negative impact is the very limited employment opportunities that this sector offers to poor women who are not educated, compared to those offered by the industrial and the agricultural sectors. On the other hand, the picture is different, if we focus on the gender gap in earnings in open semi-industrialized economies. Economic growth was higher where the gender gap in earnings was higher. This shows that various forms of growth do not diminish gender gaps in the labour market, even though the absolute incomes of women may increase. Again in open economies where capital is highly mobile, policies that successfully promote greater autonomy for women can lead to an increase in national income; but those that increase women's bargaining power in the workplace can have a negative impact on national output if the response of capital is to move to other locations.

The International Monetary Fund and the World Bank encourage developing countries to use export-led growth to expand their economies. Such globalized economies require a labour force of a size that must include women, but women's employment varies greatly by region. For example, 74 percent of women are in the work force in East Asia, the greatest proportion among all regions of the world, and they participate for the longest part of their lives in comparison to other regions. In the Middle East and North Africa, however, only about 34 percent participate, while women in the Middle East drop out of the labour force in great numbers when they marry and have children. In many cases, cultural barriers, especially in the relationship between women and men within households, impede increased economic participation, or undermine the quality of that participation. For example, even women who do work face differential treatment such as wage gaps and segregation into traditionally female industries. Women have historically borne the burden of non-monetized labour, such as child care and domestic work. Increased participation in the work force also implies increased hazards for women, however. Women's jobs outside the home tend to be the worst compensated, least secure, and most dangerous available in the economy, especially in periods of recession in most developing countries. For example, gaps in labour laws, or ignorance and lack of enforcement of the labour codes in practice allow for the exploitation of women. Women have only a precarious claim on the rights to minimum wage, work-week length, leave time, health care under the national social security system, and privacy protections. Often, they are subject to physical and/or sexual abuse, according to **Human Rights Watch**. Unfortunately, even the global nature of business does not confer universal rights for these women.

WOMEN IN INFORMAL SECTOR

In most developing countries there is a large informal economy, where economic activity lacks recognition and protection under formal legal or regulatory frameworks. It typically consists of small-scale manufacturing, services or vending in urban areas, domestic work or agricultural work on small plots of land. In many of the lowest-income countries it accounts for the large majority of workers. There is often a high proportion of women workers. This work is very diverse, from small enterprises to survival activities, including not only the self-employed and family workers but also wage labour in many forms. Typically such activities are of low productivity, and poverty levels among informal workers are high. But there is also a large reservoir of entrepreneurship and innovation. Informal work is less prominent in industrialized countries, but by no means absent, and includes the informalization of previously secure wage employment.

At the Lisbon European Council in March 2000, the European Union set itself a new strategic goal for the next decade: to become the most competitive and dynamic knowledge-based economy in the world, capable of sustainable economic growth with more and better jobs and greater social cohesion. The goal must be to make these informal activities part of a growing formal sector that provides decent jobs, incomes and protection, and can trade in the international system. This will be an essential part of national strategy to reduce poverty. That means increasing assets and productivity, appropriate regulatory frameworks, raising skills and ensuring that policy biases are removed. Policies to deal with the lack of recognition of qualifications and skills, and the exclusion of informal workers from social security and other protections are particularly important. The same are policies to improve the distribution of assets, and especially to increase access for self-employed women and men and small businesses to financial resources, technology and markets, and to increase opportunities for investment. But most workers and economic units in the informal economy have difficulty accessing the legal and judicial system to enforce contracts, and their access to public infrastructure and benefits is limited. A variety of bureaucratic and other restrictions create barriers and difficulties which hinder formalization, growth and sustainability.

The relation between both formal and informal sectors is explained by the fact that small workshops produce production inputs to the big factories. The scope of this cooperation and integration is very difficult to evaluate as it varies from time to time and from one industry to another and from one season to another. Many argue that in the process of globalization demand for female employment has increased in the informal sector, through subcontracts with the formal sector. The role and importance of the informal sector in economic activity has increased in the developing countries especially for women; however, a high ratio of these women are working without any contracts.

WOMEN AND FLEXIBILITY AT WORK

While flexibility can be attractive for workers when it meets the needs desire of the workers, but in reality this flexibility does not benefit women workers because it has created an environment of part-time work, sub contracting, temporary, and casual employment. These forms of work are increasing in industrialized countries and although they affect both men and women, it is substantially women who are employed in this insecure sector. Far from legislating to protect workers from such insecurity, some governments have actually encouraged this type of flexibility as being good for industry. This requirement for flexibility also extends to working hours where in practice it means that women are often required to meet unreasonable attendance schedules at short notice.

CONCLUSION

Globalization offers women unprecedented opportunities, but equally new and unique challenges. Gender inequality exacerbated by the effects of globalization. The paper argues that globalization creates many challenges for women in different economic sectors and a substantial number of women have been adversely affected by globalization, both absolutely as well as in relation to men. Women have additional vulnerabilities, especially malnutrition, sexually transmitted diseases, pregnancy complications, domestic violence, sexual abuse. In many cultures, women are the first to take care of the vulnerable, sick, and dying and the last to receive preventative or life saving treatment. In order to alleviate these problems, public education programs can promote healthy lifestyles, eliminate gender discrimination, access to services, and prioritize the help for women.

The paper argues that for many women, globalization has resulted in an improvement in their economic and social status. Many women workers have been absorbed in to the global production system and the wage employment gives them higher incomes than their previous situations and also gave them a greater potential economic independence and often raises social status. Progress toward eliminating gender inequality in the future depends on finding and embracing the occasions, mostly in the political and legal realm, where the global approach strengthens women's security and welfare, and fighting the issues, mostly in the economic realm, where women are made worse off by the new global system. This paper concludes that the new global system has not been to the benefit of the women. The negative impact of globalization particularly in terms of gender inequality is much more than its positive impacts.

NOTE

1. From the Women & the Economy Website: www.unpac.ca/economy/index2.html

REFERENCES

Allmendinger, J. (1989): Educational system and labour market outcomes. *European Sociological Review* 3. 231–250.

Brown, T. (1999). Challenging globalization as discourse and phenomenon. *International Journal of Lifelong Education*, 18(1), 3–17.

European Commission (2001), Employment in *Europe Report*, European Commission, Brussels, Belgium, http://europa.eu.int/comm/dgs/employment_social/pub_en.htm

ILO (2001), *World Employment Report*, International Labour Office, Geneva, Switzerland, www.ilo.org

ILO (2001) *Decent Work for Women*, Bureau for Gender Equality Breaking through the glass ceiling, International Labour Office, Geneva, Switzerland, www.ilo.org/public/english/bureau/gender

National Council for Women (2001), *Women and Globalization* Seminar, Cairo, May 2001.

Scott, Catherine V. (1995), *Gender and Development*. Boulder, Colorado: Lynne Rienner.

UNDP (1999), *Human Development Report*, 1 New York, Oxford University Press.

UNDP (2001), *Human Development Report*, United Nations Development Program, New York, USA, www.undp.org

UNI (2001), *UNI for People in the Changing Economy*, Union Network International (UNI), Nyon, Switzerland, www.union-network.org

UNIFEM (2000), *Progress of The World's Women*, UNIFEM Biennial Report. Dianne Elson, Coordinator. New York.

UNCTAD (1999), *Trade, Sustainable Development and Gender*. UN, New York and Geneva, 1999.

World Bank (2001), *Gender and the Digital Divide*, The World Bank Group, Gender and the Digital Divide Seminar Series, www.worldbank.org/gender/info/digitaldivide

✗ NO
Women: Harmed or Helped?
JAGDISH N. BAGHWATI

[. . .] GLOBALIZATION HELPS WOMEN: TWO EXAMPLES

One can go around the world and find discrimination against women. It arises at several levels and in different ways. Gender studies has brought this pervasive phenomenon to center stage. [. . .] my focus here is not on the documentation of this phenomenon or its explanation. Rather, it is on the central question: has globalization accentuated, or has it been corrosive of, the discriminations against women that many of us deplore and wish to destroy?

Japanese Multinationals Going Abroad

That globalization can help rather than harm women emerges dramatically when one examines how globalization has affected the women of Japan. In the aftermath of the great outward expansion of Japan's multi-nationals in the 1980s and early 1990s, Japanese men executives were sent to the United States, England, France, and other Western nations (Japanese women then rarely made it through a very low glass ceiling). These men brought with them their Japanese wives and children. In New York, they lived in Scarsdale, Riverdale, and Manhattan. And the wives saw at first hand that Western women, though they have some way to go, were treated better. So did the young children become not docile Japanese who are taught the value of social conformity and harmony but rambunctious little Americans who value instead the individualism that every immigrant parent confronts when the children return home from school and say, "That is the way *I* want to do it." Schools are where cultural conditioning occurs subliminally, even explicitly. The women and children who then returned to Japan became agents for change. They would never be the same again.

Feminism, women's rights, other human rights, due process for citizens and immigrants, and a host of other attributes of a modern society began slowly to replace the traditional ways of Japanese culture, and globalization in the shape of Japanese corporations' expansion abroad had played a critical role.

That influence has also come, of course, from other (non-economic) forms of globalization such as the vast increase in Japanese students in Western universities in recent years. [. . .] As they returned to Japan [. . .] they brought American responses to the increasing trade feuds with the United States. Thus, when the Hosokawa-Clinton summit in Washington failed in 1993, the Japanese prime minister's staff essentially said, "If you object to our trade practices, see you in court!" But President Clinton's staff thought we could still deal with the Japanese in the old ways, through bilateral confrontations and deals. As I explained in an article in *Foreign Affairs* at the time, we thought we were fighting the samurai, but we were fighting GIs.[1]

Price and Prejudice: Trade and the Wage Gender Gap

But the favorable effect on women's issues in Japan because of globalization in the form of extensive outward flow of Japanese multinationals to the West is not the only example one can find. My favorite example is the study of globalization in trade on the gender wage gap between 1976 and 1993 in the United States by the economists Sandra Black and Elizabeth Brainerd.[2]

Such wage discrimination can be explained in alternative ways. One persuasive theory, due to the Nobel laureate Gary Becker, is that men are paid more than women by employers, even though they have no greater merit and productivity within the firm, simply because of prejudice.[3] But this prejudice has its price: any firm that indulges it is going to be at a competitive disadvantage vis-à-vis firms that hire without this prejudice and pay men no more than they pay women.

Now, if we have a closed economy and all domestic firms share this prejudice, it will not make any one firm less competitive: all firms will be equally handicapped. But when we introduce foreign competition, the foreign firms that do not share this prejudice will be able to gain in competitiveness over domestic firms that indulge the prejudice. Liberalized trade, which enables foreign firms to compete with the domestic firms in open markets, therefore puts pressure on domestic firms to shed their prejudice. The gender wage gap will then narrow in the industries that must compete with imports produced by unprejudiced firms elsewhere.

But consider a related but different and more potent argument. If markets open to trade, competition will intensify, whatever the reason that enables foreign firms to compete with our firms in our domestic and international markets. Faced with increased competition, firms that were happy to indulge their prejudice will now find that survival requires that any and all fat be removed from the firm; cost cutting will mean that the price paid for prejudice will become unaffordable. Again, the gender wage gap will narrow.

The remarkable thing is that Black and Brainerd find that this did actually happen, confirming the predictive power of sophisticated economic reasoning. Firms in the United States that had been subject to relatively less competitive pressure but which then experienced competitive pressure due to openness to trade showed a more rapid reduction in their gender wage gap.

WOMEN'S FEARS

Yet some influential women's groups and prominent feminist scholars have expressed fears concerning the impact of globalization on their agendas and interests, among them the following.

Global Care Chains

Consider the recent argument, which has gained some currency, by the sociologist Arlie Russell Hochschild regarding the so-called global care chains and their deleterious effect on women.[4] These refer to the phenomenon where women migrants from poor countries have children who are being looked after by girl siblings, grandmothers, or other female relatives while the migrants, as maids and nannies, look after the children of women in the cities of the rich countries. Hochschild argues that this global care chain puts all women at every point in the chain at a disadvantage.

Why? For the migrant women: "Studies suggest that migrants . . . remain attached to the homes and people they leave. . . . Indeed, most of the migrant workers . . . interviewed talked of going back but, in the end, it was their wages that went home while they themselves stayed on in the USA and Italy. Many of the migrants . . . seemed to develop a 'hypothetical self'—the idea of the person they would be if only they were back home. About their own motherhood they seemed to feel two ways: on one hand, being a 'good mother' was earning money for the family, and they were used to a culture of shared mothering with kith and kin at home; at the same time, they felt that being a good mother required them to be with their children and not away from them." Being in a care chain, the author concludes, is "a brave odyssey . . . with deep costs."[5]

Regarding the children back home, the phenomenon was also considered distressing, with the migrants' affections "diverted to their young charges" away from "their own young." Hochschild quotes Sauling Wong as lamenting that "mothers are diverted from those who, by kinship or communal ties, are their more rightful recipients." Moreover, in socio-logical and psychological terms, the care chain raised added questions: "Can attention, solicitude and love be 'displaced' from, say, [the migrant] Vicky Diaz's son Alfredo, onto, say, Tommy, the son of her employers in Los Angeles? And is the direction of displacement upwards in privilege and power?"[6]

But even if these sentiments had emerged from a proper sample rather than from interviews of not necessarily representative migrants, they would have to confront the fact that as long as the choice to migrate had been made voluntarily, the psychic costs—and possibly gains, as in the case of our own maid of many years from Haiti, who escaped from an abusive husband—were outweighed by the psychic and economic gains. It is important to emphasize also the fact of psychic gains that can accrue because the migrating woman enjoys the liberating environment, both economic and social, that working away from her family, in a feudal and male-dominated environment back home, will imply. I have seen it with our maid, who has grown over the years in self-respect and dignity.

Besides, Hochschild seems to transfer to the migrant workers the values of her own culture: the great emphasis on the nuclear family is often alien to the culture of the poor countries with their extended families, as is well known to students of economic development. Children are often close to, and get looked after by, siblings, aunts, and grandmothers; migration or no migration, that is utterly normal even if it is a phenomenon that will pass as economic development takes off. [. . .] The idea of the global care chain as a chain that binds rather than liberates is almost certainly a wrongheaded one. It fits into the preconception that Hochschild seems to be afflicted with regarding economic globalization as well, as when she says:

> The declining value of child-care anywhere in the world can be compared with the declining value of basic food crops, relative to manufactured goods on the international market. Though clearly more necessary to life, crops such as wheat, rice, or cocoa fetch low and declining prices while the prices of manufactured goods (relative to primary goods) continue to soar on the world market. Just as the market price of primary produce keeps the Third World low in the community of nations, so the low market value of care keeps the status of the women who do it—and, by association, all women—low.[7]

I am afraid this is nothing short of gibberish. The assertions about the declining prices of primary products are familiar decades-old assertions that are untrue but keep recurring in uninformed circles. But even concerning child care, on what evidence does she arrive at the notion that it has a declining value? In truth, as women have gone into the workplace, the demand for child care, whether at home or in centers outside the home, has only grown, and the price of such child care has risen. In fact, one sees a shortage of high-quality child care facilities everywhere as women struggle to find them so they can be freed from all-too-explicit and facile charges of child neglect and the guilt that follows from them.

But it is not just the (economic) *price* of child care that has risen, creating a demand in turn for subsidy to child care. The (social) *value* of child care also becomes more manifest as mothers seek it from others instead of providing it themselves freely at home because of their traditional role.

In fact, there is another important consequence to ponder as women have entered the workforce in great numbers. This has meant that the subsidy they were implicitly providing to child care at home is no longer available. So, from a social viewpoint, one can argue that this traditional subsidy now must be replaced by an explicit subsidy to child care if children, who need nurture and care, are to turn into good adults and citizens. This also means that child care's importance, its social value, is now visible, not hidden by the submerged and subsidized provision of it by women confined to the home.

Unpaid Household Work

Women's Edge, which is a leading NGO promoting gender agendas, has registered several complaints, among them: "The economic theories the WTO espouses and the macro-economic policies that the WTO oversees fail to take into account women's unpaid household work (maintaining the household, growing food for the family, caring for children and relatives). . . . The United Nations estimates that if monetized, the value of unpaid women's household work would equal $11 trillion . . . per year."[8]

National income statisticians have long recognized this neglect, and it is not the only non-market activity that has been considered: volunteer work outside the family, whether by women or men, is yet another example. What is unclear, however, is why we should get the WTO to worry about getting national income accounts adjusted for this and other deficiencies!

Does the fact that women often do unpaid work affect the efficiency of resource allocation in an economy? Surely it does. It implies that the true cost of the output, chiefly child rearing, from that unpaid work is being underestimated. Therefore, this output will be overproduced relative to the case where the women were being paid at market wages. But then there is also an offsetting argument suggesting that the output will be underproduced instead. This is because child care and child rearing have socially desirable spillover effects for which the market does not reward women as it should. If the latter argument is weightier than the former, this would provide an argument for subsidizing child care.

Of course, since the participation of women in the workforce is both good in itself, as it provides women with a choice to work in the home or outside, and is also good for us, since it has several economic payoffs such as bringing into play the talents and contributions of a hitherto neglected half of the workforce, there is a further argument for a subsidy to women in the form of child care support.

But these and other implications of women's unpaid work are matters of domestic policy. It defies common sense to attack either the WTO or the freeing of trade for the absence of such policy initiatives by nation-states that are members of the WTO or that are seeking gains from trade by freeing trade. Yet Women's Edge and other groups do make that illogical leap, and others, when they make assertions such as "Trade agreements need to recognize women's competing demands and ensure that women benefit from trade to the same extent that men do."[9] The "same extent"? Can we manage to achieve such parity of results from trade liberalization for any group, whether women, Dalits (India's untouchables), or African-Americans or Hispanics in the United States? Can we manage such equality of outcomes for *any* policy reform? And yet these are assertions by serious groups: Women's Edge *is* at the cutting edge of the women's NGOs.

Other Aspects of Women's Work

Yet another issue these groups raise is that in some traditional societies, women produce crops for home consumption and men produce cash crops. If cash crops expand due to trade liberalization and access to world markets, their argument goes, men will benefit but not women; the women might even be harmed. Consider also the claim that "in sub-Saharan Africa . . . a switch to export-promotion crops . . . has often diverted resources from domestic consumption. Men have controlled the extra cash earned from this strategy and the nutritional status of women and children declined."[10]

But what the author is saying is that intra-family decision making can lead to increased incomes being spent on frills rather than on food. Indeed, it can. But then [. . .] there is a case here not for bypassing the opportunity to bring increased incomes but for social policy to accompany the increased prosperity such that the untoward effects on nutrition and the health of women and children are avoided. A situation where incomes are stagnant, or even undermined by the imposition of costly trade protection and other harmful economic policies, can also put pressure on men to indulge their taste for frills at the expense of the nutritional status and health of their families; I would submit that it is equally likely to do so. It is smarter to have income-enhancing policies go hand in hand with progressive social ones (which will be more likely to emerge and take hold if we empower women by providing them with the economic opportunities that a growing and prosperous economy will create) instead of reducing incomes so that they are divided and spent better for women.

Trade Agreements and the WTO Pursue Trade and Profits, Not Development and Women's Welfare

The National Organization for Women (NOW) and Feminist Majority, the former an important organization that has done notable work to advance women's rights in the domestic sphere in the United States, have argued:

> Current international trade agreements, liker NAFTA, violate the rights of women workers. Women workers in many factories, located in Export Processing Zones (EPZs [zones set aside to attract export-oriented firms]), have reported physical abuse, sexual harassment, and violence, and mandatory pregnancy testing as a condition for employment. Women workers in EPZs are forced to work long hours for extraordinarily low wages in poor working conditions. In Ciudad Juarez, Mexico, over 200 women have been murdered, many of them on their way to and from their work in the EPZs.[11]

But these groups fail to ask: what are the conditions of work in Mexico outside the EPZs? Are not the Mexican unskilled workers suffering yet worse conditions in local, trade-unrelated industries and occupations? Do women enjoy shorter hours of work as they, and men, struggle to survive on the farms and in rural occupations? If two hundred women have been murdered on their way to and from work, is the blame to be assigned to the foreign firms that provide the employment or to the Mexican state that, not just here but through much of Mexico, is unable to provide security to women as they move to and from work? [. . .] In short, what has freer trade got to do with it?

This problem does not exist in a vast majority of EPZs because the young female workers live on campus instead of commuting back to their families at night (and perhaps having to walk through unguarded fields since the buses do not carry them all the way). But where it does, a socially responsible policy toward their employees would be for the larger firms in the EPZs, when the state fails to provide such security to women workers, to take steps, in concert with other large firms, to impress on the host government that the firms' continuing presence in the EPZs will be imperiled if such security is not immediately provided for their workers. Indeed, since the basic safety of its workers has to be part of what a firm must accept as an obligation at the factory level, it must also be regarded as a firm's obligation to ensure their safety in getting to and from work, even if that provision must be made by the host government rather than the firm itself.

Again, Oxfam has argued in its earlier-cited 2002 report on the world trading system that unregulated multinationals are "producing poverty-level wages and severe forms of exploitation, with female workers suffering the worst excesses."[12] Fortunately, the notion that multinationals are the cause of low wages rather than an antidote to them by increasing the demand for labor in the poor countries, or that they exploit workers, male or female, when they actually pay higher wages than the average in alternative occupations, will not stand scrutiny[. . .].[13] So the proposition that female workers "suffer the worst excesses" makes little sense when the excesses themselves are illusory and the bulk of the evidence is to the contrary.

Yet another influential women's group, the International Gender and Trade Network (IGTN) agrees that "trade serves as one of the instruments for achieving the goals that we seek: prosperity, stability, freedom, and gender equality." But then it claims that "there is no guarantee that free trade is the best policy for women" and that "[t]he current WTO trade process is predatory, mercenary and destructive to livelihoods."[14]

In reaching such hard-line conclusions, IGTN makes the standard mistake of assuming that the WTO, and presumably free-traders, sub-scribe to the doctrine that trade is a goal rather than an instrument. Thus they assert: "The current world trade regime poses the wrong questions. Instead of asking what kind of multilateral system maximizes foreign trade and investment opportunities, it should ask what kind of multilateral system best enable[s] the people of our nations to pursue their own social priorities and developmental objectives."[15] But this ignores massive evidence that freeing of trade is pursued because it is argued, on both theoretical and empirical grounds, that it produces prosperity and, [. . .] has a favorable impact on poverty as well. As an economist normally accused of being "the world's foremost free trader," I have always argued for freer trade, not as an objective but rather (in the context of the poor nations such as India, from where I come) as an often powerful weapon in the arsenal of policies that we can deploy to fight poverty. [. . .]

I must add, in all fairness, that IGTN also makes the valid, and important, criticism that the WTO has been corrupted by various lobbies (in the rich countries) into being no longer a pure trade institution: "the WTO does not fundamentally pursue free trade. . . . We believe that it has taken on board non-trade issues. The role of the WTO should be reduced to enable it to deal solely with trade."[16] Indeed, [. . .] the multinationals, chiefly the pharmaceutical and software firms, lobbied successfully to get the United States, and then other rich-country governments, to back the WTO's Agreement on Trade-related Aspects of Intellectual Property Rights, turning the WTO into a royalty collection agency. And now the labor lobbies want to introduce labor standards into the WTO as well, emulating the corporate lobbies. The fact of the matter is that every lobby in the rich world—there are far too few in the poor countries—now wants to capture the WTO and turn it into an institution that advances its own agenda, using the WTO's ability to implement trade sanctions. Ironically, one could view the attempts of women's groups to include the gender agenda and gender-impact preconditions in the WTO as yet one more instance of such an ambition, whose result would be to further cripple with overload the efficiency and objectives of an essentially trade-related institution.

Obsession with Export Processing Zones

A number of women's groups are obsessed with EPZs, seeing them as the brutal face of globalization and, in ways discussed below, as the source of much of the devastation that globalization wreaks on women in the poor countries.

But note first that the EPZs, while they have played a part in the outward-oriented strategy of several countries, are rarely as dominant as critics imagine. Besides, their relative importance in overall exports often diminishes over time because the advantages offered by EPZs gradually become available nationwide. Thus, Taiwan's exports from its three EPZs—at Nantze, at Kaohsiung Harbor, and near Taichung—were no more than 10 percent of her overall exports in the 1960s; by the early 1980s, their share had fallen yet further, to 6 percent. [. . .]

In the case of inward-looking countries, as they begin to gradually shift to an export orientation, the EPZs represent attempts at introducing a set of reformist policies, such as zero tariffs, that cannot be introduced widely because of political obstacles in the country at large. This initial step leads to a steady loosening of the rest of the country through demonstration in the EPZs of the advantages of such a policy reform. The success of the EPZs leads to acceleration of reforms in the rest of the country, which then leads to better performance by the entire country. This is the story of China, where the coastal province of Guangdong turned into a gigantic export platform and then the rest of the country followed, however haltingly.

Next, the preference for young women workers in the EPZs is deplored as a tactic by which employers get pliable, docile, and uncomplaining workers who are unwilling to unionize to improve their wages and working conditions. Besides, the fact that many are let go and are replaced by other young women cripples their *ability* to unionize as well. Typically, Spike Peterson and Anne Runyon argue, "In many countries, women's proportion of formal-sector employment has significantly increased—with women sometimes displacing men—as employers seek the cheapest, most reliable workers. In this case, women are gaining employment, but typically under *conditions that exacerbate worker vulnerabilities and exploitation*" (italics added).[17]

But this critique is not the slam dunk that it seems. For example, the decline in unionization in the United States over nearly a half century is principally due to several trade-unrelated factors.[18] Improvements in minimum wages, the general rise in wages, and governmentally enacted legislation for workplace safety—the OSHA regulations—have reduced the value of unions for many workers. If workers in the EPZs feel that while they may not be doing as well as they would like, these jobs are still better than others they might obtain, their interest in unionizing may be less than compelling. That, rather than the lack of bargaining power because workers are female or temporary or both, could well be the decisive factor.

In some cases, workers who stay longer with firms will be less likely to want to join unions than less permanent workers: the former may have a more cooperative and conciliatory attitude toward their employers than the latter. Moreover, sociological studies of female workers in Central America, for instance, report interviews with women such as "Maria, who has worked for the plant for seventeen years"; "the company for which she works is known for maintaining and rewarding its better and stable workers."[19] It is therefore perhaps an exaggeration to argue that firms in EPZs necessarily see more profit in keeping workers on a short leash. Besides, as Nicholas Kristof and Sheryl WuDunn [. . .] have noted, the young women they interviewed wanted to accumulate money, worked hard and long hours by choice, and returned home by choice.[20]

Evidently, there is a diversity of experiences here. What does seem to emerge persistently from many studies is that the work in the EPZ factories is subject to more discipline and may not be suited to all. Assembly lines, for instance, impose more discipline—one worker off the line for ten minutes can disrupt the work of all during that time—than work that can be done at one's own machine. [. . .]

Thus, in the Taiwan EPZs cited earlier, the women talked of "bells, buzzers, punch-cards, supervisors and strict monetary penalties," but this was necessary because a manager observed that, in electronics, "products are either perfect or useless" and a disciplined labor force mattered. [. . .]

In Bangladesh, there was evidence that "[u]nmarried girls employed in these garment factories [which, in 1995, were employing 1.2 million workers, 90 percent of them female] may endure onerous working conditions, but they also experience pride in their earnings, maintain a higher standard of dress than their unemployed counterparts and, most significantly, develop an identity apart from being a child or wife . . . legitimate income-generating work could transform the nature of girls' adolescent experience. It could provide them with a degree of autonomy, self-respect, and freedom from traditional gender work."[21]

Indeed, this account of the liberating effect of EPZ-offered work to young girls in Bangladesh underlines the necessity of judging EPZs in light of alternatives available in these poor countries. I was impressed particularly by the account by a sociologist of a woman named Eva who had left the free trade zone in the Dominican Republic and now "work[ed] as a housekeeper for a private villa adjoining a hotel complex in La Romana. She left because she could no longer stand the pressure of working in the free trade zone. . . . She earns 1000 pesos every two weeks, and not only cleans, but washes, cooks, and serves dinner when the Dominican family for whom she works or one of their guests is in town. Though she has worked for five years, she receives no paid holidays or social security benefits, *which even free trade zone workers enjoy*" (italics added).[22]

Nonetheless, since unions are not commonplace at all in many EPZs, even when permitted, and often young girls are at work, we do need mechanisms other than the absent unions to ensure that basic safety (extending to protections against rape and sexual harassment) and related health regulations are put in place by the governments and enforced. If unions believe that temporary workers lack bargaining power, then simply having a union is not going to change that bargaining power: unions without bargaining power would be paper tigers. By contrast, the power of the government in providing the necessary regulations is immensely greater.[23] And the regulations to protect and support women should evidently be applicable nationwide, not just to EPZs, where in fact female workers are likely to be doing better!

WTO Rulings and Women

Women's Edge has also objected to the WTO Appellate Body's rulings that preferences given to the Caribbean nations on their exports of bananas to the European Union violated WTO agreements and that the European Union's restrictions on the sale of hormone-fed beef were in violation of the agreed rules requiring that a scientific test must be met if such restrictions are imposed.[24] They complain that the gender effects were not analyzed by the WTO. But their critique amounts to little more than saying that those who are affected by these decisions, whether in terms of the removal of protection or preference (e.g., the banana case) or by authorized retaliation through tariffs (e.g., the hormone-fed beef case), happen to include women. But then, almost any policy change will directly affect some women.

These WTO Appellate Body decisions raise many issues, some critical to the economic well-being of the poor countries, and fixing the system for them would automatically benefit both women and men in the workforce and as consumers. But the notion that the WTO is somehow damnably deficient in not highlighting gender issues and micro-level gender impact each time it pronounces a decision seems to be off the wall.

A telling example of such feminist concern occurred after the EU lost its case for restrictions on American hormone-fed beef. Women's Edge complained about the effects of the ensuing tariff retaliation against Dutch tomatoes and other EU exports. This retaliation by the United States against the EU was authorized by WTO rules because the EU could not eliminate the WTO-illegal ban. Women's Edge argued:

> The 100 percent tariffs imposed on Dutch tomatoes will affect Janice Honisberg, a woman business owner [who imports Dutch tomatoes]. She estimates that her company will lose 40 percent of its revenues as a result of the tariff and she will be forced to layoff half of her 65 employees, the majority of whom are women from low-income communities in Washington D.C. and Chicago.[25]

Tariff retaliation is a much-debated issue among economists, lawyers, and international relations scholars. To put into this important debate the sorry fate of Honisberg and her staff is to lose all proportion; it is as if a dam had burst, flooding villages and cities and destroying human life, and yet the fate of just a few women concerned you!

Aside from the gross disproportionality of such a focus, it is also misplaced. The WTO Appellate Body was exactly right to find against the legitimacy of the hormone-fed beef legislation of the European Union in light of the agreement at the Uruguay Round, which precluded such restrictions unless backed by a scientific test. And many of us are right to ask for a renegotiation of that agreement because of problems such as the hormone-fed beef concerns that were not anticipated at the time of that agreement. But to demand that this agreement, and every other, be reexamined and redesigned specifically from the viewpoint of women's welfare seems about as compelling as saying that the removal of potholes from New York's roads be subjected to a prior examination of whether women are more likely to fall into them (as they well might if they wear high heels).

The proper response to demands for attention to women's welfare in a society has to be to consider ways in which women in that society and economy may be more vulnerable to the consequences of policy changes such as trade liberalization, projects such as the building of roads and railways or the provision of irrigation or drinking water, and indeed the myriad ways in which change comes. Rather than setting up roadblocks on every policy change, big and small, and demanding that each policy change be made conditional on an examination of its impact on women—a tall order in many cases, since the indirect estimates at that level of detail can only be guesstimates at best—it is more useful to think of policies that alleviate the *totality* of distress to women from the multitude of policy changes.

Women, as a class, are not destined to lose from progress any more than other groups are. To block off progress, ostensibly to help them, at every turn of the policy screw is to indulge in a policy response that is both inappropriate and likely to be counterproductive to their well-being—and men's as well.

IMF, World Bank, and Women

An equal opprobrium is assigned by several women's groups to the effects on women of the stabilization programs of the IMF, which assist countries having macroeconomic difficulties such as balance-of-payments crises, and the structural adjustment programs of the World Bank, which are generally longer-term and assist countries that are implementing economic reforms. In both cases, these institutions impose "conditionality," that is, conditions such as commitment to reducing the budget deficit or tightening monetary policy, which must be met by the assisted country.

The concerns of the women's groups are twofold. First, the typical conditionalities in these programs hurt women because when the belt is tightened, the resulting unemployment disproportionately hurts women, who will be fired ahead of the men or who are simply among the workforce that is laid off. Second, the belt-tightening often involves reducing social expenditures on health and education, which in turn forces women back into the home to provide such services instead.

But these criticisms are misdirected. The IMF hands out loans when there is a stabilization crisis. Almost always this means that the country in crisis must bring its overall expenditures in line with its income. If the IMF did not come in with loans—and this counterfactual cannot be ignored—then it is likely that matters would be worse, since the country would then have no option except to live immediately within its means. In fact, IMF support often eases the ability of the country in the stabilization crisis to borrow more funds and to make the transition to a better macroeconomic situation yet easier. This should generally assist, rather than harm, women.

It is hard to argue also that it is the IMF that systematically prefers slashing expenditures to raising revenues and that this expenditure cutting is biased against health and education expenditures. Regarding the former, it is well known, for example, that for many years the IMF was reluctant to ask countries to reduce tariffs, not because it did not believe, as it should, that the high tariffs frequently encountered in the poor countries at the time and even now were harmful, but because the IMF was worried about the potential loss of tariff revenue when a stabilization crisis required more revenue and less expenditure.[26]

As regards expenditure-cutting bias against social expenditures, the IMF and all of us would have loved to get the crisis-afflicted countries to reduce their armaments expenditures instead, for instance. But these priorities, in the end, are set by these governments themselves; the IMF sticks generally to targets that have to do with the budget deficit, that is, the difference between income and expenditure of the government, which in turn must affect the overall national imbalance that attends a stabilization crisis.

The question of removing tariffs on imports and subsidies to electricity, fertilizers, freight, and so on has been more a question of structural reforms addressed by the World Bank. These reforms have certainly been promoted in an effort to change the economic policies that have been recognized as having failed. But it is a mistake to think that these reforms have been necessarily imposed from Washington via the World Bank. Often, as I argue in Chapter 18, these reforms have been advocated and embraced by intellectuals, economists, and policy makers in these countries on their own initiative. Recognition of one's folly is often a powerful factor making for change. Foreign pressure, particularly when aid funds are at stake, can make a difference. But again, the assumption that conditionality, whether of the IMF or the World Bank, is unbending and effective is also erroneous.

GLOBALIZATION: WORKING ABROAD, PROSTITUTION FOR TOURISTS, AND TRAFFICKING

There are, however, three critical phenomena, tangentially related to globalization, that pose unambiguous threats to women's well-being.

- Women going abroad as domestic servants—often to the Middle East, where local women are typically living in the Middle Ages and under Islamic laws as interpreted by illiterate and conservative religious leaders in countries such as Saudi Arabia—have been subjected to abuse and need protection.

- The growth of tourism has inevitably been accompanied by a rise in female and even male prostitution in countries such as Thailand.

- Trafficking in women has grown, especially with the economic distress that has attended attempts at transition in countries such as Russia and from financial crises in afflicted Asian countries.

The perils afflicting women as empires expanded and commerce increased offer a historical parallel, of course, although the precise pathologies have been diverse. Thus, Margaret Macmillan, writing in *Women of the Raj*, recollects the plight of the women who followed the men into India, in words that have resonance today:

> [The employees of the East India Company] took Indian mistresses; worse, from the point of view of the Company's staunch Protestant directors, they married Catholics, daughters or widows of the Portuguese. To save the souls of its men, the Company, for a time, played matchmaker. In the later part of the seventeenth century it shipped batches of young women from Britain to India. The cargo, divided into "gentlewomen" and "others," were given one set of clothes each and were supported for a year—quite long enough, it was thought, for them to find themselves husbands. *Some did not; and the Company tried to deny that it had any obligation to look after them further.* Most unfairly it also warned them to mind their morals: "Whereas some of these women are grown scandalous to our nation, religion and Government interest," said a letter from London to the Deputy Governor of Bombay in 1675, "we require you to give them fair warning that they do apply themselves to a more sober and Christian conversation." *If that warning did not have the right effect, the women were to be fed on bread and water and shipped back to Britain.*[27]

A more recent and less excusable example is that of the Korean "comfort women" who were forced into servicing the Japanese armed forces in the Second World War as they brutally moved westward into Korea and China—an issue that has led to continual demands for compensatory reparations by Japan.

The modern afflictions—abuse of female workers abroad, tourism-induced prostitution, and trafficking across borders—that can attend normal, empire-unrelated globalization require attention and both international and domestic action. They simply illustrate how even benign changes—such as the opportunity to earn more as a domestic, an opportunity prized and seized by hundreds of thousands of women in the Philippines, Bangladesh, India, Pakistan and Indonesia—can have some downside effects for women who are left unprotected against probable abuses by their employers. More disturbingly, these opportunities can be exploited by unscrupulous elements—traffickers and mafia such as the Japanese *yakuza*—to indulge in dreadful crimes against women such as trafficking in them for unremunerated prostitution and virtual slavery.

Fortunately, the unceasing activities of individual activists and NGOs, among them the Thailand-based ECPAT (End Child Prostitution, Child Pornography and Trafficking in Children for Sexual Purposes) and the Delhi-based STOP (Stop Trafficking, Oppression, and Prostitution of Children and Women, which works to end the traffic in women and children from Bangladesh and Nepal) have increased awareness of these problems at the international level for some years now. Many conventions have been signed and several ratified, to prevent trafficking, for instance, and the enormous gaps between laws and conventions and between laws and enforcement have been the target of continual critical scrutiny and agitation. Progress is slow, not just because of lack of political will but because of the complexity of the enforcement required. But it is relentless.

So while there are serious issues to be addressed in these specific areas, where the welfare and well-being of women can be imperiled and must be protected, I would conclude from the analysis in this chapter that the broader criticisms that many women's groups have voiced about the negative effects of globalization on women are not convincing.

NOTES

1. "Samurais No More," *Foreign Affairs*, May–June 1994, 7–12.

2. Sandra Black and Elizabeth Brainerd, "Importing Equality? The Impact of Globalization on Gender Discrimination," November 2000; available at http://econpapers.hhs.se/paper/izaizadps/dp556.htm.

3. Becker analyzes discrimination reflecting employers' prejudice, as explored by Black and Brainerd, and also prejudice by fellow workers and by customers. See Gary Stanley Becker, *The Economic Approach to Human Behavior* (Chicago: University of Chicago Press, 1978).

4. Arlie Russell Hochschild, "Global Care Chains and Emotional Surplus Value," in Anthony Giddens and Will Hutton, eds., *On the Edge: Living with Global Capitalism* (London: Vintage, 2001), 130–46.

5. Ibid., 136.

6. Ibid., 135.

7. Hochschild, "Global Care Chains," 144.

8. "Women and Trade," Testimony for Hill Briefing on Women and the WTO, June 28, 1999, by Marceline White, Women's Edge, 2.

9. "Women and Trade: Investing in Women: FTAA Investment Policies and Women," Trade Fact Sheet, Women's Edge, October 21, 2001.

10. Ibid., 3.

11. Reported in "How Today's Trading System Hurts Women," *Human Rights for Workers,* June 3, 2002. This newsletter, put out by Robert Senser (http://www.senser.com), is very useful.

12. Oxfam, *Rigged Rules and Double Standards* (Oxford: Oxfam, 2002), 85; also quoted in "How Today's Trading System Hurts Women."

13. Whether workers are exploited in ways other than poverty-level wages being paid to them is a wider question that is also considered in Chapter 12.

14. "Women Declare That Trade Is an Instrument of Development Not Profit," press release by the regional representatives attending the Strategic Planning Seminar in Cape Town, South Africa, August 12–18.

15. Ibid.

16. Ibid.

17. V. Spike Peterson and Anne Sisson Runyan, *Global Gender Issues,* 2nd ed. (Boulder: Westview, 1999), 82.

18. See the latest analysis of the reasons for this decline by Robert Baldwin, *The Decline of US Labor Unions and the Role of Trade* (Washington, D.C.: Institute for International Economics, 2003). This study argues that trade has contributed only modestly to the general decline in unionization though greater incidence is noted for uneducated labor.

19. H. Safa, "Free Markets and the Marriage Market: Structural Adjustment, Gender Relations, and Working Conditions Among Dominican Workers," *Environment and Planning* 31 (1999): 294. This is a fascinating sociological analysis of the effects of structural changes in the economy on gender roles and relations.

20. Their work is cited in Chapter 12.

21. Barbara S. Mensch, Judith Bruce, and Margaret E. Greene, *The Uncharted Passage: Girls' Adolescence in the Developing World* (New York: Population Council, 1998), 39–40. I thank Judith Bruce for extensive comments on an early draft of this chapter.

22. Safa, "Free Markets and the Marriage Market," 294.

23. Its efficacy would increase if NGOs were also present to bring violations of these regulations to public attention. In this context, the legal standing given by an activist Indian supreme court to NGOs to bring such violations to court on behalf of those lacking the ability themselves is a useful innovation.

24. See the WTO Dispute Settlement Report, "European Communities—Regime for the Importation, Sale and Distribution of Bananas—Recourse to Article 21.5 by Ecuador," WT/DS27/RW/ECU 99-1443.

25. "Women and Trade," Testimony for Hill Briefing on Women and the WTO, June 28, 1999, by Marceline White, Women's Edge, 4.

26. But the IMF did think that, ultimately, these countries should replace their reliance on tariffs for revenue with other more efficient methods of taxation.

27. Margaret Macmillan, *Women of the Raj* (New York: Thames and Hudson, 1996), 16–17.

POSTSCRIPT

The authors on both sides of this debate take the term "globalization" for granted, assuming that it is in fact taking place. Not everyone has accepted this fundamental assumption. Michael Veseth, for example, has questioned whether globalization is as far developed as analysts generally assume. In examining a number of "global" firms, Veseth found that their actual behaviour often was not genuinely global in nature. This finding led him to conclude that "actual global firms are relatively rare and the process of globalization is far less developed than most people imagine." Instead, globalization has become popular as a focus of discussion because it is vague and hence a variety of policies and projects can be attached to the concept. (See Michael Veseth, *Selling Globalization: The Myth of the Global Economy* [Boulder: Lynne Rienner Publishers, 1998.]) It could be argued that inequality, whether between nations, social classes, or gender, has been a common feature throughout history. Given the complex factors that contribute to the process of globalization, how much can the increase in gender inequality be attributed directly to globalization? It is possible that many of factors that might contribute to increased inequality can be attributed to other factors such as the weakening of labour unions or the declining role of governments in the social sector, which are indirect results of globalization. For a better understanding of the concept of "globalization" and the various forms that it takes see Jan Aart Scholte's *Globalization: A Critical Introduction* (New York: St. Martin's Press, 2000) and Lui Hebron and John Stack, Jr., *Globalization: Debunking the Myths* (New York: Prentice-Hall, 2009).

Suggested Additional Readings

Bakan, Joel. *The Corporation: The Pathological Pursuit of Profit and Power.* Toronto: Penguin Canada, 2004.

Barndt, Deborah. *Tangled Routes: Women, Work and Globalization on the Tomato Trail.* Lanham: Rowman Littlefield, 2002.

Black, Sandra, and Elizabeth Brainerd. "Importing Equality? The Impact of Globalization on Gender Discrimination." November 2000. Available at http://econpapers.hhs.se/paper/izaizadps/dp556.htm.

Cagatay, Nilüfer. *Gender, Poverty and Trade.* UNDP Background Paper, New York, October 2001.

Cohen, Marjorie Griffin. "New International Trade Agreements: Their Reactionary Role in Creating Markets and Retarding Social Welfare." In Bakker, Isabella (ed.), *Rethinking Restructuring: Gender and Change in Canada.* Toronto: University of Toronto Press, 1996.

Durano, Marina Fe B. *Gender Issues in International Trade.* International Gender and Trade Network, Discussion Paper, Washington DC, 2000. Available at http://www.genderandtrade.net/Archives/Marina's%20paper.htm.

Ehrenreich, Barbara, and Arlie Russell Hochschild (eds.). *Global Woman: Nannies, Maids, and Sex Workers in the New Economy.* New York: Metropolitan Books, 2002.

Giddens, Anthony, and Will Hutton, eds. *On the Edge: Living with Global Capitalism.* London: Vintage, 2001.

Keller-Herzog, Angela. *Discussion Paper: Globalization and Gender Development Perspectives and Interventions.* Prepared for Women in Development and Gender Equity Division, Policy Branch, CIDA, December 1996. Available at http://www.ifias.ca/gsd/trade/gagdindex.html.

Kelly, Rita Mae, Jane Bayes, and Brigitte Young, (eds.). *Gender, Globalization, and Democratization.* Lanham: Rowman and Littlefield, 2001.

Kofman, Eleonore, Annie Phizucklea, Parvati Raghuran, and Rosemar Sales. *Gender and International Migration in Europe: Employment, Welfare, and Politics.* London and New York: Routledge, 2001.

Marchand, Marianne, and Anne Sisson Runyan, (eds.). *Gender and Global Restructuring.* London and New York: Routledge, 2000.

Morris, Marika. *Women, Poverty and Canadian Public Policy in an Era of Globalization.* Canadian Research Institute for the Advancement of Women, Presentation made on May 29, 2000. Available at: http://www.criaw-icref.ca/factSheets/Poverty_and_globalization.htm.

Naples, Nancy A., and Manisha Desai (eds.). *Women's Activism and Globalization: Linking Local Struggles and Transnational Politics.* New York: Routledge, 2002.

White, Marceline. "GATS and Women." *Foreign Policy in Focus* 6, no. 2 (January 2001). Available at http://www.fpif.org/briefs/vol6/v6n02gats.html.

InfoTrac® College Edition

Search for the following articles in the InfoTrac® database:

Ahmed, Fauzia Erfan. "The Rise of the Bangladesh Garment Industry: Globalization, Women Workers, and Voice." *NWSA Journal* 16, no. 2 (Summer 2004): 34–45.

Channa, Subhadra Mitra. "Globalization and Modernity in India: A Gendered Critique." *Urban Anthropology & Studies of Cultural Systems & World Economic Development* 33, no. 1 (Spring 2004): 37–71.

Federici, Silvia. "Women, Land-struggles and Globalization: An International Perspective." *Journal of Asian and African Studies* 39, no. 1–2 (Jan–March 2004): 47–52.

Kingfisher, Catherine. "Western Welfare in Decline: Globalization and Women's Poverty." *Journal of Sociology & Social Welfare* 31, no. 4 (December 2004): 208–11.

Lenz, Ilse. "Globalization, Gender, and Work: Perspectives on Global Regulation." *The Review of Policy Research* 20, no. 1 (Spring 2003): 21–43.

Web Resources

For current URLs for the following websites, visit www.crosscurrents.nelson.com.

CENTRE FOR THE STUDY OF GLOBALISATION AND REGIONALISATION
http://www.warwick.ac.uk/fuc/soc/CSGR
The website of this leading academic research centre on globalization at the University of Warwick contains a collection of working papers on various dimensions of globalization.

THE GLOBALIZATION WEBSITE
http://www.sociology.emory.edu/globalization/issues02.html
This site based at Emory University contains a number of resources and links on the topic of the impact of globalization of women.

ONE WORLD/UK GUIDE ON GENDER
http://uk.oneworld.net/guides/gender
This is an important gateway website maintained by a large network on NGOs. It contains extensive materials relating to development, human rights, and globalization. See particularly their guide on gender issues, which contains links to many resources on women and globalization.

ASSOCIATION FOR WOMEN'S RIGHTS IN DEVELOPMENT
http://www.awid.org
The Association for Women's Rights in Development (AWID) is an international network of NGOs connecting, informing, and mobilizing people and organizations committed to achieving gender equality, sustainable development, and women's human rights. Their site contains many resources relating to the impact of globalization on women.

Was the "Battle in Seattle" a Significant Turning Point in the Struggle against Globalization?

✔ YES
STEPHEN GILL, "Toward a Postmodern Prince? The Battle in Seattle as a Moment in the New Politics of Globalisation," *Millennium: Journal of International Studies* 29, no. 1 (2000): 131–40

✘ NO
JAN AART SCHOLTE, "Cautionary Reflections on Seattle," *Millennium: Journal of International Studies* 29, no. 1 (2000): 115–21

Significant turning points in history have come to be symbolized by a particular event or set of events. The Boston Tea Party became identified as the beginning of the American Revolution, and the storming of the Bastille is still celebrated as the spark of the French Revolution. In more recent times, specific events have also been interpreted as significant signposts in a changing world order. The dismantling of the Berlin Wall symbolically marked the end of the Cold War. The launch of the Persian Gulf War was seen by some as a harbinger of a "New World Order."

For many, the "Battle in Seattle" has come to symbolize one such critical turning point. The immediate context was the Third Ministerial Conference of the World Trade Organization (WTO), which was scheduled to meet in Seattle from November 30 to December 3, 1999. Two previous ministerial conferences had taken place in Singapore in 1996 and in Geneva in 1998, with little public fanfare. But as delegates from 130 nations descended on Seattle for deliberations, the conference took on a totally different character.

Thousands of demonstrators took to the streets of Seattle, virtually shutting down the city and seriously disrupting WTO deliberations. As demonstrators and police clashed in increasingly violent confrontations, the "Battle in Seattle" captured headlines around the world. When the conference ended without agreement on a new Millennium Round of talks to further liberalize world trade, activists declared that they had achieved a significant victory.

The "Battle in Seattle" was in many ways reminiscent of the anti-Vietnam and anti-nuclear demonstrations of the 1960s and 1970s. However, unlike these movements, which focused on issues relating to war and peace, the Seattle demonstrations focused on issues of economic justice, corporate power, and inequality. Unlike the anti-Vietnam demonstrations of the 1960s, which were driven more by disillusioned youth, the anti-globalization demonstrations in Seattle have been described as multi-generational, multi-class, and multi-issue—environmentalists, animal-rights supporters, union members, human-rights activists, and anarchists representing a broad spectrum of causes and goals.

Since Seattle, it has become virtually impossible to hold a significant meeting of world leaders to discuss global economic issues without triggering massive demonstrations. Subsequent international meetings in Quebec City, Genoa, and Cancún featured similarly dramatic confrontations between demonstrators and policymakers.

Why has the arcane world of international economics and trade become the focus of popular mass protest? Some see these events as signifying an important setback for globalization. As resistance to globalization deepens, we are entering a new phase of de-globalization. But others suggest that we are seeing a significant shift in the politics of globalization as new voices and forces, which have been excluded from global economic governance, demand access to decision-making structures. What we are witnessing is the emergence of a "global civil society." This term refers to growth in independent NGOs, social movements, and other nonprofit sector actors that increasingly operate across national borders. It is argued that these actors are increasingly seeking access to international policy discussions, including those involving trade and finance. As a result, a process that was once the exclusive domain of power elites is being democratized.

In the following readings, we encounter two different interpretations of the meaning of Seattle. Stephen Gill of York University sees the events in Seattle as a harbinger of new political alignments and forces that are seeking to "develop a global and universal politics of radical (re)construction around values such as democratic human development, human rights, and intergenerational security." Jan Aart Scholte of Warwick University is more cautious in his interpretation of these same events. Although Scholte is hopeful that a more humane global economic order will emerge, he emphasizes that the concept of global civil society has serious limits and that developments in Seattle could be ephemeral.

✔ YES
Toward a Postmodern Prince? The Battle in Seattle as a Moment in the New Politics of Globalisation
STEPHEN GILL

The modern prince, the myth-prince, cannot be a real person, a concrete individual. It can only be an organism, a complex element of society in which a collective will, which has already been recognised and has to some extent asserted itself in action, begins to take concrete form.[1]

This essay analyses recent protests against aspects of neoliberal globalisation, as for example at the World Trade Organisation (WTO) Ministerial Meeting in Seattle in late 1999 and in Washington, DC, in spring 2000 to coincide with the IMF and World Bank Annual Meetings. I first examine the reason for the failure of the Seattle talks, and secondly, evaluate the protests and their political significance. Finally, I analyse some emerging forms of political agency associated with struggle over the nature and direction of globalisation that I call the "the postmodern Prince." This concept is elaborated in the final section of this essay. It is important to stress at the outset, however, that in this essay the term "postmodern" does not refer, as it often does, to a discursive or aesthetic moment. In my usage, "postmodern" refers to a set of conditions, particularly political, material, and ecological, that are giving rise to new forms of political agency whose defining myths are associated with the quest to ensure human and intergenerational security on and for the planet as well as democratic human development and human rights. As such, the multitude and diverse political forces that form the postmodern Prince combine both defensive and forward-looking strategies. Rather than engaging in deconstruction, they seek to develop a global and universal politics of radical (re)construction.

The battle in Seattle took place both inside and outside the conference centre in which the meetings took place; the collapse of the discussions was partly caused by the greater visibility of trade issues in the everyday lives of citizens and the increasing concern over how international trade and investment agreements are undermining important aspects of national sovereignty and policy autonomy, especially in ways that strengthen corporate power. These concerns—expressed through various forms of political mobilisation—have put pressure upon political leaders throughout the world to re-examine some of the premises and contradictions of neoliberal globalisation.

WHY THESE TALKS FAILED

Why specifically did the Seattle talks fail? The first and most obvious reason was US intransigence, principally in defence of the status quo against demands for reform by other nations concerned at the repercussions of the liberalisation framework (the built-in agenda) put in place by the GATT Uruguay Round.[2] The GATT Uruguay Round was a "Single Undertaking," a generic all-or-nothing type of agreement that meant signatories had to agree to all its commitments and disciplines, as well as to the institutionalisation of the WTO. The wider juridical-political framework for locking in such commitments can be called the new constitutionalism of disciplinary neoliberalism. This encompasses not only trade and investment, but also private property rights more generally (and not just intellectual property rights). It also involves macroeconomic policies and institutions (for example independent central banks and balanced budget amendments) in ways that minimise, or even "lock out" democratic controls over key economic institutions and policy frameworks in the long term.[3]

In this context, the US mainly wanted to sustain commitments to existing protections for intellectual property rights and investment and stop any attempts to weaken the capacity of existing agreements to open new markets for American corporations. The US position was based on intelligence work by government agencies, academics, and corporate strategists co-ordinated by the CIA.[4]

So it would be easy to say that protests outside the Seattle Convention Centre and confronted by the Seattle riot police, the FBI, and the CIA had little or no effect on the failure of the talks, other than the fact that many delegates could not get into the building because of the disruptions outside. However, this would be to misunderstand the link between public concern and the negotiating positions of states in the WTO. Indeed, it is becoming clear that the central reasons for the failure of the Seattle Ministerial were linked to the fact that the establishment of the WTO has gone well beyond the traditional role of the GATT in ways that have begun not only increasingly to encroach on crucial domestic policy areas and national sovereignty, but which also have repercussions for international law. In addition, key areas of concern to the public such as food safety, biotechnology, the environment, labour standards, and broader questions of economic development add to the popular disquiet and mobilisation over cultural, social, and ethical questions linked to the globalisation project.

In this regard—and this is very relevant to the concerns of the protesters as well as many governments—the new services negotiations that will occur in Geneva as a result of the Single Undertaking have a wide mandate and the new trade disciplines will have potentially vast impact across major social institutions and programs, such as health, education, social services, and cultural issues. This will allow for wider privatisation and commercialisation of the public sector and indirectly, of the public sphere itself, for example in social programs and education.[5] The logic of the negotiations will likely inhibit many government programs that could be justified as being in the public interest, unless governments are able to convince WTO panels that these programs are not substantially in restraint of trade and investment on the part of private enterprise. Indeed, because the built-in agenda will proceed in Geneva, many divisions among governments, especially between North and South, are emerging. The North-South divisions also revolved around dissatisfaction on the South's part at concessions made in the earlier GATT Uruguay Round, coupled with their frustration in failing to open Northern markets for their manufactured and agriculture exports.

With this agenda in mind, the protesters—although drawn from a very diverse range of organisations and political tendencies—believe there is centralisation and concentration of power under corporate control in neoliberal globalisation, with much of the policy agenda for this project orchestrated by international organisations such as the WTO, the IMF, and the World Bank. Thus, it was not surprising that the battle in Seattle moved to Washington, DC, in mid-April where the same set of progressive and environmental activists and organisations, including trade unions, protested the role of the IMF, the World Bank, and the G-7.

What is significant here is that the new counter-movements seek to preserve ecological and cultural diversity against what they see as the encroachment of political, social, and ecological mono-cultures associated with the supremacy of corporate rule. At the time of writing, the protests were set to move on to lay siege to the headquarters of Citicorp, the world's biggest financial conglomerate.

THE CONTRADICTIONS OF NEOLIBERAL GLOBALISATION AND THE SEATTLE PROTESTS

Implicitly or explicably, the failure of the talks and indeed much of the backlash against neoliberal globalisation is linked to the way that people in diverse contexts are experiencing the problems and contradictions linked to the power of capital and more specifically the projects of disciplinary neoliberalism and new constitutionalism. So what are these contradictions and how do they relate to the Seattle protests?

The first is the contradiction between big capital and democracy. Central here is the extension of binding legal mechanisms of trade and investment agreements, such as the GATT Uruguay Round and regional agreements, such as NAFTA. A counter-example, which pointed the way towards Seattle in terms of much of its counter-hegemonic political form, was the failed OECD effort to create a Multilateral Agreement on Investment. The MAI was also partly undermined by grass-roots mobilisation against corporate globalisation, as well as by more conventional political concerns about sovereignty. The protesters viewed agreements such as NAFTA and organisations such as the WTO as seeking to institutionalise ever-more extensive charters of rights and freedoms for corporations, allowing for greater freedom of enterprise and world-wide protection for private property rights. The protesters perceived that deregulation, privatisation, and liberalisation are a means to strengthen a particular set of class interests, principally the power of private investors and large shareholders. They are opposed to greater legal and market constraints on democracy.

Put differently, the issue was therefore how far and in what ways trade and investment agreements "lock in" commitments to liberalisation, whilst "locking out" popular-democratic and parliamentary forces from control over crucial economic, social, and ecological policies.

The second set of contradictions are both economic and social. Disciplinary neoliberalism proceeds with an intensification of discipline on labour and a rising rate of exploitation, partly reflected in booming stock markets during the past decade, whilst at the same time persistent economic and financial crises have impoverished many millions of people and caused significant economic dislocations. This explains the growing role of organised labour—for example American-based trade unions such as the Teamsters—in the protests, as well as organisations representing feminists, other workers, peasants, and smaller producers worldwide. In this regard, the numbers do not lie: despite what has been the longest boom in the history of Western capitalism, the real incomes of average people have been falling. So if this happens in a boom, what happens in a bust? This question has been answered already in the East Asia crisis when millions were impoverished.

Third, for a number of years now, discipline has become linked to the intensification of a crisis of social reproduction. Feminist political economy has shown how a disproportionate burden of (structural) adjustment to the harsher, more competitive circumstances over the past twenty years has fallen on the shoulders of the less well-paid, on women and children, and on the weaker members of society, the old and the disabled. In an era of fiscal stringency, in many states social welfare, health, and educational provisions have been reduced and the socialisation of risk has been reduced for a growing proportion of the world's population. This has generated a crisis of social reproduction as burdens of adjustment are displaced into families and communities that are already under pressure to simply survive in economic terms and risk becomes privatised, redistributed, and generalised in new forms.[6]

The final set of contradictions are linked to how socio-cultural and biological diversity are being replaced by a social and biological mono-culture under corporate domination, and how this is linked to a loss of food security and new forms of generalised health risk. Thus, the protesters argued that if parts of the Seattle draft agenda were ratified, it would allow for a liberalisation of trade in genetically modified crops, provisions to allow world water supplies to be privatised, and the patenting of virtually all forms of life including genetic material that had been widely used across cultures for thousands of years. The protesters also felt particularly strongly about the patenting of seeds and bio-engineering by companies like Novartis and Enron, and other firms seen to be trying to monopolise control over food and undermine local livelihood and food security.[7]

Hence protesters opposed the control of the global food order by corporate interests linked to the new constitutionalism. These interests have begun to institutionalise their right "to source food and food inputs, to prospect for genetic patents, and to gain access to local and national food markets" established through the GATT Uruguay Round and WTO.[8] Transnational corporations have managed to redefine food security in terms of the reduction of national barriers to agriculture trade, ensuring market rule in the global food order. The effect is the intensification of the centralisation of control by "agri-food capital via global sourcing and global trading," in ways that intensify world food production and consumption relations through

> unsustainable monocultures, terminator genes, and class-based diets [in ways] premised on the elimination of the diversity of natural resources, farm cultures, and food cultures, and the decline of local food self-sufficiency and food security mechanisms.[9]

Together, these contradictions contribute to what might be called a global or "organic crisis" that links together diverse forces across and within nations, specifically to oppose ideas, institutions, and material power of disciplinary neoliberalism. Much of the opposition to corporate globalisation was summed up by AFL-CIO President John Sweeny, who alongside President Clinton, was addressing the heads of the 1,000 biggest transnational corporations at the annual meeting of the self-appointed and unelected World Economic Forum in Davos in February 2000. Sweeny stated that the protests from North and South represented "a call for new global rules, democratically developed" to constrain "growing inequality, environmental destruction, and a race to the bottom for working people," warning that if such rules were not forthcoming "it will generate an increasingly volatile reaction that will make Seattle look tame."[10] Indeed, Clinton's remarks made at Davos

> seemed designed as a reminder that these fears—even expressed in unwelcome and sometimes violent ways, as they were in Seattle—have a legitimacy that deserves attention in the world's executive suites and government ministries.[11]

We know by now, of course, that the violence in Seattle was almost completely carried out by the heavily armed police militias who took the battle to the protesters. In Washington, in April 2000, police pre-emptively arrested hundreds of demonstrators, in actions justified by the local police chief as a matter of prudence. Another example of this was the repression of peaceful protests at the Asia-Pacific Economic Co-operation meeting in Vancouver in 1998. The protests focused on the contradiction of separating free trade from political democracy, dramatised by the presence of the Indonesian dictator, President Suharto. In sum, state authorities will quickly act to restrict basic political rights and freedoms of opposition by alternative members of civil society—rights supposedly underpinned by the rule of law in a liberal constitutional framework—when business interests are threatened. At Seattle, the anonymous, unaccountable, and intimidating police actions seemed almost absurd in the light of the fact that the protests involved children dressed as turtles, peaceful activists for social justice, union members, faith groups, accompanied by teachers, scientists, and assorted "tree huggers," all of whom were non-violent. Indeed, with the possible exception of a small number of anarchists, virtually none of the protesters was in any way violent. In Washington, the police protected the meetings wearing heavy armour from behind metal barricades, in the face of pro-testers carrying puppets and signs that read "spank the Bank." Moments such as these, however, illustrate not only comedy of the absurd but also the broader dialectic between a supremacist set of forces and an ethio-political alternative involved in a new inclusive politics of diversity.

Indeed, since the Seattle debacle the protesters have been able to extend their critique of what they see as the political mono-culture by showing how one of its key components, the "quality press" and TV media, reported what occurred. In the US, for example, the mainstream media found it impossible to represent the vio-lence as being caused by the authorities in order to provoke and discredit the opposition as being Luddite, anti-science, and unlawful. Seen from the vantage point of the protesters, "the *Washington Post* and the *New York Times* are the keepers of 'official reality,' and in official reality it is always the protesters who are violent."[12]

TOWARD A POSTMODERN PRINCE?

In conclusion, I advance the following hypothesis: the protests form part of a world-wide movement that can perhaps be understood in terms of new potentials and forms of global political agency. And following Machiavelli and Gramsci, I call this set of potentials "the postmodern Prince," which I understand as some-thing plural and differentiated, although linked to universalism and the construc-tion of a new form of globalism, and of course, something that needs to be understood as a set of social and political forces in movement.

Let us place this hypothesis in some theoretical context. Machiavelli's *The Prince* addressed the problem of the ethics of rule from the viewpoint of both the prince (the *palazzo*, the palace) and the people (the *piazza*, the town square). Machiavelli sought to theorise how to construct a form of rule that combined both *virtù* (ethics, responsibility, and consent) and fear (coercion) under conditions of *fortuna* (circumstances). *The Prince* was written in Florence, in the context of the political upheavals of Renaissance Italy. Both Machiavelli and later Gramsci linked their analyses and propositions to the reality of concrete historical cir-cumstances as well as to the potential for transformation. These included pressing contemporary issues associated with the problems of Italian unification, and the subordinate place of Italy in the structures of international relations. And it was in a similar national and international context that Gramsci's *The Modern Prince* was written in a Fascist prison, a text that dealt with a central problem of politics: the constitution of power, authority, rule, rights, and responsibilities in the creation of an ethical political community. Nevertheless, what Gramsci saw in *The Prince* was that it was "not a systematic treatment, but a 'live' work, in which political ideology and political science are fused in the dramatic form of a 'myth.'"[13] The myth for Machiavelli was that of *condottiere*, who represented the collective will. By contrast, for Gramsci *The Modern Prince* proposed the myth of the democratic modern mass political party—the communist party—charged with the construction of a new form of state and society, and a new world order.

In the new strategic context (*fortuna*) of disciplinary neoliberalism and globalisation, then, a central problem of political theory is how to imagine and to theorise the new forms of collective political identity and agency that might lead to the creation of new, ethical, and democratic political institutions and forms of practice (*virtù*). So in this context, let me again be clear that by "postmodern Prince" I do *not* mean a form of political agency that is based on postmodern philosophy and the radical relativism it often entails. What I am intending to communicate is a shift in the forms of political agency that are going beyond earlier modernist political projects. So the "postmodern Prince" involves tendencies that have begun to challenge some of the myths and the disciplines of modernist practices, and specifically resisting those that seek to consolidate the project of globalisation under the rule of capital.

Thus, the battles in Seattle may link to new patterns of political agency and a movement that goes well beyond the politics of identity and difference: it has gender, race, and class aspects. It is connected to issues of ecological and social reproduction, and of course, to the question of democracy. This is why more than 700 organisations and between 40,000 and 60,000 people—principally human-rights activists, labour activists, indigenous people, representatives of churches, industrial workers, small farmers, forest activists, environmentalists, social justice workers, students, and teachers—all took part collectively in the protests against the WTO's Third Ministrial on 30 November 1999. The protesters seem aware of the nature and dynamics of their movement and have theorised a series of political links between different events so that they will become more than what James Rosenau called "distant proximities" or "simply isolated moments of resistance against globalisation."[14]

In sum, these movements are beginning to form what Gramsci called "an organism, a complex element of society" that is beginning to point towards the realisation of a "collective will." This will is coming to be "recognised and has to some extent asserted itself in action." It is beginning to "take concrete form."[15] Indeed the diverse organisations that are connected to the protests seek to go further to organise something akin to a postmodern transitional political party, that is one with no clear leadership structure as such. It is a party of movement that cannot be easily decapitated. This element puzzled mainstream press reporters at

Seattle since they were unable to find, and thus to photograph or interview, the "leaders" of the protests. However, this emerging political form is not a signal of an end to the protests. It is also not a signal of an end to universalism in politics as such, since many of the forces it entails are linked to democratisation and a search for collective solutions to common problems. It seeks to combine diversity with new forms of collective identity and solidarity in and across civil societies. Thus, the organisers of the April 2000 Washington demonstrations stated that "Sweeny's prediction" made at Davos was in fact a description of events that were going on right now, but that are largely ignored by the media:

> The Zapatista uprising in Mexico, the recent coup in Ecuador, the civil war in the Congo, the turmoil in Indonesia, and the threat of the U'Wa people to commit mass suicide, are all expressions of the social explosion that has arisen from the desperation caused by the politics of the World Bank, IMF, and their corporate directors. . . . Fundamental change does not mean renaming their programs of other public relations scams. Fundamental reform means rules that empower the people of the world to make the decisions about how they live their lives—not the transitional CEO's or their purchased political leaders.[16]

In this regard, the effectiveness of the protest movements may well lie in a new confidence gained as particular struggles come to be understood in terms of a more general set of inter-connections between problems and movements world-wide. For instance, the Cartagena Protocol on Biosafety on genetically modified life forms was signed in late January 2000 in Montreal by representatives from 133 governments pursuant to the late 1992 UN Convention on Biological Diversity for the trade and regulation of living modified organisms (LMOs). The draft Protocol ensures that sovereign governments have rights to decide on imports of LMOs provided this is based on environmental and health risk assessment data. The Protocol is founded on the "precautionary principle," in effect meaning that where scientific uncertainty exists, governments can refuse or delay authorisation of trade in LMOs. Apart from pressure from NGOs, the negotiations were strongly influenced by scientists concerned about genetic and biological risks posed by the path of innovation. The process finally produced a protocol with significant controls over the freedoms of biotechnology and life sciences companies. Indeed, linkages and contradictions between environmental and trade and investment regulations and laws are becoming better understood by activists world-wide, for instance, how the Biosafety Protocol and the rules and procedures of the WTO may be in conflict.

Nevertheless, it must be emphasised that, although they may represent a larger proportion of the population of the world in terms of their concerns, in organised political terms the protest groups are only a relatively small part of an emerging global civil society that includes not only NGOs but also the activities of political parties, churches, media communication corporations, and scientific and political associations, some progressive, others reactionary. Transnational civil society also involves activities of both transnational corporations, and also governments that are active in shaping a political terrain that is directly and indirectly outside the formal juridical purview of states. Indeed, as the UN Rio conference on the environment and its aftermath illustrated, corporate environmentalism is a crucial aspect of the emerging global civil society and it is linked to what Gramsci called *transformismo* or co-optation of opposition. For example, "sustainable development" is primarily defined in public policy as compatible with market forces and freedom of enterprise. When the global environment movement was perceived as a real threat to corporate interests, companies changed tack from suggesting the environmentalists were either crackpots or misguided to accepting a real problem existed and a compromise was necessary. Of course a compromise acceptable to capital was not one that would fundamentally challenge the dominant patterns of accumulation.

I have not used the term postmodern in its usual sense. Rather, I apply it to indicate a set of conditions and contradictions that give rise to novel forms of political agency that go beyond and are more complex than those imagined by Machiavelli's *The Prince* or Gramsci's *The Modern Prince*. Global democratic collective action today cannot, in my view, be understood as a singular form of collective agency, for example, a single party with a single form of identity. It is more plural and differentiated, as well as being democratic and inclusive. The new forms of collective action contain innovative conceptions of social justice and solidarity, of social possibility, of knowledge, emancipation, and freedom. The content of their mobilising myths includes diversity, oneness of the planet and nature, democracy, and equity. What are we discussing is, therefore, a political party as well as an educational form and a cultural movement. However, it does not act in the old sense of an institutionalised and centralised structure of representation. Indeed this "party" is not institutionalised as such, since it has a multiple and capillary form. Moreover, whilst many of the moments and movements of resistance noted above are at first glance "local" in nature, there is broad recognition that local problems may require global solutions. Global networks and other mobilizing capabilities are facilitated with new technologies of communication.

A new "postmodern Prince" may prove to be the most effective political form for giving coherence to an open-ended, plural, inclusive, and flexible form of politics and thus create alternatives to neoliberal globalisation. So, whilst one can be pessimistic about globalisation in its current form, this is perhaps where some of the optimism for the future may lie: a new set of democratic identities that are global, but based on diversity and rooted in local conditions, problems, and opportunities.

NOTES

I would like to thank Cemal Acikgoz, Isabella Bakker, Adam Harmes, and Ahmed Hashi for their comments and help in preparing this essay.

1. Antonio Gramsci, *Selections from the Prison Notebooks of Antonio Gramsci*, trans. Quintin Hoare and Geoffrey Nowell Smith (New York: International Publishers, 1971), 129.

2. Scott Sinclair, "The WTO: What happened in Seattle? What's Next in Geneva?" *Briefing Paper Series: Trade and Investment* 1, no. 2 (Ottawa: Canadian Centre for Policy Alternatives, 2000), 6.

3. Stephen Gill, "Globalisation, Market Civilisation, and Disciplinary Neoliberalism," *Millennium: Journal of International Studies* 23, no. 3 (1994): 399–423.

4. See "CIA Spies Swap Cold War for Trade Wars," *Financial Times*, 14 August 1999, 1.

5. Editorial, "New Trade Rules Education," *Canadian Association of University Teachers Bulletin*, 7 September 1999, 1. The *Bulletin* added that Educational International representing 294 educational unions and associations world wide expressed great concern about how WTO initiatives would undermine public education.

6. See the essays in Isabella Bakker, ed., *The Strategic Silence: Gender And Economic Policy* (London: Zed Books, 1994).

7. Paul Hawken, "The WTO: Inside, Outside, All Around The World" [http://www.co-intelligence.org/WTOHawken.html] (26 April 2000).

8. Phillip McMichael, "The Crisis of Market Rule in the Global Food Order" (paper presented at the British International Studies Annual Meeting, Manchester, 20–22 December 1999).

9. Ibid., 2.

10. John Sweeny, "Remember Seattle," *Washington Post*, 30 January 2000, B7.

11. Ann Swardson, "Clinton Appeals for Compassion in Global Trade; World Forum Told Don't Leave 'Little Guys' Out," *Washington Post*, 30 January 2000, A18.

12. Posted on http://www.peoples@psot4.tele.dlk (26 April 2000) on behalf of the NGO network "Mobilization for Global Justice" that organised the Washington protests. Their website [http://www.a16.org] passed 250,000 visitors at the time of the protests.

13. Gramsci, *Selections from the Prison Notebooks*, 125.

14. James Rosenau, "Imposing Global Order: A Synthesised Ontology for a Turbulent Era," in *Innovation and Transformation on International Studies*, Stephen Gill and James H. Mittleman, eds. (Cambridge: Cambridge University Press, 1997), 220–35.

15. Gramsci, *Selections from the Prison Notebooks*, 129.

16. Posted by the NGO network "Mobilization for Global Justice" on http://www.peoples@post4.tele.dk (26 April 2000).

✗ NO
Cautionary Reflections on Seattle
JAN AART SCHOLTE

"The Battle of Seattle": stage one on a global popular revolution? Nail in the coffin of neoliberalism? Harbinger of a more secure, equitable, and democratic world order? While I count myself a proponent of far-reaching reform of globalisation, my reactions to recent events in the city of my youth are somewhat cautious.[1]

The demonstrations of late 1999 in Seattle against the World Trade Organisation (WTO) are the latest in a string of street protests against prevailing global economic regimes. The windows of McDonald's in Geneva suffered a similar fate to the panes of Pike Street when the WTO Ministerial Conference met on the shores of Lac Leman in 1998. Most of the Annual and Spring Meetings of the International Monetary Fund (IMF) and the World Bank have witnessed opposition rallies since several thousand people crowded the squares of Berlin in 1988. Throughout the 1990s, protesters also raised their voices outside the yearly summits of the Group of Seven (G7), most notably when tens of thousands of campaigners for the cancellation of Third World debt encircled the Birmingham G7 Summit in 1998. In early 2000, the annual Davos gathering of the World Economic Forum (WEF) became the latest occasion for "civil society" to raise the banners against "globalisation."

This popular mobilisation has made an impact. The launch of the Millennium Round in Seattle was abandoned in part due to public unease as expressed in the streets. Similarly, co-ordinated opposition from many non-governmental organizations (NGOs) played an important role in halting moves toward a Multilateral Agreement on Investment (MAI) in late 1998. Grassroots pressure for debt relief has helped prompt some reductions of bilateral and multilateral claims on poor countries. Lobbying by NGOs, trade unions, and reform-oriented think tanks has also encouraged greater attention by global and regional institutions to alleviating the social costs of economic restructuring in the face of globalisation. In 1999 the IMF even went so far as to recast its "Enhanced Structural Adjustment Facility" as the "Poverty Reduction and Growth Facility." Following pressure from civil society, the IMF, the Organisation for Economic Cooperation and Development (OECD), the WTO, and the World Bank have all intensified public relations efforts, including marked increases in disclosure about their decisions and policy processes.

These developments are welcome. Civic action has pushed issues of social justice and democracy high up the agenda of global economic governance. We may hope that these new priorities retain and indeed increase their current prominence and generate concrete benefits.

Yet "victory" in the "Battle of Seattle" is no occasion for exuberance or complacency about the future of globalisation or the role of civil society in shaping its course. Halting a new round of trade liberalisation is not the same thing as building a better world order. Nor have civic initiatives in the Seattle scenario provided full confidence in the contributions of civil society to progressive global politics.

The following comment elaborates three cautionary notes. First, we should not overestimate the significance of Seattle in terms of policy change. Second, when assessing Seattle we should not romanticise civil society as an inherently powerful and progressive force. Third, we should look beyond the dismantlement of neoliberal globalisation to the construction of something better.

SMALL HARVESTS

My first cautionary note relates to the scale of change represented by the disruption of the proceedings in Seattle. The Millennium Round has only been deferred, not dropped altogether. Social movements have sought major reform of the WTO since its inception in 1995. Development activists pursued change in the General Agreement on Tariffs and Trade (GATT) for several decades before that. These long efforts have booked only modest gains to date. Thanks in good part to pressure from certain civic groups, the WTO has since 1996 added competition issues, development concerns, environmental problems, and labour standards to its agenda. However, little has happened on these matters beyond occasional meetings of committees and working groups.[2] The core mission of the WTO has remained that of the widest and fastest possible liberalisation of cross-border flows of goods and services.

Thanks in part to pressure from churches, NGOs, and trade unions, the Bretton Woods institutions have in recent years made some greater policy revisions than the WTO; nonetheless, so far, they too have retained a mainly neoliberal orientation.[3] The IMF's recent stress on poverty has brought a striking change of rhetoric, as did the World Bank's adoption in 1999 of the so-called Comprehensive Development Framework. However, we have yet to see what concrete improvements in social and environmental conditions these changes will bring. To date, "structural adjustment" in a globalising world economy has for the Bretton Woods agencies continued in the first place to mean liberalisation, privatisation, and deregulation.

Meanwhile, civic campaigns for change have had little to say—let alone achieved much—in respect of global finance. The previously mentioned campaigns for debt reduction in the South constitute an exception in this regard, though the actual sums of relief have thus far remained fairly small. Following crises in Asia, Latin America, and Russia, much discussion spread in the late 1990s regarding a new global financial architecture, but present prospects point toward emergency rewiring rather than major reconstruction.

In short, social movements of the kind represented on the streets of Seattle have achieved only marginal reforms of global economic governance to date. Instead of the unadulterated neoliberalism that prevailed in the 1980s and early 1990s, we now have neoliberalism with some fringes of social and environmental policy. Advocates of change have succeeded in placing neoliberal approaches to globalisation under more critical public scrutiny, but the supertanker is slow to turn.

LIMITS OF CIVIL SOCIETY

My second cautionary note relates to limitations in the practices of civil society regarding global economic governance.[4] Many civic activists have assumed rather uncritically that civil society efforts inherently contribute to human betterment. Some academic accounts of global civil society have reinforced these presumptions. Such romanticism does little to advance actual reform of globalisation and indeed can encourage detrimental complacency. Measured—and at times even sceptical—assessments of global civil society are needed to maximise its contributions and sustain its integrity.

By no means does this sober stance deny the significant positive potentials of civil society for progressive global politics. For one thing, community-based organizations, labour unions, and NGOs can play substantial roles in citizen education about globalisation. Civic groups can also give voice to stakeholders who tend not to be heard through official channels. Actors in global civil society can furthermore fuel policy debates by advancing alternative perspectives, methodologies, and proposals. Pressure from civic circles can thus increase transparency and accountability in the governance of globalisation. Moreover, at a time when official channels do not provide adequate mechanisms for democracy in globalisation, civic activism can help legitimise (or delegitimise) prevailing rules and governance institutions. In all of these ways, civil society can strengthen social cohesion, countering various other aspects of contemporary globalisation that have tended to weaken it. In principle, then, a lot of good can come out of global civic mobilisation.

Events in Seattle bore out these potential benefits in a number of ways. With regard to civic education, for example, the commotion (and more particularly the media attention that it attracted) made a larger public aware of the WTO and some of the downsides of the current neoliberal global trade regime. In terms of giving voice, the streets of Seattle (briefly) handed the microphone to grassroots associations that are not often heard in policy processes surrounding global trade. With respect to fuelling debate, the demonstrations in Seattle made it plain that alternatives to currently prevailing regimes are conceivable and perhaps desirable. This pressure has also compelled proponents of the neoliberal trading order to formulate their own case more clearly, precisely, and—we may hope—self-critically. The activists of Seattle have also impressed on regulators of world trade the need to open up and be accountable to citizens. Finally, the "Battle of Seattle" illustrated the importance of civil society in legitimating—or in this case delegitimating—multilateral laws and institutions. Global economic governance cannot rest on technocratic expertise alone: it requires popular consent as well.

Yet, events in Seattle also illustrated various limitations on civil society involvement in global economic governance. For one thing, we must not exaggerate the scale of the benefits just mentioned. Much more civic education is needed about the WTO and globalisation in general. We have yet to see whether Seattle will have launched a lasting, searching, inclusive public debate about the nature of the global economy and its governance. While the managers of global economic institutions have clearly been shaken by the Seattle episode, this experience does not so far appear to have substantially raised their attention to direct public accountability.

The coalition of resistance forces in Seattle may have also proved to be ephemeral. Does this movement have the necessary levels of resources and commitment for a long-haul campaign of global economic reform and/or transformation? A core of activists has devoted itself to the cause full-time, but wider public backing has to date generally been episodic and shallow. For example, a flurry of civic actions has surrounded the IMF/World Bank Annual and Spring Meetings for the last dozen years, but between these gatherings the day-to-day pressure for change (occasional upsurges in one or the other programme country aside) has been largely restricted to a handful of professional NGO campaigners.

In Seattle, as elsewhere, campaigners for change in the global economy have faced major resource disadvantages in their struggle with forces for neoliberal continuity. Oxfam and Fifty Years Is Enough have not begun to match the World Economic Forum and the Institute of International Finance in terms of staff, funds, equipment, office premises, and access to information. Thus far, proponents of change in the global economic order have also rarely developed effective symbolic capital, that is, ideas, images, and slogans that can mobilise a large constituency in a sustained way.

Nor should we forget that most of the nonofficial actors in Seattle did not subscribe to the street protesters' rejection of neoliberal global trade. As at earlier WTO meetings in Geneva and Singapore, far and away the largest sector of civil society present in Seattle was the business lobby. Likewise, bankers have far outnumbered other non-governmental groups at meetings of the multilateral financial institutions. Business associations and individual firms have influenced the shape of contemporary global economic governance much more than reformers and radicals in other quarters. If we take the scope of civil society to include commercial lobbies and policy think tanks as well as trade unions, NGOs, and community groups, then organised non-governmental forces have on balance actually *favoured* the neoliberal status-quo, not opposed it.

This situation points to a more general problem of equitable and democratic representation in global civil society as it has developed to date. In terms of class, for instance, the non-state actors that influence global economic governance have drawn disproportionately from propertied, professional, computer-literate, and English-speaking circles. In terms of countries, the people who have congregated in Seattle, Geneva, and Washington have come disproportionately from the North. In terms of civilisational inputs, most organized civic engagement with global economic institutions has come from Western circles, with Buddhist, Hindu, Islamic, and other cultures largely left out of the loop. In terms of gender and race, women and people of colour have been severely underrepresented in the academic, business, and trade union sectors of global civil society. In addition, urban residents have tended to obtain far easier access to civic campaigns on global economic governance than people from the countryside.

In short, there is a significant danger that global civic activism can reproduce the exclusions of neoliberal globalisation, even in campaigns that mean to oppose those inequities. How can we ensure that civil society indeed gives voice to all, and not just to those who speak the right language and can afford an airfare to Seattle?

Other deficits in democratic practice can also undermine the credentials of civic campaigners for global economic change. For example, global associations—no less than a government department or a business corporation—can be run with top-down managerial authoritarianism. In addition, policy making in global civic organizations can be quite opaque to outsiders: who takes the decisions, by what procedures, and for what reasons? Civic groups may be further deficient in respect to transparency when they do not publish financial statements or even a declaration of objectives, let alone full-scale reports of their activities. Moreover, the leadership of many NGOs is self-selected, raising troubling questions of accountability and potential conflicts of interest. In short, there is nothing inherently democratic in global civil society, whether we are talking about the WEF or the demonstrators of Seattle.

LOOKING AHEAD

My final cautionary note regarding recent events in Seattle concerns the way forward. Regrettably, campaigners for change in the global economy have on the whole held underdeveloped visions of the alternative worlds that they desire. Thus far, the energies of anarchists, consumer advocates, development campaigners, environmentalists, trade unions, and women's movements have, on balance, concentrated far more on undermining the neoliberal agenda than on mapping a different course. To be sure, certain critics have articulated some fairly specific ways forward, but many opponents have not moved beyond protest to proposal, offering reconstruction as well as destruction, specifying what they are for as well as what they are against. The demonstrators of Seattle spoke forcefully about what they rejected, but they offered comparatively few details about what they wanted in place of the Millennium Round, the WTO regime, and the current global economy more generally.

In particular, calls for "deglobalisation" have not been satisfactory in this regard. Many critics of neoliberalism have sought to unravel globalisation and to regain a purportedly better pre-global past. These circles have included economic nationalists (among them some old-style socialists) and a number of environmentalists. Many religious revivalists and xenophobic groups have also wanted to turn back the clock on globalisation.

These negative stances are understandable in light of the pains of neoliberal economic restructuring for many social circles. However, calls to reverse gear are misguided. For one thing, proponents of deglobalisation have greatly romanticised the local community and national sovereignty, neither of which have produced utopia in the past. Reactive opponents of neoliberalism have also tended to discount some of the benefits of globalisation, including indeed the possibility of developing transborder solidarities of the oppressed in global civil society. Moreover, deglobalisation is impracticable. The ideational, productive, regulatory, and technological forces behind globalisation have reached such magnitude that any return to a pre-global status quo ante is currently out of the question.[5]

The challenge, then, is to reorient globalisation, to steer the process in a different direction. Like many critics, the demonstrators in Seattle, Davos, and elsewhere have often conflated globalisation with neoliberalism. They have denounced "globalisation" when their actual target is the neoliberal approach to globalisation. Other policy frameworks could handle global economic governance in more effective, equitable, and democratic ways. The problem is not globalisation, but the way we handle it.

Progressive elements in global civil society therefore face a far greater challenge than disrupting summits on global economic governance. If neoliberal globalisation has unacceptable adverse consequences, and deglobalisation is not a viable option, then new forms of globalisation need to be developed. Fortunately some academic and civil society practices are beginning to explore these potentials.[6] If the energy of protest could be coupled with the inspiration of innovation, than more humane global futures could result.

NOTES

1. See Jan Aart Scholte, *Globalization: A Critical Introduction* (Basingstoke: Macmillan, 2000), especially chap. 12.

2. Jan Aart Scholte, Robert O'Brien, and Marc Williams, "The WTO and Civil Society," *Journal of World Trade* 33, no 1 (1999): 107–24.

3. See Paul J. Nelson, *The World Bank and Non-Governmental Organizations: The Limits of Apolitical Development* (Basingstoke: Macmillan, 1995); Jonathan A. Fox and L. David Browns, eds., *The Struggle for Accountability: The World Bank, NGOs and*

Grassroots Movements (Cambridge, MA: MIT Press, 1998); and Robert O'Brien et al., *Contesting Global Governance: Multilateral Economic Institutions and Global Social Movements* (Cambridge: Cambridge University Press, 2000).

4. The following points draw on Jan Aart Scholte, "Global Civil Society," in *The Political Economy of Globalization*, Ngaire Woods, ed. (Basingstoke: Macmillan, 2000), 173–201.

5. This assessment is elaborated in *Globalization: A Critical Introduction*, chap. 4.

6. See, for instance, Samir Amin, *Capitalism in the Age of Globalization: The Management of Contemporary Society* (London: Zed Books, 1997); James H. Mattelman, *The Globalization Syndrome: Transformation and Resistance* (Princeton, NJ: Princeton University Press, 2000); Jan Nederveen Pieterse, ed., *Global Futures: Shaping Globalization* (London: Sage, 2000); and Michael Edwards and John Gaventa, eds., *Global Citizen Action: Perspectives and Challenges* (Boulder, CO: Lynne Rienner, forthcoming).

POSTSCRIPT

One problem in understanding the significance of events such as the "Battle in Seattle" is sorting out the different groups participating in the demonstrations and their wide range of tactics and strategies. The more radical anti-globalization groups seemed focused primarily on disruptive techniques aimed at bringing the work of the WTO to a halt. Others were concerned with finding ways to hold the WTO accountable by demanding a greater popular voice in decision-making processes surrounding trade policies.

Events such as those in Seattle have led some to draw attention to the "dark side" of global civil society. In an article cited below, David Robertson argues that if NGOs want to hold institutions such as the WTO accountable to the public and make their work more transparent, then NGOs themselves must be prepared to do the same. He notes that many NGOs do not hold elections for officers and do not reveal their sources of funding or their expenditures. What makes them, he asks, any more representative of the population than the governments participating in WTO negotiations? Robertson suggests that NGOs should sign a code of conduct before they are given greater accessibility and participation. What would such a code of conduct contain? Would it even be feasible or desirable?

Suggested Additional Readings

Bhagwati, Jagdish. "Responding to Seattle." *Challenge* 44, no. 1 (January–February 2001): 6–19.

Clarke, Tony. "Taking on the WTO: Lessons from the Battle of Seattle." *Studies in Political Economy* 62 (Summer 2000): 7–16.

Hoad, Darren. "The World Trade Organisation: The Events and Impact of Seattle 1999." *Environmental Politics* 9, no. 4 (Winter 2000): 123–29.

Kaldor, Mary. "'Civilising' Globalisation? The Implications of the 'Battle in Seattle.'" *Millennium: Journal of International Studies* 29, no. 1 (2000): 105–14.

Kiely, Ray. "Globalization: From Domination to Resistance." *Third World Quarterly* 21, no. 6 (December 2000): 1059–71.

Levi, Margaret, and David Olson. "The Battles in Seattle." *Politics & Society* 28, no. 3 (September 2000): 309–30.

McMichael, Philip. "Sleepless since Seattle: What Is the WTO About?" *Review of International Political Economy* 7, no. 3 (September 2000): 466–75.

Robertson, David. "Civil Society and the WTO." *World Economy* 23, no. 9 (September 2000): 1119–35.

InfoTrac® College Edition

Search for the following articles in the InfoTrac® database:

Bendle, Mervyn. "Trajectories of Anti-Globalism." *Journal of Sociology* 38, no. 3 (September 2002): 213–23.

Buttel, Frederick H. "Some Observations on the Anti-Globalisation Movement." *Australian Journal of Social Issues* 38, no. 1 (February 2003): 95–116.

Scholte, Jan Aart. "Civil Society and Democracy in Global Governance." *Global Governance* 8, no. 3 (July–September 2002): 281–304.

Thomas, Neil. "Global Capitalism, the Anti-globalisation Movement and the Third World." *Capital & Class* 92 (Summer 2007): 45–79.

Worth, Owen, and Carmen Kuhling. "Counter-hegemony, Anti-globalisation and Culture in International Political Economy." *Capital & Class* 84 (Winter 2004): 31–43.

Web Resources

For current URLs for the following websites, visit www.crosscurrents.nelson.com.

BBC News: The Battle for Free Trade
http://news.bbc.co.uk/1/hi/special_report/1999/11/99/battle_for_free_trade/534014.stm
This page offers a collection of written and audio-visual reports on the events in Seattle as covered by the BBC.

Global Issues: WTO Protests in Seattle
http://www.globalissues.org/TradeRelated/Seattle.asp
This page contains a collection of resources on the Seattle protests, with special emphasis on the media coverage of the events.

Trade Observatory
http://www.tradeobservatory.org
The Institute for Agriculture and Trade Policy sponsors this site which contains many documents and updates on the World Trade Organization and issues related to trade and globalization.

Is Development Assistance Ineffective?

✔ **YES**
WILLIAM EASTERLY, "Was Development Assistance a Mistake?"

✗ **NO**
MICHAEL CROSSWELL, "The Development Record and the Effectiveness of Foreign Aid" *Praxis:* Fletcher Journal of Human Security, Volume XIV (1999): 1–23

At the beginning of the new millennium in 2000, the United Nations called for its members to increase efforts to assist the most impoverished of its member countries. To achieve this, the United Nations adopted the Millennium Development Goals. Among the eight goals were commitments to cut the number of people living in extreme poverty and hunger by half, reduce infant mortality by two-thirds, and provide universal primary education for all children of the world by the year 2015.

To achieve these ambitious goals, the United Nations called for a rapid "scale-up" of the amount of official development assistance (ODA) provided by the high-income nations of the world. At the beginning of the new millennium, donor nations provided only about 0.25 percent of their total GNP as official development assistance. In order to hope to meet its ambitious Millennium Development Goals, the United Nations called on donor countries to commit themselves to reaching a target of 0.7 percent of GNP in development assistance by no later than 2015.

"Development aid" is the term generally used to refer to various forms of assistance given by governments and non-governmental agencies in order to provide support to the economic and social development of low-income countries. The largest share of this assistance comes from the member nations of the Organisation of Economic Co-operation and Development (OECD). The OECD has adopted the term "Official Development Assistance" (ODA) to refer specifically to the assistance provided through "official" channels. This aid is intended to achieve economic and social goals and is provided on a "concessional" basis, which is lent on better terms than commercial markets provide. The assistance is channelled either "bilaterally" through the official international aid agencies of donor governments, such as the Canadian International Development Agency or the United States Agency for International Development (USAID), or "multilaterally" through international governmental organizations, such as the UN Development Programme (UNDP), the

World Food Programme (WFP), or the International Bank for Reconstruction and Development, commonly known as the World Bank. In addition, during the past several decades, governments have chosen to provide an increasing share of the ODA through non-governmental agencies such as Oxfam or World Vision, who also raise funds directly from the public.

Development assistance has its roots in the era immediately following World War II. In 1945, Western countries led by the United States established the International Monetary Fund (IMF) and the International Bank for Reconstruction and Development as the two main international institutions providing assistance for debt relief and economic development. The initial focus was revitalizing the world economy and rebuilding the economies of Europe devastated by the war. In 1947, the U.S. Secretary of State, General George C. Marshall, established the Marshall Plan, an ambitious program to provide funds to do this. The underlying goal was primarily political; by rebuilding the war-ravaged economies of Europe, a firmer basis would be established for democratic regimes throughout Europe. As the European economies became revitalized in the 1950s, the Marshall Plan was extended to newly independent countries in Asia, Africa, and the Middle East. The West wanted to strengthen ties to these developing countries while containing the looming threat of Soviet expansionism.

In its early years, foreign aid served a number of mixed motives. Assistance to countries of Asia, Africa, and Latin America would enhance democratization and lessen Soviet and communist influences. At the same time, aid programs served the economic interests of the donor nations themselves. Canada and the United States both launched large food aid programs intended to find an outlet for their large grain surpluses which were depressing world wheat prices. Donors regularly "tied" the use their aid funds to the purchase of goods and services within the donor country itself, thus providing a boost to their own economies.

As a result of this mixture of motives, foreign aid from the beginning has been controversial. Critics have suggested that such aid programs had more to do with promoting the political and economic interests of the donors than promoting the genuine development of the recipient countries themselves. Reformers increasingly used the terms of international development assistance or international co-operation in order to emphasize that these transfers of funds were intended to promote specifically developmental goals and to serve the goals of the recipient nations. They argued that many of the conditions imposed by donors imposed significant costs on the developing countries and made aid less effective in the long run. From a reformist perspective, the main issue was not that aid itself was a flawed instrument. Rather, the frequent intrusion of donor self-interest undermined the true purpose of development assistance. If donors could focus more directly on development objectives in the formulation of their aid policies, then the contribution of development assistance to the alleviation of poverty and inequality would be vastly enhanced.

Others have been much more skeptical of the value of development aid at all. Some critics on the left have argued that aid serves only to perpetuate the dependency of recipient countries and foster patterns of development that favour the interests of Western capitalist countries. They argue for a greater emphasis on giving developing countries greater access to the markets of industrial countries rather than increasing the flow of development assistance. In contrast, critics from the right argue that aid programs have tended to foster a vast aid bureaucracy which serves often to discourage necessary economic reforms and encourages corruption within developing countries themselves. During the years of the Reagan and Bush administrations, this view of aid prevailed within the American government, leading to a gradual decline in aid-giving. With the end of the Cold War and the accompanying decline in political motivations driving aid program, the levels of aid-giving to developing countries continued to decline.

However, since the attacks of September 11th, the United States and many other donors have expressed renewed interest in aid programs, arguing that the fostering of economic development and the reduction of poverty are important deterrents to terrorism. As a result, all Western countries including the United States endorsed the UN Millennium Development Goals. At the same time, they have insisted that any increases in the level of aid funding should be accompanied by a clear demonstration that the funds are being used effectively. This has resulted in renewed discussions regarding the effectiveness of development aid in meeting its objectives of fostering development.

In the following readings, we have two contrasting perspectives on this issue. William Easterly makes the case that development assistance is rarely successful. While not advocating the totally abolition of aid programs, Easterly contends that such programs can only achieve very limited goals. In contrast, Michael Crosswell examines the record of American foreign aid programs between the 1960s and late 1990s, and finds that the record was not as blemished as many critics of development assistance contend.

✔ YES

Was Development Assistance a Mistake?

WILLIAM EASTERLY

Development assistance is the combination of money, advice, and conditions from rich nations and international financial institutions like the World Bank and International Monetary Fund designed to achieve economic development in poor nations. This article argues that development assistance was based on three assumptions that, with the benefit of hindsight (although a wise few also had foresight), turned out to be mistaken.

1. WE KNOW WHAT ACTIONS ACHIEVE ECONOMIC DEVELOPMENT

Development economists have long known the answers on how to achieve development. The only problem is that those answers have kept changing over time.

To oversimplify, the evolution of Conventional Wisdom was as follows (see also Lindauer and Pritchett 2002; the World Bank 2005; and Rodrik 2006). In the '50s through the '70s, development (i.e., economic growth) was a simple matter of raising the rate of investment to GDP, including public investments like roads, dams, irrigation canals, schools, electricity and private investment. However, private investment was usually not trusted to do enough or do the right things, and so there was a strong role for the state to facilitate and direct investment, guided in turn by the development experts.

Unfortunately, the debts accumulated to finance these investments turned out not to be repayable, so there were two debt crises in the 1980s. The middle-income countries had borrowed at commercial banks at market rates; the low-income countries had loans from official agencies at concessional rates. Both entered into a long process of rescheduling and writing off that led to a lost decade for both groups of debtors. Understandably inferring that unrepayable loans were a sign of unproductive investments, especially in Latin America and Africa, development wisdom shifted away from mobilizing and guiding capital accumulation. Attention shifted toward the success of the East Asian tigers, who combined export orientation and macroeconomic stability. This became the inspiration for structural adjustment packages of the IMF and World Bank and the "Washington Consensus," which called for removing price distortions, opening to trade, and correcting macroeconomic imbalances (mainly budget deficits). The slogan of the new wave was "adjustment with growth."

Alas, loans to finance structural adjustment met the same fate in the low-income countries as the earlier loans to finance investment—there was little or no growth, the loans couldn't be repaid, and the low-income debt crisis stretched out into the new millennium with every year a new wave of debt forgiveness (most recently, the 100 percent cancellation of the structural adjustment loans in the Multilateral Debt Relief Initiative of 2006). In the middle-income countries of Latin America, there was for the most part adjustment and debt repayment, but little growth compared to expectations in the 1990s. The hope that the "East Asian miracle" could be replicated elsewhere with the same policies proved illusory. The "Washington Consensus" then gave way to "Second Generation" reforms that stressed the importance of institutions like property rights, contract enforcement, democratic accountability, and freedom from corruption.

Although each shift in the Conventional Wisdom was provoked by the failure of the previous Conventional Wisdom, the argument was usually that previous recommendations were "necessary but not sufficient." As Dani Rodrik (2006) points out, this has the effect of placing all the blame on the recipient rather than on the development experts, of making ever longer the list of "sufficient conditions" for development, and of thus making the Conventional Wisdom non-falsifiable.

A lot of these shifts were provoked by broad stylized facts and compelling country examples rather than by formal empirics. Development knowledge could draw upon more formal empirics like growth regressions. However, the hope that arose in the early 1990s that the New Growth Literature could at last empirically find the answers eventually collapsed from a surplus of answers. Durlauf, Johnson, and Temple (2005) pointed out that 145 different right hand side variables were significant as determinants of growth in various studies with around 100 degrees of freedom. When the problems of unrestricted specification were reduced by testing the outcomes of the key Washington Consensus variables on growth, the results tended to confirm the casual empiricism described above—countries as a group moved towards "better policies," yet average growth for that group declined for unknown reasons (Easterly 2001).

In the new millennium, a remarkably broad group of academics and policy-makers seem to agree that, after all that, maybe we don't know how to achieve development, although they are reluctant to say so exactly. The World Bank (2005) was either giving up or offering instantaneous non-falsifiability: "different policies can yield the same result, and the same policy can yield different results, depending on country institutional contexts and underlying growth strategies." Similarly the Barcelona Development Agenda (2004) agreed a Who's Who of leading economists concluded that: "there is no single set of policies that can be guaranteed to ignite sustained growth. Nations that have succeeded at this tremendously important task have faced different sets of obstacles and have adopted varying policies regarding regulation, export and industrial promotion, and technological innovation and knowledge acquisition."

Lindauer and Pritchett (2002) call it most honestly: "it seems harder than ever to identify the keys to growth. For every example, there is a counter-example. The current nostrum of one size doesn't fit all is not itself a big idea, but a way of expressing the absence of any big ideas."

This does not mean that economists know NOTHING about development, or know nothing about the many little pieces that contribute to development. Good economic analysis of problems in finance, macroeconomics, taxation and public spending, health, agriculture, etc. has held up well. Economists are reasonably confident that some combination of free markets and good institutions has an excellent historical track record of achieving development (as opposed to, say, totalitarian control of the economy by kleptocrats). It is just that we don't know how to get from here to there, which specific actions contribute to free markets and good institutions, how all the little pieces fit together, that is how to achieve development.

2. OUR ADVICE AND MONEY WILL MAKE THOSE CORRECT ACTIONS HAPPEN

By the same judgment by stylized facts and country cases that has guided the evolution of the conventional wisdom, development assistance has failed to achieve development. $568 billion in today's dollars flowed into Africa over the past 42 years, yet per capita growth of the median African nation has been close to zero. The top quarter of aid recipients (heavily overlapping with Africa) received 17 percent of their GDP in aid over those 42 years, yet also had near-zero per capita growth. Successful cases of development happening due to a large inflow of aid and technical assistance have been hard to find—South Korea is often cited, but took off after aid was reduced and the Koreans disregarded the advice of the aid donors (see Fox 2000). Other more recent examples frequently cited (Ghana, Uganda, Mozambique) were cases of recovery after steep collapse, and depend on rapid growth episodes that usually prove to be temporary (Hausman, Rodrik and Pritchett 2005). Botswana might be a better example of a long-term success story initially financed by aid, although the most well known case study of Botswana (Acemoglu, Johnson and Robinson 2004) doesn't even mention foreign aid. The cases of rapid growth currently most celebrated—India, China, and Vietnam—receive little aid as percent of their GDP.

With aid, one has an even more serious problem than with other growth regressions of endogeneity of the right hand side variable—it's very likely that low growth countries got more aid because they had low growth. This calls for more formal econometric methods to disentangle the aid outcome from the counterfactual, utilizing instruments such as population size and geo-strategic factors. Unfortunately, more formal empirics on the effect of aid on growth has suffered from the same problem as other growth regressions—too many possible specifications and not enough observations (to begin with, aid did not even make Durlauf, Johnson, and Temple 2005's list of 145 statistically significant variables appearing in growth regressions). Aid and control variables have included such exotic species as aid policy and Ethnic Fractionalization Assassinations. Not surprisingly, positive aid and growth results have not proven robust.

255

The early expectations that aid would raise growth failed to pay attention to elementary economics—that a lump-sum transfer does not change the incentives at the margin to invest in the economy. With today's globalized financial markets, the paradox first pointed out by Peter Bauer (1976) is more compelling than ever—any poor country where incentives to invest are attractive does not need aid, while a poor country without incentives to invest will not have aid go into investment. The international capital market imperfections and alleged inevitability of low savings rates in poor countries used to justify aid in the past have not held up well in today's world with private capital flowing into Zambian government bonds and with Chinese peasants saving far more than Americans.

Nor was there much better news on development assistance (money cum advice) changing the policies that were supposed to raise growth in Conventional Wisdom II. Easterly (2005) found that structural adjustment lending also had no effect on the kind of macro policies and price distortions that it was supposed to correct. Van de Walle (2001, 2005) provides case study evidence that African countries did little reform in response to structural adjustment packages or aid, and aid may have even undermined policy reform. As noted earlier, there was a general worldwide trend towards better policies (as judged by Conventional Wisdom II), but the degree of movement across countries was not correlated with the intensity of aid or structural adjustment lending in those countries.

There has also been surprisingly insufficient attention in aid agencies to the political incentives facing recipient governments, as Moss, Pettersson, and Van de Walle (2007) suggest:

> Large aid flows can result in a reduction in governmental accountability because governing elites no longer need to ensure the support of their publics and the assent of their legislatures when they do not need to raise revenues from the local economy, as long as they keep the donors happy and willing to provide alternative sources of funding.

Djankov et al. (2006) and Knack (2001) in fact find empirically that aid worsens democracy, bureaucratic quality, the rule of law, and corruption.

The confidence that aid would raise growth was also naïve about the knowledge and incentive problems that afflict the foreign aid agencies. Foreign aid is a public entity spending the money of rich people on the needs of poor people. Unlike most market transactions, the recipient of the aid goods has no ability to signal their dissatisfaction by discontinuing the trade of money for goods. Unlike provison of domestic public goods in democracies, the recipient of aid-financed public services has no ability to register dissatisfaction through voting. With little or no feedback from the poor, there is little information as to which aid programs are working. Nor is there much incentive for the aid agency to find out what works with little accountability (see Easterly 2006). These problems may account for many of the more well-documented foibles of the aid system—an emphasis on aid loans made rather than results of those loans, a surplus of reports that nobody reads, a fondness for grand frameworks and world summits, moral exhortations to everyone rather than any agency taking responsibility for any one thing, foreign technical experts to whom nobody is listening, health clinics without medicines, schools without textbooks, roads and water systems built but not maintained, aid-financed governments that stay in power despite corruption and economic mismanagement, and so on.

Having development be the goal of development assistance made these incentive and knowledge problems worse for the aid agencies than if they had focused on more specific tasks like, for example, combating childhood diseases. With many aid agencies operating in each country, and with development of that country depending on many other factors besides aid agencies, and with the inability to map actions to development anyway, it was very hard to hold an individual aid agency accountable for a good or bad development outcome. Hence, development assistance as it is now conceived is inherently unaccountable and unable to process feedback.

3. WE KNOW WHO "WE" ARE

Despite the frequency of statements like "we must end world poverty," it is seldom clarified who is this "we" taking responsibility for world poverty. Is it World Bank or UN officials? National government leaders? Celebrities? Perhaps "development experts" is the most likely in writings by "we" development experts. The expert tradition is so strong that the World Bank's (2005) response to the failure of expert analysis on how to achieve development is to intensify the use of expert analysis on how to achieve development:

A vital lesson for policy formulation and policy advice is the need to be cognizant of the shadow prices of constraints, and to address whatever is the *binding constraint* on growth, in the right manner and in the right sequence. This requires recognizing country specificities, and more economic analysis and rigor than does a formulaic approach to policy making.

The other possibility, that development experts are greatly overrated as a means to achieve development, goes against the self-interest of everyone in this profession (including this author). Yet maybe it is true; after all, development experts played no role in the development of the developed countries. Anne Krueger (2007) notes: "Development economics was a new field . . . because earlier economic growth in the developed countries had more or less 'just happened': while development of roads, railroads, education systems . . . had been undertaken by governments, it had not been done as part of a conscious 'development' policy."

Economists should not find so hard to take the idea of a spontaneous bottom-up order emerging out of the decentralized actions of many actors, as opposed to a strategic vision offered by a few experts. The invisible hand may operate in other areas besides the free market—institutions may emerge much more from the social norms and spontaneous arrangements of many actors than from the diktat of some expert from above (see Dixit 2003).

Yet "what must we do?" is a question that people can't help asking about a problem so tragic as world poverty, and experts are the ones who say they have the answers. The 20th century's first development economist may have been Lenin, who wrote a famous pamphlet in 1902 called "What is to be done?," and said that the revolutionary intelligentsia had the answer. A long line of such diverse thinkers as Edmund Burke, Karl Popper, Friedrich Hayek, Isaiah Berlin, and James C. Scott have criticized the idea that experts can re-design society, all the way back to the French Revolution, and the catastrophic outcomes of the more extreme attempts to do so supported these criticisms. Yet the unquenchable demand for experts who can call tell "us" the right answers shows no sign of ending soon.

CONCLUSION

In sum, we don't know what actions achieve development, our advice and aid doesn't make those actions happen even if we knew what they were, and we are not even sure who "we" are that is supposed to achieve development. I take away from this that development assistance was a mistake.

Yet it doesn't necessarily follow that foreign aid should be eliminated. Once freed from the delusion that it can accomplish development, foreign aid could finance piecemeal steps aimed at accomplishing particular tasks for which there is clearly a huge demand—to reduce malaria deaths, to provide more clean water, to build and maintain roads, to provide scholarships for talented but poor students, and so on. It could seek to create more opportunities for poor individuals, rather than try to transform poor societies. The knowledge and incentive problems for each such focused effort seem more solvable than that of "development assistance," although not exactly easy. As far as the experts, they would also do well to remember the principles of division of labor and gains from specialization, focusing on problems such as inflation stabilization, financial regulation, or red tape facing businesses, they probably have a lot to offer. Economists also still have a more general role making the case for individual freedoms that allow the spontaneous, bottom-up processes to work.

The inability of the experts and the aid donors to provide the answers to development fortunately has not stopped development from "just happening" on its own anyway. Economic growth without much influence by experts or much contribution by foreign aid is happening around the world in places like China, India, Chile, Botswana, Turkey, and Vietnam, generally involving homegrown, gradual movement towards freer markets. Even though some of these success stories could later flop, history suggests their place will be taken by new permanent exits from poverty. This should be enough to reassure those who care about world poverty to have some hope rather than despair.

REFERENCES

Acemoglu, Daron, Simon Johnson, and James A. Robinson. 2004. "An African Success Story: Botswana," in *In Search of Prosperity: Analytical Narrative on Economic Growth*, Dani Rodrik, ed., 80–119. Princeton NJ: Princeton University Press.

Barcelona Development Agenda (2004), Forum Barcelona 2004, http://www.barcelona2004.org/esp/banco_del_conocimiento/docs/CO_47_EN.pdf (Accessed December 27, 2006).

Bauer, Peter T. 1976. *Dissent on Development: Studies and Debates in Development Economics.* Cambridge, MA: Harvard University Press.

Dixit, Avinash K. 2003. *Lawlessness and Economics: Alternative Modes of Governance.* Princeton: Princeton University Press.

Djankov, Simeon, José García Montalvo, and Marta Reynal-Querol. 2006. "The Curse of Aid," http://ssrn.com/abstract=893558.

Durlauf, Steven N., Paul A. Johnson, and Jonathan R. W. Temple. 2005. "Growth Econometrics," in *Handbook of Economic Growth*, Philippe Aghion and Steven Durlauf, eds., Volume 1A, 555–678. Amsterdam: North Holland.

Easterly, William. 2006. *The White Man's Burden: Why the West's Efforts to Aid the Rest Have Done So Much Ill and So Little Good.* New York: Penguin Press.

Easterly, William. 2005. "What Did Structural Adjustment Adjust? The Association of Policies and Growth with Repeated IMF and World Bank Adjustment Loans." *Journal of Development Economics* 76(1): 1–22.

Easterly, William. 2001. "The Lost Decades: Explaining Developing Countries' Stagnation in Spite of Policy Reform 1980–1998." *Journal of Economic Growth* 6(2): 135–57.

Fox, James. 2000. "Applying the Comprehensive Development Framework to USAID Experiences." OED Working Paper Series No. 15.

Hausmann, Ricardo, Lant Pritchett, and Dani Rodrik. 2005. "Growth Accelerations." *Journal of Economic Growth* 10(4): 303–29.

Knack, Stephen. 2001. "Aid Dependence and the Quality of Governance: Cross-Country Empirical Tests." *Southern Economic Journal* 68(2): 310–29.

Krueger, Anne O. 2007. "Understanding Context and Interlinkages in Development Policy: Policy Formulation and Implementation." Presented at AEA Meetings, Chicago.

Lindauer, David L., and Lant Pritchett. 2002. "What's the Big Idea? The Third Generation of Policies for Economic Growth." *Economia* 3(1): 1–22.

Moss, Todd, Gunilla Pettersson, and Nicolas van de Walle. 2007. "An Aid-Institutions Paradox? A Review Essay on Aid Dependency and State Building in Sub-Saharan Africa," in *Reinventing Foreign Aid*, William Easterly, ed., Cambridge MA: MIT Press (forthcoming).

Rodrik, Dani. 2006. "Goodbye Washington Consensus, Hello Washington Confusion?" http://ksghome.harvard.edu/~drodrik/Lessons%20of%20the%201990s%20review%20 _JEL_.pdf

van de Walle, Nicolas. 2001. *African Economies and the Politics of Permanent Crisis, 1979–1999.* Cambridge, UK: Cambridge University Press.

van de Walle, Nicolas. 2005. *Overcoming Stagnation in Aid-Dependent Countries.* Washington, DC: Center for Global Development.

World Bank. 2005. *Economic Growth in the 1990s: Learning from a Decade of Reform.* Washington DC: World Bank.

✗ NO

The Development Record and the Effectiveness of Foreign Aid

MICHAEL CROSSWELL

Critics of foreign aid argue that little or no progress has been made in the developing world. The Heritage Foundation's initial survey of economic freedom claimed: "Not only has U.S. development aid been wasted, it has actually retarded economic development in the countries that receive it. Not one country receiving foreign aid has succeeded in developing sustained economic growth." A recent Cato Institute attack alleged that "few programs have consumed as many resources with as few positive results as foreign aid . . . the recipients of that largesse have, by and large, failed to grow economically and develop democratically." On the basis of these sorts of claims, congressional critics have attacked foreign aid complaining that "poor countries are still poor." Others might concede that economic growth has been achieved in parts of the developing world, but argue that the poor have not benefited, owing to increased inequality in income. Additionally, some critics claim that few countries have graduated from foreign aid, and dependence on U.S. and other foreign aid has been perpetuated. Some have argued that foreign aid has largely been "poured down ratholes," and is now an obsolete relic of the Cold War. (With this view of the role of foreign aid during the Cold War, why would one expect development progress?) Looking towards the future, these critics see only dim prospects for successful development, and therefore little or no role at all for foreign aid.[1]

Each of these arguments follows the same logical structure: recipients of foreign aid have failed to make development progress; therefore foreign aid has failed. There is nothing wrong with the logic. If the premise held, the conclusion would follow.

In fact, the premise is false. This paper examines the extent of progress (and lack of progress) in development, paying particular attention to the criticisms cited above. It demonstrates that these critiques are largely without empirical foundation. Development performance on the whole has been positive, with much more success than failure, and much more progress than stagnation or decline. Prospects for further success are good.

Generally speaking, development progress does not by itself demonstrate the effectiveness of foreign aid. There is still the hypothetical possibility that while much progress has been achieved, foreign aid had little or nothing to do with it. More extensive analysis, including case studies, is needed to isolate the role of foreign aid.[2]

Nonetheless, the fact of widespread development progress provides powerful circumstantial evidence for the effectiveness of foreign aid. And it clearly refutes the arguments (cited above) made by the most politically prominent critics of foreign aid.

THE DEVELOPMENT RECORD

The findings in this paper are based on an examination of the record over three decades of ninety countries, currently comprising three billion people (see Table 1, at end). With South Africa as the only exception, all were considered developing countries during the 1960s and 1970s, and all have been foreign aid recipients. Together they received $120 billion in U.S. bilateral economic aid between 1962 and 1990. Since the explicit concern is with foreign aid recipients, the analysis excludes countries that were largely outside the sphere of development cooperation prior to 1990—such as China, the countries of Eastern Europe and the New Independent States, Iraq, Iran, Syria, Lebanon, and Libya. Also excluded are numerous smaller countries, many of them islands.

1. Have foreign aid recipients achieved sustainable economic growth? Readily available data offer both long-term and short-term perspectives on growth performance (Table 1).

Looking at the period from 1965 to 1990, forty-one countries, comprising over 2.1 billion people, achieved significant positive average annual rates of economic growth in per capita income, ranging from 1.3 to 8.4 percent.[3] The average growth rate for these countries was 3.3 percent.

Of the remaining countries, some have realized greater success more recently. If we look at the 1985–95 period, an additional sixteen countries (280 million people) achieved significantly positive growth.[4]

Combining the two groups, fifty-seven of ninety countries, embracing nearly 2.4 billion people (80 percent of the total population of three billion) have been able to sustain economic growth at meaningful rates for a reasonably long period of time.[5]

2. Are poor countries still poor? Have poor countries failed to make economic progress? Of the forty-one countries that achieved significant growth over the 1965–90 period, twenty-five (accounting for 1.8 of 2.1 billion people) were "poor" in 1965, using a per capita income criterion of $1000 in 1990 prices.[6] The average annual growth rate in per capita income for these countries was 3.5 percent. All of these countries have received large amounts of foreign aid, either in absolute terms or on a per capita basis. Of the twenty-five, about half are now middle-income countries (using a $1000 threshold), and several others are about to cross the threshold.

Does the more recent growth performance of poor countries indicate a lack of economic progress? About three-quarters of the people in poor developing countries live in countries that achieved significant economic growth over the past decade.

The World Bank's 1997 World Development Report provides 1985–95 average annual growth rates in per capita income for forty-two countries (not counting China and the Newly Independent States) with per capita incomes below $1000, comprising 2.1 billion people. Of these, fifteen countries totaling 1.65 billion people achieved significant positive average annual growth in per capita income, ranging from 1.3 to 6.0 percent.[7] The average growth rate in per capita income for these countries was 3.3 percent. Thus, while only about a third of poor countries are making at least fair economic progress, this group accounts for the bulk of the population of poor countries, and for the bulk of global poverty.

3. Has economic growth reduced poverty? The available data–covering thirty-three countries that account for over two billion people and the major share of global poverty–confirm that economic growth has almost always resulted in declines in the proportion of the population below the poverty line. In thirty-five of thirty-seven episodes of economic growth, the proportion of the population in poverty fell. The lone exceptions to the rule are Brazil (1980–90), where growth was very weak, less than 1 percent per annum on a per capita basis; and Honduras (1986–89). The data also confirm that economic decline has resulted in increased rates of poverty. This occurred during specific intervals in nine countries.[8]

How strong and direct are the impacts of economic growth on poverty? Analysis both by the United States Agency for International Development (USAID) and the World Bank confirms that the more rapid the rate of growth, the sharper the decline in poverty; and that the impacts of economic growth on poverty are direct, substantial, and not subject to lags. USAID analysis indicates that economic growth in per capita income at 2 percent a year over two decades can be expected to reduce the share of the population falling below the poverty line by half (e.g. from 50 percent to 25 percent). With continued development cooperation, this kind of growth is well within the reach of most USAID recipients, and has been achieved by many, particularly the largest recipients. More recent World Bank analysis of a larger data set indicates that a 1 percent increase in income per capita is associated with a 29 percent decline in the share of the population below the poverty line. Further, the impacts of economic growth (or economic decline) on poverty have been fairly direct and immediate. Many observations are for periods of two to six years, implying that growth affects poverty in the near term.[9]

Has inequality increased with economic growth? More often than not (at least twenty-three out of thirty-three cases, with four others uncertain), income distribution has improved with growth and contributed to declines in poverty. Thus, the basis for lack of confidence that growth reduces poverty–the belief that income distribution systematically tended to worsen with growth–is not consistent with the data. World Bank analysis of a larger sample that includes Eastern

Europe, the Newly Independent States, and some industrial countries indicates that changes in income distribution over time tend to be small, with no systematic tendency for inequality to worsen with growth.[10]

4. *Has social well-being improved overall?* Indicators of social well-being, progress has been substantial and nearly universal. The effects of poverty are revealed in high infant mortality, low life expectancy, illiteracy, high rates of fertility, and other social indicators. By and large, improvements in these indicators signal improvements in the lives and well-being of poor people. In developing countries over the past thirty-five years, infant mortality has fallen from 162 to sixty-nine per thousand births; life expectancy has risen from fifty to sixty-five years; and literacy has climbed from 35 to 67 percent. Data for individual countries confirm that poor countries have shared in this progress. Fertility has declined sharply, particularly in Asia and Latin America, and also in some African countries.[11]

5. *Have women and girls fully participated in development progress?* Various indicators suggest that development progress has benefited girls and women at least as much as boys and men. A recent study of trends in primary and secondary enrollment ratios by region (six regions, with Asia divided into three regions) between 1970 and 1992 found that "in every region, girls' enrollment has increased at least as fast as boys' over the period, narrowing or almost closing the gap between their enrollment ratios." Internal USAID analysis carried out independently arrived at the same conclusion.

Similar analysis of trends in life expectancy between 1950 and 1990, disaggregated by region, found a positive and widening gap favoring women. Life expectancy for women was higher than for men in all major regions in 1950; and the subsequent gains were greater for women than for men in all regions and sub-regions. The large declines in fertility in most countries making development progress also suggest major improvements in the well-being of women.[12]

6. *Has economic freedom increased?*[13] Estimates covering sixty-seven of the countries reviewed here indicate that economic freedom increased in fifty countries, declined in ten, and remained essentially unchanged in seven. The Fraser Institute estimated levels of economic freedom for 1975 and 1995, on a scale from 1 (worst) to 10 (best). The average change was an improvement of nearly one point, from 3.9 to 4.8. Of the twenty-six countries with *relatively large* improvements in economic freedom (1.5 points or better), eighteen have been significant recipients of U.S. aid over the past twenty years and six others were significant USAID recipients in an earlier era.[14] Of the six countries where economic freedom declined by more than one point, USAID provides little or no development aid to three (Zaire, Algeria, and Venezuela). In the others (Haiti, Honduras, Nicaragua) there have been improvements in economic freedom since the Fraser study was completed (see Table 4).

Contributor Acknowledgements

These pages constitute an extension of the copyright page. We have made every effort to trace the ownership of all copyrighted material and to secure permission from copyright holders. In the event of any question arising as to the use of any material, we will be pleased to make the necessary corrections in future printings. Thanks are due to the following authors, publishers, and agents for permission to use the material indicated.

Issue 1

Reprinted by permission of *Foreign Affairs,* Vol. 72 Issue 3, Summer 1993. Copyright 1993 by the Council on Foreign Relations, Inc. www.ForeignAffairs.org.

Douglas Alan Ross, "Ten Years After: The Inevitable Waning of Huntington's Civilization Clash Theory?" © Nelson Education Ltd.

Issue 2

Alexander Wendt "Is a World State Inevitable?". Reprinted by permission of Alexander Wendt and Macalester College.

Shannon, Vaughan P. "Wendt's Violation of the Constructivist Project: Agency and Why a World State is Not Inevitable", *European Journal of International Relations*, Vol. 11(4): 581–587. © 2005, SAGE Publications and EXPRC-European Consortium for Political Research. Permission granted by Rights Link/CCC.

Issue 3

R. Charli Carpenter "Gender Theory in World Politics: Contributions of a Nonfeminist Standpoint", *International Studies Review* 4, 3 (2002), 153-65. Reprinted by permission of Wiley-Blackwell, Oxford.

Terrel Carver "Gender/Feminism/IR", *International Studies Review* 5, 2 (2003), p. 287–302. Reprinted by permission of Wiley-Blackwell, Oxford.

Issue 4

Reprinted by permission of *Foreign Affairs*, Vol. 87 Issue 2, 2008. Copyright 2008 by the Council on Foreign Relations, Inc.

www.ForeignAffairs.org

Reprinted by permission of *Foreign Affairs*, Vol. 87 Issue 4, 2008. Copyright 2008 by the Council on Foreign Relations, Inc.

www.ForeignAffairs.org

7. Has political freedom increased? Between 1975 and 1996 political freedom improved in fifty-two countries, and worsened in twenty-four. Freedom House conducts annual surveys of political freedom, based on scores for civil liberties and political rights, each gauged on a scale from 1 (best) to 7 (worst). The average change for the entire sample was an improvement of 1.7 points (on a scale from 2 to 14, reflecting the sum of the two scores), from 9.5 to 7.8. Thirty-one countries achieved major improvements (three points or more) over the period. Most were significant USAID recipients over the past two decades, or earlier.[15] Only eight countries showed large declines in political freedom (three points or greater): Colombia, Gambia, Kenya, Liberia, Malaysia, Nigeria, Sri Lanka, and Turkey. USAID no longer maintains full programs in any of those countries (see Table 5).

8. What about graduation? At least twenty-five countries, comprising over 675 million people, can be considered advanced (using economic and social indicators) and graduates with respect to dependence on foreign aid for development purposes.[16] All were labeled developing countries in the 1960s, and as recently as the late 1970s; most received substantial amounts of foreign aid; and all are substantially independent of *developmental* foreign aid now. Some still receive aid, but for specific foreign policy purposes other than development such as peace, narcotics, and global issues. Indeed, some have joined the ranks of donor countries, including Greece, Israel, Korea, Portugal, Singapore, Spain, Taiwan, Thailand, and Turkey.

WHERE DO WE STAND NOW AND WHAT ARE THE PROSPECTS FOR CONTINUED PROGRESS?

The developing world is increasingly heterogeneous, with countries arrayed across a wide spectrum from relief to development to advanced status. From the standpoint of performance and progress over the past decade, the world can be divided into five large groups (see Table 1):

- *Advanced developing countries:* about twenty-five countries (mentioned previously) comprising 675 million people, which are (practically speaking) aid graduates, and in some cases have become donors.

- *Countries that are "middle-income," and where advanced status and graduation are not far off,* such as Botswana, the Dominican Republic, Ecuador, Egypt, El Salvador, Guatemala, Jamaica, Jordan, Morocco, Paraguay, Peru, the Philippines, South Africa, and Swaziland. This group comprises about 260 million people, and includes some major aid recipients. Most should be expected to achieve advanced status and graduate over the next decade or so.

- *Countries that are by and large still poor, but have made significant economic progress* over the past decade or longer, with average annual growth rates in per capita income ranging from 1.3 to 6.0 percent. These include Bangladesh, Bolivia, Ghana, India, Indonesia, Mozambique, Nepal, Pakistan, Sri Lanka, Uganda, and Vietnam. Together they account for about 1.5 billion people, and two-thirds of global poverty (not counting China). Their prospects for continued growth are good, but in many instances fragile, as evidenced most vividly by Pakistan. Continued progress in this group would mean major reductions in global poverty.

- *Poor countries making at best intermittent progress.* This includes most of Sub-Saharan Africa, plus a small number of countries such as Cambodia, Haiti, Honduras, Nicaragua, and Yemen. This group of forty countries accounts for 570 million people, less than one-fifth of the total population of the ninety countries under review here, and less than the population of the group of advanced countries.

  A subset of this latter group would be countries in crisis or stalemate—including Afghanistan, Burma, Congo, Liberia, Rwanda, Somalia, and Sudan—about 160 million people. These are the countries most commonly cited in critiques of foreign aid. However, they are only a small part of the bigger picture.

  Overall, this group can be seen as the "last frontier" for development progress. Social indicators have improved in most cases, but institutional capabilities are still weak, and economic progress has been limited and sporadic. Most of these countries started the "development race" from a position of relative and absolute backwardness, particularly in terms of institutional capabilities and human resources. The challenge here is to move from "at best intermittent" to "steady" progress, including the move from relief to development for countries in crisis.

- *The transitional (postcommunist) countries* (not elsewhere discussed in this paper). These twenty-five countries, comprising about 400 million people, are arguably off the "Third World" continuum described above. Indeed, they embody their own continuum, covering a wide spectrum of economic performance and prospects; income, poverty and human resource development; and proximity to graduation. The predominant challenge in these transitional countries is one of discarding and replacing "maldeveloped" (rather than underdeveloped) institutions, both economic and political. The foreign aid track record in these countries is considerably shorter, but there has already been some success, including recent and prospective graduation.

If we look at these groups over time, we see that most of the countries which are "ahead" in 1997 were "ahead" in 1965; and those which have made the least progress are by and large those which were the least developed in 1965 (see Table 3).

For instance, the top twenty-six countries in terms of 1965 per capita income include twenty-two of the countries considered graduates in the tally above. (Only Colombia, Thailand, and Tunisia moved into the top group.) Remaining countries in the middle-income group that are poised for graduation over the next decade or so were mostly in the middle of the pack in 1965. Finally, of the fifty-one countries that are considered "poor" today (the third and fourth groups), all but seven were in the bottom fifty in 1965.

These considerations help debunk some of the less informed characterizations of foreign aid that have emanated from conservative think tanks. These critics often compare advanced countries receiving little aid with poor countries receiving larger amounts of aid, and conclude that aid retards development. Similarly, they portray development progress as purely a function of political will, ignoring the wide disparities in initial conditions, including human resources and institutional capabilities, that are critical to development progress. For example, the Heritage Foundation has compared Hong Kong with Tanzania, arguing that Hong Kong received relatively little aid and has made great progress, while Tanzania has received a great deal of aid and is still poor. This ignores the huge differences in initial conditions between Hong Kong and Tanzania in the early 1960s in terms of human resource development and institutional capabilities, as represented by a per capita income twenty-two times higher in Hong Kong than in Tanzania in 1965, and similarly large gaps in social indicators.[17]

HAS U.S. FOREIGN AID GONE DOWN "RATHOLES?"

While there has been a great deal of success in the developing world, one could still make the argument that U.S. foreign aid has been largely allocated to countries that have manifestly failed in developmental terms. The set of ninety countries examined here accounts for the major portion of U.S. foreign economic aid allocated to countries between 1962 and 1990. To what extent was this aid "poured down ratholes?"

One approach is to start by ranking the ninety countries examined above in terms of how much U.S. economic aid they received over the 1962–90 period (see Table 6). It turns out that the top thirteen recipients account for two-thirds of the aid; the top twenty received three-quarters; and the top thirty-one recipients absorbed 85 percent of U.S. foreign aid. The countries are (in order) Egypt, Israel, India, Pakistan, Vietnam, Bangladesh, Indonesia, the Philippines, Turkey, El Salvador, Korea, Brazil, Honduras, Jordan, Costa Rica, Sudan, Morocco, Colombia, the Dominican Republic, Peru, Bolivia, Jamaica, Portugal, Guatemala, Sri Lanka, Chile, Zaire, Tunisia, Panama, Kenya, and Thailand. The range is from almost $17 billion for Egypt and Israel (each) to about $900 million for Kenya and Thailand (each). In the latter cases, that amounts to around $30 million per year (each) on average. To what extent are these "major recipients" of U.S. aid to be considered successes or failures?

Only two of these countries—Congo and Sudan—have made little if any progress despite thirty years of aid. With the end of the Cold War the U.S. is no longer compelled to provide development aid to such countries. It is aid driven by political and Cold War considerations which is now "antiquated." But these two countries are the exception rather than the rule, accounting for only 2.5 percent of the aid to the thirty-one top recipients discussed here, and barely 2 percent overall.

Egypt and Israel are unique cases, each making significant strides in the development progress. But the effectiveness and productivity of aid has to be judged in terms of its contribution to peace in the Middle East, and the value we place on that. Political support for such aid remains exceptionally strong.

Vietnam is also unique. U.S. foreign aid was obviously unsuccessful in developmental and political terms during the 1960s and 1970s. The conditions under which the aid was provided were particularly difficult, with only limited implications for the general issue of aid effectiveness. Vietnam has made striking progress since the mid-1980s.

Looking at the remaining twenty-six countries and the four groups identified previously:

- Ten belong in the group of advanced countries that are virtual graduates: Brazil, Chile, Colombia, Costa Rica, Korea, Panama, Portugal, Thailand, Tunisia, and Turkey. Overall the group of advanced countries received about 30 percent of total aid accounted for in this review, with Israel receiving about 14 percent.

- Eight (the Dominican Republic, El Salvador, Guatemala, Jamaica, Jordan, Morocco, Peru, and the Philippines) belong in the group of fourteen middle-income countries for which advanced status and graduation are reasonable expectations over the next decade or so. (The others are Botswana, Ecuador, Egypt, Paraguay, South Africa, and Swaziland.) Overall this group received about 28 percent of the total aid accounted for in this review, with Egypt receiving about 14 percent.

- Six belong in the group of eleven poor countries that have made clear progress, with major positive implications for global poverty: Bangladesh, Bolivia, India, Indonesia, Pakistan, and Sri Lanka. As noted, performance in Pakistan (which is no longer a U.S. aid recipient) has faltered in recent years. The other countries in the group are Ghana, Mozambique, Nepal, Uganda, and Vietnam. Overall this group received about 28 percent of the aid accounted for in this review.

- Only two of the major recipients, Kenya and Honduras, belong to the group of poor countries making limited progress; and they are among the more successful countries of this group. Overall this group received 14 percent of the aid accounted for in this review.

In summary, looking at the thirty-one countries that received at least $30 million of U.S. aid per year on average, and which account for the bulk (85 percent) of total aid between 1962 and 1990, the overall performance of this group provides no basis for arguing that foreign aid systematically has been wasted. The successful record of most of these countries suggests that U.S. foreign aid has been well allocated across countries. Except for allocations to Sudan, Zaire, and Vietnam—all heavily influenced by Cold War politics, hence "antiquated" and not relevant to the future—there is little to suggest that U.S. foreign aid has been ineffective.

Looking at the complete sample, 86 percent of $120 billion in aid went to countries that we have characterized as advanced/graduates; middle-income countries not far from graduation; and poor countries making clear progress. Only 14 percent went to poor countries making at best intermittent progress.

Finally, we can look at the countries among the ninety that might be considered clear development failures from the perspective of the first half of the 1990s, and ask what share of the $120 billion in U.S. foreign aid for 1962–90 went to such countries. One plausible list might include Afghanistan, Burma, the Central African Republic, Chad, Congo, Haiti, Liberia, Nigeria, Rwanda, Sierra Leone, Somalia, Sudan, Yemen, and Zambia. These countries account for only six percent of the total recipients of U.S. foreign aid. Given legitimate room for uncertainty about the scope for development progress—at various times prospects looked utterly dismal in Bangladesh, Ethiopia, Indonesia, Korea, and Uganda, and, to name just a few—this is not an unreasonable share. It certainly contradicts the claim that the bulk of U.S. foreign aid has been poured down "ratholes."

CONCLUDING NOTES

The development challenge as viewed in the 1960s had mainly to do with about ninety countries today embracing about three billion people. Of this group, about twenty-five countries (675 million people) have reached advanced status and—for practical development purposes œ graduated. Another fourteen or so middle-income countries (260 million people) are not far from advanced status and graduation. An additional eleven poor countries (accounting for 1.5 billion people and two-thirds of global poverty) have been making steady progress in both economic and social terms. This leaves forty poor developing countries (570 million people, less than 20 percent of three billion) where results have been mixed, both over time, across countries, and across "sectors." Only a minority of this latter group could be characterized as development failures from the perspective of the mid-1990s.

There are also some twenty-five countries (400 million people) engaged in the transition from communism, where the challenges are somewhat different, the track record of foreign aid is much shorter, and the range of variation (e.g. from graduates to failed states) is large. Many of these countries, particularly in Eastern Europe, will probably have little or no claim on foreign aid ten years from now.

This arguably constitutes a positive record, especially considering the vast majority of people whose lives have clearly improved as a result of development progress. The countries and people experiencing the most difficulties and least progress constitute a distinct minority. Further, most of these countries started (in 1960) from positions of extreme backwardness, particularly in terms of human resources and institutional capabilities. It is not surprising they would be last to "take off."

Looking ahead, there is plenty of room to build on this record, including substantial progress in reducing global poverty and in graduation, *simply by maintaining recent trends*. In particular, achieving advanced status and graduation in the middle-income group, and maintaining momentum in the very populous group of poor countries that have made clear, steady progress would constitute major success. The goal, of course, is not simply to maintain trends, but to improve them, particularly in the group of poor countries that have made only intermittent progress. In support of this goal, there is an increasingly better knowledge base about the requisites for development progress œ especially human resource development, sound policies, and improved institutions—based on successful experience. There is increasing consensus on what constitutes good policies and institutions, and mounting awareness of which countries are making adequate self-help efforts. With globalization, the rewards for good policies and strengthened institutions, and the costs of poor policies and weak institutions are increasingly large and visible.

The predominantly successful U.S. development record does not prove the effectiveness of foreign aid. However, it provides powerful, positive circumstantial evidence, and it refutes the sorts of claims cited in the introduction. Critics who want to continue to make the case that foreign aid has been ineffective need to consider more carefully the evidence on development performance, and fund new arguments that do not rest on gross mischaracterizations of the development record.

NOTES

1. Bryan T. Johnson and Thomas P. Sheehy, *The Index of Economic Freedom* (Washington, D.C.: The Heritage Foundation, 1995), 1; and Doug Bandow, "HELP OR HINDRANCE: Can Foreign Aid Prevent International Crises?" *Policy Analysis* No. 273, April 25, 1997 (Washington, D.C.: Cato Institute), 2.

2. See, for example: *Assessing Aid*, World Bank, 1998, (New York: Oxford University Press Inc.); Robert Cassen, *Does Aid Work?* (Oxford: Clarendon, 1994); Anne Krueger, Constantine Michalopoulos, and Vernon Ruttan, *Aid and Development* (Baltimore and London: Johns Hopkins University Press, 1989).

3. They include Algeria, Belize, Botswana, Brazil, Burkina Faso, Burundi, Cameroon, Columbia, Congo (until 1997, known as Zaire), Costa Rica, Cypress, the Dominican Republic, Ecuador, Egypt, Greece, Hong Kong, India, Indonesia, Israel, Kenya, Korea,

Lesotho, Malaysia, Mali, Mauritius, Mexico, Morocco, Pakistan, Panama, Paraguay, the Philippines, Portugal, Singapore, South Africa, Spain, Sri Lanka, Swaziland, Taiwan, Thailand, Tunisia, and Turkey.

4. These recipients are Argentina, Bangladesh, Bolivia, Cambodia, Chile, El Salvador, Ghana, Guinea, Guinea-Bissau, Jamaica, Mozambique, Nepal, Papua New Guinea, Uganda, Uruguay, and Vietnam.

5. In defense of 1.3 percent average annual growth on a per capita basis as a reasonable threshold for successful growth, the United States grew at the same rate over the 1985–95 period according to the World Bank 1997 World Development Report. For congressional critics of foreign aid, the U.S. growth rate is arguably a reasonable reference point. Further, according to World Development Indicators 1998, growth in per capita consumption at 1.3 percent would enable the Asia region (which accounts for most of global poverty) to meet a target of reducing the proportion of their populations in poverty by half between 1995 and 2015. Further analysis and evidence that relatively modest rates of growth can achieve substantial reductions in poverty in low-income countries is contained in Martin Ravallion and Shaohua Chen "What Can New Survey Data Tell Us about Recent Changes in Distribution and Poverty?" *The World Bank Economic Review,* Volume 11, No. 2, May 1997.

6. These twenty-five are Botswana, Burkina Faso, Burundi, Cameroon, Colombia, Congo, the Dominican Republic, Ecuador, Egypt, India, Indonesia, Kenya, Korea, Lesotho, Malaysia, Mali, Morocco, Pakistan, Paraguay, the Philippines, Sri Lanka, Swaziland, Thailand, Tunisia, and Turkey (see Table 1).

7. They include Bangladesh, Bolivia, Egypt, Ghana, Guinea, Guinea-Bissau, India, Indonesia, Mozambique, Nepal, Pakistan, the Philippines, Sri Lanka, Uganda, and (during the specific period 1986–95) Vietnam. Recent growth performance in Cambodia has also been good.

8. Economic growth reduced poverty in Bangladesh, Bolivia, Brazil (during 1960–80), Chile, Colombia, Costa Rica, Ghana, Guatemala, India, Indonesia, Jamaica, Kenya, Korea, Malaysia, Morocco, Nigeria, Pakistan, Paraguay, the Philippines, Singapore, Sri Lanka, Taiwan, Thailand, Tunisia, and Uganda. For some of these countries, there are data for more than one time period. Economic decline increased poverty in Argentina, Colombia (1978–88), Costa Rica (1977–83), Côte d'Ivoire, Panama, Peru, Uruguay, and Venezuela. These results are based on data contained in the *World Development Report 1990* and subsequent World Bank reports. The results are compiled and analyzed in Michael Crosswell, USAID, "Growth, Poverty, and Income Distribution."

9. For instance, the proportion of the population in poverty fell from 36 to 24 percent in Costa Rica between 1983 and 1986; from 28 to 17 percent in Indonesia between 1984 and 1987; and from 50 to 43 percent in India between 1977 and 1983. See World Development Report 1990. Estimates of the elasticity of poverty with respect to growth are contained in Ravallion and Chen, op cit.

10. See Michael Crosswell, "Growth, Poverty and Income Distribution," (USAID mimeo, 1996); Catherine Gwin and Joan M. Nelson, ed., "Equity and Growth in Developing Countries: Old and New Perspectives on the Policy Issues," *Perspectives on Aid and Development, Policy Essay No. 22,* 1997 (Washington, D.C.: Overseas Development Council) by Michael Bruno, Martin Ravallion, and Lyn Squire.

11. See Table 2 and James Fox, "Gaining Ground: World Well-Being, 1950–95," *USAID Evaluation Special Study No. 79,* June 1998 (Washington, D.C.: USAID).

12. See John Knodel and Gavin W. Jones, "Does Promoting Girls Schooling Miss the Mark?" *Population and Development Review,* Volume 22, Number 4, December 1996; Donald Sillers, "Strategies for Increasing Girls' Primary Enrollment Rates: Should We Attack Gender Gaps or Expand Educational Access for All," (Washington, D.C.: USAID). Analysis of changes in life expectancy by gender is from James Fox, USAID.

13. The central elements of economic freedom are personal choice, protection of private property, and freedom of exchange. The goal of this study is to construct an index that is (a) a good indicator of economic freedom across countries and (b) based on objective components that can be updated regularly and used to track future changes in economic freedom. The components include ability to hold foreign currency; capital mobility; ability to trade with foreigners; marginal rate of taxation; the extent of transfers and subsidies; whether there are exchange controls and controls on credit markets; whether the government employs conscription to raise an army; the fraction of the economy consumed by the public sector; the extent of variation in the rate of inflation; and the extent to which the government employs inflation taxes. http://www.fraserinstitute.ca/press_releases/unformatted/econ_free95.html Source: James Gwartney, Robert Lawson, and Walter Block, "Economic Freedom of the World 1975–95."

14. Listed in order of the size of the improvement: Jamaica, Mauritius, Peru, Thailand, Ghana, Pakistan, Israel, Uganda, Turkey, Colombia, the Dominican Republic, Botswana, Philippines, El Salvador, Tunisia, Egypt, India, and Sri Lanka have been significant USAID recipients over the past two decades. Portugal, Chile, Argentina, Spain, Korea, and Taiwan were significant recipients in earlier years. The others are Singapore and Malaysia.

15. Among major improvers, Benin, Bolivia, Ecuador, Ghana, Guinea-Bissau, Guyana, Haiti, Honduras, Jordan, Madagascar, Mali, Mozambique, Nepal, Nicaragua, Panama, Peru, the Philippines, Senegal, South Africa, and Uganda have been significant USAID recipients over the past two decades. Chile, Cyprus, Korea, Paraguay, Portugal, Spain, Taiwan and Uruguay have also been USAID recipients.

16. These countries include Algeria, Argentina, Belize, Brazil, Chile, Colombia, Costa Rica, Cyprus, Greece, Hong Kong, Israel, Korea, Malaysia, Mauritius, Mexico, Panama, Portugal, Singapore, Spain, Taiwan, Thailand, Tunisia, Turkey, Uruguay, and Venezuela.

17. See *The Index of Economic Freedom* op cit., p. 1 where the authors argue, "If Hong Kong had been flooded with aid, as was Tanzania, it probably would be closer to Tanzania's status as the world's second poorest country."

TABLE 1
ECONOMIC PROGRESS

Country	Population (millions) mid-1995	GNP Per Capita 1995, in current dollars	GNP Per Capita 1990, in current dollars	GNP Per Capita 1995 in 1990 dollars	Average Annual Growth in GNP Per Capita (%) 1985–95	Average Annual Growth in GNP Per Capita (%) 1965–90	Purchasing Power Parity Estimate of GNP Per Capita 1995, in current dollars	Purchasing Power Parity Estimate of GNP Per Capita 1990, in current dollars	Purchasing Power Parity Estimate of GNP Per Capita 1995, in 1990 dollars	Group
Singapore	3,0	26.73	11.16	2.312	6,2	6,5	22.77	14.92	3.09	1
Hong Kong	6,2	22.99	11.49	2.554	4,8	6,2	22.95	16.23	3.607	1
Israel	5,5	15.92	10.92	5.748	2,5	2,6	16.49	11.94	6.285	1
Spain	39,2	13.58	11.02	6.091	2,6	2,4	14.52	10.84	5.991	1
Taiwan	21,1	11.3	7.31	1.316	6,9	7,1	n/a	n/a	n/a	1
Cyprus	0,7	10.26	8.02	2.103	4,6	5,5	14.8	9.95	2.609	1
Portugal	9,9	9.74	4.9	2.34	3,7	3,0	12.67	7.95	3.797	1
Korea	44,9	9.7	5.4	972	7,6	7,1	11.45	7.19	1.294	1
Greece	10,5	8.21	5.99	3.003	1,2	2,8	11.71	7.34	3.68	1
Argentina	34,7	8.03	2.37	2.555	1,9	−0,3	8.31	4.68	5.045	1
Uruguay	3,2	5.17	2.56	2.098	3,3	0,8	6.63	6	4.916	1
Chile	14,2	4.16	1.94	1.756	6,1	0,4	9.52	6.19	5.602	1
Malaysia	20,1	3.89	2.32	870	5,7	4,0	9.02	5.9	2.213	1
Brazil	159,2	3.64	2.68	1.19	−0,7	3,3	5.4	4.78	2.123	1
Mauritius	1,1	3.38	2.25	1.024	5,7	3,2	13.21	6.5	2.957	1
Mexico	91,8	3.32	2.49	1.248	0,1	2,8	6.4	5.98	2.998	1
Venezuela	21,7	3.02	2.56	3.291	0,5	−1,0	7.9	6.74	8.665	1
Turkey	61,1	2.78	1.63	858	2,2	2,6	5.58	5.02	2.643	1
Panama	2,6	2.75	1.83	1.293	−0,4	1,4	5.98	4.12	2.91	1
Thailand	58,2	2.74	1.42	484	8,4	4,4	7.54	4.61	1.571	1
Belize	0,2	2.63	1.99	1.048	4,4	2,6	5.4	4	2.106	1
Costa Rica	3,4	2.61	1.9	1.342	2,9	1,4	5.85	4.87	3.44	1
Colombia	36,8	1.91	1.26	714	2,8	2,3	6.13	4.95	2.804	1
Tunisia	9,0	1.82	1.44	655	1,8	3,2	5	3.979	1.81	1
Algeria	28,0	1.6	2.06	1.225	−2,6	2,1	5.3	4.68	2.784	1
Total/average	686,3	7.275	4.356	1.924	3,3	3,1	10.022	7.057	3.539	
South Africa	41,5	3.16	2.53	1.832	−1,0	1,3	5.03	5.5	3.982	2
Botswana	1,5	3.02	2.04	272	6,0	8,4	5.58	4.3	572	2
Peru	23,8	2.31	1.16	1.22	−1,6	−0,2	3.77	2.72	2.86	2
Paraguay	4,8	1.69	1.11	361	1,1	4,6	3.65	3.12	1.014	2
El Salvador	5,6	1.61	1.11	1.227	2,9	−0,4	2.61	1.89	2.089	2
Jordan	4,2	1.51	1.24	n/a	−2,8	n/a	4.06	4.53	n/a	2
Jamaica	2,5	1.51	1.5	2.08	3,7	−1,3	3.54	3.03	4.203	2
Dominican Republic	7,8	1.46	830	470	2,1	2,3	3.87	2.86	1.62	2
Ecuador	11,5	1.39	980	491	0,8	2,8	4.22	3.72	1.865	2
Guatemala	10,6	1.34	900	756	0,3	0,7	3.34	2.92	2.453	2
Swaziland	0,9	1.17	810	470	0,6	2,2	2.88	2.385	1.384	2
Morocco	26,6	1.11	950	538	0,8	2,3	3.34	2.67	1.512	2
Philippines	68,6	1.05	730	529	1,5	1,3	2.85	2.32	1.68	2
Egypt	57,8	790	600	220	1,1	4,1	3.82	3.1	1.135	2
Total/average	267,7	1.651	1.178	805	1,1	2,2	3.754	3.219	2.028	
Indonesia	193,2	980	570	190	6,0	4,5	3.8	2.35	782	3
Bolivia	7,4	800	630	751	1,7	−0,7	2.54	1.91	2.277	3
Sri Lanka	18,1	700	470	230	2,7	2,9	3.25	2.37	1.16	3
Pakistan	129,9	460	380	205	1,2	2,5	2.23	1.77	955	3
Ghana	17,1	390	390	555	1,5	−1,4	1.99	1.72	2.447	3
India	929,4	340	350	219	3,1	1,9	1.4	1.15	718	3

(Continued)

TABLE 1   (CONTINUED)

Country	Population (millions) mid-1995	GNP Per Capita 1995, in current dollars	GNP Per Capita 1990, in current dollars	GNP Per Capita 1995 in 1990 dollars	Average Annual Growth in GNP Per Capita (%) 1985–95	Average Annual Growth in GNP Per Capita (%) 1965–90	Purchasing Power Parity Estimate of GNP Per Capita 1995, in current dollars	Purchasing Power Parity Estimate of GNP Per Capita 1990, in current dollars	Purchasing Power Parity Estimate of GNP Per Capita 1995, in 1990 dollars	Group
Vietnam	73,5	240	n/a	n/a	4,2	n/a	n/a	n/a	n/a	3
Uganda	19,2	240	220	404	2,8	−2,4	1.47	800	1.468	3
Bangladesh	119,8	240	210	176	2,1	0,7	1.38	1.05	882	3
Nepal	21,5	200	170	150	2,4	0,5	1.17	950	839	3
Mozambique	16,2	80	80	84	3,6	−0,2	810	620	652	3
Total/average	1.545,3	425	347	296	2,8	0,8	2.004	1.469	1.218	
Papua New Guinea	4,3	1.16	860	839	2,1	0,1	2.42	1.5	1.463	4
Lesotho	2,0	770	530	160	1,5	4,9	1.78	1.7	514	4
Congo	2,6	680	1.01	471	−3,2	3,1	2.05	2.69	1.254	4
Cote d'Ivoire	14,0	660	750	662	−4,3	0,5	1.58	1.54	1.359	4
Cameroon	13,3	650	960	459	−7,0	3,0	2.11	2.02	965	4
Honduras	5,9	600	590	521	0,2	0,5	1.9	1.61	1.421	4
Senegal	8,5	600	710	825	−1,2	−0,6	1.78	1.36	1.581	4
Guyana	0,8	590	330	458	0,8	−1,3	2.42	1.465	2.032	4
Guinea	6,6	550	440	n/a	1,4	n/a	1.8	500	n/a	4
Zimbabwe	11,0	540	640	538	−0,6	0,7	2.03	1.97	1.655	4
Mauritania	2,3	460	500	581	0,5	−0,6	1.54	1.24	1.441	4
Zambia	9,0	400	420	678	−1,0	−1,9	930	810	1.308	4
Nicaragua	4,4	380	n/a	n/a	−5,8	−5,3	2	1.495	5.833	4
Benin	5,5	370	360	369	−0,4	−0,1	1.76	1.13	1.159	4
Central African Rep.	3,3	340	390	442	−2,0	−0,5	1.07	900	1.02	4
Gambia	1,1	320	260	218	0,3	0,7	930	915	769	4
Togo	4,1	310	410	420	−2,8	−0,1	1.13	990	1.015	4
Kenya	26,7	280	370	231	0,1	1,9	1.38	1.12	700	4
Cambodia	10,0	270	n/a	n/a	2,0	n/a	n/a	n/a	n/a	4
Yemen	15,3	260	n/a	n/a	n/a	n/a	n/a	1.56	n/a	4
Nigeria	111,3	260	290	283	1,2	0,1	1.22	1.42	1.385	4
Haiti	7,2	250	370	352	−5,2	0,2	910	960	913	4
Guinea-Bissau	1,1	250	180	n/a	1,8	0,1	790	840	819	4
Mali	9,8	250	270	177	0,6	1,7	550	560	367	4
Burkina Faso	10,4	230	330	239	−0,1	1,3	780	560	405	4
Madagascar	13,7	230	230	372	−2,0	−1,9	640	740	1.195	4
Niger	9,0	220	310	569	−2,1	−2,4	750	590	1.083	4
Chad	6,4	180	190	251	0,5	−1,1	700	440	580	4
Sierra Leone	4,2	180	240	240	−3,4	0,0	580	580	580	4
Rwanda	6,4	180	310	242	−5,0	1,0	540	610	476	4
Malawi	9,6	170	200	160	−0,7	0,9	750	670	536	4
Burundi	6,3	160	210	91	−1,3	3,4	630	600	260	4
Tanzania	29,6	120	110	116	0,9	−0,2	640	540	568	4
Zaire	43,8	120	220	384	−8,5	−2,2	490	950	1.657	4
Ethiopia	56,4	100	120	126	−0,5	−0,2	450	310	326	4
Sudan	26,7	n/a	400	477	0,6	−0,7	n/a	1.18	1.407	4
Somalia	9,5	n/a	120	123	−2,3	−0,1	n/a	540	554	4
Myanmar	45,1	n/a	n/a	n/a	0,4	1,2	n/a	n/a	n/a	4
Liberia	2,7	n/a	n/a	n/a	−3,0	n/a	n/a	n/a	n/a	4
Afghanistan	23,5	n/a	n/a	n/a	n/a	n/a	n/a	n/a	n/a	4
Total/average	583,4	374	401	377	−1,2	0,1	1.243	1.072	1.1 35	

Notes: Most data are from the World Bank's *World Development Report 1992* and *World Development Indicators 1997*. Data for Taiwan are from sources published by the Taiwan authorities. Per capita incomes for 1965 are based on 1990 per capita incomes deflated by 1965–90 growth rates. Growth rates in italics are for 1970–95.

TABLE 2
SOCIAL PROGRESS

Country	Life Expectancy 1965	Life Expectancy 1995	Infant Mortality Rate 1965	Infant Mortality Rate 1995	Total Fertility Rate 1965	Total Fertility Rate 1995	Index 1965	Index 1995	Change in Index 1965–95
Singapore	66	76	27	4	4,7	1,7	7,8	11,0	3,2
Hong Kong	67	79	26	5	4,5	1,2	8,0	11,6	3,6
Israel	73	77	27	8	3,8	2,4	8,9	10,5	1,6
Spain	72	77	38	7	2,9	1,2	9,3	11,4	2,1
Taiwan	66	76	26	7	4,8	1,8	7,7	10,9	2,8
Cyprus	70	78	27	8	3,1	2,2	9,2	10,7	1,5
Portugal	65	75	65	7	3,1	1,4	8,2	11,1	2,9
Korea	57	72	62	10	4,9	1,8	6,4	10,5	4,2
Greece	71	78	34	8	2,3	1,4	9,7	11,3	1,6
Argentina	66	73	58	22	3,1	2,7	8,4	9,8	1,4
Uruguay	69	73	47	18	2,8	2,2	9,0	10,2	1,2
Chile	60	72	98	12	4,8	2,3	6,1	10,2	4,1
Malaysia	58	71	55	12	6,3	3,4	5,6	9,3	3,7
Brazil	57	67	104	44	5,6	2,8	5,2	8,9	3,7
Mauritius	61	71	65	16	4,8	2,2	6,7	10,1	3,4
Mexico	60	72	82	33	6,7	3,0	5,0	9,3	4,3
Venezuela	63	71	65	23	6,1	3,1	5,9	9,3	3,4
Turkey	54	67	169	48	5,7	2,7	3,8	8,9	5,1
Panama	64	73	56	23	5,7	2,7	6,4	9,8	3,3
Thailand	56	69	88	35	6,3	1,8	4,9	9,9	5,0
Belize	66	70	51	36	6,3	3,9	6,3	8,5	2,2
Costa Rica	65	77	72	13	6,3	2,8	5,8	10,2	4,3
Colombia	59	69	86	34	6,5	2,8	5,0	9,2	4,2
Tunisia	52	69	145	39	7,0	2,9	3,2	9,1	5,9
Algeria	50	70	154	34	7,4	3,5	2,6	8,8	6,2
Average	63	73	69	20	5,0	2,4	6,6	10,0	3,4
South Africa	52	64	124	50	6,1	3,9	4,1	7,8	3,7
Botswana	48	68	112	56	6,9	4,4	3,5	7,7	4,2
Peru	51	66	130	47	6,7	3,1	3,5	8,6	5,0
Paraguay	65	68	73	41	6,6	4,0	5,6	8,2	2,6
El Salvador	55	67	120	36	6,7	3,7	4,0	8,4	4,4
Jordan	51	70	120	31	8,0	4,8	2,8	7,9	5,1
Jamaica	66	74	49	13	5,7	2,4	6,7	10,2	3,5
Dominican Republic	56	71	110	37	7,2	2,9	3,9	9,2	5,3
Ecuador	56	69	112	36	6,8	3,2	4,1	8,9	4,8
Guatemala	49	66	112	44	6,7	4,7	3,7	7,5	3,8
Swaziland	58	58	144	69	6,5	4,6	4,0	6,6	2,6
Morocco	50	65	145	55	7,1	3,4	2,9	8,2	5,2
Philippines	56	66	72	39	6,8	3,7	4,8	8,3	3,5
Egypt	49	63	145	56	6,8	3,4	3,1	8,0	4,9
Average	54	67	112	44	6,8	3,7	4,1	8,2	4,2
Indonesia	44	64	128	51	5,5	2,7	3,9	8,6	4,7
Bolivia	45	60	160	69	6,6	4,5	2,7	6,8	4,1
Sri Lanka	64	72	63	16	4,9	2,3	6,9	10,1	3,2
Pakistan	46	60	149	90	7,0	5,2	2,6	5,9	3,3
Ghana	48	58	120	73	6,8	5,1	3,4	6,1	2,7
India	45	62	150	68	6,2	3,2	3,1	7,9	4,7
Vietnam	50	68	134	41	6,0	3,1	3,9	8,8	4,9
Uganda	47	42	119	98	7,0	6,7	3,2	3,4	0,2

(Continued)

TABLE 2 (CONTINUED)

Country	Life Expectancy 1965	Life Expectancy 1995	Infant Mortality Rate 1965	Infant Mortality Rate 1995	Total Fertility Rate 1965	Total Fertility Rate 1995	Index 1965	Index 1995	Change in Index 1965–95
Bangladesh	45	58	144	79	6,8	3,5	2,8	7,2	4,4
Nepal	41	55	171	91	6,0	5,3	2,6	5,5	2,9
Mozambique	38	47	179	113	6,8	6,2	1,7	3,9	2,2
Average	207	220	138	72	6,3	4,3	3,4	6,7	3,4
Papua New Guinea	44	57	140	64	6,2	4,8	3,2	6,4	3,2
Lesotho	49	61	142	76	5,8	4,6	3,8	6,7	2,8
Congo	44	51	129	90	5,7	6,0	3,7	4,7	1,0
Cote d'Ivoire	42	55	149	86	7,4	5,3	2,1	5,6	3,5
Cameroon	46	57	143	56	5,2	5,7	4,0	5,9	1,9
Honduras	50	67	128	45	7,4	4,6	3,0	7,6	4,6
Senegal	41	50	160	62	6,4	5,7	2,5	5,3	2,8
Guyana	58	66	94	60	6,0	2,4	5,2	8,8	3,7
Guinea	35	44	191	128	5,9	6,5	1,9	3,2	1,3
Zimbabwe	48	57	103	55	8,0	3,8	2,9	7,3	4,4
Mauritania	38	51	178	96	6,5	5,2	1,9	5,2	3,2
Zambia	45	46	121	109	6,6	5,7	3,3	4,2	0,9
Nicaragua	51	68	121	46	7,2	4,1	3,3	8,0	4,7
Benin	42	50	166	95	6,8	6,0	2,2	4,5	2,3
Central African Republic	41	48	157	98	5,7	5,1	3,1	5,0	1,9
Gambia	34	46	201	126	6,5	5,3	1,2	4,2	3,0
Togo	42	56	153	88	6,5	6,4	2,6	4,8	2,2
Kenya	48	58	112	58	8,0	4,7	2,7	6,7	4,0
Cambodia	45	53	134	108	6,2	4,7	3,4	5,5	1,3
Yemen	40	53	194	100	7,0	7,4	1,5	3,7	2,2
Nigeria	42	47	162	119	6,9	5,5	2,2	4,3	2,1
Haiti	46	57	158	72	6,1	4,4	3,1	6,6	3,4
Guinea-Bissau	35	38	192	136	5,2	6,0	2,4	3,0	0,6
Mali	38	50	207	123	6,5	6,8	1,4	3,5	2,1
Burkina Faso	39	49	190	99	6,4	6,7	1,9	3,9	2,0
Madagascar	44	52	201	89	6,6	5,8	1,9	4,9	3,0
Niger	37	47	180	119	7,1	7,4	1,4	2,9	1,5
Chad	37	48	183	117	6,0	5,9	2,1	4,1	2,0
Sierra Leone	33	40	208	179	6,4	6,5	1,1	2,1	0,9
Rwanda	44	39	141	133	7,5	6,2	2,3	2,9	0,7
Malawi	39	43	200	133	7,8	6,6	0,7	3,0	2,2
Burundi	43	49	142	98	6,4	6,5	3,0	4,1	1,1
Tanzania	43	51	138	82	6,6	5,8	2,9	5,0	2,1
Zaire	52	52	141	92	6,0	6,7	3,9	4,2	0,3
Ethiopia	43	49	165	112	6,7	7,0	2,4	3,5	1,1
Sudan	40	54	160	77	6,7	4,8	2,2	6,0	3,8
Somalia	39	49	165	128	6,7	7,0	2,1	3,2	1,1
Myanmar	48	59	122	83	5,8	3,4	4,1	7,2	3,2
Liberia	45	54	176	172	6,4	6,5	2,6	3,2	0,7
Afghanistan	38	44	206	158	7,0	6,9	1,1	2,4	1,3
Average	43	52	159	99	6,5	5,7	2,6	4,8	2,8

Notes: Data are from the World Bank's *World Development Report* , 1992 and 1996, supplemented by data from the UN Development Program's *Human Development Report* for various years. Data for Belize and Taiwan are from national and other sources. The "index" gauges social development according to ranges of 2.3 to 8.0 births per woman for fertility; 208 to 260 deaths per 1,000 births for infant mortality; and 33 to 73 years for life expectancy. A minimal value earns a score of 0, and a maximum value a score of 10. The weights are 40 percent for fertility, 30 percent for life expectancy, and 30 percent for infant mortality.

TABLE 3

SELECTED INDICATORS FOR DEVELOPING COUNTRIES, CIRCA 1965

	Infant Mortality Rate 1965	Total Fertility Rate 1965	Life Expectancy 1965	GNP Per Capita 1990, in current dollars	GNP Per Capita 1965, in 1990 dollars	GNP Per Capita Average Growth 1965–1990	Net OSA Per Capita, Annual average 1965–68 in current dollars	Net OSA Per Capita, Annual average 1965–68 in 1990 dollars	Group
Spain	38	2,9	72	11.02	6.091	2,4	2,87	12,05	1
Israel	27	3,8	73	10.92	5.748	2,6	37,33	156,79	1
Venezuela	65	6,1	63	2.56	3.291	−1,0	7,08	29,74	1
Greece	34	2,3	71	5.99	3.003	2,8	4,00	16,80	1
Argentina	58	3,1	66	2.37	2.555	−0,3	−1,99	−8,36	1
Hong Kong	26	4,5	67	11.49	2.554	6,2	0,63	2,65	1
Portugal	65	3,1	65	4.9	2.34	3,0	n/a	n/a	1
Singapore	27	4,7	66	11.16	2.312	6,5	3,96	16,63	1
Cyprus	27	3,1	70	8.02	2.103	5,5	7,93	33,31	1
Uruguay	47	2,8	69	2.56	2.098	0,8	3,50	14,70	1
Mexico	82	6,7	60	2.49	1.803	1,3	2,28	9,58	1
Chile	98	4,8	60	1.94	1.756	0,4	15,56	65,35	1
Costa Rica	72	6,3	65	1.9	1.342	1,4	11,37	47,75	1
Taiwan	26	4,8	66	7.31	1.316	7,1	5,32	22,34	1
Panama	56	5,7	64	1.83	1.293	1,4	16,85	70,77	1
Algeria	154	7,4	50	2.06	1.225	2,1	9,09	38,18	1
Brazil	104	5,6	57	2.68	1.19	3,3	2,44	10,25	1
Belize	51	6,3	66	1.99	1.048	2,6	34,07	143,09	1
Mauritius	65	4,8	61	2.25	1.024	3,2	7,01	29,44	1
Korea	62	4,9	57	5.4	972	7,1	8,21	34,48	1
Malaysia	55	6,3	58	2.32	870	4,0	4,52	18,98	1
Turkey	169	5,7	54	1.63	858	2,6	6,10	25,62	1
Colombia	86	6,5	59	1.26	714	2,3	5,74	24,11	1
Tunisia	145	7,0	52	1.44	655	3,2	18,79	78,92	1
Thailand	88	6,3	56	1.42	484	4,4	1,77	7,43	1
Jamaica	49	5,7	66	1.5	2.08	−1,3	9,45	39,69	2
South Africa	124	6,1	52	2.53	1.832	1,3	n/a	n/a	2
El Salvador	120	6,7	55	1.11	1.227	−0,4	4,94	20,75	2
Peru	130	6,7	51	1.16	1.22	−0,2	4,79	20,12	2
Guatemala	112	6,7	49	900	756	0,7	3,38	14,20	2
Morocco	145	7,1	50	950	538	2,3	6,81	28,60	2
Philippines	72	6,8	56	730	529	1,3	2,85	11,97	2
Ecuador	112	6,8	56	980	491	2,8	4,64	19,49	2
Dominican Republic	110	7,2	56	830	470	2,3	15,77	66,23	2
Swaziland	145	6,5	58	810	470	2,2	28,65	120,33	2
Paraguay	73	6,6	65	1.11	361	4,6	6,56	27,55	2
Botswana	112	6,9	48	2.04	272	8,4	26,91	113,02	2
Egypt	145	6,8	49	600	220	4,1	2,04	8,57	2
Jordan	120	8,0	51	1.24	n/a	n/a	27,41	115,12	2
Bolivia	160	6,6	45	630	751	−0,7	8,87	37,25	3
Ghana	120	6,8	48	390	555	−1,4	8,44	35,45	3
Uganda	119	7,0	47	220	404	−2,4	2,77	11,63	3
Sri Lanka	63	4,9	64	470	230	2,9	2,94	12,35	3
India	150	6,2	45	350	219	1,9	2,36	9,91	3
Pakistan	149	7,0	46	380	205	2,5	4,05	17,01	3
Indonesia	128	5,5	44	570	190	4,5	1,50	6,30	3
Bangladesh	144	6,8	45	210	176	0,7	n/a	n/a	3

(Continued)

TABLE 3   (CONTINUED)

	Infant Mortality Rate 1965	Total Fertility Rate 1965	Life Expectancy 1965	GNP Per Capita 1990, in current dollars	GNP Per Capita 1965, in 1990 dollars	GNP Per Capita Average Growth 1965–1990	Net OSA Per Capita, Annual average 1965–68 in current dollars	Net OSA Per Capita, Annual average 1965–68 in 1990 dollars	Group
Nepal	171	6,0	41	170	150	0,5	1,08	4,54	3
Mozambique	179	6,8	38	80	84	−0,2	n/a	n/a	3
Vietnam	134	6,0	50	n/a	n/a	n/a	25,30	106,26	3
Papua New Guinea	140	6,2	44	860	839	0,1	42,33	177,79	4
Senegal	160	6,4	41	710	825	−0,6	12,68	53,26	4
Zambia	121	6,6	45	420	678	−1,9	9,13	38,35	4
Cote d'Ivoire	149	7,4	42	750	662	0,5	9,74	40,91	4
Mauritania	178	6,5	38	500	581	−0,6	7,46	31,33	4
Niger	180	7,1	37	310	569	−2,4	6,18	25,96	4
Zimbabwe	103	8,0	48	640	538	0,7	−0,35	−1,47	4
Honduras	128	7,4	50	590	521	0,5	5,22	21,92	4
Congo	129	5,7	44	1.01	471	3,1	25,34	106,43	4
Cameroon	143	5,2	46	960	459	3,0	6,85	28,77	4
Guyana	92	5,5	58	330	458	−1,3	17,07	71,69	4
Zaire	141	6,0	52	220	384	−2,2	6,24	26,21	4
Madagascar	201	6,6	44	230	372	−1,9	7,07	29,69	4
Benin	166	6,8	42	360	369	−0,1	7,14	29,99	4
Haiti	158	6,1	46	370	352	0,2	1,06	4,45	4
Nigeria	162	6,9	42	290	283	0,1	2,25	9,45	4
Chad	183	5,9	37	190	251	−1,1	5,74	24,11	4
Rwanda	141	7,5	44	310	242	1,0	3,62	15,20	4
Sierra Leone	208	6,4	33	240	240	0,0	5,01	21,04	4
Burkina Faso	190	6,4	39	330	239	1,3	3,83	16,09	4
Kenya	112	8,0	48	370	231	1,9	6,15	25,83	4
Gambia	201	6,5	34	260	218	0,7	9,18	38,56	4
Mali	207	6,5	38	270	177	1,7	4,16	17,47	4
Lesotho	142	5,8	49	530	160	4,9	14,16	59,47	4
Malawi	200	7,8	39	200	160	0,9	7,26	30,49	4
Ethiopia	165	5,8	43	120	126	−0,2	1,52	6,38	4
Somalia	165	6,7	39	120	123	−0,1	0,50	2,10	4
Tanzania	138	6,6	43	110	116	−0,2	2,98	12,52	4
Burundi	142	6,4	43	210	91	3,4	2,77	11,63	4
Afghanistan	206	7,0	38	n/a	n/a	n/a	2,74	11,51	4
Cambodia	134	6,2	45	n/a	n/a	n/a	1,90	7,98	4
Guinea	191	5,9	35	440	n/a	n/a	3,73	15,67	4
Guinea-Bissau	192	5,3	35	180	n/a	0,1	n/a	n/a	4
Liberia	176	6,4	45	n/a	n/a	−3,0	31,89	133,94	4
Myanmar	122	5,8	48	n/a	n/a	1,2	0,56	2,35	4
Nicaragua	121	7,2	51	n/a	n/a	−5,3	8,79	36,92	4
Sudan	160	6,7	40	n/a	n/a	−0,7	1,64	6,89	4
Yemen	194	7,0	40	n/a	n/a	n/a	0,76	3,19	4

Notes: Data for economic and social indicators are from previous tables. Data for 1965–68 aid per capita are from the Organization for Economic Cooperation and Development, *Resources for the Developing World, 1962–68, 1970.*

TABLE 4

TRENDS IN ECONOMIC FREEDOM, 1975–95

Country[a]	Index of Economic Freedom Score			Country	Index of Economic Freedom Score		
	1975	1995	Change 1975–95		1975	1995	Change 1975–95
1 Singapore	3,8	8,2	4,4	34 Indonesia	4,9	5,8	0,8
2 Portugal	2,1	5,8	3,7	35 Chad	3,8	4,5	0,7
3 Chile	2,7	6,2	3,5	36 Paraguay	5,3	5,9	0,6
4 Argentina	3,1	6,2	3,1	37 Jordan	4,3	4,8	0,5
5 Jamaica	3,0	6,1	3,1	38 Togo	3,0	3,5	0,5
6 Spain	3,5	6,3	2,8	39 Morocco	3,4	3,9	0,5
7 South Korea	3,8	6,7	2,8	40 Rwanda	3,1	3,5	0,4
8 Mauritius	3,6	6,1	2,5	41 Kenya	3,7	4,0	0,3
9 Peru	3,0	5,5	2,5	42 Nepal	3,1	3,4	0,3
10 Thailand	4,4	6,9	2,5	43 Nigeria	3,0	3,3	0,3
11 Ghana	2,0	4,4	2,4	44 Tanzania	2,9	3,2	0,3
12 Pakistan	2,8	5,2	2,4	45 Mali	3,9	4,1	0,3
13 Israel	2,2	4,2	2,0	46 Benin	3,4	3,7	0,3
14 Taiwan	4,9	6,8	1,9	47 Guatemala	5,9	6,2	0,3
15 Uganda	1,2	3,1	1,8	48 Senegal	3,7	4,0	0,3
16 Turkey	2,4	4,2	1,8	49 Uruguay	5,9	6,2	0,3
17 Colombia	3,5	5,3	1,8	50 Brazil	2,7	2,8	0,2
18 Dominican Republic	3,2	5,0	1,8	51 Sierra Leone	3,6	3,8	0,1
19 Botswana	3,8	5,6	1,8	52 Zambia	3,0	3,1	0,1
20 Philippines	4,2	6,0	1,8	53 Malawi	3,9	4,0	0,1
21 El Salvador	4,2	6,0	1,8	54 Hong Kong	9,1	9,0	0,0
22 Tunisia	2,7	4,3	1,6	55 Cameroon	4,1	4,0	−0,1
23 Malaysia	5,5	7,1	1,6	56 Niger	3,7	3,6	−0,1
24 Egypt	2,7	4,2	1,5	57 Madagascar	3,3	3,9	−0,6
25 India	2,9	4,4	1,5	58 Ivory Coast	3,9	3,2	−0,6
26 Sri Lanka	3,3	4,8	1,5	59 Panama	7,5	6,8	−0,7
27 Costa Rica	5,4	6,8	1,4	60 Congo	4,4	3,5	−0,9
28 Greece	3,6	4,9	1,3	61 Zaire	3,0	1,9	−1,1
29 Cyprus	3,8	4,9	1,2	62 Algeria	3,4	2,1	−1,2
30 Bangladesh	3,1	4,2	1,1	63 Haiti	4,5	3,2	−1,3
31 Ecuador	4,4	5,4	1,0	64 Honduras	7,1	5,5	−1,6
32 Mexico	4,8	5,7	1,0	65 Venezuela	6,5	3,9	−2,6
33 Bolivia	5,2	6,1	0,9	66 Nicaragua	6,0	2,7	−3,2
				Average	3,9	4,8	0,9

[a]Rank ordered by change in economic freedom score.

Source: *Economic Freedom of the World 1975–95*, by James Gwartney, Robert Lawson, and Walter Block.

TABLE 5
TRENDS IN POLITICAL FREEDOM, 1975–96

Country	Political Rights 1975	Political Rights 1996	Civil Liberties 1975	Civil Liberties 1996	Combined Rating 1975	Combined Rating 1996	Improvement 1975–96
48 Oman	7	6	6	6	13	12	1
49 Trinidad	2	1	2	2	4	3	1
50 Argentina	2	2	4	3	6	5	1
51 Botswana	2	2	3	2	5	4	1
52 Burkina Faso	6	5	4	4	10	9	1
53 Greece	2	1	2	3	4	4	0
54 Algeria	6	6	6	6	12	12	0
55 Mexico	4	4	3	3	7	7	0
56 Guatemala	4	3	3	4	7	7	0
57 Morocco	5	5	5	5	10	10	0
58 Zambia	5	5	4	4	9	9	0
59 Dominican Republic	4	3	2	3	6	6	0
60 Zaire	7	7	6	6	13	13	0
61 Burundi	7	7	7	7	14	14	0
62 Tunisia	6	6	5	5	11	11	0
63 India	2	2	3	4	5	6	−1
64 Pakistan	3	4	5	5	8	9	−1
65 Rwanda	7	7	5	6	12	13	−1
66 Costa Rica	1	1	1	2	2	3	−1
67 Swaziland	6	6	4	5	10	11	−1
68 El Salvador	2	3	3	3	5	6	−1
69 Papua New Guinea	3	2	2	4	5	6	−1
70 Mauritania	5	6	6	6	11	12	−1
71 Somalia	7	7	6	7	13	14	−1
72 Venezuela	2	2	2	3	4	5	−1
73 Afghanistan	7	7	6	7	13	14	−1
74 Egypt	6	6	4	6	10	12	−2
75 Jamaica	1	2	2	3	3	5	−2
76 Sudan	6	7	6	7	12	14	−2
77 Indonesia	5	7	5	5	10	12	−2
78 Myanmar	7	7	5	7	12	14	−2
79 Sri Lanka	2	3	3	5	5	8	−3
80 Nigeria	6	7	4	6	10	13	−3
81 Malaysia	3	4	3	5	6	9	−3
82 Kenya	5	7	4	6	9	13	−4
83 Colombia	2	4	2	4	4	8	−4
84 Liberia	6	7	3	6	9	13	−4
85 Turkey	2	4	3	5	5	9	−4
86 Gambia	2	7	2	6	4	13	−9
Average	1,6	5,0	3,8	4,5	4,0	9,4	7,8

Source: Freedom House.

TABLE 6
ALLOCATION OF U.S. ECONOMIC ASSISTANCE, RANK ORDERED

Rank	Country	U.S. Economic Assistance 1962–90 Million US$	Country Share of Total Percent	Cumulative Share of Total Percent
1	Egypt	16.936	14,16	14,16
2	Israel	16.878	14,11	28,27
3	India	9.600	8,03	36,30
4	Pakistan	6.885	5,76	42,05
5	Vietnam	6.013	5,03	47,08
6	Bangladesh	3.439	2,88	49,95
7	Indonesia	3.396	2,84	52,79
8	Philippines	3.289	2,75	55,54
9	Turkey	3.202	2,68	58,22
10	El Salvador	3.089	2,58	60,80
11	Korea	2.857	2,39	63,19
12	Brazil	2.246	1,88	65,07
13	Honduras	1.621	1,36	66,42
14	Jordan	1.597	1,34	67,76
15	Costa Rica	1.567	1,31	69,07
16	Sudan	1.552	1,30	70,37
17	Morocco	1.544	1,29	71,66
18	Colombia	1.473	1,23	72,89
19	Dom Rep	1.432	1,20	74,09
20	Peru	1.410	1,18	75,27
21	Bolivia	1.342	1,12	76,39
22	Jamaica	1.262	1,06	77,44
23	Portugal	1.208	1,01	78,45
24	Guatemala	1.197	1,00	79,45
25	Sri Lanka	1.134	0,95	80,40
26	Chile	1.077	0,90	81,30
27	Zaire	1.061	0,89	82,19
28	Tunisia	1.018	0,85	83,04
29	Panama	946	0,79	83,83
30	Kenya	897	0,75	84,58
31	Thailand	891	0,74	85,33
32	Haiti	787	0,66	85,98
33	Cambodia	776	0,65	86,63
34	Liberia	772	0,65	87,28
35	Somalia	712	0,60	87,87
36	Ethiopia	699	0,58	88,46
37	Ecuador	632	0,53	88,99
38	Senegal	616	0,51	89,50
39	Ghana	615	0,51	90,01
40	Nicaragua	602	0,50	90,52
41	Afghanistan	536	0,45	90,97
42	Nigeria	528	0,44	91,41
43	Tanzania	460	0,38	91,79
44	Yemen	450	0,38	92,17
45	Zambia	449	0,38	92,54

(Continued)

TABLE 6   (CONTINUED)

Rank	Country	U.S. Economic Assistance 1962–90 Million US$	Country Share of Total Percent	Cumulative Share of Total Percent
46	Nepal	424	0,35	92,90
47	Niger	418	0,35	93,25
48	Mexico	415	0,35	93,59
49	Mali	406	0,34	93,93
50	Mozambique	394	0,33	94,26
51	Zimbabwe	380	0,32	94,58
52	Cameroon	340	0,28	94,87
53	Taiwan	311	0,26	95,13
54	Guinea	308	0,26	95,38
55	Burkina Faso	306	0,26	95,64
56	Botswana	302	0,25	95,89
57	Malawi	295	0,25	96,14
58	Lesotho	282	0,24	96,37
59	Cyprus	282	0,24	96,61
60	Uganda	235	0,20	96,81
61	Chad	221	0,18	96,99
62	Greece	220	0,18	97,17
63	Algeria	200	0,17	97,34
64	Sierra Leone	192	0,16	97,50
65	Spain	191	0,16	97,66
66	Argentina	191	0,16	97,82
67	Venezuela	188	0,16	97,98
68	Paraguay	185	0,15	98,13
69	Myanmar	174	0,15	98,28
70	Mauritania	172	0,14	98,42
71	Uruguay	170	0,14	98,56
72	Madagascar	168	0,14	98,70
73	Guyana	167	0,14	98,84
74	Swaziland	152	0,13	98,97
75	Togo	149	0,12	99,10
76	Rwanda	146	0,12	99,22
77	South Africa	123	0,10	99,32
78	Belize	117	0,10	99,42
79	Gambia	106	0,09	99,51
80	Burundi	99	0,08	99,59
81	Cote d'Ivoire	88	0,07	99,66
82	Benin	85	0,07	99,73
83	Mauritius	77	0,06	99,80
84	Malaysia	70	0,06	99,86
85	Central African Republic	55	0,05	99,90
86	Guinea-Bissau	55	0,05	99,95
87	Congo	31	0,03	99,98
88	Hong Kong	17	0,01	99,99
89	Papua New Guinea	10	0,01	100,00
90	Singapore	2	0,00	100,00
Total		119.610		

Source: USAID, U.S. Overseas Loans and Grants, 1995.

POSTSCRIPT

Following the end of the Cold War, a degree of "aid fatigue" seemed to settle in among donor nations. With the end of superpower struggle for influence in developing countries, the political motivation for aid-giving diminished. At the same time, Western governments expressed dismay that the billions of dollars that they had poured into programs had not produced more substantial and tangible results. Thus, the decade of the 1990s was marked by a decline in aid-giving among many donors. The proclamation of the UN Millennium Goals was intended as initiative to turn this situation around and prod donor nations to make a renewed commitment to aid levels.

The adoption of the Millennium Development Goals has led to renewed discussions of issues surrounding the effectiveness of development aid. This has led to a growing movement among donor governments, the United Nations, and nongovernmental agencies to give attention to ways that development aid can be made more effective. It is argued that the political will to meet the Millennium Development Goals will not be met if the publics within donor nations are not convinced that such development aid is effective. At the same time, the MDG target of halving poverty will not be successful unless both donors and recipients take the necessary measures to ensure that aid programs are effective.

The OECD has taken leadership in calling representatives from both donor and recipient countries to address ways to ensure the most effect use of aid funds. These countries met together in 2003 and again in 2005 when they adopted the Paris Declaration on Aid Effectiveness, which sets out a clear set of principles for working together to improve the effectiveness of aid. In September 2008, they met again in Accra, Ghana, to review the progress that had been made to date. The progress of efforts to address the question of aid effectiveness can be followed at the OECD's official website: http://www.oecd.org/.

Suggested Additional Readings

Cassen, R., and Associates. *Does Aid Work?* Oxford: Clarendon Press, 1994.

Collier, P., and D. Dollar. "Can the World Cut Poverty in Half? How Policy Reform and Effective Aid Can Meet the International Development Goals." *World Development* 29, no. 11 (2001): 1787–1802.

Collier, P., and D. Dollar. "Development Effectiveness: What Have We Learnt?" *Economic Journal* 114, no. 496 (2004): F244–F271.

Gibson, Clark C., Krister Anderson, Elinor Ostrom, and Sujai Shivakumar, eds. *The Samaritan's Dilemma.* Oxford: Oxford University Press, 2005.

Guillaumont, P. and L. Chauvet. "Aid and Performance: A Reassessment." *Journal of Development Studies* 37, no. 6 (2001): 66–87.

Hancock, Graham. *Lords of Poverty: The Power, Prestige, and Corruption of the International Aid Business.* New York: The Atlantic Monthly Press, 1989.

Hansen, H., and F. Tarp. "Aid Effectiveness Disputed." *Journal of International Development* 12 (2000): 375–98.

Lensink, R., and H. White. "Assessing Aid: A Manifesto for the 21st Century?" *Oxford Development Studies* 28, no. 1 (2000): 5–18.

InfoTrac® College Edition

Search for the following articles in the InfoTrac® database:

Adelman, Carol C. "The Privatization of Foreign Aid: Reassessing National Largesse." *Foreign Affairs* 82, no. 6 (November–December 2003): 9.

Djankov, Simeon, Jose G. Montalvo, and Marta Reynal-Querol. "Does Foreign Aid Help?" *The Cato Journal* 26, no. 1 (Winter 2006): 1–27.

Easterly, William. "The Cartel of Good Intentions." *Foreign Policy* (July–August 2002): 40–49.

de Mesquita, Bruce Bueno. "How Foreign Aid Can Help the Poor—And Why It Doesn't." *Commentary* 118, no. 2 (September 2004): 101.

Muzinich, Justin, and Eric Werker. "A Better Approach to Foreign Aid." *Policy Review* 149 (June–July 2008): 19–28.

Naim, Moises. "Rogue Aid: What's Wrong with the Foreign Aid Programs of China, Venezuela, and Saudi Arabia?" *Foreign Policy* 159 (March–April 2007): 96–97.

Osborne, Evan. "Rethinking Foreign Aid." *The Cato Journal* 22, no. 2 (Fall 2002): 297–316.

Siddiqi, Moin. "Does Foreign Aid Work for Africa?" *African Business* 341 (April 2008): 62–63.

Web Resources

For current URLs for the following websites, visit www.crosscurrents.nelson.com.

CENTER FOR GLOBAL DEVELOPMENT

http://www.cgdev.org/

The Center for Global Development is an independent think tank focusing on issues relating to global poverty and inequality. Under research topics, you will find a section on aid effectiveness that contains a number of reports and news updates relating to the campaign to improve aid effectiveness.

THE PRIVATE SECTOR DEVELOPMENT BLOG
http://psdblog.worldbank.org/psdblog/
The Private Sector Development Blog, while claiming not to represent the official views of the World Bank, is written by employees of the World Bank group and is maintained by the World Bank Group's Rapid Response knowledge service. The site focuses on issues relating to business environment reform and privatization policy in developing countries. However, it also has useful information regarding discussions of aid effectively from a private sector perspective.

THE NORTH-SOUTH INSTITUTE
http://www.nsi-ins.ca
The North-South Institute is an independent, non-governmental, and non-partisan research institute focused on international development. Their annual reviews of international issues often discuss questions relating to aid effectiveness.

OVERSEAS DEVELOPMENT INSTITUTE
http://www.odi.org.uk/
Based in London, the Overseas Development Institute is one of the world's leading think tanks on international development and humanitarian issues. Their site contains a number of briefing papers and studies relating to development assistance and its effectiveness.

INSTITUTE OF DEVELOPMENT STUDIES/UNIVERSITY OF SUSSEX
http://www.ids.ac.uk/
The Institute of Development Studies (IDS) provides an extensive amount of resources concerning research on development issues. See particularly their section in aid.

Will Debt Relief Address the Needs of Highly Indebted Countries?

✔ **YES**
ROMILLY GREENHILL, "The Unbreakable Link—Debt Relief and the Millennium Development Goals," Jubilee Research/New Economics Foundation (February 2002)

✗ **NO**
DENISE FRONING, "Will Debt Relief Really Help?" *The Washington Quarterly* 24, no. 3 (Summer 2001): 199–211

For many in the developing world, particularly in Africa and Latin America, the 1980s have come to be referred to as the "lost decade." By the beginning of the decade, it was evident that the call for a new international order, launched with much fanfare in the late 1960s, had become bogged down in fruitless debate. Instead of moving toward a more prosperous and hopeful future, many in the developing world found themselves facing deepening economic crises, deteriorating environmental conditions, and, in Africa, recurring famines. But the main story of the decade became the mounting debt crisis faced by a growing number of less developed countries (LDCs). By the end of the 1980s, this debt was estimated to be about U.S. $1.4 trillion. (All amounts henceforth are given in U.S. dollars.) Efforts to repay it have led to a net transfer of resources from the South to the North. In 1988 alone, $32.5 billion more was transferred to the North, mostly in the form of debt service payments, than was received in the South in aid and loans. Instead of moving toward a new and more equitable international economic order, North–South relations in the 1980s became preoccupied with crisis management and the politics of debt.

The international response to the debt crisis can best be described in terms of two phases, labelled after two successive American secretaries of the treasury who took leadership of the North's reaction to the debt crisis. The first phase, the Baker Plan, unveiled by then–U.S. Treasury Secretary James Baker, called for an additional $40 billion to be lent to the fifteen largest, mostly middle-income, debtors. Half of the funds would come from the World Bank and regional development banks, while the other half would come from "voluntary" loans from commercial banks. Access to these loans would be conditional on acceptance of International Monetary Fund–approved (IMF) programs. New sources of funding were also promised for the smaller, lower-income African states whose debts, owed mainly to donor governments and international financial institutions (IFIs), were in many cases more onerous.

However, the Baker Plan soon lost momentum, and support from many donors fell short of promised levels. Private financial flows dropped as commercial banks withdrew from all but the most risk-free loans. Resentment in the South mounted as governments struggled with the political consequences of implementing many of the austerity measures demanded by the IMF. LDC governments complained that the IMF-imposed structural adjustment programs, which typically included sharp cuts in government services and subsidies, undermined their political legitimacy without really resolving their economic crisis. Throughout the 1980s, "IMF riots" became commonplace in many LDCs. More countries were falling into arrears, not only to banks, governments, and their export credit agencies, but also to the IFIs, such as the IMF and the World Bank, whose debt payments cannot be rescheduled.

In 1989, James Baker's successor, Nicholas Brady, launched a new initiative to deal with the debt crisis. The centrepiece of the Brady Plan was to make up to $35 billion available to finance debt-reduction deals negotiated between selected debtor countries and their creditor banks. The plan was adopted by the IFIs and the G-7 industrialized countries as their primary approach to the debt crisis. But from the beginning, critics charged that the plan was fundamentally flawed and woefully inadequate. The South Commission, chaired by the former president of Tanzania, Julius Nyerere, pointed out that the plan dealt only with debt owed to commercial banks and that reduction of even this debt was still up to those banks. Further, the commission argued that the pool of funds available was clearly inadequate to achieve any real measure of debt reduction. In reviewing Northern efforts to deal with the debt crisis, the commission's report, The Challenge to the South (Oxford: Oxford University Press, 1990), concluded: "The upshot is that debt has become a form of bondage, and the indebted economies have become indentured economies—a clear manifestation of neo-colonialism. This state of affairs cannot go on. The debt and its service must be reduced to a level that allows growth to proceed at an acceptable pace" (p. 227).

At the end of the 1990s, it was increasingly evident that the fears of the South Commission had come true, especially in the case of African countries. In its 1986 World Development Report, the World Bank predicted with confidence that by the mid-1990s developing-country debt would, in the worst-case scenario, amount to about $864 billion, and that the amount owed by African low-income countries would be only about $29 billion. However, by 1994, according to the World Bank's own figures, the external debt of all developing countries stood at nearly $2 trillion, while the debt of sub-Saharan African countries was $210 billion (Susan George, "Rethinking Debt," Development 2 [1996]: 54).

The continuing debt crisis has led some people to question whether more radical debt-relief measures are needed to address the problems facing developing countries. One voice in this movement has been the Jubilee 2000 campaign, a grassroots movement started in the United Kingdom to mobilize support for debt

remission. The co-founders of Jubilee 2000, William Peters and Martin Dent, liken their campaign to the struggle against slavery in an earlier century. They developed their case for debt relief by drawing on the Hebraic concept of the jubilee as a model for debt forgiveness today.

In part as a result of the work of the Jubilee campaign, debt forgiveness has become a major international issue in recent years; the Pope and celebrities such as Bono of the pop band U2 have become spokespeople for the cause. There has also been a number of promising developments recently. One of these is the World Bank's Highly Indebted Poor Countries (HIPC) Initiative. Announced in 1996 and implemented in September 1997, HIPC aims debt-relief funding at the poorest and most heavily indebted countries. After initial projects in Uganda and Bolivia, the World Bank expanded the initiative; it is now known as the Enhanced Highly Indebted Poor Countries Initiative. The overall goal is to combine HIPC debt relief with more traditional forms of debt forgiveness and forgive up to $55 billion, a little more than half the total outstanding debt of these countries. Mozambique qualified for an additional $600 million of debt relief in April 2000, bringing its total to $4.3 billion of debt forgiven. Burkina Faso was approved for an additional $700 million in June 2000 after meeting previous guidelines. The World Bank has also established a Trust Fund for the HIPC to assist multilateral development banks with the costs they incur when forgiving debt. Since then, some individual countries have announced measures to forgive a substantial portion of developing-country debt.

Despite this progress, many feel that not enough has been done to address the debt issue. With the passing of the Jubilee year of 2000, less attention has been focused on debt forgiveness. The Jubilee 2000 campaign has been renamed the Jubilee Debt Campaign. Increasingly, the international community has turned its focus to the United Nations Millennium Development Goals announced in 2000. In the Millennium Declaration passed by the United Nations General Assembly, the leaders of the world committed themselves to reducing the number of those who live in poverty and hunger by half by the year 2015. They also set other goals, such as the achievement of universal primary education, the reversal of the spread of HIV/AIDS and malaria, and the reduction of child and maternal mortality rates by half in the same time period.

In the first reading, Romilly Greenhill looks at the issue of debt relief in the context of these new goals. In this report prepared for the Jubilee campaign, she examines the achievements of the HIPC debt-relief initiative and finds that the results have fallen far short of the hopes of debt campaigners. She then focuses on what it will take to achieve the goals set by the United Nations in the Millennium Declaration. Greenhill concludes that it is only through 100 percent debt cancellation and a significant increase in aid-giving that there is any hope of achieving these goals. Denise Froning provides another perspective by looking at some of the problems with reliance on debt forgiveness. She examines the internal problems of developing countries that need to be addressed and also looks at the changes needed in the policies of industrialized countries.

✔ YES

The Unbreakable Link—Debt Relief and the Millennium Development Goals
ROMILLY GREENHILL

At the start of the new millennium, the world's leaders met in the United Nations General Assembly to set out a new global vision for humanity. In their Millennium Declaration, the statesmen and women recognised their 'collective responsibility to uphold the principles of human dignity, equality and equity at the global level.'[1] They pledged to 'spare no effort to free our fellow men, women and children from the abject and dehumanising conditions of extreme poverty.'[2]

From these fine words, a set of goals was born: to eliminate world poverty by the year 2015; to achieve universal primary education; to promote gender equality and empower women; to reduce child mortality; improve maternal health; to combat HIV/AIDS and other diseases; and to ensure environmental sustainability. According to Clare Short, the UK's Secretary of State for International Development, these goals have the potential to 'transform the lives of hundreds of millions of poor people, and make the planet a better and safer place for our children and grandchildren.'[3]

Since then, the Millennium Development Goals—as they were subsequently named—have been adopted by all major donor agencies as guiding principles for their strategies for poverty eradication. The OECD 'confirmed their commitment to reducing poverty in all its dimensions and to achieving the seven International Development Goals.'[4] The IMF and World Bank have co-ordinated their efforts behind this set of goals, and the UK Government has made them the centrepiece of its overall aid strategy. More importantly, the adoption of the targets has motivated a fundamental shift within development thinking—away from a narrow focus on inputs, towards a fundamental concern with outcomes for the poor of the world.[5]

Moreover, since the adoption of the MDGs in the year 2000, events have conspired to reinforce the urgent need for poverty reduction in the world. According to Gordon Brown, the aftermath of September 11th has shown that 'the international community must take strong action to tackle injustice and poverty . . . [and to] achieve our 2015 Millennium Development Goals.'[6]

But meeting the 2015 targets requires resources. Ernest Zedillo, in his report of the High Level Panel for Financing for Development, has assessed that total additional resources of $50bn per year will be needed to meet these targets worldwide, over and above the current level of spending in key areas. This estimate is based on detailed costings in some of the key goal areas by UN bodies such as UNICEF, the World Health Organisation, and others such as the World Bank.[7]

The UN Millennium Declaration was not the only remarkable event of the year 2000. Equally notable—though perhaps more poignant—was the winding down of

the Jubilee 2000 campaign, described by Kofi Annan as 'the voice of the world's conscience and indefatigable fighters for justice.'[8] The Jubilee 2000 coalition had campaigned for the cancellation of the un-payable debts of the poorest countries by the end of 2000, under a fair and transparent process. Their petition—the largest ever—had been signed by 24 million people worldwide.

BOX 1
PROGRESS IN THE HIPC INITIATIVE AS OF END 2001

1. Completion Point Countries (4)

Bolivia
Mozambique
Tanzania
Uganda

2. Decision Point Countries (20)

Benin
Burkina Faso
Cameroon
Chad
Ethiopia
The Gambia
Guinea
Guinea-Bissau
Guyana
Honduras
Madagascar
Malawi
Mali
Mauritania
Nicaragua
Niger
Rwanda
Sao Tome and Principe
Senegal
Zambia

3. Other Countries (18)

Angola
Burundi
Cape Verde
Central African Republic Comoros
Comoros
Congo DR
Congo Rep
Cote D'Ivoire
Ghana
Lao PDR
Liberia
Myanmar
Sierra Leone
Somalia
Sudan
Togo
Vietnam
Yemen

The central message of the Jubilee 2000 campaign was that human rights should not be subordinated to money rights. Poor countries prepared to commit resources to meeting the basic needs and economic rights of their populations should not be prevented from doing so because of the need to pay back debts to rich creditor countries and institutions.

The Jubilee 2000 campaign had won a commitment to a $110bn write off of un-payable debts. This was to be achieved partly through an extension of the World Bank's Heavily Indebted Poor Countries (HIPC) initiative, and partly through addi-tional bilateral commitments from creditors such as the UK.

But it is now clear that the HIPC initiative is not delivering enough either to pro-duce the promised 'robust exit' from unsustainable debts or to meet internationally agreed poverty reduction goals. As shown in Box [1], by the end of 2001–a full year after the millennium deadline called by the Jubilee 2000 coalition–only four coun-tries had passed through all the hoops of the HIPC initiative. Out of the 42 countries included in the process, almost half of these had not even reached 'decision point', after which they receive some interim relief on their debt service payments. Moreover, even when relief is provided, research by Jubilee Plus[9] has shown that debt burdens remain unsustainable. HIPC is a failure.

For this reason, debt campaigners have argued that debt relief can no longer be based on arbitrary debt-to-export ratios, designed by rich country creditors and multilateral institutions so as to minimise their own losses. Instead, poor coun-tries should be able to call for debt relief when it is clear that debt repayments are crowding out payments for services fundamental to human rights.

Debt campaigners were encouraged, therefore, by indications that the upcoming UN Financing for Development Conference would be prepared to consider linking debt relief to each country's capacity to raise the finance needed to achieve the millennium development goals.[10] But hopes were dashed when this proposal was rejected by the G7 countries, including the EU, Japan, and Canada. In the usual round of horse-play which precedes these conferences, the G7 countries have been forced to make con-cessions in this area, merely in order to keep the rich countries on board.[11]

We believe that this is wrong.

We show in this report that if poor country governments are to have sufficient resources to meet the MDGs, as well as to meet other essential expenditure needs and pro-poor investments, the 42 HIPC countries as a whole cannot afford to make any debt service payments. In fact, we find that even if all the debts of these 42 countries are cancelled, the HIPCs will need an additional $30bn in aid each year if there is any hope of meeting goal 1 while for the other goals, a total of $16.5bn will be needed. [. . .]

DEBT SERVICE PAYMENTS TAKE RESOURCES FROM THE MDGS

Calculating the resources needed to meet the MDGs in each country is no easy task. Data on the number of poor people in each country, the current level of indi-cators such as HIV and malaria prevalence, or even the number of children in

school, is often not available, or not reliable. Moreover, working out the exact amount that will need to be spent across different countries to meet common objectives requires making heroic assumptions about costs in each country. Some of the goals—such as 'reversing the loss of environmental resources' are inherently very difficult to evaluate.

In this report, we make use of country specific estimates prepared by key international bodies such as the World Bank, UNICEF, World Health Organisation, and Water Vision 21. These estimates form the basis of the $50bn estimated by Ernest Zedillo and are widely used by the international community in their assessments of the resource requirements of the MDGs.[12] For goals and targets for which no estimates have been prepared, we use the total figures provided in the Zedillo Report. [...]

It should be emphasised that our approach is not new. Others, including CAFOD,[13] Christian Aid, Joe Hanlon,[14] and Eurodad[15] have undertaken similar exercises. Here, our aim is mainly to update these analyses with the most recent global estimates of the costs of meeting the 2015 targets, and the most recently available figures of current spending on both debt services and key social expenditures.

Goal 1: Eradicate Extreme Poverty and Hunger

- Halve, between 1990 and 2015, the proportion of people whose income is less than one dollar a day

- Halve, between 1990 and 2015, the proportion of people who suffer from hunger

Eradicating mass poverty is often seen as the most fundamental of the MDGs. In the simplistic world of the donor community, extreme poverty is defined as living on less than one dollar a day. This is a very problematic assumption, not least because people's well-being, or ill-being, depends on much broader factors than absolute income. Moreover, using an absolute international poverty line does not reflect differences in relative poverty across countries. While it represents gross numbers, or incidence, of those who are counted as poor, it says nothing about the depth of poverty or the inequalities amongst the poor, or between the poor and rich. But, as DFID argues, the $1 target 'represents an internationally agreed operational method of identifying the number of people who by any standards have unacceptably low incomes.'[16]

Of all the MDGs, this goal is also the most difficult to relate to debt service payments. It is clear that debt repayments are taking resources that could be spent to reduce poverty, but quantifying the exact linkages is much more difficult. [...]

Goal 2: Achieving Universal Primary Education

- Ensure that, by 2015, children everywhere, boys and girls alike, will be able to complete a full course of primary schooling

Access to primary education is a basic human right. Education benefits individuals, their families, and also society as a whole, by enabling greater participation in

democratic processes. Education serves to empower individuals, helps them to take advantage of economic opportunities, and improves their health and that of their family.

Yet, in 2000, **one in three** children across the developing world did not complete the 5 years of basic education which UNICEF belives in the minimum required to achieve basic literacy.[17] We are clearly a long way from achieving the Millennium Development Goal of achieving Universal Primary Education by 2015.

UNICEF has calculated the amount that countries will need to spend in order to meet the MDGs.[18] They found that almost all of the HIPCs will need to increase spending on education—with larger countries such as Ethiopia needing to spend an extra $203m, and the poorer HIPCs such as Burkina Faso and Niger needing an extra $60m.

We added these estimates to current level of spending on education, taken from the World Development Indicators 2001.[19] From this, we were able to calculate the total spending that would be required in each of the HIPCs each year if the MDGs are to be met. [. . .]

The HIPC countries will only need to spend $6.5bn each year in order to ensure that every child gets an education sufficient to ensure basic literacy. While large relative to the incomes of HIPCs, on a global scale this figure is miniscule—representing, for example, less than half of one percent of the projected US defence budget of $1,600bn over the next five years. And only $1.2bn of this is additional to what governments are currently spending—although [. . .] countries like Burkina Faso will need much larger increases in spending than some of the other HIPCs.

Goal 4: Reducing Child Mortality

• Reduce, by two-thirds, between 1990 and 2015, the under-five mortality rate

Goal 5: Improving Maternal Health

• Reduce by three quarters, between 1990 and 2015, the maternal mortality ratio

Goal 6: Combating HIV/AIDS, Malaria and Other Diseases

• Have halted by 2015, and begun to reverse, the spread of HIV/AIDS

• Have halted by 2015, and begun to reverse, the incidence of malaria and other related diseases

A tragedy is unfolding in Africa. Within the last 24 hours, 5,500 Africans were killed by HIV/AIDS. One in five of all adults in Africa are infected by the virus, while 17 million Africans have died from AIDS since the start of the epidemic. AIDS has so far left 13 million children orphaned, a figure which will grow to 40 million by 2010 if no action is taken.[20]

Moreover, AIDS is not the only killer. Other diseases such as malaria, TB, childhood infectious diseases, maternal and prenatal conditions and micronutrient deficiencies abound. Average life expectancy in Africa has *fallen* since 1980, from 48 to 47–and in individual countries, the fall is much more extreme. Life expectancy in Zambia is now only 38 years, down from 50 years in 1980, while Sierra Leone has a life expectancy of only 37 years. And even these figures mask the catastrophic impact on children. In Africa, 161 children out of every 1,000 children will die before their fifth birthday; in Niger, this figure is as high as one in four.[21]

Yet, the Global Commission on Macroeconomics and Health has estimated that **eight million** lives could be spared each year if a simple set of health interventions needed to meet the MDGs were put in place.

The Commission, which is chaired by Professor Jeffrey Sachs of Harvard University, was launched by Gro Harlem Bruntland, Director General of the World Health Organisation, in 2000. In a recent report on Macroeconomics and Health, it stated that 'the vast majority of the excess disease burden [in poor countries] is the result of a relatively small number of identifiable conditions, each with a set of existing health interventions that can dramatically improve health and reduce the deaths associated with these conditions. **The problem is that these interventions don't reach the world's poor.** Some of the reasons for this are corruption, mis-management and a weak public sector, but in the vast majority of countries, there is a more basic and remediable problem. **The poor lack the financial resources to obtain coverage of these essential interventions, as do their** governments.'[22] [. . .]

The Commission recommends that some of the increase in spending needed should come from domestic revenues. But as they note, 'for the low-income countries, we still find a gap between financial means and financial needs, which can be filled only by the donor world if there is to be any hope of success in meeting the MDGs.[23] But 'there is another method to raise more revenues for health in low income countries: deeper debt relief, with the savings allocated to the health sector.'[24]

The need for more debt relief is evident. The Commission Report has shown that vast improvements in the lives of millions of people in poor countries are achievable, with an increase in expenditure totalling only 0.1% of GDP of the rich donor and creditor countries. Yet, despite this overwhelming imperative, the poorest countries are still paying debt service of $8bn per year.

Target 10: Halve, by 2015, the Proportion of People Without Sustainable Access to Safe Drinking Water

Like education and health care, access to safe water is a basic right. Safe water is vital for proper health and hygiene, including the prevention of water borne

diseases. Distances travelled to fetch water result in a huge loss of time for poor people, particularly women and children. Yet, **one billion** people currently lack safe drinking water and almost **three billion**—half the world's population—lack adequate sanitation. **Two million** children die each year from water-related diseases. As the Vision 21 Framework for Action states, this situation is 'humiliating, morally wrong and oppressive.'[25]

This is the more so, given that the resources required to ensure universal access to basic water and sanitation are comparatively small. Water Vision 21, a report produced by partners in the Water Supply and Sanitation Collaborative Council, has estimated that providing access to safe water and sanitation will only cost $25 per rural dweller—$15 to provide access to safe water, $10 for rural sanitation and hygiene promotion—and $75 per urban dweller, of which $50 is for urban water and $25 for peri-urban sanitation. These are additional to the costs currently borne by households and communities. These are one-off costs of providing access to basic water, and do not include the continuing costs, for example of operations and maintenance of current water supplies.

In order to meet the MDG of halving the proportion of people without sustainable access to safe drinking water, our calculations [. . .] find that in total, the HIPCs would have to spend only $2.4bn per year on water and sanitation—less than Europe spends on alcohol over ten days.

Target 11: By 2020, to have Achieved a Significant Improvement in the Lives of at Least 100 Million Slum Dwellers

Slums are defined by the World Bank as 'neglected parts of cities where housing and living conditions are appallingly poor.'[26] Hundreds of millions of the urban poor in developing countries currently live in unsafe and unhygienic environments where they face multiple threats to their health and security. The tenth millennium development target commits the international community to over-turning this unacceptable situation, and improving the lives of at least 100 million slum dwellers by 2020.

The World Bank has calculated that programmes of upgrading that would provide services to all slum areas in all developing countries could be implemented at a cost of approximately 0.2% to 0.5% of GDP.[27] When the costs of investment in infrastructure, land acquisition and necessary institutional support are added, the total comes up to around 1% to 2% of GDP. Because the MDG only refers to improving the lives of 100 million slum dwellers worldwide, we take the lower of these estimates, and assume that the HIPCs will need to spend 1% of GDP annually on improving slum conditions. In total, this comes to **$1.7bn** for all the 39 HIPCs considered.

OTHER GOALS AND TARGETS

Goal 3: Promoting Gender Equality and Empowering Women

- Eliminate gender disparity in primary and secondary education preferably by 2005 and to all levels of education no later than 2015

Target 9: Integrate the Principles of Sustainable Development into Country Policies and Programmes and Reverse the Loss of Environmental Resources

Providing basic health, education and water to the populations of poor countries is clearly vital and should be given preference over debt service payments. But at the same time, other dimensions of development–such as promoting gender equality and protecting environmental resources, are also needed if development is to be sustainable in the long run.

Unfortunately, however, these goals are inherently difficult to cost, and are therefore difficult to compare with debt service payments. Promoting gender equality and empowering women will, according to the Zedillo report, require a total yearly sum of $3bn, but we cannot tell how this will be allocated across the HIPCs and non HIPCs. Ensuring environmental sustainability will require a much greater change in resource use and energy use, particularly the need for contraction and convergence in energy use between rich and poor countries.

TOTAL REQUIRED TO MEET MDGS

Our analysis shows that the total funds required each year to meet MDGs 2 to 7 are not exorbitant. In order to meet the UN Millennium Declaration's intention to 'free our fellow men, women and children from the abject and dehumanising conditions of extreme poverty, to which more than a billion of them are currently subjected',[28] a mere $30.6bn per year is required.

This figure may be small in global terms. But [. . .] it represents 18% of GDP for the 42 HIPCs as a whole, and a staggering 355% of their debt service. [. . .]

LINKING DEBT SERVICING TO THE MILLENNIUM DEVELOPMENT GOALS

Even without servicing their external debts, it is clear that the 39 HIPCs face a formidable challenge if they are to raise the level of resources required to meet the MDGs.

While it is true that governments can raise their own revenues by taxing their domestic populations, in most of the HIPC countries the extreme poverty experienced means that governments find it very difficult to raise the kind of resources needed.

Debt servicing worsens this position by diverting preciously needed resources, which could be used for saving lives, and educating children, towards rich country creditors.

Moreover, governments cannot be spending all their revenues on social expenditures. Crucial expenditures such as maintaining law and order, public administration, essential infrastructures such as roads, policing and defence are also needed. Following Joe Hanlon, who bases his analysis on work done by Jeffrey Sachs, we argue that the HIPCs should be spending 10% of GDP on other essential expenditures.[29]

Given the current ability of the HIPC governments to raise revenues, and given the essential expenditures needed to meet the MDGs and for other essential expenditures, we now ask: how much can the HIPCs afford to pay to their rich country creditors in debt service payments? [. . .]

Our analysis shows that, as whole, the HIPCs have no spare resources available that could be used for debt servicing. In fact, even with 100% debt cancellation, the HIPCs will require an additional $16.5bn if goals 2 to 7 are to be met, and this is without the additional $30bn needed for goal 1. [. . .]

Our conclusion, therefore, is simple. All of the 39 HIPCs here—and the three not included in our data set—will need 100% debt cancellation if the MDGs are to be met.

COUNTER ARGUMENTS

This conclusion has far reaching implications, and in particular shows that the current process for debt service reduction, the HIPC initiative—which will bring down debt service payments by only around 27% in nominal terms—is woefully inadequate.

We know that our conclusion will not be welcomed by everyone, in particular the rich country creditors and multilateral institutions who collect the meagre interest payments paid by poor countries. Accordingly, we now deal with two popular counter arguments: firstly, that it is impossible to ensure that the money saved in debt service payments is not siphoned off elsewhere; and secondly, that we should be increasing grants, rather than providing debt relief.

Objection 1: How Can We Ensure that the Savings Made in Debt Service Payments will in Fact be Channelled towards Meeting the MDGs?

This is a common objection to any form of debt relief mechanism, and generally reflects a patronising view of poor country leaders as being corrupt and incompetent. Certainly corruption is an issue, and as such has been the target of much action by Jubilee 2000 campaigners in heavily indebted nations. However, it is

somewhat ironic that multilateral and bilateral creditors are concerned about corruption when discussing debt relief—yet pay little attention to issues of corruption when making new loans.

Moreover, experience in the use of HIPC resources to date has shown that, if civil society is involved, mechanisms can be developed to ensure that all debt relief funds are dedicated to key expenditure areas as required to meet the MDGs. Encouragingly, Uganda's experiences with costing her Poverty Eradication Action Plan—the Ugandan Poverty Reduction Strategy Paper—have shown that debt relief can be channelled towards those expenditures most likely to have an impact on poverty targets.

Objection 2: We Should Provide More Aid, not Reduce Debts

The colossal financing needs of the poorest countries if the MDGs are to be met have not gone unnoticed by world leaders. Gordon Brown's new proposed trust fund, into which major donors would contribute funds towards the overall target of $50bn per year, is a commendable example of the concern of some of the leaders of rich countries to meet these goals. So, why not forget about debt relief, and just provide for more aid?

As we have already argued, there is little point in providing more aid to poor countries if it is just to be swallowed up in debt service payments. But more importantly, there are many arguments to suggest that debt relief will be much more effectively used than increased aid.

Firstly, global aid flows are, despite the 0.7% of GDP commitment, in long term decline. The US recently termed ODA as an 'obsolete form of development assistance.' Even the UK currently gives less than half the 0.7% aid target.

Secondly, debt relief acts as de facto budget support—meaning that it is money that can be used by the government according to its own strategic priorities, just like its own revenues. Traditional project aid—through which donors provide funds for a particular purpose, such as building a road or an individual food security project—faces multiple difficulties. These include donor co-ordination; priorities being determined by donors' strategic interests rather than by recipient governments; tying of aid to procurement from the host country; and transactions costs. More importantly, however, debt relief is highly predictable—it is the securest form of revenue, stretching over a 20 year period.

In many countries, debt relief also has greater ownership within debtor countries, particularly amongst civil society groups. People see the savings from debt relief as 'their' money to be spent wisely, rather than donors' money which is seen as having little to do with domestic needs.

CONCLUSION: THE NEED FOR A SABBATH ECONOMICS

Our conclusion is clear. If the Millennium Development Goals are to be met, all of the HIPCs will need full cancellation of all of their debts. This is not an act of charity, but a moral imperative. While eight million die each year for want of the

funds spent by the rich countries on their pets; when millions of children stay out of school for want of half a percent of the US defence budget; and when the amount spent on alcohol in a week and a half in Europe would be adequate to provide sanitation to half the world's population, something is very wrong.

Maybe it is time, once again, to call on biblical principles. The 'Jubilee' principle—which provides ways of reversing the relentless flow of resources from the poor to the rich, and narrowing the gap between—formed the foundation of one of the most successful global campaigns ever. But there are others. The central tenets of 'Sabbath Economics' are that the world is abundant and provides enough for everyone—but that human communities must restrain their appetites and live within limits. For Sabbath Economics, disparities in wealth and power are not natural, but come about through sin, and must be mitigated within the community through redistribution.[30]

We do not have to believe in God—or indeed any religion—to accept these principles. It is enough for us to recognise that more than a billion people do not need to live in poverty while their debts continue to be repaid. The current HIPC initiative does not and cannot do enough to bring down the unsustainable debt burden of the world's poorest countries. If the Millennium Development Goals are to be met, there is no alternative but to provide a new framework for debt relief— one which respects the human rights of the poor.

NOTES

1. United Nations Millennium Declaration, Resolution 55/2.

2. ibid.

3. Foreword to 'Halving world poverty by 2015: economic growth, equity and security' DFID 2001.

4. OECD/DAC Guidelines on Poverty Reduction: In the Face of Poverty.

5. Sir John Vereker, Permanent Secretary of the UK's Department for International Development, at a speech at the All Party Group on Overseas Development (APGOOD), January 23rd 2002.

6. Statement from the Rt Hon Gordon Brown MP to the IMFC on Saturday November 17th 2001.

7. Report of the High Level Panel on Financing for Development, United Nations.

8. Cited in 'The world will never be the same again' Jubilee 2000 Coalition, December 2000.

9. See 'Flogging a Dead Process', a Report by Jubilee Plus, September 2001.

10. UN General Assembly, Preparatory Committee for the International Conference on Financing for Development, 4th Session: Revised draft outcome prepared by the Facilitator, 7 December 2001.

11. Source: *Financial Times*, Monday January 28th, 'US blocks move for big rise in aid to poor countries', by Carola Hoyos and Allan Beattie.

12. It should be noted that in most cases, we have used the most conservative estimates of the required spending, for example by excluding the capital costs of education spending.

13. For example, 'Further and deeper debt cancellation is vital for development' Presentation at the UN's Financing for Development Preparation Committee, by Henry Northover, October 2001; and 'The Human Development Approach to Debt Sustainability Analysis for the World's Poorest' CAFOD Policy Paper.

14. Cancelling debt to promote development: Paper by Joseph Hanlon, Policy Advisor to Jubilee 2000 Coalition.

15. Putting Poverty Reduction First: Why a poverty approach to debt sustainability must be adopted. Eurodad, October 2001.

16. DFID: Halving world poverty by 2015: economic growth, equity and security.

17. Is EFA affordable? Estimating the Global Minimum cost of 'Education for All', UNICEF Innocenti working paper no. 87.

18. UNICEF did this by: estimating the number of children enrolled in school in 2000; estimating the number of children who will be in school in each year between 2000 and 2015 assuming that enrolment rates don't change, based on projected levels of population growth; estimating the number of children who will need to be in school each year if enrolment ratios move from current levels to 100% by 2015, in a linear fashion; calculating the number of new school places that will be needed each year, by subtracting the total number of children who will need to be in school to reach 100% by 2015, from the baseline scenario; multiplying the number of additional children to be added into school by country specific educational costs relative to expenditure levels in the year 2000; and then dividing the additional costs by 15 to get average annual costs. It should be noted that we take the lower range of UNICEF's estimates, excluding, for example, the capital costs of building classrooms and the recurrent costs of improving educational quality.

19. It should be noted that these include all forms of educational spending, i.e. including secondary and tertiary spending. However, in most countries secondary and tertiary spending are small in comparison with primary spending.

20. Source: 'Reality Check: The Need for Deeper Debt Cancellation and the Fight Against HIV/AIDS' Drop the Debt Report, April 2001.

21. Source: World Development Indicators 200128 Report of the Commission on Macroeconomics and Health, Page 4.

22. Report of the Commission on Macroeconomics and Health, Page 4.

23. Source: Decision Point paper for Ethiopia, World Bank.

24. ibid., page 62.

25. Vision 21: A Shared Vision for Hygiene, Sanitation and Water Supply p. 1.

26. World Bank: Cities Alliance for Cities Without Slums: Action Plan, page 1.

27. ibid.

28. United Nations Millennium Declaration, op. cit.

29. This is broken down into 2% on public administration; 3% on police and defence; and 5% on essential infrastructures such as roads.

30. Myers, C. (2001) 'The Biblical Vision of Sabbath Economics'.

✗ NO

Will Debt Relief Really Help?
DENISE FRONING

In 2000, debt relief for what the International Monetary Fund (IMF) and World Bank term Heavily Indebted Poor Countries (HIPCs) was the cause of the moment in development theory, attracting international attention and broad agreement that it was the single most important piece of the poor-country development puzzle. Widespread consensus emerged that international lenders must forgive the HIPCs' debt burden. In the ebb and flow of development trends, debt relief thus had its moment in the sun, and rich countries rightly agreed to forgive some of the debt—although the World Bank and the IMF did not.

This relief, although limited to bilateral debt, will help. But when the G-7 and other advocates of development move on to the latest fad in the quest for solutions to the problems of the world's poorest countries—whether disease, education, or some yet unmentioned ill—all the attendant causes of debt relief will still need to be addressed.

All of these problems are long-term concerns. None of these countries will be wealthy tomorrow, nor will they solve all their troubles immediately. For G-7 nations, perhaps especially the United States, accustomed to focusing on the next quarter's profits rather than long-term returns, the temptation will likely be to give up too soon. That decision would be a mistake.

The fact is that these poor countries face far too many problems in addition to overwhelming debt, many of which are precisely what caused the debt accumulation in the first place. Many factors—disease, poverty, lack of education, lack of institutions, lack of transportation infrastructure, lack of food, lack of business, lack of security, lack of foreign investment, and lack of prospects—continue to stifle the economic growth of these countries, and they will continue to do so after debt relief. Without a change in these circumstances, debt relief will be only a short-term palliative, and these countries will find themselves back in the same predicament that they now face.

WHAT IS THE PROBLEM?

Bad policies and their attendant outcomes, both within and outside these countries, contribute to the "problem of poverty." Poor countries must improve domestically in a number of areas; their poverty cannot be attributed entirely to external factors. Although these countries face some valid domestic woes, many of the excuses for poverty are invalid. A lack of natural resources, for instance, does not fully account for the poverty the HIPCs face. Africa, where most of the world's 41 HIPCs are located, is awash in natural wealth, from diamonds, gold, and oil to arable agricultural land.[1] As George Ayittey observes, the continent has abundant natural potential. This potential, however, remains largely unrealized. Citing examples such as

Russia, some have argued that such resources are more a curse than a blessing, but that argument does not explain the lack of development. Country after country has become rich based on these very resources.

Some maintain that lack of progress among HIPCs is due in part to geographical location and the affliction of disease that accompanies that location. The impact of disease, from malaria to cholera to AIDS, is indeed debilitating; but even if disease were entirely eliminated, the lack of institutions (or the persistence of corrupt ones) would keep the people of these countries poor.

I do not belittle the effects of disease or suggest that people should abandon attempts to mitigate the health crisis in the HIPC countries. Rather than quibble about which cause of poverty should be considered paramount, however, we must first acknowledge that the troubles of these countries are legion and that each must be addressed for lasting development to take place. For example, a couple of years ago, before the debt-relief craze, corruption was the cause du jour. The World Bank and other august institutions held conferences, everyone nodded their heads sagely, and learned people everywhere agreed that corruption was corrosive and that something must be done. Although work to address this particular problem undoubtedly continues, the international focus on corruption has shifted to other contributing factors of poverty; yet corruption's effects remain as debilitating as ever.

The construction of sound institutions, as one example, ought not to be abandoned because other problems exist. In fact, admitting that the impediments are many and related reduces the risk of "fad" development, in which whatever currently fashionable panacea that captures popular attention reigns while other crucial issues are forgotten.

Bad Leaders

Ayittey makes the important distinction between the African people and the leaders of African nations. It is not the African people who squander development opportunities. Too often, it is African leaders, as Ayittey has observed, who seize both native wealth and foreign aid while plunging their countries into war and plundering their money, both through the exploitation of resources like diamonds and by stealing massive amounts of foreign aid.[2] As the Freedom House annual survey of political freedom points out, "Only 21 African countries (40 percent) are electoral democracies."[3] The African people do not choose these leaders, but they must suffer the consequences of these leaders' poor decisions.

Corruption

Despite its trendiness as an issue, corruption is a truly debilitating factor in the poorest countries. Indeed, much of Africa reflects the results of corruption undermining efforts to foster emerging market economies. Corruption is a cancer on the

most legitimate efforts at development in many African countries, affecting regulation as well as property rights and discouraging economic progress. Although hardly unique to Africa or to developing nations, corruption is all the more damaging to them; it creates obstacles to development that an already established, large-scale economy might survive but that can prove fatal to fledgling efforts at market development in small economies.

Part of Africa's development problem, as economist John Mukum Mbaku writes, is bureaucrats who are often

> members of the politically dominant group and have significant influence over the allocation of resources. Under these conditions, civil servants behave like interest groups whose primary objective is to put pressure on the political system in an effort to redistribute wealth to themselves. "In countries with poorly constructed, inefficient, and non-self-enforcing constitutional rules, opportunistic behavior (including rent seeking) [is] usually quite pervasive. . . . Excessive regulation of economic activities creates many opportunities for rent seeking, including bureaucratic corruption."[4]

Mukum Mbaku's solution: reform the laws to remove the state from direct control over the economy—a system which leads to profit skimming, if not outright profit seizure.

Corruption compounds itself. Sometimes because of profit seizure, lower-level bureaucrats themselves are underpaid and regard taking bribes as necessary for their survival. The whole system becomes rotten in layers, with the entire structure threatening to tumble down if one attempts to reform one part of it.

Bad Institutions

Ayittey delineates four institutional pillars[5] that are essential for lasting development in Africa: an independent judiciary, an independent central bank, free media, and neutral armed forces. In HIPCs and other poor countries, these pillars are often missing, which is why foreign assistance—even by those agencies whose sole purpose is giving aid—has proved ineffective overall. World Bank analysis of past loans and credits concludes that assistance "has a positive impact on growth [only] in countries with good fiscal, monetary, and trade policies."[6] In countries with poor policies, aid has had a negative impact. Robert Barro's analysis reveals that countries with "good fiscal, monetary, and trade policies" are more likely to experience positive economic growth whether they receive assistance or not.[7] Meanwhile, regardless of how much assistance they have received, countries with poor economic policies have not experienced sustained economic growth.[8] Clearly, sound economic policies, not foreign assistance, are the key to development.

HOW RICH NATIONS EXACERBATE THE PROBLEM

For poor countries to succeed in the international economy, they must have access to the markets of developed countries. Yet the United States levies the most onerous of its tariffs–as high as 45 percent–against some of these impoverished nations.

The U.S. weighted-average tariff rate of only 2 percent on worldwide imports is low by global standards,[9] but rather than apply this rate evenly among nations, the United States applies tariffs according to the type of product imported. The goods that face the highest U.S. tariffs are precisely those that the poorest countries produce: agricultural goods, textiles, and apparel. Combined with the impact of quotas, the U.S. tariff structure presents a significant obstacle to any country struggling to create even an initial presence in the world economy.

U.S. weighted-average tariff rates vary widely when plotted along lines of the exporting countries' economic wealth. Countries whose inhabitants earn an annual per capita gross domestic product (GDP) of more than $25,000 face an average U.S. tariff rate of 2 percent. Twenty-five countries with annual per capita GDPs of less than $1,000–approximately the amount that a minimum-wage worker in the United States earns in one month–face tariff rates greater than the U.S. average.

This disparity in U.S. tariff rates exists because poor countries tend to export many of the commodities that are subject to high tariffs in the United States and other wealthy markets. Low-income nations develop industries in which they have a comparative advantage and which provide goods and services that meet the basic needs of their people. The agricultural, textile, and apparel industries are labor-intensive and do not require sophisticated machinery or large amounts of capital to make a profit. The resource they do require, and the resource–sometimes the only resource–that developing countries have, is people.

The United States imposes absurdly high duties on the very goods for which poor countries most need a market, effectively pricing HIPCs out of the market. For example, Gambia, which has a GDP per capita of about $325 per year, faces duty rates on exports to the United States ranging from 8.8 percent on woven cotton fabrics to 11.8 percent on textile outerwear to 15.4 percent on women's clothing; the tariff on women's clothing is almost eight times the U.S. average tariff rate of 2 percent. The notion that women's skirts from Gambia are going to flood the U.S. market, overwhelm American textile factories, and send Ann Taylor out of business is clearly preposterous. In fact, if Gambia exported its entire economy to the United States, it would amount to less than 0.005 of 1 percent of total U.S. GDP.

Other examples of U.S. protectionism against HIPCs are just as absurd and needlessly damaging. Burkina Faso, a landlocked nation subject to droughts and desertification (both of which make agriculture a difficult endeavor, to say the least), has an annual GDP per capita of about $215. Its main exports are cotton

and gold, and the United States is not one of its principal markets. Nonetheless, Burkina Faso faces a 33.3 percent tariff on whatever outerwear it might attempt to send to the United States. If Burkina Faso—which faces high costs in exporting everything because of its poverty and landlocked nature—somehow manages to get a coat to the United States, that coat is instantly taxed at a third against its cost.

Likewise, Malawi produces a total GDP of only $1.8 billion—just 0.02 percent the size of the U.S. economy—but faces a U.S. tariff rate of 32.8 percent on exports of suits and coats (raincoats excluded). Presumably, raincoats fall under "outerwear," which faces a 15.3 percent tariff when entering the U.S. market.

Ironically, the United States has said it wants to help these very countries! The entire economies of these HIPCs, much less their total exports, are a raindrop in the ocean of the U.S. economy. The same situation is true for other wealthy nations like those of the European Union (EU). It would cost nothing for developed nations such as the G-7 countries to eliminate all duties and quotas on HIPCs, but that act could mean a lot to the Malawian who can expect to earn $160 this year—the proverbial "less than a dollar a day."

An opportunity to use the resources they do possess—people—to build the sort of labor-intensive industries that are the only comparative advantage of poor countries could lead to long-term development. These high tariffs and continuing quotas, however, discourage development of such industries. Who in these poorest countries can afford to risk precious money to build a factory producing goods for which no market exists?

On the other hand, by gaining access to the world market, where the demand and remuneration are much higher than in domestic markets, poor countries can acquire more capital. This capital in turn fuels further production, increases savings, and fosters the development of new industries that can create further economic growth.

WHAT IS THE SOLUTION?

Breaking the cycle of indebtedness will require several actions.

Forgive Debt

Among those actors who must act on debt forgiveness are the World Bank and IMF, which refuse to forgive the debt HIPCs owe to them even though multilateral debt accounts for as much as 80 percent of overall debt in some of these countries. The policies of these lenders perpetuate the debt cycle, forcing indebted countries to continue to depend on new aid in order to pay off old debts. This situation will never lead to sustainability.

The debt crisis in poor countries is real. A long-term solution requires total forgiveness of existing bilateral and multilateral debt, which is unlikely to be repaid in any event, and ending the debt cycle by eliminating bilateral and multilateral

assistance. Countries must foster their own economic policies that attract private-sector credit and investment and that have proven to be the best means of achieving long-term, sustainable economic growth.

Remove Barriers to Globalization

Dani Rodrik cites "a long list of admission requirements" imposed on countries that try to join the world economy today.[10] He's right: a thicket of protectionist policies has sprung up around the global market, impeding developing countries' progress toward wealth. Of course, regardless of the protectionist behavior of other nations, rich or poor, it is crucial to HIPC development that the HIPCs themselves unilaterally lower their own barriers to trade and foster sound institutions internally. These measures will benefit the HIPCs regardless of what other countries do.

Nonetheless, the impediments to which Rodrik refers do exist. Therefore, rich countries should give the HIPCs time to implement the Uruguay Round obligations to which they have committed themselves in the World Trade Organization (WTO), recognizing that poor countries face very high costs in their efforts to liberalize. Among the WTO's 140 members are 109 developing or transition economies. The cost of implementing just three WTO agreements—the sanitary and phytosanitary measures, the customs valuation, and the TRIPS (Trade-Related Aspects of Intellectual Property Rights) agreements—is $150 million for each developing country.[11]

For such countries where, as Rodrik remarks, $150 million may amount to a full year's development budget, implementation is a huge task. Clearly, for these countries to comply with the TRIPS or other agreements in any reasonable amount of time (reasonable from any perspective, rich or poor), they need some assistance. Thus, wealthy countries should increase their commitment to providing educational advice on how to implement such agreements and should be receptive to creative alternatives with respect to implementation by those countries that may lack the infrastructure developed countries take for granted. Also, rich countries must be patient and recognize that obstacles will have to be resolved along the way.

Encourage Trade through Regional Customs Arrangements

Encouragement can include strengthening the free-trade role of such existing customs unions as the Southern African Development Community (SADC). For many of the HIPCs, multilateral agreements on the WTO scale may simply be too big an aspect of modern globalization to undertake at present. Without giving up on the multilateral endeavors to which they have already committed, they may need to focus on more manageable liberalization, through bilateral or regional negotiations.[12] Multilateral advancement of free trade is ideal, but in an imperfect world, the perfect often must give way to the achievable.

Establishing a common trading system such as a regional trade union will allow these poor countries to pool their limited resources to establish a customs framework. At the same time, each country can gain expertise in building the institutional elements of a modern economy without bearing the cost of modernizing on its own. Regional customs arrangements also alleviate the trade burden for landlocked countries, including some HIPCs, which face dramatically higher trading costs because they must transport goods through a neighboring country to reach a port.

Notably, however, these regional customs unions often have not met their own trade liberalization commitments for various reasons. Sometimes, members delay pledged liberalization due to war or the fear that trade constitutes a threat to their own industries—as Tanzania did when withdrawing from COMESA (the Common Market for Eastern and Southern Africa). In such circumstances, the HIPCs and other poor countries must take responsibility for their own actions and honor the free-trade commitments they have already made, which will foster economic growth in the long run even if trade flows do not rise significantly in the short term.

Eliminate All Tariffs and Quotas on HIPCs

Rich countries should lower the entry fees HIPCs pay to join the global economy by removing trade barriers imposed on these countries. Both the United States and the EU have passed legislation intended to increase market access for developing countries. The EU recently proposed duty-free access to its market for 48 poor countries in its "Everything But Arms" plan; the United States enacted the Trade and Development Act of 2000 to increase access to the U.S. market for poor African and Caribbean countries.

Both of these initiatives, however, offer only limited market access improvements in sectors that would most benefit these developing countries: textiles and some agricultural goods in the U.S. market; sugar, rice, and bananas in the EU. Moreover, both efforts serve domestic protectionist interests far more than they promote economic development in poor countries. For example, under the EU's proposal, tariff reductions on rice and sugar would not even begin until 2006. Because 2006 is also the year in which the EU's agricultural subsidy program, or Common Agricultural Policy (CAP), is due for its next review, the likelihood that those tariffs will be eliminated or even reduced is questionable.

Aside from denying market access to developing countries, the CAP is very costly to the world economy, around $75 billion annually.[13] Two-thirds of the cost ($49 billion) is borne by Europeans in the form of higher prices, inefficient production, and economic distortions. The remaining $25 billion—roughly equal to the total output of Burkina Faso, Gambia, Malawi, Cameroon, Guinea-Bissau, Madagascar, Mali, and Mozambique—falls on countries outside the EU in the form of lost agricultural export opportunities in Europe.

The United States also maintains barriers in the textile and apparel sector that impose enormous costs on U.S. citizens as well as on developing countries. The annual cost imposed on foreign countries by U.S. textile and apparel barriers ranges from $4 billion to $15.5 billion.[14]

The European CAP and U.S. textile and apparel barriers impose a significant burden on the world economy and are clearly an impediment to trade liberalization. As illustrated above, the cost to rich nations of eliminating these barriers for HIPCs is minimal; but for many low-income countries, agricultural and textile exports are a vital source of income and an important path to development.

Institute Economic Freedom

Ultimately, establishing sound institutions is crucial to development. For development to take place, a country must first establish a rule of law on which its people can rely. Laws must ensure protection of personal property rights, as Barro established in his studies.

Other actions to maximize economic freedom are also essential, including minimizing the level of corruption and reducing the regulation that stifles economic development and hinders individual liberty. Hernando de Soto details the very real way in which red tape can prevent the legal purchase of property in some developing countries, requiring a number of steps that can reach into the hundreds through a number of agencies and last for years.[15] Free-trade flows are also a key component of development.

The benefits of economic freedom are not just ivory-tower musings. They appear as tangible evidence in the real world. Regardless of geography or culture or the unique conditions of different nations and regions, economic freedom, and through it the seeds of prosperity, can develop globally. Examples include Chile in Latin America, Hong Kong and Singapore in the Asian tropics, and Estonia among the former Communist republics of Eastern Europe, not just the already vibrant Western economies.

Critics often dismiss such examples of success as isolated incidents that are exceptions to the rule. They say, for example, that Hong Kong and Singapore are too small to be representative, or that Taiwan and South Korea succeeded economically in a different era, and so on. These criticisms are excuses, not reasoned arguments. The fact that so few countries in the tropics have developed is indeed a sign of more things wrong than right in the region, but to dismiss Hong Kong and Singapore is counterproductive when examples of success are needed instead. In addition, the notion of an "exception proving a rule" is scientifically backward: theories are proven wrong when an exception is found, not vice versa. The development of Hong Kong and Singapore, two tropical countries, disproves the theory that development of the Western kind cannot occur in the tropics.

The next argument that inevitably arises about Hong Kong and Singapore—that they are not viable tropical success stories because of their territorial size—is equally invalid. As Jagdish Bhagwati observes,

The exceptionalism cited to explain away the East Asian performance has taken some strange forms. For instance, it used to be asserted that Hong Kong and Singapore were small "city states" and therefore somehow not subject to the economic laws applying to other "normal" nations. Of course, many nations around the world are even smaller on dimensions such as population.[16]

Such exceptionalism was likewise applied to "exceptionally large" countries like India to justify development failures without regard to the success of the United States, a large country in every sense of the word.[17] Is the economic growth of the United States then to be regarded as an exception? Where does one draw the line? Is Switzerland too small to be anything other than an exception to development success? Is Chile? Or Estonia?

In truth, countries will succeed or fail regardless of their size. Their performance depends far more on implementing successful institutions and addressing their unique problems, as well as taking advantage of the unique attributes that each finds in its own situation. In a variation on the Anna Karenina principle,[18] each troubled country is troubled in its own way.

The standard excuses for lack of HIPC development, then, fall short. Tropics are not the reason: there are examples of tropical success stories. Lack of resources is not the reason: the tropics possess abundant natural resources, far more in fact than many other regions. Countries in the tropics do have the problem of disease. Along with the admitted problems of their tropical location, however, their natural wealth offers a potential solution. A country like Nigeria that has an abundance of oil could spend all its petroleum proceeds on vaccines if its government so chose. But it does not. Instead, the money vanishes into private bank accounts. Why? Corruption and lack of sound institutions, as well as the lack of a viable rule of law that could, if present, minimize the siphoning of profits into private hands.

REASON TO HOPE

Success stories exist, often in places few would predict. Upon its establishment in 1949, the Republic of China on Taiwan had a poor, agricultural economy that was inefficient and overregulated, and its people were not politically free. In the 1960s, however, the government began to institute economic reforms. It guaranteed private property and set up a legal system to protect it, reformed the banking and financial sectors, stabilized taxes, gave public lands to private citizens, and allowed the free market to expand. Taiwan has become one of the world's fastest growing economies in recent years; in the 1990s, its growth rate was 11 percent.

Taiwan also has developed a functional democracy and has conducted successful multiparty elections in both the legislative and executive branches of government after years of rule by a repressive, one-party system. It is proof that a nation that was under an authoritarian regime little more than a quarter-century ago can evolve into an economically thriving democracy.

For those who are convinced by the argument that Taiwan's development took place at a time in which the costs of globalization were lower, Chile, whose GDP per capita has grown steadily since the government imposed economic reforms (except during a recession in the mid-1980s), offers a more recent example. Although the costs of this economic liberalization were often high, Chile demonstrates that institutions of economic freedom can impel political liberalization as well, for it was Augusto Pinochet's military regime that first began to institute the reforms that continued and intensified under subsequent democratic governments. Today, Chile has a market-oriented economy characterized by a high level of foreign trade.

An even more recent example of poor-country growth took place in the 1990s, when the costs of joining the world economy were about as high as they are now: Estonia, which emerged from half a century of Soviet domination in 1991 only to find that its standard of living, which in 1939 had been on par with Scandinavian cousin Finland, now lagged far behind. (Even today, Estonia's GDP per capita is one seventh the level of Finland's.) Lacking an education in Western-style economic or political theory and having been taught in the Soviet system, Estonians began building sound economic institutions, privatizing state-owned industries, establishing a sound legal framework to attract foreign investment, liberalizing trade barriers, balancing the budget, and stabilizing the currency (by tying it to the German mark). In 10 short years, Estonia has become a model of economic development.

Of course, some could argue that Estonia's location—near its Scandinavian neighbors, which were already developed countries—has eased its progress; certainly, having a high volume of trade with Finland has proven beneficial. Yet some could also argue that Estonia's location—next to an unpredictable giant that just 50 years earlier overran it and destroyed its economic prosperity along with its sovereignty—is a distinct liability. Fundamentally, Estonia, like Chile, Singapore, Taiwan, and the rest of the world's economic success stories, has maximized its assets and sought to minimize its liabilities. All countries must do the same, no matter how insurmountable the liabilities may seem, in order to develop.

Three countries in three distinct regions, with three different cultural backgrounds, and in three different time frames: all examples of the possibilities of growth through sound institutional reform. Addressing the plight of the HIPCs may seem an overwhelming endeavor, but that does not mean it cannot be done. Far from it; anyone who sees a solution to a particular HIPC problem should be encouraged to tackle it, for these countries need assistance in many areas.

I myself advocate the fundamental necessity of institution building. Economic freedom is vital and, in the end, the only truly humane solution, for history demonstrates that only under such a system do people have the chance to use free will to achieve maximum prosperity. But creating economic freedom also means building sound, corruption-resistant, independent institutions that minimize the ability of anyone, native or foreign, rich or poor, to meddle in individual lives. Only then will debt relief really help.

NOTES

1. George Ayittey, *Africa in Chaos* (New York: St. Martin's Press, 1998).

2. Ayittey, "How the West Compounds Africa's Crisis," *Intellectual Capital*, June 29, 2000, located at <http://207.87.15.232/issues/Issue387/item9858.asp>.

3. Adrian Karatnycky, *Freedom in the World: 2000–2001*, located at <http://www.freedomhouse.org/research/freeworld/2001/essay1.htm>.

4. John Mukum Mbaku, "Bureaucratic Corruption in Africa: The Futility of Cleanups," *Cato Journal* 16, no. 1, located at <http://www.cato.org/pubs/journal/cj16n1-6.html>.

5. Ayittey, "How the West Compounds Africa's Crisis."

6. Craig Burnside and David Dollar, "Aid, Policies, and Growth," World Bank, Policy Research Department, Macroeconomic and Growth Division, June 1977.

7. See Robert J. Barro, "Rule of Law, Democracy, and Economic Performance," in Gerald P. O'Driscoll, Kim R. Holmes, and Melanie Kirkpatrick, eds., *2000 Index of Economic Freedom* (Washington, D.C.: Heritage Foundation and Dow Jones & Co., 2000), 31–51.

8. David Dollar and Lant Pritchett, "Assessing Aid: What Works, What Doesn't and Why," *World Bank Policy Research Report*, 1998, 2.

9. U.S. International Trade Commission, information available at <http://www.usitc.gov>.

10. Dani Rodrik, "Trading in Illusions," *Foreign Policy* (March/April 2001), located at <http://www.foreignpolicy.com/issue_marapr_2001/rodrick.html>.

11. J. Michael Finger, remarks at workshop on "Developing Countries and the New Round of Multilateral Trade Negotiations," Harvard University, November 5–6, 1999.

12. Traci Phillips, "Copyrights and Wrongs," *Marquette Intellectual Property Law Review* 4 (2000), in *Foreign Policy* (January–February 2001), located at <http://www.foreignpolicy.com/issue_janfeb_2001/gnsjanfeb2001.html>.

13. Brent Borell and Lionel Hubbard, "Global Economic Effects of the EU Common Agricultural Policy" in *Reforming the CAP* (Institute of Economic Affairs, 2000), 21.

14. Robert Feenstra, "How Costly Is Protectionism?" *Journal of Economic Perspectives* 6, no. 3 (Summer 1992): 163. See also Laura Baughman et al., "Of Tyre Cords, Ties and Tents: Window-Dressing in the ATC?" *World Economy* 20, no. 4, 409.

15. Hernando de Soto, *The Mystery of Capital* (New York: Basic Books, 2000).

16. Jagdish Bhagwati, *The Wind of the Hundred Days* (MIT Press, 2000), 31.

17. See generally Bhagwati, *The Wind of the Hundred Days*.

18. The opening line of Leo Tolstoy's *Anna Karenina*: "Happy families are all alike; every unhappy family is unhappy in its own way."

POSTSCRIPT

An interesting dimension of the issue of debt relief has been the success of the Jubilee 2000 movement in winning some concessions. In the past, advocacy campaigns on complex technical issues such as international trade and finance have met with limited results. Campaigns such as the International Campaign to Ban Landmines have been successful because they focus on an issue of physical harm that is readily identifiable; as well, the link between cause and effect can be easily drawn. In many cases, the answer to the question of whom to "blame" can be fairly easily identified.

The situation is quite different in the case of debt relief. Given the complexity of the issue, it is sometimes difficult to identify who was responsible for the accumulation of the debts. The Jubilee campaigners have often focused on the notion of international debt as a form of "bondage" or "slavery" in an effort to prod the conscience of the North to respond to the issue. But not everyone agrees that the industrialized countries need to share this responsibility by offering debt forgiveness. Peter Bauer, in his article "Ethics and the Etiquette of Third World Debt" (*Ethics and International Affairs* 1 [1987]: 73–84), provides a neoclassical economic case against debt relief. Bauer believes that the debt problems are largely the creation of LDC governments themselves, who must take the responsibility for dealing with them. In fact, he argues, it is unethical to offer debt relief to those who were responsible for creating the debt in the first place, since this may only cause them to continue their irresponsible behaviour. Does the question of who is to blame for the debt crisis have a direct bearing on how the burden should be shared? From the discussion above, is it clear who is "responsible" for these debts? How should the response to this question shape our decision on whether to support debt forgiveness?

Suggested Additional Readings

Addison, Tony, and Mansoob Murshed. "Debt Relief and Civil War." *Journal of Peace Research* 40, no. 2 (March 2003): 159–76.

Ayittey, Geroge B.N., and Michelle Denise Carter. "Should Western Donors Impose Strict Conditions for African Debt Relief." *CQ Researcher* 13, no. 29 (August 29, 2003): 713–15.

Bulow, Jeremy, and Kenneth Rogoff. "Cleaning Up Third World Debt Without Getting Taken to the Cleaners." *Journal of Economic Perspectives* 4, no. 1 (Winter 1990): 31–42.

Collins, Carole, et al. "Jubilee 2000: Citizen Action across the North–South Divide." In Michael Edwards and John Gaventa, (eds.), *Global Citizen Action*. Boulder: Lynne Rienner, 2001; 135–48.

Dent, Martin, and Bill Peters. *The Crisis of Poverty and Debt in the Third World.* Aldershot: Ashgate, 1999.

Easterly, William. "How Did Heavily Indebted Poor Countries Become Heavily Indebted? Review Two Decades of Debt Relief." *World Development* 30, no. 10 (October 2002): 1677–96.

Garg, Ramesh C. "The Case for Debt-Forgiveness for Latin America and the Caribbean Countries." *Intereconomics* 28, no. 1 (January–February 1993): 30–34.

Jaggar, Alison M. "A Feminist Critique of the Alleged Southern Debt." *Hypatia* 17, no. 4 (Fall 2002): 119–44.

Keet, Dot. "The International Anti-Debt Campaign: A Southern Activist View for Activists in 'the North'. . . and 'the South.'" *Development in Practice* 10, no. 3/4 (August 2000): 461–78.

Stiglitz, Joseph. "Odious Rulers, Odious Debts." *Atlantic Monthly* 292, no. 4 (November 2003): 39–41.

Thomas, M.A. "Getting Debt Relief Right." *Foreign Affairs* 80, no. 5 (September–October): 36–45.

InfoTrac® College Edition

Search for the following articles in the InfoTrac® database:

Addison, George Mavrotas, and Mark McGillivray. "Aid, Debt Relief and New Sources of Finance for Meeting the Millennium Development Goals." *Journal of International Affairs* 58, no. 2 (Spring 2005): 113–38.

"Forgive Poor Countries' Outstanding Debt." *Christianity Today* 52, no. 6 (June 2008): 17.

Rowden, Rick. "A World of Debt." *The American Prospect* 12, no. 12 (July 2, 2001): S29.

Sachs, Jeffrey D. "Resolving the Debt Crisis of Low-Income Countries." *Brookings Papers on Economic Activity* 1 (Spring 2002): 257–86.

Sharma, Sohan, and Surinder Kumar. "Debt Relief—Indentured Servitude for the Third World." *Race and Class* 43, no. 4 (April–June 2002): 45–56.

"The G8's African Challenge: The G8 and Africa: Will More Aid and Debt Relief Succeed Where Previous Development Efforts Have Failed?" *Global Agenda* (Sept. 6, 2005).

Web Resources

For current URLs for the following websites, visit www.crosscurrents.nelson.com.

HEAVILY INDEBTED POOR COUNTRIES CAPACITY BUILDING PROGRAMME
http://www.hipc-cbp.org/
Debt Relief International runs a program to build the capacity of the governments of the HIPCs to manage their own debt strategy and analysis, without having to rely on international technical assistance.

GLOBAL POLICY FORUM
http://www.globalpolicy.org/socecon/develop/debt/index.htm
This site contains a large number of documents and articles relating to debt relief.

THE WORLD BANK GROUP: HIPC
http://www.worldbank.org/hipc
The HIPC site, maintained by the World Bank, offers official documents and reports relating to debt relief.

PART FOUR

GLOBAL COOPERATION AND HUMAN SECURITY

Should Human Security Be the Core Value of Canadian Foreign Policy?

Is the United Nations New Human Rights Council a Failure?

Do We Need an International Criminal Court?

Are Truth Commissions Useful in Promoting Human Rights and Justice in Transitional Societies?

Do We Need a World Environmental Organization?

Should There Be a Right to Intervene to Prevent Acute Environmental Damage?

Should Human Security Be the Core Value of Canadian Foreign Policy?

✔ **YES**
LLOYD AXWORTHY, "Human Security: Safety for People in a Changing World," Ottawa: Department of Foreign Affairs and International Trade, 1999

✗ **NO**
WILLIAM W. BAIN, "Against Crusading: The Ethics of Human Security and Canadian Foreign Policy," *Canadian Foreign Policy* 6, no. 3 (Spring 1999): 85–98

During much of the twentieth century, most policymakers and academics had a common understanding of the concept of security as the basis for foreign policy. It was generally assumed that the study of security had to do with the ways in which force or threats to use force were employed to ensure the physical safety of a country's citizens and the protection of that country's core values. Thus, security was closely associated with the state's role in providing "national security."

This approach is based on several realist assumptions:

1. The international system is characterized by a state of anarchy—that is, a lack of overarching authority. As a result, states must pursue their own self-interest, even if at times it conflicts with the larger collective interest.

2. The danger of a foreign attack is a constant and overriding threat to the physical well-being of the state and its inhabitants. States must therefore be vigilant to recognize threats as they emerge and take appropriate action to counter them.

3. Ensuring national security is rooted in the effective management of military force and the balance of power.

4. Since the state is the ultimate guarantor of security, the security of individuals is subsumed in the broader quest for "national security."

In this traditional formulation, the notion of threat was primarily associated with military threats posed by other states, or in some cases threats posed by non-state actors such as terrorist groups. As policymakers and analysts assessed the changes taking place in the post–Cold War international order, there was growing dissatisfaction with the traditional concept of national security. Many began to

question the definition of security itself. They have argued that we should move beyond some abstract notion of the state and "national interests" and instead focus on "security" as it affects the well-being of individual human beings and groups where they actually live.

Typical of this approach was the *Human Development Report, 1994*, issued by the United Nations Development Programme. In this report, a case is made for developing a concept of "human security" that is universal, human-centred, and multidimensional. The report maintains that security, rather than being a military concept, has many components: economic, nutritional, environmental, personal, community, and political. In reconceptualizing security, the report proposes that states move away from the unilateralism that typifies traditional national security policies toward a more collective and cooperative approach. This change would give rise to a new form of diplomacy in which states would increasingly cooperate not only with other states and international governmental organizations but also with non-governmental organizations (NGOs) and other civil society actors.

The "human security" agenda reflects what Nicholas Wheeler calls a "solidarist" approach to international society. Solidarists argue that a state's claim to sovereignty and non-intervention is limited by the duty of all states to maintain a minimal standard of humane treatment of all citizens within their borders. Where such basic humane standards are not maintained, others have a responsibility, if not a duty, to come to the aid of those suffering.

Lloyd Axworthy took up the human security concept when he became the minister of foreign affairs and made it the focal point of the Liberal government's foreign policy. As a result, a whole set of issues gained prominence on the Canadian foreign policy agenda: human rights and democratization, landmines, peace-building, and the ways in which the plight of war affects children, to name only a few. To Axworthy, the human security agenda builds naturally on the liberal internationalist principles that have long shaped Canadian foreign policy.

Although Axworthy has since left his government post, the human security agenda officially remains a key element in the Canadian foreign policy agenda. But how useful is the focus on human security? Should this continue to be the lens through which we view the world and shape our foreign-policy interests?

Two perspectives on these questions are presented here. In the first reading, Lloyd Axworthy lays out his vision of human security and the role it should play in Canadian foreign policy. In the second reading, William W. Bain offers a more skeptical perspective. He argues for a more pluralist understanding of international society that gives greater priority to the notions of sovereignty and non-interference and respects the right of states to pursue their own vision of the good life. Bain doubts that the kind of moral principles that underlie the

concept of human security have in fact become universally accepted. He fears that a foreign policy driven by a human security agenda would mean an overly moralized policy. Such a crusading spirit could lead to charges of cultural imperialism abroad and cynicism at home if Canada cannot live up to its promises to deliver. A more prudent approach to foreign policy, Bain argues, is more in keeping with the traditions of Canadian foreign policy than with this crusading spirit.

✔ YES

Human Security: Safety for People in a Changing World
LLOYD AXWORTHY

I. THE NEED FOR A NEW APPROACH TO SECURITY

Since the end of the Cold War, security for the majority of states has increased, while security for many of the world's people has declined.

The end of the superpower confrontation has meant greater security for states touched by that rivalry. Yet during this decade we have seen new civil conflicts, large-scale atrocities, and even genocide. Globalization has brought many benefits, but it has also meant a rise in violent crime, drug trade, terrorism, disease, and environmental deterioration. It clearly does not follow that when states are secure, people are secure.

Security between states remains a necessary condition for the security of people. The principal objective of national security is the protection of territorial integrity and political sovereignty from external aggression. While declining in frequency, the threat of inter-state war has not vanished, and the potential consequences of such a war should not be underestimated. Technological advances and proliferation of weaponry mean that future wars between states will exact a horrific toll on civilians. At the same time national security is insufficient to guarantee people's security.

A growing number of armed conflicts are being fought within, rather than between, states. The warring factions in these civil wars are often irregular forces with loose chains of command, frequently divided along ethnic or religious lines. Small arms are the weapon of choice and non-combatants account for eight out of ten casualties. Once considered merely "collateral damage," civilians are being thrust into the epicentre of contemporary war.

Greater exposure to violence is not limited to situations of armed conflict. It is also directly related to the erosion of state control. This decline is most evident in failed states, where governments are simply incapable of providing even basic security for people threatened by warlords and bandits. Challenges to state control can also be seen in the expansion of organized crime, drug trafficking, and the growth of private security forces.

Security for people is also affected by a broadening range of transnational threats. In an increasingly interdependent world we routinely experience mutual, if unequal vulnerability. Opening markets, increased world trade, and a revolution in communications are highly beneficial, but they have also made borders more porous to a wide range of threats. A growing number of hazards to people's health—from long-range transmission of pollutants to infectious diseases—are

global phenomena in both their origins and their effects. Economic shocks in one part of the world can lead rapidly to crises in another, with devastating implications for the security of the most vulnerable.

These broad trends are clearly not new to the 1990s; each has been intensifying over recent decades. During 40 years of superpower rivalry, however, nuclear confrontation and ideological competition dominated the security agenda. As a result, these other challenges have only been widely acknowledged in more recent years. Outside the confines of the Cold War, the opportunity exists to develop a comprehensive and systematic approach to enhancing the security of people.

II. BACKGROUND TO THE CONCEPT OF HUMAN SECURITY

While the term "human security" may be of recent origin, the ideas that underpin the concept are far from new. For more than a century—at least since the founding of the International Committee of the Red Cross in the 1860s—a doctrine based on the security of people has been gathering momentum. Core elements of this doctrine were formalized in the 1940s in the UN Charter, the Universal Declaration of Human Rights, and the Geneva Conventions.

The specific phrase "human security" is most commonly associated with the 1994 UNDP *Human Development Report*, an attempt to capture the post-Cold War peace dividend and redirect those resources towards the development agenda. The definition advanced in the report was extremely ambitious. Human security was defined as the summation of seven distinct dimensions of security: economic, food, health, environmental, personal, community, and political. By focusing on people and highlighting non-traditional threats, the UNDP made an important contribution to post-Cold War thinking about security.

The very breadth of the UNDP approach, however, made it unwieldy as a policy instrument. Equally important, in emphasizing the threats associated with underdevelopment, the Report largely ignored the continuing human insecurity resulting from violent conflict. Yet by the UNDP's own criteria, human insecurity is greatest during war. Of the 25 countries at the bottom of the 1998 Human Development Index, more than half are suffering the direct or indirect effects of violent conflict. The UNDP definition of human security was proposed as a key concept during the preparatory stages of the 1995 Copenhagen Summit on Social Development. But it was rejected during the Summit and has not been widely used thereafter.

Over the past two years the concept of human security has increasingly centred on the human costs of violent conflict. Here, practice has led theory. Two initiatives in particular, the campaign to ban landmines and the effort to create an International Criminal Court, have demonstrated the potential of a people-centred approach to security. Anti-personnel landmines are a clear example of a threat to the security of people. While contributing only marginally to the security of

states, mines have a devastating impact on ordinary people attempting to rebuild their lives in war-torn societies. The International Criminal Court establishes a mechanism to hold individuals accountable for war crimes and crimes against humanity, and holds the promise of preventing the future abuse of people by governments and other parties to conflicts. Both measures are practical, powerful applications of the concept of human security.

III. DEFINING HUMAN SECURITY—A SHIFT IN THE ANGLE OF VISION

In essence, human security means safety for people from both violent and non-violent threats. It is a condition or state of being characterized by freedom from pervasive threats to people's rights, their safety, or even their lives. From a foreign policy perspective, human security is perhaps best understood as a shift in perspective or orientation. It is an alternative way of seeing the world, taking people as its point of reference, rather than focusing exclusively on the security of territory or governments. Like other security concepts—national security, economic security, food security—it is about protection. Human security entails taking preventive measures to reduce vulnerability and minimize risk, and taking remedial action where prevention fails.

The range of potential threats to human security should not be narrowly conceived. While the safety of people is obviously at grave risk in situations of armed conflict, a human security approach is not simply synonymous with humanitarian action. It highlights the need to address the root causes of insecurity and to help ensure people's future safety. There are also human security dimensions to a broad range of challenges, such as gross violations of human rights, environmental degradation, terrorism, transnational organized crime, gender-based violence, infectious diseases, and natural disasters. The widespread social unrest and violence that often accompanies economic crises demonstrates that there are clear economic underpinnings to human security. The litmus test for determining if it is useful to frame an issue in human security terms is the degree to which the safety of people is at risk.

IV. A NECESSARY COMPLEMENT TO NATIONAL SECURITY

Human security does not supplant national security. A human security perspective asserts that the security of the state is not an end in itself. Rather, it is a means of ensuring security for its people. In this context, state security and human security are mutually supportive. Building an effective, democratic state that values its own people and protects minorities is a central strategy for promoting human security. At the same time, improving the human security of its people strengthens the legitimacy, stability, and security of a state. When states are externally aggressive, internally repressive, or too weak to govern effectively, they threaten the security of people. Where human security exists as a fact rather

than an aspiration, these conditions can be attributed in large measure to the effective governance of states.

From a human security perspective, concern for the safety of people extends beyond borders. Although broadening the focus of security policy beyond citizens may at first appear to be a radical shift, it is a logical extension of current approaches to international peace and security. The Charter of the United Nations embodies the view that security cannot be achieved by a single state in isolation. The phrase "international peace and security" implies that the security of one state depends on the security of other states. A human security perspective builds on this logic by noting that the security of people in one part of the world depends on the security of people elsewhere. A secure and stable world order is built both from the top down, and from the bottom up. The security of states, and the maintenance of international peace and security, are ultimately constructed on the foundation of people who are secure.

V. AN ENABLING ENVIRONMENT FOR HUMAN DEVELOPMENT

The two concepts of human security and human development are mutually reinforcing, though distinct. The UNDP report itself, while proposing a very broad definition of human security, was clear that the two concepts were not synonymous. Together, human security and human development address the twin objectives of freedom from fear and freedom from want.

People's freedom to act can be constrained by both fears; and for the poorest and most vulnerable members of society, poverty and insecurity are linked in a vicious circle. Breaking that cycle requires measures to promote human development, through access to reliable employment, education, and social services. But it also requires measures to promote human security by offering protection from crime and political violence, respect for human rights including political rights, and equitable access to justice. The absence of such guarantees of human security constitutes a powerful barrier to human development. Regardless of levels of income, if people lack confidence in society's ability to protect them, they will have little incentive to invest in the future. A development optic highlights this positive dimension of the concept—namely the opportunity that human security provides to liberate the potential for growth.

Human security provides an enabling environment for human development. Where violence or the threat of violence makes meaningful progress on the developmental agenda impractical, enhancing safety for people is a prerequisite. Promoting human development can also be an important strategy for furthering human security. By addressing inequalities which are often root causes of violent conflict, by strengthening governance structures, and by providing humanitarian assistance, development assistance complements political, legal, and military initiatives in enhancing human security.

VI. FOREIGN POLICY IMPLICATIONS

Human security provides a template to assess policy and practice for their effects on the safety of people. From a foreign policy perspective, there are a number of key consequences.

First, when conditions warrant, vigorous action in defence of human security objectives will be necessary. Ensuring human security can involve the use of coercive measures, including sanctions and military force, as in Bosnia and Kosovo.

At the same time, the human costs of strategies for promoting state and international security must be explicitly assessed. This line of argument dates back to the 19th-century movement to ban the use of inhumane weapons, but, as we have seen in the recent campaign to ban anti-personnel landmines, it continues to have contemporary relevance. Other security policies, such as comprehensive economic sanctions, should take into account the impact on innocent people.

Third, security policies must be integrated much more closely with strategies for promoting human rights, democracy, and development. Human rights, humanitarian, and refugee law provide the normative framework on which a human security approach is based. Development strategies offer broadly based means of addressing many long-term human security challenges. One of the dividends of adopting a human security approach is that it further elaborates a people-centred foreign policy.

Fourth, due to the complexity of contemporary challenges to the security of people, effective interventions involve a diverse range of actors including states, multilateral organizations, and civil society groups. As the challenges to the safety of people are transnational, effective responses can only be achieved through multilateral cooperation. This is evident in the array of new international instruments developed in the last decade to address transnational organized crime, drug trafficking, terrorism, and environmental degradation. These threats link the interest of citizens in countries which enjoy a high level of human security with the interests of people in much poorer nations, who face a wider range of threats to their safety.

Fifth, effective responses will depend on greater operational coordination. For example, successful peace-support operations are multi-dimensional, and depend on the close coordination of political negotiators, peacekeepers, human rights monitors, and humanitarian aid personnel among others. Furthermore, development agencies are now engaged in promoting security sector reform, while security organizations have helped channel development assistance in post-conflict countries. Managing these overlapping mandates and objectives is one of the principal challenges for a human security agenda.

Sixth, civil society organizations are seeking greater opportunity and greater responsibility in promoting human security. In many cases, non-governmental organizations have proven to be extremely effective partners in advocating the security of people. They are also important providers of assistance and protection

to those in need of greater security. At the same time, the business sector, potentially a key actor in enhancing human security, could be more effectively engaged.

VII. TOWARDS AN AGENDA FOR HUMAN SECURITY

Human security offers a new angle of vision and a broad template for evaluating policies. It also yields a concrete set of foreign policy initiatives. Focusing systematically on the safety of people highlights the need for more targeted attention to key issues that are not yet adequately addressed by the international community. Current examples of such gaps include the unchecked proliferation of small arms and the inadequate protection of children in circumstances of armed conflict.

Human security is enhanced by reducing people's vulnerability and by preventing the conditions which make them vulnerable in the first place. Assisting people in highly insecure situations, particularly in the midst of violent conflict, is a central objective of the human security agenda. Refugees have long been the focus of international attention. The same focus on vulnerability highlights the immediate needs of the internally displaced, and demobilized combatants. At the same time, a human security agenda must go beyond humanitarian action, by addressing the sources of people's insecurity. Building human security, therefore, requires both short-term humanitarian action and longer-term strategies for building peace and promoting sustainable development.

Two fundamental strategies for enhancing human security are strengthening legal norms and building the capacity to enforce them. New standards are needed in areas such as restricting the illegal trafficking in small arms, banning the use and recruitment of children as soldiers, prohibiting exploitative child labour, providing greater protection for the internally displaced, and ensuring the applicability of legal standards to non-state actors and to violence below the threshold of armed conflict.

There is little point in defining new norms and rights, however, if societies have no capacity to enforce existing norms or to protect already recognized rights. For this reason, improving democratic governance within states is a central strategy for advancing human security. So is strengthening the capacity of international organizations, in particular the United Nations, to deliver on their agreed mandates. Yet the range of protection tasks assigned to UN-mandated operations is increasing, at the same time as the UN's capacity to organize and fund such operations is dwindling.

Building institutional capacity without strengthening respect for norms would undermine a human-centred standard of security. Strengthening norms without building the capacity to protect them only invites disillusionment with the possibility of constraining power by the rule of law. Both are essential strategies if we are to move towards a more humane world.

✗ NO

Against Crusading: The Ethics of Human Security and Canadian Foreign Policy

WILLIAM W. BAIN

Recent efforts to include the ethic of human security as one of the core objectives of Canada's foreign policy lack the necessary coherence required to be a useful guide for the conduct of statecraft. Canada's foreign policy seeks to achieve three key objectives: (1) to promote prosperity and employment; (2) to protect security within a stable international framework; and (3) to protect abroad Canadian values and culture (Canada 1995: 10). In the practice of statecraft these objectives are not always reconcilable and, consequently, they sometimes—though not always—demand conflicting action. Ottawa has traditionally emphasized its eco-nomic and security interests above other goals, even though Canada has been at the forefront of the effort to promote the global observance of human rights, the rule of law, and good governance. More recently, the discourse of Canada's for-eign policy, especially as it is articulated by Foreign Minister Lloyd Axworthy, may indicate a significant change in this order of priorities and in the moral sub-stance of Canada's interests abroad. But the practical implementation of Ottawa's emerging doctrine of human security may impede efforts to secure other equally fundamental, but conflicting, values and it may commit Canada to principles that it is not entirely prepared to fulfill.[1]

The ethic of human security challenges and possibly undermines the moral foundation of international society as it has existed for nearly four hundred years. Exponents of human security reject the sovereign state as the paramount moral community of international society; they do not believe that these communities ought to be the principal referents of security. Rather, the ethic of human security accords moral priority to the security of individual human beings. Therefore, the difference between human security and our traditional understanding of national security presupposes an important change in the moral character of world poli-tics; indeed, it may foreshadow a change which is nothing short of revolutionary. By investigating the ethical foundation of Ottawa's nascent doctrine of human security we can gain important insight into Canada's basic values and how these values impact its foreign policy and sense of purpose in world politics. It will become evident as a result of this investigation that Canada's doctrine of human security emphasizes certain norms which are often at odds with the prevailing norms of present-day international society, norms which also constitute an important part of Canada's traditional foreign policy objectives. Moreover, this doctrine may engender excessive moralism; that is, a tendency to encounter the world as if Canada were engaged in a moral crusade. Indeed, a foreign policy

which is guided, at least in part, by a universal doctrine such as human security is difficult to reconcile with the practical realities and fundamentally pluralist nature of international society. In its effort to include human security as one of its core foreign policy objectives, Ottawa must recognize the circumstantial character of world politics and how this contingent condition affects the achievement of certain values. Recognizing this state of affairs entails relying upon prudent judgment, rather than indiscriminate universal principles, to guide Canada's foreign relations. An approach which carefully weighs competing and conflicting moral claims permits the greatest opportunity to criticize others for unjust practices, to stand in solidarity with those resisting oppression, to refrain from recklessly imposing our values on others, and to achieve the key objectives of Canada's foreign policy.

ALTERNATIVE ETHICS OF SECURITY IN THE POST–COLD WAR WORLD

The tremendous change brought about by the end of the cold war compelled scholars and practitioners of world politics to question and to reconceptualize the meaning of security. It is often said that focusing upon nuclear deterrence, military balances, zero-sum games, competing power blocs, and interstate relations is overly narrow or even out of date in the post-cold war world.[2] Replacing this cold war security discourse are several discourses which centre upon issues such as the environment, equity, human potential, multilateralism, religion, ethnicity, gender, identity, and cooperative and common security. Following from this ongoing process of critical reflection and redefinition is an approach which not only rejects the traditional cold war understanding of security, but proposes instead an ambitious set of principles that, if implemented fully, would signal a revolutionary change in the practice of diplomacy.

Given the lofty goals proposed by the advocates of human security, we might be inclined to view the concept as mere rhetoric or we might be tempted to dismiss it as unrealizable, albeit well-intentioned, ideals in much the same way as the aspirations of the inter-war idealists were disparaged by those who subscribed to a more "realistic" approach to world politics.[3] But human security is an idea which is much larger than Minister Axworthy and his aspirations for Canada's foreign policy. It is an idea which enjoys considerable support throughout the world. And the discourse of world politics indicates clearly that the idea of human security amounts to a great deal more expedient, idealistic, naïve, and foolish rhetoric. For example, the principles and imperatives of human security command a prominent place in the activities of the UN, they are at the centre of the Report of the Commission on Global Governance, and they are a pervasive theme in the discourse of global civil society.[4] Similarly, the purpose and value of global initiatives such as the Ottawa Treaty, which prohibits anti-personnel mines, the proposed International Criminal Court, efforts to define the rights of the child, and

326

attempts to confront the global problem posed by the spread of AIDS are all intelligible and are frequently justified in the discourse of human security. These developments indicate that, far from being more rhetoric, at least some people associate human security with a set of ends which are good in themselves; that is, their enjoyment needs no further justification. And while advocates of human security often differ in areas of emphasis and in matters of prescription, they share a common belief that human security is a better way to engage the complexities of an emerging world that is challenged less by interstate threats than by threats which are contained within states or which transcend the jurisdiction of particular states.

The ethical foundation of human security differs in several important ways from the ethic of national security which has heretofore dominated both theoretical and practical understanding of security. The ethic of human security incorporates into the security discourse a cluster of values which broadens significantly the scope and substance of the word "security." In articulating the idea of human security, Minister Axworthy proposes an understanding which recognizes the elementary importance of "human rights and fundamental freedoms, the right to live in dignity, with adequate food, shelter, health and education services, and under the rule of law and good governance" (Axworthy 1996c: 3–7). In addition to these values, he suggests that human security also embraces a commitment to democratic development and ensuring quality of life and equity for all human beings. Collectively, these values are to form an integral part of a Canadian foreign policy, which is designed to confront the post-cold war world.

Human security has gained currency in large part because of the dilemmas presented by the practice of national security.[5] National security is concerned with the safety of particular political communities: sovereign states. Individual security is assumed to follow from national security by virtue of our membership in a particular political community. Thus, national security presupposes the assumption that states are worth preserving; that is, sovereign states are thought of as moral communities in their own right. In fact, preserving the fortunes of the political community is such a deeply held norm that national security is one of the few norms that, in certain circumstances, may justifiably pre-empt other fundamental norms of international society. But the practice of world politics reveals a more troubling side of national security: some states do not provide adequate security for their citizens and they fail to deliver the most basic social goods. Failed or unjust states, such as Somalia, Liberia, Rwanda, and the former Yugoslavia, are typically bastions of tyranny, sources of great misery, and are often themselves the most immediate threat to their citizens' security. In states such as these, the term "national security" is nothing more than a misnomer; it refers to a juridical entity rather than a sociological nation. Ironically, the constitutive norms of international society sustain this condition in a rather perverse way: the rights of sovereign equality, nonintervention, and political independence

help to ensure the survival of what are otherwise unviable states.[6] That some states do not provide adequate security for their citizens, yet manage to ensure their own survival, casts doubt upon their worth as moral communities and upon the doctrine of national security.

Recognizing the principal difficulty of national security—individual security does not necessarily follow from the security of the political community—underscores the key normative difference between national security and human security. Whereas national security postulates states as the principal recipients of security, human security confers moral priority on the security of individual human beings. Human security, or what Minister Axworthy calls "real" security, is concerned foremost with the protection of the individual (1996b: 2). An ethic of human security does not permit us to remain detached from, or indifferent to, human suffering on account of deeply ingrained injunctions against interfering in the domestic affairs of sovereign states. For Canada, this means that a commitment to human security requires a "broadening of the focus of security policy from its narrow orientation of managing state-to-state relationships, to one that recognizes the importance of the individual and society for our shared security" (Canada 1995: 25). Thus, in a departure from the classical ethic of national security, human security discloses a cosmopolitan ethic which posits the community of humankind as resting above the society of states.

IS HUMAN SECURITY A SOUND FOUNDATION FOR CANADA'S FOREIGN POLICY?

A tension exists between the practical implications of a foreign policy which seeks to secure the values of human security and the prevailing moral disposition of the society of states. The moral substance of international society is disclosed in a constellation of constitutive norms which reflect the common values and interests of its constituent members. These norms are not given by any philosophical treatise; they are not discovered by power of human reason; and they are not theorized by the spectators of world politics in relation to how they think the world ought to be. The norms of international society are products of human activity: they are the distillation of centuries of diplomatic, military, economic, and other international practice. And because these norms are artifacts of human experience they are historically situated: over time they have varied in their incarnation, strength, importance, and interpretation.

Although international society is embedded in, and is a product of, history, it should not be confused with any purposive enterprise or any evolutionary view of human progress: international society is not justified by the achievement of specific ends, such as welfare or human dignity. The definite mark of international society "[lies] not in the shared purposes of its members states ... but in their acknowledgement of formal rules of mutual accommodation" (Nardin 1983: 309). The constitutive norms of international society represent moral injunctions which

circumscribe the exercise of power. And by imposing limits on the exercise of power these norms stand opposed to certain policies, even when they represent the most expedient way of fulfilling the requirements of the national interest. The constitutive norms of international society restrict the means that states may employ to obtain national advantage and the ends for which states may aspire (Morgenthau 1948: 80). Thus, in a key and basic way, the norms of international society provide the basis for mutual coexistence; collectively they admit that there are different conceptions of the "good life." In recognizing different conceptions of the good life, international society affords individual states the opportunity to pursue their own notion of the good life without being subject to interference on the part of others. Located at the heart of this notion of society is an ethic of pluralism: "the conception that there are many different ends that men may seek and still be fully rational, fully men, capable of understanding each other" (Berlin 1991: 11).

To argue that international society is fundamentally pluralist in its organization is not to say that the theory of pluralism is the only basis of human organization and association. For example, medieval Europeans ordered themselves on the principle that all European states constituted the *respublica Christiana*—the Christian Commonwealth of Europe. In this mode of association, human relations are intelligible in one universal pattern, a pattern which determines the place of all persons, their rights and duties, their function and purpose. It is a pattern which presupposes the acceptance of a singular common good, or common good life, to be shared by all. And while there is no logical or empirical reason not to believe that a universal association or commonwealth could again exist in contemporary world politics, the history and discourse of world politics suggest that large groups of human beings do not believe that they live in such a world today. In terms of foreign policy, we continuously debate the most profitable course of action; we complain that we give too much or not enough; we blame others for failing to fulfill their obligations and they, in turn, respond that they have done so; and in our relations with others, we are concerned to answer the question: to whom do we owe our primary obligations—to members of our own political community or to those persons who are not members?

These moral conversations may indicate that many of us do not properly understand the common good and purpose of our world or that perhaps we know too little or that we are too feeble-minded to comprehend its significance. These conversations may indicate also that the ends and purposes of human beings are many; that they speak to ends that are of the category "good" but which do not necessarily entail one another and are not reconcilable in one systematic, uniform, and all-encompassing pattern.[7] We find that these different ends of human life may "come into conflict, and lead to clashes between societies, parties, individuals, and not least within individuals themselves; and furthermore that the ends of one age and country differ widely from those of other times and other

outlooks" (Berlin 1969: 102). And because the ends of human beings are many, the world in which they live is not intelligible in the context of a single moral theory. Rather we live in a world in which moral voices and perspectives coexist and sometimes conflict; over the course of history they advance and retreat; and we discern and evaluate their importance in the context of varying degrees of strength or weakness. Thus, it might be the case our present world discloses some degree of universalism and that our world may once again be ordered on principles of a universalist ethic. However, it seems as if the ethic of pluralism, at least for the moment, best describes the dominant ethic of international society.

It is precisely this ethic of pluralism which potentially conflicts with human security. Human security does not allow full expression of different conceptions of the good life: it does not recognize that there are ways of organizing our lives which are both different and moral. The doctrine of human security imposes upon all a universal good life that is determined by values whose meaning is derived mainly from Canadian and western experience and which rest above the diversity and particularisms of individual political communities. Thus, a Canadian foreign policy based upon the doctrine of human security would not stop at securing the moral and material interests of Canadians; rather it would transcend this proper purpose in an attempt to secure the interests of humanity in its entirety. This universal mission is revealed inasmuch as "Canadians hold deeply that we must pursue our values internationally. They want to promote them for their own sake, but they also understand that our values and rights will not be safeguarded if they are not enshrined throughout the international environment" (Canada 1995: 34). And in asserting that Canadians speak with one moral voice, Minister Axworthy suggests that "[i]t is critical that this voice be heard internationally as it both validates our worth as a country and promotes the value of human dignity around the globe" (1996a: 1). But in a society of states which values pluralism, this view wrongly identifies the aspirations of Canada with the aspirations of the world.

This excessive moralism which may infect Canada's sense of purpose in world politics is an unsuitable foundation for a nation's foreign policy. For a foreign policy of this type does not acknowledge the circumstantial nature of human relations; and it is indicative of an attitude or mood which does not differ significantly from the indiscriminate cold war injunction, "stop communism," which led the US to oppose all communist regimes everywhere without assessing their origin or their specific character. And it was the pursuit of this (indiscriminate) universalist mission that entangled the US in the catastrophe of Vietnam. Like all realms of human relations, world politics is marked by contingency, chance, change, and unpredictability. But Minister Axworthy's notion of human security takes scant notice of this conditional state of affairs. Rather it is imbued with inchoate references and ill-considered commitments to a multitude of abstract ideals and universal principles of which the implications have not been sufficiently thought through. A foreign policy which endorses abstract principles before appraising the

circumstances which impose upon the statesperson, is bound to fail. The actions of the stateperson are bound by practical limits: "human activity, with whatever it may be concerned, enjoys a circumscribed range of movement. The limits which define this range are historic, that is to say, they are themselves the product of human activity" (Oakeshott 1996: 116). And that is why words such as "possibility," "necessity," "requirement," "likely," "compromise," "restraint," and "contingent," constitute the substance of the vocabulary of statecraft. But abstract principles are divorced from the practical world of statecraft. They are ahistorical, they take no notice of human experience, they are not susceptible to limitation, they are ignorant of circumstance, and they are not amenable to compromise. Indeed, human conduct which is guided wholly by abstract principle has difficulty recognizing that the achievement of one end may, in some circumstances, conflict with another desirable end (Mill 1988: 138).

The danger of permitting abstract principle to guide foreign policy is evident, for example, in Canada's human rights policy. Human rights are a central part of Canada's foreign policy agenda: they are accorded the status of a "threshold" issue which colours significantly Canada's international relations. Indeed, Minister Axworthy submits that "[r]espect for human rights is a critical component of the Canadian identity and therefore must play an important role in our foreign policy agenda" (1997: 1). But in these pronouncements it is difficult to find any moral reason to qualify how Canada's human rights policy is to be implemented. There is acknowledgement that Canada's "ability to effect change can be limited," and that its efforts are sometimes construed as unjustified interference in the internal affairs of others (Axworthy 1997: 1–7). There is also recognition that Canada's ability to force change is limited by a paucity of economic leverage and international clout. However, these conditions speak to instrumental problems: they refer only to limitations of the means with which to achieve the end and not to the achievement of the end itself. Canada's foreign policy establishment, in its commitment to secure human rights, is noticeably silent on questions concerning moral conflict: it does not acknowledge that fundamental values sometimes clash. And it seems as if Canada's doctrine of human security does not recognize that the pursuit of human rights may sometimes impede securing other fundamental values; that obtaining the good of human rights may entail a loss of order, or of security, or some other value; and that an occasion may arise when human rights ought to be subordinated to the achievement of other fundamental values.

In the absence of these qualifications, Canada's stated human rights objectives are not the result of careful deliberation which weighs interest, power, obligations, rights, competing claims, and the circumstances in which they are embedded. A human rights policy which is guided wholly by abstract principle quickly transforms itself into a doctrine of universal human salvation. And it is in this spirit of universal salvation that Canada charts a course which asserts

that: "it is important that we pursue the issue of human rights internationally. It is important as an extension of our own beliefs" (Axworthy 1997: 1). A foreign policy of this type is less about securing Canadian interests than it is about validation and affirmation of national righteousness. This is when the conduct of foreign policy ceases to be a useful instrument of statecraft: it becomes the servant of justice for the sake of doing justice.

A foreign policy which seeks justice, but is unaware of circumstance, rival claims, and conflicting obligations, can see no diversity or difference in human experience. Universalism and uniformity are all that is intelligible in a mission to extend our beliefs and to validate our worth as a country. It is at this point that we seek to repress difference, not because difference contributes to disorder or insecurity, but because it is identified with error. Thus, the chief duty of government and the purpose of foreign policy becomes one of suppressing as error all opposition to the enterprise of securing the greater justice of human rights for all.[8] And in its missions to secure a particular notion of justice for all of humanity, Canada runs the risk of inflicting injustice of a greater magnitude than that which it seeks to remedy. Instead of recognizing the circumstantial nature of world politics and the diversity of human existence, Canada seems intent on pursuing a universalist mission in an attempt to perfect the inherently imperfect nature of the human condition.

But we must be quick to note that recognizing and celebrating diversity does not require us to remain silent in the face of injustice. We are not required to accept an extreme relativist position which precludes all communication with members of other cultures and civilizations. We are not muted prisoners of our own cultural practices, unable to understand the practices of others. Because human beings are moral creatures, we are able to comprehend injustice, even when it occurs in circumstances quite different from our own. And because we are able to communicate with members of other cultures, we are able to criticize unjust practices and stand in solidarity with other human beings against injustice. Canada ought to criticize oppressive governments and it ought to stand in solidarity with those who are resisting oppression.

But in criticizing others for human rights abuses, for example, Canada must remain acutely aware of how this criticism affects the realization of other fundamental values, both for Canadians and for others. Occasion may arise when the achievement of order, security, or peace may be threatened by an overly progressive human rights policy. A foreign policy which is conscious of circumstances is aware of something which foreign policy guided by abstract principle is not: the norms of international society sometimes demand conflicting action. There is no predetermined way to disentangle these conflicting obligations. Good and right in international society are not derived from any particular norm such as order or justice. We can comprehend no universal and common chief good for which all the world's statespersons strive to secure. And we cannot resolve conflicting moral demands by

appealing to a single authoritative norm; we cannot discern a definite and permanent hierarchy in which the norms of international society are arranged; nor is it evident that these norms are equal to each other at all times and in all circumstances. The norms of international society are an eclectic group which merely reflect the contradictions, tensions, and imperfections of the creatures that created them.

RECONCILING HUMAN SECURITY AND CANADA'S FOREIGN POLICY OBJECTIVES

The moral dilemmas and conflicts of world politics are not resolved in the abstract, but in the practice of statecraft. In the practice of world politics, the circumstances of our world, at times, oblige some norms to yield to others. The practice of statecraft suggests that, in extreme cases, the rights of sovereign states may be abrogated or suspended when it is in the interest of international society as a whole. Likewise, when human rights injunctions clash with the imperatives of national security, human rights usually lose. And in the absence of an authoritative norm to guide the practice of statecraft, the statesperson must rely upon a particular type of judgment, a type of judgment we call prudence, to resolve conflicting obligations.

Prudence, which is often described as the supreme virtue of politics, is a species of practical wisdom: it discloses a mode of common sense which is the antithesis of abstract intellectualism. Prudence is the name we give to that type of wisdom which is associated with careful consideration, deliberation, restraint, and foresight. It is a type of sound judgment which guides the statesperson through the difficult choices and which makes some sense of conflicting demands and obligations. And through all the complexity, mystery, and uncertainty of our world, it is the prudent statesperson who is able to choose the best course of action under these trying conditions. Thus, the prudent statesperson demonstrates the ability to make the right decision at the right time—the ability to solve real problems, to get things done, to select the most profitable course among the many possible paths on which to travel. However, prudence ought not to be mistaken for ordinary common sense; rather it is a kind of wisdom with which few are endowed. For prudence is not a technical subject: we do not become prudent simply by reading philosophy or by observing world politics from the sidelines. And prudence is not learned mechanically or by rote. The practice of statecraft, like human conduct in general, is indeterminate, uncertain, and susceptible to chance, and it is quite unlike exact sciences which require no deliberation (Aristotle 1963: 49). Therefore, it is not possible to stipulate in advance a prudential principle, apply it to our subject, and expect successful political action to follow. Rather, prudence is imparted and learned by way of practice and experience.

The prudent statesperson must consider a multitude of parties and circumstances in the conduct of statecraft. Prudential statecraft refuses to judge and solve problems in the abstract. In contrast, abstract principles know only absolute truth:

they cannot discriminate between the circumstances which distinguish a problem's moral significance. The prudent statesperson is obligated to attend first to the interests of his/her own citizens—those to whom he/she is directly accountable. Performing this task is the chief duty of the stateperson. And in a democratic society, fulfilling this duty may sometimes require that the stateperson ignore popular opinion. But the stateperson's work is not finished after the requirements of the national interest have been satisfied. He/she must also consider the legitimate interests of other claimants and he/she must contemplate the interests of innocent third parties before deciding upon a particular course of action. Indeed, considering the legitimate interests of others is a basic and necessary ingredient of successful foreign policy; for a "nation that is too preoccupied with its own interests is bound to define those interests too narrowly. It will do this because it will fail to consider those of its interests which are *bound up in a web of mutual interests* with other nations. In short, the national interest when conceived only from the standpoint of the self-interest of the nation is bound to be defined too narrowly and therefore to be self-defeating [italics in original]" (Niebuhr, 1958: 40). The virtuous statesperson must assess all legitimate claims and decide which one, under the circumstances, appears to be closest to the truth. The prudent statesperson, in carefully weighing different claims and circumstances, adjusts to the contours of the problem (Vico 1965: 34). In contrast, the moral crusader applies to the problem a universal principle in the effort to obtain a solution.

It is not yet clear how Ottawa intends to reconcile its doctrine of human security with the circumstantial nature of human relations; for there appears to be little allowance for contingency, unpredictability, accident, and chance. Human security is a universalist doctrine which takes little notice of the pluralist nature of international society; instead it posits a community of humankind above the society of states. And this cosmopolitan commitment supposes that Canadian values are those of the entire world without ascertaining if this sense of right is a truth held by others. As such, human security is an unsuitable objective of Canada's foreign policy. However, this does not mean that Canada must abandon its commitment to issues concerning human rights, democracy, the rule of law, and good governance. Canada may legitimately, and ought to, criticize Indonesia's human rights record in East Timor, China's suppression of pro-democracy activists, child labour practices in India, military rule in Burma, war crimes in Yugoslavia, and genocide in Rwanda.

But caution must be exercised while expressing opposition to the practices of others. Canada must avoid undermining other constitutive norms of international society while pursuing these ends. This means that Canada may recognize injustice and may express solidarity with those who are resisting oppression; that is to say, that we can share with them an opposition to injustice and therefore "march in their parade" (Walzer 1994). This also means that purposive efforts to remedy injustice

may be, in some cases, better left to those directly engaged. When we move from a position of moral solidarity to one of direct engagement, we inevitably retreat into our own particular morality (Walzer 1994). It is at this point that universalist schemes of human salvation manifest themselves and begin to erode the pluralist nature of international society. A prudent foreign policy allows us to "march in the parade" without indiscriminately imposing our values on others. A policy which abstains from moral crusading is important both for the moral development of others and for Canada. Canada has demonstrated that it is not always prepared to undertake the responsibilities that the ethic of human security entails. For example, when faced with choosing between human rights and economic interests, Canada has often demonstrated a willingness to secure the latter at the expense of the former. We see in the past that Canada has softened its human rights agenda in order to advance its economic interests abroad.[9] But in the absence of a willingness to consistently fulfill the requirements of a policy of human security, and in the absence of a forthright acknowledgment that the fundamental objectives of Canadian foreign policy may sometimes conflict, any ongoing commitment to a policy sustained by self-righteousness invites charges of hypocrisy and threatens to fray the moral fabric that is distinctly Canadian.

Surely this advice will meet profound dissatisfaction, and even indignation, from the prophets of human security and other similar universalist doctrines. They will criticize the prudent course as being conservative and slow to work. They are right. But Canada ought to be most reticent and cautious before it begins to subvert international society as it presently exists. International society has provided the basis for some countries—Canada among them—to strive for and achieve some notion of the good life. And enshrined in international society is an ethic that permits Canada to pursue an understanding of the good life which is distinctly its own. Thus, Canada ought to pursue its foreign policy objectives in such a way that it preserves and, indeed, sustains the pluralism of international society. However, a Canadian foreign policy based upon the principles of human security would not be favourably disposed toward securing this good. Rather it would likely suffer from an unacknowledged contradiction which may hinder the practical conduct of statecraft by infusing Canada's international relations with excessive moralism. And insofar as Ottawa fails to acknowledge that Canada's foreign policy objectives may sometimes demand conflicting action, it invites allegations of hypocrisy which threaten to undermine Canada's credibility, both at home and abroad.

The potential danger of a foreign policy which does not acknowledge that conflicting demands may confound the best attempts to secure basic values is evident in recent events concerning Canada and the Asia-Pacific region. Canada's efforts to increase its economic presence in the region are often met with strident criticism because of Indonesia's human rights record in East Timor, China's treatment of pro-democracy activists, and child labor practices in India and Pakistan. Likewise, attempts to pursue Canada's human rights agenda regularly provoke

attitudes of apathy and skepticism at home, and accusations of cultural imperialism from abroad. Canada's leaders are likely to evoke feelings of uncertainty and disbelief when, on the one hand, Minister Axworthy openly questions the value and relevancy of APEC because it does not address human rights issues and, on the other hand, Prime Minister Jean Chrétien emphasizes that APEC "means business" by indicating that it is primarily a free-trade group in which human rights concerns are to be raised "on the margin in private bilateral talks" (Sallot 1997). And we are apt to encounter confusion when foreign policy statements are less about Canada's interests abroad than with concerns at home. Canada may do harm to its international reputation and credibility, and it may unnecessarily complicate its foreign relations, to the extent that human security "must play a important role in our foreign policy agenda" because it "validates our worth as a country" and affirms Canada's national identity. The inevitable contradictions and hypocrisies of a foreign policy which is not grounded in the substance of international affairs, but is directed toward fostering national unity or some other domestic concern, is likely to breed mistrust, doubt, and suspicion. Thus, we should not be surprised that demonstrators protesting the recent APEC summit in Vancouver accused Ottawa of putting "profits before people," "indulging murderers," and being "indifferent to human suffering." The anti-APEC protesters, in their anger, passion, and skepticism, are pointing to the principal difficulty of committing Canada to a policy of human security: Canada is not always prepared to achieve the ambitious set of ideals that human security entails.

In abandoning its moralist pretensions and in tempering its aspirations with regard to human security, Ottawa need not abandon its commitment to human rights, democracy, the rule of law, and good governance. Canada ought to pursue these objectives in such a way that the statesperson, after carefully deliberating over competing and conflicting moral claims, determines a course of action which is most appropriate given the particular circumstances that distinguish the problem. This means that we ought to pursue human rights, democracy, the rule of law, and good governance when the circumstances permit us to do so. It is this middle ground, that area between relativism which accords validity to all truth claims and a universalism which imposes one pattern of life on all, for which Canada's foreign policy ought to aim. This area is, admittedly, difficult to find; it is something which is constantly shifting: its boundaries are blurred and uncertain and its content is always open to change, challenge and revision. However, the substance of this middle ground is sufficiently stable so that we are able to speak of it in a meaningful way. The middle ground of which we speak is that area in which we secure the greatest possible amount of the many obtainable goods, but which does not permit injustice of a magnitude that would be rightly called intolerable. We ought to aim at achieving those goods which are associated with human security insofar as the circumstances permit us to do so; but in doing so, we ought to aim also at maintaining values such as political independence and

noninterference—goods which are essential to the maintenance of the society of states. Thus, we see that the middle ground between relativism and universalism is an area whose procedural basis rests upon the virtue of compromise.

But in aiming for this middle ground, we ought to be forthright in acknowledging that occasions may arise when we ought not pursue certain policies for the sake of other fundamental values. Recognizing that fundamental values clash; that it may not be possible to secure all things considered to be good at all times and in all places; and that sometimes it is best to accept a state of affairs which does not satisfy all the requirements of justice, is only to realize that finding the middle ground is often difficult. And it is difficult to maintain ourselves in this area precisely because our values may clash and because our moral injunctions may demand conflicting action. That is why a foreign policy which is based upon prudential ethics does the greatest justice to Canada and to its neighbors. Thus, in the effort to secure these goods while, at the same time, preserving the good of pluralism, Canada's foreign policy toward Asia Pacific, and elsewhere, ought to be guided by the wisdom of Vico's learned sage, "who through all the uncertainties of human action keeps his eye steadily focused on eternal truth, manages to follow in a roundabout way whenever he cannot travel in a straight line so as to be as profitable as the nature of things permit" (Vico 1965: 35).

REFERENCES

Annan, Kofi (1998). *Annual Report of the Secretary-General on the Work of the Organization* The Fifty-Third Session of the General Assembly (New York: United Nations).

Aristotle (1963). *Ethics* John Warrington ed. & trans. (London: J.M. Dent and Sons).

Axworthy, Lloyd (1997). *Notes for an Address by the Honourable Lloyd Axworthy, Minister of Foreign Affairs, at the Consultations with Non-Governmental Organizations in Preparation for the 53rd Session of the United Nations Commission on Human Rights* (Ottawa: February 5).

_____ (1996a). *Notes for an Address by the Honourable Lloyd Axworthy, Minister of Foreign Affairs, at the Consultations with Non-Governmental Organizations in Preparation for the 52nd Session of the United Nations Commission on Human Rights* (Ottawa: February 13).

_____ (1996b). *Notes for an Address by the Honourable Lloyd Axworthy, Minister of Foreign Affairs, to the 52nd Session of the United Nations Commission on Human Rights* (Geneva, Switzerland: April 3).

_____ (1996c). *Notes for an Address by the Honourable Lloyd Axworthy, Minister of Foreign Affairs, to the 51st General Assembly of the United Nations* (New York, NY: September 24).

Baldwin, David (1997). "The Concept of Security" *Review of International Studies* 23: 1–26.

Berlin, Isaiah (1969). "Historical Inevitability" *Four Essays on Liberty* (Oxford: Oxford University Press).

_____ (1991). "The Pursuit of the Ideal" *The Crooked Timber of Humanity* Henry Hardy ed. (London: Fontana Press).

Canada (1995). *Canada in the World* (Ottawa: DFAIT).

Carr, E. H. (1946). *The Twenty Year Crisis: 1919–1939* (London: Macmillan).

Commission on Global Governance (1995). *Our Global Neighbourhood* (Oxford: Oxford University Press).

Gilles, David (1996). *Between Principle and Practice: Human Rights in North-South Relations* (Montreal: McGill-Queen's University Press).

Jackson, Robert H. (1990). *Quasi-States: Sovereignty, International Relations and the Third World* (Cambridge: Cambridge University Press).

_____ (1995). *Human Security in a World of States* Paper Presented at the Annual Conference of the International Studies Association (Toronto: March 18–22).

Krause, Keith and Michael Williams (1996). "Broadening the Agenda of Security Studies: Politics and Methods" *Mershon International Studies Review* 40: 229–54.

Lipschutz, Ronnie D. ed. (1995). *On Security* (New York: Columbia University Press).

Mill, John Stuart (1988). *The Logic of the Moral Sciences* (La Salle, IL: Open Court).

Morgenthau, Hans J. (1948). "The Twilight of International Morality" *Ethics* 58:2.

Nardin, Terry (1983). *Law, Morality, and the Relations of States* (Princeton: Princeton University Press).

Niebuhr, Reinhold (1958). "America's Moral and Spiritual Resource" in Earnest W. Lefever ed. *World Crisis and American Responsibility* (New York: Association Press).

Oakeshott, Michael (1996). *The Politics of Faith and the Politics of Scepticism* Timothy Fuller ed. (New Haven: Yale University Press).

Roberts, Adam and Benedict Kingsbury eds. (1993). *United Nations, Divided World: The UN's Role in International Relations* (Oxford: Clarendon Press).

Sallot, Jeff (1997). "Axworthy Warns APEC of Irrelevancy" *The Globe and Mail* (24 November): A1, A6.

Vico, Giambattista (1965). *On the Study Methods of Our Time* Elio Gianturco trans. (Indianapolis: Bobbs-Merrill Company, Inc.).

Waltzer, Michael (1994). *Thick and Thin: Moral Argument at Home and Abroad* (Notre Dame: University of Notre Dame Press).

NOTES

This essay was first presented at the Annual Meeting of the International Studies Association, Washington DC, February 16–20, 1999. The author would like to thank Barbara Arneil, Megan Gilgan, K. J. Holsti, Robert Jackson, Brian Job, Samuel LaSelva, Heather Owens, Hamish Telford, Mark Zacher, and the two anonymous reviewers for their helpful comments and suggestions.

1. The category "human rights," unless indicated otherwise, refers to the restrictive civil and political conception rather than the more permissive conception which includes economic, social, and cultural rights. The more inclusive category "fundamental values" refers to a cluster of issues such as peace, order, security, and justice.

2. For example see Lipschutz (1995); Krause and Williams (1996); and Baldwin (1997).

3. For example see Carr (1946).

4. For example see Roberts and Kingsbury (1993); Annan (1998); Commission on Global Governance (1995). It should be noted that global civil society, or transnational society, performs a very important role in promoting human security and shaping the content of national and international security discourse. But the importance and significance of this role does not indicate a parallel foreign policy which exists apart from state activity. Rather global civil society and states are part of the same process of foreign relations, although they serve different purposes and functions. For the purpose of this article it is most appropriate to focus upon states and the issues that affect them because the ultimate authority to conduct foreign relations is endowed in states and it is states, in spite of role and influence of global civil society, who bear ultimate responsibility for the success or failure of foreign policy.

5. The following discussion on security is derived from and heavily influenced by Jackson (1990) and Jackson (1995).

6. For a detailed explication of this argument see Jackson (1990).

7. This discussion is derived from Berlin (1969).

8. This thought is derived from Oakeshott (1996: 60–64).

9. For example, see Gillies (1996).

POSTSCRIPT

It is worth noting that Canada has taken a lead role in promoting the human security agenda among other states. Following a bilateral meeting between Lloyd Axworthy and the foreign minister of Norway in 1998 to launch the idea, a larger forum was held that included foreign ministers from Austria, Chile, Ireland, Jordan, the Netherlands, Slovenia, South Africa, Switzerland, and Thailand.

Although Bain questions whether the concept of human security is in keeping with Canadian foreign policy traditions, one can certainly argue that Canada's promotion of the idea follows the country's traditional role as a middle power. Axworthy, a former political scientist and university professor, has long been an advocate of the notion of "soft power." According to this view, Canada's power in the international community lies not in its military might, but in its ability to promote powerful ideas. Canadian efforts to build an international coalition of "like-minded" states around humanitarian issues in the 1990s can be seen a perpetuation of Canada's traditional role as a middle power.

In his critique of human security, Bain is fearful that Canada may pursue a moralistic and interventionist foreign policy. In examining cases where Canada has pursued human security as the goal, is there evidence that Canada has tried to impose its claims on other states?

It is also worth noting that Bain suggests that "abandoning its moralist pretensions and . . . tempering its aspirations" does not mean that Ottawa should "abandon its commitment to human rights, democracy, the rule of law, and good governance." But it should pursue these objectives only "when the circumstances permit us to do so." If Bain's advice had been taken during the past decade, how different would Canadian foreign policy be? What issues might Canadian foreign policymakers have chosen not to promote?

Suggested Additional Readings

Axworthy, Lloyd. "Human Security and Global Governance: Putting People First." *Global Governance* 7, no. 1 (January 2001): 19–23.

Hampson, Fen Osler, and Dean F. Oliver. "Pulpit Diplomacy: A Critical Assessment of the Axworthy Doctrine." *International Journal* 54, no. 3 (1998): 379–406.

Hampson, Fen Osler, et al. *Madness in the Multitude: Human Security and World Disorder.* Don Mills: Oxford University Press, 2002.

Jockel, Joe, and Joel Sokolsky. "Lloyd Axworthy's Legacy: Human Security and the Rescue of Canadian Defence Policy." *International Journal* 56, no. 1 (Winter 2000–2001): 1–18.

Khong, Yuen Foong. "Human Security: A Shotgun Approach to Alleviating Human Misery?" *Global Governance* 7, no. 3 (July–September 2001): 231–36.

McRae, Robert, and Don Hubert. *Human Security and the New Diplomacy: Promoting People, Promoting Peace.* Montreal: McGill-Queen's University Press, 2001.

Nef, Jorge. *Human Security and Mutual Vulnerability: An Exploration into the Global Political Economy of Development and Underdevelopment.* Ottawa: International Development Research Centre, 1995.

Paris, Roland. "Human Security: Paradigm Shift or Hot Air?" *International Security* 26, no. 2 (Fall 2001): 87–102.

Suhrke, Astri. "Human Security and the Interests of States." *Security Dialogue* 30, no. 3 (1999): 265–76.

InfoTrac® College Edition

Search for the following articles in the InfoTrac® database:

Bernard Jr., Prosper. "Canada and Human Security: From the Axworthy Doctrine to Middle Power Internationalism." *American Review of Canadian Studies* 35, no. 2 (Summer 2006): 233–62.

Khong, Yuen Foong. "Human Security: A Shotgun Approach to Alleviating Human Misery?" *Global Governance* 7, no. 3 (July–September 2001): 231–36.

King, Gary, and Christopher J. L. Murray. "Rethinking Human Security." *Political Science Quarterly* 116, no. 4 (Winter 2001): 585–611.

Oberleitner, Gerd. "Human Security: A Challenge to International Law?" *Global Governance* 11, no. 2 (April–June 2005): 185–204.

Ward, Thomas J. "The Political Economy of NGOs and Human Security." *International Journal on World Peace* 24, no. 1 (March 2007): 43–64.

Web Resources

For current URLs for the following websites, visit www.crosscurrents.nelson.com.

FREEDOM FROM FEAR: CANADA'S HUMAN SECURITY
http://www.humansecurity.gc.ca

This site, from the Department of Foreign Affairs and International Trade Canada, offers a definition of the term "human security" and discusses Canada's approach to human security.

HUMAN SECURITY NETWORK
http://www.humansecuritynetwork.org

The Human Security Network supports and encourages initiatives that protect human security.

CANADIAN CONSORTIUM ON HUMAN SECURITY

http://www.humansecurity.info/#

Based at the University of British Columbia, this website maintained by a network of scholars researching human security provides updates on recent research developments and activities in the field.

GEORGE MACLEAN, "THE CHANGING PERCEPTION OF HUMAN SECURITY: COORDINATING NATIONAL AND MULTILATERAL RESPONSES"

http://www.unac.org/en/link_learn/Canada/security/perception.asp

This paper defines and illustrates how human security can create a more peaceful global climate. It also looks at modern threats to human security.

UNESCO SECURIPAX FORUM

http://www.unesco.org/securipax/

The online UNESCO Forum on Human Security contains a large collection of UN publications and materials by other agencies on human security.

Is the United Nations New Human Rights Council a Failure?

✔ **YES**

BRETT D. SCHAEFER, "The United Nations Human Rights Council: A Disastrous First Year"

✘ **NO**

YVONNE TERLINGEN, "The Human Rights Council: A New Era in UN Human Rights Work?" *Ethics & International Affairs* 21, no. 2 (Summer 2007): 167–78

Article I of the Charter of the United Nations states that one of its founding purposes was "to achieve international co-operation in solving international problems of an economic, social, cultural, or humanitarian character, and in promoting and encouraging respect for human rights and for fundamental freedoms for all without distinction as to race, sex, language, or religion."

To give flesh to this commitment, the UN adopted the Universal Declaration of Human Rights in 1948. This declaration states that "all human beings are born free and equal" and goes on to outline a variety of human-rights norms, including a ban on torture, the guarantee of religious and political freedom, and the right of basic economic well-being. Since 1948, the General Assembly of the United Nations has adopted more than 60 human-rights instruments. These have included such documents as the International Covenant on Civil and Political Rights; the International Covenant on Economic, Social and Cultural Rights; the Convention on the Political Rights of Women; and Convention of the Rights of the Child.

Although the UN has committed itself to the promotion of human-rights norms, the enforcement of such norms has proven problematic. Efforts to enforce human-rights standards in other countries can be taken as interference with the sovereign rights of a nation and hence a violation of the Charter itself. At the same time, external pressures such as trade boycotts or diplomatic sanctions may only succeed in hurting those rights who are being violated in the first place. As a result, the United Nations has focused on two strategies: promoting the adoption of human-rights standards among nations and bringing pressure to bear on those governments that do not live up to the standards they have adopted.

To achieve this, the various conventions and covenants promulgated by the United Nations have been formulated as legally binding treaties. These treaties were first signed by the member countries of the United Nations and then ratified

by their respective governments. By ratifying the treaty, the signatory commits itself to implanting the standards of the treaty in its national laws and promises to submit regular reports to the UN outlining its progress in implementing the new norms.

In order to facilitate this process, the UN established the United National Commission on Human Rights in 1946. Created as a 53-member functional commission of the Economic and Social Council (ECOSOC), the UNCHR focused primarily on promoting human rights and assisting member nations develop treaties embodying these principles. In the first twenty years of its existence, it adhered strictly to the principle of sovereignty and non-interference in the internal affairs of member states. As a result, it played no real role in either investigating or condemning human-rights violators.

In 1967, the Commission shifted its policy toward one of great interventionism. With the wave of decolonization that spread through Asia and Africa, there were growing concerns expressed about the ongoing human-rights violations in South Africa under its policy of apartheid. The Commission stated its intention to investigate and produce reports on human-rights violations. To implement this, the Commission pursued two approaches in the following decades. First, it created geographically oriented working groups to focus on investigating human-rights violations within a specific region or country. Second, it created theme-oriented working groups to investigate and report on specific types of abuses. To further enhance the promotion of human rights, the post of UN High Commissioner for Human Rights was created to coordinate the work of the Commission.

Despite these efforts, the Commission suffered a steady decline in credibility among many member nations and activists promoting effective implementation of human rights. While it was successful in helping to promote human rights as an issue, the Commission was increasingly seen as a failure in its efforts to implement of human rights within member states themselves. Critics of the Commission complained that often major perpetrators of human-rights abuses were voted as members of the Commission. Procedural tactics prevented discussion of specific human-rights situations in countries like Sudan and China. Commission members were often accused of being selective in their judgment, overlooking wrongdoing among their own friends and allies while criticizing those whose human-rights records were less tarnished. Critics noted that the Commission met for only six weeks annually, giving it little time to delve into specific complaints in any detail. Furthermore, it was not available to deal with emerging crisis situations that arose at other times. Although piecemeal reforms were carried out, the credibility of the Commission continued to decline even at a time when the global commitment to human rights was strengthening among many of its members.

Fearing that the failure of the Commission threatened the credibility of the United Nations itself, the UN Secretary-General proposed a complete overhaul of the UN human rights structure through the creation of a new Human Rights

Council. By upgrading the status of the body from a commission to a council, human-rights issues would become equal to security and development issues. As a standing body, the Human Rights Council could meet on a regular basis and not be limited to only six weeks of the year. The membership of the Council would be made more accountable and representative by electing its membership by a two-thirds vote in the General Assembly.

In September 2005, the UN World Summit endorsed the Secretary-General's proposal and referred to the General Assembly negotiation of the final details. In March 2006, the General Assembly formally voted to establish the new Human Rights Council. Only the United States, the Marshall Islands, Palau, and Israel voted against the establishment of the new body. The United States voted against the resolution because it did not believe that sufficient measures had been taken to ensure that abusive nations would not be made members of the Council.

Supporters of the resolution believed that the replacement of the Commission of Human Rights with a new Human Rights Council would give fresh start to the hopes of creating a more effective international human-rights regime. The General Assembly held the first election of select members May 2006 and the Council immediately began its work. Within a short time, the Council became embroiled in a number of controversies. A new body had been created, but it seemed that many of the same issues that plagued the Commission continued to dog the new Human Rights Council.

The following readings give two perspectives on the successes and failures of the first year of operation of the new Human Rights Council. Brett Schaefer expresses the skepticism that American conservatives have about the ability of the UN to promote human rights. He finds the first year of the new Council to be a disaster and advocates that the U.S. refuse to participate in or fund the Council. Yvonne Terlingen, a human-rights activists, recognizes that the Council has not lived up to many of its expectations in the first year. Yet, she calls for an informed and critical support of the Council in hopes of encouraging it to make the changes needed to be successful.

✔ YES

The United Nations Human Rights Council: A Disastrous First Year

BRETT D. SCHAEFER

The United Nations Human Rights Council (HRC) was established in 2006 to replace the discredited U.N. Commission on Human Rights (CHR). Despite minimal safeguards against capture of the HRC by human rights abusers—the source of the commission's ineffectiveness—HRC supporters, including U.N. High Commissioner for Human Rights Louise Arbour, were quick to declare that the new body represented the "dawn of a new era" in promoting human rights in the United Nations.[1] U.N. General Assembly President Jan Eliasson, who oversaw the reform negotiations, called the council "a new beginning for the promotion and protection of human rights" and declared that the council would be "principled, effective and fair."[2] After nearly a year in existence and four regular sessions and four special sessions, the HRC has clearly been none of these.

The United States was one of only four countries that voted against the U.N. General Assembly resolution that created the council.[3] The U.S. cast its vote out of concern that the new council would lack safeguards against the problems that afflicted the CHR. Regrettably, this concern has proved to be well founded:

- The council has mirrored the commission's obsessive focus on Israel to the detriment of other, more severe human rights situations.

- It has become a platform for human rights abusers to deflect criticism rather than being held to account.

- The abusive states are leading an effort to undermine the few effective aspects of the council, such as the special procedures dedicated to examining human rights abuses in specific countries, and are supporting efforts to weaken the universal periodic review of the human rights practices of all U.N. member states.

The U.S. chose not to run for a seat on the HRC in 2006 and 2007. This was the right decision. Until the council proves effective, the U.S. should not lend its credibility to the flawed body by participating.

However, the U.S. should use its influence to make the body effective by encouraging states with good human rights records to run for seats on the council and by speaking up on situations before the council. The U.S. should encourage the council to maintain procedures that have proven effective and strive to block efforts by human rights abusers to weaken those procedures. It should also seek to make the universal periodic review of council member states as frequent and objective as possible.

The council will make many of these decisions in the upcoming June session. Success in these areas should lead the U.S. to continue its engagement with the

council. Failure would demonstrate that the council is simply incapable of effectively advancing fundamental human rights, in which case the U.S. should publicly wash its hands of the council and withhold its portion of the council's budget from its contributions to the U.N.

HUMAN RIGHTS FAILURE AT THE U.N.

Since the birth of the United Nations, protecting and advancing fundamental human rights has been one of the organization's primary objectives. The drafters of the U.N. Charter included a pledge by member states "to reaffirm faith in fundamental human rights, in the dignity and worth of the human person, in the equal rights of men and women."[4] U.N. treaties, such as the Universal Declaration on Human Rights, which the General Assembly passed in 1948, form the core of international standards for human rights.

Yet the U.N.'s recent record in promoting fundamental human rights is riddled with failure and inaction. For nearly six decades, the U.N. Commission on Human Rights epitomized this failure as the premier U.N. human rights body charged with reviewing the human rights performance of states and promoting human rights around the world.[5] Sadly, the commission devolved into a feckless organization that human rights abusers used to block criticism and into a forum for attacks on Israel.[6] The disrepute of the CHR grew so great that even former U.N. Secretary-General Kofi Annan acknowledged, "We have reached a point at which the commission's declining credibility has cast a shadow on the reputation of the United Nations system as a whole, and where piecemeal reforms will not be enough."[7]

After lengthy deliberations and negotiations, the U.N. General Assembly voted to replace the commission with a new Human Rights Council in March 2006.[8] Regrettably, during the negotiations, the General Assembly rejected many of the reforms and standards that had been proposed to ensure that the council would not repeat the mistakes of the commission.[9] For instance, the U.S. wanted a much smaller body than the 53-member commission to enable it to act more easily; a high threshold for election to the council (a two-thirds vote of the General Assembly); and a prohibition on electing nations to the council that are under U.N. Security Council sanction for human rights abuses. Extensive negotiations in the General Assembly produced a 47-member council that is only marginally smaller than the commission, approved a simple majority vote for election rather than the two-thirds requirement, and did not ban human rights violators from sitting on the council.

Because the resolution creating the HRC lacked serious membership criteria, the U.S. voted against it. "Absent stronger mechanisms for maintaining credible membership, the United States could not join consensus on this resolution," explained then-U.S. Ambassador to the U.N. John Bolton. "We did not have sufficient

confidence in this text to be able to say that the HRC would be better than its predecessor."[10] Well-known human rights abusers Burma, China, Cuba, Ethiopia, Libya, Saudi Arabia, Sudan, Syria, and Zimbabwe voted in favor of the new council.

After the resolution passed over U.S. objection, the U.S. announced that it would not run for a seat on the council in 2006 but would consider running in the future if the council proved effective.[11] Thus, the U.S. reserved judgment until the council had a chance to prove its merit. As Ambassador Bolton noted, "The real test will be the quality of membership that emerges on this council and whether it takes effective action to address serious human rights abuse cases like Sudan, Cuba, Iran, Zimbabwe, Belarus, and Burma."[12] The council has failed on both counts.

MANY HUMAN RIGHTS ABUSERS ELECTED TO THE COUNCIL

The resolution that created the HRC established no hard criteria for membership other than quotas for each of the regional groups in the U.N. and a requirement that council members be elected by a simple majority of the General Assembly (currently 97 of 192 votes). No state, no matter how poor its human rights record, is barred from membership. Even states under Security Council sanction for human rights abuses are not excluded.

The resolution instructs U.N. member states that "when electing members of the council, Member States shall take into account the contribution of candidates to the promotion and protection of human rights."[13] Candidates are also asked to submit "voluntary pledges and commitments" on their qualifications for the council based on their past and future adherence to and observance of human rights standards. The toothlessness of this instruction quickly became evident when notorious human rights abusers Algeria, Cuba, China, Iran, Pakistan, Saudi Arabia, and Russia ran for election, asserting their strong commitment to human rights and pledging their commitment to such standards in the future.[14]

The May 2006 election showed that simply creating a new council had not convinced the General Assembly to spurn the candidacies of human rights abusers. Despite their poor human rights records and disingenuous pledges, the General Assembly elected Algeria, China, Cuba, Pakistan, Russia, and Saudi Arabia to the council.[15]

Contrary to the bold predictions that the new council would be a significant improvement over the commission, the council's membership in 2006 was only marginally better than the commission's membership in 2005. The highly touted requirement for a majority vote was undermined by the secret ballot voting process that shielded governments from accountability for their votes and facilitated horse trading and negotiations. This yielded only minimal improvement in the ratio of "free" to "partially free" to "not free" countries.(See Table 1.) Less than half of the commission's members in 2005 were considered "free" by Freedom

House. China, Cuba, Egypt, Pakistan, Sudan, and Zimbabwe—some of the world's worst human rights abusers—routinely used their positions on the commission to block scrutiny of their own practices and to launch spurious attacks on other countries for political reasons (e.g., Israel) or for speaking openly about their human rights violations (e.g., the U.S.).

As Ambassador Bolton noted, for the council to perform better than the commission, it must start with better membership. The first council election produced a council in which 25 countries out of 47 members (53 percent) were ranked "free" by Freedom House—a marginal improvement over the commission. Some of the more disreputable human rights abusers—Burma, North Korea, Sudan, and Zimbabwe—did not run for seats. Iran and Venezuela ran for seats but were unsuccessful, although Venezuela received enough votes (101) to have won a seat if other states had not won more support.[16] Despite these minor successes, a number of states with dismal human rights records won seats, including Algeria, Azerbaijan, Cameroon, Cuba, China, Pakistan, Saudi Arabia, Tunisia, and Russia.

The second council election, held on May 17, 2007, marked a regression from 2006.[17] The number of "free" countries on the council declined, and the number of "not free" countries increased. The only significant victory was blocking Belarus from winning a seat. Yet until about a week before the election, Belarus and Slovenia were the only two candidates for the two open Eastern European seats. Only enormous pressure from human rights groups and the U.S. persuaded Bosnia and Herzegovina to run, denying Belarus a seat on the council.[18] However, Angola, Egypt, Qatar, and Bolivia—states with dismal human rights records—were elected easily.[19]

An additional concern is that, unlike the robust competition for seats in the 2006 election, only two regions—Eastern European States and the Western Europe and Other States—offered more candidates than available seats in the 2007 election.[20] The decision of the African, Asian, and Latin American and Caribbean regions to offer only enough candidates to fill their open seats marked a disturbing return to the practices of the commission and defeated the purpose of competitive elections in the General Assembly, which were supposed to offer a larger choice of possible candidates in order to select the best possible members for the council.

THE HRC'S DISAPPOINTING RECORD

During its first year, the Human Rights Council has proven just as feckless in confronting human rights abuses and just as vulnerable to politically motivated attacks on Israel as its predecessor. Council decisions reveal that the bulk of its membership has declined to scrutinize major violators of human rights and has instead focused disproportionately on censuring Israel.[21]

Specifically, according to UN Watch, a Geneva-based nongovernmental organization (NGO) focused on the work of the Human Rights Council, "To date, there

have been 12 country-specific HRC resolutions: nine censures of Israel and three non-condemnatory resolutions on Sudan." Even the commission had a better record. Over a 40-year period, only 30 percent of its resolutions condemning specific states for human rights violations focused on Israel.[22]

MEMBERSHIP OF U.N. HUMAN RIGHTS BODIES

2005 Commission on Human Rights		2006 Human Rights Council		2007 Human Rights Council	
Countries (53)	2005 Freedom House Ranking	Countries (47)	2006 Freedom House Ranking	(Countries 47)	2007 Freedom House Ranking
African States		*African States*		*African States*	
Burkina Faso	Partly Free	Algeria	Not Free	Angola	Not Free
Congo	Party Free	Cameroon	Not Free	Cameroon	Not Free
Egypt	Not Free	Djibouti	Partly Free	Djibouti	Partly Free
Ethiopia	Partly Free	Gabon	Partly Free	Egypt	Not Free
Eritrea	Not Free	Ghana	Free	Gabon	Partly Free
Gabon	Partly Free	Mali	Free	Ghana	Free
Guinea	Not Free	Mauritius	Free	Madagascar	Partly Free
Kenya	Partly Free	Morocco	Partly Free	Mali	Free
Mauritania	Not Free	Nigeria	Partly Free	Mauritius	Free
Nigeria	Partly Free	Senegal	Free	Nigeria	Partly Free
South Africa	Free	South Africa	Free	Senegal	Free
Sudan	Not Free	Tunisia	Not Free	South Africa	Free
Swaziland	Not Free	Zambia	Partly Free	Zambia	Partly Free
Togo	Not Free				
Zimbabwe	Not Free				
Asian States		*Asian States*		*Asian States*	
Armenia	Party Free	Bahrain	Partly Free	Bangladesh	Partly Free
Bhutan	Not Free	Bangladesh	Partly Free	China	Not Free
China	Not Free	China	Not Free	India	Free
India	Free	India	Free	Indonesia	Free
Indonesia	Party Free	Indonesia	Free	Japan	Free
Japan	Free	Japan	Free	Jordan	Partly Free
Malaysia	Party Free	Jordan	Partly Free	Malaysia	Partly Free
Nepal	Party Free	Malaysia	Partly Free	Pakistan	Not Free
Pakistan	Not Free	Pakistan	Not Free	Philippines	Partly Free
Qatar	Not Free	Philippines	Partly Free	Republic of Korea	Free
Republic of Korea	Free	Republic of Korea	Free	Saudi Arabia	Not Free
Saudi Arabia	Not Free	Saudi Arabia	Not Free	Sri Lanka	Partly Free
Sri Lanka	Party Free	Sri Lanka	Partly Free	Qatar	Not Free

Panel 1

Eastern European States

Country	Rating
Hungary	Free
Romania	Free
Russia	Not Free
Ukraine	Party Free

Latin American and Caribbean States

Country	Rating
Argentina	Free
Brazil	Free
Costa Rica	Free
Cuba	Not Free
Dominican Republic	Free
Ecuador	Party Free
Guatemala	Party Free
Honduras	Party Free
Mexico	Free
Paraguay	Party Free
Peru	Free

Western Europe and Other States

Country	Rating
Australia	Free
Canada	Free
Finland	Free
France	Free
Germany	Free
Ireland	Free
Italy	Free
Netherlands	Free
United Kingdom	Free
United States of America	Free
Free	42%
Partly Free	30%
Not Free	28%

Panel 2

Eastern European States

Country	Rating
Azerbaijan	Not Free
Czech Republic	Free
Poland	Free
Romania	Free
Russia	Not Free
Ukraine	Free

Latin American and Caribbean States

Country	Rating
Argentina	Free
Brazil	Free
Cuba	Not Free
Ecuador	Partly Free
Guatemala	Partly Free
Mexico	Free
Peru	Free
Uruguay	Free

Western Europe and Other States

Country	Rating
Canada	Free
Finland	Free
France	Free
Germany	Free
Netherlands	Free
Switzerland	Free
United Kingdom	Free
Free	53%
Partly Free	28%
Not Free	19%

Panel 3

Eastern European States

Country	Rating
Azerbaijan	Not Free
Bosnia and Herzegovina	Partly Free
Slovenia	Free
Romania	Free
Russia	Not Free
Ukraine	Free

Latin American and Caribbean States

Country	Rating
Bolivia	Partly Free
Brazil	Free
Cuba	Not Free
Guatemala	Partly Free
Mexico	Free
Nicaragua	Partly Free
Peru	Free
Uruguay	Free

Western Europe and Other States

Country	Rating
Canada	Free
France	Free
Germany	Free
Italy	Free
Netherlands	Free
Switzerland	Free
United Kingdom	Free
Free	49%
Partly Free	30%
Not Free	21%

Sources: U.N. Commission on Human Rights, "Membership," at www.unhchr.ch/html/menu2/2/chrmem.htm (May 25, 2007); U.N. Human Rights Council, "Human Rights Council Elections at www.ohchr.org/english/bodies/hrcouncil/elections.htm (May 25, 2007); and Freedom House, "Freedom in the World Country Rankings, 1972–2006," at www.freedomhouse.org/uploads/frw/FIWANScores.xls (May 25, 2007), and "Freedom in the World 2007," at www.freedomhouse.org/uploads/press_release/frw07_charts.pdf (May 25, 2007).

In its first four regular sessions and four special sessions, the council failed to address ongoing repression in Belarus, China, Cuba, North Korea, and Zimbabwe and many other dire human rights situations around the world. Nor did the HRC censure the government of Sudan for its role in the genocide in Darfur. Instead, it adopted three mild decisions expressing "concern" regarding the human rights and humanitarian situation in Darfur and dispatched a "High-Level Mission to assess the human rights situation in Darfur and the needs of the Sudan in this regard."[23] However, the council did find the time to hold three special sessions on Israel and pass nine strong resolutions condemning Israel.

During more than 10 weeks worth of meetings in its first year, the council:

- Passed 12 resolutions on the human rights situations in only two countries. Nine were one-sided condemnations of Israel. Three were soft, non-condemnatory resolutions on Sudan.

- Did not adopt a single resolution or decision condemning human rights abuses in 19 of the 20 "worst of the worst" repressive human rights situations as identified by Freedom House in 2007. The 19 other situations—which do not include Sudan—are Belarus, Burma, China, Tibet (China), Côte d'Ivoire (Ivory Coast), Cuba, Equatorial Guinea, Eritrea, Laos, Libya, Western Sahara (Morocco), North Korea, Chechnya (Russia), Saudi Arabia, Somalia, Syria, Turkmenistan, Uzbekistan, and Zimbabwe.[24]

- Convened its first three special sessions on Israel. In the first special session, it adopted a one-sided resolution condemning Israel but ignoring the provocations of Palestinian armed groups.[25] In a second special session on August 11, 2006, it adopted a resolution that strongly condemned Israel for "violations of human rights and breaches of international humanitarian law in Lebanon" but ignored provocations by Hezbollah.[26] The council convened its third special session on November 15, again on Israel.[27]

- Convened its fourth special session in mid-December 2006 on the human rights situation in the Darfur region of Sudan. The tone and conclusions of the session were markedly different from those of previous special sessions in that the council took pains not to ascribe any wrongdoing to the Sudanese government. The resulting resolution was non-condemnatory, merely expressing "concern regarding the seriousness of the human rights and humanitarian situation." The resolution did not even mention the word "violations," and a European alternative expressing "grave concern" was rejected.[28]

- Requested a report during the fourth special session on the situation in Darfur. The investigatory mission was led by Nobel Peace Laureate Jody Williams. The Sudanese government denied the mission entry to Darfur, forcing it to investigate from Ethiopia and Chad. As expected, the mission's report strongly condemned the Sudanese government for orchestrating and participating in "large-scale international crimes in Darfur."[29] Allies of Sudan

on the council subsequently rejected the report as invalid because the investigatory team had not gone to Darfur. The council finally adopted a weak resolution that "took note" of the Williams report but did not adopt its recommendations or condemn the Sudanese government for its actions in Darfur.[30]

- Decided in its fourth regular session to discontinue consideration of the human rights situations in Iran and Uzbekistan under the 1503 procedure,[31] which involves confidential proceedings to encourage government cooperation. The confidential nature of the proceedings makes it difficult to determine the reasoning for discontinuing consideration of the human rights situations in Iran and Uzbekistan.[32] This decision is an appalling abdication by the council of its responsibilities, considering that many human rights organizations and the U.S. Department of State have argued convincingly that severe human rights abuses and government-sanctioned oppression and mistreatment demand scrutiny by the council. Despite evidence of extensive human rights abuse, 25 of the council's 47 members voted to end scrutiny of Iran and Uzbekistan.[33]

- Adopted two resolutions that condemn "defamation of religions" but specifically mention only Islam. After a Danish newspaper published cartoons of the prophet Mohammed in 2005, the Organization of the Islamic Conference (OIC) led an effort to persuade the commission and then the council to adopt a resolution against the defamation of Islam. In June 2006, the council responded by passing a resolution merely requiring expert reports. However, it passed a second resolution in March 2007 that expressed "deep concern at attempts to identify Islam with terrorism, violence and human rights violations" and urged states to "to take all possible measures to promote tolerance and respect for all religions and their value systems and to complement legal systems with intellectual and moral strategies to combat religious hatred and intolerance."[34] Worryingly, the resolution asserts that the right to freedom of expression may be limited out of "respect for religions and beliefs."

All council members pledge their commitment to human rights standards when they run for election. As a council member, a country is supposed to "uphold the highest standards in the promotion and protection of human rights."[35] Yet the council's actions reveal a profound lack of commitment to either human rights or freedom.

Some of this disappointing performance can be blamed on the negligible difference in quality between the council's membership and the commission's membership. The situation is aggravated by the shift in proportional representation of regions from the commission, which had greater representation of Western democracies, to the council, in which Africa and Asia control a majority. This has

dramatically increased the influence of groups like the Non-Aligned Movement (NAM) and the OIC. Members of the NAM also held a majority of seats in the council's first year. The OIC held 17 seats, more than the one-third (16 seats) required to call a special session. Unsurprisingly, both groups have repeatedly used their influence to attack Israel and to protect abusive states from council scrutiny.

However, the most frustrating aspect of the council's first year has been the reluctance of free, democratic states, including South Africa and India, to support human rights efforts on the council. As UN Watch noted:

> [A]lthough slightly more than half of the council's 47 members are free democracies, only a minority of these countries—about a dozen—have consistently voted in defense of the values and principles that the council is supposed to promote. Instead, the body has been dominated by an increasingly brazen alliance of repressive regimes seeking not only to spoil needed reforms but to undermine the few meaningful mechanisms of UN human rights protection that already exist. Their goal is impunity for systematic abuses. Unfortunately, too many democracies have thus far gone along with the spoilers, out of loyalty to regional groups and other political alliances.[36]

A UN Watch analysis of significant actions taken by the council during its first year concluded that only 13 of the council's 47 members were net positive contributors to its human rights agenda. Four free democracies—Indonesia, Mali, Senegal, and South Africa—were among the 17 receiving the worst score of –16 points out of a possible –20 points. India did minimally better, receiving a score of –15 points.[37]

THE CASE AGAINST PARTICIPATION

The council's disappointing record led the U.S. to decline to seek election to the council for the second year in a row in 2007. As State Department Spokesman Sean McCormack explained:

> We believe that the Human Rights Council has thus far not proved itself to be a credible body in the mission that it has been charged with. There has been a nearly singular focus on issues related to Israel, for example, to the exclusion of examining issues of real concern to the international system, whether that's in Cuba or Burma or in North Korea.
>
> So we are going to remain as observers to the Human Rights Council and we hope that over time, that this body will expand its focus and become a more credible institution representative of the important mission with which it is charged. But nonetheless, the United States will remain actively engaged not only in the UN system but also outside of the UN system in promoting human rights.[38]

The U.S. decision not to run for a seat on the Human Rights Council drew sharp criticism from human rights groups, U.N. advocates, and political opponents. These groups claim that the U.S. is undermining the council's credibility and that it would be a stronger, more effective advocate for human rights if the U.S. were on it. For instance, Representative Tom Lantos (D–CA), chairman of the House Committee on Foreign Affairs, strongly criticized the Administration's decision:

> [I]n an act of unparalleled defeatism, the Administration announced that for a second year in a row, the United States will step aside to allow a cabal of military juntas, single-party states and tin-pot dictators to retain their death grip on the world's human rights machinery.[39]

There is little evidence to support Representative Lantos's claim, which incorrectly assumes that simply having the U.S. on the council would have changed its decisions. Because council membership is based on geographic representation, the U.S. would simply displace one of the seven countries representing the Western Europe and Other States region, which already vote largely as the U.S. would vote. Thus, any gain from a U.S. vote on the council would be marginal.

Nor would winning a seat on the council necessarily give the U.S. greater voice or influence. Any U.N. member state can comment on and speak to issues before the council, and the U.S. has frequently expressed its support of or opposition to various resolutions and decisions.

WHAT THE U.S. SHOULD DO

Any hope that the Human Rights Council would rectify the poor record of the U.N. Commission on Human Rights in holding human rights abusers to account has proven illusory. The council does not incorporate the protections and standards that would lead to a more effective body. It has the potential to become a stronger body than its discredited predecessor, but this depends entirely on the actions of its members.

To help to achieve this goal, the U.S. should:

- **Refuse to run for a seat on the council until it proves worthy of U.S. membership.** Human rights activists' argument that U.S. membership could make the council more effective is doubtful. The U.S. has been a close observer and active contributor to council deliberations and proceedings, even though it is not a member. Yet, despite the best efforts of the U.S. and other countries, the council has fallen far short of expectations. U.S. participation would undoubtedly increase the council's prestige but is unlikely to increase its effectiveness.

  The U.S. should not lend its legitimacy to such a flawed body until the council begins to take its responsibilities seriously. A premature decision to run for a seat would only mask the deplorable state of the current council. As State

Department spokesman Sean McCormack noted, "We would hope that if we do come to the day when we decide to run for the Human Rights Council, it will have gotten to the point where it is a credible institution and that we could, in fact, lend our diplomatic weight to the council as a participant."[40]

- **Press for positive actions in the council, particularly regarding its special procedures, the universal periodic review, and interactions with NGOs.** During the upcoming June session, the council is scheduled to decide a number of key issues, including clarifying rules for NGO participation; deciding whether or not to maintain some or all of the "Special Procedures" (the special rapporteurs and representatives, independent experts, and working groups) inherited from the commission; and determining the specific details for the universal periodic review of all U.N. member countries' human rights practices.

  Even though the council has proven generally ineffective in advancing fundamental human rights, some U.N. human rights activities are useful, particularly the independent experts who investigate human rights issues in specific countries. The council is currently reviewing the special procedures system to decide how to change the system, if at all. Predictably, the human rights abusers on the council are trying to use a code of conduct to limit the independence of country-specific experts and trying to minimize or eliminate their ability to criticize individual countries for human rights problems,[41] as well as to eliminate country mandates for special rapporteurs to investigate human rights in countries like Belarus, Burma, Cuba, and North Korea. These same states are trying to limit NGO input into council deliberations. The council is also discussing the details of how the universal periodic review of human rights in all U.N. member states will work. Unsurprisingly, the abuser states are trying to weaken the reviews.

  The U.S. should oppose these efforts to weaken the council's special procedures, institutions, and other activities that help to advance fundamental human rights and hold abusive regimes to account.

  Weigh the human rights records of aid recipients more heavily when allocating U.S. development assistance. The U.S. spends billions of dollars in development assistance each year, but this assistance has a dismal record in catalyzing economic growth. Despite the poor record of development assistance and the mounting evidence that financial assistance is far less important to development than sound economic policy and a strong rule of law, support for development assistance remains strong in the U.S. Congress.

  The U.S. should focus development assistance on countries with good policies and use it to support U.S. policy priorities.[42] Advancing fundamental human rights is and should be a U.S. priority. The U.S. should try to change the dynamics of the HRC by focusing development assistance on countries with demonstrable records of improving human rights practices and supporting human rights on the council.

Clearly state that unless the HRC demonstrates improvement in confronting and advancing fundamental human rights, the U.S. will cease to interact with the council and will withhold its portion of HRC funding. The U.S. should not wait indefinitely for the council to improve. Instead, it should disengage from the council if the council fails to demonstrate greater willingness to confront human rights abusers or to adopt a meaningful universal periodic review process, if the council eliminates the practice of assigning experts to assess the human rights situations in individual countries, or if the General Assembly continues to elect human rights abusers to the council. Such failures would clearly indicate that the human rights abusers are running the council agenda and that further U.S. engagement, as a member or as an observer, could not repair the damage. Rather than continuing to interact with a fatally flawed body, the U.S. should refuse to participate in council processes and withhold U.S. contributions to the body.[43]

CONCLUSION

Advancing fundamental human rights is and should be a U.S. priority. However, in its inaugural year, the Human Rights Council has proven itself to be ineffective in addressing and advancing human rights. The Bush Administration correctly decided not to seek a seat on the council.

U.S. participation in international bodies should not be automatic; rather, the U.S. should base its participation on the effectiveness and relevance of the body to U.S. policy priorities. On this basis, the Human Rights Council is a grave disappointment that is unlikely to be greatly improved by U.S. membership. The May 17 election of council membership does not inspire confidence that the council will improve its performance in the coming year.

The U.S. should continue its efforts to improve the HRC's membership, special procedures, and institutions, but it should refuse to lend the council the credibility of U.S. membership until the council takes its responsibilities seriously by censuring major human rights abusers, exposing their reprehensible actions to public scrutiny, and eschewing its disproportionate focus on Israel. The U.S. should use its influence to oppose efforts to weaken the council's special procedures, universal periodic review, and other activities that contribute to the promotion of fundamental human rights. The U.S. should also use its foreign assistance to encourage improved human rights practices among council members and aid recipients more broadly.

However, the U.S. should not wait indefinitely for the council to improve. If the council does not significantly improve its performance in the coming year or if abusive states succeed in gutting the council of its effective elements, the U.S. should sever ties with the council and withhold financial support for the body.

NOTES

1. UN Watch, "Dawn of a New Era? Assessment of the United Nations Human Rights Council and Its Year of Reform," May 7, 2007, at 20 www.unwatch.org/atf/cf/ %7b6deb65da-be5b-4cae-8056-8bf0bedf4d17%7d/dawn_of_a_new_era_hrc%20report_final.pdf (May 24, 2007).

2. U.N. General Assembly, Department of Public Information, "General Assembly Establishes New Human Rights Council by Vote of 170 in Favour to 4 Against, with 3 Abstentions," GA/10449, March 15, 2006, at www.un.org/News/Press/docs/2006/ga10449.doc.htm (May 24, 2007).

3. Ibid.

4. Charter of the United Nations, preamble, at www.un.org/aboutun/charter/index.html (May 24, 2007).

5. United Nations, "UN in Brief," chap. 3, at www.un.org/Overview/uninbrief/chapter3_humanrights.html (May 24, 2007).

6. See Brett D. Schaefer, "The United Nations Human Rights Council: Repeating Past Mistakes," Heritage Foundation Lecture No. 964, September 19, 2006, at www.heritage.org/Research/WorldwideFreedom/upload/hl_964.pdf (May 24, 2007).

7. Kofi Annan, "Secretary-General's Address to the Commission on Human Rights," Office of the Spokesman for the U.N. Secretary-General, April 7, 2005, at www.un.org/apps/sg/sgstats.asp?nid=1388 (May 24, 2007). See also Mark P. Lagon, Deputy Assistant Secretary for International Organization Affairs, U.S. Department of State, "The UN Commission on Human Rights: Protector or Accomplice?" testimony before the Subcommittee on Africa, Global Human Rights and International Operations, Committee on International Relations, U.S. House of Representatives, April 19, 2005, at www.state.gov/p/io/rls/rm/44983.htm (May 24, 2007).

8. Press release, "Explanation of Vote by Ambassador John R. Bolton, U.S. Permanent Representative to the United Nations, on the Human Rights Council Draft Resolution, in the General Assembly," U.S. Mission to the United Nations, March 15, 2006, at www.un.int/usa/06_051.htm (May 24, 2007).

9. See Schaefer, "The United Nations Human Rights Council."

10. U.N. General Assembly, "General Assembly Establishes New Human Rights Council."

11. Press statement, "The United States Will Not Seek Election to the UN Human Rights Council," U.S. Department of State, April 6, 2006, at www.state.gov/r/pa/prs/ps/2006/64182.htm (May 24, 2007).

12. Press release, "Explanation of Vote by Ambassador John R. Bolton."

13. U.N. General Assembly, "Human Rights Council," Resolution A/RES/60/251, 60th Sess., April 3, 2006, at www.ohchr.org/english/bodies/hrcouncil/docs/A.RES.60.251_En.pdf (May 24, 2007).

14. For pledges and candidates for election to the Human Rights Council in 2006, see U.N. General Assembly, "Human Rights Council," at www.un.org/ga/60/elect/hrc (May 24, 2007). For pledges and candidates for election to the Human Rights Council in 2007, see U.N. General Assembly, "Human Rights Council Election," May 17, 2007, at www.un.org/ga/61/elect/hrc (May 24, 2007). See also Brett D. Schaefer, "Human Rights Relativism Redux: UN Human Rights Council Mirrors Discredited Human

Rights Commission," Heritage Foundation WebMemo No. 1069, May 10, 2006, at www.heritage.org/Research/InternationalOrganizations/wm1069.cfm.

15. Schaefer, "Human Rights Relativism Redux" and "The United Nations Human Rights Council."

16. See Human Rights Watch, "Human Rights Council: Latin America & Caribbean States: 8 seats, 11 Declared Candidates," at www.hrw.org/un/elections/lac/lac.htm (May 24, 2007).

17. The resolution calls for one-third of the HRC to be elected annually. The 47 members elected in 2006 were randomly assigned terms of one, two, or three years to set the stage for this process. Each member elected in 2007 will hold its term for the full three years. For a list of members and their terms, see U.N. Human Rights Council, "Membership of the Human Rights Council," at www.ohchr.org/english/bodies/hrcouncil/membership.htm (May 24, 2007).

18. According to one news report, Bosnia and Herzegovina decided to run only after the U.S. strongly implied to other European countries that the U.S. would run for a council seat next year if Belarus did not win a seat. If true, this is a perverse and shortsighted strategy that would undermine America's principled position not to run for a seat until the council proves its merit in return for only a one-time defeat of Belarus. Maggie Farley, "U.S. Appears Willing to Join U.N. Human Rights Panel," Los Angeles Times, May 18, 2007, at www.latimes.com/news/printedition/asection/la-fg-rights18may18,1,2886241.story (May 24, 2007).

19. See Anne Bayefsky, "The Oppressors' Club," National Review, May 18, 2007, at http://article.nationalreview.com/?q=NDM2NTQ2ODZmNDU3MTA2ZTBiNDFiNGExZ WRjMWM2YjQ (May 24, 2007).

20. For a list of the candidates for the Human Rights Council in 2007, see U.N. General Assembly, "Human Rights Council Election."

21. For instance, the July resolution on Israel and Palestine was passed by a vote of 29 to 11 with five abstentions, the August decision on the Israeli invasion of southern Lebanon was passed by a vote of 27 to 11 with 8 abstentions, and the November decision on Darfur involved a vote of 25 to 11 with 10 abstentions. Canada, the Czech Republic, Finland, France, Germany, the Netherlands, Poland, Romania, Ukraine, and the United Kingdom voted against these resolutions. Switzerland and Japan voted for at least one. Press release, "Human Rights Council Decides to Dispatch Urgent Fact-Finding Mission to the Occupied Palestinian Territories," U.N. Human Rights Council, July 6, 2006, at www.unog.ch/unog/website/news_media.nsf/(httpNewsByYear_en)/ 6382E27860145DA7C12571A3004D1F19 (May 24, 2007); press release, "Second Special Session of Human Rights Council Decides to Establish High-Level Inquiry Commission for Lebanon," U.N. Human Rights Council, August 11, 2006, at www.unog.ch/unog/website/news_media.nsf/(httpNewsByYear_en)/F16C6E9AE98880 A0C12571C700379F8C (May 24, 2007); and press release, "Human Rights Council Notes with Concern Serious Human Rights and Humanitarian Situation in Darfur," November 28, 2006, at www.unog.ch/unog/website/news_media.nsf/(httpNewsBy Year_en)/62C6B3F928618CCEC12572340046C4BB (May 24, 2007).

22. This figure increased over time. In 2005, the commission adopted four resolutions against Israel and four resolutions against all other countries. UN Watch, "Dawn of a New Era?"

23. U.N. Human Rights Council, "Decision 2/115: Darfur," November 28, 2006, at http://ap.ohchr.org/documents/E/HRC/decisions/A-HRC-DEC-2-115.doc (May 24,

2007), and "Decision S-4/101: Situation of Human Rights in Darfur," December 13, 2006, at www.ohchr.org/english/bodies/hrcouncil/specialsession/4/docs/Dec_S_4_101_en.doc (May 24, 2007).

24. Freedom House, The Worst of the Worst: The World's Most Repressive Societies, 2007 (New York: Freedom House, 2007), at www.freedomhouse.org/uploads/press_release/worstofworst_07.pdf (May 24, 2007).

25. U.N. Human Rights Council, "Human Rights Situation in the Occupied Palestinian Territory," Special Session Resolution S-1/1, July 6, 2006, at www.ohchr.org/english/bodies/hrcouncil/docs/specialsession/A.HRC.RES.S-1.1_en.pdf (May 25, 2007).

26. U.N. General Assembly, "Report of the Human Rights Council on Its Second Special Session," August 17, 2006, at www.ohchr.org/english/bodies/hrcouncil/docs/specialsession/A.HRC.S-2.2_en.pdf (May 24, 2007).

27. See U.N. General Assembly, "3rd Special Session on Israeli Military Incursions in Occupied Palestinian Territory," Web site, November 15, 2006, at www.ohchr.org/english/bodies/hrcouncil/specialsession/3/index.htm (May 25, 2007).

28. UN Watch, "Dawn of a New Era?" p. 12.

29. U.N. Human Rights Council, "Report of the High-Level Mission on the Situation of Human Rights in Darfur Pursuant to Human Rights Council Decision S-4/101," A/HRC/4/80, March 9, 2007, at www.ohchr.org/english/bodies/hrcouncil/4session/reports.htm (May 25, 2007).

30. U.N. Human Rights Council, "Report to the General Assembly on the Fourth Session of the Human Rights Council," A/HRC/4/ L.11/Add.1, March 30, 2007, at www.ohchr.org/english/bodies/hrcouncil/docs/4session/A_HRC_4_L.11_Add1.doc (May 25, 2007).

31. The Working Group on Situations (WGS) examines the particular situations referred to it by the Working Group on Communications under the 1503 procedure. The WGS then makes recommendations to the council on how to proceed. In these cases, it recommended that the council discontinue consideration of the situations in Iran and Uzbekistan. The WGS is composed of representatives from five countries, including Zimbabwe, despite that country's own massive abuses that merit council consideration. See Office of the U.N. High Commissioner for Human Rights, "Working Group on Situations," at www.ohchr.org/english/issues/situations/index.htm (May 25, 2007).

32. Press release, "Human Rights Council Concludes Fourth Session," U.N. Human Rights Council, March 30, 2007, at www.unhchr.ch/huricane/huricane.nsf/view01/21184A0A02055F5BC12572AE005D09C6 (May 25, 2007).

33. Human Rights Watch, "UN: Rights Council Fails Victims in Iran, Uzbekistan," March 27, 2007, at http://hrw.org/english/docs/2007/03/27/uzbeki15577.htm (May 25, 2007).

34. U.N. Human Rights Council, "Report to the General Assembly on the Fourth Session of the Human Rights Council."

35. U.N. General Assembly, "Human Rights Council."

36. UN Watch, "Dawn of a New Era?" p. 1.

37. UN Watch scored 20 "key actions" of the council in its first year. The positions taken by countries on these key actions were assigned a value: 1 point for taking a positive position for human rights in the council, 0 points for taking a neutral position, and −1 point for taking a negative position. Ibid., pp. 5–8 and 26–27.

38. Sean McCormack, "Daily Press Briefing," U.S. Department of State, March 6, 2007, at www.state.gov/r/pa/prs/dpb/2007/mar/81471.htm (May 25, 2007).

39. Press release, "Lantos Blasts Administration Decision Not to Take Part in United Nations Human Rights Council," Committee on Foreign Affairs, U.S. House of Representatives, March 6, 2007, at www.internationalrelations.house.gov/press_display.asp?id=313 (May 25, 2007).

40. Press statement, "The United States Will Not Seek Election to the UN Human Rights Council."

41. UN Watch, "Dawn of a New Era?" pp. 16–17.

42. See by Brett D. Schaefer and Anthony B. Kim, "U.S. Aid Does Not Build Support at the U.N.," Heritage Foundation Backgrounder No. 2018, March 26, 2007, at www.heritage.org/Research/InternationalOrganizations/upload/bg_2018.pdf.

43. The HRC is funded through the U.N. regular budget, so the U.S. cannot directly withhold funding. Instead, it could withhold an amount equal to the U.S. portion of the council's budget (about $3 million annually) from the U.N. regular budget. This withholding would have little direct effect on the council's budget because the withholding would be spread across all U.N. activities funded through the regular budget, but it would clearly signal U.S. displeasure with the council. Congress should also take this as a lesson to move toward more direct funding of U.N. activities, ideally through voluntary budgets, so that the U.S. can tailor its financial support to bolster U.N. activities that perform well or support U.S. interests and to lessen support for activities that perform poorly or do not support U.S. interests.

✗ NO
The Human Rights Council: A New Era in UN Human Rights Work?
YVONNE TERLINGEN

Kofi Annan did more than any UN Secretary-General before him to stress the close link between human rights and peace and security. In his inaugural address to the newly created Human Rights Council in Geneva on June 19, 2006, he said: "... lack of respect for human rights and dignity is the fundamental reason why the peace of the world today is so precarious, and why prosperity is so unequally shared." With the creation of the Human Rights Council, "a new era in the human rights work of the United Nations has been proclaimed."

The previous year, at the September 2005 World Summit in New York, Annan persuaded all of the world's leaders to agree that human rights constitute one of the three pillars—along with peace and security and economic and social development—that form the base of all the UN's work. The summit's Outcome Document captured the results of the highly ambitious if not wholly successful UN reform agenda that Annan had initiated in his second term. Landmark outcomes from the vantage point of human rights include recognition by all states that the international community has a "responsibility to protect ... should peaceful means be inadequate and national authorities manifestly fail to protect their populations" from genocide, war crimes, and crimes against humanity; that the regular budget resources of the Office of the High Commissioner for Human Rights must be doubled; and that a new Peacebuilding Commission will be created to "advise on and propose integrated strategies for post-conflict peacebuilding and recovery."

Most important, world leaders decided that a new, more authoritative human rights body—a Human Rights Council—should be created to replace the fifty-nine-year-old Commission on Human Rights. After intense and at times highly divisive negotiations, which were eventually resolved by General Assembly President Jan Eliasson of Sweden, the assembly adopted Resolution 60/251 by an overwhelming majority on March 15, 2006, resolving to create a Human Rights Council. In the 170–4 vote, only the United States, Israel, the Marshall Islands, and Palau voted against (with Iran, Venezuela, and Belarus abstaining). Nevertheless, U.S. Representative John Bolton graciously promised that "the United States will work cooperatively ... to make the Council as strong and effective as it can be," and added: "We remain committed to support the UN's historic mission to promote and protect the basic human rights of all the world's citizens."

WHY A NEW HUMAN RIGHTS BODY?

The council's predecessor, the Commission on Human Rights, created in 1946, achieved a more substantive body of human rights work than is often recognized. The commission drafted major international human rights standards, including

the two international human rights covenants, which, together with the earlier adopted Universal Declaration of Human Rights (1948), form what is known as the International Bill of Human Rights. The commission advanced human rights protection globally through increasingly substantive thematic and country-specific work, inventing a unique system of Special Procedures—that is, a body of independent and objective human rights experts and working groups that includes, and is sometimes generally referred to as, Special Rapporteurs. As the commission's—and now the council's—"eyes and ears," these Special Rapporteurs monitor and rapidly respond to reported human rights violations anywhere in the world, visiting countries, carrying out studies, intervening on behalf of individuals, and reporting back with recommendations for action. Now numbering forty-one, this body of country-specific and thematic experts began to grow in the 1980s, when they were first established to address enforced disappearances and other gross human rights violations in Chile and Argentina. Their current mandates include torture, violence against women, issues of health and housing, and specific country situations, such as Myanmar, Sudan, and North Korea. They perform the crucial function of providing objective information to underpin the UN's human rights work. They have provided early warning of human rights crises and have pressured states to turn their human rights commitments into reality. Nongovernmental organizations (NGOs) concerned with human rights, whether big or small, national or international, have gained access to the commission in a manner unequaled elsewhere in the UN system.

Nonetheless, the commission suffered increasing criticism from NGOs for failing to address important issues on their merits. States complained of double standards, especially in the selection of countries for public scrutiny. Some states from the South rightly wondered why the Commission on Human Rights—on which the "Permanent Five" members of the Security Council (China, France, the Russian Federation, the United Kingdom, and the United States) were virtually guaranteed a permanent seat—never adopted a resolution condemning well-known and gross abuses in, for instance, Tibet, Chechnya (the commission did so exceptionally in 2000 and 2001 but subsequent draft resolutions were rejected), or in Guantanamo Bay. Of particular annoyance to the United States was its unexpected failure to win a seat on the commission in 2002 and the election of the Libyan ambassador to chair the commission in 2003 (in which capacity she served rather well). Even the High Commissioner for Human Rights and the UN Secretary-General himself, in his landmark March 2005 report "In Larger Freedom," spoke of the commission suffering a "credibility deficit." In outlining his reform agenda, Annan severely criticized the commission:

> Yet the Commission's capacity to perform its tasks has been increasingly undermined by its declining credibility and professionalism. In particular, States have sought membership of the Commission not to strengthen human rights but to protect themselves against criticism or to criticize

others. As a result, a credibility deficit has developed, which casts a shadow on the reputation of the United Nations system as a whole.

In that report the Secretary-General proposed to replace the commission with a smaller Human Rights Council, a decision that appears to have been taken rather hastily. The idea was no more than an afterthought in the December 2004 report of the High-Level Panel on Threats, Challenges, and Change, which Annan had specifically commissioned to lay the groundwork for the recommendations in his own report. In fact, the High-Level Panel's chief recommendation had gone in the opposite direction: it advocated that the fifty-three-member Commission on Human Rights be turned into a body with universal membership, adding at the very end that "in the longer term, Member States should consider upgrading the Commission to become a 'Human Rights Council' that is no longer subsidiary to the Economic and Social Council [ECOSOC] but a Charter body standing alongside it and the Security Council. . . ."

Making this far-reaching human rights proposal immediately his own was certainly a bold initiative, and bold is what NGOs had asked Annan to be. The Secretary-General's decision was, however, made at a time of profound suspicion and distrust between North and South, sharpened by the U.S.-led invasion of Iraq and its aftermath. Certainly, this was not an easy time, as experience shows, to build an entirely new human rights body that must be better than its predecessor.

KEY FEATURES OF THE NEW HUMAN RIGHTS COUNCIL

Annan conceived the council as having "a more authoritative position corresponding to the primacy of human rights in the Charter." He expressed the hope that the Human Rights Council, like the Security Council, the General Assembly, and ECOSOC, could be elevated to the status of a "principal organ" of the United Nations. Human rights would thus logically, in institutional terms, get their proper place next to peace and security and development as one of the three pillars of the UN. Although many countries wished the Human Rights Council to have that principal organ status, putting it on an equal footing with the Security Council was not a particularly welcome idea to some key developing countries. They did not look favorably upon linking the UN's main human rights body to the all-powerful Security Council, which can take binding decisions. Rather, the Human Rights Council was eventually created as a subsidiary organ of the General Assembly, but the assembly agreed to review the council's status within five years of its formation. Meanwhile, the council was given a firm mandate "to address situations of violations of human rights, including gross and systematic violations," and to "respond promptly to human rights emergencies." Arrangements and practices observed by the commission for NGO participation, based on ECOSOC Resolution 1996/31, were retained. General Assembly Resolution 60/251 places much emphasis on the principles of cooperation and genuine dialogue in

the council's work; recognizes the need for "objectivity and non-selectivity" in considering human rights issues; and proclaims that "double standards and politicization" must be eliminated.

Although there had been growing support for the High-Level Panel's proposal to make the Commission on Human Rights a universal membership body—which would help enhance its authority by the sheer force of its members—the Secretary-General, probably with an eye on the United States, proposed to create a "smaller standing Human Rights Council." The United States had consistently advocated a smaller, leaner human rights body, arguing that a membership of twenty states would be ideal. Eventually, a compromise was reached and a body of forty-seven members (just under the commission's fifty-three) was decided upon.

What many diplomats did not realize until late in the negotiations was that any new UN body would have to be created along customary UN lines of equitable geographical distribution. In the case of the council, this comes down to thirteen for the African Group (which had fifteen in the commission), thirteen for the Asian Group (which had twelve), six for Eastern Europe (which had five), eight for the Latin American and Caribbean Group (which had eleven), and seven for the Western European and Others Group (known as WEOG, which previously had ten seats).

In the commission, African and Asian states had about the same number of votes as the Latin American and WEOG groups combined, but the lineup is very different in the council. The African and Asian members now have a comfortable majority (at least twenty-six out of forty-seven votes) in the UN's main political human rights body; and they are definitely using it to set the agenda, as is clear on a range of issues, including the selection of countries for immediate attention by "special session" (see below) and the reluctance of many African and Asian members to act on country situations apart from Israel. WEOG and the Latin American Group have lost their power to win a vote on these and other issues unless their proposals attract the support of at least three African and Asian states. The changed political dynamics point to the need for European and Latin American countries to adopt a cross-regional approach to address human rights issues of common concern.

Membership is for three years and shall end after a country has served two consecutive terms. Thus, the principle of rotation has been established, so that even the permanent members of the Security Council have lost their de facto claim to perpetual membership. All council members are obliged to "uphold the highest standards in the promotion and protection of human rights" and "shall fully cooperate with the Council"—obligations unfortunately not taken seriously by some of its current elected members. Elections are held in secret and the votes of an absolute majority of the General Assembly's members—that is, at least 97 out of 192—are needed for election regardless of how many UN member states are present and voting. Candidates' contributions to human rights as well as their pledges and commitments shall be taken into account in the vote. Interestingly,

all regions except Africa put up more candidates than there were seats for the region, and countries with highly problematic human rights records—such as Sudan and Zimbabwe—did not stand for the first elections, held in May 2006. Iran and Venezuela-two of the three countries that abstained in the vote to establish the council—were not elected. The election outcome shows that the results would hardly have been different had the United States won its campaign for a two-thirds majority voting requirement for council membership. (Disregarding the vote in the highly competitive Eastern European Group, only Saudi Arabia and Sri Lanka would not have been elected under a two-thirds majority requirement.) Although not obliged to do so, all candidates made written pledges outlining their human rights agendas, a major advance even though the quality of the pledges varies greatly from country to country.

Louise Arbour, the High Commissioner for Human Rights, argued that a system of Universal Periodic Review (UPR)—put forward by Annan as Universal Peer Review—was the only logical answer to the criticism (largely considered justified) that the commission's old practice of selecting specific countries for scrutiny was marked by "selectivity and double standards." Under this novel system of UPR, unique in the UN's human rights regime, the human rights record of all UN member states, including such powerful countries as China, the Russian Federation, and the United States, shall henceforth be examined by the council. Just how effective the UPR will be in holding all states to account, however, is yet to be seen.

A major drawback of the former commission was that it only sat once a year, for six weeks in spring, and was ill placed to react in a timely manner to human rights crisis situations. The new council sits for ten weeks per year, and shall meet at least three times a year, including for a main session. Moreover, it can easily convene in special session: it is sufficient that only a third of its members make the request, and the council has shown a great appetite for it.

HOW IS THE HUMAN RIGHTS COUNCIL DOING?

The council has had a difficult start. The simultaneous outbreak of renewed hostilities in the Middle East—traditionally the most sensitive issue on the former commission's agenda—complicated its early steps. As expected from a political body, strong political divisions among countries and groups are reflected in the council's debate, and its proceedings to date cannot be characterized as exemplifying the spirit of "constructive international dialogue and cooperation" that Resolution 60/251 so proudly proclaims. Nonetheless, there are also some definite signs of hope.

The council's first session, June 19–30, 2006, marked a substantive beginning, with two major new human rights instruments adopted. The International Convention for the Protection of All Persons from Enforced Disappearances was adopted by acclamation. (Fifty-seven states have already signed the convention

after the General Assembly adopted the text by consensus at its sixty-first session.) The draft Declaration on the Rights of Indigenous Peoples, negotiated for more than eleven years, was adopted by vote with thirty for, two against, and twelve abstentions. (Unfortunately, the text is now running into difficulties in the current, sixty-first, General Assembly). In addition, a working group was established to draft a protocol to the Covenant on Economic, Social, and Cultural Rights to create an individual complaints procedure.

The council also took the first steps in the massive operation to build its entirely new human rights architecture. It decided to let all of its twenty-eight thematic and thirteen country-specific Special Rapporteurs continue their crucial work for one year, pending review. It created two working groups: one to review the system of these Special Rapporteurs, the other to establish the new UPR system to monitor all states' human rights performance, as required by Resolution 60/251. Both groups have started their daunting task and must deliver results within one year, by June 2007. While the council is engaged in tense negotiations to establish the UPR and review the system of Special Procedures before the June 2007 deadline, its thematic and country work is taking a back seat.

The first regular session discussed five "substantive issues" and adopted a resolution on Palestine. Given the rapidly deteriorating situation in the Occupied Palestinian Territories, the council voted for the first time in its young history to hold a special session on that situation. For whatever reason, the European Union thought it necessary to call for a vote and then proceeded to vote against the proposal, which was easily passed with twenty-nine for, twelve against, and five abstentions.

The Special Session on the Occupied Palestinian Territories was held on July 6, 2006, and was the first in a series of three special sessions all called for by the Group of Arab States, who were twice joined by the Organization of the Islamic Conference (OIC), to deal with actions by Israel. As a result, the council decided, by vote, to send the Special Rapporteur on the Palestinian Territories on a fact-finding mission. The second special session, held on August 11, 2006, responded to the worsening human rights crisis in Lebanon and established, also by vote, a high-level commission of inquiry. The third, on November 15, 2006, adopted a resolution (by a vote of thirty-two for, eight against, and six abstentions) expressing the council's shock at Israeli killings of Palestinian civilians at Beit Hanoun and calling for a high-level fact-finding mission.

On their merits, all three situations were urgent and grave and deserved the special attention of the council. But their outcome was in some respects unworthy of a council expected to act in a "fair and equal manner," as Resolution 60/251 requires. Particularly regrettable was the one-sided resolution that the council adopted—by a vote of twenty-seven for, eleven against, and four abstentions—on Lebanon (A/HRC/S-2/1). The highly politicized resolution strongly condemned "grave Israeli violations of Human Rights and breaches of International

Humanitarian Law in Lebanon," but entirely ignored the massive human rights abuses committed by Hezbollah in using indiscriminate rocket attacks against Israeli civilians. This was a clear example of the "selectivity" and "double standards and politicization" that Resolution 60/251 seeks to eliminate. Moreover, the nearly exclusive focus of these special sessions on Israel, at the cost of disregarding equally if not more egregious human rights situations elsewhere in the world, started to raise serious questions regarding the council's credibility.

More recently, however, the council has begun to steer a more balanced course. Prompted by exceptionally strong statements by Secretary-General Annan as well as the High Commissioner for Human Rights, the council eventually convened a long overdue Special Session on Darfur on December 12–13, 2006, resulting in a decision calling for action in Darfur. Particularly encouraging is that no fewer than thirty-three members, representing all regions of the council, cosponsored the call for the Darfur special session—a higher number than the three previous calls for a special session, which were twenty-one, sixteen, and twenty-four, respectively. Moreover, the thirty-three included a significant number of African countries: Algeria, Gabon, Ghana, Mauritius, Nigeria, South Africa, and Zambia. Although the decision adopted (S-4/101) was not as strong as many observers felt it should have been (it failed to identify the Sudanese government and the Janjaweed as responsible for the serious human rights abuses), it is nevertheless the only resolution or decision adopted unanimously by the council in any special session to date. (In a move of defiance of the council's will, the Sudanese government in February 2007 refused to grant visas to the high-level fact-finding mission that the council despatched to Darfur. Equally regrettable, in December, Israel refused access to the fact-finding mission created to investigate the Beit Hanoun killings.)

In all four special sessions the council decided to send inquiry commissions to investigate the situations and report back, suggesting that the council is serious about looking at new ways to address pressing human rights situations rather than simply sitting in Geneva and adopting condemnatory resolutions.

Meanwhile, the council also continued its work in regular sessions, holding no fewer than three regular sessions in 2006 (June, September/October, and November/December). These sessions concentrated on procedural decisions, institution building, and some thematic issues. Generally, these regular sessions have not yet resulted in concrete outcomes to protect human rights in specific countries, even in such pressing situations as Sri Lanka. The resumed second regular session addressed Israeli actions in the occupied Syrian Golan and the Palestinian Territories. It took two consensus decisions, on Nepal and Afghanistan, urging these countries to cooperate with the High Commissioner for Human Rights and asking her to report on these countries to future sessions. At the end of that session, on November 28, the council also took a decision (2/115) on Sudan (Darfur), which was pushed through by Algeria as chair of the African Group, notwithstanding attempts by one African

and many other countries to strengthen the text. The decision was unacceptably weak, failing to identify the Sudanese government's responsibility for the gross violations committed; and it lacked any operational mechanism—such as an immediate call for action by the High Commissioner or follow-up by the council itself—to address the particularly grave situation in Darfur. Dissatisfaction with the bland decision prompted an immediate and successful call for a Special Session on Darfur, as described above.

A human rights threat of symbolic proportions, as posed by Guantanamo Bay, has not yet surfaced in the council. Chronic and widespread human rights violations, such as in North Korea, Iraq, and Myanmar (Burma), also stand out to be addressed. The case of Myanmar will be an immediate test for the Human Rights Council's resolve to address such serious situations. Two of its members, Indonesia and Russia, which are also members of the Security Council, told the Security Council on January 12, 2007, that they favored action on Myanmar in the Human Rights Council after both countries failed to vote for a Security Council resolution that would have called for the release of all political prisoners in Myanmar. (In the Security Council vote, Russia vetoed the resolution and Indonesia abstained.) This once more illustrates that the Human Rights Council cannot postpone acting on these and other serious country situations any longer. If it fails to do so, the Third Committee of the General Assembly, which also deals with human rights, will increasingly become the focus for country-specific human rights resolutions, detracting from the council's primacy as the UN's foremost human rights body.

This brief overview shows that calling for a special session is now the de facto way to generate council action to protect human rights in specific countries. Many other human rights situations have been discussed in the council in the context of the reports presented by the Special Rapporteurs, however, and these have generated many more proposed country visits—illustrating how essential the Special Rapporteurs are to the council's work. One of the most positive developments so far is the substantive "interactive dialogue" with Special Rapporteurs that the council held at its second regular session in September 2006. As these UN debates go, they were unprecedented in their vitality, the depth of interaction with the Special Rapporteurs, and the level and nature of participation. Many missions participated at the ambassadorial level, and national human rights institutions and NGOs took part in the debate. This is unprecedented in Geneva, and NGOs remain unable to speak in similar dialogues with the Special Rapporteurs in the General Assembly's Third Committee in New York. Unfortunately, these debates have so far failed to lead to concrete outcomes to promote and protect human rights in the countries discussed and thus give effect to the recommendations made by the council's own thematic and country-specific Special Rapporteurs. This will be a key challenge for the council in the future.

Another remarkable development is that the council is in fact becoming the "standing" body to address human rights situations whenever necessary, as Annan had in mind. The result of the flurry of calls for special sessions—whatever one may think of the highly politicized selection criteria—combined with the ongoing substantive regular sessions is that the council was in session every single month of 2006 since it opened its doors on June 19, 2006. The much greater frequency of sessions (compared to the once-yearly session of the commission) has created a range of options to swiftly react to human rights situations in countries that need urgent attention, including keeping the situations under review for the next session, depending on whether the governments concerned take steps to improve their human rights performance. Another interesting development is the recent proposal made by the president of the council, Luis Alfonso de Alba of Mexico, to use the presence of ministers at the high-level debate to start roundtable discussions on topical human rights issues, and to schedule thematic debates throughout the year to allow more in-depth attention to a specific theme related to the council's work. Regrettably, these proposals for innovation have, so far, broadly met with skepticism. Nevertheless, the council now has different tools at its disposal that will be developed over time, and some members are thinking about how to use them creatively.

WHERE TO GO FROM HERE?

It is generally agreed that institution building has to be the council's highest priority. There must be an understanding of the time and effort that council members need to spend on this highly complex task, in which non-council members and NGOs are also playing a substantive role. Two imperatives stand out for the council's new human rights architecture. The first is to build an effective system of Universal Periodic Review to assess human rights performance in all countries. The second is to preserve and strengthen the system of Special Rapporteurs and to defeat attempts by some members to weaken their independence.

Concentrating on institution building alone, however, is not the way to create a better human rights body. As was the case with the commission, many members of the council have shown a tendency to put politics, and sometimes regional politics, above human rights. Many council discussions have been marked by suspicion and distrust, and the voices of some members have been stifled by regional or other group positions, leading Annan to caution the council last November that "States that are truly determined to uphold human rights must be prepared to take action even when that means, as it sometimes will, giving offense to other States within their own region."

The former UN Deputy Secretary-General, Louise Frechette, precisely identified the current predicament in an interview of January 17, 2007:

> To a certain extent we have sought institutional responses, institutional fixes, through reform to problems that are more fundamental and more

political. . . . The Human Rights Commission was deemed to be ineffective by a lot of countries. The answer was to transform it into a new institution called the Human Rights Council. But it's not performing all that much better than the Human Rights Commission because the world is composed of countries that have very different views on human rights. And unless there's real political action to really strengthen the solidarity of all the countries that do believe in human rights across the North–South divide, you shouldn't be surprised that you have the exact same results. I think there's not enough attention paid to building this political consensus among countries that share the same views, and too much on the machinery.

As Frechette makes clear, the Human Rights Council must find new ways to work across regions. It must identify common human rights concerns and adopt confidence-building measures to address them on their merits, such as creating ad hoc cross-regional groups. A future challenge also is to link the work of the Human Rights Council to that of the Security Council. Once well established, the Human Rights Council should also hold one of its sessions in New York. For the new council, this is a crucial period of construction and exploring new ways of operating. At the same time, those suffering human rights violations in all regions of the world need protection now. They and human rights defenders cannot wait. The council needs informed and critical support to help it to be impartial and effective. Civil society and opinion makers worldwide can do much to remind all forty-seven council members that they have been elected, individually, to promote and protect the highest human rights standards, not to play power politics.

POSTSCRIPT

The above debate leaves us with a number of interesting questions. Is it possible to create a new Human Rights Council that will be a credible, effective, and legitimate force for change in international human rights? It is possible for the new Council to avoid the flaws and charges of politicization and selectivity that plagued the Commission on Human Rights? Is successful implementation of human rights a question of finding the right institutional structure or a matter of member nations having sufficient will power?

One issue that emerges from this discussion is how best to promote reform in the United Nations. Should leading member states refuse to participate in an organization that they feel is flawed and dysfunctional? The United States and Great Britain have pursued this policy in the past when they withdrew from UNESCO because insufficient reforms were being carried out. Should other nations like Canada take up Schaefer's advice to the U.S. to not participate in the Council until it is assured that genuine reforms are in place?

The Canadian government and several prominent Canadians such as Louise Frechette and Louise Arbour have played prominent roles in the UN human-rights machinery. Thus, Canada has played the role of a reformer, supporting the UN human-rights institutions while advocating for reform. This seems to fit Terlingen's call for "informed and critical support," but what does this mean in practice? How can this approach best be implemented in policy?

Suggested Additional Readings

Godet, Blaise. "Reforming Human Rights." *Harvard International Review* 29, no. 4 (2008): 74–76.

Kurtz, Paul, Austin Dacey, Norm Allen Jr., and Hugo Estrella. "Restoring Universal Human Rights at the United Nations." *Free Inquiry* 28, no. 5 (2008): 4–5.

Lauren, Paul Gordon. "To Preserve and Build on it Achievements and to Redress its Shortcoming: The Journey from the Commission on Human Rights to the Human Rights Council." *Human Rights Quarterly* 29, no. 2 (May 2007): 307–45.

Pubantz, Jerry. "Constructing Reason: Human Rights and the Democratization of the United Nations." *Social Forces* 84, no. 2 (December 2005): 1291–1303.

Rahmani-Ocora, Lada. "Giving the Emperor Real Clothes: The UN Human Rights Council." *Global Governance* 12, no. 1 (January–March 2006): 15–20.

Scheipers, Sibylle. "Civilization vs. Toleration: The New UN Human Rights Council and the Normative Foundation of the International Order." *Journal of International Relations & Development* 10, no. 3 (September 2007): 219–43.

Wedgwood, Ruth. "Two Steps Backward in Geneva." *American Interest* (May 2008): 143–47.

InfoTrac® College Edition

Search for the following articles in the InfoTrac® database:

"A Screaming Start: The UN and Human Rights (Has the UN's Human-rights Machinery Really Improved?)." *The Economist (US)* 376, no. 8577 (April 26, 2008): 78.

Alston, Philip. "Reconceiving the UN Human Rights Regime: Challenges Confronting the New Human Rights Council." *Melbourne Journal of International Law* 7, no. 1 (2006): 185–224.

Rahmani-Ocora, Ladan. "Giving the Emperor Real Clothes: The UN Human Rights Council." *Global Governance* 12, no. 1 (January–March 2006): 15–20.

Web Resources

For current URLs for the following websites, visit www.crosscurrents.nelson.com.

UN HUMAN RIGHTS COUNCIL

http://www2.ohchr.org/english/bodies/hrcouncil/

This is the official homepage of the UN Human Rights Council. It provides access to many of the background documents regarding the work of the Council as well as updates on its latest activities.

UN WATCH

http://www.unwatch.org/

The UN Watch is an NGO based in Geneva that monitors the activities of the United Nations, particularly in the area of human rights, and lobbies for reforms. The site has a section dedicated to the Human Rights Council and contains links to many reports and articles on the reasons for establishing the Council and assessing its progress to date.

UNITED NATIONS HUMAN RIGHTS/OFFICE OF THE HIGH COMMISSIONER OF HUMAN RIGHTS

http://www.ohchr.org/

The High Commissioner of Human Rights is the principal official within the United Nations mandated to promote human rights within the UN system. This

site contains many reports on both the activities of the High Commissioner as well as other happenings within the UN human rights system.

GLOBAL POLICY FORUM

http://www.globalpolicy.org/reform/topics/hrcindex.htm

The Global Policy Forum provides a section on the Human Rights Council which contains an extensive archive of articles both on the foundation of the Council and on the many controversies surrounding its operation.

Do We Need an International Criminal Court?

✔ YES

DOUGLASS CASSEL, "Why We Need the International Criminal Court,"
Christian Century 116, no. 15 (May 12, 1999): 532–36

✗ NO

ALFRED P. RUBIN, "Some Objections to the International Criminal Court,"
Peace Review 12, no. 1 (March 2000): 45–50

How are notions of justice and human security to be implemented in a world composed of nation-states? One answer to that question is the argument that the state should remain the primary arena where issues such as justice, human rights, and civil liberties are defined and protected. The best hope for pursuing justice then is in the maintenance of orderly and stable relations between states. In a society of states, this order can best be achieved by observance of two fundamental legal and moral principles: respect for national sovereignty of all states and non-intervention in the domestic affairs of another sovereign state. These principles were largely built on the belief, rooted in the turmoil of the sixteenth and seventeenth centuries, that the greatest threat to peace and the pursuit of justice stemmed from the widespread intervention in the affairs of other states. They assumed that the priority should be placed on promoting peace and justice between states rather than addressing the issues of peace and justice within states; issues of domestic justice are placed beyond the concerns of the international community.

This way of thinking has had an important impact on the way that human justice has been viewed in the international system. As Hedley Bull notes, "the basic concept of coexistence between states, expressed in the exchange of recognition of sovereign jurisdiction, implies a conspiracy of silence entered into by governments about the rights and duties of their respective citizens" (*The Anarchical Society: A Study of Order in World Politics* [London: Macmillan, 1977]: 83). It is this conspiracy of silence that has increasingly come to bother many people. While some have seen in the notion of sovereignty the promise of security and protection from the wanton harm of outsiders, others have experienced sovereignty as a cloak of protection for oppression and injustice. The worst crimes against humanity and the most oppressive human-rights abuses, they argue, have taken place under the legal protection of national sovereignty. In fact, studies of contemporary conflicts show that in the twentieth century, more people have been killed in intrastate fighting than in interstate wars. For many people, the greatest threat to personal security is not a foreign military force but their own government.

How do we address this situation? Some have suggested that the world needs a permanent international criminal court. Such an idea is not new. As long ago as 1474, Peter van Hagenbach was tried by the Court of the Holy Roman Empire for the torture of civilians. At the Congress of Vienna in 1815, states debated whether there should be trials for those engaged in the slave trade. And, in 1872, Gustave Moynier, a founder of the International Committee of the Red Cross, drew up a proposal for an international criminal court to try violators of the Geneva Conventions of 1864.

Although discussions of the concept of an international criminal court continued in the twentieth century, actual efforts at implementing such a plan proceeded largely on an ad hoc basis. Following the atrocities of World War II, the International Military Tribunal at Nuremberg and the International Military Tribunal for the Far East were established to prosecute war criminals. But these efforts have long been subject to criticism for being driven by political imperatives rather than representing a triumph of the rule of law. Some critics argued that they were nothing more than "victor's tribunals."

During the Cold War, the ideological struggle between the East and the West created little political will to move forward with the idea of an international criminal court. However, the end of the Cold War and the experience of conflicts in Yugoslavia and Rwanda with devastating civilian casualties and human-rights abuses created new momentum for such a project. In 1994, an Ad Hoc Committee on the Establishment of the International Criminal Court, composed of state representatives, was set up to begin working on a draft statute. This work eventually led to the convening in Rome of a UN Diplomatic Conference of Plenipotentiaries on the Establishment of an International Criminal Court in June 1998. These negotiations in turn led to the adoption, in July 1998, of a treaty calling for the creation of an International Criminal Court (ICC). A total of 120 countries voted in favour, 21 abstained, and 7 were opposed. The United States and Israel joined China, Iran, Iraq, Libya, and Sudan in opposing the treaty.

The Rome Statute declares that the signatories recognize that international crimes "threaten peace and security" and affirms that these crimes "must not go unpunished." At the same time, signatory states promise to ensure "an end to impunity" for individual perpetrators. Proponents of the treaty see its provisions as a significant advancement of the norms of human justice in the international system. The ICC would provide a means of non-military intervention to protect the welfare of individuals. Advocates argue that it is a significant advancement in the development of cosmopolitan values. However, the Rome Statute has strong critics who are skeptical about whether anything like a commonly understood notion of international criminal law exists between nations. Further, the growing intrusion into national sovereignty is seen as having potentially dangerous side effects in the future.

In the first essay, Douglas Cassel, a professor of international law, makes the case for the International Criminal Court. Then Alfred P. Rubin, also a professor of international law, argues against implementing the ICC.

✔ YES
Why We Need the International Criminal Court
DOUGLASS CASSEL

This has been a good century for tyrants. Stalin killed millions but was never even charged with a crime. Pol Pot slaughtered well over 1 million but never saw the inside of a prison cell. Idi Amin and Raoul Cedras are comfortably retired. Despite recent legal complications, Chile's General Augusto Pinochet, too, will probably escape trial. Ditto for Slobodan Milosevic, who has chosen to close out the century by brutalizing Kosovo.

There have been few exceptions to this pattern of impunity. The most notable exceptions are the Nazis who faced judgment at Nuremberg. Joining the short list of adjudged are the Greek colonels, the Argentine junta, the genocidal regime in Rwanda and some leaders in the former Yugoslavia. But the odds have overwhelmingly favored those who commit atrocities. Will the 21st century be any better?

The answer may well depend in large part on the success—or failure—of the world's first permanent court with global jurisdiction over the most serious international crimes. Last summer in Rome, by a vote of 120 nations in favor, seven opposed and 21 abstentions, a United Nations diplomatic conference adopted a treaty to establish an International Criminal Court (ICC) in The Hague in the Netherlands. It will hear cases of genocide, war crimes and crimes against humanity that national governments are unable or unwilling to prosecute.

The ICC will differ from the existing World Court, officially called the International Court of Justice, also located in The Hague. The World Court hears only lawsuits between governments and cannot prosecute individuals. As a permanent global court, the ICC will likewise differ from the special International Criminal Tribunals created by the UN Security Council to address atrocities in the former Yugoslavia and Rwanda.

Nearly all the world's democracies—Europe plus such countries as Argentina, Australia, Canada, Costa Rica, South Africa and South Korea—supported the Rome treaty. Seventy-eight nations have now signed the treaty, indicating their intention to join it. Once 60 countries complete the ratification process (to date only Senegal has done so), the treaty will go into effect and the ICC will be created.

Late blooming 20th-century tyrants have little to fear; the ICC will have power to try only crimes committed after it is established. The current carnage in Colombia, Congo and Sierra Leone, for example, will either go unpunished or be addressed in some other way.

Only two democracies—Israel and the United States—opposed the ICC, thereby joining a rogue's gallery of regimes like China, Iran, Iraq, Libya and Sudan. Israel's opposition is regrettable but understandable: the Jewish state has lost so many lopsided UN votes that it fears giving power to an international prosecutor.

The U.S., too, professes to fear frivolous or politically motivated prosecutions of American soldiers and officials. However, the ICC has so many built-in safeguards against unwarranted prosecutions that the odds of abuse are minimal. Otherwise, the ICC would hardly have garnered support from Britain, France and other countries with extensive military and peacekeeping forces overseas.

Washington's real grievance is that it cannot control the court. In 1995, on the 50th anniversary of the Nuremberg trials, President Clinton became the first U.S. president to announce support for an ICC. But the U.S. insisted on an ICC that would be an arm of the UN Security Council, which would make prosecutions subject to a U.S. veto and insulate Washington from unwanted trials.

The rest of the world found this vision uninspiring. Still, in a fruitless effort to induce U.S. participation, backers of the ICC at Rome offered numerous concessions, including a significant role for the Security Council. The council will be empowered to refer cases to the ICC. Indeed, at least in the early years, council referral is likely to be the primary route by which cases reach the court. While cases can also be referred by states that are party to the treaty or by the prosecutor, the obstacles to doing so will initially be so high that the ICC will depend heavily on the council. The council can also block investigations by voting to defer them for one year, renewable indefinitely.

But these and other concessions were not enough to dispel Washington's fears that if American troops commit war crimes in another country, that country could have those troops tried in The Hague (unless the U.S. would agree to investigate the case itself). Also, other nations with veto power on the Security Council could block a resolution to defer a case. In short, U.S. control is less than fully assured under the ICC, which pleased neither the Pentagon nor Senate Foreign Relations Committee Chair Jesse Helms, who declared that any treaty to create a court that could conceivably prosecute Americans would be "dead on arrival" on Capitol Hill.

U.S. opposition to the ICC is of a piece with its vote a year earlier against the treaty to ban antipersonnel landmines, its refusal to pay UN dues, its economic sanctions on allies that do business in Cuba and its implicit foreign policy of demanding a "superpower exemption" from international rules. It lends further support to the views held by "elites of countries comprising at least two-thirds of the world's people," according to Harvard scholar Samuel Huntington, writing in *Foreign Affairs*, that Uncle Sam is "intrusive, interventionist, exploitative, unilateralist, hegemonic, hypocritical, and applying double standards." Small wonder that following the 120-7 humiliation of the U.S. in Rome, delegates applauded for 15 minutes.

U.S. opposition to the ICC not only undermines American credibility and diplomacy but also strains the human rights banner Washington purports to carry. The rest of the world cannot fail to notice that the U.S. supports the prosecution of Yugoslavs and Rwandans for human rights crimes but not the prosecution of Americans. If human rights is no more than a flag of convenience, its rallying power diminishes.

But American participation, while important, is not indispensable. The world's democracies are likely to go ahead without us. Americans who care more for the dignity of humanity than for the color of their passports should support the ICC, despite its shortcomings, as a first step toward international justice for crimes against humanity.

But does "justice" for atrocities require a court, let alone a criminal court, much less an international criminal court? Volumes have been devoted to defining justice. For ICC purposes, however, we can focus on an operational definition. Justice calls for identification, exposure, condemnation and proportionate punishment of individuals who violate fundamental norms recognized internationally as crimes, and it calls for reparations to victims, by means of fair investigations and fair trials by an authorized judicial body. Thus defined, justice requires criminal courts, including—as experience has shown—at least the possibility of prosecution before international courts.

Like other efforts to capture "justice" in words, this account covers both too little and too much. As Martha Minow has observed, some crimes are so horrific or massive that no amount of punishment can be proportional. And no form of court-ordered reparation can truly repair the loss of even a single loved one, much less of an entire people. At best, successful prosecutions can deliver only a measure of justice.

On the other hand, criminal punishment may not always contribute to a just society. As argued eloquently by Donald Shriver in these pages (August 26, 1998), "living with others sometimes means that we must value the renewal of community more highly than punishing, or seeking communal vengeance for, crimes." And while "some forms of justice sow the seeds of justice, some do not. Without peaceful public acceptance of their decisions, courts risk irrelevance at best and social chaos at worst."

The case for an ICC must acknowledge the wisdom of such insights. Yet these comments do not so much counsel against the existence of the ICC as remind us of its inherent limitations. Criminal justice is not, by itself, sufficient to heal either victims or societies.

Still, without at least the credible prospect of criminal punishment, victims and societies are unlikely to wield the leverage necessary to pry out the truth, which is an essential prerequisite to genuine repentance, forgiveness and reconciliation. Pervasive impunity is therefore the enemy of justice in all its dimensions.

How might the ICC contribute to justice?

First, in particular cases, it may identify, expose, condemn and punish perpetrators and provide reparations to victims. It may do so either by its own prosecutions or by stimulating prosecutions in national courts, brought by governments reluctant to see their officials and soldiers hauled off to The Hague for trial. Either way, an effective ICC could lift the blanket of impunity that now covers atrocities almost everywhere. By so doing, it could provide a measure of justice to some victims. That by itself would justify creation of the ICC.

But such a court would have even broader impact. It would serve to reinforce moral norms. There is no more powerful social condemnation of evil than to label it as a serious crime, for which serious punishment may be imposed. The preamble adopted in Rome elevates ICC crimes to the status of the "most serious crimes of concern to the international community as a whole." The ICC's every indictment, arrest, conviction and sentence may serve to remind governments, the media and the public that there is "zero tolerance" for crimes against humanity.

The pedagogical and practical import of such moral messages is illustrated by the current case of General Pinochet. In strictly legal terms, he has suffered no more than deprivation of liberty and freedom of movement for some months. He may never actually be prosecuted. But his hopes of becoming a respected senior statesman and to go down in history as his country's savior have been dashed. He will now be remembered, above all, as a torturer who got nabbed. Not only has he suffered loss of honor and reputation, but Chile will now understand its history differently. In Chile and elsewhere, a generation of youth has been taught that his alleged crimes, most of which took place before they were born, are so unconscionable that he is pursued for them even today.

Such messages sensitize global consciousness. This, in turn, has practical consequences. Governments may find it more difficult to grant visas, confer political asylum or otherwise treat alleged torturers as if their crimes could be forgotten. Voices of conscience may be empowered; their demands to treat future Pinochets as pariahs will be legitimized. Of course, to the extent the ICC proves to be ineffective, its moral message will be undermined. An impotent ICC may serve merely to stoke the fires of cynicism. This is one reason why the extensive compromises made at Rome are troubling.

To succeed, however, the court need not be perfect. Consider the case of former Bosnian Serb leader Radovan Karadzik. In 1995 he was indicted for genocide by the International Criminal Tribunal for the former Yugoslavia. Yet he remains at large, because NATO troops in Bosnia to date have not dared to arrest him. Does his case show that genocide is tolerated in practice?

Prior to the Dayton peace agreements, that may indeed have been the message. Until then, few of the suspects indicted by the International Tribunal had been arrested. Karadzik still strutted the world stage as head of the Bosnian Serb "government." But he was barred from Dayton, because he had been indicted and would have to be arrested if he left Yugoslavia. The agreements reached at Dayton also excluded him from any future position in government because, again, he had been indicted. Since then he has lost his official position, and remains hunkered down in Serb territory, unable to travel. Dozens of other suspects have now been arrested or have surrendered.

A similar point may be made on the question of the court's deterrent value. The prospect of prosecution will not deter a Pol Pot or a Slobodan Milosevic. But not all dictators are fanatics like Pol Pot. And at times, calculating manipulators like

Milosevic may be restrained by the threat of indictment. How often this happens may depend on how credible the threat is. That, in turn, depends on how the compromises made at Rome play out in practice.

Two of the Rome compromises are especially troublesome. The first imposes a "state consent" requirement on the ICC's jurisdiction (except in cases referred by the Security Council). In cases referred by states or by the prosecutor on his or her own motion, the ICC will not be free to prosecute crimes regardless of where they are committed. It will have jurisdiction only by consent of either the state where the crime was committed or the state in which the accused is a citizen. States that ratify the Rome treaty are parties to the court and automatically consent to its jurisdiction. Other states may consent on a case-by-case basis.

The treaty negotiations suggest the significance of this limitation. Germany proposed that the ICC have "universal" jurisdiction, that is, be able to prosecute crimes wherever they are committed. This made legal sense. For centuries individual states have had the right to prosecute piracy, regardless of where it takes place. Treaties now allow states to prosecute genocide, torture and serious war crimes—all within ICC jurisdiction wherever they are committed. If individual states have universal jurisdiction over such heinous international crimes, why can they not agree to delegate it to an international court?

This legally sensible proposal did not, however, attract much diplomatic support. Most states were unwilling to give the court a worldwide license to prosecute.

South Korea proposed a compromise: Let the ICC hear any case that has the consent of any one of four states—the state where the crime took place, the state of nationality of the defendant, the state of nationality of the victim, or the state having custody of the suspect. While far short of universality, this proposal would have given the ICC jurisdiction in most cases. But the U.S. strenuously objected. Allowing so many states to invoke ICC jurisdiction would allow the court to bypass the Security Council.

In a last-ditch effort to bring the U.S. on board without gutting the court's jurisdiction, the Canadian chair of the Rome conference whittled the four states in South Korea's proposal down to two: the territorial state and the state of nationality of the accused. Over U.S. objections, this proposal became part of the final text of the treaty.

To understand the effect of this provision, consider a hypothetical case involving Saddam Hussein. If he commits atrocities in Kuwait, either of two states could consent to ICC jurisdiction: Kuwait, where the crimes were committed, or Iraq, the state of Saddam's nationality. Since Kuwait would be likely to consent, in such cases—international wars—state consent is not a major obstacle.

But suppose Saddam commits atrocities against Kurds or political dissidents inside Iraq. Then the territorial state and the state of his nationality are one and the same: Iraq, which he controls. In such cases—regimes that repress ethnic minorities or others within their own borders—the ICC may be unable to act.

This kind of situation poses a serious threat to the effectiveness of the court. Except on referral by the Security Council, the ICC could not, for example, prosecute Milosevic for atrocities committed in Kosovo, nor Pol Pot for killing Cambodians, nor Pinochet for "disappearing" Chileans.

Another potentially crippling compromise allows the ICC to hear cases (again, except for those referred by the Security Council) only when the states involved are unable or unwilling to do so. The U.S. likes this provision; it can avoid ICC jurisdiction simply by conducting its own good-faith investigation—even if the result is a decision not to prosecute, or an acquittal.

But what if, say, a Milosevic promises to investigate alleged war crimes by his troops in Kosovo? Unlike the International Criminal Tribunal for Yugoslavia, which has primary jurisdiction, the ICC would have to defer to a Yugoslav national investigation unless the ICC prosecutor can prove that it is a sham. But how can the prosecutor impeach a national investigation before it starts? In most cases, the ICC will have to wait until the individual nation has a chance to show its true colors. In the meantime, what may happen to fingerprints, blood samples, autopsies and witnesses? ICC prosecutor and judges will have to keep careful watch lest national prosecutors merely go through the motions, stall and possibly ruin the ICC's case.

Despite such weaknesses and uncertainties, the agreement on the ICC reached in Rome is the best we are likely to get for the foreseeable future. It deserves support as an essential first step. Once created, it will have a chance to prove itself. If it fails, the need to strengthen it will be demonstrated.

Neither the Clinton administration nor the U.S. Senate is likely to accept the ICC. This is no reason, however, for American supporters to sit on their hands.

It should be stressed that the ICC has significant safeguards against abuse. For example, its judges must have expertise in criminal or international law, and can be elected only by a two-thirds majority of states which are parties to the treaty, most of which will be democracies. Its prosecutor cannot begin an investigation of an American without first notifying the U.S. and allowing it to take over the investigation and any prosecution. Even if the U.S. consents, the ICC prosecutor still cannot begin an investigation without reasonable grounds and the prior approval of a three-judge panel, which may be appealed to a five-judge panel. Once the investigation is complete, no trial can be held without another prior approval by the three-judge panel. Even then there are extensive fair-trial safeguards. No judicial system is airtight, but this one comes close.

Supporters can also dispel Pentagon claims that because American troops undertake so many overseas missions they are uniquely exposed to ICC prosecution. In Bosnia as of mid-1998, for example, our troops represented less than 20 percent of NATO forces and only 10 percent of the International Police Task Force.

Bringing international criminals to justice is no easy task. But the ICC gives humanity in the coming century a chance to administer justice that wasn't available in the 20th century. Let us not miss the opportunity.

THE PINOCHET PRECEDENT

Chile's General Augusto Pinochet would be a prime candidate for trial before the International Criminal Court—if the court existed. Since it does not, a makeshift substitute—extraditing him from Britain for trial in Spain—has been attempted.

In 1973, assisted by the U.S., Pinochet overthrew the democratically elected government of socialist Salvador Allende. His military regime then set out to eliminate and terrorize its political opponents. According to reports based on official Chilean investigations, Pinochet's regime was responsible for over 2,000 assassinations, more than 1,000 disappearances and countless cases of torture.

Numbers cannot tell the full story. As noted by Lord Steyn in the British extradition proceedings, "The case is not one of interrogators acting in excess of zeal." Rather, as Lord Steyn described the alleged torture, "The most usual method was the 'grill,' consisting of a metal table on which the victim was laid naked and his extremities tied and electrical shocks were applied to the lips, genitals, wounds or metal prosthesis."

Nor is Pinochet accused merely of failing to prevent crimes by underlings. Chile's intelligence agency responsible for torture, the notorious DINA, "was directly answerable to General Pinochet rather than to the military junta." According to the Spanish charges, DINA killed, disappeared and tortured victims "on the orders of General Pinochet."

To date Pinochet has enjoyed both de facto and de jure impunity in Chile. In 1978, after the worst was over, he awarded himself and his men an amnesty for any crimes that might have been committed by their regime. When he finally restored civilian rule in 1990, he warned against "touching a hair on the head of one of my men." The new constitution also made him senator for life, immune from prosecution. For added insurance, military courts retain jurisdiction over any alleged crimes by the military.

Pinochet was so safe from prosecution in Chile that he presumed he was safe anywhere. He was wrong. Assisted by human rights activists, Spanish Judge Baltasar Garzon has in recent years accumulated enough evidence to charge the general not only for murdering Spanish citizens but also for committing crimes against a far larger number of Chileans.

As Pinochet recuperated from back surgery in London last October, Judge Garzon asked British authorities to arrest him for extradition to Spain. Britain obliged. As of this writing, the general has been under house arrest in England for six months. Three British courts have now ruled on the case. Most recently a committee of Law Lords, Britain's highest court, voted six to one against the general's claim that as a former head of state he is immune from prosecution. The United Nations Convention Against Torture, they ruled, requires member states either to extradite or prosecute alleged torturers. Sitting heads of state are immune, but former heads are not.

Since Britain did not join the convention until 1988, however, the lords authorized the government to extradite Pinochet only for torture committed after 1988. British Home Secretary Jack Straw decided in April that the post-1988 cases submitted by the Spanish judge justify extradition. However, lengthy legal proceedings, followed by a final opportunity for Straw to reconsider, could take months or even years.

Whatever the ultimate outcome, the rulings in this case by the highest courts of Britain and Spain make clear that international law now permits third countries to prosecute torturers whose home country is unwilling or unable to bring them to court. But the case also shows the unreliability of this approach. What if Britain had not joined the torture convention? Or if Downing Street were still occupied by Tories and not Tony Blair? Would Britain have arrested Pinochet? Whatever the outcome, the Pinochet case thus underlines the need for an ICC.

✗ NO
Some Objections to the International Criminal Court
ALFRED P. RUBIN

Perhaps it is unwise to comment on the structure of the proposed International Criminal Court (ICC) while the negotiations to define it still continue. Nevertheless, there are underlying inconsistencies between the dominant conceptions of the ICC's operations and the realities of the international legal (and political and economic) order. These inconsistencies cannot be remedied by tinkering with the details. As currently conceived by its supporters, the ICC cannot work as envisaged without massive changes in the international legal order. But those changes cannot be accomplished without losses that nobody realistically expects and few really want.

The ICC assumes there is such a thing as international criminal law. But what is its substance? Who exercises law-making authority for the international legal community? Who has the legal authority to interpret the law once supposedly found?

While ample precedents for the international equivalent of common law can be found in the claims and property areas, the criminal law is different. Some acts by individuals have been historically deemed to violate it, whatever it is—piracy, war crimes, international traffic in slaves, and now genocide and perhaps aggression and other atrocities. But until now those "crimes" have not been defined by international law as such. They have been defined instead by the municipal laws of many states and in a few cases by international tribunals set up by victor states in an exercise of positive law making. Thereby, the tribunal's new rules were "accepted," under one rationale or another, by the states in which the accused were nationals.

Some Nazis were convicted at Nuremberg of planning aggressive war, but the Nazi attack on Poland in 1939 was preceded by the Molotov-Ribbentrop Pact. The notion that the Soviets did not help plan the "aggressive war" was regarded by many as hopelessly unconvincing, so it was agreed among the Nuremberg prosecutors not to allow any mention of that treaty at the trial. As to "war crimes," Grand Admiral Doenitz, Hitler's successor in Germany, was convicted at Nuremberg among other things of authorizing unrestricted submarine warfare in violation of a 1936 treaty. Admiral Nimitz, the American hero, sent a letter to the tribunal pointing out that he had issued almost identical orders in the Pacific on December 7, 1941. Of course, Nimitz was not tried for anything by anybody.

As for "crimes against humanity," it was agreed to define those as acts connected with Word War II itself. Thus, the Soviet Union's deliberate starvation of the Ukraine and the establishment of the Gulag Archipelago were not within the Nuremberg charge. Nor were American acts of wartime hysteria, such as the mass

displacement of Americans of Japanese heritage from the three West Coast states but not from Hawaii. The nuclear bombing of Nagasaki was not mentioned either, although it could be said to have raised serious questions about American observance of the laws of war even assuming the Hiroshima bomb was a legitimate wartime act. In sum, the victors did not apply to themselves the rules they purported to find in the international legal order. The deeper question is whether rules asserted by victors and applied only to losers represent "law" at all.

Another theory has been that if all or nearly all "civilized" states define particular acts as violating their municipal criminal laws, then those acts violate "international law." Far from being new to the international arena, that conception attempts to revive jus gentium theory, which failed when Lord Mansfield, Sir William Scott, and Joseph Story, among many others, developed conflict-of-law and choice-of-law theory in a civil claims context so as to make it unnecessary to determine which states are "civilized" and which rules are universal.

Occasionally, the same theory has been urged under the argument that some acts violate "general principles of law recognized by civilized states," and thus violate general international law. But to define states that agree with us as "civilized" and those that disagree as not worth considering would eliminate most of the human race from the rubric "civilized." That might be correct as far as we are concerned, but it will not likely represent any universal "law." And it does not make even acknowledged wicked acts "criminal" in any known sense.

Suppose it was possible to define as universal crimes acts defined and punished as criminal by various municipal legal orders. If that were done it still would not confer "standing" in the international community to expand any single state's municipal jurisdiction, to create a "universal" jurisdiction over the acts of foreigners abroad, no matter how horrendous.

Early attempts to resolve these problems abound. For example, in the United States, the first statute criminalizing "piracy" was enacted in April 1790. It made criminal by U.S. law any "offense which if committed within the body of a county, would by the laws of the United States be punishable by death" and various lesser acts such as running away with goods "to the value of $50" (not saying whether lesser valuations or greater valuations would be included in the definition), yielding up a "vessel voluntarily to any pirate" (not defining "pirate"), or mutiny (without using the word). The statute was found defective in early cases and was supplemented with another in 1819 which made criminal by U.S. law "the crime of piracy as defined by the law of nations" and apparently asserted universal jurisdiction over those committing "piracy" as so defined by subjecting them to the American criminal process if they were "afterwards . . . brought into or found in the United States," even if they were foreigners acting solely against foreign interests or persons.

That statute was upheld by the Supreme Court in 1820, but reduced in its effect, as to both definition and jurisdiction, and eventually abandoned, although it still appears in the U.S. Code. The principal problem was that Joseph Story and some

other judges felt they knew how the "law of nations" defined "piracy" but very few others did. Despite Story's objections, in all but "piracy cases," "common law crimes" were abandoned in the United States federal courts because prosecutors refused to bring such cases.

A similar fate met attempts to establish an international criminal court to hear cases involving the international traffic in slaves. When such a court was proposed by the British in the 1830s and 1840s, it was rejected by the U.S. A close examination of the British proposal showed how it would authorize British warships to arrest vessels of any nationality in only some parts of the world, but did not authorize American or other warships to arrest British vessels near the British Isles. Indeed, when Haiti established its own anti-slave-trade legislation based on identical assertions of universal jurisdiction in 1839, the British objected, claiming that the universal law of the sea allowed no universal jurisdiction in any case outside of the exercise of belligerent fights in wartime.

Turning to attempts to incorporate universal jurisdiction in an ICC by treaty construction, consider that the Genocide Convention and the four 1949 Geneva Conventions on the protection of the victims of armed conflict leave the traditional jurisdictional arrangements of general international law untouched. All four Geneva Conventions refer to some "grave breaches," generally acts that individuals might commit or order that seem to harm persons or property that need not be harmed in order for the conflict to proceed in the usual miserable ways. The obligation is on the High Contracting Parties severally to enact municipal legislation. The Conventions provide in identical language in each Convention that "The High Contracting Parties undertake to enact any legislation necessary to provide effective penal sanctions for persons committing, or ordering to be committed, any of the grave breaches of the present Convention defined [sic] in the following Article."

In fact, the various wicked acts are not "defined" in the Geneva Conventions. For example, each of the Conventions lists "willful killing" as such a "grave breach." But soldiers routinely "willfully kill" the enemy. All known legal orders excuse or authorize "willful killing" in self-defense or to defend a protected class of others, such as family members. The 1949 Conventions do not attempt to draw the necessary distinctions between a "willful killing" that is legally a "grave breach" to be made the subject of criminal sanctions in all contracting states, and one that remains legally within a soldier's privilege.

Nor do they define who is a "soldier" for those purposes. The attempt to define who is entitled to prisoner-of-war treatment if captured by an enemy might be interpreted as such a definition, but not necessarily, and itself leads to serious complications. Indeed, in the Prisoners of War Convention itself (Convention III of 1949), questions about status are to be resolved by "a competent tribunal" (Article 5) with no clue as to who should convene the tribunal or determine its criteria. And there is much more that is doubtful about the interpretation of the key provisions of this part of the Prisoners of War Convention, indeed of all four Conventions.

Similarly, the Genocide Convention of 1948, although calling "genocide" a "crime under international law," restricts the definition and enforcement of this "crime" to the municipal tribunals of the various parties who alone are "to provide effective penalties for persons guilty of genocide." And persons charged with genocide "shall be tried by a competent tribunal of the State in the territory of which the act was committed, or by such international penal tribunal as may have jurisdiction with respect to those Contracting Parties which shall have accepted its jurisdiction." Clearly those who sought to establish in 1948 a universal jurisdiction by means of the positive law failed.

It has been argued that at least the 1949 Geneva Conventions resolve the universal jurisdiction issue by providing that "[e]ach High Contracting Party shall be under the obligation to search for persons alleged to have committed, or to have ordered to be committed, such grave breaches, and shall bring such persons, regardless of their nationality, before its own courts." But there are many problems with this interpretation. First, so severe have been the practical difficulties that there have been no cases in the 50 bloody years since 1949 in which any High Contracting Party has fulfilled that "obligation." Second, even if the "obligation" were taken seriously, it would be impossible in many cases for the accused to defend themselves. How could General Schwarztkopf, for example, produce the evidence to show that before he ordered the bombing during the Gulf War of what later appeared to be a civilian bomb shelter, his best intelligence—derived from intercepts and possibly infiltrators or other eye-witnesses—was that the supposed bomb shelter was actually an illegal overlay of civilians above a military communications site?

It can be argued that the law has progressed from the days of Nuremberg and the 1948 and 1949 Conventions: that universal jurisdiction is now an accepted custom. But is it? What states, under what circumstances, have accepted the custom? Even where it has been enacted, has it been accepted outside of a positive commitment? Accepted as law? We should have serious doubts about the assertions of customary law that are occasionally used in this context.

What about the ICC Convention itself as a positive law document under which states agree to submit to the Court and to have it exercise jurisdiction over specified offenses? That would seem to fit the caveat in the Genocide Convention and make the "world community" the "victor," setting up a victor's tribunal for which Nuremberg and Tokyo would be the precedents. Indeed, similar tribunals with non-combatant "victors" were set up regarding events in the former Yugoslavia and Rwanda. But that has not and would still not solve the deeper problems as they appear on the surface.

To illustrate the difficulties, let us agree that to be "law" the rule to be applied must be applied universally. Some villains will escape, of course, as they do in municipal legal orders' criminal subsets. But are the jurisdictional rules and the substantive rules themselves applicable? Would they apply, for example, to Russian soldiers in Chechnya? To Chechens who infiltrate Russia and blow up

civilian housing? If conceptually the rules did apply regardless of Russian or Chechen legislation defining their soldiers' status and privileges, which might otherwise exempt their own personnel from liability, the next question is whether Russian or Chechen officials would agree that American or other police have the authority to investigate or make arrests in Russian or Chechen controlled territory. Is their agreement necessary?

In East Timor it was thought to be necessary, and the formal government of Indonesia did agree to the introduction of foreign forces in its territory, apparently to apply some notion of law (although precisely what law, how it is to be applied and by whom are open questions) while East Timor remained part of the Indonesian state. If so, then this returns us to the world of positive law and national discretion. If not, before what forum is the point to be argued? By whom? What if the Russians or Chechens still disagree? Would Americans agree to Russian or Chechen investigators or police, unauthorized by American law, making arrests of American military personnel in U.S. territory and placing them before their own or some "international" tribunals to be tried under their concept of "criminal law"?

But, it may be argued, we are not speaking of Russian or Chechen officials. We are speaking of representatives of the international community. Surely we cannot object to an evolution of the international legal order to allow international inspectors and police to make arrests for offenses defined by positive law. But Iraq has made exactly that objection to the United Nations. And Iraq turns out not to be friendless, regardless of the American notion of the Iraqi legal argument and however villainous Saddam Hussein may be. We are left with the notion that positive submission is probably required both to define the evil acts and to enforce their proscription against individuals. But that positive submission has not yet been given by anybody outside various victors' or similar situations (such as with the former Yugoslavia). As a matter of positive law, once the agreement has been given it is subject to interpretation and it cannot be reasonably supposed that the state whose leaders are accused of violating the undefined law will agree with those officials of any institution on all their interpretations of the "law."

These theoretical difficulties obviously arise in practice, and no amount of new theory can resolve the problems as I see them. The issue is not the politicization of tribunals. It is the value systems in the minds of honorable judges. For example, in 1970 Mohammed Bedjaoui, later President of the International Commission of Jurists, argued that newly independent states retain a discretion to renounce their debts and nationalize foreign-owned property based on the primacy of national self-determination over property rights in the international legal order. Who can say definitively that he was wrong? Despite the ringing assertions of "reasonableness" we have heard on all sides since the days of Cicero, arguments over value systems, about which reasonable people do in fact disagree, are not the same as having political biases.

In practice, the issues arise in yet another form. Not only are the value systems in the minds of the ICC's officials very much in question, but the questions extend to the entire process. For example, when is an indictment to be handed down or carried out? If it is to be immediately upon discovering convincing evidence of an indictable atrocity, then is a general to be arrested in the midst of a battle? By whom? And what of the battle? Assuming, as I suppose we must, that Article 2.4 of the United Nations Charter makes international armed conflict itself unthinkable, what about internal battles? Or have we reached a stage in world development in which all existing constitutions are to be protected by the international community from revolutionary change? Who is to determine that rebels, using the best tools available to them, are to fail because there are legal questions surrounding the use of some of those tools that seem to outside parties to be disproportionate in the death and destruction they bring to innocents?

Is war and revolution to be reduced to the status of a game with an impartial umpire blowing a whistle when his or her conception of the rules is violated? Then is the world supposed to stop while the case is brought to a tribunal that might in fact find that the umpire blew the whistle prematurely? And if the umpire blows the whistle after the battle ends, is the victorious military leader to be tried? Was Admiral Nimitz or President Truman or "Bomber" Harris or Josef Stalin responsible for the transgressions of which they have been accused?

The notion that any society should be ruled by the "best," regardless of the will of ordinary folks, has been with us since at least the days when Plato wrote his *Republic*. But who is to discover the "best"? Who is to convince the traditional holders of authority to yield that authority to others whom yet others regard as the "best"? I forbear to cite examples when this approach has been tried, including the attempt by Dionysus II to apply it in his Kingdom of Sicily with Plato himself present. It has always failed.

The reasons why it has failed were eloquently illustrated in a naively arrogant book by Sherard Osborn, a British Navy Captain publishing in 1857 about events during the 1830s when he served British interests in the Malay Peninsula:

> Such are the cruelties perpetrated by these wretched native monarchies . . . and yet philanthropists and politicians at home maunder about the unjust invasion of native rights, and preach against the extension of our rule. As if our Government, in its most corrupt form, would not be a blessing in such a region, and as much if not more, our duty to extend, as a Christian people, than to allow them to remain under native rulers, and then to shoot them for following native habits.

Those who agree with the moral rationales for 19th-century European imperialism and ignore the other things that went with it, such as the exercise of force to implement that fancied moral and political superiority, might support the ICC. I cannot.

POSTSCRIPT

When analyzing the debate over the ICC, it is instructive to examine the very different approaches taken to this issue by Canada and the United States. Under the umbrella of its commitment to promoting human security, Canada has been a strong supporter of the concept underlying the ICC from the beginning. The Canadian government chaired the "Like-Minded Group," a coalition of nearly 60 countries advocating the ICC. Canada was active in the negotiations leading up to the establishment of the ICC and contributed to the UN trust fund that helped many developing countries partici-pate in the deliberations. On June 29, 2000, Canada became the first country to adopt legislation to implement the provisions of the Rome Statute in its national law. The Crimes Against Humanity and War Crimes Act was adopted by the Canadian Parliament in order to bring Canadian law into conformity with the ICC. In February 2003, a Canadian lawyer was elected as the first presiding chief justice of the ICC.

In contrast, the American government has persistently expressed doubts about the ICC. Despite a variety of concerns, President Clinton finally signed the treaty in the dying days of his administration in December 2000. But he recommended that the incoming administration not ratify the treaty in the Senate. Almost immediately upon taking office, the Bush administration expressed its concerns about the ICC. President Bush focused particularly on the fear that American government officials and military personnel might be unfairly tried for war crimes for political reasons. He thus sought an exemption for American personnel participating in overseas mis-sions. Finally, in May 2002, the U.S. government informed UN Secretary-General Kofi Annan that the United States would not seek to ratify the treaty and that is was renouncing any legal obligations flowing from its signing of the treaty. Subsequently, the United States requested that the Security Council grant exemptions from prosecution to U.S. military personnel before the U.S. government approves participation in any UN peacekeeping missions. In addition, President Bush signed into law the American Servicemembers Protection Act. This law gives the president the authority to use military force to free any Americans held by the ICC in the Hague, to suspend military assistance to any country ratifying the ICC treaty, and to restrict U.S. participation in UN peacekeeping operations unless prior immunity to prosecution is granted to U.S. military personnel.

As of October 2008, 108 states have become members of the ICC. A further 40 countries have signed, but not yet ratified the Rome Statue. However, a number of key countries continue to be critical of the ICC and have indicated that they have no intention of joining. This includes the United States, China, and India.

Suggested Additional Readings

Anderson, John B. "An International Criminal Court–An Emerging Idea." *Nova Law Review* 15 (1991): 433–47.

Arsanjani, Mahnoush. "The Rome Statute of the International Criminal Court." *American Journal of International Law* 93, no. 1 (1999): 22–43.

Bass, Gary J. *Stay the Hand: The Politics of War Crimes Tribunal.* Princeton: Princeton University Press, 2000.

Bassiouni, Cherif. "From Versailles to Rwanda in Seventy-Five Years: The Need to Establish a Permanent International Criminal Court." *Harvard Human Rights Law Journal* 10 (1997): 11–62.

Cogan, Jacob. "International Criminal Courts and Fair Trials: Difficulties and Prospects." *Yale Journal of International Law* 27 (Winter 2002): 111–41.

Gallarotti, Giulio M., and Arik Y. Preis. "Toward Universal Human Rights and the Rule of Law: The Permanent International Criminal Court." *Australian Journal of International Affairs* 53, no. 1 (April 1999): 95–112.

Rieff, David. "Court of Dreams." *New Republic* 219, no. 10 (1998): 16–18.

Rubin, Alfred P. "Challenging the Conventional Wisdom: Another View of the International Criminal Court." *Journal of International Affairs* 52 (Spring 1999): 783–95.

Sewall, Sarah B., and Carl Kaysen, eds. *The United States and the International Criminal Court: National Security and International Law.* Lanham, Md.: Rowman & Littlefield Publishers, 2000.

Stromseth, Jane E. (ed.). *Accountability for Atrocities: National and International Responses.* Ardsley, N.Y.: Transnational Publishers, 2003.

InfoTrac® College Edition
Search for the following articles in the InfoTrac® database:

Hale, Christopher. "Does the Evolution of International Criminal Law End with the ICC? The 'Roaming ICC': A Model International Criminal court for a State-centric World of International Law." *Denver Journal of International Law and Policy* 34, no. 3–4 (Summer–Fall 2007): 429–99.

Roach, Steven C. "Courting the Rule of Law? The International Criminal Court and Global Terrorism." *Global Governance* 14, no. 1 (January–March 2008): 13–20.

Scharf, Michael P. "The ICC's Jurisdiction over the Nationals of Non-Party States: A Critique of the U.S. Position." *Law and Contemporary Problems* 64, no. 1 (Winter 2001): 67.

Tochilovsky, Vladimir. "Globalizing Criminal Justice: Challenges for the International Criminal Court." *Global Governance* 9, no. 3 (July–September 2003): 291–99.

Tucker, Robert W. "The International Criminal Court Controversy." *World Policy Journal* 18, no. 2 (Summer 2001): 71–81.

Web Resources

For current URLs for the following websites, visit www.crosscurrents.nelson.com.

COALITION FOR AN INTERNATIONAL CRIMINAL COURT
http://www.iccnow.org
This website, established by a coalition of NGOs supporting the ICC, contains not only textual material but also audio documentaries and links.

HUMAN RIGHTS WATCH: INTERNATIONAL CRIMINAL COURT
http://www.hrw.org/campaigns/icc/
This is the website of the NGO Human Rights Watch's campaign, which supports the ICC.

HUMAN RIGHTS FIRST
http://www.humanrightsfirst.org
This lawyers' site dealing with human rights offers a good collection of materials on the ICC and other international tribunals.

ROME STATUTE OF THE INTERNATIONAL CRIMINAL COURT
http://untreaty.un.org/cod/icc/index.html
The official UN website for the ICC contains the text of the statute, information regarding current status of ratification, and related documentation.

INTERNATIONAL CRIMINAL COURT: RESOURCES IN PRINT AND ELECTRONIC FORMAT
http://www.lib.uchicago.edu/~llou/icc.html
The University of Chicago Library offers an annotated list of materials on the topic of the ICC.

Are Truth Commissions Useful in Promoting Human Rights and Justice in Transitional Societies?

✔ **YES**
JOANNA R. QUINN, "Truth Commissions and Restorative Justice"

✗ **NO**
RICHARD ASHBY WILSON, "Challenging Human Rights as Restorative Justice"

In October 2000, when the first freely elected president of Yugoslavia (now Serbia and Montenegro) took office, the first thing he did was announce the creation of a truth commission. The purpose of this commission was to investigate the crimes and human-rights abuses that had taken place during the wars of Yugoslav succession. In the nine months following this announcement, at least eleven other truth commissions were established in various parts of the world, from East Timor to Sierra Leone and from Panama to Bosnia.

The recent interest in truth commissions has stemmed partly out of the experiences of Latin America and South Africa in searching for ways to assist their societies in making a transition from a period of protracted civil conflict and human-rights abuses to a stable, functioning democracy based on rule of law and observance of human rights. These efforts have been supported by the international community, and other countries have been encouraged to see them as models.

Supporters of truth commissions argue that they are necessary in helping transitional nations overcome the limitations of a more traditional criminal justice approach embodied in the concept of war-crimes tribunals and international criminal courts discussed in Issue Fifteen. The International Criminal Court or an ad hoc war-crimes tribunal cannot deal with situations where massive or systemic human-rights abuses have occurred over a period of time. Because of the high demand for proof in criminal trials, the number of those who are actually prosecuted and found guilty still represents only a very small fraction of those culpable. International tribunals can be expensive, move slowly, and produce only limited results. In war-torn societies that are trying to rebuild fragile institutions, it is too much to expect that the domestic judicial system will pick up the slack. In Rwanda, for example, there were over 100 000 prisoners waiting for years in jail to be tried for their involvement in tribal genocide. Ten years after the genocide occurred, only a small percentage of those implicated in the events had been successfully prosecuted. In the

end, the emphasis on criminal prosecution may have a limited role in preventing new outbreaks of strife and violence.

These difficulties have led some to advocate the use of additional human-rights initiatives, especially the establishment of truth commissions. Such commissions can play an important role in fostering reconciliation, forging mutual understanding, and aiding victims. By providing the victims of a conflict with a platform to tell their stories, they reveal the terrible human cost of human-rights abuses, war, and dictatorship. Often, people from one side come to see the suffering and pain experienced by those on the other side of the conflict. Such meetings can provide the basis to move beyond the formal "peace process" at the highest levels to a deeper process of reconciliation within the society. By moving beyond narrow, legalistic definitions of guilt, truth commissions may foster a broader national process of introspection that encourages all sectors of a society to examine their role in past conflicts. By focusing on recovering the "truth" about its past, a society can reform its institutions in order to prevent recurrences of abuses. Because truth commissions downplay the notion of punishment and retribution, governments can then pursue more proactive strategies aimed at promoting reconciliation along ethnic, racial, linguistic, or religious lines.

In many transitional societies, truth commissions are attractive for some very pragmatic reasons. In some cases, oppressive leaders have sought immunity from prosecution in return for surrendering power or making peace. Often, large numbers of civil servants or military officials implicated in abuses remain in office. It is simply not possible to purge a government of everyone implicated in a previous regime without causing a collapse of the government and its bureaucracy. In other cases, the extent of the human-rights abuses has been so extensive that prosecution of all those implicated is not possible without overwhelming the already fragile national judicial system. The placing of such a high burden on the judicial system may further weaken its credibility and legitimacy.

Because of these factors, there is a growing interest in how the international community can facilitate the establishment and functioning of truth commissions. According to a database established by the United States Institute of Peace, at least 24 truth commissions have been established since 1982, the majority of them since 1990. Nearly a dozen countries have also established commissions of inquiry or similar bodies that function somewhat like truth commissions.

Despite this growing interest, truth commissions are not without their share of controversy. Within the international human-rights community itself, there is growing debate over the value of truth commissions in helping transitional societies in the long term. On one side are those who argue that truth commissions embody an approach to national reconciliation based on the principle of "restorative justice." By downplaying the importance of prosecution and punishment and placing an emphasis on forgiveness, truth commissions provide a basis for national reconciliation that will lead to more stable, just societies in the future.

On the other side, a growing number of analysts have challenged the concept of restorative justice as a basis for truth commissions. These analysts argue that it is important not to overlook the role that retribution plays in establishing justice. Unless the perpetrators of past war crimes and human-rights abuses are seen to suffer some punishment for their actions, it is difficult to build a society that respects human rights in the future.

This debate is taken up in the following two articles. Joanna Quinn is a Canadian scholar who has studied truth commissions in Haiti and Uganda. She argues that the principles of restorative justice are important to an understanding of the positive role that truth commissions play in aiding transitional societies in re-establishing social order. In response, Richard Wilson, who has studied and written extensively on the Truth and Reconciliation Commission in South Africa, argues that the emphasis on forgiveness and reconciliation that underlies truth commissions may in fact undermine the legitimacy of the human-rights and domestic judicial systems that are necessary to the task of nation-building.

✔ **YES**

Truth Commissions and Restorative Justice

JOANNA R. QUINN

In recent years, a debate has emerged about what should be done in societies where egregious human rights violations have taken place. Societies like these are often at a stand-still, needing to do something to move forward, but worried in case the choice they make might somehow not be enough. Throughout most of the world, it is common practice to subject the perpetrators of crimes, both large and small, to trials in which they are held accountable for what they have done. Yet these kinds of proceedings are simply unable to address many of the other aspects of the crimes which have been committed, including the impact on victims and their families, as well as implications for the larger society.

RETRIBUTIVE VS. RESTORATIVE JUSTICE

The distinction that must be made here is between retributive and restorative justice. The first of these, trials, are a form of *retributive justice*. The term *retribution* is defined by the *Canadian Oxford Dictionary* as "punishment for a crime, injury, etc.; vengeance." Centred around principles such as accountability and punishment, retributive mechanisms bring the person charged with a particular crime before a judge or panel of judges who hear evidence as to the crime committed, whereupon a decision as to the person's guilt or innocence is taken, and a proportional response or sentence is meted out. Such legal prosecutions follow from the rule of law, the parameters of which have long been established. "In the Western liberal legal tradition, the rule of law . . . entails the presumption of innocence, litigation under the adversary system, and the ideal of a government by laws, rather than by persons."[1]

Retributive justice can take many forms. In the Western world, trials are commonly held to deal with criminal charges. In such cases, decisions are often made by a combination of judge and/or jury to determine not only a person's guilt or innocence, but also decide what penalty he or she should incur. These trials are held under the jurisdiction of national laws.

Another more recent development in retributive justice is the advent of retributive tribunals. Starting with the Nuremberg trials, which were held post–World War II to deal with Nazi war crimes, and again with the appointment of the International Criminal Tribunal for the Former Yugoslavia (ICTY) and the International Criminal Tribunal for Rwanda (ICTR), as well as the recent initiation of the International Criminal Court (ICC), the international community has begun to take a significant interest in the prosecution of perpetrators of crimes of mass atrocity, genocide, and war crimes. Often, such bodies derive their authority from

international agreements and international treaties; the ICC, for example, came into being through the signing by state parties of the Treaty of Rome. In these cases, too, panels of judges hear evidence before deciding a person's guilt or innocence and determining an appropriate sentence.

Such bodies, however, are both labour- and knowledge-intensive. Often, a dichotomy of responses is carried out. In the first and very common scenario, hundreds of people are needed to run these complex organizations: courtrooms staffed by clerical and security staff, judges assisted by legal staff, and prisons. In other cases, the legal system is simply unable to deal with the onslaught of cases that would inevitably be brought before it. The Cambodian case provides a useful illustration. In 2000, its weak court system comprised judges 80 percent of whom did not hold law degrees and many of whom had never received formal education at all, let alone training in legal matters.[2] Another difficulty is that the sheer magnitude of the period of mass atrocity would make it nearly impossible to deal effectively with the cases at hand. In Rwanda, for example, approximately 120,000 Rwandans remained in prison in 2000, six years after the genocide of approximately 800,000 Rwandans in 1994. It is estimated that if the regular court system tried to deal with these cases, it would take upwards of 180 years. Those constructing the model of restorative justice must recognize and deal with these constraints and the perceptions of the system and its limitations.

Other societies have taken a different approach; they have opted instead to use a form of *restorative justice*. As I define it, restorative justice is a process of active participation in which the wider community deliberates over past crimes, giving centre stage to both victim and perpetrator in a process that seeks to bestow dignity and empowerment upon victims, with special emphasis placed upon contextual factors.[3] Quite unlike in the retributive system described above, however, the applicability of punishment is absent from this type of justice. And unlike in the process of retribution, wherein the perpetrator is the sole focus of the proceedings, in restorative processes the victim receives special attention.

Any number of instruments may be employed to bring about restorative justice. In most cases, the instrument itself is developed with regard to the specificities of the situation in which it is to be employed; as opposed to retributive trials and tribunals, instruments of restorative justice are not merely cookie-cutter solutions. Among the methods available to states grappling with past atrocity are reparation, which might include apology or restitution, like that granted to Canadians and Americans of Japanese descent who were interned during World War II. In 1988, the American government gave those Japanese who had been interned US$20,000 per survivor as a form of compensation under the Civil Liberties Act, while in the same year, the Canadian government awarded $21,000 per survivor under the Japanese Canadian Redress Agreement.

Another response to mass human rights abuses by the state has been the truth commission. In the spirit of restorative justice, the truth commission often avoids

retribution and sentencing. Rather, it pushes for the provision of an apology or reparation to the citizens of a country who have been wronged by human rights abuses. This tendency is due in part to the relative cost associated with other forms of reparation, resources that are often thought to be better allocated to other social programs in a transitional society. Certainly, truth commissions may not be appropriate in every context. They do, however, have the potential to generate many benefits for societies in transition.

TRUTH COMMISSIONS

A relatively new instrument of justice following a period of atrocity, the truth commission provides a forum in which a society can learn about the abuses of the past. Generally, a truth commission's main task is to collect information about such abuses and to compile this information to produce a coherent account of the history of that society. This can be particularly important in societies where abuses have been government-sponsored and have therefore gone unrecorded in any official way. It is often the case that these abuses are unsubstantiated or even denied by the governments in question. For this reason, a truth commission can play a vital role in uncovering and chronicling the events of a society's collective past.

By my definition, a truth commission is made up of four components: it is (a) a non-judicial investigatory body established, sanctioned, or empowered by the state (or by a dominant faction within the state) to (b) determine the truth about widespread human rights violations that occurred in the past in order to (c) discover which parties may be blamed for their participation in perpetrating such violations over (d) a specified period of time. These four characteristics adequately address the various needs of the truth commission.

The first-ever truth commission was convoked in Uganda in 1974, although it completely failed to promote either truth or acknowledgement. Since that time, more than twenty truth commissions have been appointed by national governments, among them highly successful commissions in Argentina, Chile, and South Africa. Truth commissions may be variously concerned with other aspects of reparation, including property and/or loss of income. Truth commissions are, however, effectively prohibited from dealing with aspects *other* than past human rights abuses because of the relative cost associated with other forms of retributive justice, monies that might better be allocated to other facets of the transitional society.

Among the most highly celebrated (and successful) truth commissions is the Truth and Reconciliation Commission (TRC) that was held in South Africa to consider the human rights abuses that had taken place during apartheid. It was established under the 1995 Promotion of National Unity and Reconciliation Act by the South African parliament. The Act gave the TRC the power to grant individualized amnesty, as well as search and seizure powers, subpoena powers, and witness-protection powers. The

TRC had three separate yet inter-related capacities: the Human Rights Violations Committee, the Amnesty Committee, and the Reparations and Rehabilitation Committee. The TRC took testimony from 23,000 victims and witnesses, 2000 of whom appeared in public hearings. The TRC process seems to have been able to bring about a societal recognition and responsibility for the abuses perpetrated under apartheid-era governments. It was also pivotal in publicizing truth commissions around the world.

Another commission of note is the National Commission on Truth and Reconciliation (NCTR) that took place in Chile between May 9, 1990, and February 9, 1991. During that nine months, the Commission received evidence from more than 3400 victims and their families, considered such evidence, and finally prepared a report. The NCTR compiled lists of victims and the details of their cases. Testimony was heard, evidence gathered, and decisions made; in the end, all of the evidence was referred to the courts, except for the testimony of those who had been granted a blanket amnesty. The acknowledgement of the suffering of the people of Chile brought about in Chilean society appears to have played a vital role in helping Chile to regain democracy.

The success of truth commissions appears to depend upon the creation of a common and official "truth narrative" that can lead to the outward and public acknowledgement of past events. This hearing of the experiences of oneself and others might well validate the experience of those involved in past crimes. The discussion of group and individual experiences and the recognition of others' experiences as valid are required. This acknowledgement of past events is a critical step in the process of reconciliation between victims and perpetrators. And it is influential in bringing a sense of healing to the community.

HOW TRUTH COMMISSIONS CAN PROMOTE RESTORATIVE JUSTICE

The very definition of the relative "success" of truth commissions, however, is based on a different set of evaluative criteria than that of its retributive justice counterpart, acknowledgement trials. In a restorative context, the process is not at all perpetrator-centric. As such, truth commissions are focused less on prosecuting and sentencing those who have committed past atrocity. Rather, the aim of restorative mechanisms of all stripes, but particularly of truth commissions, is to determine the truth about such events, by means of a collaborative and often very public process.

Critics often argue that people who have lived through abuse are hungry for justice and revenge. They contend that only by holding people accountable can any kind of societal reconciliation take place. Certainly, if conducted properly, national accountability trials can showcase the ability of a country's judicial system to function, which can in turn have a deterrent effect on the future commission of human rights abuses. Sadly, however, the underpinnings necessary for traditional judicial function are often simply not in place, as in the case of Cambodia, mentioned above.

Truth commissions have many advantages over more traditional forms of retributive justice. I have identified six reasons that the restorative process is preferable, each of which is discussed in greater detail below.

First, restorative justice does not merely deal with a particular case among the many thousands that may exist; it is a process with a significantly broader focus, which allows it to begin to work at a broader societal level. This is so because of the broad mandate of most truth commissions. The Ugandan truth commission, for example, was mandated to "inquire into all aspects of violations of human rights, breaches of the rule of law and excessive abuses of power committed against any persons" between 1962 and 1986.[4] Whereas trials traditionally focus on only one case and collect information pertaining to that one case, truth commissions are able to consider a broad spectrum of cases and to collect information pertaining to them all. In a ground-breaking use of applied technology, the Haitian truth commission collected information regarding more than 8,000 individual cases of abuse. The commission was then able to compile this information into a database that could be used to cross-reference the details of each crime committed and to provide an overall picture of the many thousands of abuses that had taken place. The scope of most trials is such that an investigation of this magnitude is not possible.

Second, truth commissions can also have a popular educative effect. Because their activities concern such a broad spectrum of the wider society, its activities are often widely publicized. In turn, this gives the commission the opportunity to effect a great degree of change within that society. One outcome of truth commission activity after a period of atrocity that is often felt is that people begin to learn about the sanctity of their rights and the state's responsibility to uphold them. Especially where the state itself has sponsored and carried out human rights abuses, people often have no idea of the rights to which they are entitled. One additional benefit that can be brought about by truth commission activity is that the society can begin to build a shared understanding and public record of the events that took place. This is particularly important because often people are aware only of their own circumstances; through the building of a common understanding of shared past events, people in a society can more readily come to terms with their shared history and begin to move forward.

Third, a truth commission can help strengthen and build a new judicial infrastructure. Although it is not concerned with the retributive aspects of the justice system and cannot replace a trial, a truth commission can begin to carry out some of the functions that a functioning judicial system should be able to encompass. It is particularly important, for example, that a society should feel able to trust in the judicial process. By appointing as commissioners people of integrity who are beyond reproach, and by carrying out proceedings in a way that honours everyone involved, this trust in the judicial system can be augmented. Moreover, in some cases, the truth commission may actually be afforded quasi-judicial

powers that allow it to turn the evidence collected over to authorities involved in other retributive mechanisms. In this way, the truth commission and national trials, for example, may actually work in tandem.

Fourth, as mentioned above, truth commissions are often tailored to a society's particular circumstances. This specificity allows the appointed truth commission the opportunity to address directly the crimes committed within a given society. Obviously, the situation in each society will be different. The Guatemalan Commission for Historical Clarification was agreed to in 1994 by the Guatemalan government and leftist rebels after nearly thirty years and more than 200,000 deaths and disappearances. The Guatemalan commission, when it began work in 1997, was mandated to work with the armed forces and guerrilla organizations and even appointed a liaison team to carry out a special investigation of both organizations. Conversely, the Argentine National Commission on the Disappeared was established in 1983 to uncover the details of disappearances carried out under several successive military juntas. To date, no truth commission has borne more than a slight resemblance to the next. Yet each has gone some distance to specifically attend to the abuses that were carried out within the society in question.

Fifth, and more importantly, truth commissions are often able to operate in a much less costly fashion than their retributive counterparts. After a period of mass atrocity, societies are left devastated. The impact is often felt both physically and socially. The destruction of the physical infrastructure becomes apparent in crumbling hospitals, bullet-riddled buildings, and collapsed roads and bridges. The social infrastructure, too, is ruined. People no longer feel able to trust in their friends, neighbours, or government institutions. Yet in most cases, the finite financial resources of the society enable it to tackle either the physical *or* the social problems. Truth commissions require less staff to be able to operate at full capacity and are able to address significantly more cases in a shorter period of time. As a result, the truth commission presents itself as an attractive option to many societies in the early stages of transition.

Lastly, and above all, the truth commission acts to foster aspects of reconciliation. Although truth commissions have been variously concerned with finding details of disappearances, government complicity, or guerrilla activity, among others, the main desired outcome implicit in the mandate and goals of each commission is reconciliation. That is to say, one of the underlying purposes of any truth commission is to bring the factions of society that have been at odds to a point where they are once again able to live and work together. Such individual and societal reconciliation can lead to strengthened civil society and even the re-establishment of democracy among the population.[5] By its very nature, then, the truth commission, as a mechanism of restorative (rather than retributive) justice, is significantly better able to provide the foundation for these desired effects.

CONCLUSION

One must be careful not to confuse the very different processes of retributive and restorative justice. It is clear that retributive processes such as the accountability trial are able to perform a particular function. It is also clear that, given the proper support and resources, they can do it well. Restorative mechanisms such as the truth commission, however, perform a substantially different set of tasks. Indeed, trials and truth commissions fulfill a disparate set of functions and must be recognized as being distinctly different. For a variety of reasons, detailed above, truth commissions are better suited to bring about the processes of restorative justice, including societal healing and reconciliation.

NOTES

1. Martha Minow, *Between Vengeance and Forgiveness: Facing History after Genocide and Mass Violence* (Boston: Beacon Press, 1998), 25.

2. Kay Johnson, "Will Justice Ever Be Served?" Time, 10 April 2000, 17.

3. Adapted from Sinclair Dinnen, "Restorative Justice in Papua New Guinea," *International Journal of the Sociology of Law* 25 (1997): 245–62.

4. The Republic of Uganda, *The Report of the Commission of Inquiry into Violations of Human Rights* (Kampala: UPPC, 1994), 3.

5. Consideration of the outcomes of societal reconciliation and acknowledgement are only now beginning to emerge. See, for example, Joanna R. Quinn, "Acknowledgement: The Road to Forgiveness," *Institute on Globalization and the Human Condition Working Paper Series*, McMaster University, January 2003, available at www.humanities.mcmaster.ca/~global/wps/Quinn.pdf.

✗ NO
Challenging Human Rights as Restorative Justice
RICHARD ASHBY WILSON

In the 1990s in democratizing countries of Latin America, Eastern Europe, and South Africa, human rights emerged as a universal panacea to authoritarianism. Human rights were demanded by ordinary citizens massed in the squares of Leipzig or on the streets of Bisho in South Africa, and they became the bedrock of the new constitutional order. Human rights legislation became a central component in the transformation of repressive state institutions and the establishing of the rule of law after authoritarian rule. In each society, new political leaders had to face the question of how to deal with the gross human rights violations of the past, and they set up new institutions and commissions to reaffirm human dignity and prevent the reoccurrence of mass atrocities.

One result of their increasing popularity was that human rights became detached from their legal foundations and transformed into a generalized moral and political discourse, which is then used to address all manner of power relations among individuals, groups, and states. The broad extension of human rights talk intensified as democratizing regimes, with crumbling economies and fractured social orders, grasped for unifying metaphors. Human rights seemed to provide an ideological adhesive through their emphasis on truth and reconciliation. Indeed, the ideological promiscuity of human rights—their ability to appeal to diverse and often opposed political constituencies—is one explanation for their wide-ranging globalization in the 1990s.

Now over a decade after the wave of democratic transitions, it is time to take stock and to evaluate critically the role of human rights ideas and institutions. It has became possible to move on from simply extolling human rights as a universally "good thing" to examining what happened when human rights institutions were established in the context of political compromise, where neither opposing side in a civil war had won an outright military victory and where key perpetrators of the era of repression (from Vice-President F.W. de Klerk in South Africa to Senator Augusto Pinochet in Chile) still occupied positions of political power.

This evaluation requires a political analysis of the concrete conditions faced by new political elites and, in particular, of the fractured nation identity and lack of legitimacy of state institutions. It focuses on how new political leaders often used human rights to re-imagine the nation and to manufacture legitimacy for key state institutions. By focusing on how new elites have used human rights to legitimate their own regimes, we can understand one reason why, ten years or so after the transitions, human rights have come to lack authority in the eyes of many citizens in Latin America and South Africa. In South Africa, human rights became less and less legitimate as an emergent

political elite used human rights to shore up bargains made with the outgoing authoritarian political establishment.

Even though the new vision of nation-building appeared to be characterized by liberal values of tolerance and decency, it had its own morally coercive implications, as new amnesty provisions deprived victims of their right to prosecute perpetrators. In South Africa, retributive justice[1] based upon punishment of perpetrators was defined as "un-African" by former Archbishop Desmond Tutu, chair of the country's Truth and Reconciliation Commission (or TRC), which functioned in its entirety from 1996 to 1998. Desmond Tutu's religious vision of reconciliation stressed public confession by victims, created meaning for suffering through a narrative of sacrifice and liberation, and encouraged the forsaking of revenge. Reconciliation portrayed retributive justice as blood-lust and as an affront to democratization and the new political order. In place of retribution, Tutu promoted a restorative justice view of human rights, which has as its aim the restoration of social bonds and the repairing of the torn fabric of society.

The TRC's version of reconciliation was conveyed to the population primarily through the Human Rights Violations (HRV) hearings. For two years during the historical moment in which the fledgling "new South Africa" was born, the TRC's hearings became national rituals of "reconciliation," forgiveness, and truth-telling. Reconciliation is a quasi-religious concept that became a guiding principle for new rituals of civic nationalism. HRV hearings were emotionally intense public ceremonies that generated collective moral values and sought to inculcate them in all who participated, including those watching hearings on television each night. Like all rituals, they were met with a complex mixture of compliance, acceptance, indignation, and resistance.

There were a number of positive benefits to South Africa's experiment in truth and reconciliation. Transitions from authoritarianism require the breaking of hegemonic silences and the construction of a new public space where ordinary citizens can speak openly about the consequences of state terror. Public recognition of formerly repressed stories allowed greater mutual understanding between the sections of South African society that had been separated by the racialized boundaries of apartheid. This made possible a greater "fusion of horizons," to use the phrase of philosopher Hans-Georg Gadamer, a base line of understanding, and it defined the parameters of discussion on the past. As Michael Ignatieff (2001) has contended, the recognition and acceptance of these formerly repressed truths, as well as their integration into a public narrative about the past, circumscribes the range of impermissible lies. After the South African Truth and Reconciliation Commission, one can no longer maintain, as the National Party once attempted to argue, that apartheid was a benevolent, "good neighbor" policy somehow gone awry. Nor can one deny that tens of thousands were killed by the operatives of an abhorrent political system.

However, the identification of human rights with restorative justice was not without serious drawbacks. In the South African transition, reconciliation became a symbol of the pact between the old, outgoing apartheid elite and the incoming elite, a pact that perpetuated an aspect of authoritarian legality—namely impunity—in the present. Here, reconciliation became the language not of principle and inalienable individual rights, but of compromise, political hedging, and trade-offs that included amnesty—an official pardon—for human rights offenders. This strategy of reconciling with past enemies became more widespread beyond South Africa and was reinforced in countries such as El Salvador and Sierra Leone by United Nations missions and international nongovernmental organizations seeking diplomatic solutions to conflicts. In these situations, reconciliation helps to forge a new nation-building ideology that values political expediency over legality and consolidating the rule of law. But this is done at the cost of sacrificing the individual rights and dignity of victims, and especially their right to justice as enshrined in new bills of rights in national constitutions. As Borneman (1997) contends, the most successful postauthoritarian regimes are those that place accountability and retributive justice at the center of their moral and political project.

Advocates of restorative justice often maintain that truth commissions can fulfill a need for public education on human rights and democratic values of tolerance. In the case of South Africa, the TRC's objectives of creating reconciliation and building a new inclusive and benevolent image of the nation were only partially fulfilled, as maintained in my book *The Politics of Truth and Reconciliation in South Africa* (2001). For all their media coverage, TRC hearings were often little more than a symbolic and ritualized performance with a weak impact on vengeance in urban townships. The transfer of reconciling values from an elite to the masses was uneven and ambiguous. In the case of South Africa and its impressive array of new human rights institutions, the involvement of victims did not necessarily mean a deep loyalty to nation-building or a new language of rights.

Even some members of the South African Truth and Reconciliation Commission came to recognize that reconciliation demanded too much of victims, and that the concept was excessively infused with Christian connotations of "turning the other cheek" and "love thine enemy." Commissioners consequently abandoned the practice of asking victims at the Human Rights Violation hearings whether they forgave their persecutor. Reconciliation implies a shared set of moral values that may not actually exist on the ground, especially in societies ravaged by long-standing conflicts. Thus, it has the potential to coerce individuals into compliant positions they would not adopt of their own accord. In the post-conflict order, everyone is required to co-exist peacefully and to forsake individual acts of revenge, but, beyond that, it could be argued that individuals have the right to think and feel what they like, including hatred for their former enemy. This is a central tenet of liberalism—that governments legislate actions, not beliefs.

My own ethnographic research in the townships of Johannesburg had led me to the conclusion that, contra the established view within the Truth and Reconciliation Commission, retributive understandings of justice are more salient in South African society than ideas of reconciliation and forgiveness. The main reason why the TRC could not convert many South Africans to its view of restorative justice was that, as a result of many years of state violence and counter-violence, most citizens held a punitive, "eye-for-an-eye" vision of justice. This is not a result of "African culture" but of the specific historical conditions created by apartheid and the anti-apartheid struggle. In the African townships surrounding metropolitan centers such as Johannesburg and Durban, the anti-apartheid movement had militarized the youth in response to the counter-insurgency strategy of the apartheid state. In 1990, a war erupted between the anti-apartheid African National Congress (ANC) and the Inkatha Freedom Party, the party of Zulu nationalism, which was armed and trained by apartheid state operatives. There were also battles within the ANC that followed generational lines, where youths were organized into Special Defense Units and older men were members of a separate ANC military structure—MK.

In the absence of gainful employment after the first multi-racial elections in 1994, many hardened cadres of the political struggle turned to criminality. Post-apartheid African townships became characterized by a patchwork of warring gangs who terrorized the local population. In the ten years after apartheid, South Africa had some of the world's worst crime figures for homicide, rape, and car hijackings, and it also has one of the highest incarceration rates in the world. These harsh realities ensure that revenge remains a feature of the political landscape and they hamper lofty sentiments of reconciliation.

Advocates of restorative justice such as Joanna Quinn argue persuasively that truth commissions can strengthen the new judicial infrastructure by acting inclusively and building trust. Yet I would argue that in practice, the South African TRC was not particularly effective in creating a new culture of human rights or greater respect for the rule of law. Because of its emphasis on reconciliation, the South African Truth and Reconciliation Commission did not sufficiently engage with popular understandings of justice based in widespread practices of revenge. Instead, the TRC demonized understandable feelings of retribution as dangerous to the well-being of the new "rainbow nation." This approach simply did not take into account the widespread views on justice of many South Africans. As long as human rights institutions worked to undermine criminal prosecutions and financial reparations from perpetrators, they would be resisted by some victims and denounced as a "sell-out" by informal justice institutions such as community courts.

Because Africans were neglected for so many years by the formal legal system,[2] they set up local courts to mediate and adjudicate many of their own problems. In the 1990s, this took place with little reference to the criminal justice system or

bodies such as the TRC, which was seen by many people I interviewed as weak and ineffectual. The low level of reparations and the amnesty process within the TRC combined to strengthen the view that human rights were really about the violation of principles of "natural justice." Instead of appealing to human rights commissions to solve problems of social order, many Africans turn to over 400 local courts in rural and urban areas across the country. Local legal structures deal mostly with petty crimes and domestic disputes, but they have also taken on the legacy of past political violence. In particular, they have protected returning black councilors and their families who were chased out of the townships in 1984, when their houses were burned and some family members were "necklaced." Unlike human rights commissions, many community members take the view that local courts will always find out the guilty and achieve justice through vengeful punishment, rather than "reconciliation" and amnesties. Thus, a discontinuity between legal systems has emerged in the South African transition through the opposition between local, retributive justice versus national, restorative justice.

The unintended consequences of popular justice are worth remarking upon here. Despite the opposition of local African courts to the TRC, there is a strong convergence in the aims and objectives of local and human rights institutions around co-existence. I hesitate to use the word *reconciliation*, since no one I interviewed thought that it accurately described the process of reincorporation of former "apartheid collaborators." Reconciliation is clearly the moral discourse of national-level institutions. Yet it is ironic that neighborhood courts that portray themselves as a "tribal" authority and that reject the TRC's humanitarian view of human rights for a more punitive and retributive view of justice are in the end promoting similar solutions to the TRC. They do so not through notions of reconciliation derived from Christian ethics and human rights talk, but through expressions of legitimate traditionalist authority and the possibility of punitive sanction against any who transgress its decisions.

The empirical evidence from other democratizing countries shows that retributive justice can itself lead to reconciliation (in the sense of peaceful co-existence and the legal, non-violent adjudication of conflict) in the long run. The most damaging outcome of truth commissions results from their equating of human rights with reconciliation and amnesty. This delegitimizes them enormously in relation to popular understandings of justice and can lead to greater criminalization in society. There is growing evidence from Eastern Europe and elsewhere (Borneman 1997) that it is necessary for democratizing regimes to challenge directly the impunity created during the authoritarian order if they are going to avoid an upsurge in criminality and a lack of respect for state institutions.

Ironically, human rights became the language of restorative justice and forgiveness of human rights offenders in South Africa, whereas at the same time in international contexts human rights were developing in just the opposite direction with the establishing of the International Criminal Court and a number of

successful prosecutions brought by the UN war crimes tribunals for the former Yugoslavia and Rwanda. Pursuing more criminal trials of perpetrators within South Africa not only would have had the advantage of fortifying the rule of law and indirectly addressing wider criminalization in society, but also would have linked human rights to popular understandings of justice and accorded human rights–oriented institutions much greater legitimacy in the process. This, in turn, could have helped resolve the wider legitimacy crisis of post-apartheid state institutions in a more effective manner. A policy of allowing more civil prosecutions of offenders would have made the transformation of the judiciary clearer and more evident.

This view is backed up by a salient interpretation of international human rights treaties, which holds that those responsible for gross human rights violations must be brought before a court of law and held accountable. In the pages of the *Yale Law Journal*, Diane Orentlicher (1991: 2540) reiterated the international legal imperative to punish that transcends national political contexts:

[T]he central importance of the rule of law in civilized societies requires, within defined but principles limits, prosecution of especially atrocious crimes . . . [I]nternational law itself helps assure the survival of fragile democracies when its clear pronouncement removes certain atrocious crimes from the provincial realm of a country's internal politics and thereby places those crimes squarely within the scope of universal concern . . . A state's complete failure to punish repeated or notorious instances of these offenses violates its obligations under customary international law.

I am persuaded that Orentlicher has articulated correctly the ideal relationship between international human rights and national processes of democratization and the establishment of the rule of law. The international character of human rights laws and institutions exists to reinforce national processes of delivering retributive justice for victims of human rights violations. The rule of law cannot meaningfully be said to exist if it is predicated upon impunity for gross human rights violations committed in the authoritarian past, since, as Orentlicher (1991: 2542) states:

If law is unavailable to punish widespread brutality of the recent past, what lesson can be offered for the future? . . . Societies recently scourged by lawlessness need look no further than their own past to discover the costs of impunity. Their history provides sobering cause to believe, with William Pitt, that tyranny begins where law ends.

The justice advanced by international criminal law and ad hoc human rights tribunals is retributive justice: punishment for offenders and just compensation for victims. In transitional contexts such as South Africa, human rights institutions should

ideally reinforce this understanding of justice. However, in countries emerging from authoritarian rule, human rights commissions often come to undermine accountability in favor of nation-building, thus thwarting the intention of national and international human rights courts. Truth commissions often signify individual or blanket amnesty for perpetrators and a limited "truth finding" operation as a parallel compromise solution.

In sum, we can say that in the 1980s and 1990s, human rights at the national level often became the language of pragmatic political compromise rather than the language of principle and accountability being pursued through international legal institutions. This is the main obstacle to popular acceptance of human rights in newly democratized countries. The redefinition, and some would say deformation, of human rights during democratic transitions to mean amnesty and reconciliation conflicted not only with widespread notions of justice in society, but also, it could be argued, with a state's duty to punish human rights offenders as established in international criminal law.

The appropriation of human rights by nation-building politicians and their identification with forgiveness, reconciliation, and restorative justice elevates social stability as the greatest social good. This image of human rights undermines accountability and the rule of law, and with it the breadth and depth of the democratization process. If human rights are associated instead with a principled position of accountability of key human rights offenders, then this would bring human rights into line with the views of the majority, who see justice as proportional punishment for wrongdoing. This would also connect national change to international human rights law, which increasingly takes the view that there are no conditions under which a torturer or a mass murderer should go free.

With the establishment of the International Criminal Court in 2002 and extradition proceedings against General Augusto Pinochet in Britain in 1999, which established that heads of state do not enjoy immunity from prosecution for human rights violations such as torture, the stage seems increasingly set for international human rights law to transcend national legal systems and to prosecute those involved in gross human rights violations with greater vigor. The arrest and extradition to the UN war crimes tribunal of Slobodan Milosevic in June 2001 sets an international precedent, as Milosevic is the first head of state to stand trial for human rights abuses at an international tribunal. The tide of global justice is now turning in favor of legality, prosecution, and punishment rather than diplomacy, reconciliation, and forgiveness.

Despite the protestations of some political leaders who replace the dictators, international prosecutions are seen as wholly just by many of those who lived through periods of violence, terror, and authoritarianism. In an international context where the jurisdiction of human rights institutions is intensifying and broadening, it is misguided to delegitimize human rights at the national level by detaching them from a retributive understanding of justice and attaching them to

a religious notion of reconciliation-forgiveness, regrettable amnesty laws, and an elite project of nation-building. Democratizing regimes should seek legitimacy less through nation-building efforts to forge a moral unity and communitarian ideology and more through accountability and justice, defined as proportional retribution and procedural fairness. The role of human rights commissions in all of this is to create the bedrock of accountability upon which democratic legitimacy can be built.

NOTES

1. By retributive justice, I mean the prosecution of alleged criminal acts in a recognized court according to standard procedures and rules of legal evidence, and if guilt is established, sentencing (as punishment) proportional to the gravity of the harm and the degree of responsibility of the wrongdoer. My understanding follows Robert Nozick's (1981: 363–97) "non-teleological retributivism" that does not have as its aim the moral improvement of the offender.

2. There are other important state institutions to consider apart from the TRC—namely the criminal justice system itself, which has received only a fraction of the international interest that the TRC has enjoyed. The TRC deflected attention from the more serious project of making the legal system more representative, efficient, and fair.

REFERENCES

Borneman, Jon. 1997. *Settling Accounts: Violence, Justice and Accountability in Postsocialist Europe.* Princeton: Princeton University Press.

Ignatieff, Michael. 2001. "Introduction." In Jillian Edelstein, *Truth and Lies: Stories from the Truth and Reconciliation Commission in South Africa:* 15–21. London: Granta Books.

Nozick, R. 1981. *Philosophical Explanations.* Cambridge, MA: Harvard University Press.

Orentlicher, Diane. 1991. "Settling Accounts: The Duty to Prosecute Human Rights Violations of a Prior Regime." *Yale Law Journal* 100: 2539–2615.

Wilson, Richard Ashby. 2001. *The Politics of Truth and Reconciliation in South Africa: Legitimizing the Post-Apartheid State.* Law and Society Series. Cambridge: Cambridge University Press.

POSTSCRIPT

This debate raises some interesting questions regarding the process of democratization and peace-building in conflict-torn societies and the ways in which the international community can best facilitate such efforts. Both human-rights advocates and conflict resolution specialists, through the work of non-governmental organizations (NGOs) and international organizations, have become involved in the efforts of transitional nations to transform themselves into more stable, just societies. It is clear, however, that these two groups have a different orientation to the task of nation-building.

Conflict resolution specialists are focused on a more pragmatic, interest-based approach that desires to build a sense of cooperation in divided communities. Thus, they appear more willing to make compromises and avoid sensitive issues that may cause further division and strife. Hence, the concept of restorative justice discussed by Joanna Quinn has considerable appeal to them. In contrast, human-rights advocates tend to focus on a more principle-driven, rights-based approach. To many peace groups, this approach appears to be overly legalistic and punitive in nature; they fear that an emphasis on retributive justice may prolong the conflict and continue to exacerbate tensions. As a result, there is a tendency to see human rights and peacemaking as being in competition. But do these two approaches necessarily stand in contradiction to one another? Is there a way in which a human rights focus can be integrated into peace work that will contribute to the promotion of human security? A useful starting point for answering these questions is the Winter 2002 issue of *Human Rights Dialogue* on integrating human rights and peace work, available at http://www.cceia.org.

Suggested Additional Readings

Adam, Heribert. "Trading Justice for Truth." *The World Today* 54 (January 1998): 11–13.

Dugard, John. "Reconciliation and Justice: The South African Experience." *Transnational Law & Contemporary Problems* 8, no. 2 (1998): 277–311.

Goldstone, Richard. "Exposing Human Rights Abuses: A Help or Hindrance to Reconciliation?" *Hastings Constitutional Law Quarterly* 22 (Spring 1995): 607–21.

Graybill, Lyn S. "Pursuit of Truth and Reconciliation in South Africa." *Africa Today: A Quarterly Review* 45 (1998): 103–33.

Graybill, Lyn S. *Truth and Reconciliation in South Africa: Miracle or Model?* Boulder, Colo.: Lynne Rienner, 2002.

Hayner, Priscilla B. *Unspeakable Truths.* New York: Routledge, 2003.

"Justice As a Tool for Peace-Making: Truth Commissions and International Criminal Tribunals." *New York University Journal of International Law and Politics* 28, no. 3 (1996): 485–503.

Kritz, Neil J. (ed.). *Transitional Justice: How Emerging Democracies Reckon with Former Regimes*, vols. 1–3. Washington, D.C.: United States Institute of Peace, 1996.

Little, David. "A Different Kind of Justice: Dealing with Human Rights Violations in Transitional Societies." *Ethics and International Affairs* 13 (1999): 65–80.

Minow, Martha. *Between Vengeance and Forgiveness: Facing History after Genocide and Mass Violence.* Boston: Beacon Press, 1998.

Pankhurst, Donna. "Issues of Justice and Reconciliation in Complex Political Emergencies: Conceptualizing Reconciliation, Justice and Peace." *Third World Quarterly* 20, no. 1 (1999): 239–56.

Quinn, Joanna R. "Dealing with a Legacy of Mass Atrocity: Truth Commissions in Uganda and Chile." *Netherlands Quarterly of Human Rights* 19, no. 4 (December 2001): 383–402.

Rotberg, Robert I., and Dennis Thompson (eds.). *Truth v. Justice: The Morality of Truth Commissions.* Princeton, N.J.: Princeton University Press, 2000.

Tepperman, Jonathan. "Truth and Consequences." *Foreign Affairs* 81, no. 2 (March–April 2002): 128–45.

Zegeye, Abebe, and Ian Liebenberg. "Pathway to Democracy? The Case of the South African Truth and Reconciliation Process." *Social Identities* 4, no. 3 (1998): 319–20.

InfoTrac® College Edition

Search for the following articles in the InfoTrac® database:

Garkawe, Sam. "The South African Truth and Reconciliation Commission: A Suitable Model to Enhance the Role and Rights of the Victims of Gross Violations of Human Rights?" *Melbourne University Law Review* 27, no. 2 (August 2003): 334–80.

Hayner, Priscilla B. "Fifteen Truth Commissions—1974 to 1994: A Comparative Study." *Human Rights Quarterly* 16, no. 4 (November 1994): 597–655.

Silove, Derrick, Anthony B. Zwi, and Dominique le Touze. "Do Truth Commissions Heal? The East Timor Experience." *The Lancet* 367, no. 9518 (April 15, 2006): 1222–25.

Wong, Adrien Katherine. "A Truth and Reconciliation Commission for Palestine/Israel: Healing Spirit Injuries? *Transnational Law & Contemporary Problems* 17, no. 1 (Winter 2008): 139–64.

Web Resources

For current URLs for the following websites, visit www.crosscurrents.nelson.com.

Truth Commissions Digital Collection
http://www.usip.org/library/truth.html
This site provides a complete list of truth commissions along with links to key documents and reports related to the work of each commission.

INCORE Guide to Internet Resources on Truth and Reconciliation
http://www.incore.ulst.ac.uk/cds/themes/truth.html
INCORE is a joint project between the University of Ulster and United Nations University focusing on peace and reconciliation efforts. This site has an extensive list of resources on all aspects of truth commissions and peacemaking.

Centre for the Study of Violence and Reconciliation
http://www.csvr.org.za
The website of this South African NGO contains some good studies on various aspects of truth commissions; click on Publications to access these materials.

International Internet Bibliography on Transitional Justice
http://userpage.zedat.fu-berlin.de/~theissen/biblio/index.htm
This page, prepared by Gunnar Theissen, offers an extensive list of resources on transitional justice, with a special focus on South Africa and Germany.

Do We Need a World Environmental Organization?

✔ **YES**

FRANK BIERMANN, "Green Global Governance: The Case for a World Environment Organisation," *New Economy* 9, no. 2 (June 2002): 82–86

✘ **NO**

ADIL NAJAM, "The Case against a New International Environmental Organization," *Global Governance* 9, no. 3 (July–September 2003): 367–84

In the last half of the twentieth century, international organizations began focusing the world's attention on global environmental issues. In 1968, the UN Economic and Social Council adopted a resolution calling for initiatives to address the "human environment." This led to the hosting of the Stockholm Conference on the Human Environment in 1972, the first global international conference of its size on environmental issues. Twenty years later, at the Earth Summit held in Rio de Janeiro, delegates and observers expressed disappointment in the limited progress that had been made in addressing many key environmental issues. As a further follow-up, a second Earth Summit, referred as the World Summit on Sustainable Development (WSSD), was held in Johannesburg, South Africa, in 2002.

One issue that permeated the discussions at each of these meetings was how the global community should organize to address environmental issues. The Stockholm Conference and the Rio Summit have been successful in helping to raise global awareness of environmental issues. However, the response of the international community has been largely ad hoc and fragmented in nature. The Stockholm Conference led to the creation of the United Nations Environment Programme (UNEP). Based in Nairobi, Kenya, the UNEP was intended to serve as the focal point of UN discussions on the environment and help coordinate the various environmental activities of the United Nations.

Yet, most of the more than 500 environment-related treaties that have been negotiated since Stockholm are either bilateral or regional. Many of these have their own secretariat to monitor the implementation of the agreement. In addition, more than a dozen international organizations have some environmental activities in their mandates. For example, the UN Food and Agriculture Organization (FAO) is involved in protecting depleting fisheries and promoting sustainable agriculture. The UN Development Programme (UNDP) has created a Sustainable Energy and Environment Division (SEED) to consolidate its environmental initiatives, including work on energy and atmosphere issues, natural

resources management, and management of desertification. The World Meteorological Organization co-sponsors the Intergovernmental Panel on Climate Change, which has had an important impact on debates about climate change. The World Health Organization promotes the development of guidelines regarding air and water pollution standards.

Despite these many developments, the United Nations Environment Programme has remained a relatively small player in the global environment picture. The UNEP's annual budget is less than U.S. $100 million. Its total spending since its inception is less than the annual budget of the UN Development Programme. The resources of the UNEP are minuscule in comparison to those of other international organizations, such as the World Bank or the International Monetary Fund. Its location in Nairobi, far from the agencies that it was intended to coordinate, has further contributed to the limited role that the UNEP can play in global environmental diplomacy.

These developments have led some to argue for a new approach to global environmental governance. This approach is based on the argument that existing institutions and agreements are inadequate for the environmental challenges facing the world today. The ad hoc, fragmented approach, which lacks any centralized, effective enforcement mechanism is a major impediment to effective environmental action. What is needed is a comprehensive restructuring at a global level that would put in place new institutional structures in order to overcome the current inertia on many environmental issues.

During the past two decades, a number of proposals for such a restructuring have been put forward. In 1989, the prime ministers of France, the Netherlands, and Norway proposed the creation of a new United Nations body that would have the power to both legislate on environmental regulations and impose punitive sanctions on any states failing to abide by them. While this proposal did not result in the adoption of a concrete plan, various governments, scholars, and activists have put forward similar schemes in the years that followed. Interest in some sort of global or world environmental organization increased following the establishment of the World Trade Organization (WTO). Some environmentalists hoped that the WTO could serve as a model for establishing a world environmental organization (WEO) with real enforcement powers. However, many states have been unwilling to support such a proposal, arguing that they were reluctant to surrender any of their national sovereignty in such a crucial area. At the same time, in looking at the experience of the WTO, many developing countries expressed fears that a WEO would provide one more mechanism for the interests of industrialized nations to intervene in the sovereignty of their countries.

Nevertheless, the topic of global environmental governance has remained on the international agenda. During its time in the presidency of the European Union, France actively campaigned in support of a world environmental organization. Global environmental governance was an important focus of the discussions and

negotiations leading up the WSSD in South Africa. The UNEP played a key role in facilitating these discussions.

In the following readings, we examine the debate concerning the form that future global environmental governance should take. In the first article, Frank Biermann, a leading exponent of reform, sets out the case for a world environmental organization. After reviewing the need for such a body, Biermann explains how such a world environmental organization could be structured. In particular, he looks at the World Heath Organization, the World Trade Organization, and the Security Council as possible models. In response, Adil Najam argues that too much attention has been paid to organizational restructuring as a solution to environmental problems. Making a distinction between "institutions" and "organizations," Najam argues that the international community should not get bogged down in organizational minutiae but should focus instead on how to improve the current institutional framework for environmental action. He argues that more effort should be made to support and enhance existing institutions such as the UNEP rather than creating a new, centralized environmental organization.

✔ YES
Green Global Governance: The Case for a World Environment Organisation
FRANK BIERMANN

The present discourse on 'greening' the global governance system expresses the frustration felt in many quarters with the state of international environmental policy. Many observers have pointed to the paradoxical situation that powerful international bodies oriented towards economic growth—such as the World Trade Organisation (WTO), the World Bank or the International Monetary Fund—are matched only by a modest UN sub-programme for environmental issues, the United Nations Environment Programme (UNEP). The imbalance is even more apparent when UNEP is compared to the plethora of influential UN specialised agencies in the fields of labour, shipping, agriculture, communication or culture.

As a mere programme, UNEP has no mandate to adopt treaties or any regulations upon its own initiative. It cannot avail itself of regular and predictable funding, and it is subordinated to the UN Economic and Social Council. UNEP's staff hardly exceeds 300 professionals—a trifle compared to its national counterparts such as the German Federal Environment Agency with 1,043 employees and the United States Environmental Protection Agency with a staff of 18,807.

AN IDEA WHOSE TIME HAS COME

This situation has led to a multitude of proposals to grant the environment what other policy areas have long had: a strong international agency with a sizeable mandate, significant resources and sufficient autonomy—a 'World Environment Organisation' (WEO). Ideas for such an international environmental organisation were first floated before the 1972 Stockholm Conference on the Human Environment, but the reform debate has only now gained momentum after a number of governments and senior experts have expressed their support.

Amongst the idea's supporters are the former heads of the World Trade Organisation (WTO), Renato Ruggiero, and of the UN Development Programme (UNDP), Gustave Speth, as well as the designated new WTO director, Supachai Panitchpakdi. Several academics and expert commissions have also advocated a world environment organisation. Likewise, a number of national governments have come forward with proposals for a new agency, among them Brazil, France, Germany, New Zealand, Singapore and South Africa.

The discourse has reached the early stages of intergovernmental negotiation. In February 2001, UNEP established an open-ended intergovernmental group of Ministers or their Representatives on International Environmental Governance to systematically assess the existing institutional weaknesses and define future needs

and reform options. The UN General Assembly has also created a bi-annual Global Ministerial Environment Forum to upgrade the governing council of UNEP, and an Environmental Management Group (EMG) to coordinate environmental activities within the UN system. The next major political event, which could spark new initiatives and decisions, will be the World Summit on Sustainable Development in September 2002 in Johannesburg.

The creation of several new international bodies over the past few decades—including the UN Industrial Development Organisation (UNIDO), the World Intellectual Property Organisation (WIPO), the WTO and the International Criminal Court—suggests that states are still prepared, in certain situations, to strengthen global governance by setting up organisations that can evolve into semi-autonomous actors. The launch of a WEO that would integrate existing programmes and bodies may not seem desirable or feasible for some, but given the support this idea has already mustered among some governments, it no longer seems entirely unrealistic.

THE NEED FOR A WORLD ENVIRONMENT ORGANISATION

Why do we need a new body? In short, there are three major shortcomings of the present state of global environmental governance that support the case for a WEO.

Co-ordination Deficit

First, there is a co-ordination deficit in the international governance architecture that results in substantial costs and sub-optimal policy outcomes.

When UNEP was set up in 1972, it was comparatively independent and had a clearly defined agenda. Since then, however, the increase in multilateral environmental regimes has led to a considerable fragmentation of the system. Norms and standards in each area of environmental policy are set up by distinct legislative bodies—the conferences of the parties to the environmental treaties—without much respect for repercussions and linkages with other policy fields. This situation is made worse by the organisational fragmentation of the various convention secretariats that have evolved into distinct medium-sized bureaucracies with strong centrifugal tendencies.

In addition, most specialised international organisations and bodies with some relation to environmental protection, such as the UN Food and Agriculture Organisation (FAO), have initiated environmental programmes of their own over the years. But there is not much co-ordination among these organisations and their policies.

By analogy with national politics, the current situation might come close to abolishing national environment ministries and transferring their programmes and policies to the ministries of agriculture, industry, energy, economics or trade—a policy proposal that would not find much support in most countries. An international body

with a clear strategy to ensure global sustainable development would seem to be an idea whose time has come. Just as within nation states, where environmental policy has been institutionally strengthened through the introduction of independent environmental ministries, global environmental policies could be made stronger through an independent WEO that helps to contain the special interests of individual programmes and organisations and to limit duplication, overlap and inconsistencies.

Disparate Processes

Second, a WEO would be in a better position to support regime-building processes, especially by initiating and preparing new treaties.

The International Labour Organisation (ILO) could serve as a model here. While the ILO has developed a comprehensive body of conventions that come close to a global labour code, global environmental policy remains far more disparate and cumbersome in its normsetting processes. It is also riddled with various disputes among UN specialised organisations regarding their competencies, with UNEP in its current setting being unable to adequately protect environmental interests. A WEO would also improve the overall implementation of international environmental standards, for example by a common comprehensive reporting system on the state of the environment and on the state of implementation in different countries as well as by stronger efforts in raising public awareness.

Ad Hoc Support for Developing Countries

Third, a WEO could assist in the build-up of environmental capacities in developing countries.

The demand for financial and technological North-South transfers in this area is certain to increase when climate, biodiversity and other global environmental policies are more intensively implemented in the developing world. Yet the current organisational setting for financial transfers is too ad hoc and too fragmented to meet the requirements of transparency, efficiency and participation of the parties involved.

A WEO could link the normative and technical aspects of financial and technological assistance and could overcome the fragmentation of the current system. The organisation could co-ordinate various financial mechanisms and administer the funds of sectoral regimes in trust, including the future clean development mechanism and emissions trading system under the Kyoto Protocol on climate change. These responsibilities do not need to imply the set-up of large new bureaucracies. Instead, a WEO could make use of the extensive expertise of the World Bank or the United Nations Development Programme (UNDP), including their national representations in developing countries.

A WEO might meet the interests especially of developing countries, because it would provide for a more efficient and more effective transfer of technology and financial assistance to the South. A more centralised body would also create a

more efficient negotiation system that would increase the opportunities of small developing nations to raise their voices in global fora. This would include the chance for developing countries to co-ordinate their positions better, which will strengthen their collective bargaining power. In addition, decision-making procedures based on North-South parity could ensure that the WEO would not evolve into a conduit of 'eco-colonialism' as many developing country actors suspect.

POSSIBLE MODELS FOR A WORLD ENVIRONMENT ORGANISATION

What might a WEO look like? What are the best organisational models for such a new body?

Model 1—The WHO

The least-demanding option would be to maintain the current system of decentralised, issue-specific international environmental regimes along with existing specialised organisations active in the environmental field, but to upgrade UNEP at the same time from a mere UN programme to a fully-fledged international organisation with its own budget and legal personality, increased financial and staff resources and enhanced legal powers. In this model, a WEO would function—as a co-operating, not co-ordinating unit—among the other international institutions and organisations whose member states might then be inclined to shift some environment-related competencies to the new WEO.

The elevation of UNEP to a WEO of this type could be modelled either on the World Health Organisation and the ILO—that is, independent international organisations with their own membership—or on the UN Conference on Trade and Development (UNCTAD), a UN internal body established by the UN General Assembly for debate and co-operation on international trade policy.

A WEO as a specialised UN agency could approve a set of regulations to bind all members, by qualified majority voting. Its general assembly could also adopt draft treaties negotiated by subcommittees under the auspices of the organisation. The ILO Constitution, for example, requires parties to process, within one year, all treaties adopted by the ILO General Conference to the respective national authorities (such as national parliaments) and to report back to the organisation on progress in the ratification process. This influence goes much beyond the powers of the UNEP Governing Council, which can initiate intergovernmental negotiations but cannot adopt legal instruments on its own.

Model 2—The WTO

A second, more far-reaching model would alter the current system of decentralised, issue-specific international environmental regimes by attempting a stronger integration within a common framework of a WEO. Again, UNEP would form the core of this new organisation, which would, however, be empowered to co-ordinate other

organisations and regimes. By large measure, a WEO of this type would follow the WTO model. This would require a basic Agreement on Establishing the World Environment Organisation, which would contain a number of general principles— maybe building on the 1992 Rio Declaration on Environment and Development—as well as coordinating rules that govern the organisation and its relationship with the issue-specific environmental regimes. Environmental regimes covered by the organisation could be divided into multilateral and plurilateral environmental agreements. As for multilateral agreements, ratification would be compulsory for any new member of a WEO, but plurilateral agreements would still leave members the option to remain outside. The multilateral agreements would thus form the global environmental law code under the WEO, with the existing conferences of the parties—say, to the climate convention—being transformed into subcommittees under the ministerial conference of the organisation.

This integration would enable the WEO to develop a common reporting system for all multilateral environmental agreements (e.g. an annual national report to the WEO); to develop a common dispute settlement system; to develop mutually agreed upon guidelines that may be followed—based on an interagency agreement—for the activities of the World Bank and the WTO dispute settlement system; and to develop a joint system of capacity-building for developing countries along with financial and technological transfers. The establishment of such an organisation would create a number of welfare gains by increasing the overall efficiency in the system. For example, the sometimes minuscule secretariats of multilateral environmental agreements would be integrated into the WEO.

Likewise, negotiations could be centralised geographically, which would especially benefit developing countries that are often not in a position to send diplomats with sufficient expertise to the various environmental treaty conferences around the world. A WEO at one specific seat—most likely in Africa—would allow especially smaller developing countries to build up specialised environmental embassies with a highly qualified staff able to follow various complicated negotiations. The same could be said for non-governmental organisations that could participate in global negotiations at lower cost.

Model 3—UN Security Council

A third theoretical option would be to envisage a world authority for the protection of the global environment or the global commons entrusted with enforcement powers against states that fail to implement certain standards (possibly agreed upon by majority vote). The model for this option would be the UN Security Council with its far-reaching powers under Chapter VII of the UN Charter. Such an organisation seems unlikely, however, to muster sufficient support among states in the next decades. Many proposals in this vein would necessitate an amendment of the UN Charter, which would require ratification by two-thirds of UN members including China, France, Russia, the United Kingdom and the United States.

Such far-reaching restrictions of national sovereignty seem difficult to envision. Current experiences with global environmental policy indicate that for the near future, any kind of hierarchic institutionalisation of the state system will encounter insurmountable resistance in both North and South. In practice, comprehensive, even punitive enforcement and sanctioning mechanisms administered by a WEO would be feasible only against relatively small developing countries that already perceive themselves as threatened by new forms of environmental 'colonialism'. A WEO with 'sharp teeth' thus appears counterproductive at the present. Most nations would stay away from the organisation or, conversely, demand weaker standards than those devised under current environmental regimes. The aim of environmental protection would hardly be served.

CONCLUSION

Creating a World Environment Organisation would pave the way for the elevation of environmental policies on the agenda of governments, international organisations and private actors. It could assist in developing the capacities for environmental policy in African, Asian and Latin American countries, and it would improve the institutional environment for the negotiation of new conventions and action programmes as well as for the implementation and co-ordination of existing ones. Establishing a cooperative body, akin to the World Health Organisation, should be our realistic short-term goal, keeping the option open for further international integration over the course of the century.

✗ NO
The Case against a New International Environmental Organization
ADIL NAJAM

> [World Organizations] are credited with an importance they do not possess;
> they are blamed for not doing what they are not given the means to do;
> faults that are often imaginary are ascribed to them, while their real faults
> go unnoticed; mythical explanations are invented to explain their ineffec-
> tiveness; and finally, there is very little recognition of the few significant
> results that they do achieve.[1]
>
> —Maurice Bertrand

The premise of this article is that the current debate about global environmental governance with its still dominant focus on establishing a superorganization for the environment represents a serious misdiagnosis of the issues, is unfair to the United Nations Environment Programme (UNEP), and is likely to distract attention from other more important challenges of global environmental governance.

This is not to suggest that there is no crisis of global environmental governance. The crisis, however, is one of governance, of which organizational structure is but one element and, in this case, a relatively small element at that.[2] By coopting the larger discussions on global environmental governance, the discourse on organizational tinkering—under whatever grandiose name such proposals are advertised—are distracting from the more important and immediate challenges of global environmental governance that we face as the Rio compact on environment and development crumbles around us. The thought that any of the competing plans for a World, or Global, Environmental Organization (WEO or GEO) that are being peddled might actually be taken seriously by the world's governments—as it sometimes seems possible—is even more disturbing.[3] Not only do they show very little promise of actually doing much good to the cause of improved global environmental governance, but some could actually do harm by distracting international attention from more pressing issues.

It is not the purpose of this article to reexamine, or critique, the details of different schemes for organizational restructuring. Critiques are available elsewhere in the larger literature.[4] Moreover, to do so would be to cede to the premise on which such proposals are based, and it is that very premise that needs to be questioned. It should be noted, however, that there is a certain variety in the proposals—ranging from Daniel C. Esty's GEO, which would focus only on global issues;[5] to Frank Biermann's WEO, which would also incorporate more local concerns;[6] to John Whalley and Ben Zissimos's desire to create a global bargaining-based entity;[7] to David L. Downie and Marc A. Levy's notion of a super-UNEP.[8] However, all such schemes share a strong

supposition that the problem of global environmental governance can largely be reduced to, and resolved by, playing around with the design of global environmental organizations. It is the fundamental flaws of this premise, and the dangers of taking it too seriously, that I focus on in this article.

THE DANGERS OF CONFUSING INSTITUTIONS AND ORGANIZATIONS

Although the WEO/GEO literature routinely refers to its enterprise in terms of *institutions*, it tends to use the term as if it were the plural of organization.[9] The distinction, of course, is not merely semantic; it is well established in the literature and is absolutely critical to this context.[10] Institutions, as Konrad von Moltke reminds us, are "social conventions or 'rules of the game,' in the sense that marriage is an institution, or property, markets, research, transparency or participation."[11] Therefore, institutions need not necessarily have a physical existence. Organizations, on the other hand, are much more circumscribed; according to Oran Young, they are "material entities, possessing physical locations (or seats), offices, personnel, equipment, and budgets."[12] The WEO/GEO discourse is clearly preoccupied with organizations and often ignores fundamental questions about *why* environmental degradation happens, or *why* global cooperation founders, or even *why* global environmental governance is a good idea.[13]

This confusion has the effect of trivializing global environmental governance. To place the spotlight on organizational tinkering and label it institution building is to imply that the institutional will—in terms of societal conventions and rules of the game—for global environmental cooperation already exists, and all that remains is to set up an appropriate organizational framework;[14] that global cooperation is a function of inappropriately designed organizations rather than a reflection of a fundamental absence of willingness on the part of states;[15] that the lack of implementation of international regimes stems from dispersed secretariats rather than the failure of these very same regimes "to target those actors that create the problems that regime arrangements set out to address";[16] that improved global environmental governance is a puzzle of administrative efficiency rather than a challenge of global justice.[17] None of the institutional challenges identified here are likely to be resolved by merely rearranging the organization of chairs on our planetary Titanic. Unless the core institutional questions are somehow first addressed, any new organization will fall prey to the exact same pathologies that confront existing arrangements.

The focus on organizational minutia is dangerous precisely because it distracts attention from the more real and immediate institutional challenges to global environmental governance. Two such challenges are of particular importance; both are treated only peripherally by GEO/WEO proponents, if at all.

The first relates to the near demise of the much-celebrated Rio compact on sustainable development—the supposed understanding between the developing

countries of the South and their more industrialized counterparts from the North that environment and development will be dealt with as an integrated complex of concerns within the context of current and future social justice and equity. The compact, to whatever extent it did exist, was always understood to be an expression of desire rather than reality—what Tariq Banuri has called "a triumph of hope over experience."[18] The hope, obviously misplaced, was that in time the compact would become real; that both North and South would somehow learn not simply to accept it but to operationalize it. That was not to be.[19] In fact, the optimism was shed rather quickly—the North soon became wary of the fuzziness of sustainable development while the South began to fear that the supposed definitional problems with the concept were being used as an excuse for maintaining the status quo.[20]

The implication of this for the future of global environmental governance is profound. To whatever extent the concept of sustainable development embodied the semblance of an *institutional* bargain on how environmental issues should be contextualized globally, that bargain is now functionally defunct—and so is the very tentative and always nebulous accord that might once have existed on why global environmental governance may be a good thing, for whom, and on what terms. It is not a surprise, then, that the immediate reaction of many in the South is to shirk at the first mention of a GEO or a WEO; or that the addition of development-related flourishes to these proposals fail to woo the South and are either rejected or ignored.[21] Frankly, the glib and lofty goals of finding "thoughtful ways to manage our ecological interdependence"[22] or of "[elevating] environmental policies on the agenda of governments, international organizations, and private actors"[23] or even of "equitably and effectively [managing] planet Earth"[24] are no longer credible, or necessarily appealing, to those who have lived through the last ten years of broken global promises on sustainable development. In essence, the very basis of global environmental cooperation—and thereby governance—that might have seemed to exist a decade ago, is under threat today. As Anil Agarwal, Sunita Narain, and Anju Sharma point out, no effective governance is possible under the prevailing conditions of deep distrust; organizational rearrangements might distract attention from deeper problems but are unlikely to solve them.[25] This sense of frustration by the developing countries was particularly apparent during the buildup to the 2002 World Summit on Sustainable Development (WSSD) in Johannesburg. Although the issue of global environmental governance was on the table during the preparatory phase, developing countries saw little value in discussions that remained focused on organizational redesign rather than on institutional restructuring.

The second critical challenge to the cause of improved global environmental governance pertains not to the exclusion of the concerns of Southern governments from the emerging "New Global Environmental Order" but to the meaningful inclusion of civil society concerns, especially those of the South.[26] This is

important because the very nature of the environmental problématique is different from many other international concerns (for example, defense and security) in that a greater proportion of key environmental decisions lie beyond the direct ability or authority of states. This underscores the need for a society-centric view of global environmental governance—one that includes state organs but goes beyond them.[27] This, of course, stands in contradiction to the predominantly state-centered view of global governance in the organizationally inclined literature. This is not to suggest that interstate organizations are unimportant. Far from it, they will have to be an integral—probably a central—component of improved global environmental governance. From an institutional perspective, however, the quality of such governance will be determined by how interstate organizations connect with emerging global public policy networks (GPPNs), of which civil society organizations are a key part.[28] In ignoring, downplaying, or at the very least distracting from the centrality of such integration, the organizational debate fails to rise to the challenge of what could have been a very timely discourse on meaningful institutional reform.

There are, however, other streams of scholarship on global governance that recognize that the key challenge is to create institutions that can integrate the multitude of voices that now feel alienated from the official chatter on global environmental issues. For example, those who talk in terms of GPPNs see better governance emanating not just from decisions taken at centralized interstate organizations or via coordinated legal frameworks, but also through networks of dispersed decision points spread out globally, across all sectors: state, market, and civil.[29] This leads one to a very different set of organizational questions—with the emphasis shifting from a search for better management as measured by administrative efficiency to better networking as gauged by broad-based legitimacy.[30]

The centrality that has been assumed by the GEO/WEO debate within the global environmental discourse translates to a distraction from these other pressing issues. It is not only that new organizational maneuvering is likely to be insufficient to revive the spirit of the Rio compact or to integrate with civil society networks; it is also that any new organizational arrangement is likely to remain as stymied as the current arrangement until these other issues of global environmental governance are tackled first.

NEW LAMPS FOR OLD

Ever since *Aladdin and the Magic Lamp*,[31] those of us who come from what used to be called the Orient have learned to be wary of anyone offering "new lamps for old!" Therefore, when someone offers to replace existing organizational arrangements with a new and improved architecture, one instinctively asks, "What is it that is so bad about the old or so different about the new?" In the case of global environmental organizations, the answer is, "Not much!"

Proponents of organizational rearrangement invariably begin with the standard scare tactics—global ecological systems are under growing threat. While this assessment is correct, the jump between acknowledging the ecological crisis and pointing to organizational inefficiency as the culprit is a rather wide one. Beyond assertion, there is no attempt to establish causality, or even correlation, between the continuing ecological crisis and the nature of the existing organizational arrangements. Two questions need to be asked. First, would things have been worse had the existing system *not* been in place? I argue later that the answer is that certainly they would have been worse. Second, could things be better under an alternative system?

Proponents of large-scale organizational rearrangement obviously believe that things would, in fact, be improved if the organizational architecture were rearranged. They accuse the existing arrangements of a coordination deficit, deficient authority, and insufficient legitimacy and they promise that setting up a new organization would streamline organizational coordination, accelerate financial and technology transfers, and improve the implementation and development of international environmental law.[32] What is not made clear, however, is why the pathologies that inflict the existing arrangements would simply not be transferred to any new arrangement? If coordination is the real roadblock to better environmental performance, then why should one believe that a new organization could achieve it better than UNEP? After all, UNEP's very raison d'être has been to coordinate and catalyze. Why should one assume that rich nations that have been so stingy in meeting their global fiscal responsibilities in the past—in environmental as well as other arenas—will suddenly turn generous for a new organization? If fragmentation is what makes the current arrangements unwieldy, could that not be addressed within the framework of Section 38.22(h) of Agenda 21, which called for the co-location of various treaty secretariats under the UNEP umbrella? What in the new system would make Northern governments—who have consistently reneged on their international commitments regarding financial and technology transfer—suddenly reverse this trend? In short, the most interesting questions are never asked, and certainly not answered.

The problems that these proposals seek to solve through reorganization are not organizational problems at all. If UNEP has been denied authority and resources, it is because the nation-states wish to deny it (and any successor superorganization) authority and resources. They have certainly never demonstrated the willingness to provide UNEP with the resources that would be required to do what they claim it ought to do. The coordination deficit is not something that crept in; it was something that was painstakingly designed into the system—because the countries that are most responsible for the global ecological crisis have never demonstrated the intention of owning that responsibility and because intense turf battles between UN agencies forced an unmanageable coordination mandate upon UNEP.[33] The coordination deficit is indeed real, but it is not organizational. It is

institutional and is unlikely to go away through cosmetic architectural renovations. With due apology for sounding cynical, the point to be made is that the global environmental governance crisis at hand is not about organizational minutia; it is about the now glaring lack of willingness to embrace global environmental cooperation. This lack of will has been evident in a variety of recent environmental negotiations, most notably those related to climate change and WSSD.

The problems that the proponents of organizational rearrangement identify are, for the most part, real problems. The goals they identify for the rearranged system are laudable goals. One has no qualms about either. The issue is with how the dots are connected—or, in this case, not connected. The proposals inspire no confidence that the problems confronted by the current setup will not simply transfer to a new setup, or that new arrangements would be any more likely to succeed where the current arrangements have failed. This seems to be one more incidence of "hope triumphing over experience."[34]

VIVA LA UNEP!

Although not always intentional, the immediate casualty of the misdiagnosis on the part of WEO/GEO proponents is the reputation of the UNEP. Even though some view UNEP as the central core of the ultimate superstructure for global environmental governance—and some within UNEP may well find this notion appealing—the fact is that, implicitly or explicitly, UNEP is portrayed as being at the root of the problem. After all, when the existing organizational structure is accused of being inefficient, ineffective, and insufficiently legitimate, then UNEP – which is the centerpiece of that structure—must also stand accused, even if indirectly. Indeed, one should concede that like any other UN agency, UNEP has much that can be improved. However, the stings—implied or explicit—showered on it either ignore or underplay its very significant achievements.

The tragedy is not just that such proposals are based on the assumption that the much-trumpeted weakness of UNEP lies at the heart of the crisis of global environmental governance. Nor is it just that even the critics of such schemes nearly never question this assumption. The real tragedy is that UNEP's own leadership seems to have bought into this assumption. The rampage of exaggerated external criticism and unwarranted self-doubt cannot bode well for UNEP or for the morale of its staff. Indeed, in this article I argue that while UNEP is certainly not the perfect agency, and while there is much that can and should be improved, it is not the weakling or underachiever that it is portrayed as. Arguably, it has performed relatively well in comparison to other agencies of the UN family both in terms of performance and legitimacy, and it has every right to stand proud of its remarkable achievements, which came despite all the limitations that its critics are so fond of enumerating.

Similar to much of what is being proposed in the current round, UNEP was originally conceived as the "environmental conscience of the UN system" and was charged to act as the "focal point for environmental action within the United Nations system."[35] In defining this mandate of coordination, it was charged with "perhaps one of the most difficult jobs in the entire UN system."[36] It has been hinted that UNEP may have been designed for failure, or at least for something less than success.[37] As John McCormick points out, "It had severe obstacles placed in its path from the outset. It had too little money, too few staff, and too much to do, it had the thankless task of coordinating the work of other UN agencies against a background of interagency jealousy and suspicion, and national governments were unwilling to grant UNEP significant powers."[38] Given the sprawling and bickering nature of the UN machinery, its own lack of executive status, and the dismal resources at its command, "UNEP could no more be expected to 'coordinate' the system-wide activities of the UN than could a medieval monarch 'coordinate' his feudal barons."[39] It should therefore be no surprise that UNEP has not been able to fulfill what Ken Conca has called "its hopeless mandate as system-wide coordinator on environmental matters."[40]

Yet, while there is agreement that UNEP has not been allowed to fulfill its coordination mandate,[41] it is also argued that it "can be credited with having achieved more than it was in reality empowered to do."[42] Those who have studied it in depth agree that it is "generally well-regarded,"[43] "relatively effective,"[44] and, given its meager resources and authority, it "has been a remarkable success."[45] While this is not the place to evaluate UNEP's achievements, I list here a sampling of reasons why it should be considered a successful international organization.

MAKING THE ENVIRONMENT A GLOBAL ISSUE

The single most important, and totally unappreciated, achievement of UNEP is its role in converting the environment into a global issue. It is easy to forget the hostility with which the developing countries had greeted the Stockholm conference of 1972 and the subsequent establishment of UNEP.[46] The placement of UNEP in Nairobi was not just a symbolic act; it was a strategic necessity without which the developing countries might never have accepted the creation of an environmental organ.[47] The fact that this became the first, and only, UN organ to be based anywhere in the developing world galvanized the South both in the process of getting it to locate to Nairobi and in its early and most difficult years: the 1970s into the mid-1980s.[48] Although they stood with UNEP largely out of a sense of Southern solidarity, the developing countries began buying into parts of the environmental agenda and, more important, demanding that the agenda be modified to incorporate their realities. Indeed, the call to set up the World Commission on Environment and Development (WCED) came out of a discussion at the UNEP

Governing Council. While WCED might have come up with the term *sustainable development*, the stage for it had already been set by UNEP and its Governing Council at its tenth anniversary meeting in 1982.

Advancing the Global Environmental Agenda

Those who gathered in Stockholm in 1972 could scarcely have imagined the global environmental agenda becoming as advanced and as prominent in international affairs as it is today. UNEP played a significant part in this transformation.[49] Through its various activities, and especially training programs, it helped create an environmental constituency within and outside governments that has been at the forefront of moving this agenda forward. It played a pivotal role in putting desertification, ozone depletion, and organic pollutants on the global agenda.[50] Even for issues like climate change, biodiversity, and deforestation, UNEP's contribution has been more important than it is often given credit for.

International Environmental Law

International environmental law has probably been the single fastest growing subfield of international law; and UNEP has to be among the most active and productive UN agencies in terms of advancing international law. This is not an idle statement. Apart from the agenda-setting role it played on issues such as desertification, biodiversity, and climate change, it has been the principal negotiation manager for complex global regimes on ozone depletion, trade in endangered species, trade in hazardous wastes, persistent organic pollutants, regional seas, etc. For an organization as young and as resource strapped as UNEP, this is a remarkable achievement indeed. UNEP-managed treaty negotiations—such as those on ozone-depleting substances and, more recently, on persistent organic pollutants—are generally regarded to have been among the most efficient and successful global environmental negotiations.[51]

Legitimacy

By routinely suggesting that a new organizational architecture would lend legitimacy to global environmental governance, the proponents of GEO/WEO seem to imply that UNEP has less than sufficient legitimacy as an international organization. If they were not earnest, it would be funny that some proponents of a super-organization want to scrap UNEP and replace it with something that might look more like the World Trade Organization (WTO). Massive public demonstrations from Seattle to Prague and feelings of distrust and apprehension are what come to mind when one thinks of the WTO or the World Bank (another organization that is sometimes talked about as the model to follow). UNEP, on the other hand, does not have to place barriers or bring out riot police at its annual meetings and has a tradition of good relations with civil society. Indeed, in terms of general

public legitimacy and honest efforts to involve civil society in its orbit, UNEP has fared much better than most international organizations, even though there remains room for improvement.[52]

In summary, while UNEP has its share of problems, they relate not to its mandate as much as to the resources it has been provided. The fact that some of its critics have never forgiven it for being located in a developing country does not help either. It is unfortunate that its leadership has sometimes been defensive about both its achievements and its potential, instead of building upon its rather rich legacy of performance. It is not a perfect organization, but it has been a rather good one. It would be sad if, in our zeal for organizational rearrangement, we made the allegedly perfect the enemy of the demonstrably good.

TOWARD BETTER GLOBAL ENVIRONMENTAL GOVERNANCE

It should be obvious that I am not persuaded by the need for an environmental superorganization. However, an argument against new organizational superstructures should not be confused with an argument for organizational inertia. All organizations should strive for improvement, and global environmental organizations—including UNEP—are no exception. There are a number of elements within the various proposals that do make sense—not as arguments for organizational overhaul, but as elements of an agenda to improve the existing organizational setup. Moreover, change that happens within the existing system is likely to be substantively less disruptive and politically more feasible. This final section highlights five key elements of a potential agenda for organizational improvement that can be pursued within the confines of the existing structures and would begin addressing the larger institutional challenges of global environmental governance discussed earlier.[53] It should be noted, however, that for all the reasons already discussed, some of these ideas are not going to be easy to implement. Yet, to the extent they can be implemented, they are likely to be easier to implement within UNEP's existing structure than within a new supraorganization of the GEO/WEO variety.

Enabling UNEP to Fulfill Its Mandate

There is no need to change UNEP's mandate. There is, however, an urgent need to provide it with the resources, staff, and authority it needs to fulfill its mandate. UNEP's shareholders—that is, the member states—need to invest in UNEP in proportion to the responsibilities they demand of it. One step in this direction might be to convert UNEP into a specialized agency (as opposed to a program) with the concomitant ability to raise and decide its own budget. Greater autonomy may not in itself be sufficient to translate to greater resources, but it could allow UNEP to be more innovative and even assertive in its resource mobilization strategies. However, given the political wrangling this would require, the UN General Assembly might consider maintaining UNEP's program status but providing it

with greater autonomy in budgetary matters to ensure a sufficient and consistent resource base.

Indeed, UNEP was originally modeled on the United Nations Development Programme (UNDP) and should aspire to fulfill that original intent. While this would require more assertive leadership from UNEP, it would also obviously require the UN secretary-general and member states to give UNEP the budgetary and operational prominence that it has so often been promised, thereby giving it the respect it deserves. One step could be to invest in making its flagship *Global Environmental Outlook Reports* an environmental equivalent to the World Bank's *World Development Reports*, or UNDP's *Human Development Reports*.

Realizing Sustainable Development

Over the years, many have become quite fond of arguing that the problem with sustainable development is that it is very difficult to define. While defining it in precise terms is certainly not easy, it is also not entirely necessary. The real problem with sustainable development is that the governments of the world lack the commitment to realize it. The main culprit in this regard is governments in the North that have consistently reneged on their financial commitments. However, the governments of the South are also to blame for viewing sustainable development simply as an excuse to continue with development as usual without any regard to its environmental consequences.

From an institutional perspective, realizing sustainable development would imply streamlining mechanisms for financing sustainable development and monitoring and validating progress. Because of its problems of transparency and performance, many developing countries consider that the Global Environmental Facility (GEF) lacks legitimacy.[54] Other funding mechanisms are even more strapped for cash. There is a need to reconsider the operation of GEF, broaden the scope of activities that it can finance, replenish it to higher levels, and possibly place its management more firmly within UNEP, which enjoys more credibility with developing countries and routinely deals with issues of environment and sustainable development as its primary focus. The existing trilateral management structure involving UNEP, UNDP, and the World Bank can, in fact, be maintained while UNEP is given the role of lead agency in its actual management. Doing so would also allow UNEP to better fulfill its existing mandate.

Managing MEA Proliferation

Over the last decade, the great increase in negotiations pertaining to the new or existing multilateral environmental agreements (MEAs) has caused a serious problem of MEA proliferation and attendant pathologies of negotiation fatigue, particularly among developing country delegates.[55] This has placed an immense burden on most developing countries, which simply do not have the resources to keep up with the frantic pace of increasingly complex negotiations. Moreover, the

frenzy to complete negotiation as quickly as possible has left behind a legacy of less-than-perfect agreements or resulted in too little attention being paid to questions of implementation.[56]

How do these various MEAs fit together? A certain clustering of independently negotiated treaties has begun to emerge organically as part of the evolution of international environmental law; it is timely to convert this into a deliberate schema.[57] Von Moltke, in particular, has outlined a useful list of possibilities for MEA clustering.[58] A co-location of MEA secretariats—which some WEO proponents also suggest—seems an equally pragmatic idea even though it is likely that some governments and secretariat staff might resist it. Yet it is an idea worth pursuing because it could provide efficiency gains, increase cross-treaty communication, and discourage MEA fiefdoms. Overlapping or joint meetings of related MEAs, possibly in permanent locations, would serve to ease the pressures on participating delegates and encourage more continuity in representation.

UNEP, with its good record of MEA management—both in terms of overseeing complex negotiations and of hosting MEA secretariats—again emerges as the best-suited candidate for this task. Hence, not only would this not require a new super-organization, it would also not require a major legal restructuring of UNEP's mandate. In fact, the task was already awarded to UNEP a decade ago by Agenda 21, which called upon UNEP to concentrate on (among other things) the "further development of international environmental law, in particular conventions and guidelines, promotion of its implementation, and coordinating functions arising from an increasing number of international legal agreements, inter alia, the functioning of the secretariats of the Conventions . . . including possible co-location of secretariats established in the future."[59]

Coordination, Yes; Centralization, No

Echoing UNEP's original charter, Agenda 21 had also defined UNEP as the "principal body within the United Nations system in the field of environment" (Section 38.23). However, for good reason, the UNEP was never intended to be the only UN body with relevance to the environment. Centralization makes little conceptual sense for issues related to the environment and even less for sustainable development. The fabric of environmental concerns, and even more of sustainable development concerns, is a multivariate web of interlinked issues that do not have a clear center and are unlikely to respond to centralized policymaking. A reading of Agenda 21, or of the report of the World Commission on Environment and Development before it, would make it quite clear that if there is any body that has the authority to centrally devise all sustainable development policy—or to even coordinate all sustainable development policy—that body would be the United Nations as a whole rather than any subcomponent of it. Could one imagine creating a central entity that is responsible for all issues related to sustainable development, ranging from biodiversity to international debt, from climate change to education, from

poverty alleviation to pollution? Should one imagine such a centralized entity, even if one could?

Given the fundamentally interlinked and cross-sectoral nature of these issues, UNEP's original mandate as a catalyst and coordinator was, in retrospect, well conceived. However, as already noted, UNEP has been less than successful in realizing its coordination mandate. At the same time, the coordination mandate is now spread out around the system: in addition to the Commission on Sustainable Development (CSD), the recently created Environmental Management Group (EMG) and the Global Ministerial Environment Forum (GMEF) both seem to have some elements of the coordination function in their mandates. This dilution of UNEP's coordination responsibility may not be a bad thing. Not only is coordination a thankless job but, as Mark Imber reminds us, "the primary responsibility for coordination rests with governments."[60] The agency heads that make up EMG and the senior government delegates that make up the CSD and GMEF seem far better positioned for UN-wide coordination than UNEP's secretariat staff could ever be expected to. Having multiple forums for coordination may also not be bad—there is enough cross-participation within these groups to keep duplication or contradiction manageable, while multiple forums could actually have the effect of reinforcing each other on the need for coordination.

Civilizing Global Environmental Governance

Providing the space and opportunity for meaningful participation of civil society networks in global environmental governance may well be the most important challenge from the institutional as well as the organizational standpoint.[61] Within the realm of global public policy, the environment is an issue on which civil society has been particularly active and influential.[62] However, there is a growing sense that international organizations are becoming increasingly introverted. Especially in the aftermath of recurrent civil protests arising from a deeply felt distrust of globalization—and of international organizations as the agents of globalization—both UNEP and CSD need to invest more attention to linking with civil society. In a recent report, Turiq Banuri and Erika Spanger-Siegfried lay out a detailed set of recommendations for establishing deeper linkages with civil society actors, particularly GPPNs, for leveraging the opportunities for policy innovation and cross-sectoral synergies that this would offer.[63] There is also the need to begin viewing civil society not just as stakeholders in but as motors of global environmental governance.[64] Following the tradition of human rights regimes, civil society networks could potentially become the real drivers of MEA implementation. Indeed, for political as well as logistic reasons, they may be more likely to play that role than governments or intergovernmental agencies.[65]

In conclusion, I have argued that not only is there no need for a new international environmental organization, but the discussions on this subject tend to distract attention from the actual reforms in the existing organizations that are

needed. I outlined five elements of such an organizational reform agenda but recognize that these must be embedded in the larger challenge of institutional reform. In practical terms, this means that the key change has to come not in the structural details of existing or new organizations but in the support and political will that national governments are willing to invest in these organizations.

NOTES

1. Maurice Bertrand, *The Third Generation World Organization* (Dordrecht: Martinus Nijhoff, 1989).

2. For a particularly insightful discussion of global governance, see Oran R. Young, "Global Governance: Toward a Theory of Decentralized World Order," in Oran R. Young, ed., *Global Governance: Drawing Insights from the Environmental Experience* (Cambridge: MIT Press, 1997), pp. 273–299.

3. There have been a number of different proposals floating around. See, for example, Ford C. Runge, Francois Ortalo-Magne, and Philip Van de Kamp, *Freer Trade, Protected Environment: Balancing Trade Liberalization and Environmental Interests* (New York: Council on Foreign Relations Press, 1994); Daniel C. Esty, "The Case for a Global Environmental Organization," in Peter B. Kenen, ed., *Managing the World Economy: Fifty Years After Bretton Woods* (Washington, D.C.: Institute for International Economics, 1994), pp. 287–309; Steve Charnovitz, "Improving Environmental and Trade Governance," *International Environmental Affairs* 7, no. 1 (1995): 59–91; Frank Biermann, "The Case for a World Environmental Organization," *Environment* 42, no. 9 (2000): 22–31; David L. Downie and Marc A. Levy, "The UN Environment Programme at a Turning Point: Options for Change," in Pamela S. Chasek, ed., *The Global Environment in the Twenty-First Century: Prospects for International Cooperation* (Tokyo: United Nations University Press, 2000), pp. 355–377; and John Whalley and Ben Zissimos, "What Could a World Environmental Organization Do?" *Global Environmental Politics* 1, no. 1 (2001): 29–34.

4. See Anil Agarwal, Sunita Narain, and Anju Sharma, *Green Politics* (New Delhi: Centre for Science and Environment, 1999); Calestous Juma, "The Perils of Centralizing Global Environmental Governance," *Environment Matters: Annual Review* (July 1999–June 2000), (Washington, D.C.: World Bank, 2000), pp. 13–15; Calestous Juma, "Stunning Green Progress," *Financial Times*, 6 July 2000; Konrad Von Moltke, "The Organization of the Impossible," *Global Environmental Politics* 1, no. 1 (2000): 23–28; Peter Newell, "New Environmental Architectures and the Search for Effectiveness," *Global Environmental Politics* 1, no. 1 (2001): 35–44. For a rebuttal of such critiques, see Frank Biermann, "The Emerging Debate on the Need for a World Environmental Organization," *Global Environmental Politics* 1, no. 1 (2001): 45–55.

5. Daniel C. Esty, "Stepping Up to the Global Environmental Challenge," *Fordham Environmental Law Journal* 8, no. 1 (1996): 103–113.

6. Biermann, "The Case for a World Environmental Organization."

7. Whalley and Zissimos, "What Could a World Environmental Organization Do?"

8. Downie and Levy, "The UN Environment Programme at a Turning Point."

9. See, as just one example, Frank Biermann, "Reform of International Environmental Institutions: Would a World Environment Organization Benefit the South?" paper

presented at the annual meeting of the International Studies Association, New Orleans, March 2002.

10. See Oran R. Young, *International Governance: Protecting the Environment in a Stateless Society* (Ithaca: Cornell University Press, 1994).

11. Konrad Von Moltke, *Whither MEAs? The Role of International Environmental Management in the Trade and Environment Agenda* (Winnipeg: International Institute for Sustainable Development, 2001), p. 11.

12. Oran R. Young, *International Cooperation: Building Regimes for Natural Resources and the Environment* (Ithaca: Cornell University Press, 1989), p. 32.

13. Newell, "New Environmental Architectures."

14. See Von Moltke, *Whither MEAs?*

15. See Juma, "Stunning Green Progress."

16. Newell, "New Environmental Architectures," p. 40.

17. Agarwal, Narain, and Sharma, *Green Politics.*

18. Tariq Banuri, "Envisioning Sustainable Development," unpublished note (Boston: Stockholm Environmental Institute, 2001). Based on an original quotation from Samuel Johnson.

19. To get a sampling of views on what transpired, and why, see Tariq Banuri, *Noah's Ark or Jesus's Cross?* Working Paper WP/UNCED/1992/I (Islamabad: Sustainable Development Policy Institute, 1992); Adil Najam, "An Environmental Negotiation Strategy for the South," *International Environmental Affairs* 7, no. 3 (1995): 249–287; Richard Sandbrook, "UNGASS Has Run Out of Steam," *International Affairs* 73, no. 4 (1997): 641–654; Agarwal, Narain, and Sharma, *Green Politics.*

20. Adil Najam, "From Rio to Johannesburg: The State of Sustainable Development," paper presented at the annual meeting of the International Studies Association, New Orleans, March 2002.

21. See Agarwal, Narain, and Sharma, *Green Politics*; Juma, "Stunning Green Progress"; and Newell, "New Environmental Architectures."

22. Daniel C. Esty, "The Value of Creating a Global Environmental Organization," in *Environment Matters: Annual Review* (July 1999–June 2000), (Washington, D.C.: World Bank, 2000), pp. 13–14.

23. Biermann, "The Case for a World Environmental Organization," p. 29.

24. Biermann, "Reform of International Environmental Institutions," p. 16.

25. Agarwal, Narain, and Sharma, *Green Politics*, p. 372.

26. Ibid.

27. Tariq Banuri and Erika Spanger-Siegfried, *UNEP and Civil Society: Recommendations for a Coherent Framework of Engagement* (Boston: Stockholm Environmental Institute, 2000).

28. Wolfgang H. Reinicke, *Global Public Policy: Governing Without Government?* (Washington, D.C.: Brookings Institution, 1998).

29. See Wolfgang H. Reinicke and Francis M. Deng, *Critical Choices: The United Nations, Networks and the Future of Global Governance* (Ottawa: International Development Research Centre, 2000).

30. Banuri and Spanger-Siegfried, *UNEP and Civil Society*.

31. In this famous children's tale—one of the original Arabian Nights and the subject of a Disney animation film—the villain is able to steal the magic lamp from Aladdin's unsuspecting wife by making her an offer she cannot refuse: promising to replace old lamps for new.

32. Esty, "Stepping Up to the Global Environmental Challenge"; Biermann, "The Case for a World Environmental Organization."

33. Branislav Gosovic, *The Quest for Worm Environmental Cooperation: The Case of the UN Global Environment Monitoring System* (London: Routledge, 1992).

34. To again misquote Banuri ("Envisioning Sustainable Development") misquoting Mark Twain.

35. UN General Assembly, Res. 2997 (XXVII), adopted December 1972.

36. Richard Sandbrook, "The UK's Overseas Environmental Policy," in Brian D.G. Johnson, ed., *The Conservation and Development Programme for the UK: A Response to the World Conservation Strategy* (London: Kogan Page, 1983), p. 388.

37. Konrad Von Moltke, "Why UNEP Matters," *Green Globe Yearbook of International Cooperation on Environment and Development, 1996* (Oxford: Oxford University Press, 1996), pp. 55–64.

38. John McCormick, *The Global Environmental Movement* (New York: John Wiley, 1995), p. 152.

39. Mark Imber, *Environment, Security and UN Reform* (London: St. Martin's Press, 1994), p. 83.

40. Ken Conca, "Greening the UN: Environmental Organizations and the UN System," in Thomas G. Weiss and Leon Gordenker, eds., *NGOs, the UN, and Global Governance* (Boulder: Lynne Rienner, 1996), p. 108.

41. Indeed, no UN agency (including the UNDP or even the secretary-general's Secretariat) has been allowed to meaningfully fulfill the coordination function; moreover, there is no indication that any agency (current or future) will be allowed such a liberty.

42. McCormick, *The Global Environmental Movement*, p. 153.

43. Mark Imber, "Too Many Cooks? The Post-Rio Reform of the United Nations," *International Affairs* 69, no. 1 (1993): 56.

44. Conca, "Greening the UN," p. 112.

45. Von Moltke, "Why UNEP Matters," p. 58.

46. *Development and Environment: Report and Working Papers of Experts Convened by the Secretary-General of the United Nations Conference on the Human Environment*, held at Founex, Switzerland, June 1971 (Paris: Mouton, 1972).

47. Wade Rowland, *The Plot to Save the World* (Toronto: Clarke, Irwin, 1973).

48. See, especially, Gosovic, *The Quest for World Environmental Cooperation*. Note that this period also marks the height of Southern solidarity and the movement for a New International Economic Order (NIEO). During this period, the symbolism of UNEP being in Nairobi was of significant importance to the developing countries. This resulted in their very visibly and disproportionately supporting an organization that they had originally resented.

49. Lynton K. Caldwell, *International Environmental Policy: Emergence and Dimensions*, 3d ed. (Durham: Duke University Press, 1996).

50. Downie and Levy, "The UN Environment Programme at a Turning Point."

51. Richard Benedick, *Ozone Diplomacy: New Directions in Safeguarding the Planet* (Cambridge: Harvard University Press); Mustafa K. Tolba, *Global Environmental Diplomacy: Negotiating Environmental Agreements for the World, 1973–1992* (Cambridge: MIT Press).

52. Banuri and Spanger-Siegfried, *UNEP and Civil Society*.

53. Some of these ideas are informed by the author's participation at the "Expert Consultation on International Environmental Governance," organized by UNEP in Cambridge, England, on 28–29 May 2001. A report of the meeting is available online at www.unep.org/IEG/docs/.

54. Agarwal, Narain, and Sharma, *Green Politics*.

55. Adil Najam, "The Case for a Law of the Atmosphere," *Atmospheric Environment* 34, no. 23 (2000): 4047–049.

56. Adil Najam and Ambuj Sagar, "Avoiding a COP-out: Moving Towards Systematic Decision-Making Under the Climate Convention," *Climatic Change* 39, no. 4 (1998); Adil Najam, "Developing Countries and the Desertification Convention: Portrait of a Tortured Relationship," presented at the annual meeting of the International Studies Association, New Orleans, March 2002.

57. Najam, "The Case for a Law of the Atmosphere."

58. Von Moltke, "The Organization of the Impossible."

59. Agenda 21, Section 38.22[h].

60. Imber, "Too Many Cooks?" p. 66.

61. Banuri and Spanger-Siegfried, *UNEP and Civil Society*.

62. Leon Gordenker and Thomas G. Weiss, "NGO Participation in International Policy Processes," *Third World Quarterly* 16, no. 3 (1995): 543–555; Adil Najam, "Citizen Organizations as Policy Entrepreneurs," in David Lewis, ed., *International Perspectives on Voluntary Action: Reshaping the Third Sector* (London: Earthscan, 1999), pp. 142–181.

63. Banuri and Spanger-Siegfried, *UNEP and Civil Society*.

64. Tariq Banuri and Adil Najam, *Civic Entrepreneurship: Civil Society Perspectives on Sustainable Development*, vol. 1 (Islamabad: Gandhara Academy Press).

65. Adil Najam, "The Four C's of Third Sector-Government Relations: Cooperation, Confrontation, Complementarity, and Co-optation," *Nonprofit Management and Leadership* 10, no. 4 (2000): 375–396.

POSTSCRIPT

In his critique of arguments for a world environmental organization, Najam insists that attention should be focused on institutions rather than organizations. Preoccupation with creating new, more centralized organizational structures may not lead to significant improvements in the handling of environmental issues. Some participants in this debate seem to have been influenced by such arguments and have thus sought to find a different, "third way" of approaching this issue.

Daniel Esty and Maria Ivanova have written extensively on environmental issues and have been strong advocates of a new global environmental organization. Recently, however, they have modified their position, arguing for the creation of a "Global Environmental Mechanism" instead. While they argue that there is indeed a need for better coordinated "collective action" to address environmental issues, they no longer believe that this can be achieved through the creation of new organizations in the style of traditional international bureaucracies. Instead, they advocate using new communications technologies to build networks of cooperation between existing agencies. They suggest that rather than replacing organizations such as the UNEP, a Global Environmental Mechanism could act as a coordinating hub for facilitating cooperation, information sharing, and negotiation. Their new argument can be found in an article entitled "Revitalizing Global Environmental Governance: A Function-Driven Approach," available at http://environment.yale.edu/documents/downloads/a-g/esty-ivanova.pdf.

Suggested Additional Readings

Charnovitz, S. "Improving Environmental and Trade Governance." *International Environmental Affairs* 7, no. 1 (Winter 1995): 59–91.

Conca, Ken. "Greening the UN: Environmental Organisations and the UN System." In Thomas G. Weiss and Leon Gordenker (eds.), *NGOs, the UN, and Global Governance.* Boulder: Lynne Rienner, 1996: 103–19.

Doyle, W. Michael, and Rachel Massey. "Intergovernmental Organizations and the Environment: Introduction." In Pamela S. Chasek (ed.), *The Global Environment in the Twenty-First Century.* New York: United Nations University Press, 2000: 411–26.

Esty, D.C. "The Case for a Global Environmental Organization." In P.B. Kenen (ed.), *Managing the World Economy: Fifty Years after Bretton Woods.* Washington, D.C.: Institute for International Economics, 1994: 287–309.

Esty, Daniel, and Maria H. Ivanova, eds. *Global Environmental Governance: Options & Opportunities.* New Haven, Conn.: Yale School of Forestry & Environmental Studies, 2002. Available at http://environment.yale.edu/publication-series/law_and_policy/782/global_environmental_governance/

Haas, P.M., R.O. Keohane, and M.A. Levy (eds.). *Institutions for the Earth: Sources of Effective International Environmental Protection.* Cambridge, Mass.: MIT Press, 1993.

Imber, Mark. "Too Many Cooks? The Post-Rio Reform of the United Nations." *International Affairs* 69, no. 1 (January 1993): 55-70.

Juma, Calestous. "The Perils of Centralizing Global Environmental Governance." *Environment Matters: Annual Review* (World Bank) (July 1999-June 2000): 13-15.

United Nations University. *International Environmental Governance. The Question of Reform: Key Issues and Proposals. Preliminary Findings.* Tokyo: United Nations University, Institute for Advanced Studies, 2002. Available at http://www.ias.unu.edu.

von Moltke, Konrad. "The Organization of the Impossible." *Global Environmental Politics* 1, no. 1 (February 2001): 23-28.

Whalley, John, and Ben Zissimos. "What Could a World Environmental Organisation Do?" *Global Environmental Politics* 1, no. 1 (February 2001): 29-34.

InfoTrac® College Edition
Search for the following articles in the InfoTrac® database:
Agrawal, Arun, and Maria Carmen Lemos. "A Greener Revolution in the Making? Environmental Governance in the 21st Century." *Environment* 49, no. 5 (June 2007): 36-46.

Biermann, Frank. "The Case for a World Environment Organization." *Environment* 42, no. 9 (November 2000): 22-31.

Haas, Peter M. "International Institutions and Social Learning in the Management of Global Environmental Risks." *Policy Studies Journal* 28, no. 3 (Autumn 2000): 558.

Web Resources
For current URLs for the following websites, visit www.crosscurrents.nelson.com.

THE GLOBAL ENVIRONMENTAL GOVERNANCE (GEG) PROJECT
http://www.yale.edu/gegdialogue/
This research group based at Yale University has produced papers and books dealing with issues relating to global environmental governance that can be found at this website.

INTERNATIONAL INSTITUTE FOR ENVIRONMENT AND DEVELOPMENT
http://www.iied.org
This nonprofit environmental research institute provides extensive resources on a wide range of global environmental issues.

AGIR POUR L'EVIRONNEMENT
http://www.agirpourlenvironnement.org/campagnes/c16.htm
For those who read French, this NGO based in France has many resources available as part of its campaign for the creation of a global environmental organization.

INTERNATIONAL ENVIRONMENTAL GOVERNANCE
http://www.unep.org/ieg/
The United Nations Environment Programme provides a website containing many documents and background papers on the topic of international environmental governance.

ISSUE 18

Should There Be a Right to Intervene to Prevent Acute Environmental Damage?

✔ YES

ROBYN ECKERSLEY, "Ecological Intervention: Prospects and Limits," *Ethics & International Affairs* 21, no. 3 (Fall 2007): 293–316

✗ NO

MARK WOODS, "Some Worries about Ecological-Humanitarian Intervention and Ecological Defense," *Ethics & International Affairs* 21, no. 3 (Fall 2007)

In Issue Thirteen, we explored efforts to challenge the traditional realist understanding of international security, which focuses on the security of states, by calling for a greater attention to human security, which concentrates on the security and well-being of individual human beings and groups. In this issue, we look at another debate regarding the redefinition and broadening of the notion of security; this time, the discussion includes the concept of environmental and ecological well-being as well.

Beginning in the 1980s, efforts to bring greater attention to environmental issues in international relations focused on the concept of "environmental security." Initially, analysts considered situations where environmental degradation and resources scarcities had been overlooked as potential sources of domestic and international conflict. A number of researchers, including Canadian Thomas Homer Dixon, undertook projects that brought attention to the very complex ways in which resource scarcities can be both a cause and a result of human conflicts. In framing the environment as a "security" issue, advocates of an "environmental security" approach hoped to push issues of environmental degradation higher on national political agendas. If national politicians had a clear idea of the potential threat that environmental issues posed to national security, they might be willing to devote more attention and resources to addressing these concerns. However, not everyone was enthusiastic about the conceptualization of the environment as a security issue. For one reason, environmental problems cannot be easily resolved by military action and thus are not "security" issues as traditionally defined. Moreover, some doubt that the links between conflict and war and environmental degradation are as clear cut as claimed and that environmental problems alone may lead to conflict. Despite these debates, analysts agree that environmental degradation and resource constraints can contribute to economic tensions and pressures that can in turn trigger tensions between states and other political actors.

The debate over the concept of environmental security begs a further question. In talking about environmental security, what is the object of the security being sought? Are we attempting to secure the well-being of states or people in the face of environmental crises or resource scarcities? Or are we talking about ensuring the security of the ecology of the earth itself, often in the face of threats posed by the actions of states or individuals?

In fact, the latter goal has received increased attention in the past several decades. As discussed in Issue Seventeen, there are now over 500 international treaties that address environmental issues. In addition, the range of discussions covered in these treaties has gradually broadened to include not only issues such as environmental pollution and bio-diversity, but also preservation of endangered species, wildlife protection, and climate change.

There is little doubt that environmental security, in both senses of the terms used above, has continued to receive sustained attention even in an era where headlines have been pre-occupied with the "war on terrorism." Nevertheless, progress has been limited. Despite the proliferation of treaties and conventions addressing environmental issues, international organizations often have limited means of enforcing their principles. States regularly invoke the principle of national sovereignty to defend their right to take actions for national or security reasons that may have a detrimental impact on the environment.

In light of this dilemma, Robyn Eckersley has asked whether we need not only to ensure that environmental issues are on the top of the international agenda, but also a "greening" of the fundamental principles that underlay the international system, including the concept of sovereignty itself.

Eckersley makes her case by drawing an analogy to the development of the concept of humanitarian intervention. She notes that as human rights principles have become increasingly accepted on the international level, there has been a rethinking of the inviolability of the principle of national sovereignty in the face of gross human rights violations. Thus, in the area of human security, if states demonstrate that they cannot adequately ensure security and well-being, the international community may not only have the right but perhaps the duty to intervene. Is it time that the concept of the "right to protect" be extended from just the protection of human beings to the endangered species and the environment itself? Should destruction of the ecosystem or the extinction of a species be treated as a "crime against nature," eliciting the same response that we now expect in cases of "crimes against humanity"?

This is the case that Eckersley puts forward in the first reading. She is well aware of the limits of such an argument and as a result sets out the constraints that should be placed in the use of "ecological intervention." Here she draws on the principles of just war, which are often used, at least in theory, as a means of setting limits on to when war is resorted. In the second article, Mark Woods examines the limits of Eckersley's argument. He fears that the notion of "ecological intervention" will only provide additional reasons for the use of military force by governments and not necessarily succeed in providing additional protection for the environment.

✔ YES

Ecological Intervention: Prospects and Limits

ROBYN ECKERSLEY

Violence in civil conflicts in the post–Cold War period has ignited a heated debate about the morality, legality, and legitimacy of humanitarian intervention. Recriminations continue against the failure of the United Nations Security Council to prevent massacres in Bosnia, Rwanda, and Darfur. But should the international community also be concerned about massacres perpetrated against critically endangered species? Must it stand by and allow a deliberate massacre of, say, the last surviving population of mountain gorillas by poachers? In considering this and other scenarios of grave environmental harm, this article seeks to extend the already controversial debate about humanitarian intervention by critically exploring the morality, legality, and legitimacy of ecological intervention and its corollary, ecological defense. By "ecological intervention" I mean the threat or use of force by a state or coalition of states within the territory of another state *and without the consent of that state* in order to prevent grave environmental damage.[1] By "ecological defense" I mean the preventive use of force in response to the threat of serious and immediate environmental harm flowing into the territory of a "victim" state.

If the legacy of the Holocaust was the Nuremberg trials and acceptance of a new category of "crimes against humanity," an emerging norm of humanitarian intervention, and, most recently, the creation of an international criminal court, then might the willful or reckless perpetration of mass extinctions and massive ecosystem destruction be regarded as "crimes against nature" such as to support a new norm of ecological intervention and an international environmental court?[2] If the international community condemns genocide, might it one day be ready to condemn ecocide?

In 2001 the International Commission on Intervention and State Sovereignty, an independent, international, twelve-member body established by the government of Canada to reconcile the international community's commitment to upholding humanitarian norms with the principle of state sovereignty, argued that sovereignty carries with it responsibilities, and that all states have "a responsibility to protect" their citizens.[3] In cases of serious harm, such as genocide and gross human rights violations, the commission argued that the international community has the responsibility to step in and prevent abuses where the responsible state is unable or unwilling to do so. In the words of the commission, in these circumstances, "the principle of non-intervention yields to the international responsibility to protect."[4] This article explores the analogous but more controversial argument that state sovereignty carries with it not only the right to control and develop territory but also the responsibility to protect it, and that states' responsibilities over their territories should be understood as fiduciary rather than proprietary.

The international community has already endorsed the basic idea that states have a responsibility to protect the environment in a wide range of environmental treaties, declarations, and action programs. Apart from environmental war crimes, however, states have so far declined to underpin their individual and collective environmental responsibilities with a minimal code of acceptable environmental behavior, the breach of which might in appropriate circumstances justify the use of force and/or prosecution in an international court. Yet it seems odd that the international community should accept environmental criminal prosecutions for "scorched earth" environmental atrocities committed during times of war but not in times of peace, even though some forms of environmental harm generated during peacetime may be no less grave and imminent—and there is not even the defense of "military necessity."[5] Indeed, we should expect standards of environmental protection to be higher during times of peace than times of war. The international customary law principle of state responsibility for environmental harm imposes a duty on states to pay reparations to neighboring states for transboundary environmental harm, but there are no mechanisms that enable states to force the cessation of such harm.

WHY CONSIDER MILITARY FORCE?

Although there is now a widespread literature on ecological security and an emerging literature on ecological peacekeeping, the question of military intervention to secure environmental protection has so far received only limited treatment by international lawyers and even less attention from political theorists and moral philosophers interested in global sustainability and environmental justice.[6] This is not surprising, given that most ecological problems rarely constitute a high level of threat, offer only a short period of warning, *and* require the need for a rapid military-style response.[7] While global warming, for example, has been designated a "weapon of mass destruction" because its harmful consequences are likely to be at least as severe as those of nuclear, chemical, and biological weapons, the threat is not immediate and military intervention is a singularly inappropriate means of responding to such a complex problems.[8] This is typical of most environmental problems, which are normally diffuse, transboundary, and unintended; evolve and continue over a fairly long time frame; implicate a wide range of actors; and usually require painstaking dialogue to move toward cooperation and resolution.[9] More generally, it has been shown that shared ecological problems present peacemaking opportunities.[10] Indeed, many environmental scholars see very little advantage, and considerable dangers, in "securitizing" our understanding of ecological problems in order to elevate them to the status of "high politics." Daniel Deudney, who has spearheaded this critique, has suggested that "for environmentalists to dress their programs in the blood-soaked garments of the war system betrays their core values and creates confusion about the real tasks at hand."[11] These "real" (and more mundane) tasks include more concerted

environmental capacity building (in the form of green aid packages and environ-mental technology transfer), more robust environmental treaties that equitably distribute the benefits and burdens of cooperation, and fairer international trading and credit rules.

The foregoing arguments provide very good reasons for approaching the ques-tion of the use of military force to secure environmental protection with great caution. Nonetheless, there are at least two reasons why an exploration of the case for ecological intervention (and ecological defense) is a worthwhile exercise. First, while most ecological problems are not amenable to any kind of military response, there are still *some* ecological problems and risks that do constitute environmental emergencies in the sense that they are grave and imminent and require a military or paramilitary response if they are to be avoided or minimized. Suppose, for example, that a chain reaction has commenced in an outdated nuclear reactor in Ukraine that is threatening to grow beyond control, with the imminent threat of a Chernobyl-style nuclear explosion. Suppose, too, the Ukrainian government has refused international technical assistance, even though European experts warn that Ukraine lacks the technical capacity and human resources to bring the potential emergency under control. Under such circum-stances, military intervention may be the only means of preventing an imminent transboundary ecological disaster.

We can also expect that the number of environmental disasters and emergen-cies is likely to grow rather than lessen over time, given increasing economic interconnectedness, increasing pressures on natural resources and ecosystems, rising populations, and new technologies. Anticipating such emergencies and encouraging a debate about an appropriate principled response may head off the possible proliferation of unilateral military action to protect the environment, such as when Canadian naval forces seized a Spanish fishing vessel on the high seas in 1995 in an effort to prevent overfishing of migratory stocks that were cen-tral to the viability of the Canadian fishing industry.[12]

Apart from environmental emergencies that threaten public safety, there are other categories of environmental harm that may not necessarily have trans-boundary effects but might still constitute a high level of threat and offer only a short period of warning, thereby possibly warranting a rapid military-style response. For example, if the Rwandan government were unable and/or unwilling to protect its dwindling population of mountain gorillas from illegal hunting and poaching, then a swift response by multilateral forces might be the only remaining effective measure that would prevent the total extinction of these great apes.[13]

Second, exploring the use of military force for environmental protection enables a useful stocktaking and clarification of the relationship between new ecological norms and the fundamental political and legal norm of noninterven-tion and its corollary, self-determination. Such an inquiry provides one significant

gauge of the extent to which sovereignty has been, or may be, "greened."[14] The international human rights discourse is complicated, controversial, and mostly aspirational, but support can now be found for the idea that there should be certain minimal standards of human decency, the breach of which should entail the temporary forfeiting of certain prerogatives associated with the principle of state sovereignty. In the light of three major environmental summits and an expanding body of mutually reinforcing environmental treaties, declarations, and strategies, it is timely to explore whether it is possible to piece together a basic set of non-derogable environmental norms (that is, norms that cannot be abrogated by any state) that must be observed during times of war and peace.

THE LEGALITY, MORALITY, AND LEGITIMACY OF MILITARY INTERVENTION

Given the potential mischief associated with any kind of military intervention, the case for ecological intervention should pass a fairly stiff test. Ideally, it must be consistent with, or at least find a precedent in, international law; it must qualify as a just cause (and the remaining requirements of *jus ad bellum,* such as the proportionality criterion, must also be satisfied); and it should be widely accepted as legitimate or "rightful" by most states, which means that it must transcend the cultural and political proclivities of powerful states and reflect norms that are common to developed and developing countries alike. While the requirements of legality, morality, and political legitimacy can overlap in practice and are sometimes mutually informing and constraining, they are analytically distinct and often diverge. For example, moral claims are normative claims about what ought to be done according to the demands of justice, whereas claims that certain actions are politically legitimate are based on social and political conventions that are derived from particular political communities (in this case, the society of states).[15] To expect a neat convergence among legality, morality, and legitimacy in order to justify military intervention is, therefore, rather a tall order, given that learned interpretations of international law, understandings about justice and morality, and political judgments about what is appropriate behavior are rarely clear, settled, and in perfect alignment. Yet it is the slippages and discrepancies among legal, moral, and political norms that create openings for normative innovation, and it is these openings that I wish to explore and exploit in the discussion that follows.

Shifts in morality or political understandings of appropriate behavior can sometimes lead to shifts in law (and vice versa). Humanitarian intervention has only an "emergent" rather than "settled" status as an international norm precisely because the legal, moral, and political arguments have yet to coalesce. For example, the Independent International Commission on Kosovo concluded that NATO's intervention in Kosovo was "legitimate" (in this case, meaning morally

just because it sought to put a stop to human rights abuses) though not strictly "legal," and it recommended the legal codification of the doctrine of humanitarian intervention to bridge the gap between law and justice and provide greater clarity.[16] Many developing countries, however, wish to uphold the principle of nonintervention embedded in the United Nations Charter as an important political principle because, among other reasons, it provides an important bulwark against unilateral interventions by powerful states. My strategy, then, is to assess the legality, morality, and political legitimacy of ecological intervention in order to pinpoint where the blockages and possible openings for innovation may be found. This means that my analysis will be partly legal, partly normative, and partly sociological. My task is to explore and, where possible, exploit precedents, analogies, and anomalies in order to present the case for ecological intervention in its best light, and also to assess its general prospects.

To focus the discussion, I explore the potential scope of ecological intervention and defense in relation to three different categories of environmental harm: (1) major environmental emergencies with transboundary spillover effects that threaten public safety in the wider region; (2) ecocide or crimes against nature that also involve genocide or serious human rights violations (irrespective of spillover effects); and (3) ecocide or crimes against nature that are confined within the territory of the offending state and which involve no serious human rights violations. I consider the prospects for multilateral action (by the Security Council), as well as unilateral action by one or more states.

Environmental Emergencies with Transboundary Spillover Effects

The United Nations Charter upholds the principle of the sovereign equality of its member states and expressly forbids any state to use or threaten to use force against "the territorial integrity or political independence of any State," except for the purposes of individual or collective self-defense against an armed attack.[17] The quality of the global environment was not a concern of the drafters of the Charter, and the word "environment" makes no appearance in the text. Nonetheless, the United Nations, through the General Assembly and the United Nations Environmental Program, has facilitated the development of a range of significant multilateral environmental declarations and treaties, particularly over the last three decades in response to mounting environmental problems. There are also increasing cross-references among treaties, declarations, and strategies and a growing degree of convergence in many of the principles embodied in these environmental multilateral instruments. The 1992 Rio Declaration brings together these shared understandings, including the recognition that "peace, development and environmental protection are interdependent and indivisible."[18] In the post–Cold War period, it has become increasingly recognized that environmental degradation is a potential threat to peace and security.

The Security Council has the power to determine what constitutes a threat to the peace, a breach of the peace, or an act of aggression, and to authorize military intervention under Chapter VII of the UN Charter in order to restore international peace and security. Although peace and security are undefined in the Charter, it does not require any great stretch of the imagination to classify an environmental emergency or imminent environmental disaster with international ramifications, such as an imminent nuclear explosion, as a threat to peace and security.[19] Indeed, British prime minister John Major, speaking as president of the UN Security Council, declared in 1992 that "non-military sources of instability in the economic, social, humanitarian and ecological fields have become threats to peace and security."[20] Given this acknowledgment, and the Security Council's preparedness to authorize the use of force in response to other nonmilitary sources of insecurity in the post–Cold War period, such as humanitarian crises, it would seem inconsistent for the Security Council not to respond to environmental emergencies that also undermine human security, especially when such emergencies threaten to cause significant loss of human life and suffering on a larger scale than humanitarian crises that are confined to one state. Environmental emergencies of this kind represent one situation when the principle of nonintervention ought to yield to the international responsibility to protect. Indeed, it is hard to think of a credible moral or political argument against intervention in our "Chernobyl" scenario. After all, nuclear radiation is nuclear radiation, irrespective of whether it emanates from a failed nuclear power plant or a nuclear bomb. Ecological intervention in these circumstances would uphold the principle of collective security enshrined in the UN Charter, which represents one of the most significant renovations to the Westphalian system in the twentieth century.

If the Security Council declined to act because of the exercise of the veto power by one or more permanent members, it could be argued that in a Chernobyl-like scenario neighboring states, or NATO, would be entitled to take control of the reactor as an act of self-defense in order to guarantee the health and safety of their citizens. Article 51 of the Charter explicitly preserves the right of states to use force in "self-defense" against an attack, and this has been interpreted to extend to the use of preemptive measures when a serious threat or attack is imminent and likely to be overwhelming and leave no room for choice.[21] Direct and major incursions of pollution or hazardous substances into the territory of neighboring states are analogous to an "armed attack" with chemical, biological, or nuclear weapons; they enter or threaten to enter the territory of the victim state without its consent and with equally grave consequences. Ecological defense may therefore be understood as representing an appropriate response to a wrongful *intervention* in the "territorial integrity or political independence" of the defending state within the meaning of Article 2(4) of the Charter. "Territorial integrity" can readily be interpreted to include "ecosystem integrity"; and "political independence" includes the political autonomy of nation-states to determine

their own levels of environmental quality and not have them undermined by the willful or reckless actions of other states. On this interpretation, the act of ecological defense would reinforce rather than undermine the fundamental principle of nonintervention.

The foregoing interpretations would also overcome the limitations in the current state remedies available under the customary law principle relating to transboundary environmental harm, according to which no state may use its territory in ways that cause serious injury to the territory, property, or population of another state.[22] This principle has been interpreted not to permit unilateral preemptive measures or even injunctive relief in the World Court on the part of victim states to head off serious environmental damage, but merely to permit compensation for tangible damage suffered.[23] For example, in the French nuclear tests case brought before the International Court of Justice by Australia and New Zealand against atmospheric nuclear testing in the Pacific, it was admitted by Judge Ignacio-Pinto that Australia and New Zealand could not legally prohibit another state from using its territory in ways that exposed them to the future likelihood of nuclear fallout.[24] All they could do was to wait for the incursion and then seek reparations for actual damages suffered. Such a situation provides small comfort to victim states and their residents (such as residents of Mururoa Atoll), who may suffer from radiation sickness.

Taking preemptive measures to prevent massive harm from an imminent environmental disaster emanating from a neighboring state probably represents one of the few instances where unilateral military action might be legally, morally, and politically justified in the name of environmental protection in circumstances where the UN Security Council was unable or unwilling to respond to the crisis. Such action would, of course, need to be reported to the Security Council and respect the laws of war and the just war tradition (including the requirements of necessity and proportionality in the case of self-defense).

Ecocide Involving Serious Human Rights Violations

Genocide is universally condemned and the prohibition against genocide is considered to be *jus cogens* and therefore nonderogable.[25] Serious human rights abuses, such as torture, are also widely condemned by the international community, notwithstanding the ongoing philosophical and political disagreement about the justification of human rights claims. Insofar as ecocide also produces direct, immediate, and grave consequences for humans, involving large numbers of deaths and/or significant human suffering on a par with genocide or crimes against humanity, then the moral case for ecological intervention need only ride on the coattails of the moral case for humanitarian intervention. The decimation of the marsh region, the homeland of the Ma'dan, or Marsh Arabs, by Saddam Hussein's Baathist government is a case in point. The large-scale, government-sponsored drainage of the marsh region has been ecologically catastrophic and

directly implicated in human rights abuses against the Marsh Arabs.[26] The Marsh Arabs were also the most persecuted of the Shia Muslims in Iraq. The brutal murder, torture, imprisonment, forced expulsion, and disappearance of Marsh Arabs has clearly constituted genocide and crimes against humanity.[27] Upholding the human rights of Marsh Arabs therefore provides one indirect means of protecting the marsh region, and vice versa. We might therefore call military intervention to stop ecocide that also involves genocide "eco-humanitarian intervention."

To the extent that grave environmental harm is often associated with serious human rights violations, there are obvious advantages in developing these linkages and building on existing humanitarian law, along with the existing programs of United Nations agencies. Many well-recognized human rights also have an ecological dimension, such as the right to life and security of the person (which presupposes the absence of major ecological risks that threaten human health and well-being, such as a contaminated environment produced by radiation or toxic chemicals), but new developments are also under way.[28] A further general advantage of linking ecological intervention with humanitarian intervention is that it will ensure that human rights abuses, including social discrimination, are not committed in the name of ecological intervention. Conversely, separating the observance of human rights from the preservation of ecosystems could potentially provide a license for "coercive conservation" and other misanthropic practices.[29] Given the difficult military capacity issues associated with mounting swift and successful humanitarian interventions, there is the predictable concern that a broader case for ecological intervention (where no harm to humans is imminent) might divert scarce resources away from humanitarian crises. Eco-humanitarian intervention would avoid this problem by bringing together the arguments for humanitarian and ecological intervention.

Humanitarian intervention is, as we have noted, only an "emerging" rather than settled norm. If the case for eco-humanitarian intervention is to ride on the back of the case for humanitarian intervention, then it must address the familiar challenges that confront supporters of humanitarian intervention. Most of these challenges arise less from moral disagreement about the importance of human rights and more from significant asymmetries in the power of states to decide when to intervene, which tends to match asymmetries in military and economic power. The key political challenge is how to avoid a replay of the colonial past and address the suspicion among non-Western states that humanitarian and, by extension, eco-humanitarian interventions are just Western imperial projects dressed up to appear "universal."[30]

The colonial legacy continues to shape the environmental values, priorities, and practices of developed and developing countries in multiple ways. Developing countries have shown considerable hostility toward new forms of "green conditionality" attached to trade, aid, and debt relations imposed by powerful states in

the North upon states in the South, which they view as just another verse in the same old colonial song. The double-barreled "responsibility to protect" underlying the norm of eco-humanitarian intervention—to observe certain minimal requirements of human decency as well as minimal standards of environmental conduct—is likely to be rejected by developing states as a further encroachment on their right of self-determination, including the right to develop according to their own priorities. I address these concerns in more detail below in the discussion of the duty to protect biodiversity.

International lawyers and various states are also divided over whether the UN Security Council has the legal power to authorize humanitarian intervention. Those adopting a literal reading of the Charter (what we might call the "legal classicists") argue that such intervention contravenes the plain language of Article 2(4) of the UN Charter. In contrast, "legal realists" adopt a more flexible, contextual approach that interprets the Charter in the light of contemporary geopolitical needs and realities.[31] The legal realists also point to the broad discretion conferred on the Security Council in Article 39 to determine what constitutes "a threat to the peace." Upholding human rights is also one of the basic tenets of the UN Charter, and the Security Council has on a number of occasions (Rwanda, Somalia, and Haiti) already considered that it has the power under Chapter VII to authorize the use of force to prevent major human rights violations.[32] Clearly, the case for eco-humanitarian intervention would likewise rest on a legal realist interpretation of the UN Charter.

The case for eco-humanitarian intervention by a single state or "a coalition of the willing" is likely to be mired in the same legal, moral, and political controversies as unilateral humanitarian intervention. Based on a strict interpretation of the Charter, unilateral humanitarian intervention by a single state or "a coalition of the willing" is illegal. The NATO intervention in Kosovo, for example, is widely considered to be illegal, and this view has indeed been reiterated by many states, particularly from the developing world.[33] Moreover, Michael Byers and Simon Chesterman have argued that it is extremely unlikely that workable criteria for *unilateral* humanitarian intervention could be developed to the satisfaction of more than a handful of states.[34]

In the event of strong resistance to eco-humanitarian intervention by any permanent members of the Security Council, advocates of eco-humanitarian intervention face a now familiar but unpalatable choice: resignation to a paralyzed and ineffective Security Council dominated by the geopolitical interests of the permanent members, or the pursuit of action outside the UN Charter that threatens to undermine the principles and institutions of international law. In the light of this dilemma, Byers and Chesterman argue that "coalitions of the willing" should concede that their actions are prima facie contrary to international law, but to offer a special "plea in mitigation" based on extraordinary, exculpatory circumstances. They reject the alternative, which is to offer new and creative interpretations of the

existing rules, as merely an effort to mold the law to suit the practices of a small handful of powerful states.[35] Thomas Franck has pushed this argument in favor of "exceptional illegality" one step further in pointing out how pleas in mitigation can play a positive role in the evolution of international law by helping to bridge the gap between strict adherence to the letter of the law and common notions of what is just and necessary. Jane Stromseth has likewise defended what she calls an "excusable breach" of the UN Charter as providing an important "safety valve" that reduces the tension between legality and legitimacy, although she argues that it is preferable to defend the action as a legal exception in accordance with an emerging norm of customary international law.[36]

If we accept the foregoing arguments as an appealing "middle way," then proponents of eco-humanitarian intervention, either by a particular state or a coalition of states, would need to pick their test case of "exceptional illegality" extremely carefully; that is, they would need to be confident that they are on strong moral grounds, to know they have at least the tacit support of a significant number of states, and to show that the law is seriously lagging behind morality and legitimacy. The very different reactions of the international community to NATO's intervention in Kosovo and the U.S.-led military adventure in Iraq are revealing in this respect. As Franck points out, "the reactions of the UN system to such 'off-Charter' uses of force may be bellwethers of evolution in Charter interpretations."[37] The acceptance of the case for eco-humanitarian intervention would be seriously set back by an ill-considered unilateral adventure that attracted strong international condemnation.

Ecocide, Crimes Against Nature, and the Protection of Biodiversity

Military intervention to prevent ecocide or "crimes against nature" involving no serious harm to humans represents the most challenging case because it directly appeals to a moral referent beyond humanity. Humanitarian law rests on the bedrock humanist idea that all humans matter, that they matter equally, and therefore that each person is equally entitled to physical security, sustenance, and a life of dignity and respect. For full-blooded liberal cosmopolitans, such as Jean Bethke Elshtain, the basis of humanitarian intervention should shift from rescuing victims as an act of charity or pity to upholding civic security as a matter of justice, based on the elementary international justice principle of equal regard and inviolable human dignity.[38] For communitarians, such as Michael Walzer, the duty of humanitarian intervention in response to genocide and crimes against humanity is a moral duty simply because human atrocities of this kind shock the conscience of *all* communities and are universally condemned as morally repugnant.[39] For communitarians generally (whether liberal, leftist, or conservative), we might say that the idea of crimes against humanity reminds us of our membership in a common human family and implicitly uses nonhuman species as the necessary point of differentiation. What distinguishes us humans from other

species is our moral capacities, so that mass atrocities committed by some humans against others reflect badly on us all.

If we accept that we humans are members of a broader web of life, however, then major environmental atrocities also reflect badly on us all. The ecological crisis and the rise of environmental activism have spawned a revolution in Western ethics that has challenged what David Ehrenfeld called "the arrogance of humanism," or what has since become known as anthropocentrism or human chauvinism.[40] This is the widely held idea that humans are the center of the universe, the apex of evolution, and the only beings that matter from a moral point of view. Nonanthropocentric environmental philosophers have argued that anthropocentrism legitimates a purely instrumental posture toward the nonhuman world, which diminishes nonhuman nature (along with humanity) while also rendering it completely valueless and dispensable unless it serves some useful human purpose. Nonanthropocentric moral discourses share the conviction that the dominant political ideologies that have helped to shape the modern world (most notably, liberalism and Marxism) have elevated and celebrated humanity at the expense of nonhuman nature, and that this has helped to sanction the domination and destruction of nonhuman nature. The ethical quest has been to develop a new moral vocabulary that recognizes human membership in a larger moral community and respects the value of nonhuman species "for their own sake." The political and legal quest has been to develop new policies and laws that enable the *mutual* flourishing of the human and nonhuman world, rather than the flourishing of humans at the expense of the nonhuman world. If the idea of "crimes against nature" is to have any meaning beyond eco-humanitarianism, then an ethical and political development along these lines would seem to be necessary to provide a warrant for the rescue of the endangered mountain gorillas or other endangered species and habitats.

Nonanthropocentric environmental philosophers divide over how much of nonhuman nature should be admitted into Kant's kingdom of ends, however, and whether moral considerability should be confined to individual organisms or extended to ecological communities. Utilitarian (for example, Peter Singer) and Kantian (for example, Tom Regan) liberal philosophers concerned with the welfare of animals work from an atomistic ontology and consider only individual animals, or sentient creatures, as worthy of having their interests considered in any utilitarian moral calculus or of possessing rights.[41] Both have argued that an animal need not be a fully competent moral *agent* (equipped with powers of moral reasoning) in order to be recognized as a worthy moral *subject*—that is, as a being that is entitled to moral consideration. If we accept that morally incompetent humans are nonetheless morally considerable, then there is no good reason for not accepting nonhuman others as morally considerable on the grounds that they too are ends in themselves or otherwise capable of suffering or being harmed. Failure to consider the interests of animals is symptomatic of speciesism—an

unwarranted prejudice against nonhuman others *just because they are not human.* Whereas biocentric philosophers take these arguments one step further by extending moral recognition to all living things, ecocentric philosophers work from a relational ontology and are concerned with the integrity of not only populations and species but also broader ecological communities at multiple levels of aggregation.[42] Despite their significant differences, however, animal liberationists, biocentrists, and ecocentrists all generally support the protection of species habitat and biological diversity, either for their own sake or because they are essential for the survival and well-being of animals, sentient creatures, and/or individual living organisms.

One adventurous attempt to extend moral consideration to nonhuman species in the international sphere, which builds on liberal moral arguments, is the International Great Ape Project. Supporters of this project argue that great apes—the chimpanzee, bonobo (pygmy chimpanzee), gorilla, and orangutan—should be included in the human "community of equals." Rather than invoke a new biocentric ethic, however, the project's "Declaration of Great Apes" self-consciously builds on the human rights tradition—particularly the United Nations Universal Declaration of Human Rights of 1948—in claiming that great apes belong to the same moral community as humans and are entitled to a right to life, a right to the protection of their liberty, and a right to be free from torture.[43] Robert Goodin, Carole Pateman, and Roy Pateman have extended this argument by defending the idea of "simian sovereignty" in the form of internationally protected, autonomous trust territories for great apes.[44] Building on the precedent of protectorates and mandated territories, initially set up by the League of Nations, they suggest that a body or state with an interest in the well-being of great apes could be empowered by international law to secure great ape communities by resisting incursions (whether from inside or outside the relevant state) into their homeland.[45] All of this has become thinkable, they argue, because the concept of sovereignty is becoming more flexible in the wake of globalization. Moreover, apes are recognized as having their own "authority structures," so providing great apes with limited rights of *internal* self-determination in relation to their homelands is consistent with a range of arguments for the self-determination of nations that fall short of state sovereignty. In short, human communities are shown to be not the only communities or "tribes" entitled to self-determination.

Yet the idea of human rights for apes raises a strategic and moral dilemma for those interested in the preservation of biodiversity and ecosystem health and resilience in general. On the one hand, in employing familiar moral arguments and legal precedents, the Great Ape Project provides an argument for building political support for the protection of great apes that is directly analogous with humanitarian intervention. Whether the threatened decimation of our "close relatives" is sufficiently "conscience-shocking" to warrant international condemnation and support for a military response is an open question. Indeed, we can

expect the argument to unsettle established moral hierarchies. More generally, however, the arguments underpinning the Great Ape Project have limited ecological mileage because they cannot be readily extended beyond the great ape community to species who are not "like us." The ecological reach of this argument is therefore minimal. Indeed, it could be argued that the relevant crime here on the part of gorilla poachers is still a crime against humanity (or a "crime against great apes" as a "community of equals") rather than a crime against nature, because it still rests on a *humane* rather than *ecological* ethic.

What, then, of the more controversial case for ecological intervention to prevent major assaults on biological diversity?[46] The legal concept of "common heritage of humankind" has not been extended to include biodiversity *within* the territory of nation-states, even though it has been designated a "common concern of humankind."[47] Traditionally, biodiversity has been understood to form part of the natural resource assets of states and therefore subject to the principle of permanent sovereignty over natural resources, which is widely regarded as a basic constituent of the right to self-determination.[48] The template for the general notion of state dominion over territory came from Roman private law, which gave the property owner complete and exclusive control over their property.[49] In more recent times, states have gradually expanded their dominion over territory by negotiating a range of agreements that extend their sovereign rights beyond the "territorial sea" to include maritime "exclusive economic zones" (which include most of the world's fish catch) and to plant and animal genetic resources.[50]

The principle of permanent sovereignty over natural resources has formed an important plank in the "negative sovereignty" discourse of postcolonial states. The 1962 UN Resolution on Permanent Sovereignty over Natural Resources declared that "the rights of peoples and nations to permanent sovereignty over their natural wealth and resources must be exercised in the interest of their national development and of the well-being of the People of the State concerned."[51] While this principle had originally been formulated as a *human* right belonging to peoples or nations that had been subjected to colonial rule to freely dispose of their natural wealth, since the 1972 Stockholm Conference on the Human Environment it is more typically formulated as a right belonging to sovereign *states*.[52] As it happens, most of the earth's richest areas of biodiversity lie in tropical and subtropical regions in developing states. The argument that biodiversity should be considered part of the common asset of humankind held in trust by states, rather than as exploitable resources, would be widely regarded by developing states as yet another imperialist scheme by the North to deny former colonies the right to make use of their natural resources for the benefit of their people.

The question of the *wrongful appropriation* of natural resources or biodiversity by colonial or former colonial powers, however, is analytically distinct from the question of their *appropriate* management and protection by states. In any event,

the principle of permanent sovereignty over natural resources was formulated in a waning colonial context that predates most of the significant developments in international environmental law and policy. The 1972 Stockholm Declaration and the 1992 Rio Declaration marked significant turning points in the general evolution of the development prerogatives and environmental responsibilities of states. The Rio Declaration, which represents the most up-to-date encapsulation of international environmental norms, seeks to artfully balance the principle of permanent sovereignty over natural resources with states' responsibility for avoiding transboundary environmental harm in Principle 2.[53] More significantly, the Rio Declaration also makes clear that states have environmental responsibilities in relation to their own territories. Principle 3 provides that "the right to development must be fulfilled so as to equitably meet developmental and environmental needs of present and future generations"; while Principle 4 declares that "in order to achieve sustainable development, environmental protection shall constitute an integral part of the development process and cannot be considered in isolation from it." Although the UN Convention on Biological Diversity reaffirms that states have sovereign rights over their biological resources, it also recognizes the intrinsic value of biological diversity and affirms that its conservation is a "common concern of humankind."[54]

Curiously, very little has been written by political philosophers about the *moral* basis of the state's right to control its territory and natural resources, as distinct from the people inhabiting or moving through its territory.[55] The significant exception are liberal cosmopolitans, such as Charles Beitz, who consider the distribution of natural resources among states to be even more morally arbitrary than the distribution of natural talents among individuals; such arbitrariness is seen to justify the application of Rawls's difference principle on a global scale.[56] However, international legal recognition of the territorial rights of states is based on the fact of possession and the power to assert control and to defend a territorial claim rather than on any moral entitlement—as indigenous peoples around the world have painfully learned. Indeed, the means by which most states have acquired their territory has been anything but morally exemplary. The acquisition of territory by seizure, military conquest, or negotiation under duress by powerful states has been eventually accepted and legally recognized by the international community, albeit sometimes "after a suitable mourning period."[57] Yet if it is accepted that the right of sovereign states to control *people* should be subject to certain minimal moral strictures, then why should not the right of sovereign states to control their *territories* be likewise subject to minimal moral strictures? As we have seen, the international community has made it clear in the Rio Declaration that the right of states to exploit their territory is not unlimited. States may not cause transboundary environmental harm; states must serve the development and environment needs of present *and* future generations; and environmental protection should form an integral part of the development process.

The international customary law principle of state responsibility for environmental harm, also derived from Roman law, goes some way toward regulating the external duties of states. This principle merely seeks to qualify state territorial user rights, however, rather than to protect victims or ecosystems per se. The principle is based on a presumption in favor of territorial rights, which places the onus on the victim state to prove tangible damage, causation, and a lack of due diligence. Moreover, as we saw in the French nuclear tests case, the customary rule provides no mechanisms that enable states to bring about the cessation of such harm. Indeed, reparations could simply be factored into the costs of doing business on the part of the culprit state. Nor does this customary principle prevent states from causing serious harm to their *own* environment if the consequences are confined within the territory of the state.

Environmental customary law has been increasingly overshadowed by environmental treaty law, however, and the broad trend in treaty law is to move away from a construction of the state as owner or overlord of its territory and toward that of caretaker or trustee of territory, with multiple "responsibilities to protect" vis-a-vis different classes of environmental beneficiaries.[58] Although treaty law is binding only on the parties, there is an increasing convergence of international opinion around certain key environmental norms.[59] We may think of the trustor as the international community (the bestower of recognition of territorial rights), and the primary beneficiaries as the citizens of the state (in relation to the state's internal duties) and the international community and global commons (in relation to the state's external responsibilities and matters of "common concern").[60]

Of course, clarifying the general environmental responsibilities of states is a different exercise from determining what might amount to a serious dereliction of responsibility sufficient to warrant internationally sanctioned military intervention in the absence of any serious transboundary environmental harm. If the conservation of biological diversity, including the preservation of species, is a "common concern" of humankind, then what categories of harm might serve as minimal, nonderogable standards of conduct to shore up this common concern? Given that genocide and crimes against humanity perform this role in the field of humanitarian law, then the obvious candidates in the field of environmental law are ecocide and crimes against nature. Building on humanitarian precedents,[61] ecocide may be defined as intentional and systematic acts that cause "widespread, long-term and severe damage to the natural environment."[62] This formulation has already been accepted by the international community in the case of environmental war crimes, and there seems to be no good reason not to extend it to times of peace as well to enable the prosecution of the perpetrators in an international criminal court. If the category of crimes against nature is to have any independent meaning over and above the category of ecocide, then it may be understood as intentional and systematic acts that cause the extinction of a species. The willful and systematic extermination of a species may be considered especially

"conscience-shocking" because the effects are irreversible. In both cases (ecocide and crimes against nature), it should not be necessary that the damage to the natural environment or the extinction of species constitute the *primary* purpose of the acts. Rather, it should be enough that the acts themselves are willful and systematic, and that the environmental damage or extinction is a clearly foreseeable consequence of the acts. A clear wartime case is Iraq's willful setting fire to Kuwait's oil wells, which led to immense smoke clouds, a ten-degree Celsius drop in temperature in Kuwait, and massive pollution of coastal stretches resulting from the considerable influx of crude oil into the sea.[63]

It could be argued that the prohibitions against ecocide and crimes against nature ought to constitute legal duties that are nonderogable and owed to the international community as a whole.[64] In effect, this would require the enlargement of the trustor-trustee-beneficiary relationship sketched above to include nonhuman species as direct rather than merely indirect beneficiaries of the trust relationship. If this argument is accepted, then military intervention by UN-sanctioned forces to prevent these crimes may be defended as intervention for a "just cause," assuming, of course, that the remaining criteria of *jus ad bellum* can be satisfied (for example, that intervention did not make matters worse).[65] This is a big "if," however, and it remains an open question whether these basic prohibitions—particularly crimes against nature—would attract a cross-cultural consensus among states. There are certainly many non-Western indigenous cultures and religions that value nature in noninstrumental terms, but these traditional orientations have tended to be overshadowed by state-sponsored practices of economic development. It is possible that the wide range of instrumental arguments for the protection of ecosystems and biological diversity may, over time, prove to be sufficient to ground a general agreement over "critical ecological thresholds" and/or forms of ecocide that "shock the conscience" of the international community. Until such time as these norms take hold, the gorillas in our fictitious scenario would remain at the mercy of poachers.

CONCLUSION

Advocates of the use of military force for environmental protection face a heavy political onus, especially now that skepticism toward military intervention of any kind is running high in the shadow of the Anglo-American intervention in Iraq. If anything, the norm of nonintervention has become more rather than less politically important over time with the proliferation of non-European states, which regard nonintervention as an important principle of justice in an unequal world.[66] States with limited military capacity have been unable to play any prominent rule in deciding when military intervention may be warranted.[67] There is also the danger that the case for ecological intervention might provide a license for powerful states to act as global green action heroes or military missionaries in furtherance of their own environmental values and priorities that may not be widely

shared. Moreover, the state with the greatest military power has hardly been exemplary when it comes to ratifying and implementing key international environmental treaties to protect biological diversity or to mitigate global warming (which is expected to accelerate rates of species extinction). Finally, military intervention itself can often result in heavy civilian casualties and environmental damage, which is one of the many factors that lie behind the general pacifist orientation of most environmentalists.[68] These factors conspire to make military intervention politically hazardous, even in circumstances where the moral case might otherwise seem compelling. The advantage of ecological defense over ecological intervention is that it avoids these hazards by reinforcing rather than challenging the prevailing norm of nonintervention. More generally, military intervention should always be a last resort, even in cases of imminent ecocide or crimes against nature, and the consequences should always be carefully assessed against the consequences of nonmilitary forms of intervention, whether coercive (such as trade sanctions), semi-coercive (such as "green conditionality" attached to loans), or consensual (such as ecological peacekeeping with the consent of the relevant state).

I have shown that the minimalist argument for ecological intervention—multilateral intervention in the case of environmental emergencies with transboundary spillover effects—is also the strongest because it is likely to satisfy all three tests of legality, morality, and legitimacy. "Eco-humanitarian intervention" (to prevent ecocide and crimes against nature involving serious human rights violations) is, however, like humanitarian intervention, still particularly shaky on the question of political legitimacy, especially from the point of view of many developing countries. The most challenging case of all—the military rescue of nonhuman species—conflicts with deeply entrenched international legal and political norms concerning state territorial rights. Nonetheless, the moral case cannot be dismissed, and I have suggested that some of the legal norms of territoriality have, appropriately, started to fray to the point where extending the idea of "the responsibility to protect" to include biological diversity is no longer unthinkable.

NOTES

1. This definition represents an adaptation of J. L. Holzgrefe's definition of humanitarian intervention in "The Humanitarian Intervention Debate," in Robert O. Keohane and J. L. Holzgrefe, eds., *Humanitarian Intervention: Ethical, Legal and Political Dilemmas* (Cambridge: Cambridge University Press, 2003), pp. 15–52. A less restrictive interpretation might also include nonmilitary coercive measures, such as sanctions, or ecological peacekeeping, which is usually carried out with state consent, but my primary concern here is to explore the circumstances when military force might be justifiable.

2. This is the objective of the International Court of the Environment Foundation (ICEF), a non-governmental organization founded in Rome in 1992 under the directorship of Judge Amedeo Postiglione of the Italian Supreme Court. See www.icef-court.org/icef/about.htm, accessed October 7, 2005.

3. ICISS, *The Responsibility to Protect—Report of the International Commission on Intervention and State Sovereignty* (Ottawa: International Development Research Center, 2001).

4. Ibid., p. xi.

5. I should add that no state has ever been held accountable for environmental damage during wartime and no individual has been criminally prosecuted. See Tara Weinstein, "Prosecuting Attacks that Destroy the Environment: Environmental Crimes or Humanitarian Atrocities?" *Georgetown International Environmental Law Review* 17, no. 4 (Summer 2005), p. 698.

6. For a comprehensive overview of this literature, see Lorraine Elliott, "Imaginative Adaptations: A Possible Environmental Role for the UN Security Council," *Contemporary Security Policy* 24, no. 2 (2003), pp. 47-68. See also Markku Oksanen, "Humanitarian Military Intervention Versus Nature: An Environmental Ethical Perspective" (paper presented to the workshop on A New Generation of Green Thought, Seventh Nordic Environmental Social Science Research (NESS) Conference, held at Gothenburg University, Sweden, June 15–17, 2005).

7. Mark Imber, *Environment, Security and UN Reform* (New York: St. Martin's Press, 1994), p. 19.

8. John Houghton, "Global Warming Is Now a Weapon of Mass Destruction," *Guardian*, July 28, 2003.

9. Daniel Deudney, "The Case against Linking Environmental Degradation to National Security," *Millennium* 19, no. 3 (Winter 1990), pp. 461–76.

10. Ken Conca and Geoffrey D. Dabelko, eds., *Environmental Peacekeeping* (Washington, D.C., and Baltimore, Md.: Woodrow Wilson Center Press and Johns Hopkins University Press, 2002).

11. Daniel Deudney, "Environmental Security: A Critique," in Daniel Deudney and Richard A. Matthew, eds., *Contested Grounds: Security and Conflict in the New Environmental Politics* (Albany, N.Y.: State University of New York Press, 1999), p. 214.

12. Derrick M. Kedziora, "Gunboat Diplomacy in the Northwest Atlantic: The 1995 Canada-EU Fishing Dispute and the United Nations Agreement on Straddling and High Migratory Fish Stocks," *Northwestern Journal of International Law and Business* 17, nos. 2/3 (Winter/Spring 1996), p. 1132.

13. I hasten to add that this is a hypothetical situation designed to force a confrontation with the environmental ethical issues at stake. The Rwandan government has an active program to save the mountain gorillas.

14. Karen T. Litfin, ed., *The Greening of Sovereignty in World Politics* (Cambridge, Mass.: MIT Press, 1998).

15. I use the term "political legitimacy" here to refer to sociological legitimacy, while "morality" refers to normative legitimacy. The former refers to social and political conventions of rightful conduct in a particular community (observable by an anthropologist or sociologist), while the latter refers to normative claims of justice (which may vary according to particular moral or religious frameworks).

16. Independent International Commission on Kosovo, *Kosovo Report* (New York: Oxford University Press, 2000), pp. 187–98.

17. United Nations Charter, Articles 2(4) and 51; available at www.un.org/aboutun/charter/.

18. United Nations Declaration on Environment and Development, Principle 25; available at www.unep.org/Documents.Multilingual/Default.asp? DocumentID=78&ArticleID=1163.

19. See Linda A. Malone, "'Green Helmets': A Conceptual Framework for Security Council Authority in Environmental Emergencies," *Michigan Journal of International Law* 17 (1996), pp. 515-36; and Michael Murphy, "Achieving Economic Security with Swords as Ploughshares: The Modern Use of Force to Combat Environmental Degradation," *Virginia Journal of International Law* 39 (1999), p. 1197.

20. United Nations Security Council, Note by the President of the Security Council, S/23500, January 31, 1992, p. 3; available at www.sipri.org/contents/cbwarfare/cbw_research_doc/cbw_historical/ cbw_historical/cbw-unsc23500.html.

21. The customary international law of preemptive defense, according to the "Caroline criteria," requires that there must be "a necessity of self-defence, instant, overwhelming, leaving no choice of means and no moment for deliberation," and the action taken must not be "unreasonable or excessive." See Michael Byers, "Iraq and the 'Bush Doctrine' of Pre-emptive Self-Defence," Crimes of War Project, August 20, 2002; available at www.crimesofwar.org/expert/bush-byers.html.

22. *Trail Smelter Case (United States v. Canada)*, Arbitral Tribunal, Montreal, April 16, 1938, and March 11, 1941; *United Nations Reports of International Arbitral Awards* 3 (1947), p. 1905.

23. Moreover, the victim state must show causation and a lack of due diligence on the part of the offending state, a test that rests on the prevailing understanding of what is "reasonable use of territory."

24. Nuclear Tests Case *(Australia v. France), ICJ Reports,* 1973, p. 99; *(New Zealand v. France), ICJ Reports,* 1974, p. 135. As it turned out, France voluntarily agreed to halt nuclear testing, so the ICJ was not required to make a determination on the specific claim.

25. A *jus cogens* norm may not be violated by any state, including states that object to the norm, which means that it can override ordinary customary law (which is based on consent).

26. The marsh region is located at the confluence of the Tigris and Euphrates rivers in southeastern Iraq and once formed the largest system of wetlands and lakes in the Middle East, covering an area of around 20,000 square kilometers. Not only does the marshland contain rich deposits of oil, but they also provided a refuge for political opponents of Saddam Hussein's regime. Human Rights Watch, "The Iraqi Government Assault on the Marsh Arabs," A Human Rights Watch Briefing Paper, January 2003; available at www.hrw.org/backgrounder/mena/marsharabs1.htm; accessed October 3, 2005). See also Sayyed Nadeem Kazmi and Stuart Leiderman, "Twilight People: Iraq's Marsh Inhabitants," *Human Rights Dialogue* 2, no. 11 (Spring 2004).

27. According to Human Rights Watch, the population of the Marsh Arabs in their ancestral homeland has been reduced from around 250,000 in 1991 to around 20,000 in 2003, with an estimated minimum of 100,000 internally displaced in Iraq. Human Rights Watch, "The Iraqi Government Assault on the Marsh Arabs." See also Aaron Schwabach, "Ecocide and Genocide in Iraq: International Law, the Marsh Arabs, and Environmental Damage in Non-International Conflicts," *Colorado Journal of International Environmental Law & Policy* 15, no. 1 (2004), pp. 1-28.

28. For example, the UN Sub-Commission on Prevention of Discrimination and Protection of Minorities (working with the U.S.-based Sierra Club Legal Defense Fund) has produced a Draft Declaration of Principles on Human Rights and the Environment, which is incorporated into the Sub-Commission's Final Report. Final Report on Human Rights and the Environment, Commission on Human Rights, Sub-commission on Prevention of Discrimination and Protection of Minorities, UN ESCOR, 46th Sess., UN Doc. E/CN.4/Sub.2/1994/9 (1994), pp. 74-77.

29. See, e.g., Nancy Lee Peluso, "Coercing Conservation: The Politics of State Resource Control," in Ronnie D. Lipschutz and Ken Conca, eds., *The State and Social Power in Global Environmental Politics* (New York: Columbia University Press, 1993), pp. 46-70.

30. See, e.g., Tzvetan Todorov, "Right to Intervene or Duty to Assist?" in Nicholas Owen, ed., *Human Rights, Human Wrongs: The Oxford Amnesty Lectures* (Oxford: Oxford University Press, 2001); and Mohammed Ayoob, "Humanitarian Intervention and State Sovereignty," *International Journal of Human Rights* 6, no. 1 (2002), pp. 81-102.

31. For a more detailed discussion of these differences, see Holzgrefe, "The Humanitarian Intervention Debate," in Keohane and Holzgrefe, eds., *Humanitarian Intervention*, pp. 37-49.

32. Ibid., pp. 41-43.

33. Michael Byers and Simon Chesterman, "Changing the Rules about Rules? Unilateral Humanitarian Intervention and the Future of International Law," in Keohane and Holzgrefe, eds., *Humanitarian Intervention*, pp. 177-203.

34. Ibid., p. 202.

35. Ibid.

36. Jane Stromseth, "Rethinking Humanitarian Intervention: The Case for Incremental Change," in Keohane and Holzgrefe, eds., *Humanitarian Intervention*, pp. 243-44. For example, NATO did not plead exceptional illegality for its intervention in Kosovo; rather, it justified its actions as legally exceptional in order to prevent genocide.

37. As Thomas M. Franck goes on to point out, while some illegal acts of intervention have been roundly condemned, others have been greeted with "mute, but evident satisfaction," while still others have received retrospective validation through the authorization of a United Nations presence. See Thomas M. Franck, "Interpretation and Change in the Law of Humanitarian Intervention," in Keohane and Holzgrefe, eds., *Humanitarian Intervention*, pp. 216-26.

38. Jean Bethke Elshtain, "International Justice as Equal Regard and the Use of Force," *Ethics and International Affairs* 17, no. 2 (Fall 2003), pp. 63-75.

39. Michael Walzer, *Just and Unjust Wars: A Moral Argument with Historical Illustrations*, 3rd ed. (New York: Basic Books, 2000), p. 107; *Thick and Thin: Moral Argument at Home and Abroad* (Notre Dame, Ind.: University of Notre Dame Press, 1994), pp. 15-19; and "The Politics of Rescue," *Social Research* 62 (1995), pp. 53-66.

40. David Ehrenfeld, *The Arrogance of Humanism* (Oxford: Oxford University Press, 1981).

41. Peter Singer, *Animal Liberation: A New Ethics for Our Treatment of Animals* (New York: The New Review, 1975); Tom Regan, *The Case for Animal Rights* (Berkeley: University of California Press, 1983); and Paola Cavalieri and Peter Singer, eds., *The Great Ape Project: Equality Beyond Humanity* (New York: St. Martin's Press, 1994).

42. For a defense of ecocentrism, see Robyn Eckersley, *Environmentalism and Political Theory: Toward an Ecocentric Approach* (Albany, N.Y.: State University of New York Press, 1992). For a general stocktaking of nonanthropocentric discourses, see Robyn Eckersley, "Ecocentric Discourses: Problems and Future Prospects for Nature Advocacy," in John Dryzek and David Schlosberg, eds., *Debating the Earth: The Environmental Politics Reader*, 2nd ed. (Oxford: Oxford University Press, 2005), pp. 364–81.

43. Great Ape Project, "Declaration of Great Apes"; available at www.greatapeproject.org/declaration.html; accessed October 4, 2005.

44. Robert Goodin, Carole Pateman, and Roy Pateman, "Simian Sovereignty," *Political Theory* 25, no. 6 (1997), pp. 821–49.

45. Ibid., pp. 834–35.

46. Biodiversity is used in the 1992 UN Convention on Biological Diversity to encompass all aspects of variability evident within the living world, including diversity within and between individuals; within populations; within species; and within communities and ecosystems on land and water.

47. The preamble to the 1992 UN Convention on Biological Diversity recognizes that the conservation of biological diversity is a common concern of humankind. Similarly, the preamble to the UN Framework Convention on Climate Change also acknowledges "that change in the Earth's climate and its adverse effects are a common concern of humankind." See Frank Biermann, "'Common Concern of Humankind': The Emergence of a New Concept of International Environmental Law," *Archiv des Volkerrechts* 34 (1996), pp. 426–81.

48. Franz Xaver Perrez, "The Relationship between 'Permanent Sovereignty' and the Obligation Not to Cause Transboundary Environmental Damage," *Environmental Law* 26 (1996), p. 1207.

49. Friedrich Kratochwil, "Sovereignty as Dominium: Is There a Right of Humanitarian Intervention?" in Gene M. Lyons and Michael Mastanduno, eds., *Beyond Westphalia? National Sovereignty and International Intervention* (Baltimore, Md.: Johns Hopkins University Press, 1995), p. 25.

50. See the 1982 United Nations Convention on the Law of the Sea, Article 56; the 1992 Convention on Biological Diversity, Article 15; and the Food and Agricultural Organization's International Treaty on Plant Genetic Resources for Food and Agriculture, Article 10.1. Peter H. Sand, "Sovereignty Bounded: Public Trusteeship for Common Pool Resources?" *Global Environmental Politics* 4, no. 19 (2004), pp. 47–48.

51. Article 1, GA resolution 1803 (XVII), December 14, 1962.

52. Nico Schrijver, *Sovereignty Over Natural Resources: Balancing Rights and Duties* (Cambridge: Cambridge University Press, 1997), pp. 369–70.

53. Principle 2 of the Rio Declaration provides that "States have, in accordance with the Charter of the United Nations and the principles of international law, the sovereign right to exploit their own resources pursuant to their own environmental and developmental policies, and the responsibility to ensure that activities within their jurisdiction or control do not cause damage to the environment of other States or of areas beyond the limits of national jurisdiction."

54. See note 47.

55. A. John Simmons, "On the Territorial Rights of States," in Ernest Sosa and Enrique Villanueva, eds., *Social, Political, and Legal Philosophy* (Boston: Blackwell, 2001), p. 30l.

56. See Charles Beitz, *Political Theory and International Relations* (Princeton, N.J.: Princeton University Press, 1979).

57. Simmons, "On the Territorial Rights of States," in Sosa and Villanueva, eds., *Social, Political, and Legal Philosophy,* p. 303.

58. Robyn Eckersley, *The Green State: Rethinking Democracy and Sovereignty* (Cambridge, Mass.: MIT Press, 2004).

59. Examples include the polluter pays principle; the precautionary principle; the principle of sustainable development, which incorporates the principle of intra- and intergenerational equity; and the principle of "common but differentiated responsibilities," which acknowledges the different capacities and abilities of developed and developing countries to respond to global environmental change and pursue sustainable development strategies.

60. This trustee relationship is adapted from Peter Sand, "Sovereignty Bounded," p. 55.

61. Genocide involves the intentional and systematic killing of large numbers of people on the basis of their social, political, religious, or ethnic status, whereas crimes against humanity are defined as a range of acts (such as murder, extermination, enslavement, and torture) "committed as part of a widespread or systematic attack directed against any civilian population, with knowledge of the attack." See Articles 6 and 7 of the Rome Statute of the International Criminal Court.

62. The phrase "widespread, long-term and severe damage to the natural environment" is taken from Article 8(b)(iv) of the Rome Statute of the International Criminal Court, dealing with war crimes (in this case, environmental war crimes).

63. Eva M. Kornicker Uhlmann, "State Community Interests, *Jus Cogens* and Protection of the Global Environment: Developing Criteria for Peremptory Norms," *Georgetown International Environmental Law Review* 11 (1998), p. 120.

64. In this respect, the prohibitions approximate the status of *jus cogens* or *erga omnes* obligations. The definition of *jus cogens* in section 53 of the Vienna Convention is rather general, but it has been fleshed out by Eva M. Kornicker Uhlmann as requiring the satisfaction of the following four criteria: (1) The norm must transcend the individual interests of states and serve the entire community of states or "state community interests"; (2) it must have a foundation in morality; (3) the norm must be absolute or overriding; and (4) it must command the agreement of the vast majority of states. See Kornicker Uhlmann, "State Community Interests," p. 104.

65. The remaining requirements are last resort, right intention, proportionality, proper authority, and reasonable hope of success. In the wake of the U.S.-led invasion of Iraq, we might add an assessment of the prospects for successful postintervention institution building.

66. Jennifer M. Welsh, "Taking Consequences Seriously: Objections to Humanitarian Intervention," in Jennifer M. Welsh, ed., *Humanitarian Intervention and International Relations* (Oxford: Oxford University Press, 2004), p. 66.

67. Most multilateral and unilateral humanitarian interventions have been carried out against small, weak, or failed states. No such interventions have taken place in nuclear states or powerful and rich states, and the majority of states do not have the

military capacity to act unilaterally. Smaller states do have the opportunity to influence intervention decisions, however, when they take a turn as a nonpermanent member on the Security Council.

68. Of course, these factors should always form part of the general pragmatic assessment as to whether military intervention is likely to make matters better or worse, all things considered.

✗ NO

Some Worries about Ecological-Humanitarian Intervention and Ecological Defense
MARK WOODS

In "Ecological Intervention: Prospects and Limits," Robyn Eckersley offers an emergency stopgap and glimmer of hope to halt environmental destruction: states and coalitions of states should be permitted to use military force to prevent urgent and acute environmental damage.[1] While I find her article well-written and her arguments for ecological-humanitarian intervention (EHI) and ecological defense (ED) intriguing, in what follows I will outline a number of reasons for caution and skepticism about using military force to prevent crimes against nature.

Before I begin, two brief caveats are in order. First, I applaud Eckersley's effort to bring together environmental philosophy and the ethics of war and peace. There is little discussion between people who work in these two areas, and there is much common ground of concern.[2] Second, I hope that Eckersley's article and the responses provided by Simon Dalby, Matthew Humphrey, Clare Palmer, and me are the harbingers of continued future, and fruitful, discussion.

Eckersley provides a moral, political, and legal groundwork for armed EHI and ED. Consider first the legality of such military ventures. Conventional international law has yet to fully catch up with the custom of standard, non-ecological humanitarian intervention (HI). Under the rubric of the United Nations Charter, the use of military force is permissible only in matters of self-defense (Article 51) and when authorized by the UN Security Council (Chapter VII). Eckersley (pp. 302–304) notes the general reluctance of the UN Security Council to authorize HIs. Presuming that this general legal problem for HIs can be surmounted, what legal precedents exist for armed EHIs? Beyond a passing comment that environmental criminal prosecution exists for "'scorched earth' environmental atrocities" (p. 294), Eckersley surprisingly provides no real discussion of environment-specific international treaties that regulate war and that would seem to be the most likely legal precedents for EIH (and ED).

There are three such treaties: (1) the United Nations Convention on the Prohibition of Military or Any Other Hostile Use of Environmental Modification Techniques (1976)—known as the ENMOD Convention; (2) the Protocol Additional to the Geneva Conventions of 12 August 1949 and relating to the Protection of Victims of International Armed Conflicts—known as Protocol I (1977); and (3) the Rome Statute of the International Criminal Court (July 17, 1998), which established the International Criminal Court. Rather than actually protecting the natural environment, the ENMOD Convention prohibits deliberate modification of natural processes such that they are used as weapons of war. In contrast, both Protocol I and the Rome Statute are designed to protect the environment. Article

35(3) of Protocol I prohibits any methods or means of warfare that can cause "widespread, long-term and severe damage to the natural environment"; Article 55(1) of Protocol I adds a prohibition against damages to the natural environment that "prejudice the health or survival of the [human] population"; and Article 8.2(b)(iv) of the Rome Statute defines causing "widespread, long-term and severe damage to the natural environment" as a war crime.

The existence of these environment-specific international treaties is less than reassuring. Consider first that no environment-specific treaty has ever been invoked to actually protect the environment or to bring charges against a nation-state for environmental damage. One of the clearest cases of deliberate environmental damage occurred during the 1991 Persian Gulf War when Iraqi forces released approximately 11 million barrels of oil into the northern Arabian Gulf and when the fires caused from the sabotage of more than 800 oil wells spewed approximately 6 million gallons of crude oil into the atmosphere.[3] The fact that the United States claimed these actions violated neither the ENMOD Convention nor Protocol I is telling and shows how little bite international environmental law actually has.[4] Second, the ENMOD Convention, Protocol I, and the Rome Statute apply only to interstate armed conflicts, and conflicts that might warrant EHIs are not interstate conflicts. Third, the threshold for environmental damage for all three of these treaties is "widespread, long-lasting, and severe," a threshold Eckersley notes on page 310 to define ecocide. This threshold is not defined in Protocol I or the Rome Statute. In an "Understandings Regarding the Convention" text meant to accompany the ENMOD Convention, *widespread* is defined as "encompassing an area on the scale of several hundred square kilometers"; *long-lasting* is defined as "lasting for a period of months, or approximately a season"; and *severe* is defined as "involving serious or significant disruption or harm to human life, natural or economic resources or other assets." Thus, environmental damage must cover an area almost half the size of the U.S. state of Rhode Island, last for a minimum of at least three months, and/or be severe, simply redefined as serious or significant. Is this how Eckersley wants to legally stipulate the crime of ecocide? A fourth issue for treaties designed to protect the environment from military damage is that environmental "collateral damage" is permissible when it is done in the name of military necessity and offers a military advantage. Similar to the alleged remark of a U.S. commander in Vietnam—"we had to destroy the town [Ben Tre] in order to save it"—it is not too farfetched to imagine hearing a military commander say, "we had to destroy the mountain gorillas in order to save them." In terms of precedent from environment-specific international treaties, I submit that the legal ground for Eckersley's notion of an armed EHI is less than firm.[5]

Eckersley's political legitimacy ground is also not without problems. She claims that the Rio Declaration "represents the most up-to-date encapsulation of international environmental norms" that "makes clear that states have environmental

responsibilities in relation to their own territories" (p. 308). While it does contain some laudable norms, it is important to note that the Rio Declaration has had little if any real effect on the political world of international relations. At the 1992 United Nations Conference on Environment and Development there was no agreement on an expected Earth Charter, and the main document produced at the conference—*Agenda 21*—was never implemented. Much of the conference was directed toward sustainable development (as seen in Principle 1 of the Rio Declaration) and, more importantly, on the *development* side of sustainable development.[6] The global South was wary about global North concerns with nature conservation and pollution abatement taking precedence over concerns about poverty and underdevelopment.

Eckersley's notion of an armed EHI to prevent ecocide ("widespread, long-lasting, and severe" environmental damage), transboundary spillover effects (namely pollution), and other crimes against nature (namely biodiversity loss) is a good example of Northern concern exhibited at Rio. She correctly notes that an armed EHI to protect biodiversity might be "regarded by developing states as yet another imperialist scheme by the North to deny former colonies the right to make use of their natural resources for the benefit of their own people" (p. 308). There is considerable and sometimes vociferous debate on the ground and in scholarly literature about how the protection of nonhuman nature occurs at the expense of local peoples.[7] In this debate between mainstream environmentalists and environmental justice advocates, the notion of an armed EHI seems to come down squarely on the side of the former, and Eckersley's advocacy seems akin to what environmental justice advocates pejoratively call the "Yellowstone model" of environmental injustice. After its creation in 1872, US Army Calvary was posted to guard Yellowstone National Park, in large part to prevent Bannock, Tukedeka, and other Shoshone Indians from entering the park, killing game animals, and otherwise utilizing natural resources that they had used prior to the arrival of Euro-Americans. From the perspective of environmental justice advocates and local peoples, any armed intrusion under the banner of an "EHI" would likely be viewed as yet another instance of environmental injustice.

This brings us to the last ground for Eckersley's notion of an armed EHI: moral legitimacy. In order to be morally legitimate, many people argue that a standard HI must satisfy criteria from the just war tradition (JWT).[8] In terms of a just war or the justice of going to war—*jus ad bellum*—this includes legitimate (or right) authority, just cause, right intention, macro-proportionality, likelihood of success, and last resort. In terms of fighting justly—*jus in bello*—this includes discrimination and micro-proportionality. There is much that can be said about applying these JWT criteria to an armed EHI and ecological defense (ED), but I will limit my discussion to just cause and proportionality.

As noted above, Eckersley suggests that just causes for armed EHIs and ED include stopping ecocide, transboundary spillover effects, and other crimes

against nature. While there are clear instances of ecocide, such as the ancient Roman obliteration of Carthage, trying to define instances of "widespread, long-lasting, and severe" environmental damage today seems fraught with difficulties. How widespread, long-lasting, and/or severe does the damage have to actually be before a military response threshold is passed? It is important to remember that militaries are designed first and foremost to kill. Militarizing the mitigation of transboundary spillover effects seems akin to issuing a death threat against one's neighbor because of pollution emissions. I need only look ten miles south of my home in San Diego, California, to see the tragic consequences of a similar policy: the militarization of the US-Mexico border to mitigate the transboundary spillover effects of undocumented people entering the US. Illegally crossing a political boundary to work is not an act of war that should demand a military response. Likewise, emitting harmful pollution is a crime that should demand good police and judicial work.

The final "just cause" category of crimes against nature is also problematic. Eckersley focuses her discussion of this on the protection of biodiversity (pp. 304–309). If conservation biologists are correct that current anthropogenic species extinctions are 300 to 2,700 times higher than the background extinction rate (prior to the evolutionary arrival of humans), the number of species extinctions occurring *each day* is quite staggering.[9] One would need to pick one's battles wisely to decide which of these potential extinctions warrants an armed intervention. While I agree with Eckersley that a species threatened with extinction is a tragic problem that demands an immediate response, I am not convinced that military action is the correct response.

Just cause is stretched even further when Eckersley suggests preemptive military strikes in the name of ED (pp. 299–301). Michael Walzer classically has argued that a preemptive strike is a just cause for war when a potential aggressor state has a manifest intent to injure, is actively preparing to intend danger, and doing anything other than fighting preemptively will magnify the risk to the potentially aggressed-against state.[10] The most likely just cause candidate for preemptive ED is a transboundary spillover effect, particularly air and water pollution. It is doubtful that most people who emit pollutants do so with a manifest intent to harm. Eckersley's ED would instead need to focus on militarily preventing the unintended consequences of actions that result in pollution. This prevention of a possible future danger seems more akin to a preventative strike against a gathering threat—precisely the justification the US used to invade Iraq in 2003. In the preface of the fourth edition (2006) of *Just and Unjust Wars*, Walzer correctly notes that such preventative war is not justifiable under the guise of the JWT. Eckersley's ED might fail to meet the *jus ad bellum* criterion of just cause.

Finally, consider proportionality. A possible war must pass a macro-proportionality test (*jus ad bellum*) in which more good than evil will be achieved by

going to war, and an actual war must pass micro-proportionality tests (*jus in bello*) whereby more good than evil is achieved throughout the means of war, such as individual battles, tactics, and weapons use. There is a general dearth of environmental ethics discussion of what some call the ecology of war and peace—the effects of military activities on the environment—in spite of the fact that the world's militaries are estimated to be the largest single polluter on Earth, accounting for as much as 20 percent of all global environmental degradation.[11] Conventional military activities have many negative environmental consequences.[12] Consequently, a war *on* environmental destruction, such as an armed EHI or ED, would more likely be a war *of* environmental destruction.

In conclusion, there are a number of reasons to proceed with caution and skepticism in regard to the prospects of ecological intervention. Rather than searching for new environmental reasons to use our militaries, perhaps we should instead find new environmental reasons to restrain such use.

NOTES

1. Robyn Eckersley, "Ecological Intervention: Prospects and Limits," *Ethics & International Affairs* 21, no. 3 (Fall 2007), pp. 293–316.

2. See, for example, my attempt to bring environmental ethics considerations into the just war tradition. Mark Woods, "The Nature of War and Peace: Just War Thinking, Environmental Ethics, and Environmental Justice," in Michael W. Brough, John W. Lango, and Harry van der Linden, eds., *Rethinking the Just War Tradition* (Albany: State University of New York Press, 2007), pp. 17–34.

3. Muhammad Sadiq and John C. McCain, eds., *The Gulf War Aftermath: An Environmental Tragedy* (Dordrecht: Kluwer Academic Publishers, 1993); Farouk El-Baz and R.M. Makharita, eds., *The Gulf War and the Environment* (New York: Gordon and Breach Science Publishers, 1994).

4. The UN held Iraq responsible for this environmental damage, but Iraqi liability stemmed from the wrongful occupation of Kuwait and not from Iraq's actual environmental actions.

5. In addition to the ENMOD Convention, Protocol I, and the Rome Statute, there are a variety of non-environment specific international treaties that plausibly could help protect the environment from war crimes. These treaties include: (1) Hague Convention IV Concerning the Laws and Customs of War on Land (1907), (2) Protocol for the Prohibition of the Use in War of Asphyxiating, Poisonous or Other Gases, and of Bacteriological Methods of Warfare (Geneva Convention 1925), (3) Fourth Geneva Convention (1949) relative to the protection of Civilian Persons in Time of War, (4) Hague Convention for the Protection of Cultural Property in the Event of Armed Conflict (1954), (5) Treaty Banning Nuclear Weapon Tests in the Atmosphere, in Outer Space and Under Water (Limited Test Ban Treaty 1963), (6) Convention on the Prohibition of the Development, Production and Stockpiling of Bacteriological (Biological) and Toxin Weapons and on Their Destruction (1974), (7) 1980 Convention on Certain Conventional Weapons and its Protocols, (8) Chemical Weapons Convention (1992), and (9) Convention on the Prohibition of the Use, Stockpiling, Production and Transfer of Anti-Personnel Mines and on Their Destruction (Ottawa

Convention 1997). For discussion of some of these treaties and the three environment-specific treaties, see Richard Falk, "The Inadequacy of the Existing Legal Approach to Environmental Protection," pp. 137–155; Adam Roberts, "The Law of War and Environmental Damage," pp. 47–86; and Michael N. Schmitt, "War and the Environment: Fault Lines in the Prescriptive Landscape," pp. 87–136; all in Jay E. Austin and Carl E. Bruch, eds., *The Environmental Consequences of War: Legal, Economic, and Scientific Perspectives* (New York: Cambridge University Press, 2000).

6. Wolfgang Sachs, "Global Ecology and the Shadow of 'Development'," in Wolfgang Sachs, ed., *Global Ecology: A New Arena of Political Conflict* (London: Zed Books, 1993), pp 3–21.

7. Giovanna Di Chiro, "Nature as Community: The Convergence of Environment and Social Justice," William Cronon, ed., *Uncommon Ground: Toward Reinventing Nature* (New York: W.W. Norton & Company, 1995), pp. 298–320; Charles Zerner, ed., *People, Plants, and Justice: The Politics of Nature Conservation* (New York: Columbia University Press, 2000); Steven R. Brechin, Peter R. Wilshusen, Crystal L. Fortwangler, and Patrick C. West, eds., *Contested Nature: Promoting International Biodiversity with Social Justice in the Twenty-first Century* (Albany: State University of New York Press, 2003).

8. Shi Yinhong and Shen Zhixiong, "After Kosovo: Moral and Legal Constraints on Humanitarian Intervention," in Bruno Coppieters and Nick Fotion, eds., *Moral Constraints on War: Principles and Cases* (Lanham, MD: Lexington Books, 2002), pp. 256–260; Paul Christopher, *The Ethics of War and Peace: An Introduction to Legal and Moral Issues*, 3rd ed., Upper Saddle River, NJ: Pearson Prentice Hall, 2004), pp. 244–255.

9. Martha J. Groom, "Threats to Biodiversity," in Martha J. Groom, Gary K. Meffe, and C. Ronald Carroll, eds., *Principles of Conservation Biology*, 3rd ed. (Sunderland, MA: Sinauer Associates, 2006), p. 86; Malcolm L. Hunter, Jr. and James Gibbs, *Fundamentals of Conservation Biology*, 3rd ed. (Malden, MA: Blackwell Publishing), p. 120.

10. Michael Walzer, *Just and Unjust Wars: A Moral Argument with Historical Illustrations*, 4th ed., (New York: Basic Books, 2006), p. 81.

11. Michael Renner, "Assessing the Military's War on the Environment," in Lester R. Brown et al., eds., *State of the World 1991: A Worldwatch Institute Report on Progress Toward a Sustainable Society* (Washington, DC: W.W. Norton & Company, 1991), pp. 135–152.

12. Direct impacts on the environment include: (1) formation of craters and compaction, erosion, and contamination of soils by bombs, missiles, and military vehicles and their hazardous and toxic residues, (2) other forms of land pollution ranging from latrines and garbage dumps to landmines, unexploded ordnance, and radioactive dust, (3) defoliation, deforestation, and land degradation, (4) contamination of surface waters and groundwater, (5) atmospheric emissions and resulting air pollution from military equipment and vehicles, (6) direct and collateral killing of animals and plants and loss of habitat, (7) degradation and destruction of protected natural areas, and (8) noise pollution of 140 decibels or more from low-flying aircraft and weapons that can lead to long-term hearing impairment in people and animals. Further environmental harms for people include: (a) damage and destruction of water storage and distribution systems, waste and wastewater treatment facilities, and sewer systems, (b) damage and destruction of croplands, pasturage, marine fisheries, and the resulting

loss of agricultural products or other foodstuffs, and (c) damage and destruction of other human structures ranging from buildings to power grid systems and entire towns. These environmental harms in turn can (i) disrupt or destroy the social and economic infrastructures of human communities, (ii) dislocate human populations and result in displaced peoples and refugees, and (iii) create new opportunities for pathogenic microbes and the spread of infectious diseases among human populations. See Asit K. Biswas, "Scientific Assessment of the Long-Term Consequences of War," pp. 303–315; Jeffrey A. McNeely, "War and Biodiversity: An Assessment of Impacts," pp. 353–378; both in Austin and Bruch, eds., *The Environmental Consequences of War.*

POSTSCRIPT

In her article, Robyn Eckersley makes the case for states to use force or the threat of force to "prevent grave environmental damage." Eckersley's case for "ecological intervention" faces some of the same dilemmas that have faced the proponents of humanitarian intervention, particularly since the events of 9/11.

Initially when the concept of humanitarian intervention was promoted following the end of the Cold War, some advocates suggested that the acceptance of the legitimacy of use of military intervention to protect civilians from human-rights abuses may actually curtail the use of military force by governments. By recognizing that there were higher moral purposes to which military force could be used (a sort of "military humanitarianism" as one writer called it), states would feel constrained from using force to promote more narrow selfish national purposes. Thus, it was hoped that the legitimization of the principle of humanitarian intervention might reduce the occasions when states felt justified in resorting to the use of the force against other states. However, it is now feared that in the aftermath of 9/11 and the ongoing "war on terrorism" that the principle of humanitarian intervention may now be used as pretext for more frequent interventions. Analysts point to the way the United States built in case for throwing the Taliban in Afghanistan by highlighting the human-rights abuses and treatment of women by the Taliban government in the days preceding the intervention.

Does the concept of "ecological intervention" face the same problem? Would expanding the concept of humanitarian intervention to apply to non-human cases such as environmental crises only serve to legitimate further use of military force? Eckersley seems aware of this problem by giving significant attention to developing a strict set of criteria to define when such interventions should take place. But, is this likely to restrain the use of military force or will it, as some fear, give states yet another pretext for using military force?

Suggested Additional Readings

Dalby, Simon. "Ecological Intervention and Anthropocene Ethics." (Online Exclusive.) *Ethics & International Affairs* 21, no. 3 (Fall 2007). Available at http://www.cceia.org/resources/journal/21_3/feature_and_symposium/index.html.

Eckersley, Robyn. "Ecological Security in a Global Risk Society." In Damian Grenfeld and Paul James (eds.), *Rethinking Insecurity, War and Violence: Beyond Savage Globalization?* New York: Routledge, 2008.

Eckersley, Robyn. "Greening the Nation-state: From Exclusive to Inclusive Sovereignty." In John Barry and Robyn Eckersley (eds.), *The State and the Global Ecological Crisis.* Cambridge, Mass.: MIT Press, 2005, 159–80.

Eckersley, Robyn. *The Green State: Rethinking Democracy and Sovereignty.* Cambridge, Mass.: MIT Press, 2004.

Eckersley, Robyn, and Andrew Dobson (eds.). *Political Theory and the Environmental Challenge.* Cambridge: Cambridge University Press, 2006.

Eckersley, Robyn, and John Barry (eds.). *The State and the Global Ecological Crisis.* Cambridge, Mass.: MIT Press, 2005.

Homer-Dixon, T.F. "On the Threshold: Environmental Changes as Causes of Acute Conflict." *International Security* 16, no. 2 (Fall 1991): 76–116.

Humphrey, Mathew. "On Not Being Green about Ecological Intervention." (Online Exclusive.) *Ethics & International Affairs* 21, no. 3 (Fall 2007). Available at http://www.cceia.org/resources/journal/21_3/feature_and_symposium/index.html.

Levy, M.A. "Is the Environment a National Security Issue?" *International Security* 20, no. 2 (Fall 1995): 35–62.

Mathews, J.T. "Redefining Security." *Foreign Affairs* 68, No. 2 (Spring 1989): 162–77.

Myers, N. "The Environmental Dimension to Security Issues." *The Environmentalist* 6 (1986): 51–57.

Palmer, Clare. "Ecological Intervention in Defense of Species." (Online Exclusive.) *Ethics & International Affairs*, 21 no. 3 (Fall 2007). Available at http://www.cceia.org/resources/journal/21_3/feature_and_symposium/index.html.

Ullman, R.H. "Redefining Security." *International Security* 8, no. 1 (Summer 1983): 129–53.

Westing, A.H. "An Expanded Concept of International Security." In Arthur H. Westing (ed.), *Global Resources and International Conflict.* Oxford: Oxford University Press, 1986.

InfoTrac® College Edition

Search for the following articles in the InfoTrac® database:

Foster, Gregory D. "Environmental Security: The Search for Strategic Legitmacy." *Armed Forces & Society: An Interdisciplinary Journal* 27, no. 3 (Spring 2001): 1–15.

Levy, Marc. "Exploring Environment-Security Connections." *Environment* 41, no. 1 (January 1999): 3.

McGowan, Alan H. "The Environment and National Security." *Environment* 49 (June 2007).

NE

Web Resources

For current URLs for the following websites, visit www.crosscurrents.nelson.com.

THE INSTITUTE FOR ENVIRONMENTAL SECURITY (IES)

http://www.envirosecurity.org/

The IES is an international NGO based in the Hague that promotes global awareness of issues related to environmental security.

ENVIRONMENTAL CHANGE AND SECURITY PROGRAM

http://www.wilsoncenter.org/

Look under "programs" to find the link to the Woodrow Wilson Center's Environmental Change and Security Program. A variety of resources can be found here, including a blog which deals with environmental security issues.

ENVIRONMENTAL SECURITY DATABASE

http://www.library.utoronto.ca/pcs/database/libintro.htm

The Environmental Security Database contains information on books, journal articles, papers, and newspaper clippings relating to the study of the links between environmental stress and violent conflict in developing countries, including some of work of Thomas Homer-Dixon.

APPENDIX
Debating the Issues
LUCILLE CHARLTON

One way to gain a more complete understanding of contemporary international issues is to participate in a classroom debate. Most students learn debating skills in secondary school; some may have even joined debating teams or participated in a model United Nations forum. The yes/no format of this book encourages debates on the topics presented. Debating at the college or university level requires a high level of preparation for both content and style. If you are asked to participate in a debate on these issues, the following guidelines will help you prepare for your part of the debate.

UNDERSTAND THE FORMAT OF THE DEBATE

Debates both in and beyond the classroom setting have several basic rules. One group presents the proposition or questions. The other group presents a counter-argument. Both sides have equal time to persuade the audience that their view-point is right. However, the format, time, and make-up of the team can vary according to which framework the debate is being followed. Are you debating as an individual or as a team? How much time is being allotted for each segment of the debate? Are you familiar with the rules of this debate? For example, is it acceptable to interrupt the other speakers?

Part of your preparation depends on the setting. Is this debate in the classroom or in front of a larger group? If possible, listen to some actual debates and take notes on how arguments and counter-arguments are presented.

What do you hope to achieve from this debate? Classroom debates are most often evaluated on the quality of analysis, strength of the evidence, organization, and delivery skills. A key component of any debate is to analyze your strengths and weaknesses in each of these areas.

For more information on the various debate formats, see:

http://www.csun.edu/~dgw61315/debformats.html

UNDERSTAND THE QUESTION

Most debates put forward a question or proposition that has a yes/no or agree/disagree idea. Debaters should start by researching both sides of the question. Start with the sources listed with each debate in this book, and then research other reliable sources as a part of your preparation. Debating relies on critical thinking. Evaluate sources, analyze the arguments, and synthesize materials. You may be

asked to defend a position that you do not personally agree with. In any debate, keep an open mind to all arguments.

FORMULATE ARGUMENTS AND COUNTER-ARGUMENTS

Whatever side you are asked to support, your knowledge of both sides of the argument is crucial to success. Make a list of the important points on each side of the argument. You must be ready to support your claims as well as anticipate all opposing arguments and refute them. What are the important types of evidence for each claim? Citing more than one piece of evidence to back up your points strengthens your arguments. Evaluate all evidence for strengths and weaknesses. Use only reliable sources such as peer-reviewed journals, expert researchers, and trustworthy websites. Relying on Wikipedia for information or analysis is not a good idea! Think carefully about the differences between opinion and evidence and how to use them in a debate.

Develop clear lines of reasoning. Identify any logical fallacies in your own thinking and be ready to attack your opponents if you observe any fallacies in their presentation. For a list and examples of logical fallacies, see:

http://www.csun.edu/~dgw61315/fallacies.html

http://owl.english.purdue.edu/owl/resource/659/03/

Keep careful records of all your research sources. You may need these for future debates or follow-up assignments on the topic.

Most importantly, teams must organize their presentations to avoid repetition. Decide ahead of time what the strongest arguments and evidence are. Ideally, your team should reiterate the strongest points in the closing arguments. Always conclude with a strong summary of your position.

PREPARE AND PRACTICE

Because most debates consist of teamwork, preparation and rehearsal are important. Practice keeping within time limits and changing from one speaker to another. Teams should agree in advance on how to handle unexpected arguments from the other side.

Refresh your memory of all the qualities of good public speaking:

- Good eye contact
- Appropriate mannerisms
- Natural gestures
- Vocal variety
- Voice projection appropriate for the setting
- Speaking from cues

During practice sessions, use peer review to point out negative points of your debating skills, such as the following:

- Boring delivery or monotone voice
- Hesitation or usage of "um" and "uh"
- Lack of eye contact
- Speaking too quietly or too loudly
- Obvious nervousness

In addition, check out the room and the sound equipment if necessary. Make sure your team is comfortable with the electronics.

DURING THE DEBATE

Rehearsing will help your team move smoothly through the debate. The most important task is to listen to and jot down notes on the other team's arguments. You will have to think of quick rejoinders for their arguments. Be ready to challenge their reasoning and evidence on a point-by-point basis. Stay focused and follow the rules. Don't personalize the arguments. Launching a personal attack on the opposing team will sink your credibility immediately.

AFTER THE DEBATE

Whatever the outcome, your team should take time to debrief. Analyze the content and style. Jot down points of interest from both sides of the question. What has your team gained from this experience? What could you do better the next time? Remember, the objectives of most debating exercises are to gain knowledge about a particular issue.

OTHER SOURCES TO CONSULT ON DEBATING

BASIC DEBATING SKILLS
http://www.actdu.org.au/archives/actein_site/basicskills_.html

CALIFORNIA STATE UNIVERSITY
http://www.csun.edu/~dgw61315/dgwdebate.html

MINISTRY OF EDUCATION, NEW ZEALAND
http://english.unitecnology.ac.nz/resources/units/debating/student_what.html

DEBATE CENTRAL WORKSHOP: POWERPOINT PRESENTATION
www.debate-central.org/file_download/57

Issue 5

Reprinted with permission from *Behind the Headlines*, Vol. 59, Summer 2002, p. 1–8, a publication of the Canadian International Council.

Reprinted with permission from *Behind the Headlines*, Vol. 59, Summer 2002, p. 10–16, a publication of the Canadian International Council.

Issue 6

Steven Meyer, "Carcass of Dead Policies: The Irrelevance of NATO," reprinted with permission of the author from *Parameters*, Winter 2003–2004; p. 83-97. THE VIEWS EXPRESSED ARE PERSONAL ONES AND DO NOT REFLECT THE OFFICIAL POLICY OR POSITION OF THE NATIONAL DEFENSE UNIVERSITY, THE DEPART-MENT OF DEFENSE, OR THE U.S. GOVERNMENT.

Rebecca Johnson and Micah Zenko, "All Dressed Up and No Place to Go: Why NATO Should Be on the Front Line in the War on Terror." Reprinted with permission from *Parameters* Volume 32, No. 4 (Winter 2002–2003): 48-63.

Issue 7

Courtesy of Dr. Michael Byers, University of British Columbia.

CDFAI Dispatch IV, No. II, Summer 2006, Canadian Defence & Foreign Affairs Institute. Reprinted by permission.

Issue 8

Gary Hufbauer "The Fair Play Debate: Free Trade", *The National Interest*, May/June 2008, p. 15-18. © 2008 The National Interest.

Joseph Stiglitz "The Fair Play Debate: Fair Trade", *The National Interest*, May/June 2008, p. 19-24. © 2008 The National Interest.

Issue 9

Naierossadat Daneshvar Hosseini "Globalization and Women: Challenges and Opportunities", *International Business & Economics Research Journal*, March 2006, Vol. 5, No. 3, p. 35–40.

Jagdish N. Bhagwati, "Women: Harmed or Helped?", *In Defense of Globalization*, p. 73-91. Copyright © 2004 Oxford University Press. Reprinted by permission of the publisher.

Issue 10

Reproduced by permission of SAGE Publications Ltd., London, Los Angeles, New Delhi, Singapore and Washington DC from Stephen Gill, "Toward a Postmodern